I0729492

Front cover: Code of Honor, Aquatic Park, Berkeley, 1983
Back cover: Photo by Cammie Toloui

Layout by Paul Curran
Design by Justin Marsh

Published in 2024 by Last Gasp of San Francisco

Last Gasp
777 Florida Street, Suite 201
San Francisco, CA 94110
lastgasp.com
Second printing, December 2024

ISBN 978-0-86719-927-7

Printed in China

HAIL MURRAY!

The Bay Area Punk Photography of Murray Bowles

1982-1995

Edited by Anna Brown

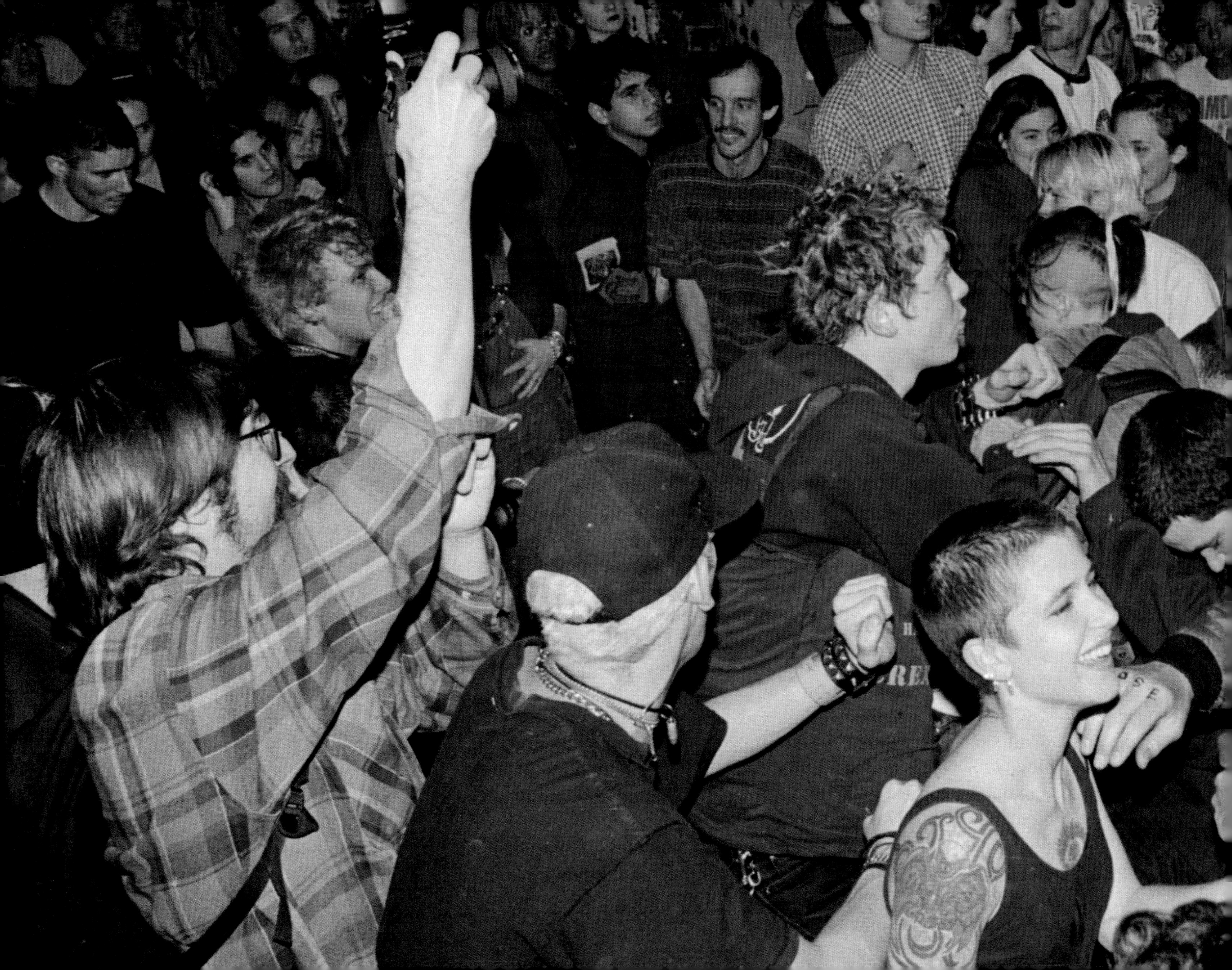

I wanted to be more than a spectator

—*Murray Bowles*

Murray at Gilman Street, 1993 (Photo by Christian Larsen)

Hail Murray

by Anna Brown

Murray Bowles documented the Bay Area punk underground for four decades, from the emergence of hardcore in the early eighties until his sudden death in 2019. He photographed thousands of shows and left behind a massive body of work—more than half a million images—yet neither his family nor his colleagues knew this part of his life, or the worldwide renown he'd reluctantly earned as the chronicler of our world.

Impossible to miss at any show, Murray was the bearded, bespectacled man in the pit, wearing blue jeans, a punk shirt, and a backpack. Holding his camera over his head with one hand, he shot pictures without looking through the viewfinder.

In his interview for the documentary film *Turn It Around*, Murray described the hazards of shooting so close to the melee: "I remember a stagediver getting his feet trapped in my camera strap and then thrashing around trying to make themself free. That's why you don't let your camera hang around your neck. It's much better to hold it in your hand."

It's amazing that he could just raise his camera, point in a certain direction, and capture something so ineffable. Murray was quick to demystify his process, explaining that he just shot with a wide angle lens and cropped later in the darkroom. The fact remains that he had an

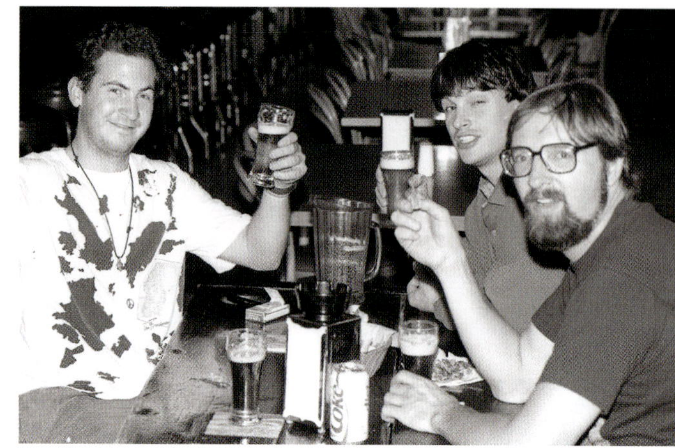

Jason, David, and Murray at Picante, Berkeley, 1991

uncanny ability to locate the most compelling subject in the room, and later in the negative. It seems perfectly true to Murray's character that his artistic practice was so much an exercise in intuition and discovery.

Every weekend without fail Murray could be found in the basements, dive bars, and scrappy punk clubs where the music was loud and the crowd was gleefully rowdy. Never much drawn to the established nightclubs where you could expect to see something polished or packaged, he preferred the unknown or up-and-coming bands, avowing that you're always better—freer, more true— before you find an audience (or they find you).

Murray subscribed to the punk ethos, *be more than a spectator*. You'd never see him camped out behind a velvet rope; even as his reputation and access grew, he was not one to flash a press pass for free admission or try to rub shoulders backstage. (In fact, I never saw him at a venue that had a backstage.) Driven by his impulse to document history, his love of his craft, and a deep commitment to his found community, he always wanted to be in the thick of it.

Murray developed film and made prints in his kitchen three to four nights a week, selling them at shows for fifteen cents, the cost of the paper. Back then few of us

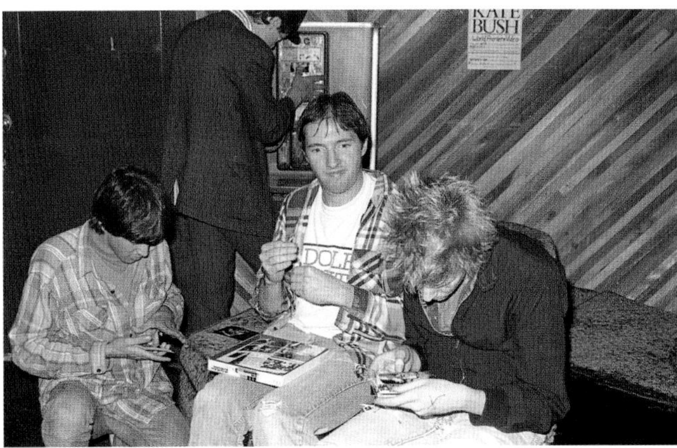

Murray selling photos, 1983

recognized how much time and dedication he devoted to this work, but it was always a highlight of the night to dig through stacks of 4x5 prints and come home with a few gems in the pocket of your leather jacket. Those of us who lived in the Bay Area still prize the personal collection of "Murray pics" we have stashed in shoeboxes or crammed into albums. For anyone new to the scene, it was a thrill to start appearing in Murray's pictures. It was a sign that you belonged. He had a way of making you feel seen, and what he saw was far more beautiful than the way you saw yourself.

Murray was born in 1951 and grew up in San Gabriel, California. He was a studious kid. Obsessed with his record player from an early age, he loved the Doors and Frank Zappa as well as all kinds of classical music. According to his sister, Kathy, it wasn't unusual to find Murray holed up in his room with the TV on mute, a record playing, and his nose in a book. After high school, she recalls, "He left for college and never came home."

Murray went to college at Harvey Mudd, in Pomona, and then got a graduate degree in computer science at UC Berkeley. He was irresistibly drawn to Silicon Valley, where in the late seventies and early eighties misfit coders like himself were creating the first operating systems that would become the foundation of today's digital world. At home in this milieu, Murray worked as a software engineer for forty years.

According to his old colleague Dave Curry, Murray was a "superprogrammer." His colleagues knew him as "a genius who could program anything," but not a big talker. (Except when it came to critiquing the shortcomings of commercial software—all modesty aside, Murray didn't suffer fools.)

Dave also remembers that Murray never concerned himself with money. On payday, Murray would put his check in a desk drawer and forget about it. They would pile up until someone reminded him to cash them. During an interview at a new project he was recruited for, Murray was asked what his current salary was, and he didn't know.

On Friday afternoons, Dave and Murray and a few other programmers would gather at The Garret—a pizza place with big tables and peanut shells on the floor—to talk shop and blow off steam. Together they would solve the world's problems over pitchers of beer.

Murray began going to punk shows in 1979 when a co-worker took him to see the Mutants at the Mab. It must have been a thrilling time to be coding the future in Silicon Valley by day, and seeing bands in sweaty basements and ad hoc punk spaces by night. These distinct and disparate histories were unfolding simultaneously, and Murray was immersed in them both.

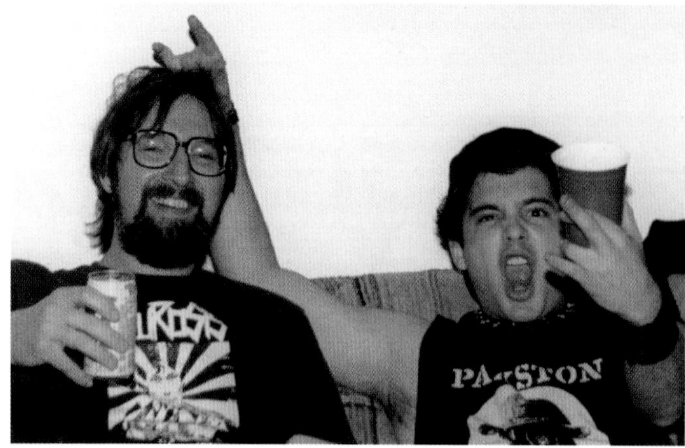

Murray and Greg, 1993 (Photo by Anna Brown)

Murray also played viola, and was a member of the Peninsula Symphony for twenty-six years. Longtime conductor Mitchell Klein recalls Murray as an accurate and exacting musician, and also "the most congenial, unobtrusive, easy, positive team player." After Murray's death, everyone in the symphony was shocked to learn that their violist was a legendary punk photographer. "He lived a clearly segmented life, and was successful in everything he did," Mitchell told me. "But Murray was not a diva. He just seemed genuinely, harmoniously happy in each of his separate worlds."

Indeed, Murray kept his worlds very separate. Just as his co-workers in Silicon Valley knew nothing about his life in the underground, his family had no idea that he had another family of sorts in the punk scene. Kathy describes how he would leave a family gathering, saying that he was "going to a show," and none of them knew what he was talking about. Meanwhile, most of the punks—arguably the people who knew him best—were clueless that he was a notorious superprogrammer and an accomplished classical musician.

Murray learned how to develop film from his grandfather, Roscoe Charles Bowles, and started out, by his own account, as "a nature photography kind of guy." Scattered throughout the archives are pictures of lakes, birds, and

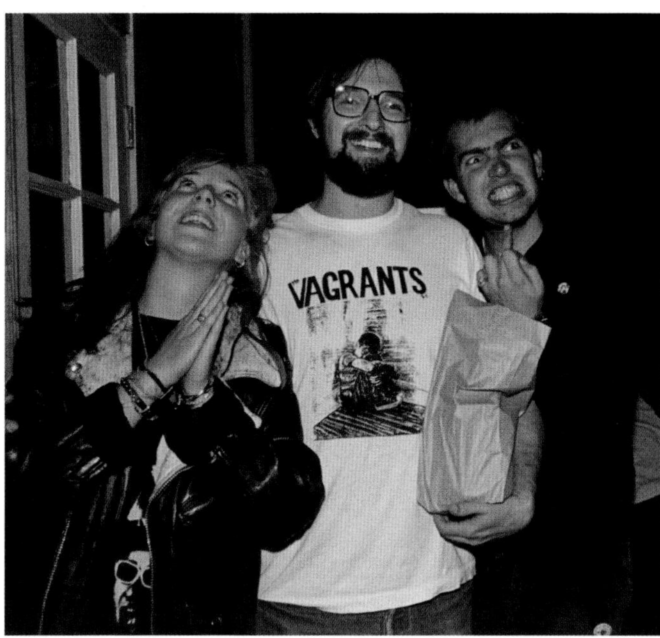

La, Murray, and Jake, 1989 (Photo by Anna Brown)

mountaintops taken on camping trips in the Sierras with his dad. When the music drew him into the basements and warehouses of the punk scene, Murray discovered an entirely different landscape, and found his vocation as its compulsive documentarian. (Compulsive, yes, but not indiscriminate. He didn't go to just any show. He generally had to like at least one band on the bill. No funk, rarely metal. Never, ever new wave.)

If we're to judge by the photo record, by the early eighties Murray was going to two or three shows every week. He got his first photo assignment from Tim Tonooka of *Ripper*, a punk zine out of San Jose. Tim showed Murray how to move around the room and shoot from different angles and perspectives, rather than staying in one place. It wasn't long before Murray developed his personal style: close-cropped action shots that exude an unselfconscious irreverence.

Murray soon met Tim Yohannan and ended up taking loads of pictures for *Maximum Rocknroll*—because, as Murray said in his usual unassuming way, "they printed anything." These images captivated young rockers from all over the world, and motivated hundreds of them to pack up their van and move to the Bay to take part in this exhilarating second wave of punk.

In true punk form, Murray was never out to make money from his photos—and indeed, he never did. He allowed countless bands to use his work in their album art, granting permission for nothing more than a photo credit. The sheer number of credits is staggering. His work

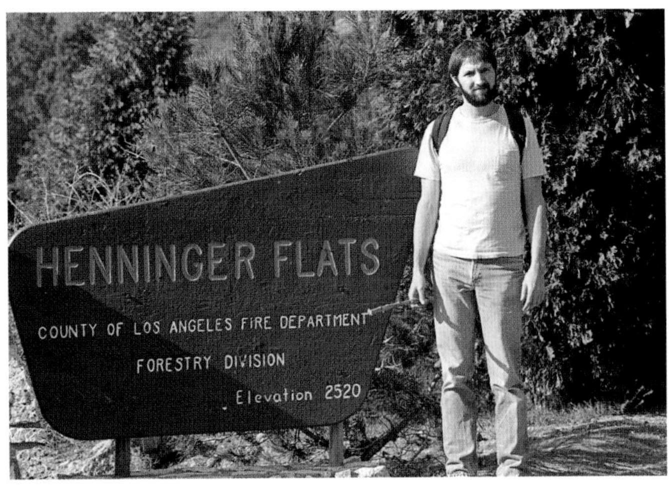
Murray on hiking trip, 1993

appeared on the covers and in liner notes of all the classic records of the era, including Jawbreaker *Unfun*, Raw Power *Screams from the Gutter*, Operation Ivy *Energy*, Neurosis *The Word as Law*, and a multitude of albums by the Minutemen, Fang, Verbal Abuse, Crimpshrine, Doughboys, SNFU, Offspring, Green Day, Corrosion of Conformity, Youth of Today, Schlong, No Use for a Name, Blatz, and Attitude Adjustment—just to name a few.

Murray gave away priceless negatives and obliged any band who asked by sending them pictures of their show for free. Even when *Rolling Stone* occasionally came calling for the "when they were young" images of bands like Green Day and Operation Ivy that only Murray had, he never used contracts or charged what his pictures were worth. Just like in his programming life, Murray's desk drawers were littered with uncashed checks from VH1.

Murray spent countless hours on his photography, but he was always open to side projects. He teamed up with pal Eric Yee to form M&E Records so they could put out the 1992 Grimple LP, *Grimple Up Your Ass*. (Grimple had arrived in the Bay from New Mexico two years earlier and quickly became one of Murray's all-time favorite bands to photograph.) Later Murray and Lenny Johnson formed East Bay Menace Records and put out a dozen LPs, including a Grimple/Logical Nonsense split and the 1995 comp, *Shit Gets Smashed*.

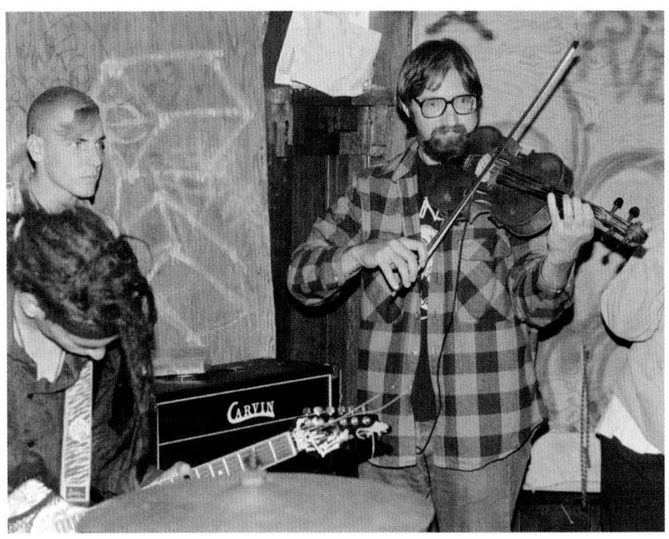
Murray performing with 23 More Minutes, 1991

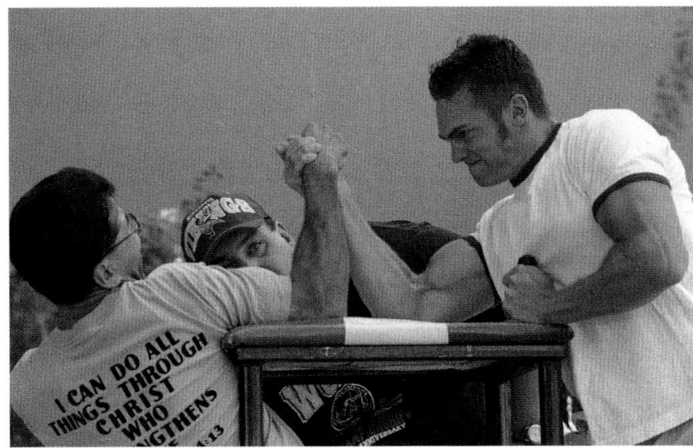

Arm wrestling contest, 2008

Over the years, Murray also found time for a bunch of musical experiments. In 1980, Murray sang for a punk band called the Clots. After the punks heard he played viola, there were viola guest spots with Grinch, 23 More Minutes, and others. Finally he played fiddle in country punk bands Ding Dang and the Shitkickers, and found he enjoyed being on the stage himself.

Over the years, Murray's eye grew more tender and his camera gravitated to more personal subjects: his friends. The archives are overflowing with images of punk rockers drinking and laughing, or lost in quiet moments of contemplation. His affection for his subjects is unmistakable. When he appears in his own negatives, it was usually because he was a little wasted and let me or another friend mess around with his camera for a while.

We took great pleasure in turning the lens on him, happy and content, surrounded by his people.

Murray never stopped searching for excitement and photographic inspiration. Around 2000, he became obsessed with competitive arm wrestling. His archives contain hundreds of photos of these contests, taken at places like the San Benito County Fair or the Huck Finn Jubilee. A world apart from punk, these images nonetheless contain some of the same visceral intensity as those of thrashers in the pit. Murray once told me, "In a way, arm wrestling is more underground than punk."

Murray's body of work is likely the largest individual collection of punk photographs in the world. It has a deep relevance—not just to Murray's friends, who saw themselves grow up in his pictures, or to music fans who crave images of bygone days, but to the world. The Bay Area scene was special in many ways, from the cheeky political attitude we were steeped in from birth, to the unique spaces that showcased the music and art: Tool & Die, the Vats (an old Hamm's brewery, squatted by San Francisco punks), New Method (a warehouse art space and show venue that housed dozens of weirdos), Barrington Hall (a debauched student co-op just off the Berkeley campus), 924 Gilman (Berkeley's famous all-ages, volunteer-run punk club), Ruthie's Inn, the Farm, Mabuhay Gardens, On Broadway, and seemingly

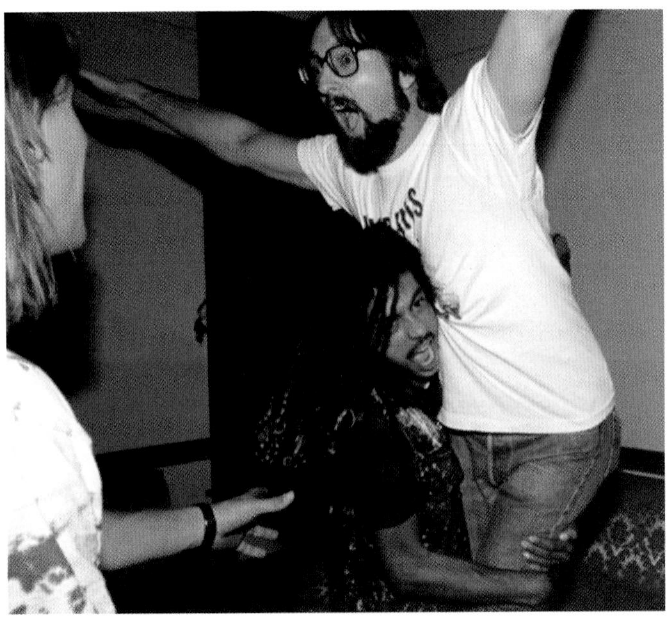

Murray and Sham, 1989

hundreds of backyards—Eggplant's house in the 'burbs, the Pill Hill Zoo House, and so many others—where punks regularly gathered to make noise and party.

If Murray's work is "about" anything, it's about the joy of punk. Going through his archives, you come away feeling that Murray's mission, in simplest terms, was to celebrate the feeling of being there on any given night or afternoon—the collective energy of a singular moment. He certainly wasn't out to glorify his experience, or any individual. He shot people as they were—flashbulb in the face, often in moments of exultation.

He rarely photographed bands from below in a way that would make them look larger than life. He wasn't looking to elevate anyone as a rockstar. Nor was he interested in sensational punk grit, or violence. As Murray said in *Turn It Around*, "I have hardly any pictures of people beating up people and stuff like that. Because I didn't want to be encouraging it, by capturing images. I tried to take pictures of people having fun or being sort of aggressive, but not being jerks."

Murray's talent was for capturing the room, which was as much about the audience as the bands playing. Indeed, it's not uncommon to scan a whole roll of film that's labeled, say, "Victim's_Family_Santa_Rosa_8_16_91," and find not a single picture of the band. Often something else would catch Murray's eye and all thirty-six shots

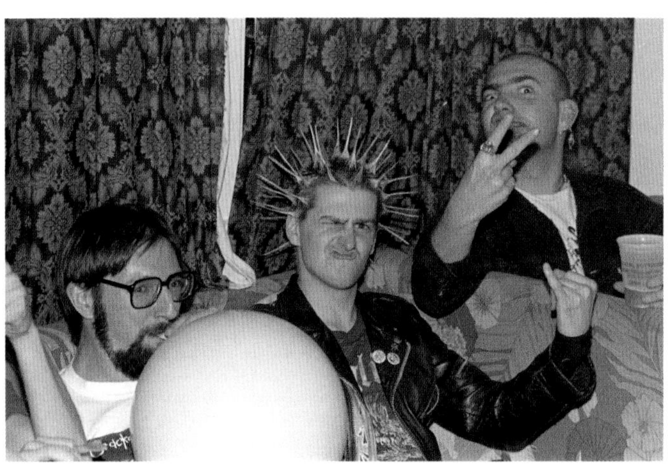

Murray with Jim and Jake at the Maxi Pad, 1991

would be of people drinking beer on the roof, of skaters in the parking lot, or some radiant stranger ruling the pit.

Murray was content to make his work and contribute to his community without any major accolades. He was deeply revered by the punks, but in thirty-five years, he only showed his work once, in 2001, at the Red Door, an East Oakland warehouse gallery. He simply took any 4x5 prints he had lying around, mounted them on foamboard, and stuck them to the wall. The East Bay punks were out in force for the opening but for the general public, Murray's work remained under the radar.

Murray published just one photozine, *If Life Is a Bowl of Cherries, What Am I Doing in the Pit?* in 1986. It was compiled and edited in a marathon session with Tim Yohannan, Martin Sprouse, and Cynthia Connolly, the only criteria being the pictures had to be taken in the Bay Area (the same criteria as this book, though we made exceptions for a few photos taken in LA). MRR printed 10,000 copies, which are now highly sought after.

Even as Murray so studiously avoided the spotlight, he couldn't escape the measure of celebrity that came with being featured in Richie Bucher's cover art for *Dookie*, Green Day's major label debut. In Bucher's illustration, the dookie bombs are falling on us all—the cops and the suits, the miscreants and clowns. The world is one big unruly shit-mosh, and Murray is there in the middle of it all, glasses, beard, one-handing his camera above his head, capturing the chaos in his signature Hail Mary style.

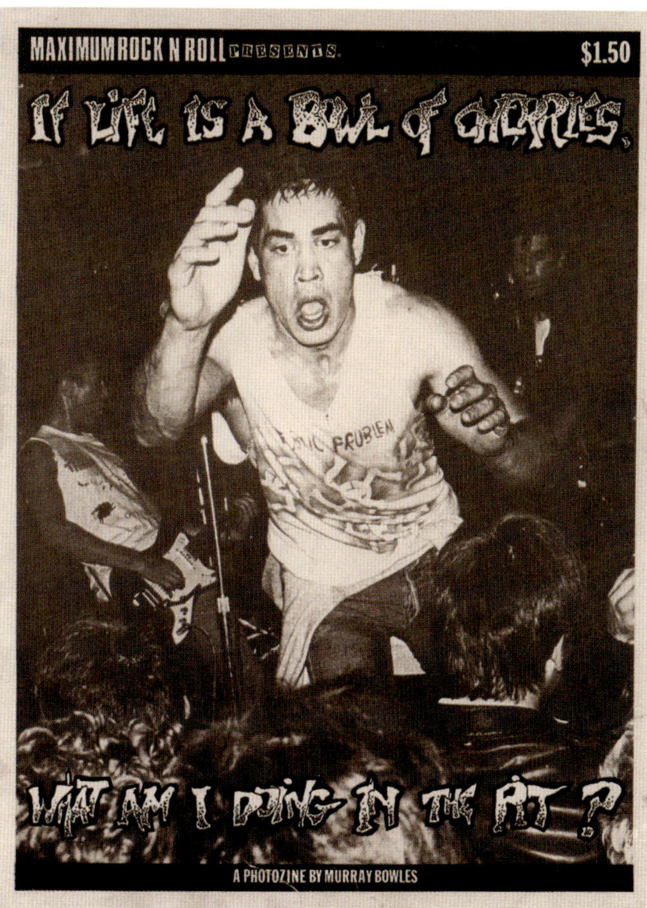

If Life Is a Bowl of Cherries, What Am I Doing in the Pit?, 1986

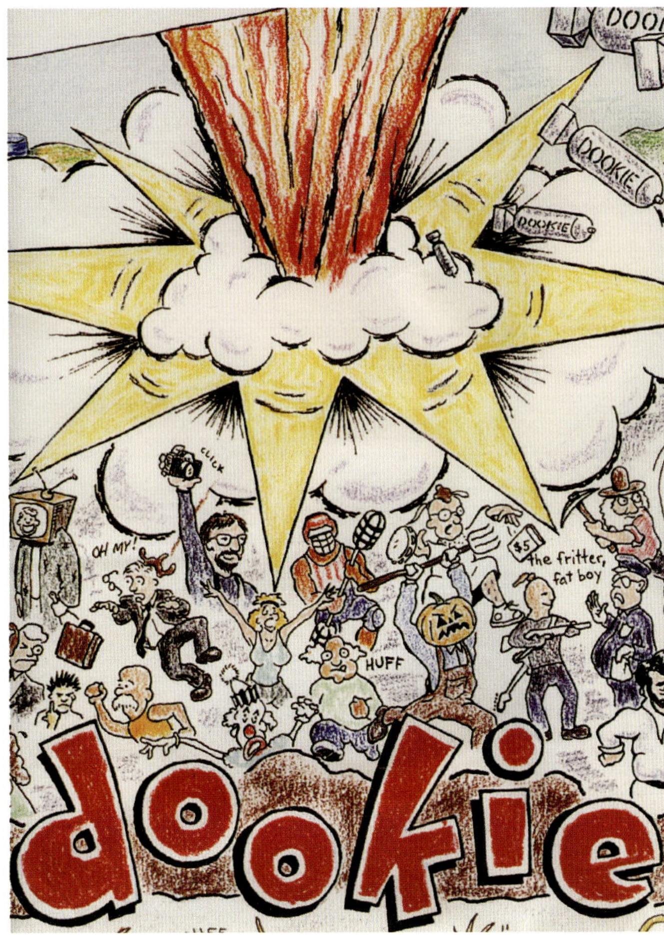

Detail: Cover of Green Day's *Dookie*, 1994, by Richie Bucher

Murray was always confounded by the way total strangers, for years after, would peg him for the cartoon photographer on the cover of *Dookie*. "People keep recognizing me, even today," he would say. "They say, 'you're that guy that…' and I'm like, 'Really? How can you tell?'" He could never quite believe that people could make the connection, but of course Bucher's image is pure Murray Bowles.

At the time of Murray's death he was excited to be working on this, his first ever perfect-bound monograph. He selected many of the photos but seemed unaware of just how mind-blowing and special his work truly was. Some of the pictures are historically significant— he captured early images of so many legendary bands, interiors of forgotten venues, long-dead personalities. Others are great works of art, up there with the best of rock and roll photography, getting at the heart of what live music does. You feel them in your gut.

I first met Murray when I was fourteen. He was outside Gilman Street, selling his pictures out of an old Ilford box. I'd only been going to shows for a few weeks, but he was already a familiar face. Murray soon became a lifelong friend. Together we went to countless shows (Davis, Guerneville, Santa Rosa, LA, even Tijuana), to art films and museums, beer gardens, and many, many parties. In the early days, Murray drove a convertible Cabriolet that fit at least four people in the back and three in the front, and he was always down for anything.

I never understood why he didn't have a book, or many books, of his work. So finally I pestered him into making one. We were hard at work gathering images when he died, leaving a giant void in our hearts and our community.

Murray and I worked on this book on and off for several years, but the negatives were endless, and we barely scratched the surface. Murray always said he would just "write a program" to organize it all. I was assured the task wouldn't fall to me. My plan was for Murray to direct and me to produce. I'm still devastated that this book wasn't finished in time for him to revel, even a bit, in his own legacy.

After Murray's death I called in my old friend Eric Yee, who with his encyclopedic knowledge of East Bay punk and tireless scanning, helped the book take shape. In selecting images, we tried to be as democratic as Murray was about taking them. Obviously, some people pictured turned out to be assholes, or worse. Inclusion of certain unsavory characters in these pages is in no way an endorsement of their actions or beliefs.

How does one approach an archive of this size? It's been a huge and terrifying endeavor. Inevitably, hard choices were made. Above all, I've tried to do justice to Murray's talent and aesthetic. I hope what comes through is a tribute to Murray—his artistic vision and the unforgettable person he was. I also looked for pictures that no one had seen, of spaces with the lowest ceilings and poles running right through the pit, and I sought to challenge some of the persistent stereotypes of what the scene was and is (all white, all dudes). This part wasn't hard, as Murray saw everyone. He was never cynical or jaded about the scene. Quite the contrary. Everything he did was a celebration of what it means to be in love with the world. What a gift it is to see it through his eyes.

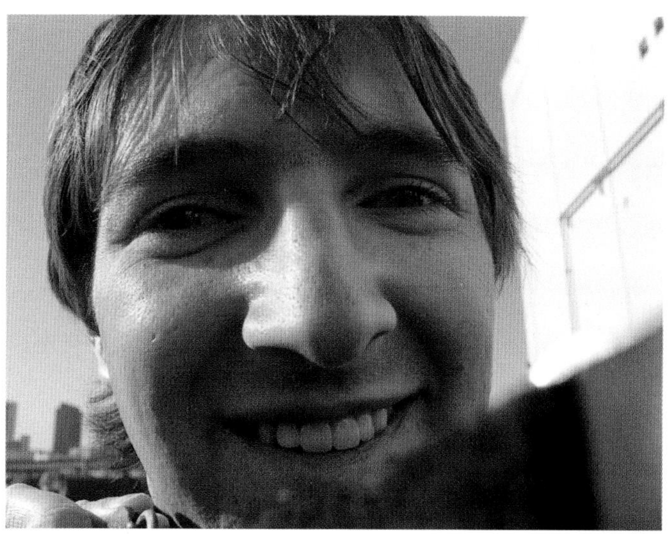

Murray self portrait at the Vats, 1984

Chronicler of the Lost

by Aaron Cometbus

Books about punk have a predictable arc: the scene is authentic and pure until the year the author drops out.

Punk documentaries are the same. To believe them, nothing will ever be as real as Detroit in '82 or London in '76. Prizes are passed out to the pioneers who gave up or died first. Everything that came after is fake and second rate, and no group can be celebrated without putting down everyone that followed in their wake.

When the photos in this book were taken we were constantly being told that we'd missed the boat. According to *RE/Search*'s V. Vale, punk had changed from a "genuine underground... however brief" to "mere style... or a violent simulation." He put hardcore in quotes. We didn't and don't.

Murray's photos put a lie to all those self-serving storylines, and the idea that punk can be carved up and cut off from the root, or claimed by any one group. They show Bay Area punk—and by extension the whole international scene—as one continuous thread, one fluid motion, one long gig. No hardcore era of violence, no Gilman era of rebirth, no stretch after the first wave where punk was just white, male, and straight.

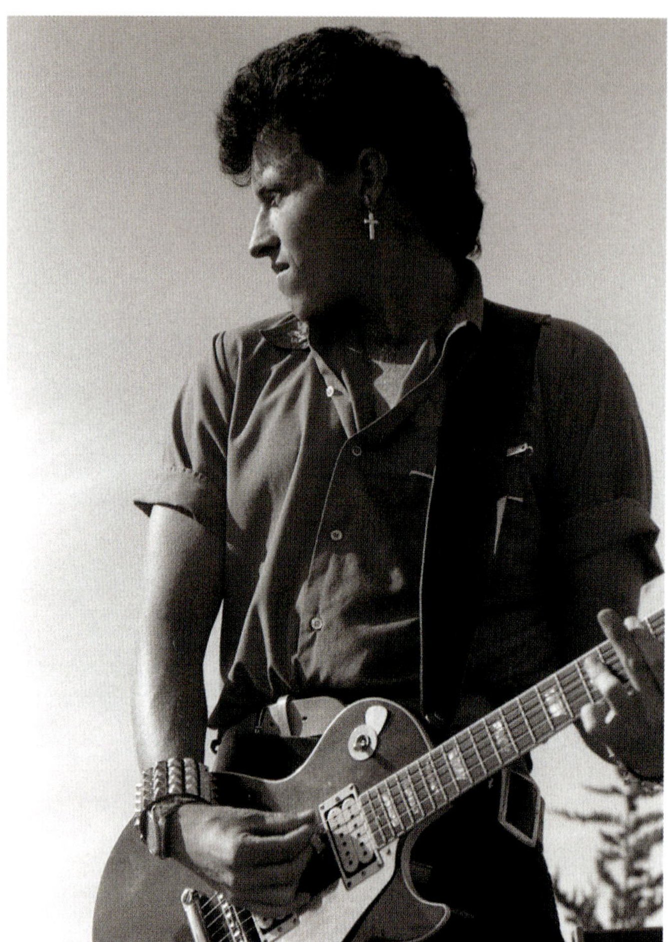

Shattered Faith, Berkeley, 1982

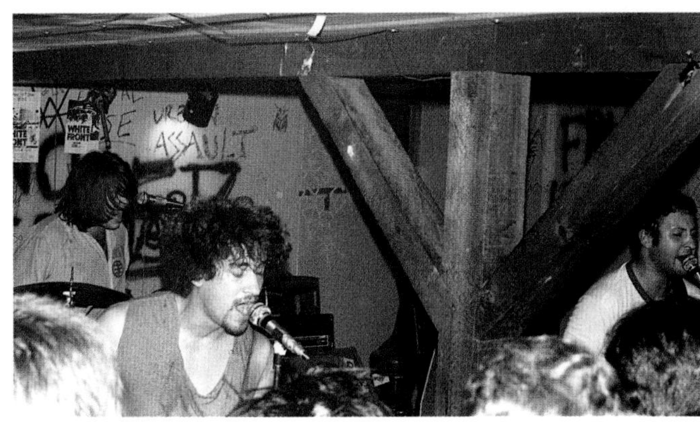

Hüsker Dü, Tool & Die, 1983

The events captured here were ecstatic and fun, *actually* all-ages affairs that brought together weirdos who wouldn't fit in anywhere else. There were always mysterious people in the mix, some much older and some just little kids—but none as mysterious and beloved as Murray, and none as unanimously accepted and entrusted with representing the scene.

That says something about Bay Area punk, but also about the man. Murray was a comforting presence. He was gentle, and his bear-like, beer-like demeanor put everyone at ease. He was composed rather than reserved, naturally quiet with a shy and slightly sly grin. He looked on benevolently and without judgment, like no adult in our lives.

He was not parental but also—apologies to some of my friends—not a permanent, overgrown kid. He was always an adult, with a job and a whole other existence we didn't discuss, though there was nothing unusual about that. We all led bifurcated lives, whether *MRR*'s Chairman Yo carrying dinosaur bones at his day job at the Lawrence Hall of Science, or the families and home lives we all tried to hide.

The mischievous gleam in his eye was not readily apparent in his person, but it was evident in every picture he took. Murray loved chaos and rambunctious fun. He loved people completely lost in the moment, with wide grins revealing missing teeth. He loved morons, recognizing a saintliness in their lack of guile and pretension—kindred spirits, I think, for Murray himself.

He was no voyeur like some photographers on the scene, and every photographer in the mainstream. He just loved recklessness and its joyous release. It's true he didn't want to encourage people hurting each other, but part of the fun of his photos is how close everyone is to hurting themselves. There are stagedives that couldn't have ended well, and the ubiquitous posts in the middle of clubs which sent a lot of punks straight from the pit to the ER.

His way of distributing his work was part of the charm. You discovered it when a stranger handed you a stack of

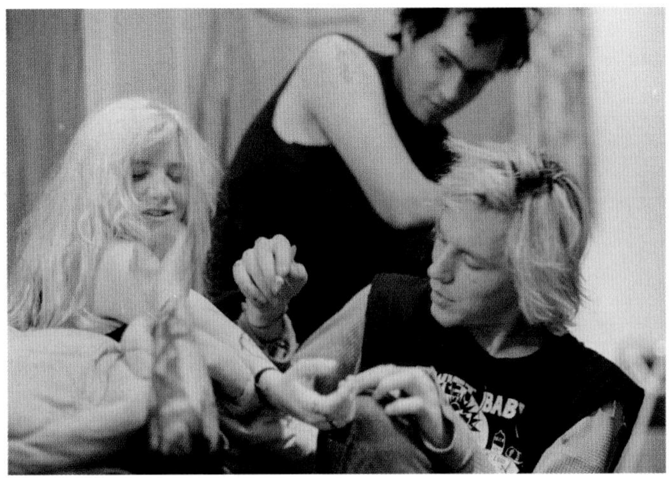

Anna, Jake, and Aaron at the Ashtray, 1989

black-and-white prints at a gig, which you pored over then instinctively passed on. It took weeks or months to figure out where these photos were originating, and that they could be purchased if you could find Murray in the crowd.

He captured a whole era we would have little proof of otherwise. The journalists and art school crowd had disappeared with the advent of hardcore, and it was fifteen years before cameras reappeared at gigs, when the possibility of commercial success reared its head once more.

He was the only one steadily taking photos at Bay Area shows in the years between. There was even a sign at Gilman hanging behind the bands, "Photo by Murray Bowles." *Maximum Rocknroll* shitworkers had erected it

so they wouldn't have to paste his name on every photo credit in the magazine.

The lack of documentation—until now—has made it easy for people to imagine the worst about that period, or to spin tall tales about why they stayed away.

Was there violence? Sure. Bob Noxious from the Fuck-Ups went through a phase where he attacked every out-of-town singer onstage. We just avoided the On Broadway

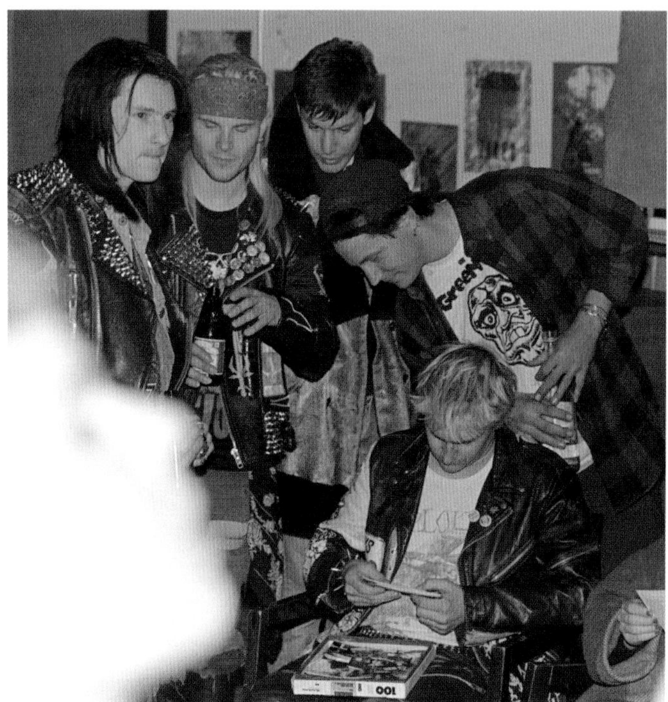

Looking through Murray photos at 7th St Warehouse, 1991

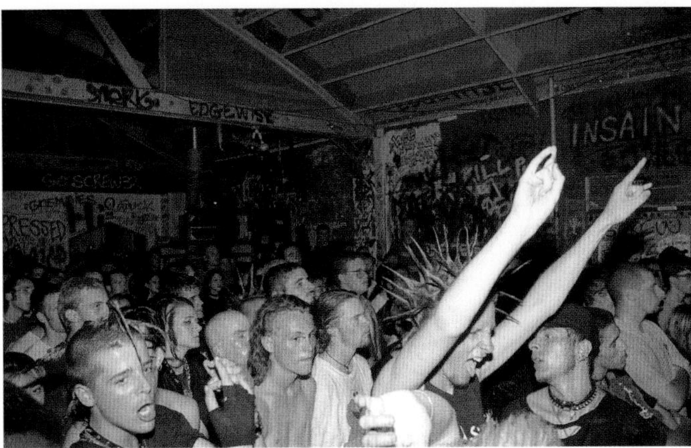

Crowd at Neurosis show, Gilman Street, 1995

He was our historical record, and part of that was capturing the marginal figures, too—the people on the edge of the crowd, the wonderful (and not so wonderful) "losers of the year" who passed through our scene without leaving a traceable name.

Some are remembered and some are not; some are dead but all are lost. Their face in a Murray pic is the only memento they left. For me, these passing figures are the ones that capture the passionate and fleeting nature of punk best.

for a while, and went to the Tool & Die instead, where there was no stage, and most of the bands were local. Like most problems, Bob passed before long.

Without risks there are no rewards, which is why Murray found it hilarious when people tried to warn him before stagediving, lest he or his camera get hurt.

His focus changed over the years, mirroring the changing focus of punk as the gaze moved from the stage to the personal and day-to-day.

He knew everyone's crushes based on which prints they bought, but he never gossiped or let on. He just made multiple copies of the pictures he knew would be popular, whether of bands or the charismatic locals Murray had a knack for catching right as they were coming into bloom.

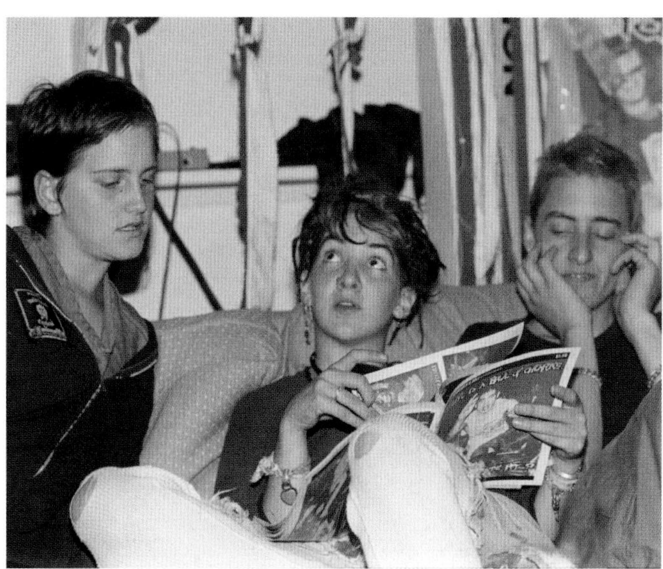

Ivy, Robin, and Tony reading *If Life Is a Bowl of Cherries*, 1992

Murray Interviewed for *MRR*

by Anna and Aaron, 2010

How did you get started on this path?

I got started as a backpacker, taking pictures of nature. I moved to the Bay Area as a student at Berkeley from 1973 to 1976. Then I began working as a computer programmer in San Jose and some of the people who worked with me were into the punk scene. Tim Tonooka from *Ripper* enlisted me to write reviews for the magazine in 1982. Some other people at my job volunteered at Target Video. Tim used to take all the pictures for *Ripper*, but one day he asked me to do it when he couldn't make it to a show. I had fun and I started bringing my camera to every show I went to. It was addictive.

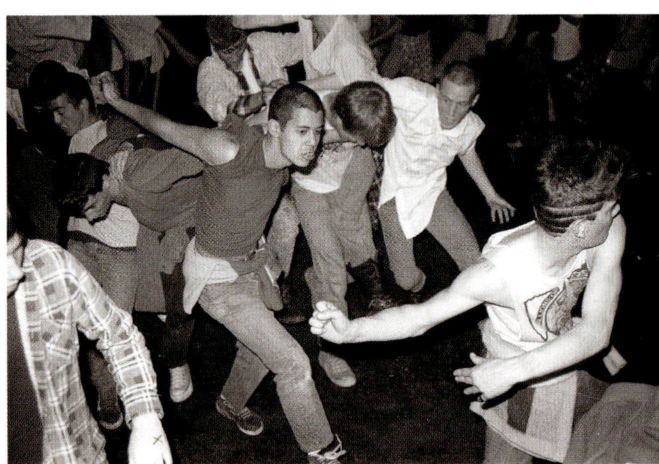

On Broadway, 1983

How did you learn photography?

My grandfather taught me the kitchen developing technique. He used to do amazing trick photography, like making us look like midgets, peering around coffee cans.

How many cameras have been destroyed at shows?

No cameras have been destroyed, but lots of flashes. They get smashed, and the batteries tend to fall out and fly all over the place.

Stagedivers must know to avoid hitting you by now.

I learned some things, like how to protect my face. That's how the point-and-shoot method evolved—you have to avoid holding the camera up to your face.

You are always in the audience, never on the side of the stage or in the front row. So your pictures capture the audience perspective, in the middle of the action.

Yeah, I have never liked those guys who shoot metal bands with the ultra wide-angle lenses and a huge flash, taking dozens of the same shot.

How did your style evolve—was it a moral or aesthetic choice?

I try to get shots of everybody. Drummers are hard because if you're in the audience lots of things get in the way. I have gotten good at shooting the singer without the microphone in their mouth. The first shows I went to were at places like the Mab. I went with the Target Video guys to all sorts of obscure shows at strange venues. Al Flipside was very influential, too. He encouraged everyone to be more than just a witness to the scene. To do something useful. Taking pictures got me more into things. I wasn't just a record collector that went to shows anymore.

How was it seeing your work published?

My pictures moved from *Ripper* to *MRR*. I did guest DJ spots on MRR Radio, and bands started contacting me for pictures. Tim Yohannan was often looking for something specific, and he would go through my pictures. I also started printing 4x5s and selling them at shows.

How did people respond? What surprised you about their reactions?

Well, it always surprises me when people want copies of crummy photos. They don't care if it's barely in focus if it's of the right people. Bands always want pictures with all the members showing, but it's really hard. I tend to take pictures of one to two people. People bought a lot of pictures of crowd shots, depending on who was there that night.

You must have learned a lot of secrets—the secret social life of the scene.

I don't know about that, but you do begin to notice who reacts in what way to other people in pictures. I sold multiple copies of certain people. Over time I moved off the stage and started focusing more on individual people and less on the stage. Stages are still kind of ideal, though. They are usually elevated, wide, and provide a natural view. But pictures of people playing pool in the back of the club, for example, can be as interesting as a band playing.

Whatever the subject is, you always give the impression that you're right there involved in the action.

Yeah, well that's the punk party line: "No boundaries between the band and the crowd." It's nice to be able to show that. At this punk house in San Jose last year there were shows where the whole scene was crowded into this tiny basement. Sometimes the bands were good; always the people were fun.

Your photos are on tons of albums, how did that happen?

It just happened. The Raw Power album was put out by someone from LA who contacted me. I think I ran into Mike Watt at Al's Bar when they were screening the world premiere of *Desperate Teenage Love Dolls* and I happened to have some pictures with me.

When your photos appeared on albums, people really started to know you and your work. How did *If Life Is a Bowl of Cherries, What Am I Doing in the Pit?* come about?

Maximum Rocknroll published *If Life Is a Bowl of Cherries* in 1987 or so. Glen Friedman was making a photo zine at the time and *Maximum* was probably influenced by that. It was Tim's idea. But in *MRR*'s effort to economize, they used cheap paper that turned yellow. I heard they ended up scrapping a whole bunch of them.

It was great, though. Weren't you proud?

Yeah, I was proud.

Any more plans for books?

Yeah, there are plans.

So who are your favorite subjects to shoot? Orlando comes to mind...

Yeah, Orlando is reliable. Bob Noxious, Mark Dagger, Jello...

Who was an impossible subject?

Well, Capitol Punishment was surprisingly hard. They always came out overexposed. Agent Orange was hard, so was Naked Raygun. With some bands there is just always more action in the music than on stage. Grimple was the ideal band to take pictures of.

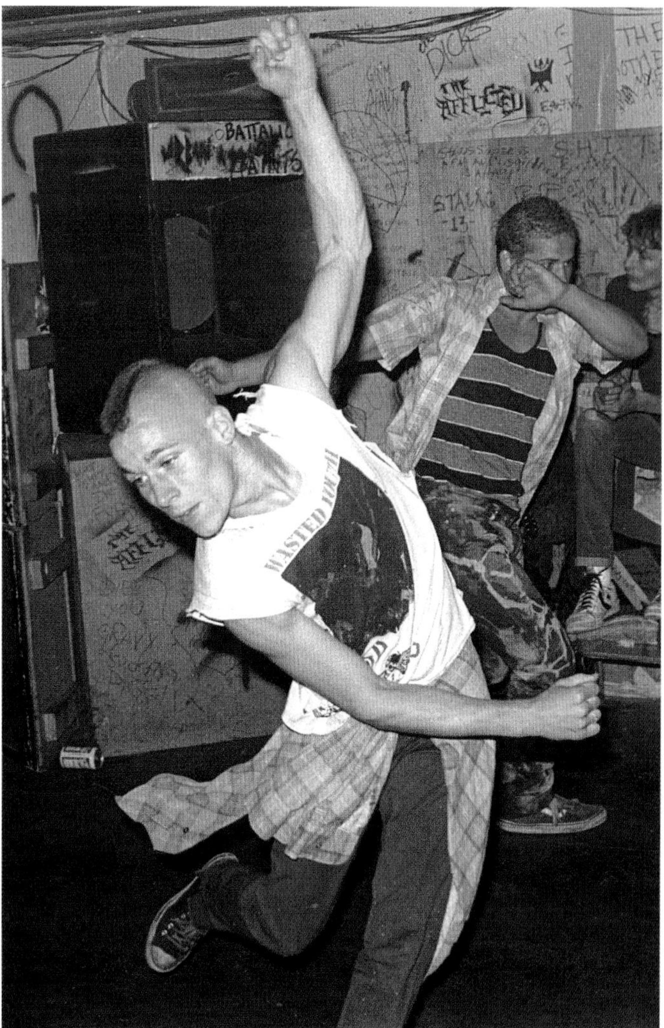

Tool & Die, 1983

Your pictures are characterized by a sense of playfulness and lack of pretense. There's something so charming about that.

Capturing people having fun is always fun. There was this real public perception of punk violence, moshing, and danger. It's nice to show it can be both ways. It can be fun to be violent.

So what are you actually taking pictures of?

The energy and interactions. The crowd as much as the band.

So shows that lack certain things aren't good.

Yeah, I don't want to take pictures of people standing around, holding cigarettes in the air. There have to be good vibes, but not mindless happiness. Emo shows are unsatisfactory.

For so many reasons.

There has to be happiness and energy.

How does that mesh with your more recent subjects of arm wrestling competitions?

Wrestling compared to punk captures some of the same intensity. Faces and motion—the physical expression of drama.

Like photographing drummers?

Kind of like that.

Talk about transitioning from photographer to musician on stage.

Well, even before I started playing with Ding Dang, two co-workers—Randy, the Target Video guy, and Rich, a record collector—and I were in the Clots. Rich and I sang. This was like 1980. Later various people heard I played viola in the symphony. So that led to collaborations with Grinch, Brian Stern, 23 More Minutes, and others. I ended up playing fiddle in Ding Dang.

How was it going from private to public? It's nice to see background people on the stage, like Marshall going from doing sound to playing in Blatz...

I'm not prone to stage fright, but being on a stage is different than playing in an orchestra. Like, making mistakes is no big deal when you're in a huge orchestra. But I guess it's not in punk, either. I got used to being a spectacle—the photo guy playing fiddle. For a while I was the new guy in the Shitkickers, but now people know me as a musician, too. It's kind of fun to play and tour and let other people take the pictures, but I still take pictures from the stage sometimes.

Do you think you were able to take such amazing candid pictures because everyone knew you and was comfortable with you?

It probably helped a lot. It's hard taking pictures where you don't know anyone. Or at a show at a teen center where everyone is really young—that's not right either. I'm not sure why people are so comfortable with me.

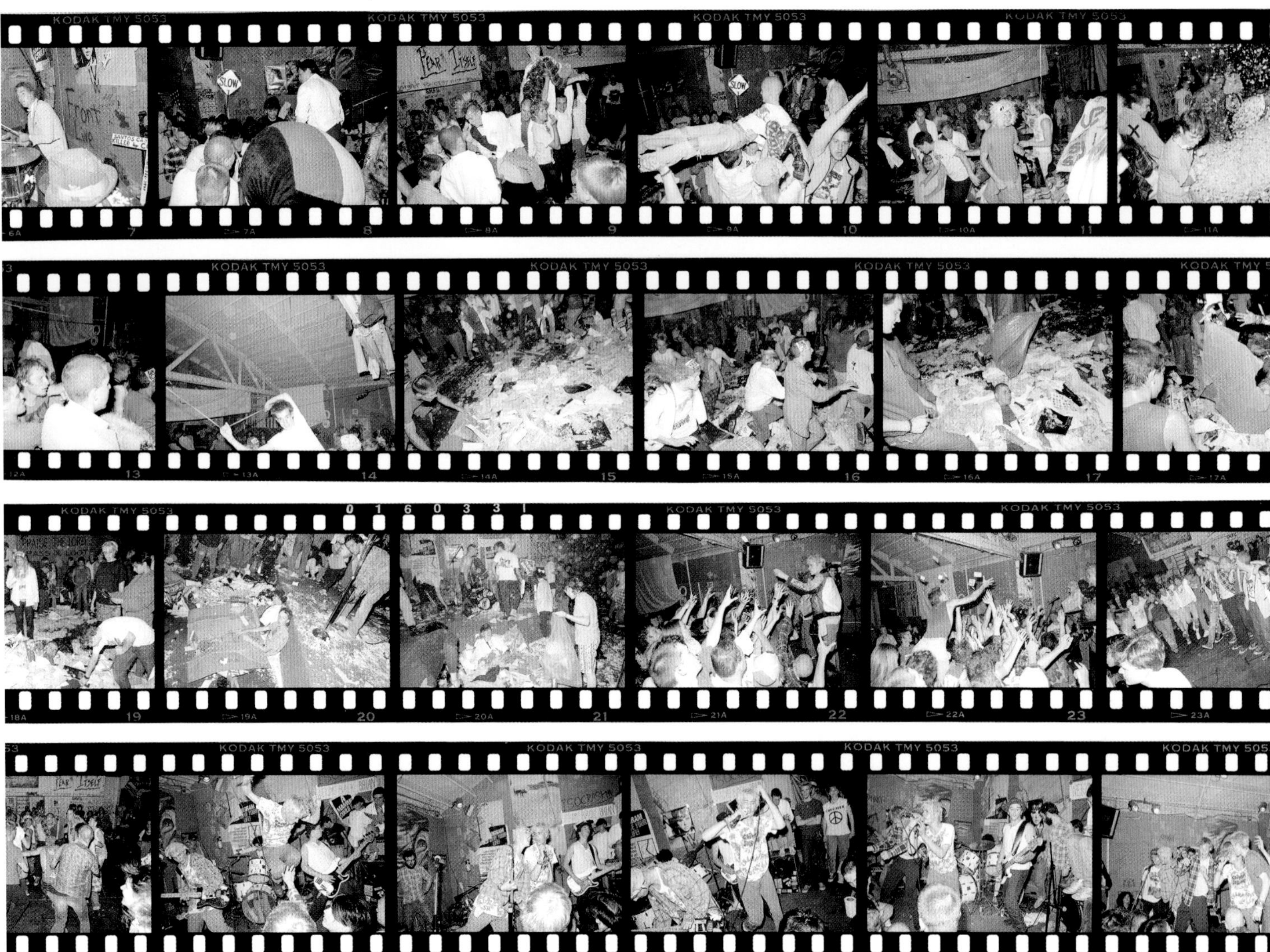

Isocracy and Operation Ivy, Gilman Street, 1987

I don't spend a lot of time looking through the viewfinder or arranging a shot.

So did taking pictures at shows change how you interacted with people?

Yeah, it kept me in the scene. It's a good way to meet people, and it gave me something to do. Now it seems pointless to go to a show without my camera, just a drink in my hand.

You must have amazing archives.

It's almost like my photos are more important to individual people than to the scene. People say to me all the time, "You have documented my life."

Did you ever accidentally capture something on film? Like in *Blow-Up*?

There's the heroic beer truck robbery at Eastern Front.

When I see Glen Friedman or Bob Gruen's work I think, "Where were you during the nineties? Did you still take pictures, but only of lousy bands no one wants to see?"

Maybe they didn't stick with the underground stuff very long.

Roberta Bayley did the same thing, Ed Colver... but you seem to have an enduring love for small, crappy bands.

Once the band gets bigger, the crowd gets diluted and the music gets watered down. Also the venues get bigger, and really annoying. They require special agreements to take pictures.

What would you like to see happen to your work?

A book is in the back of my mind. It would be easier to do new stuff, but the old stuff is more interesting to the people who can afford a coffee-table book. It would be nice to see the pictures printed on really good paper. I think it is important to document the Bay Area. Other scenes have been documented pretty well.

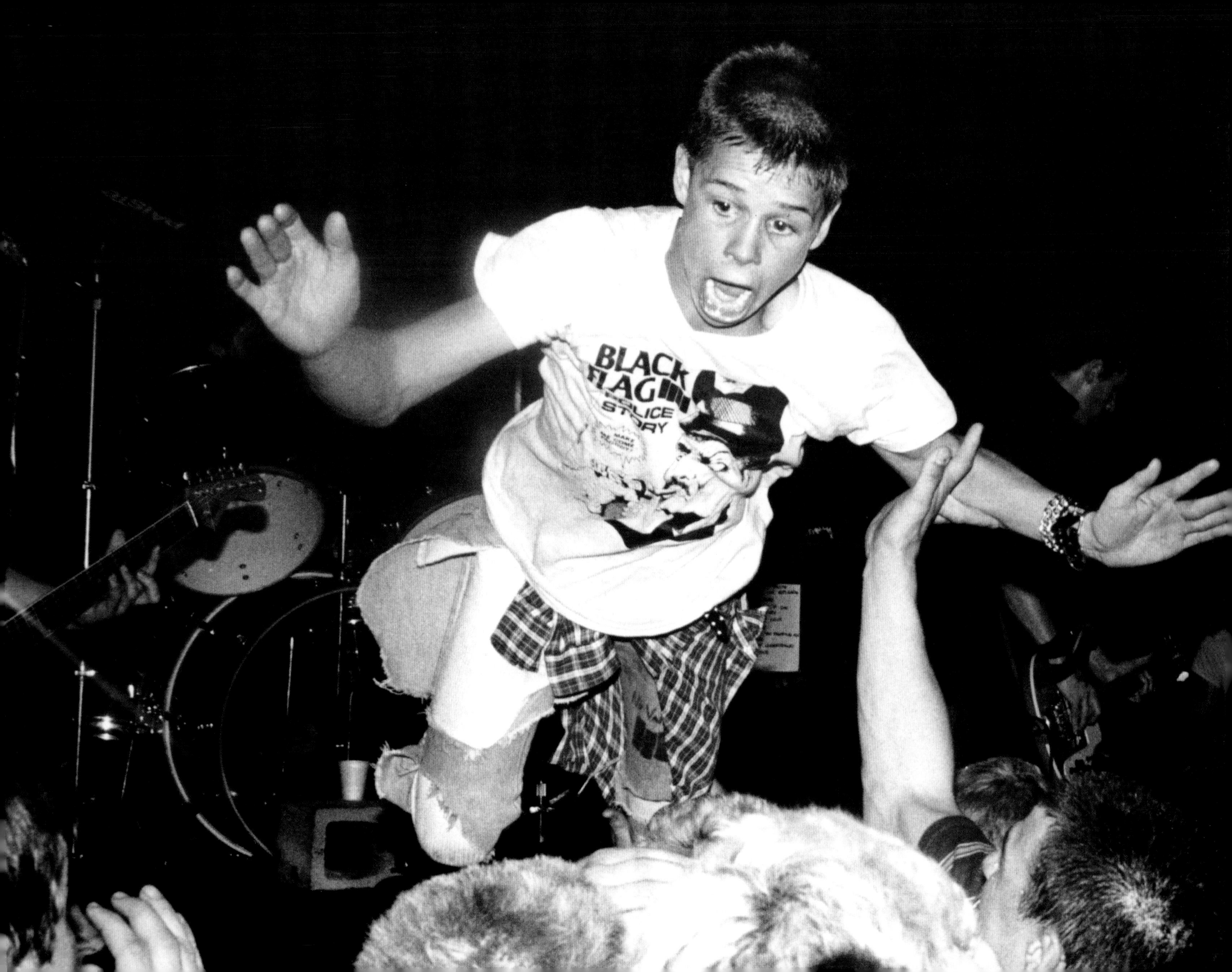
BLACK
FLAG
POLICE STORY

On Broadway, San Francisco, 1983

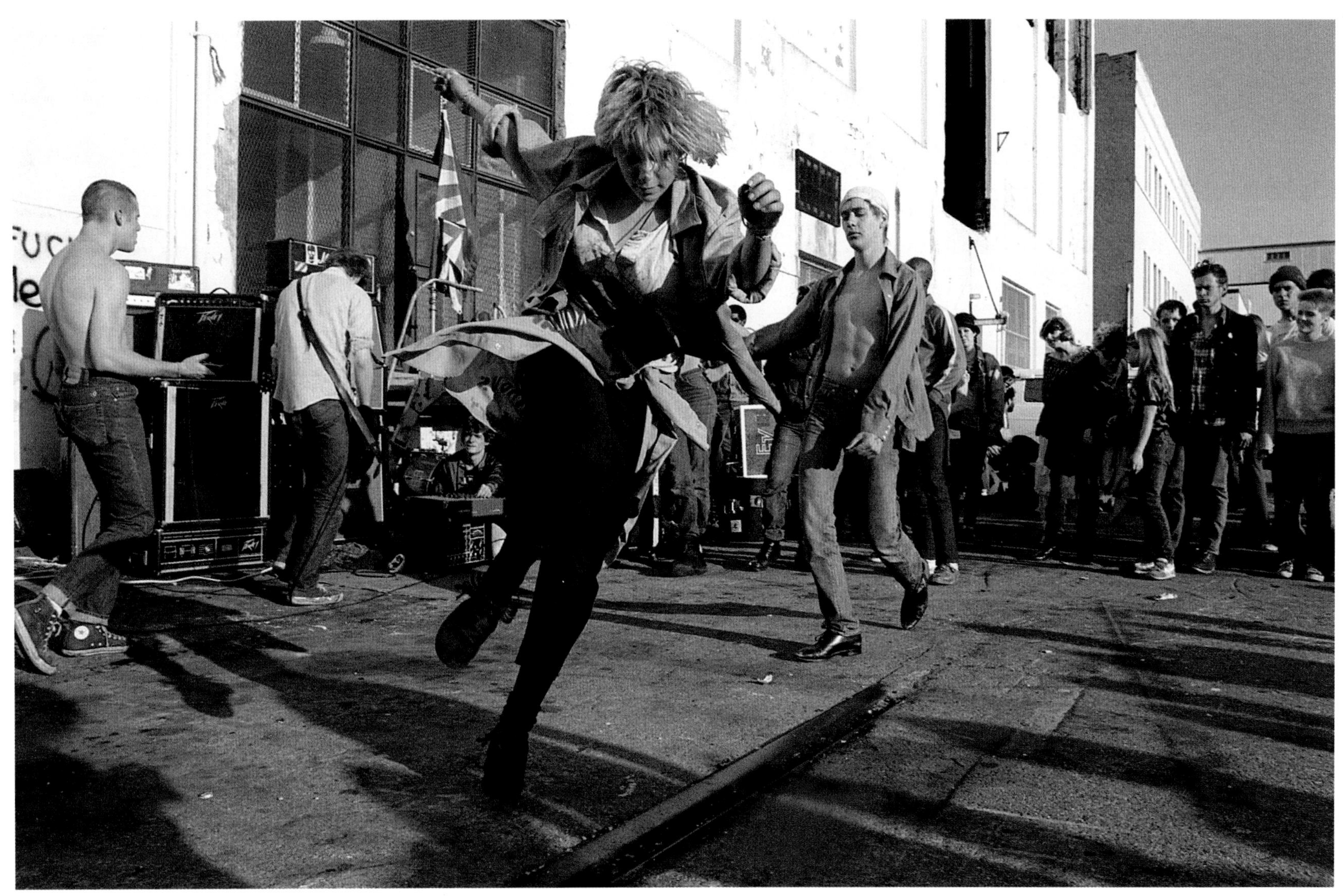

The Vats, San Francisco, 1984

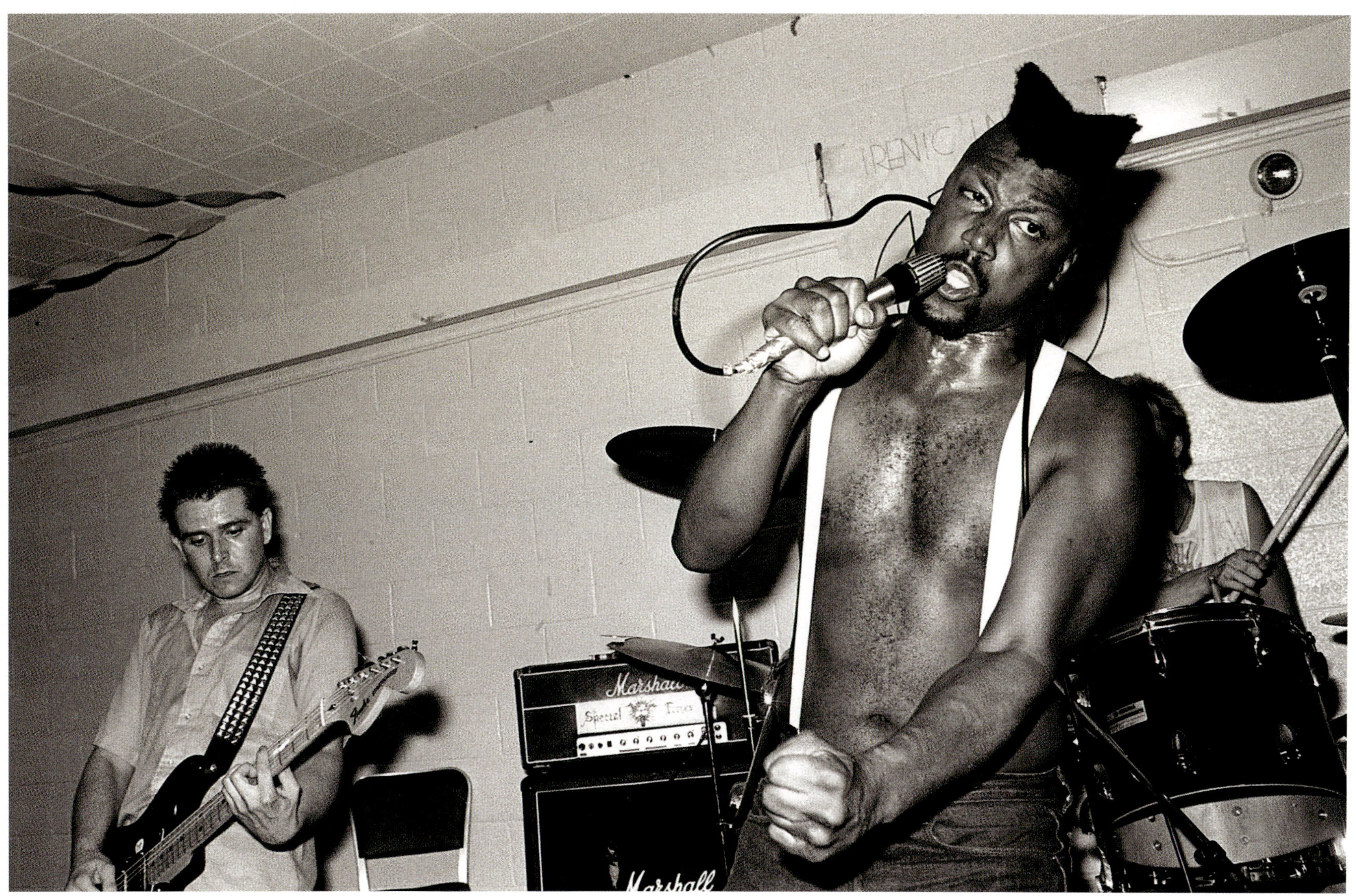

Special Forces

San Jose, 1984

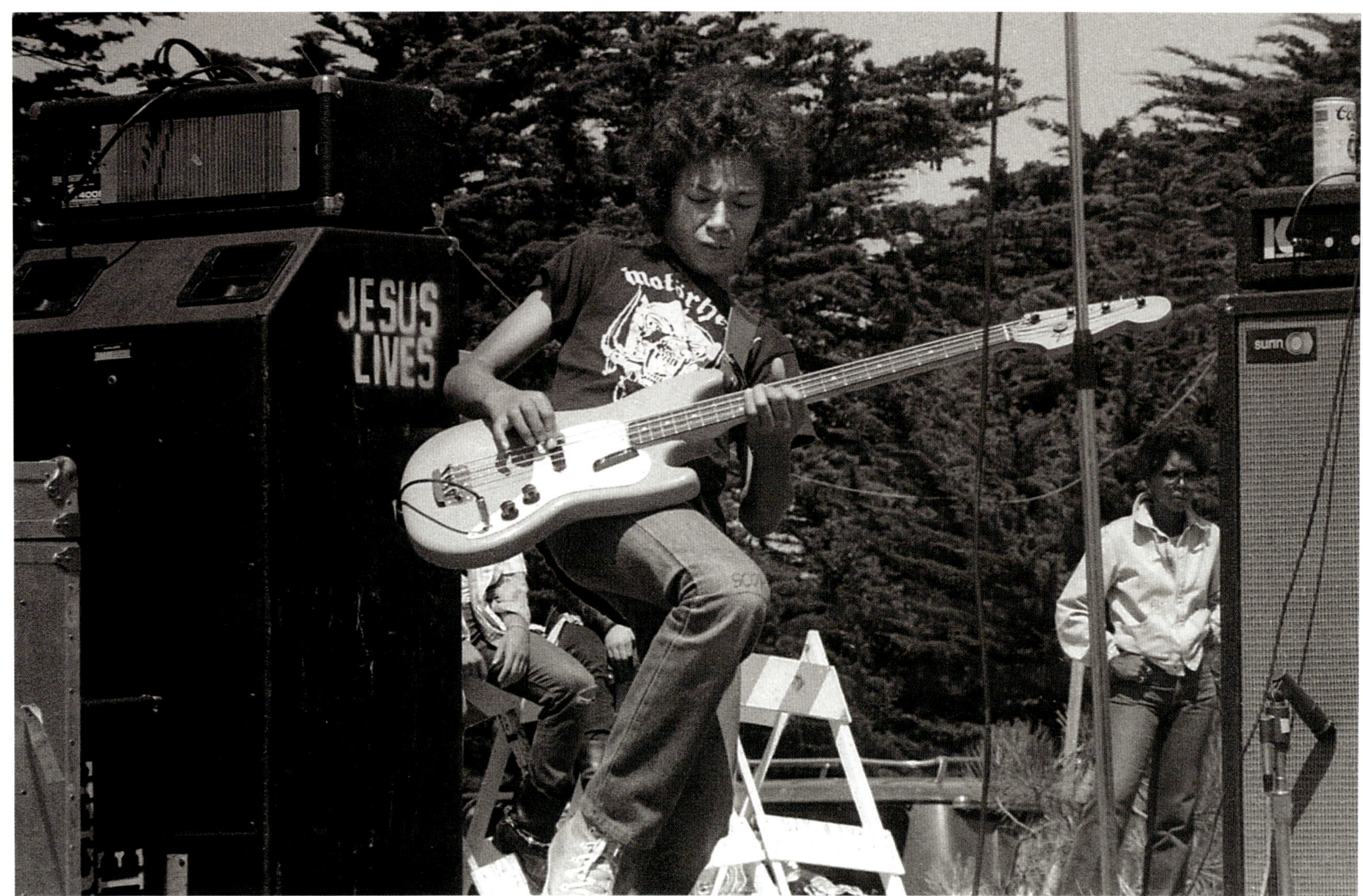

Free Beer
Aquatic Park, Berkeley, 1982

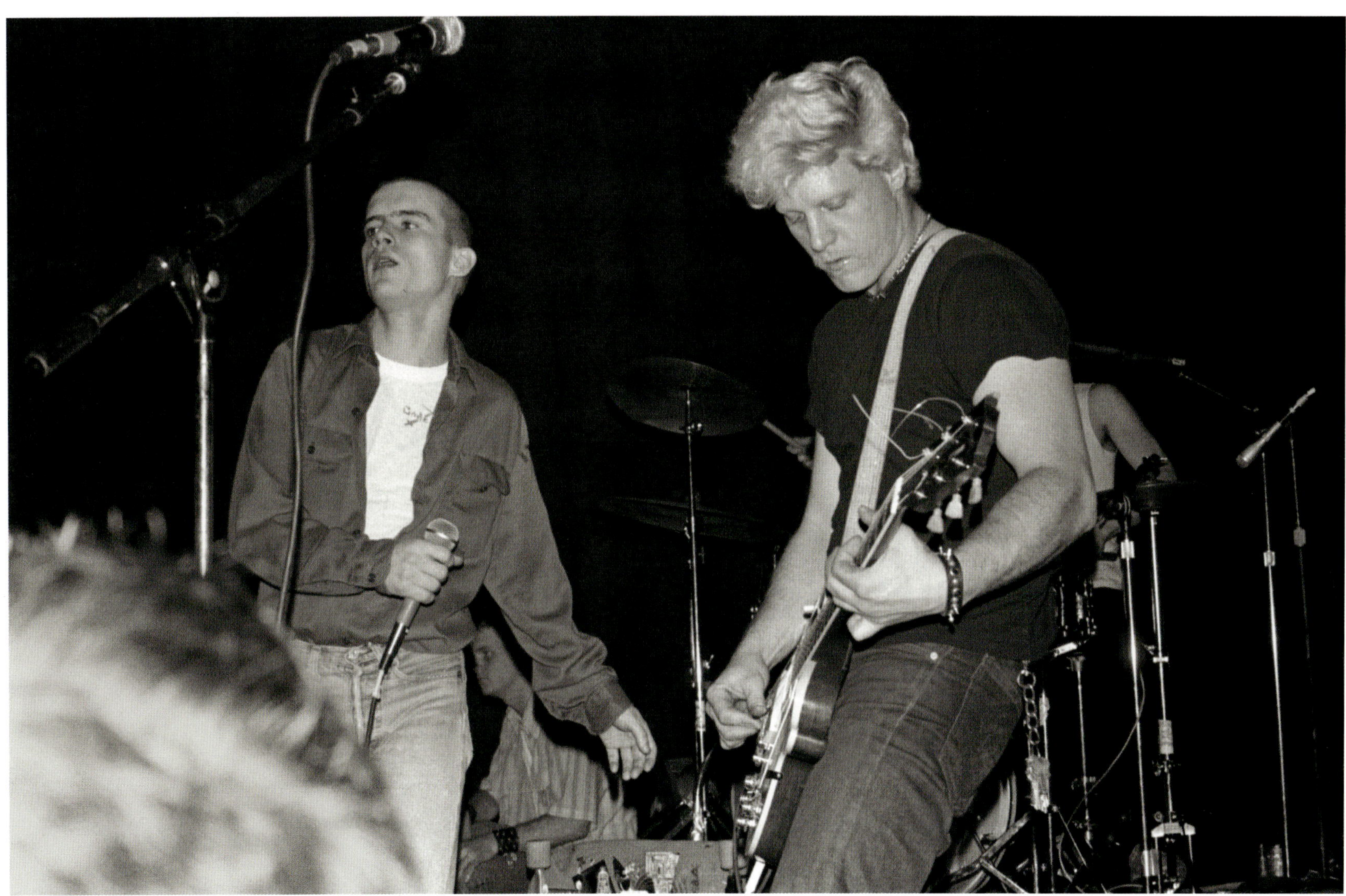

Code of Honor
On Broadway, San Francisco, 1982

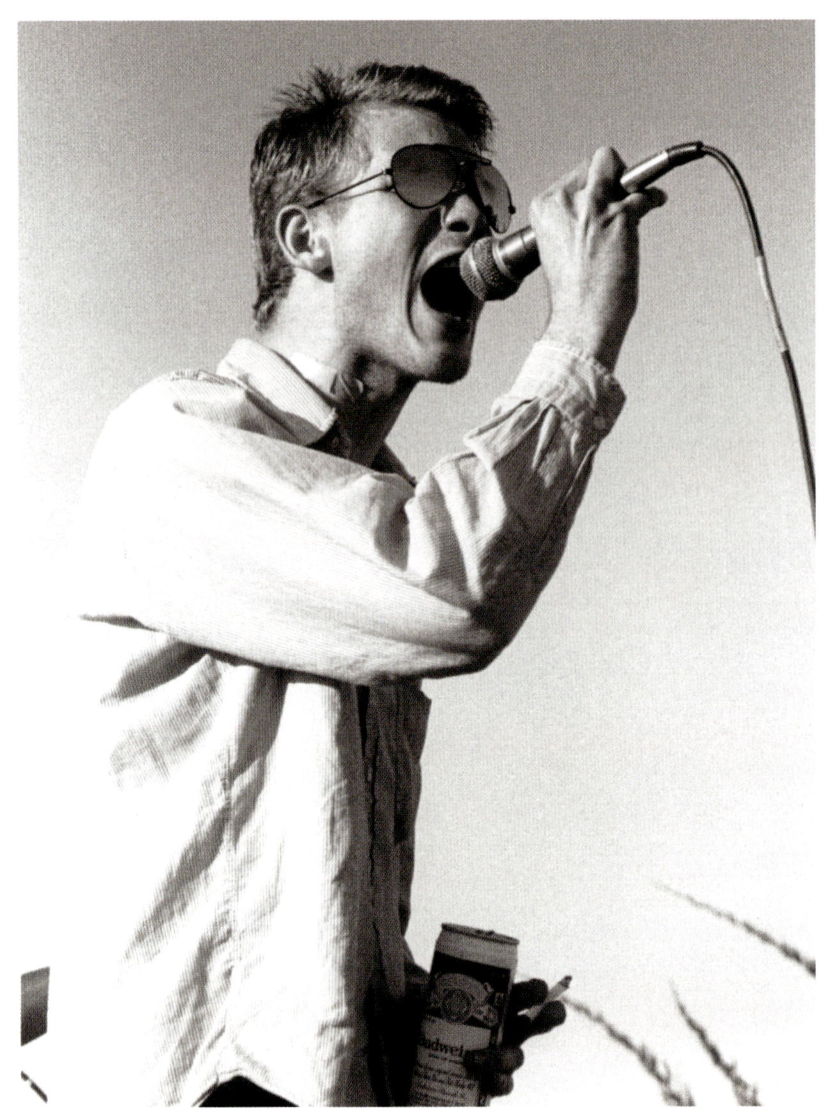

Flipper
Aquatic Park, Berkeley, 1982

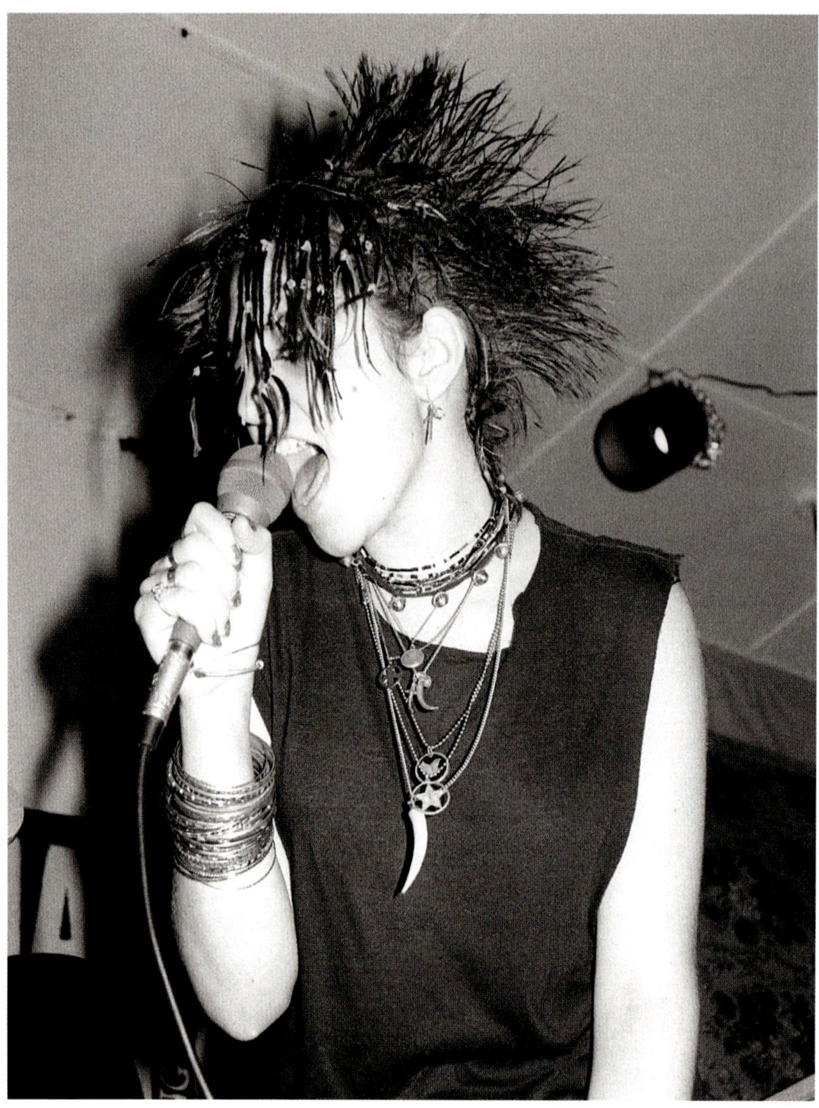

Atrocity
Club Foot, San Francisco, 1983

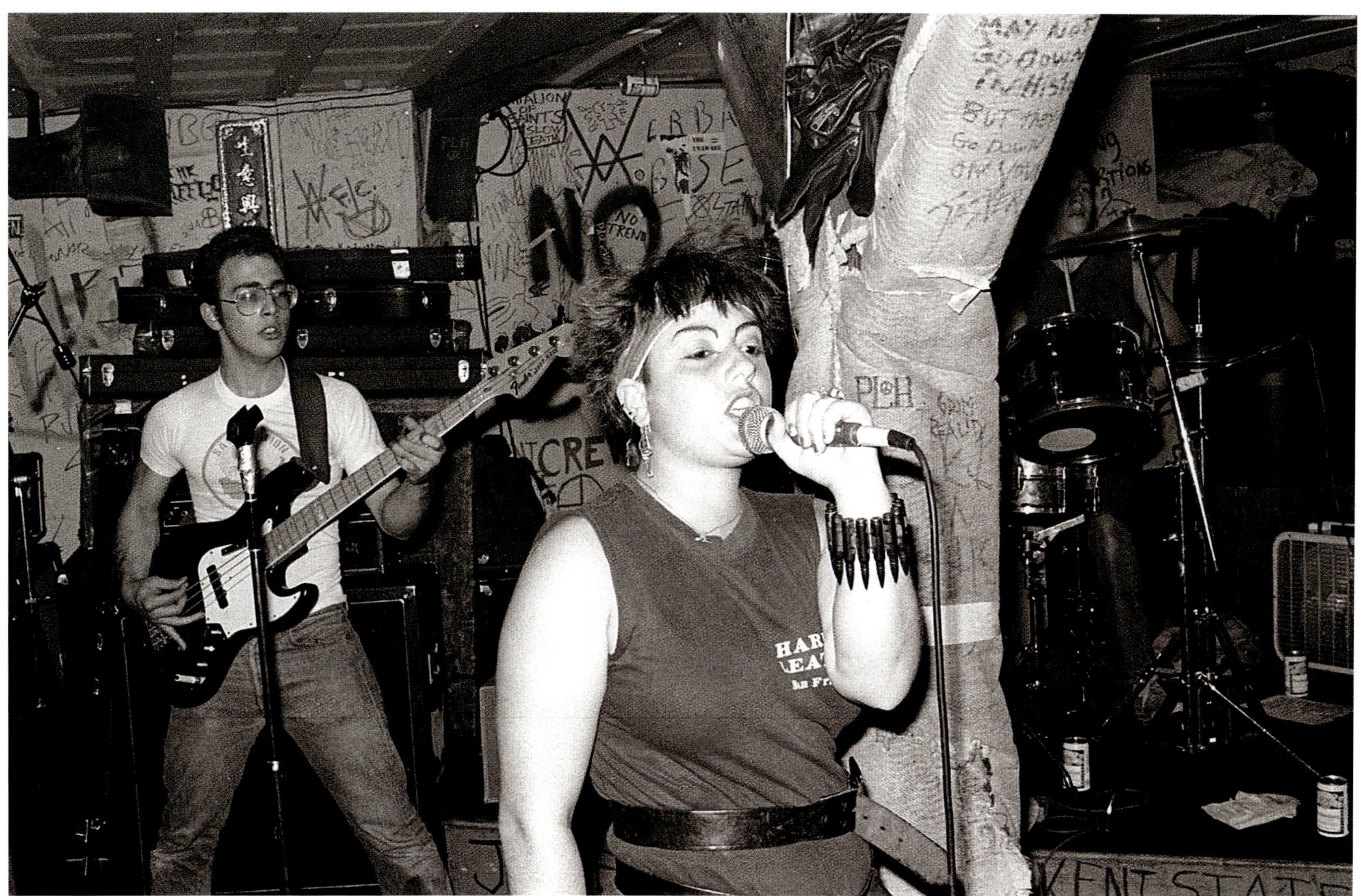

Sado-Nation

Tool & Die, San Francisco, 1983

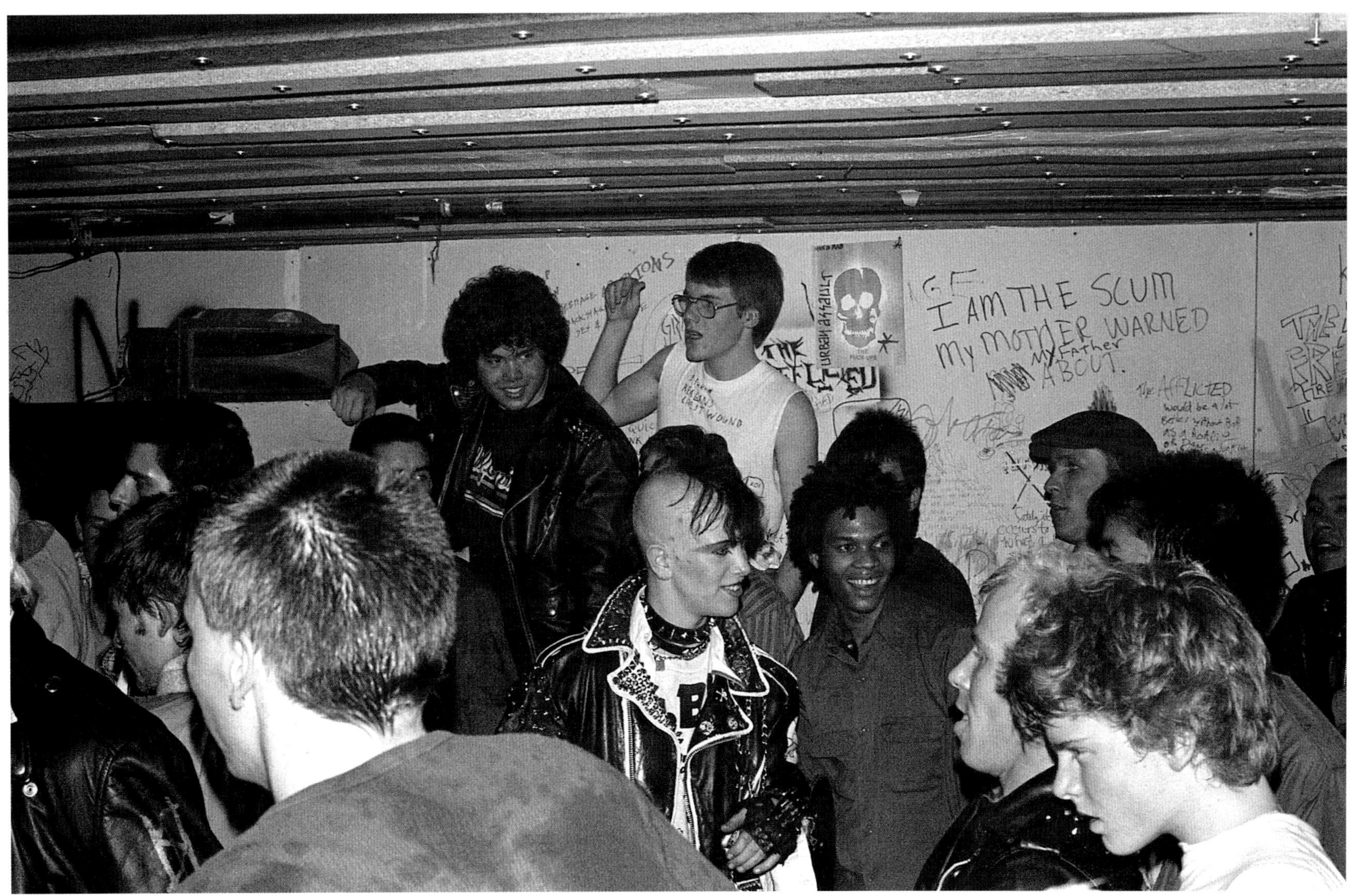

Tool & Die, San Francisco, 1983

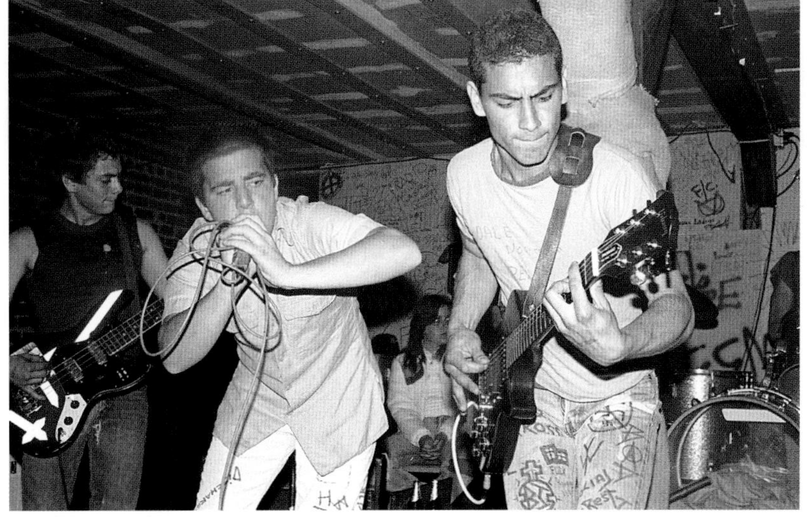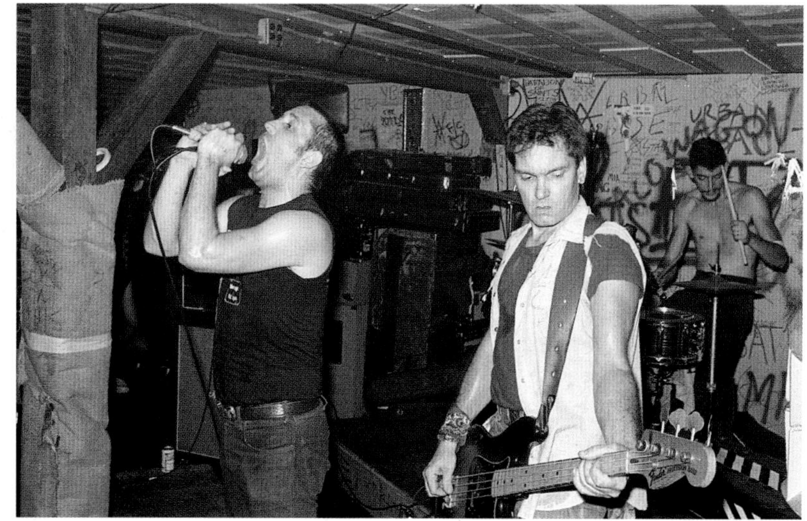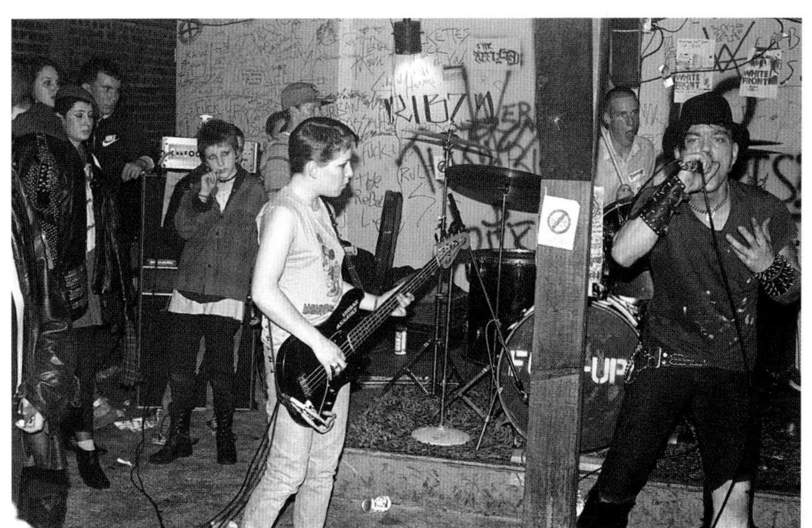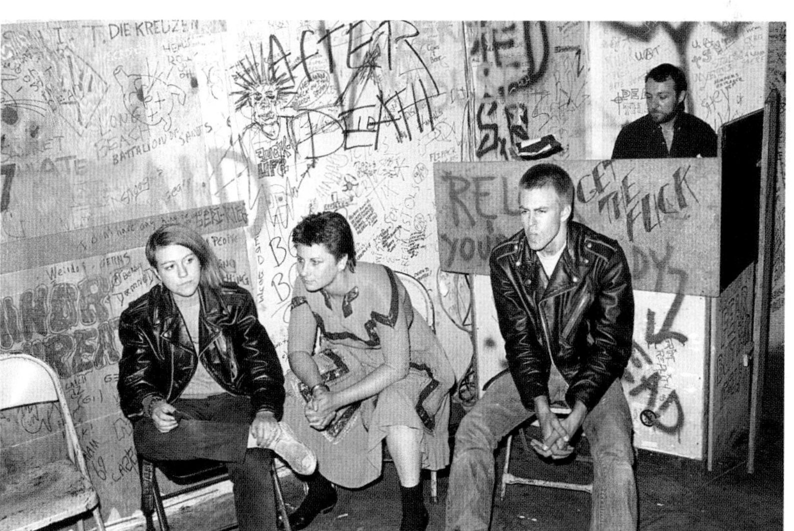

Tool & Die, 1983 (clockwise from top left) Bad Influence, Really Red, unidentified punks, Urban Assault

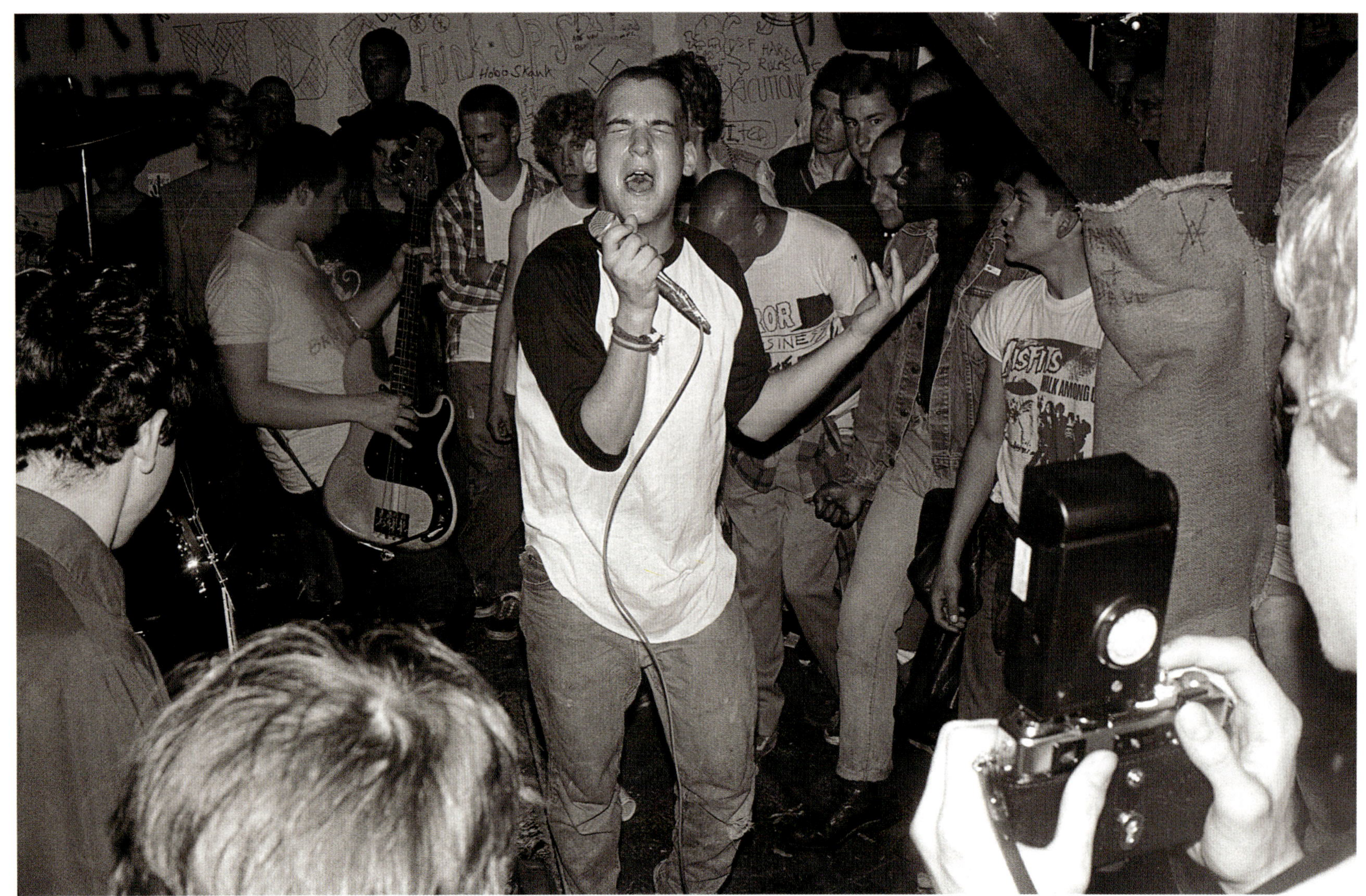

Minor Threat

Tool & Die, San Francisco, 1983

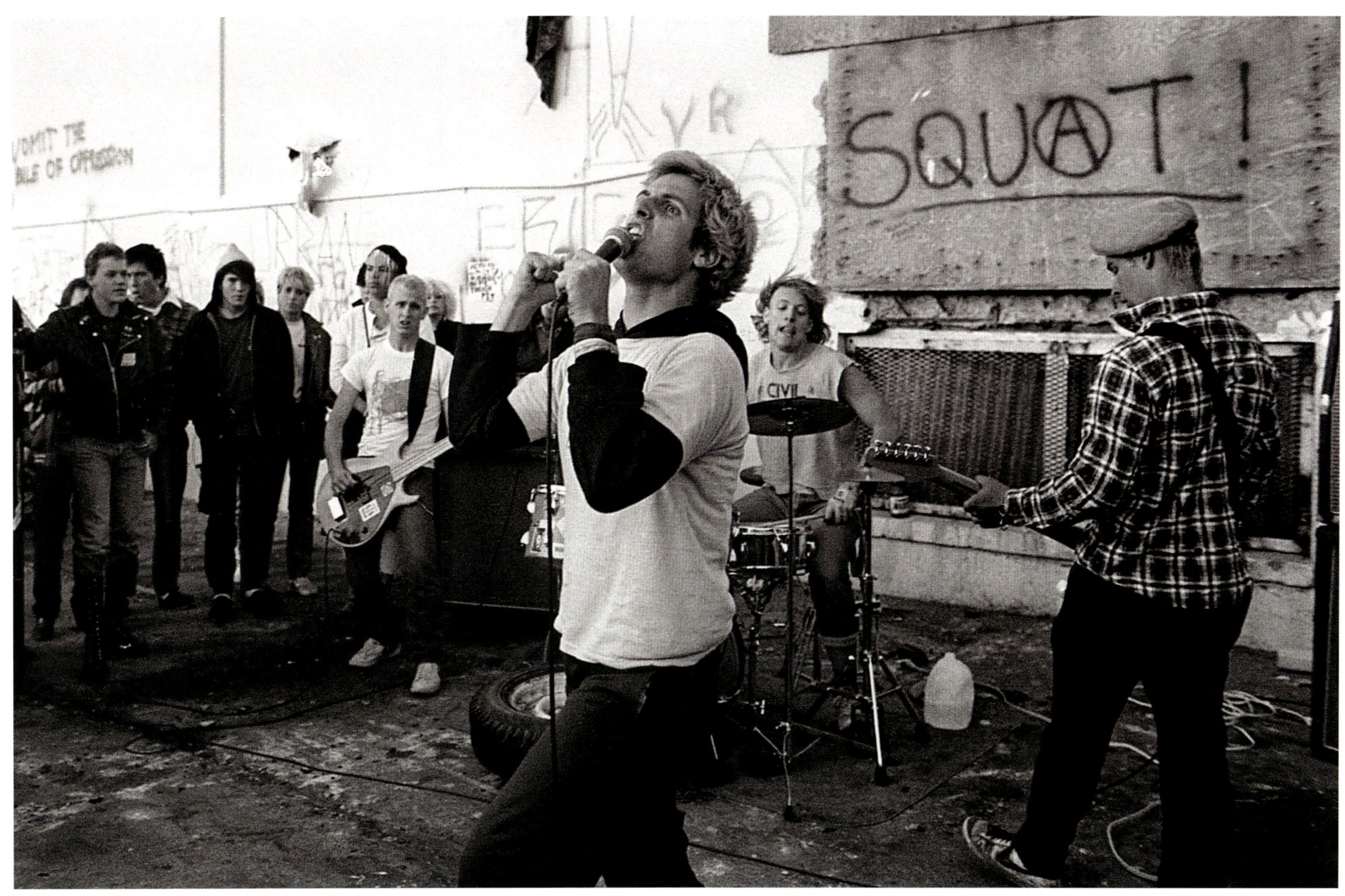

7 Seconds

The Vats, San Francisco, 1984

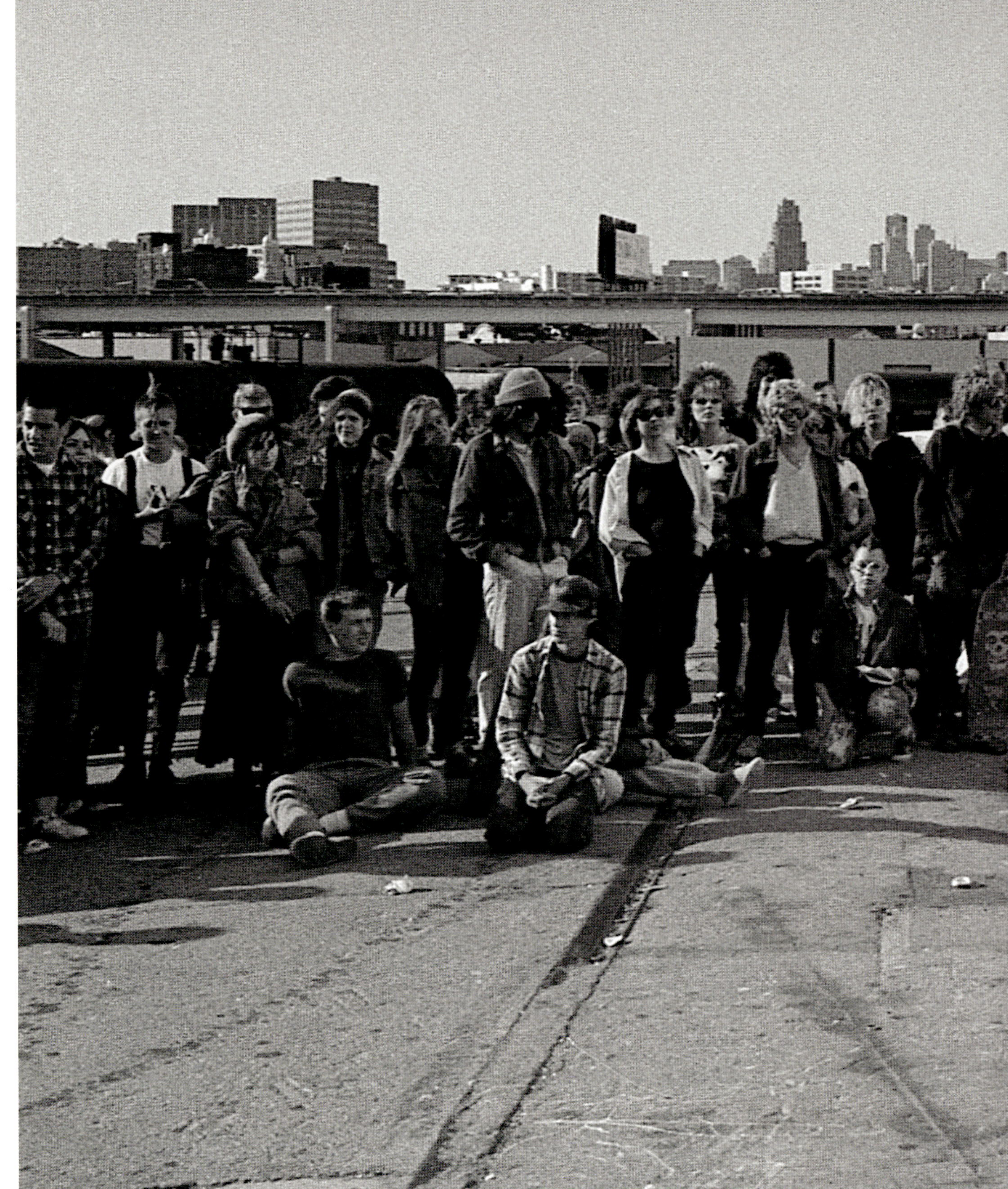

MDC
The Vats, San Francisco, 1983

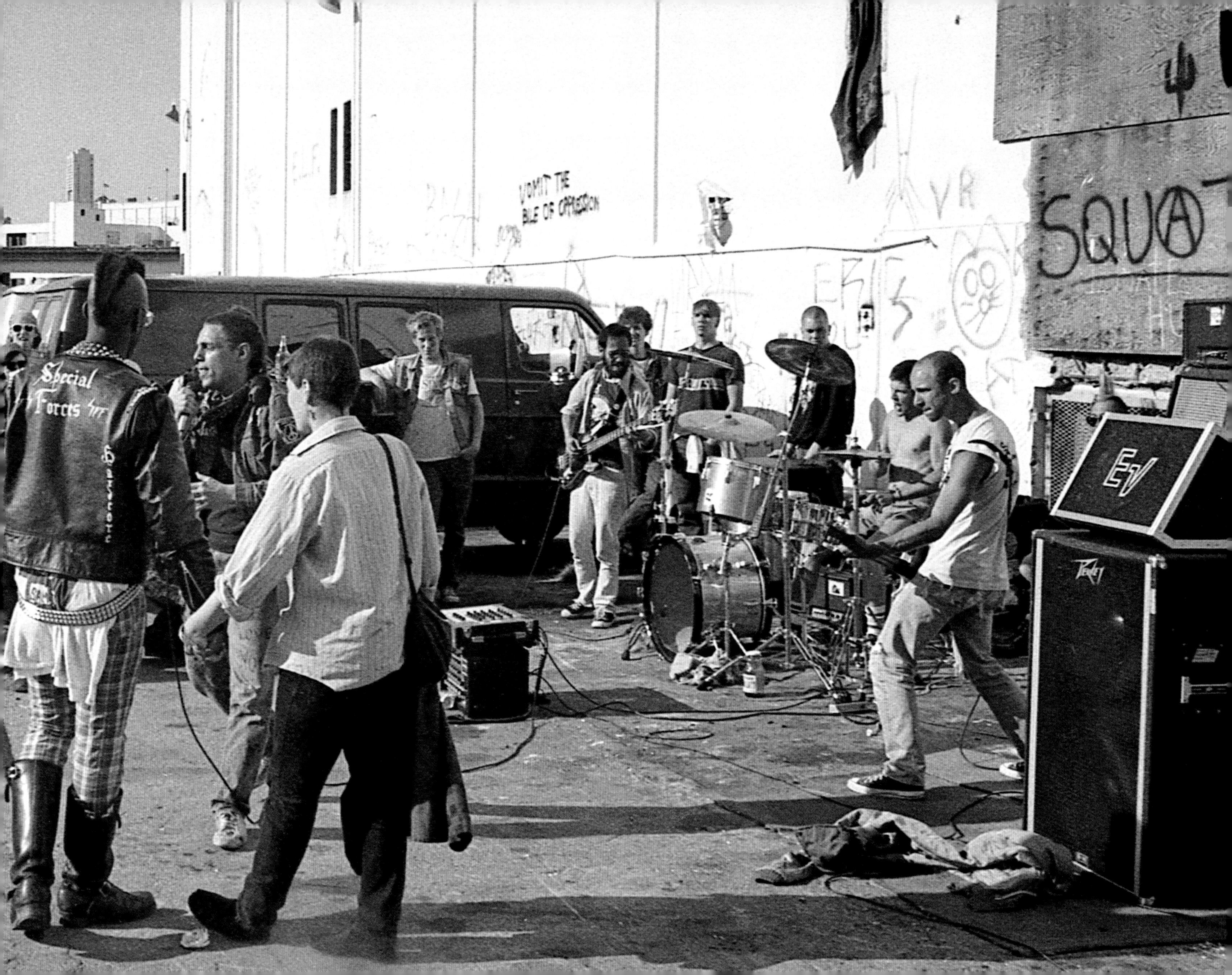

VOMIT THE
BILE OF OPPRESSION
SQUAT
EV

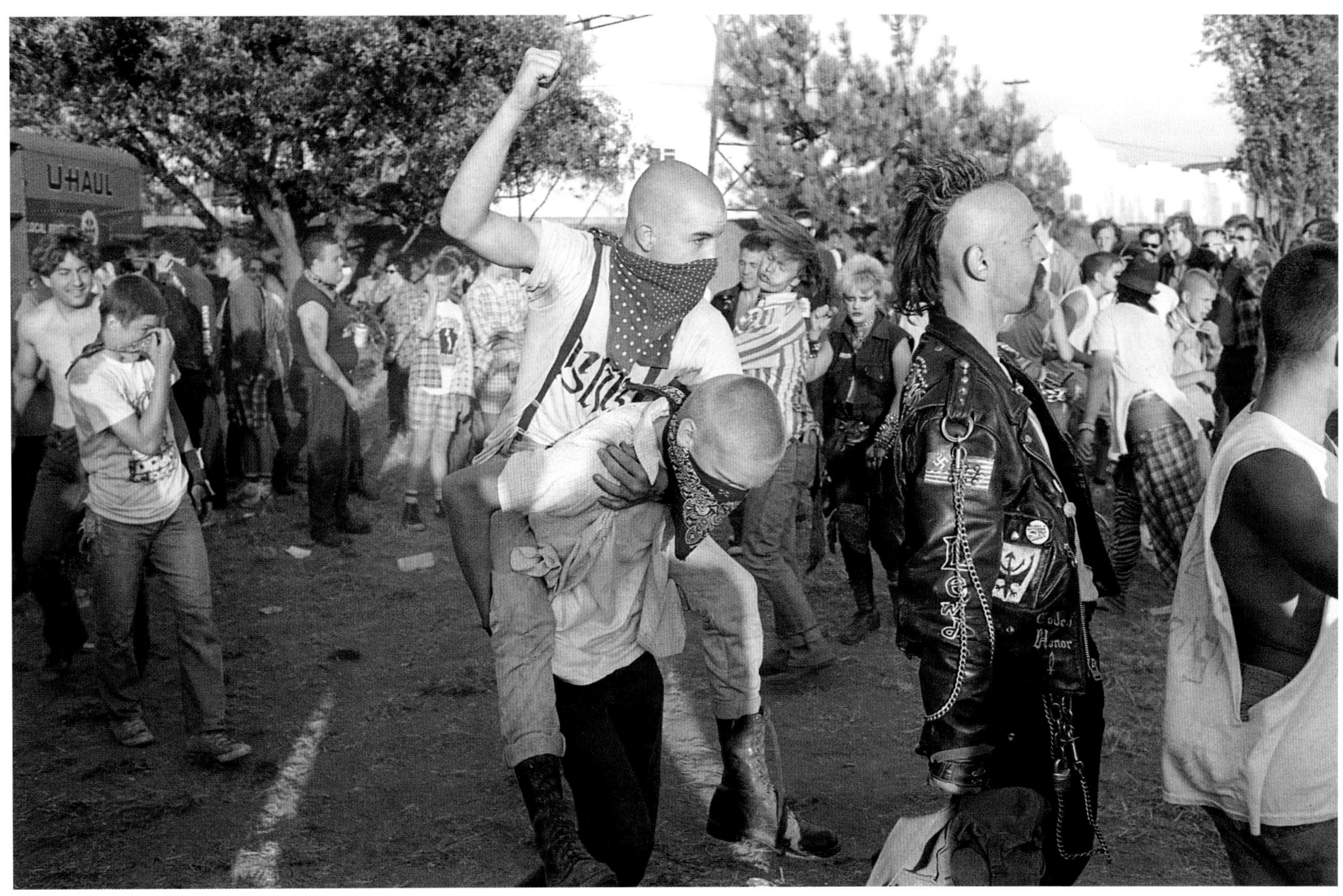

Aquatic Park, Berkeley, 1983

Opposite:
Tool & Die, San Francisco, 1983

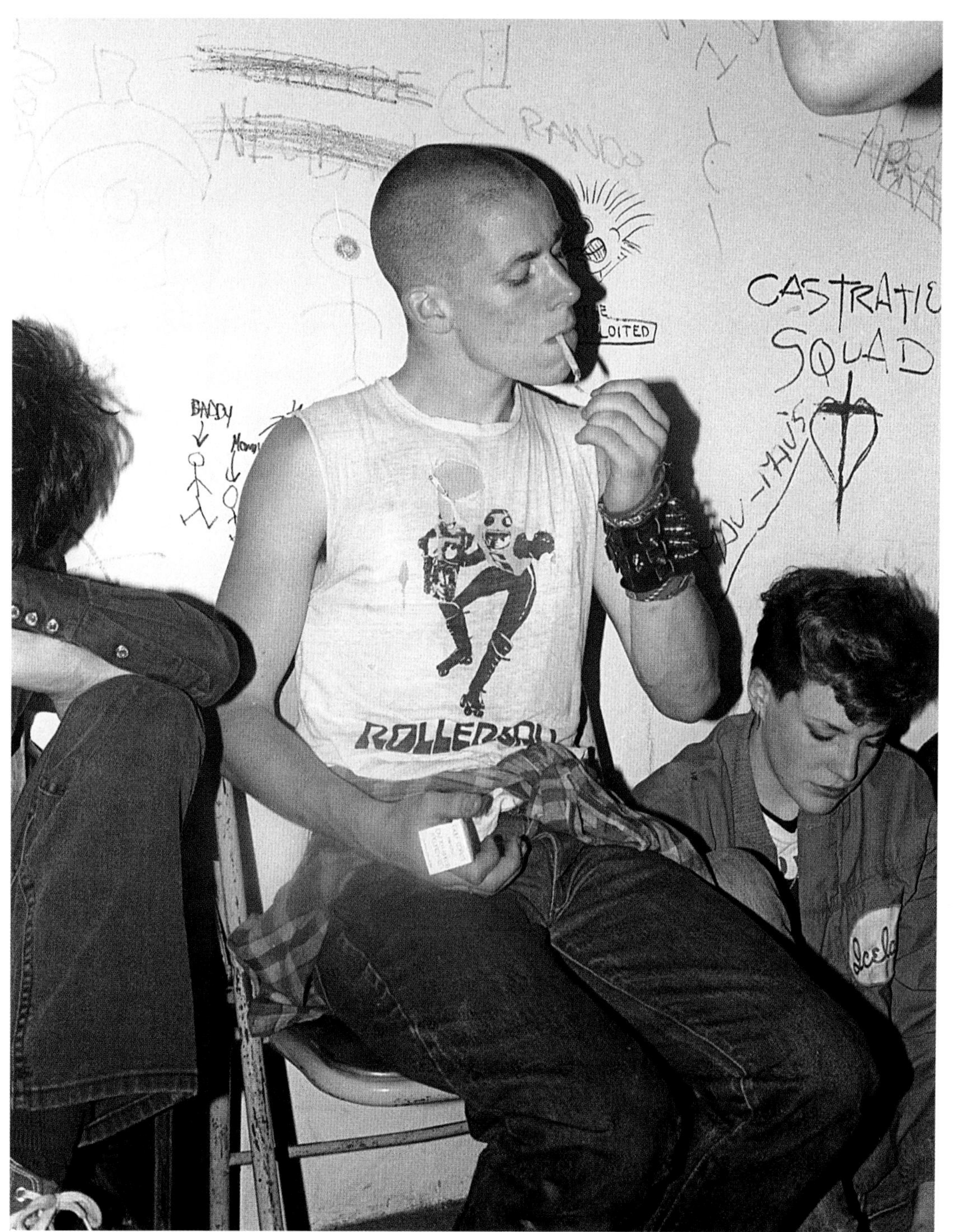
CASTRATIO
SQUAD
ROLLEDSOV

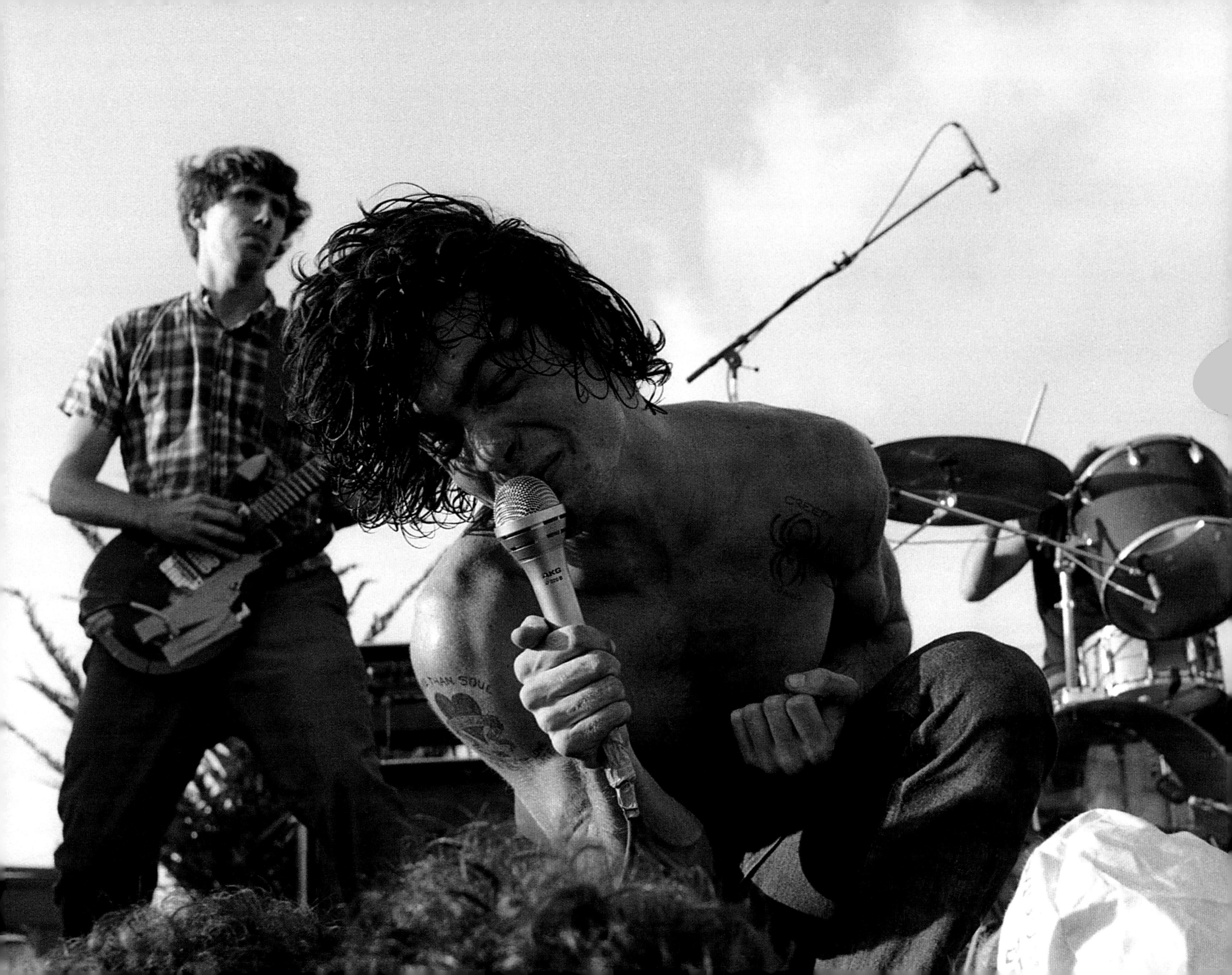

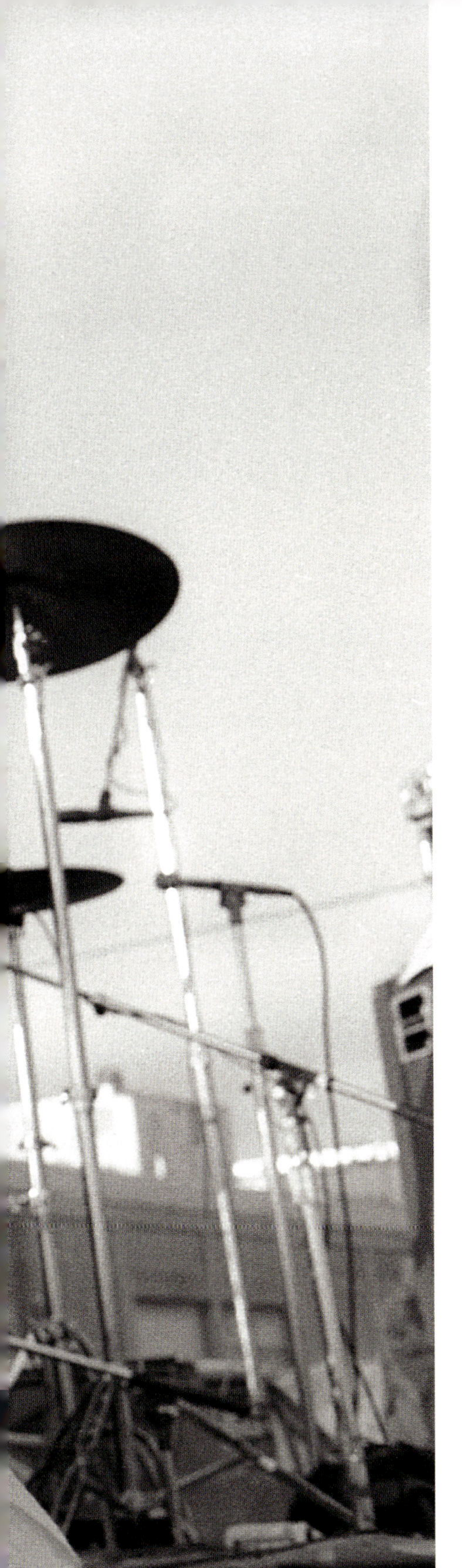

Black Flag

Aquatic Park, Berkeley, 1983

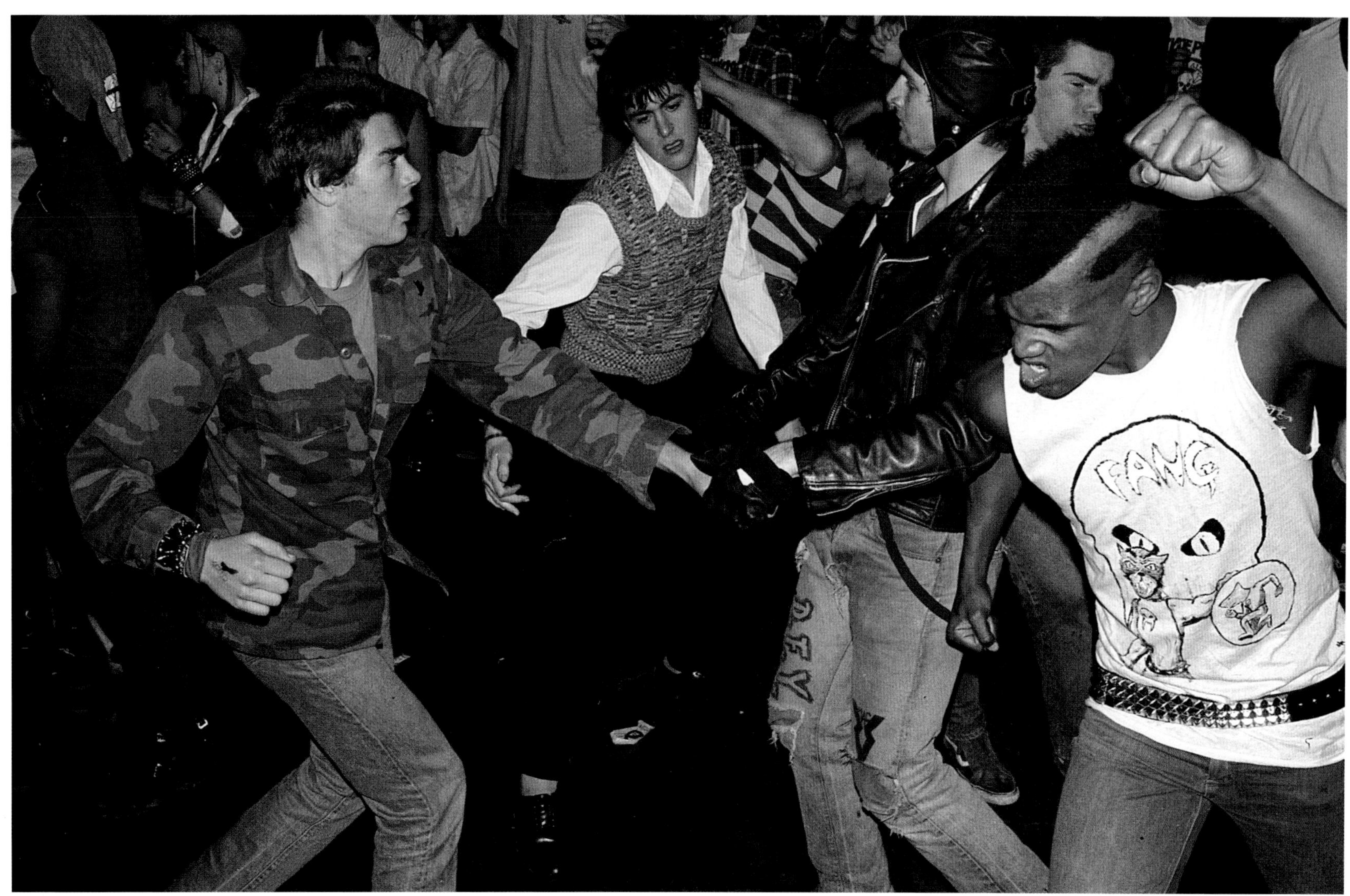

On Broadway, San Francisco, 1983

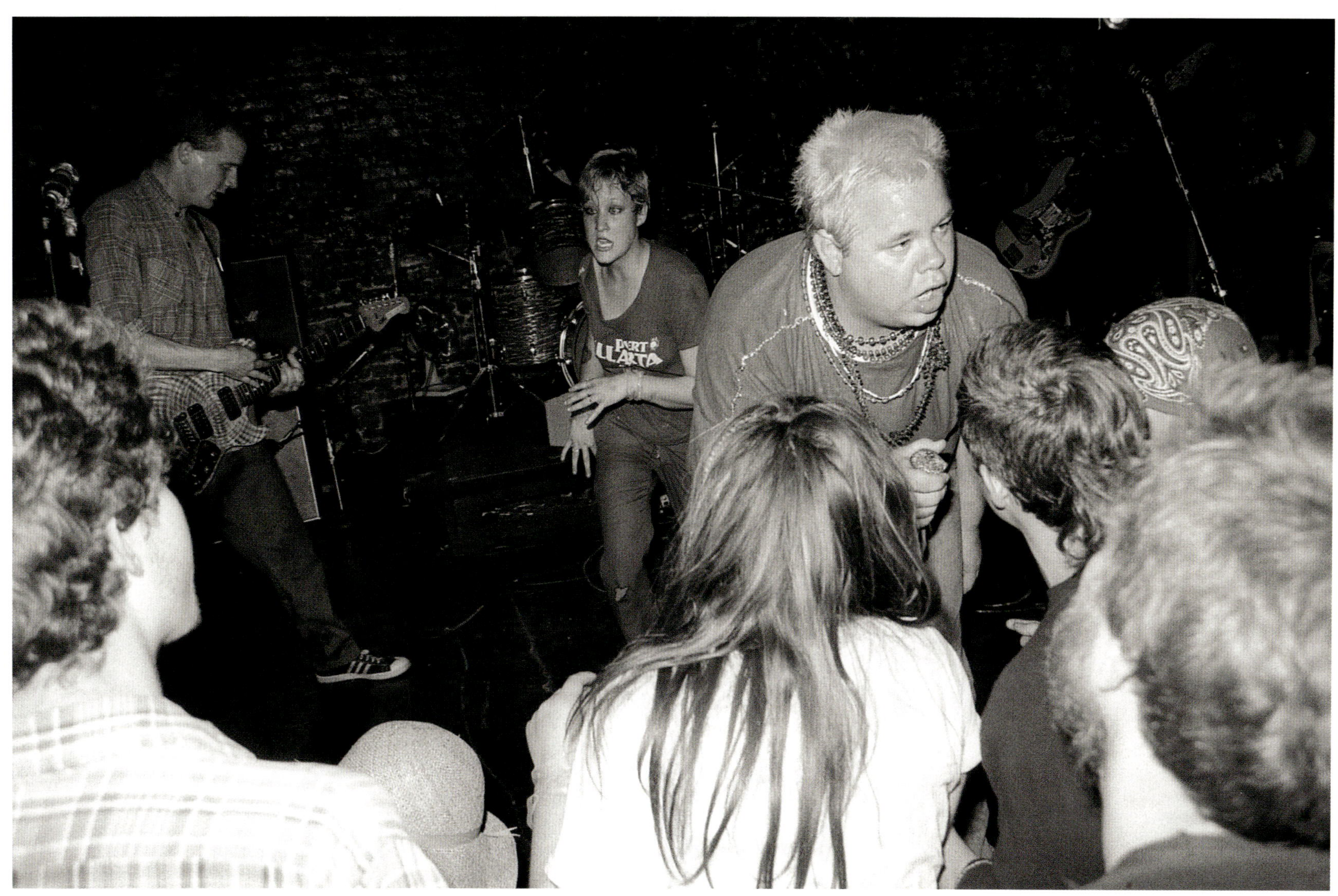

The Dicks
Mabuhay Gardens, San Francisco, 1984

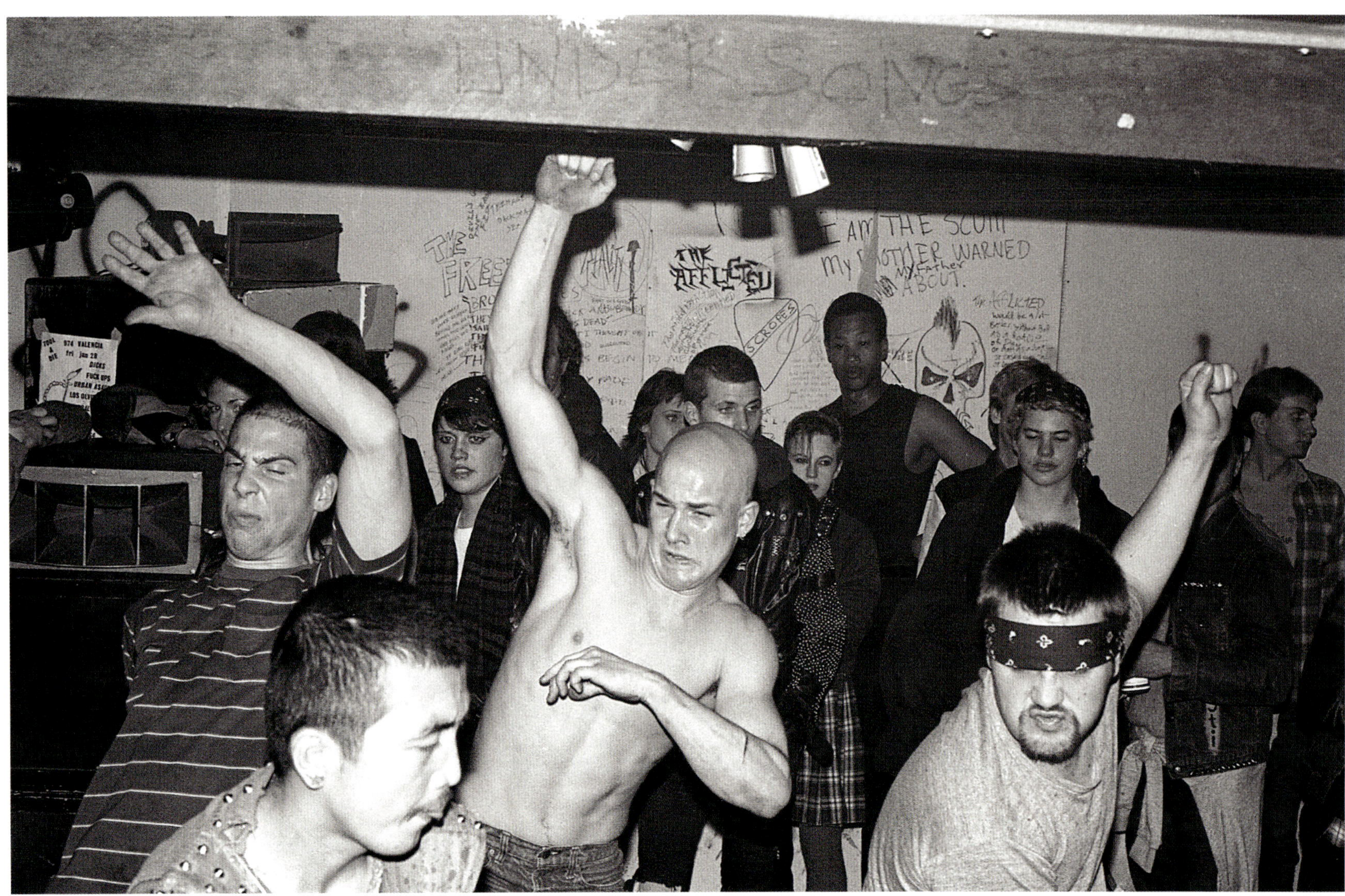

Tool & Die, San Francisco, 1983

Opposite:
St. Vitus
Aquatic Park, Berkeley, 1983

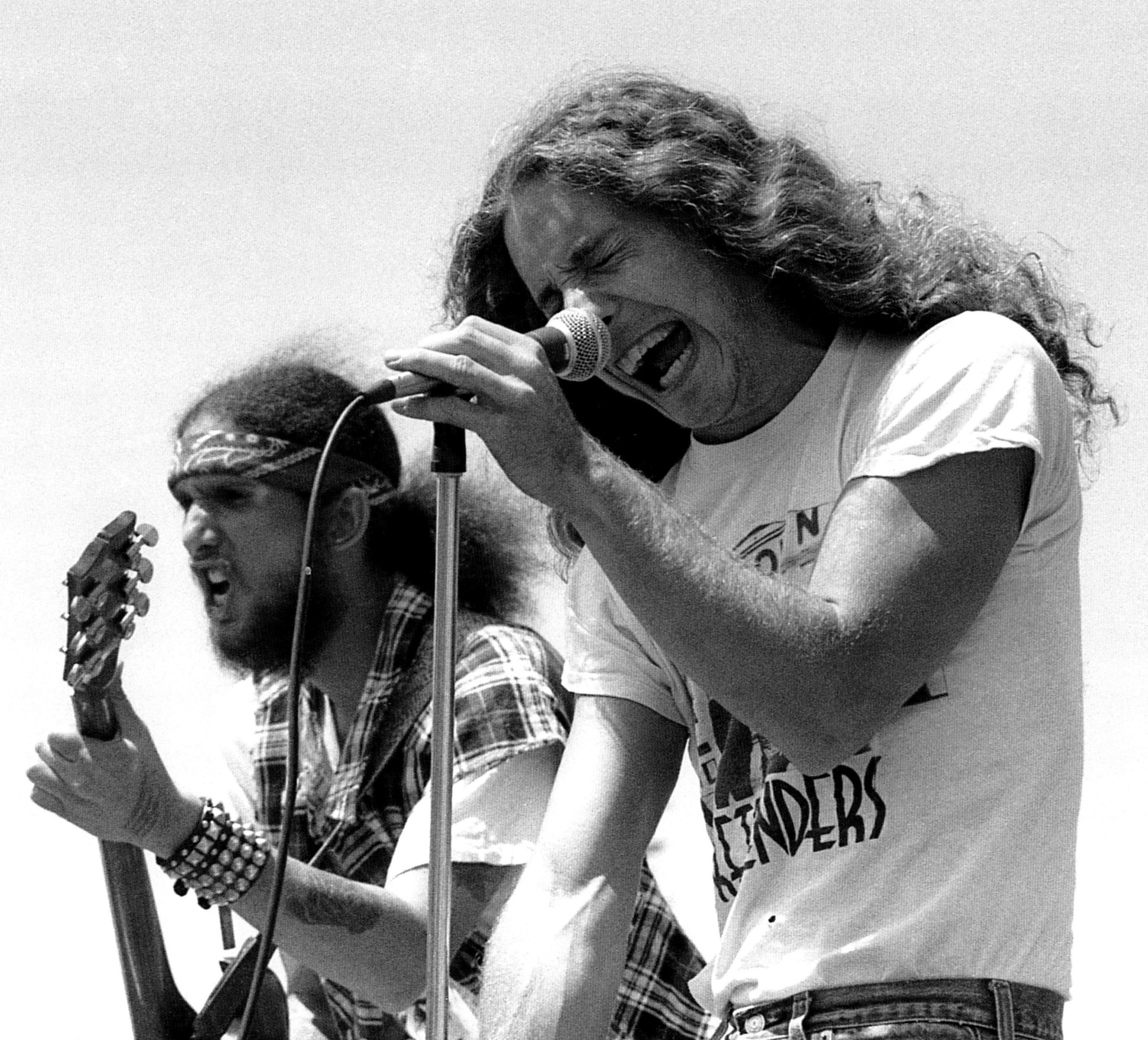

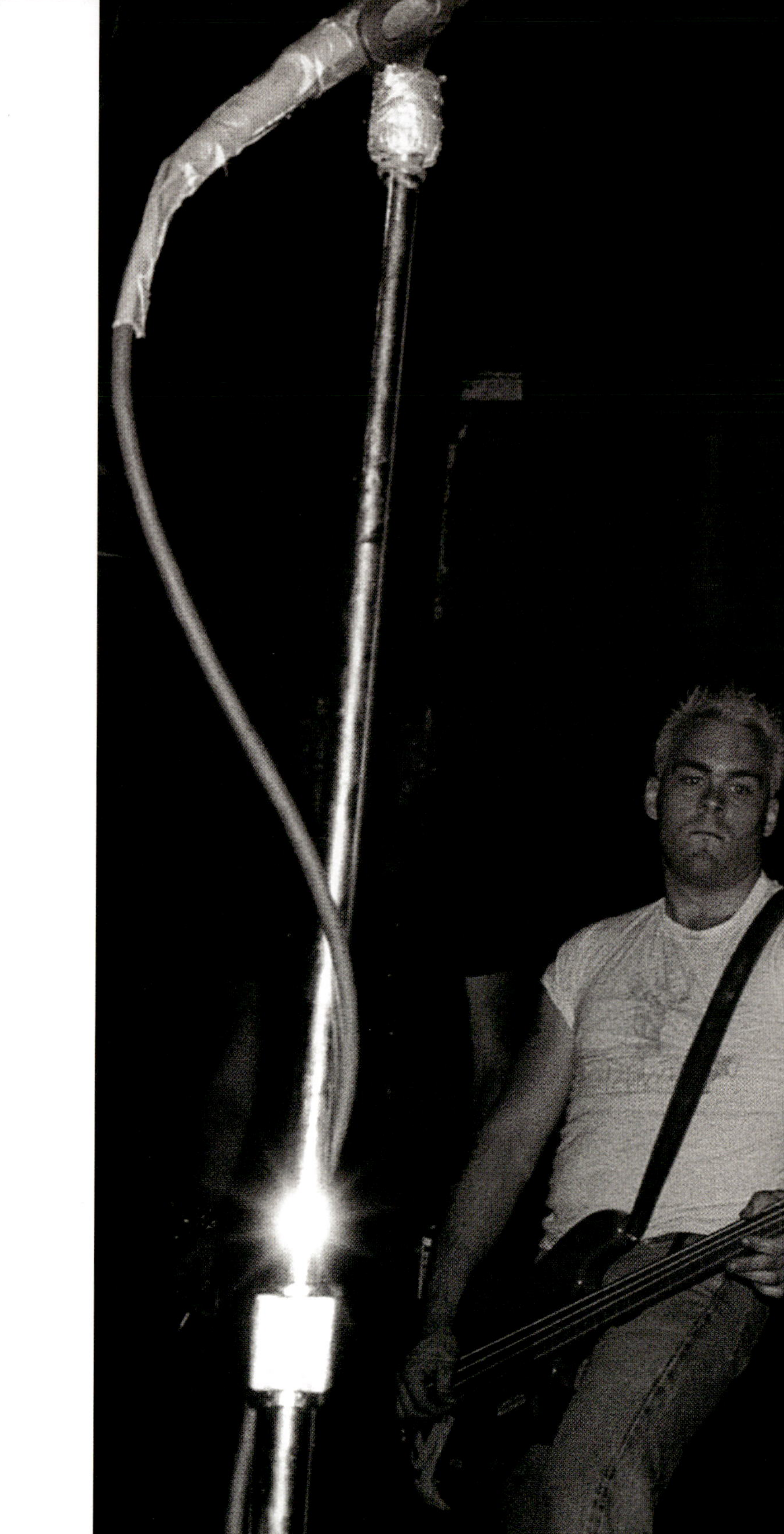

Big Boys
On Broadway, San Francisco, 1983

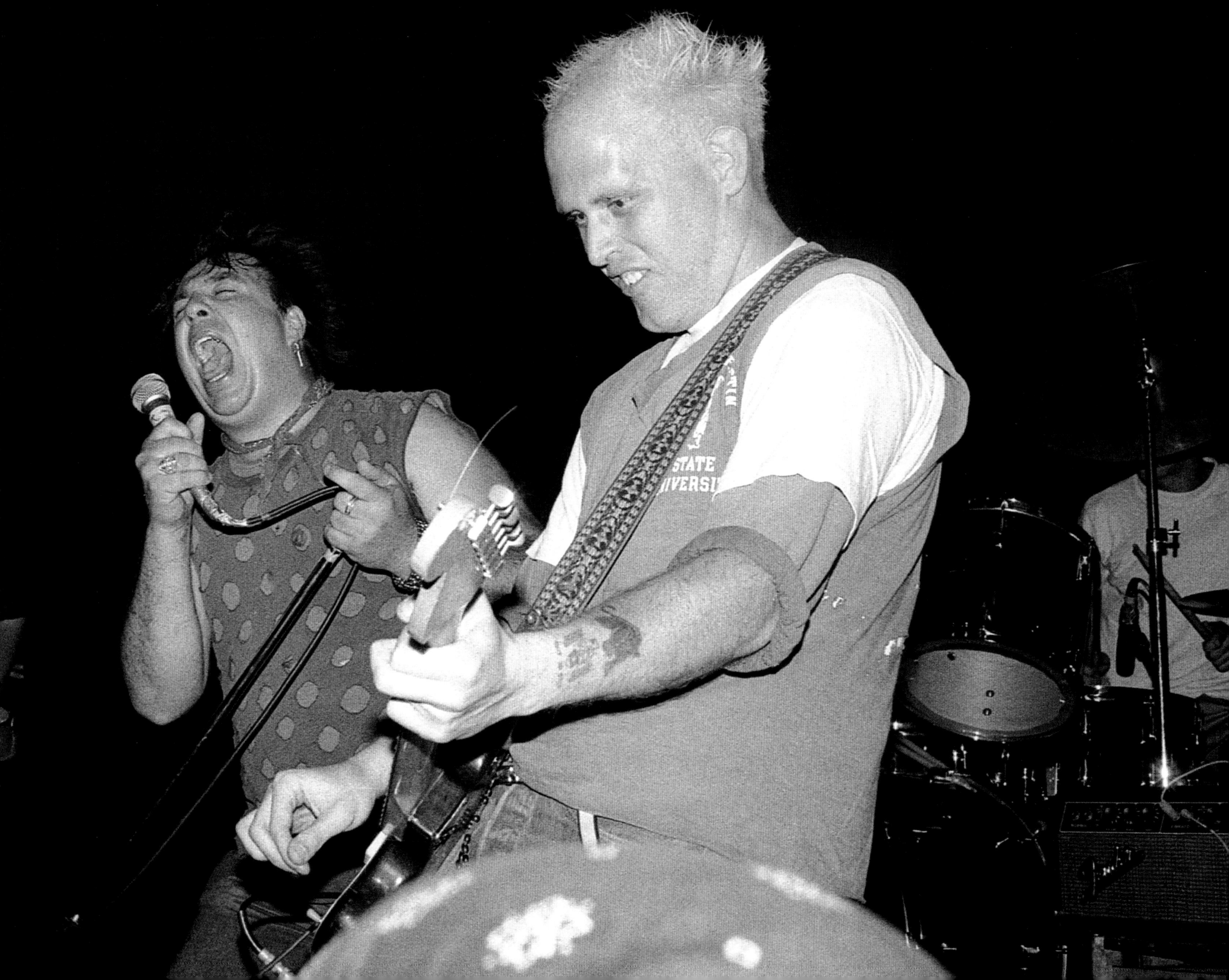

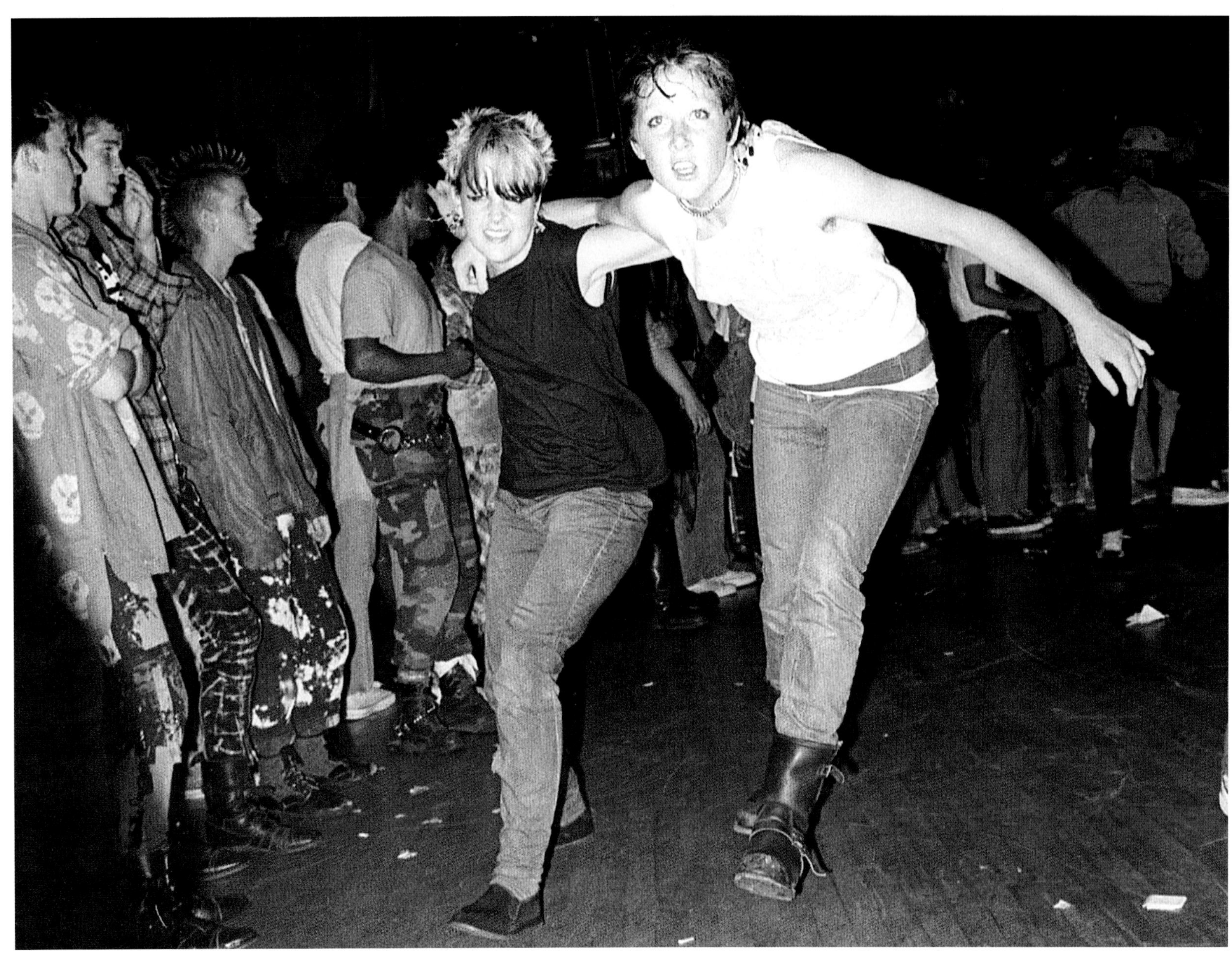

Booker T. Washington Community Center, San Francisco, 1984

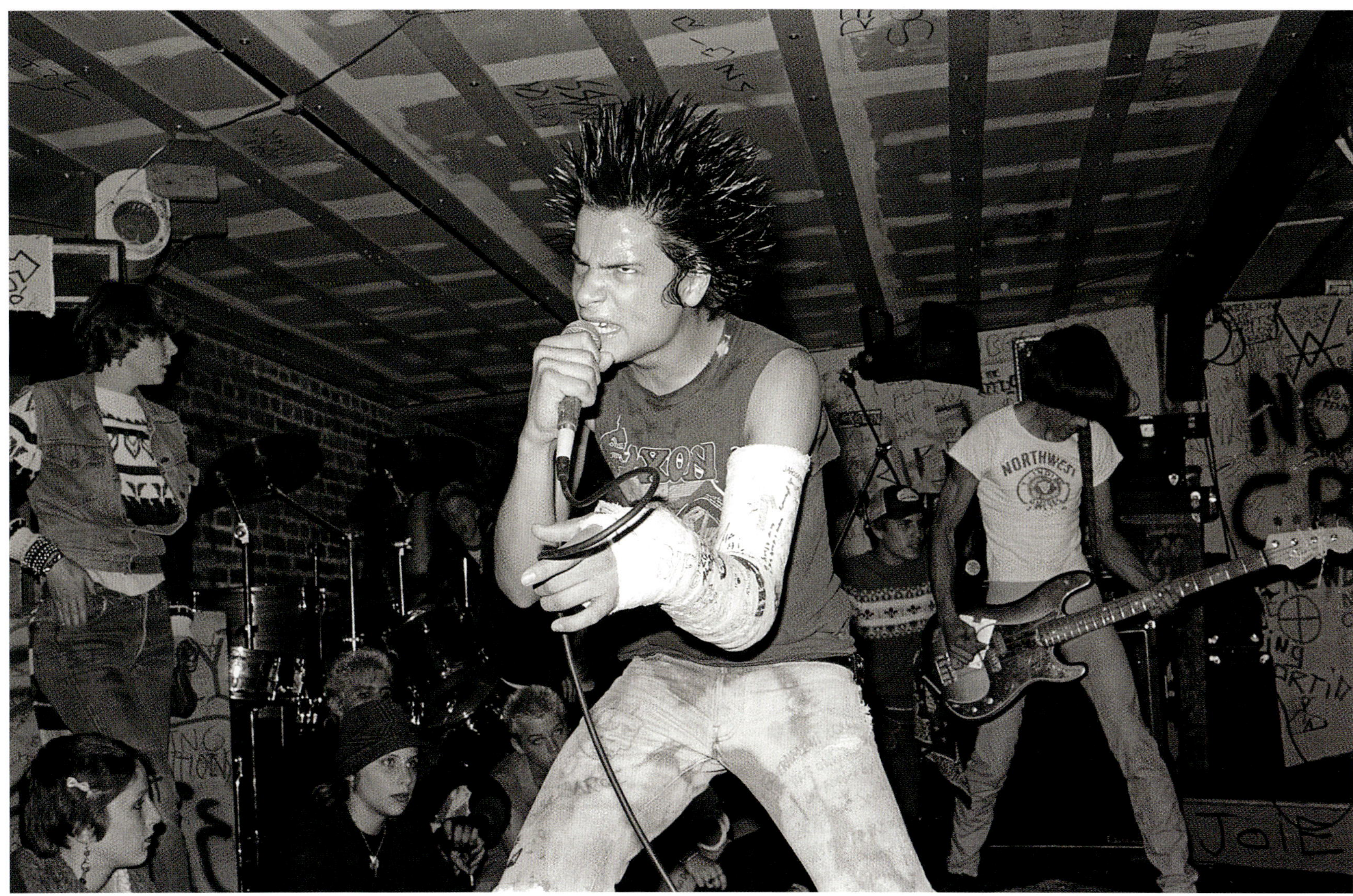

Ribzy
Tool & Die, San Francisco, 1983

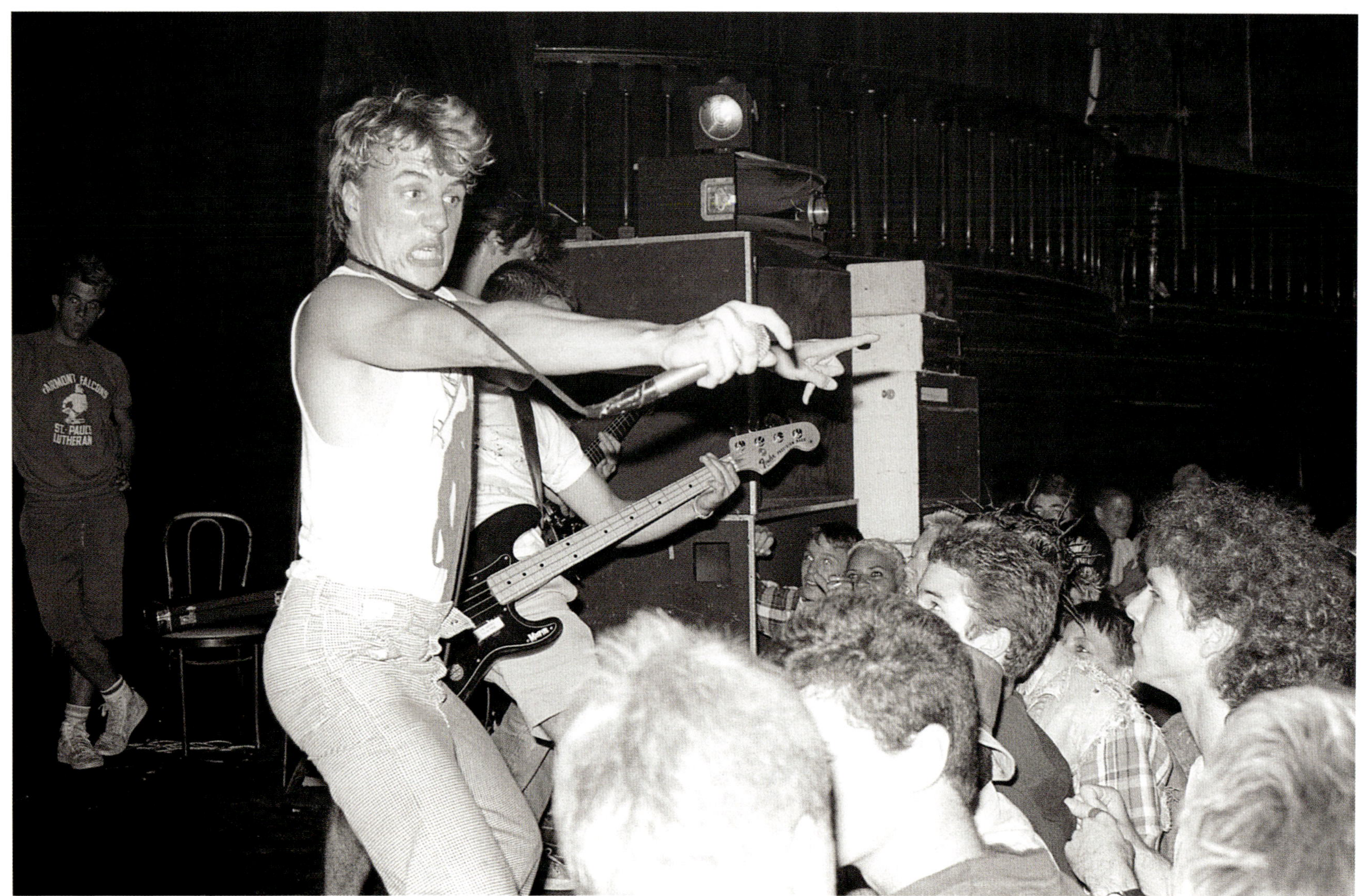

SS Decontrol

On Broadway, San Francisco, 1983

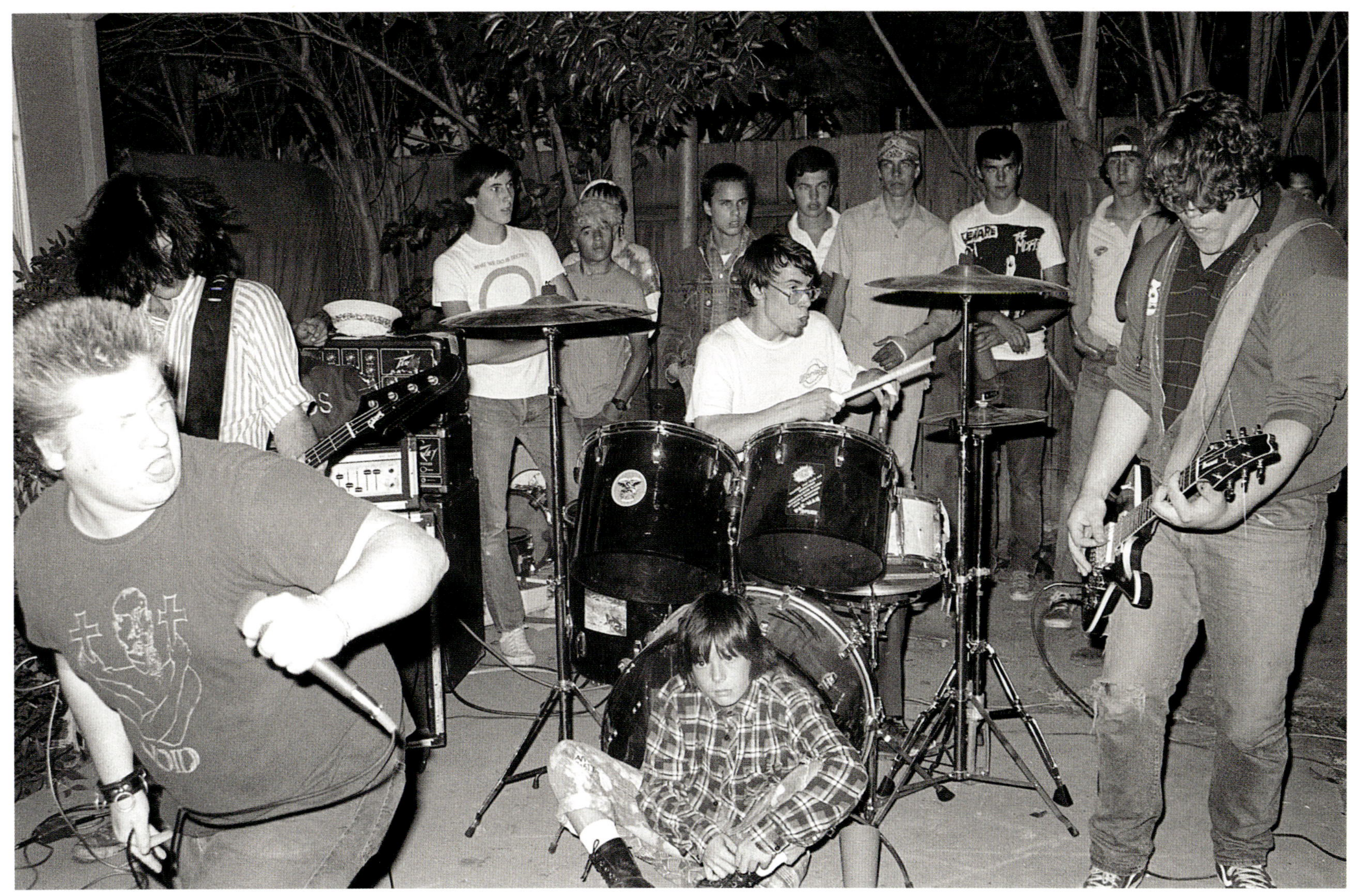

Necros

San Jose, 1983

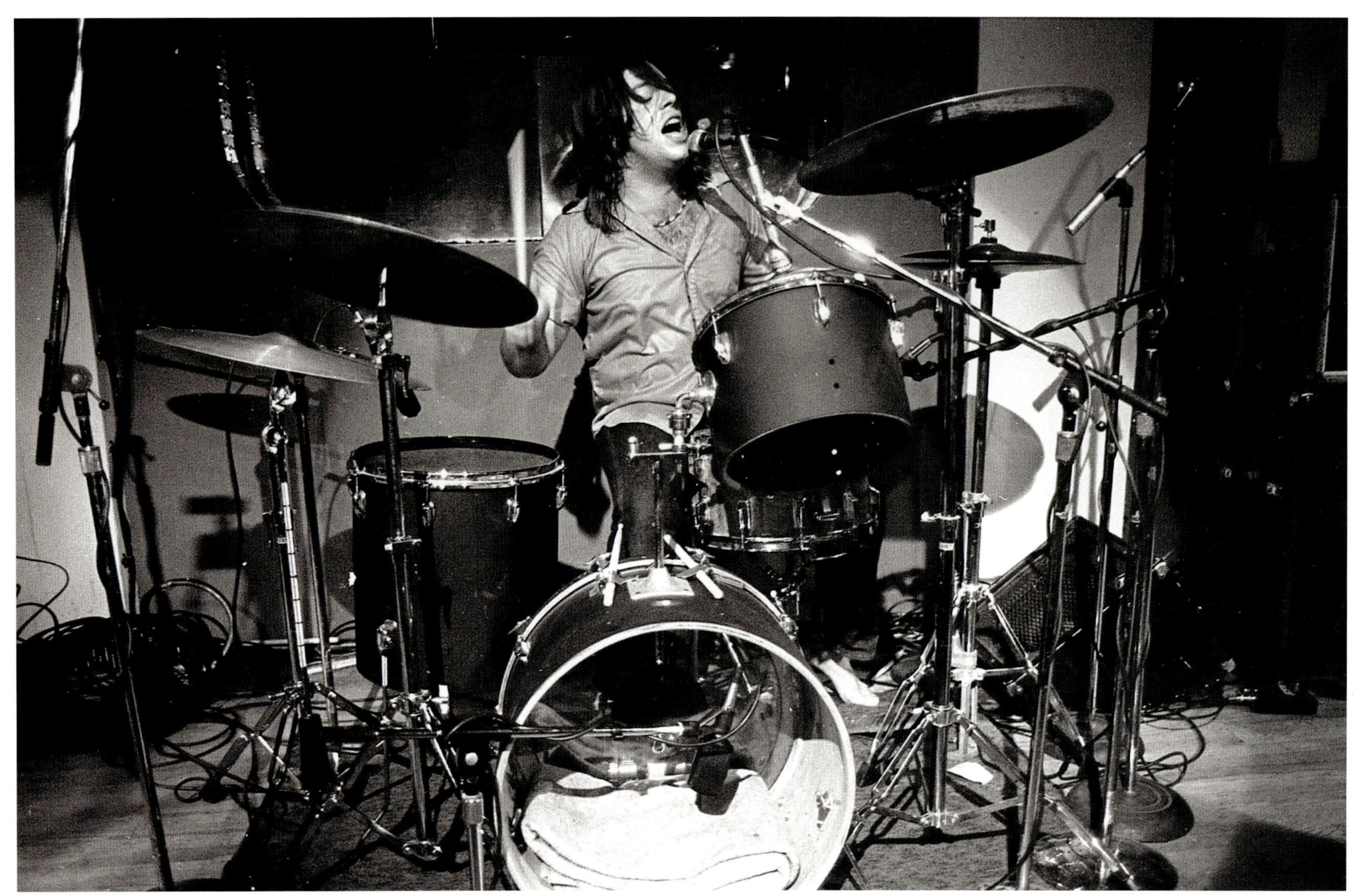

Hüsker Dü

Al's Bar, Los Angeles, 1985

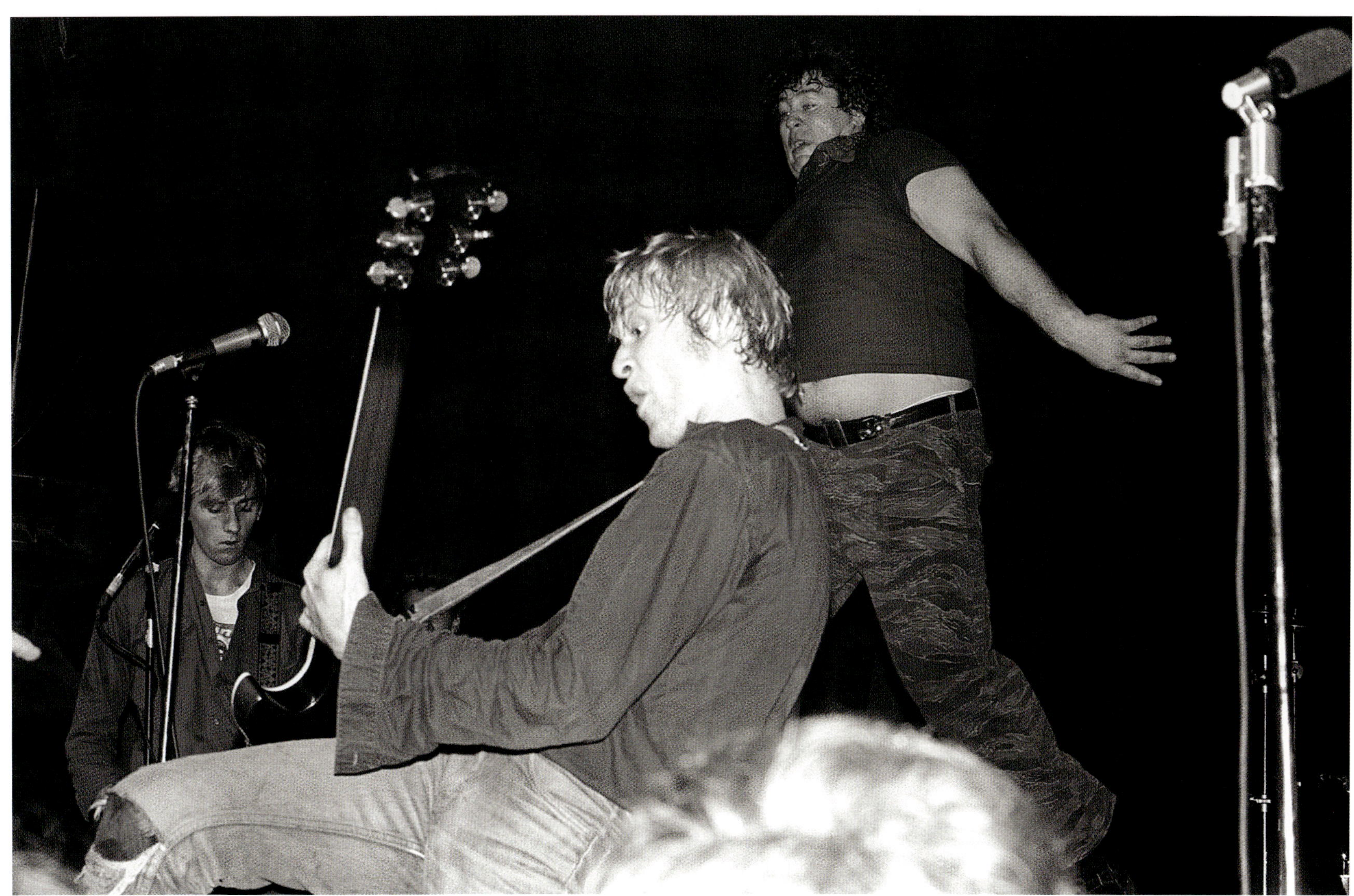

Toxic Reasons
On Broadway, San Francisco, 1983

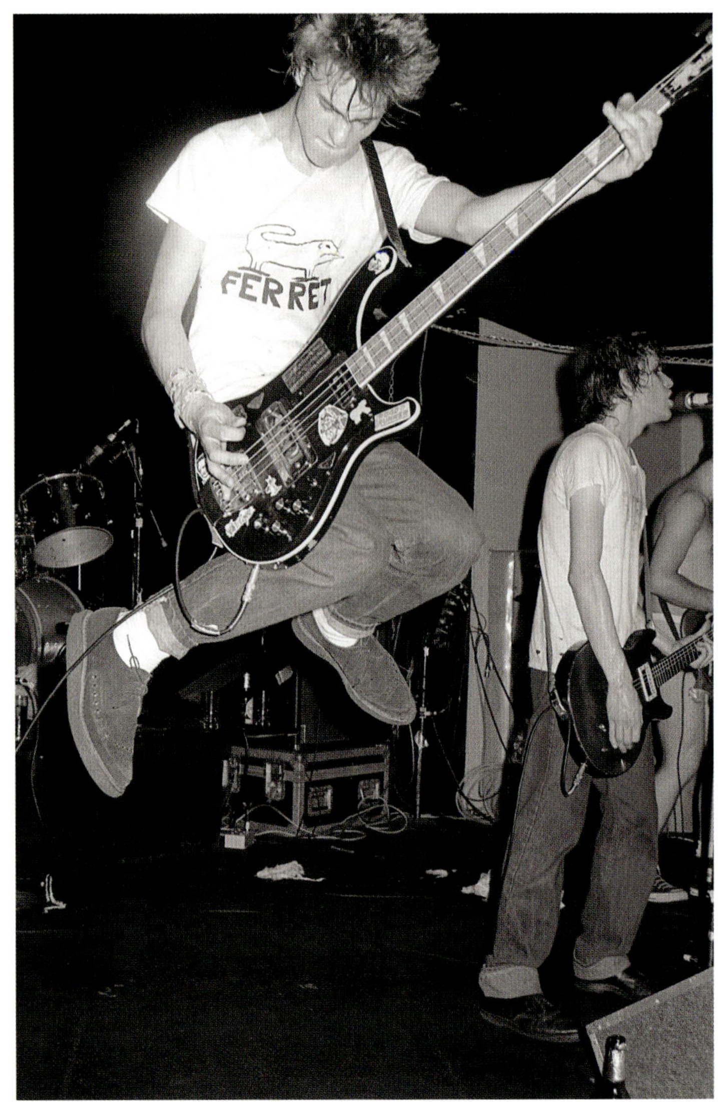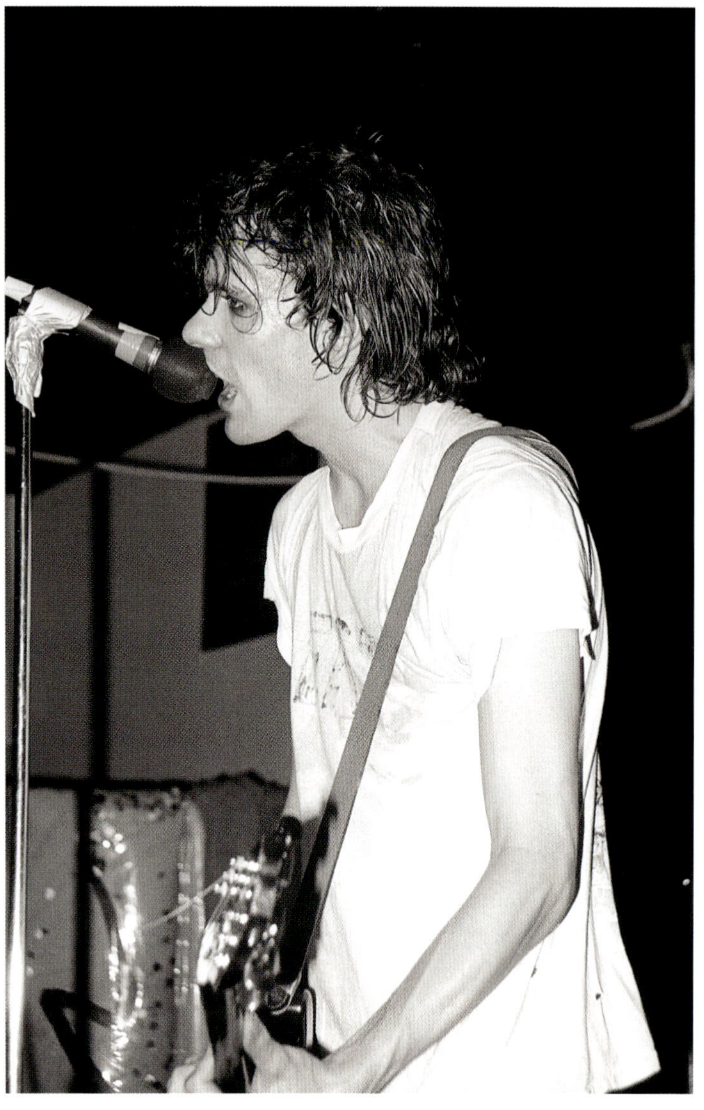

The Replacements
Berkeley Square, Berkeley, 1983

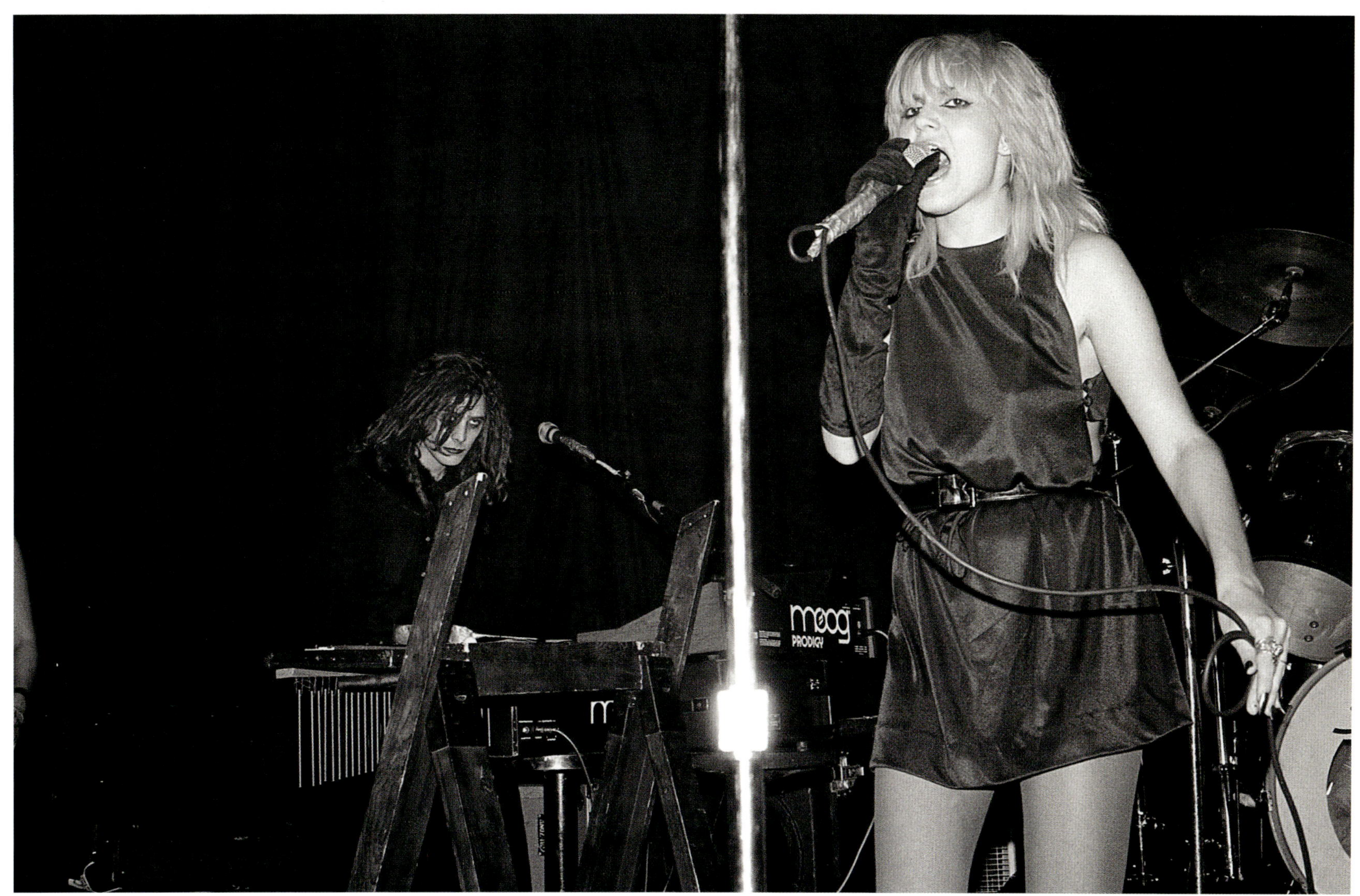

45 Grave

On Broadway, San Francisco, 1983

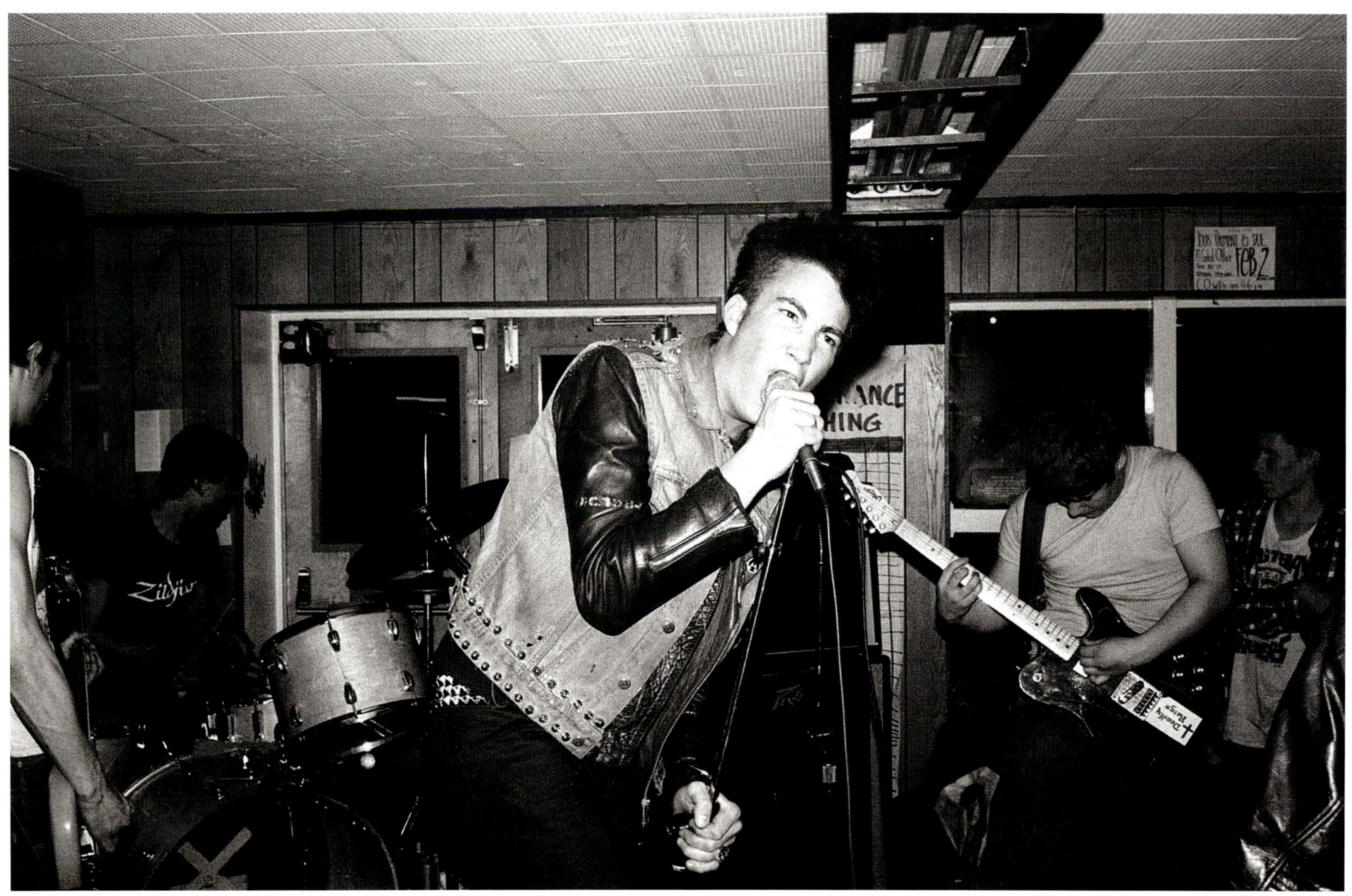

Intensified Chaos
Barrington Hall, Berkeley, 1983

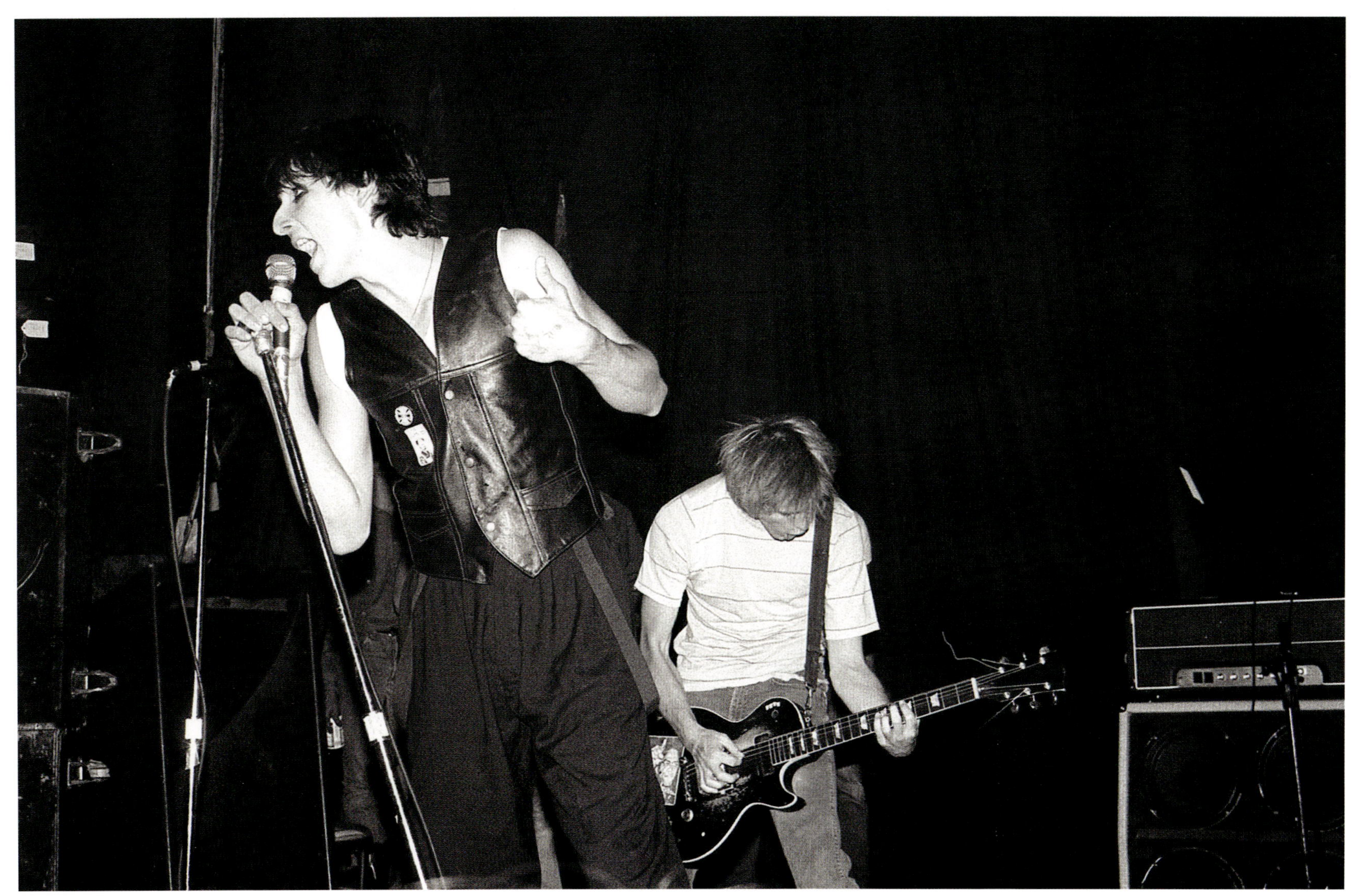

Los Olvidados
On Broadway, San Francisco, 1983

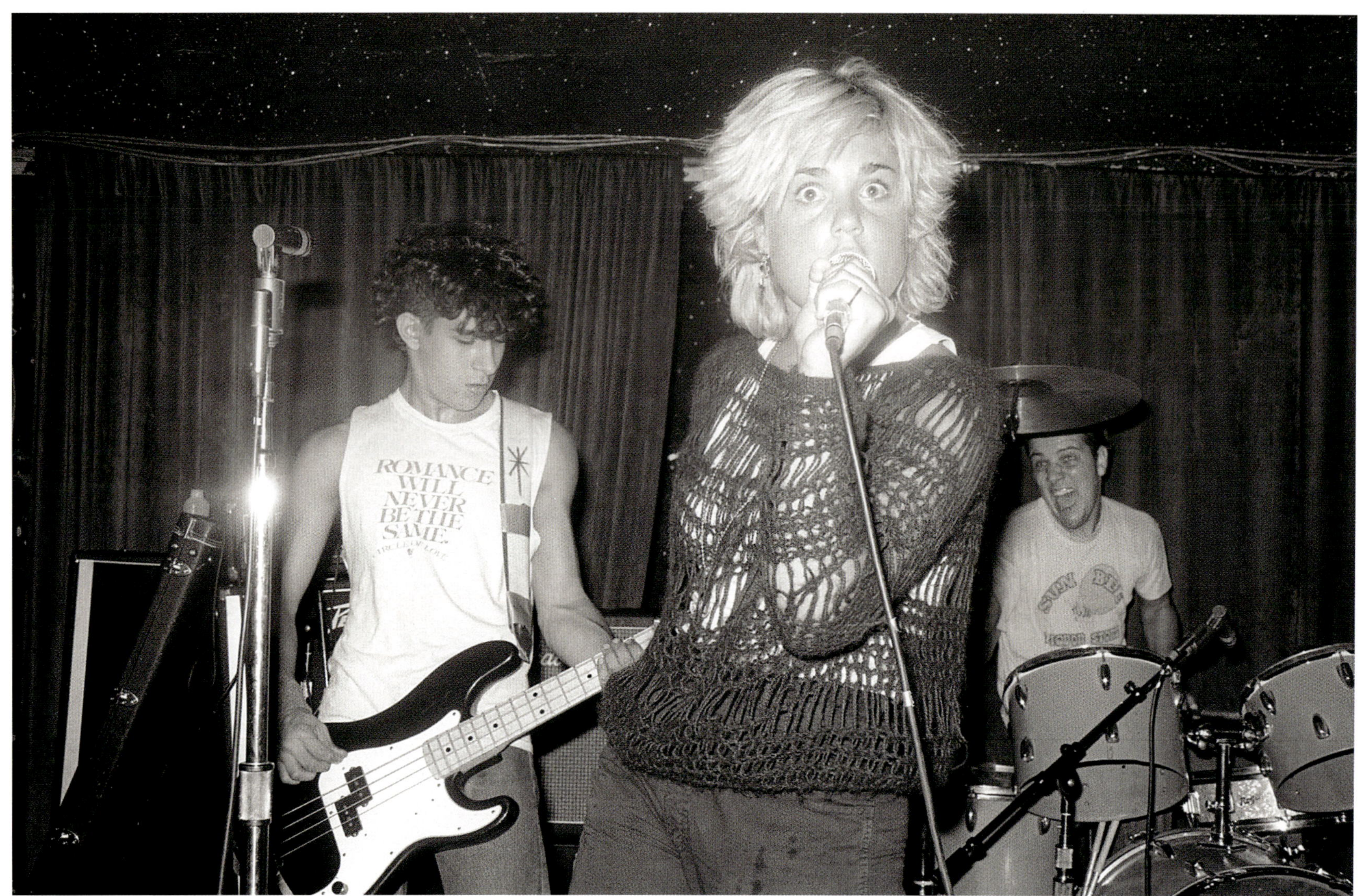

Sin 34
Ruthie's Inn, Berkeley, 1983

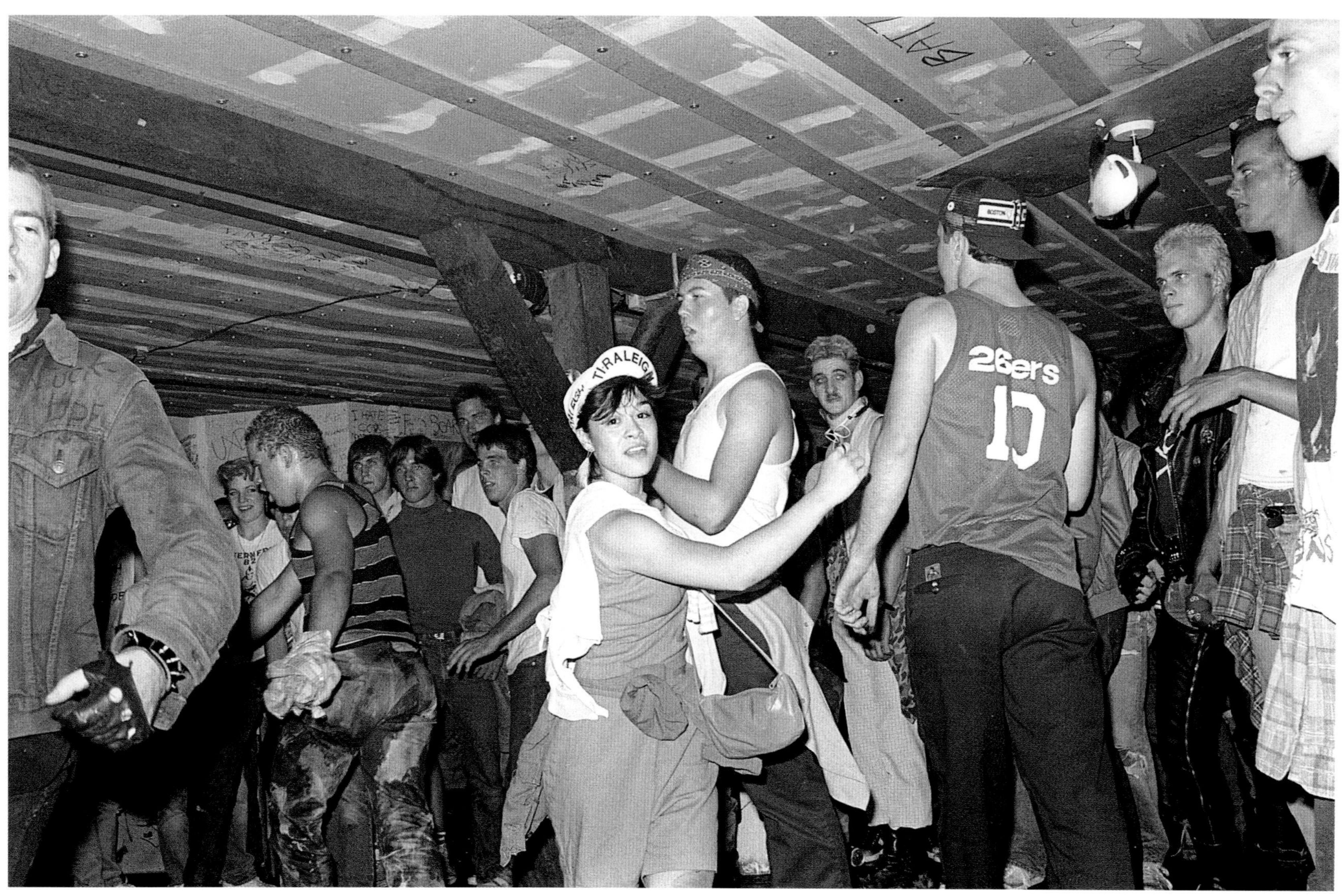

Tool & Die, San Francisco, 1983

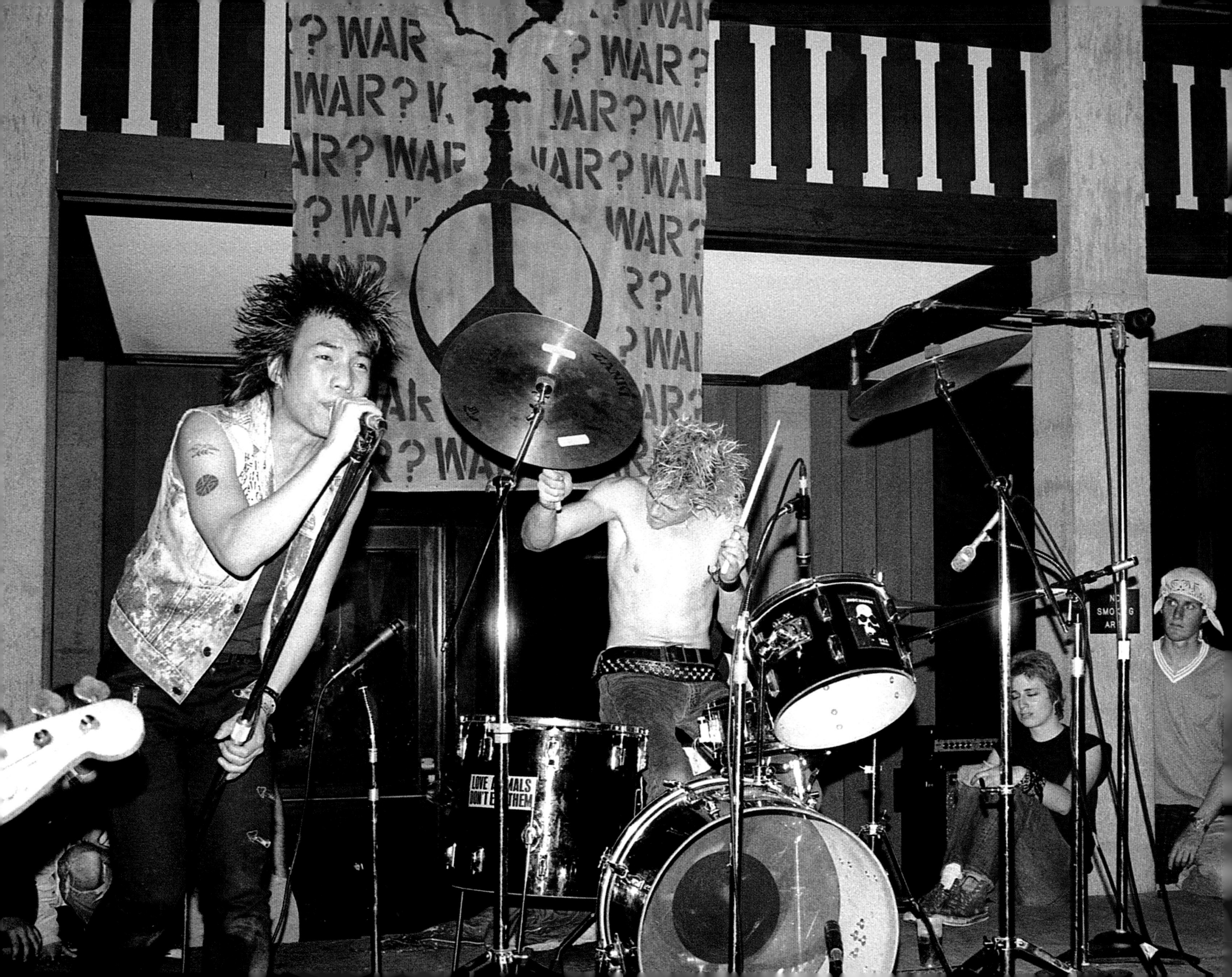
WAR?
WAR? V.
WAR? WAR?
WAR? WAR
? WAR?
WAR? WAR
? WA
R? W
WAR
ZANKI
LOVE ANIMALS
DON'T EAT THEM
NO
SMOKING
AREA

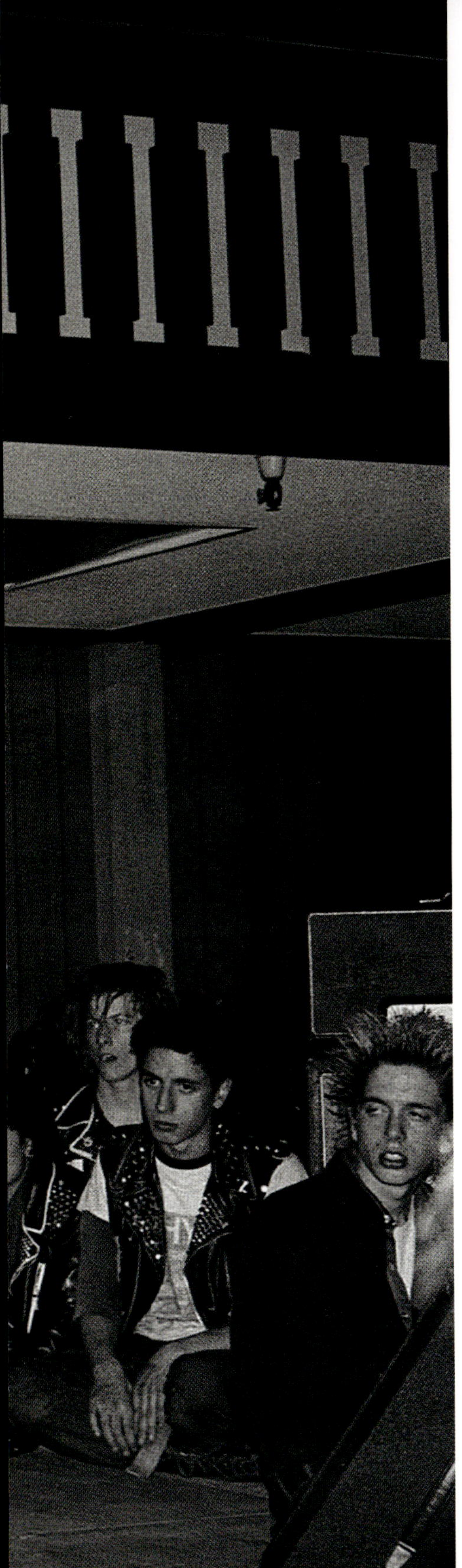

Crucifix
De Anza College, Cupertino, 1983

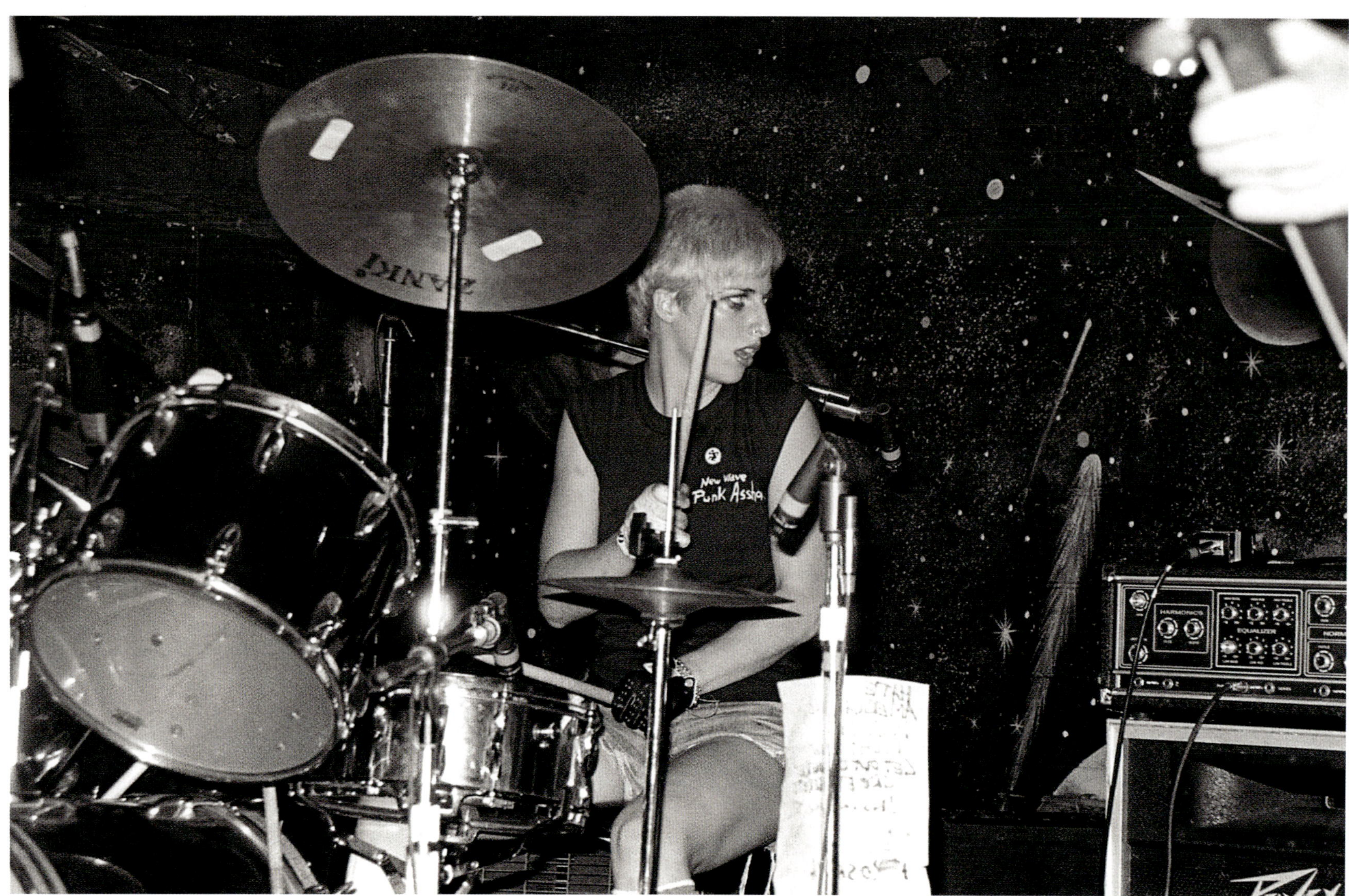

Deadly Reign

Ruthie's Inn, Berkeley, 1983

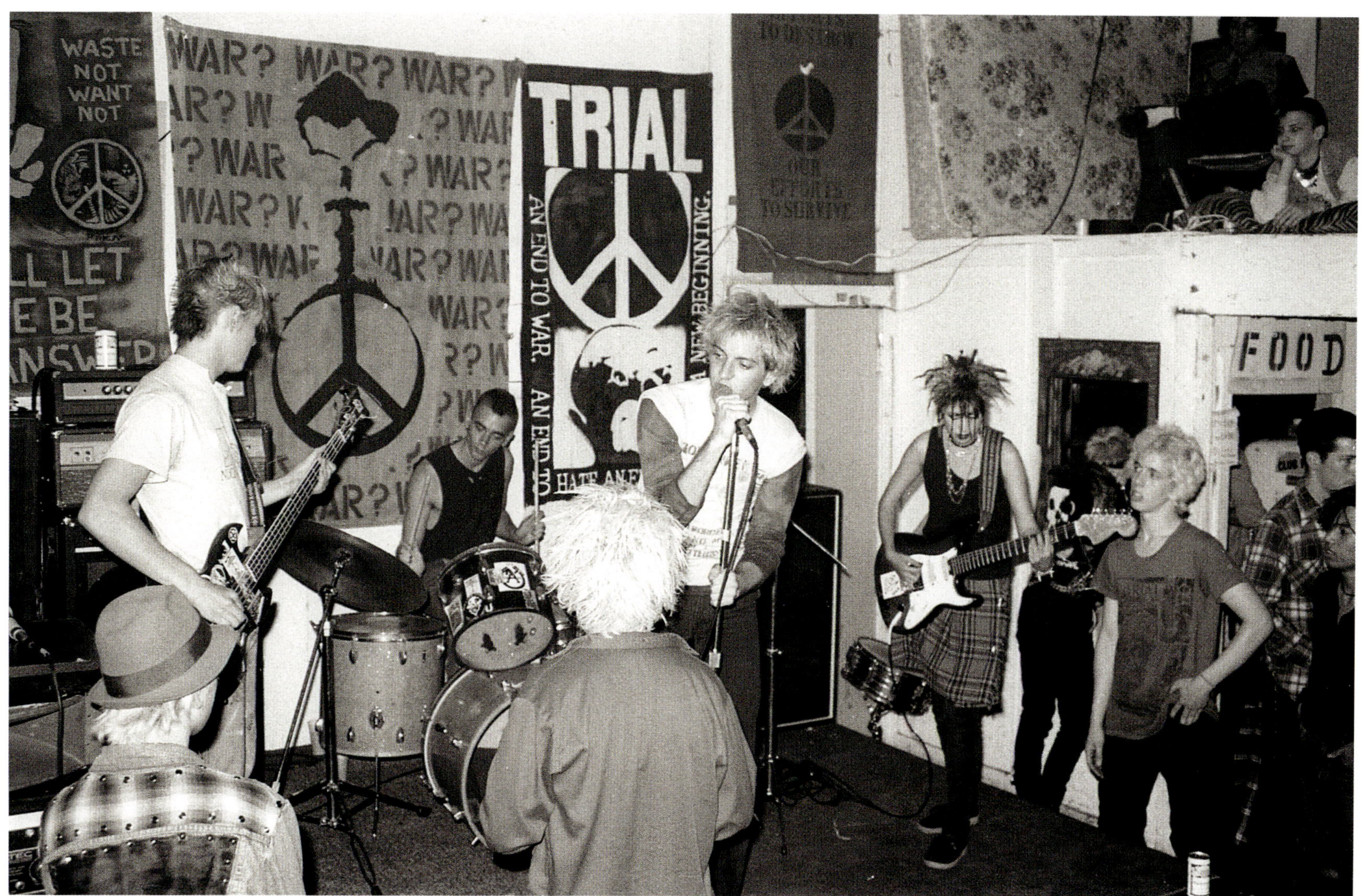

Treason

Club Foot, San Francisco, 1983

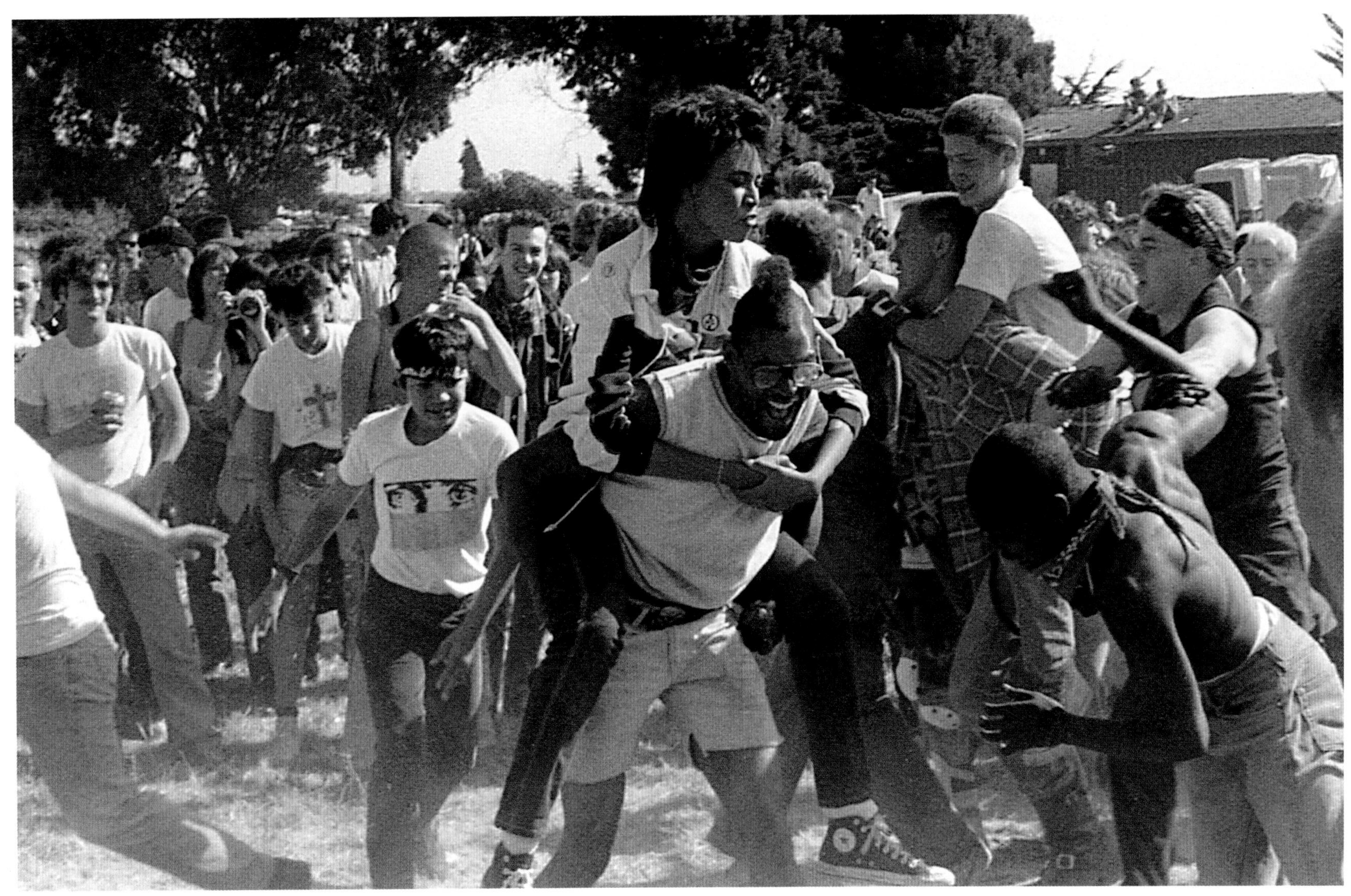

Aquatic Park, Berkeley, 1984

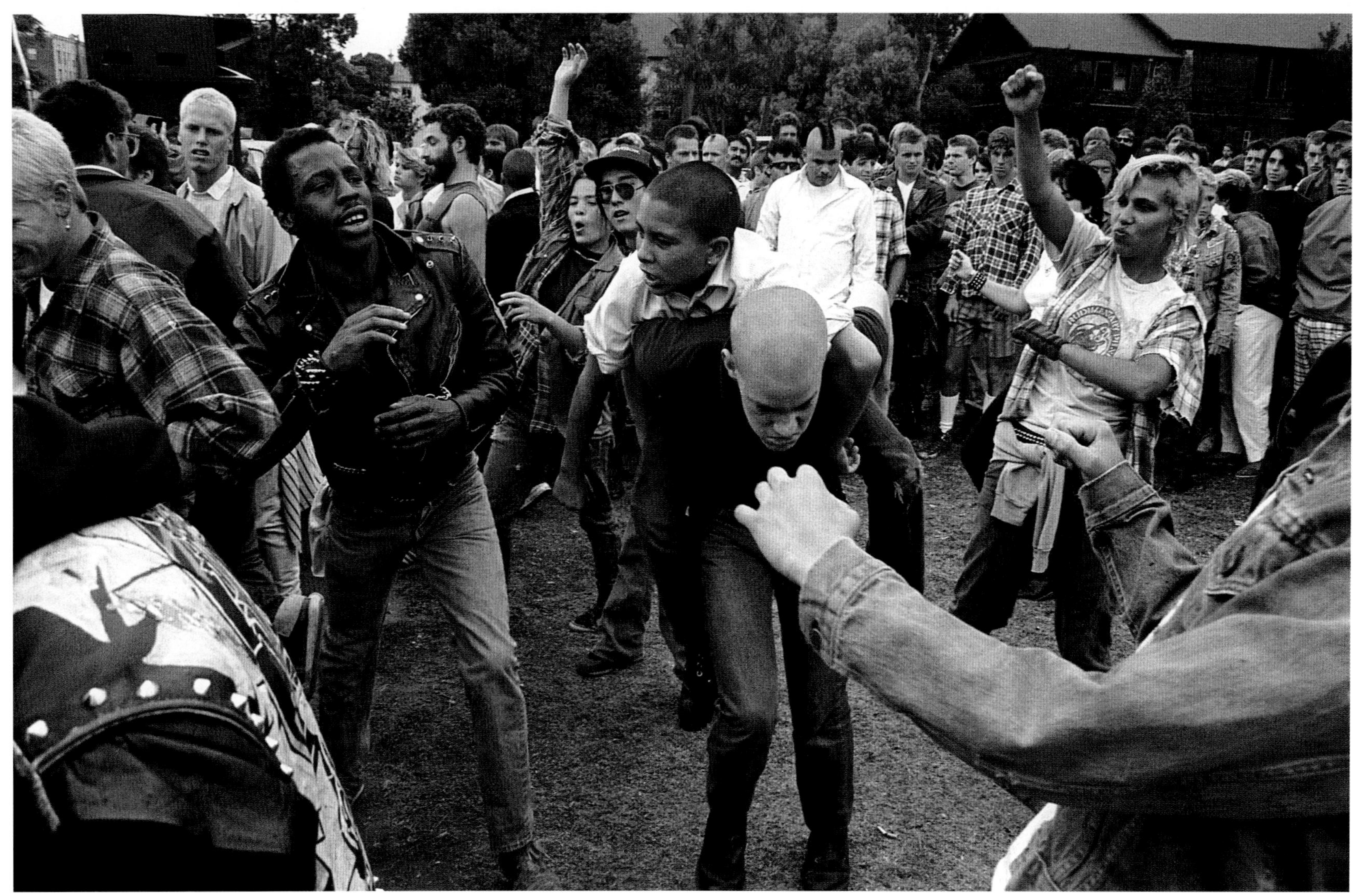

People's Park, Berkeley, 1984

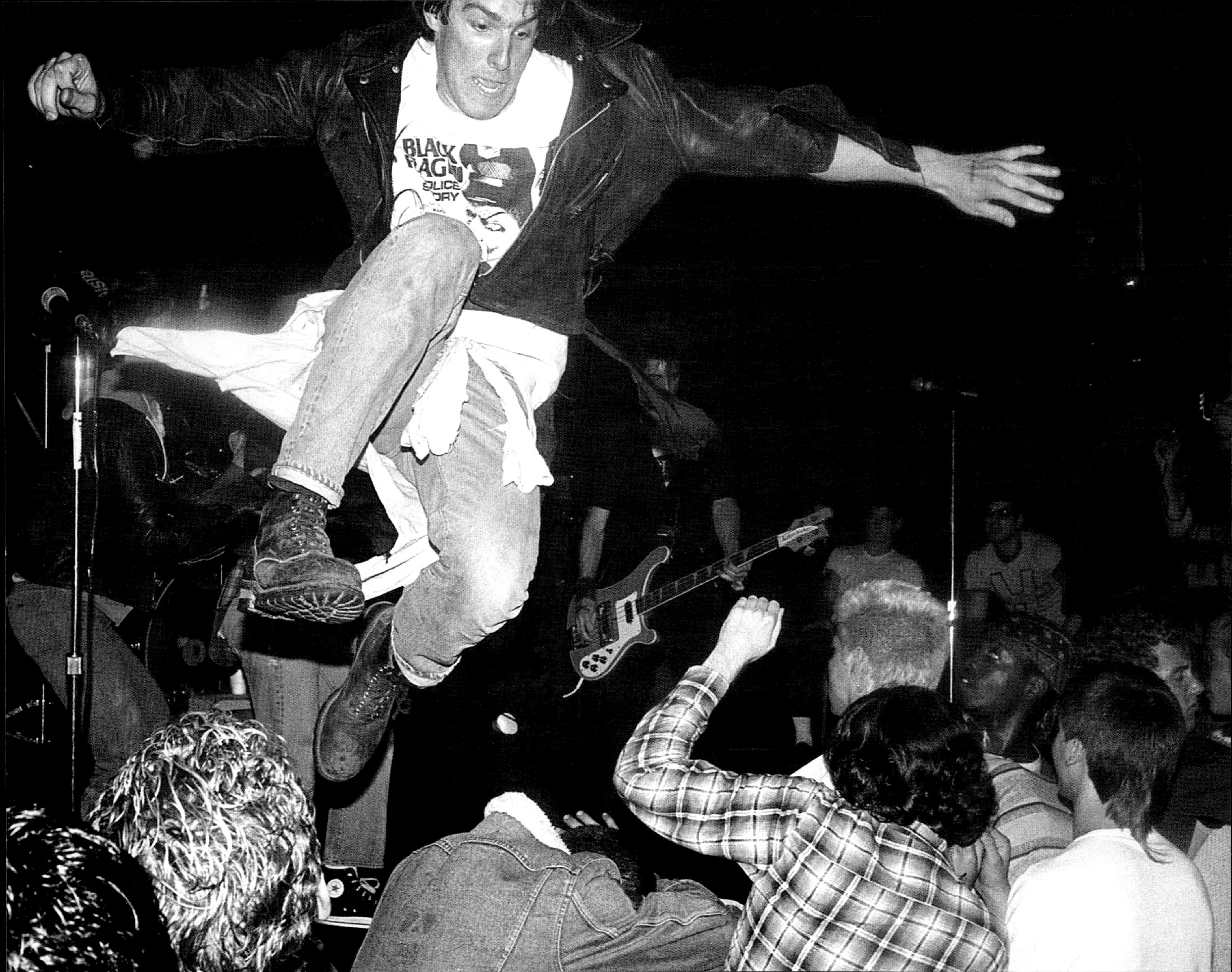

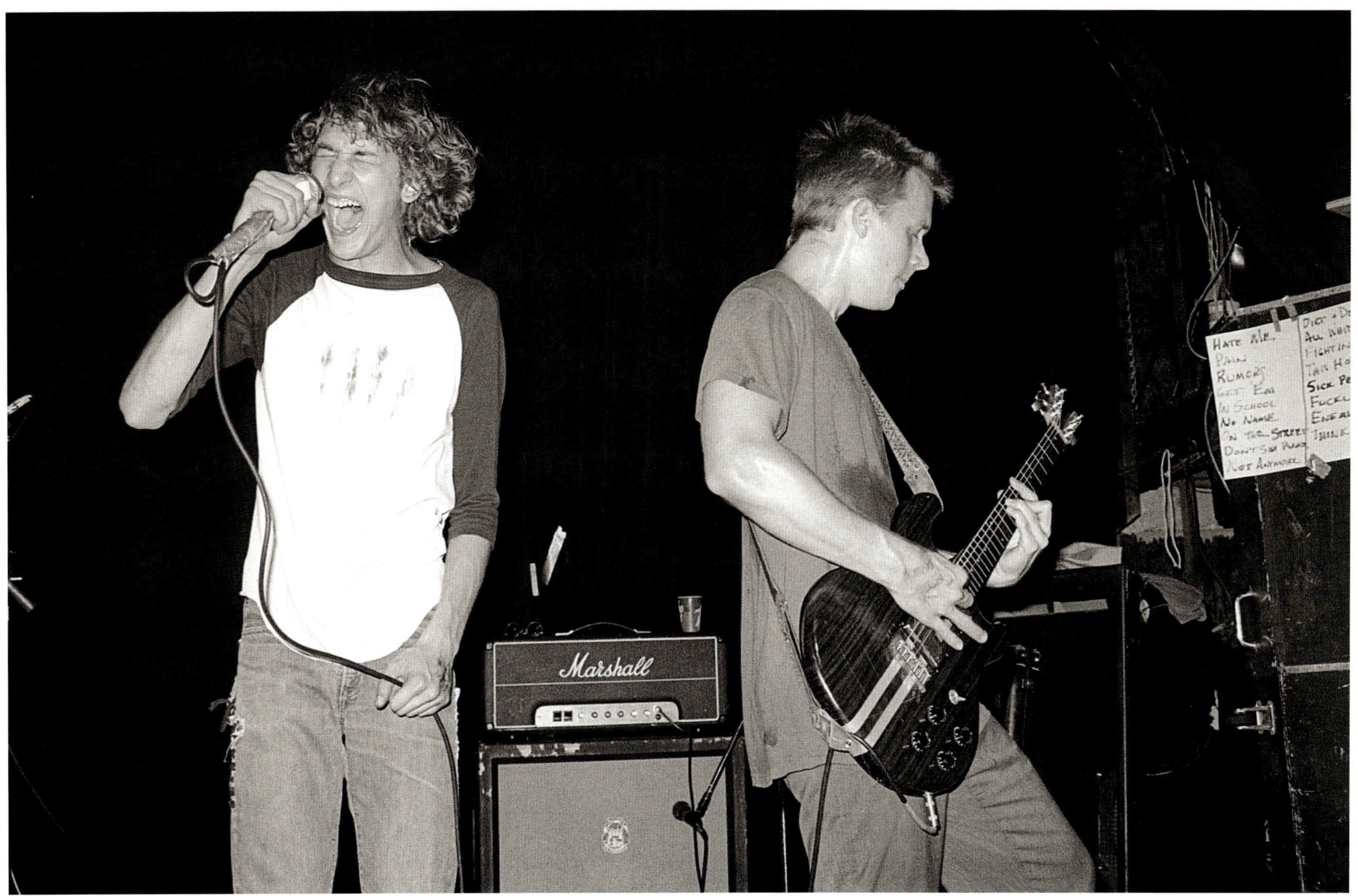

Die Kreuzen

On Broadway, San Francisco, 1983

Opposite:

On Broadway, 1983

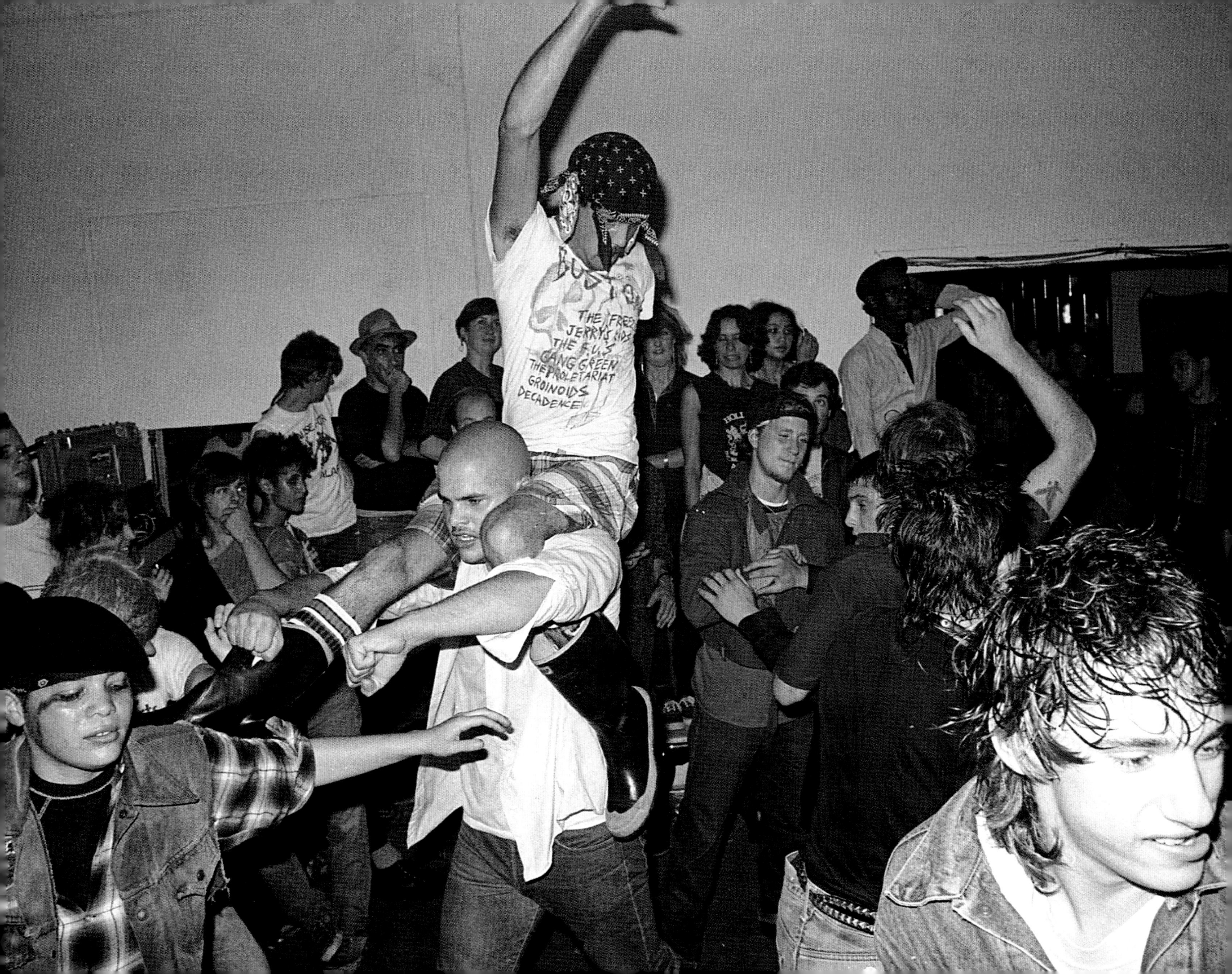
BOSTON
THE FREEZE
JERRY'S KIDS
THE F.U.'S
GANG GREEN
THE PROLETARIAT
GROINOIDS
DECADENCE

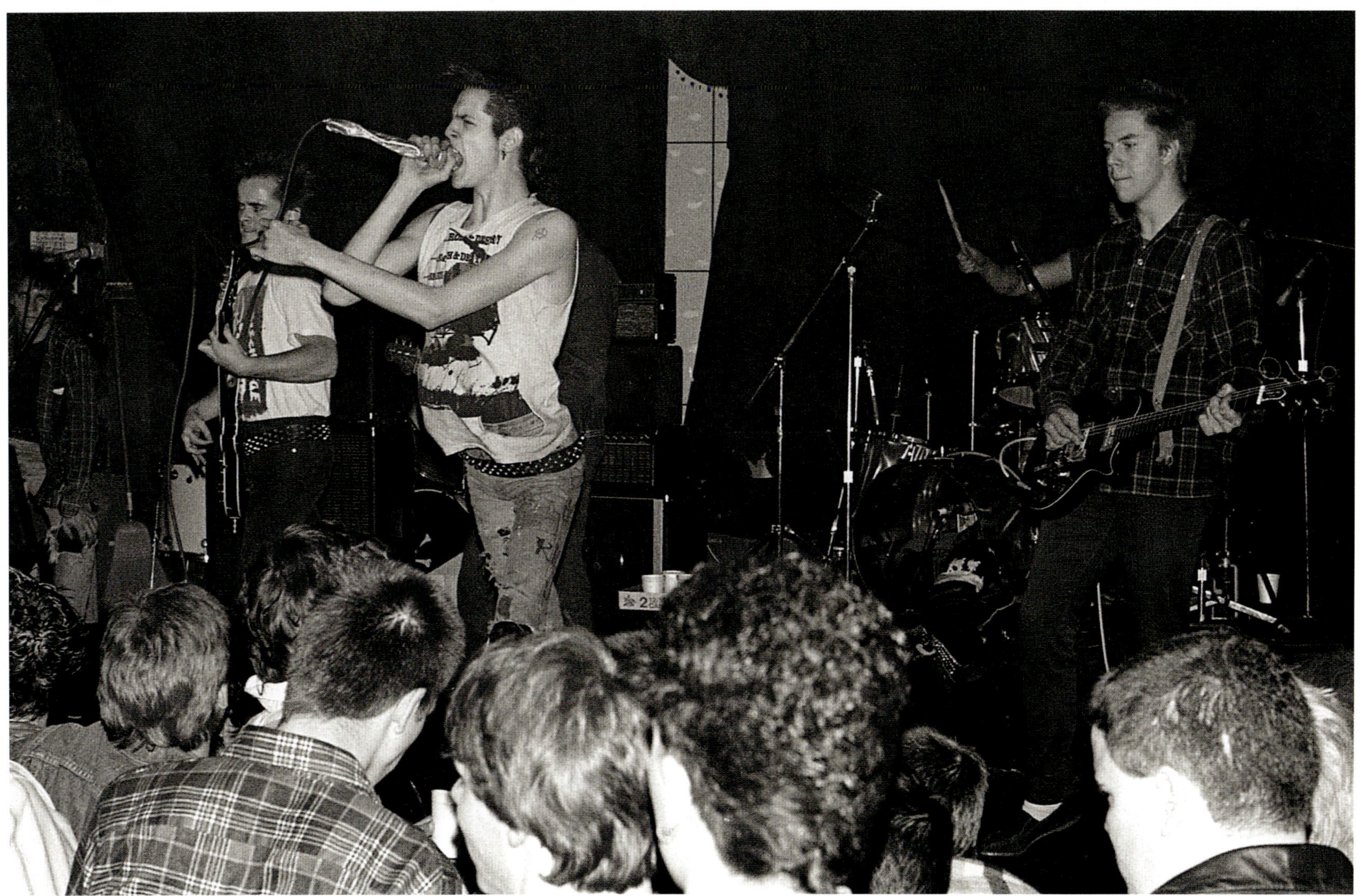

Social Unrest

On Broadway, San Francisco, 1983

Opposite:

Fiji and Tropical Island Junction, Oakland, 1984

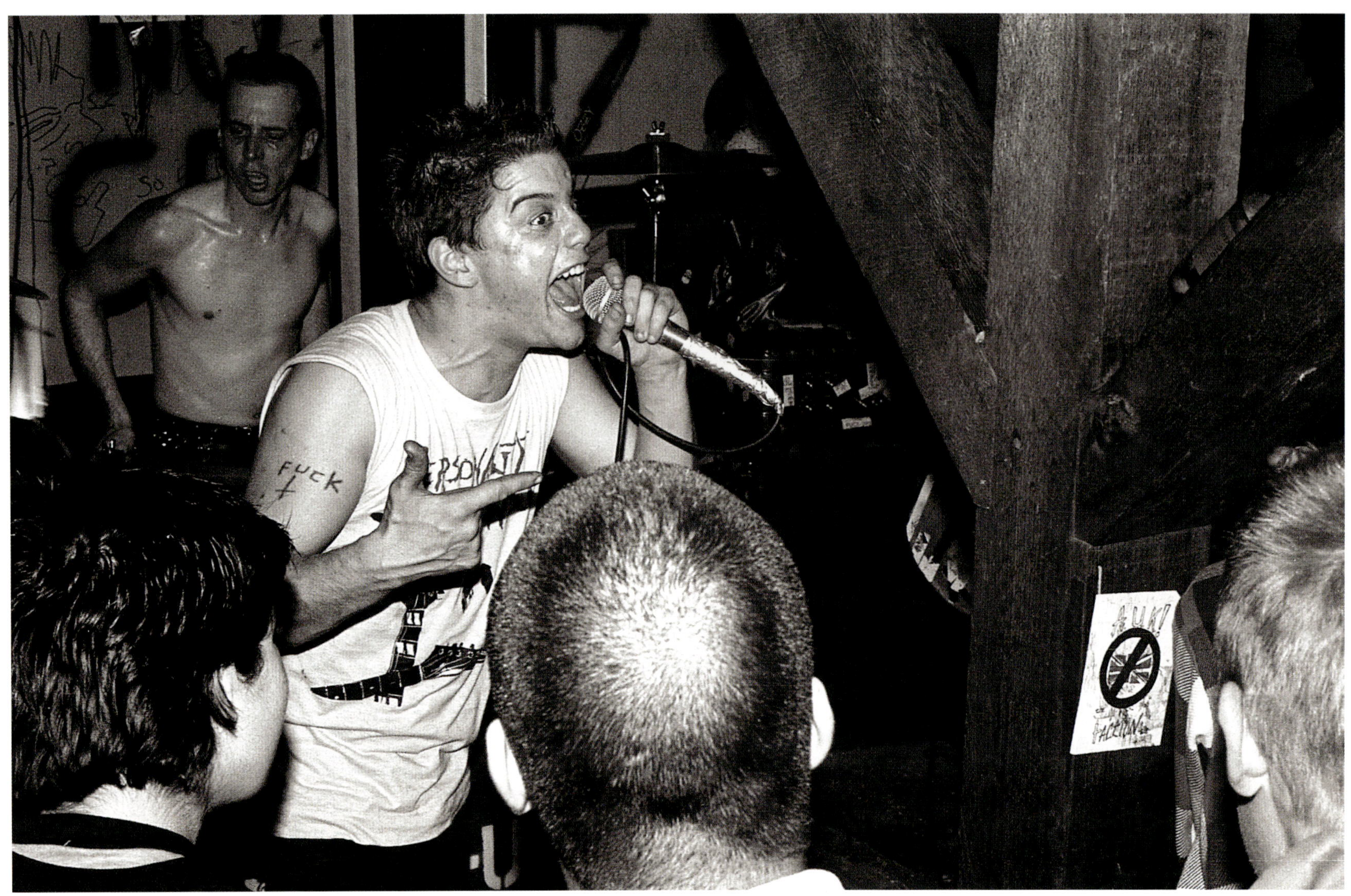

The Fuck-Ups

Tool & Die, San Francisco, 1982

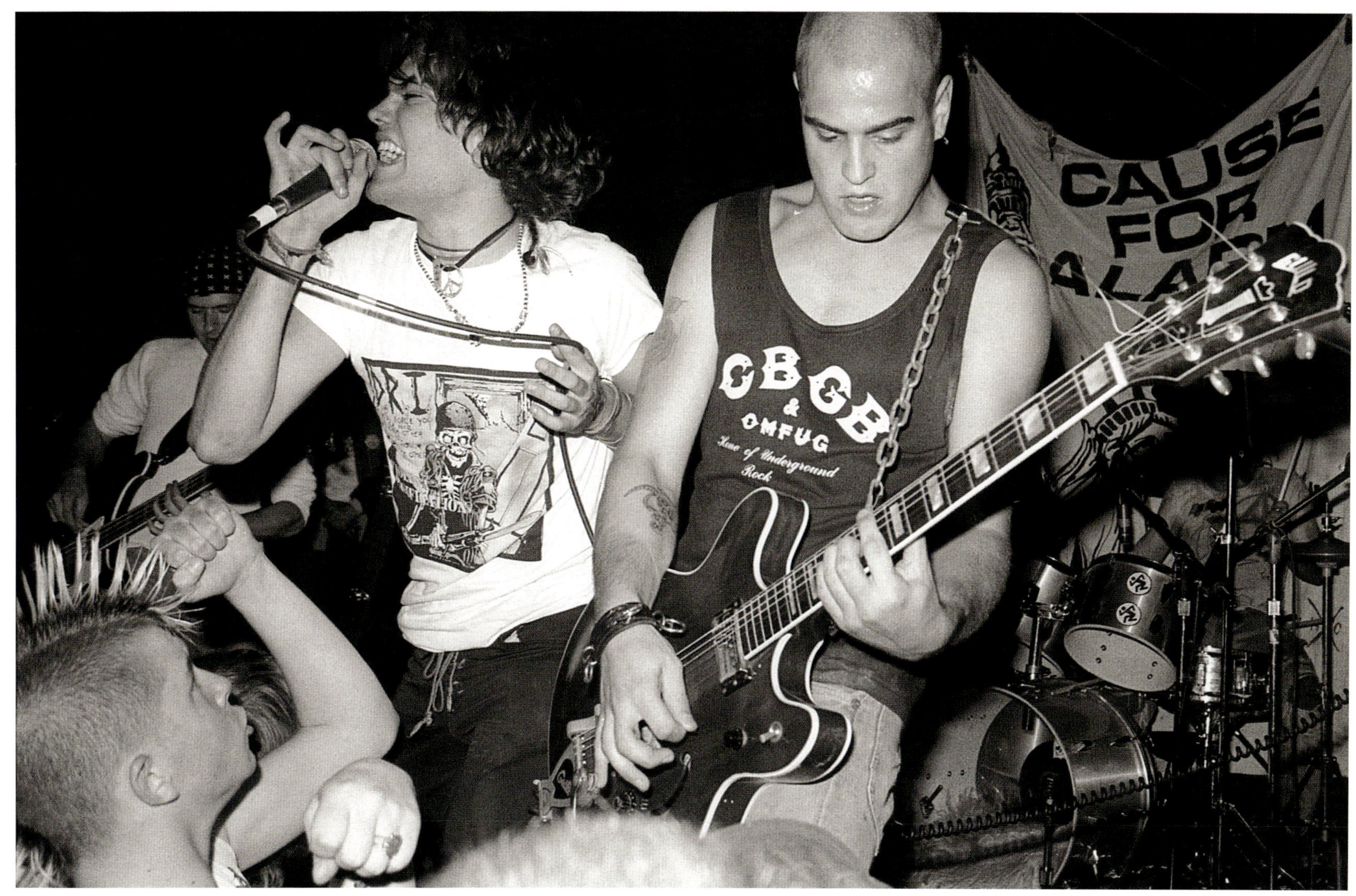

Cause For Alarm
Booker T. Washington Community Center, San Francisco, 1984

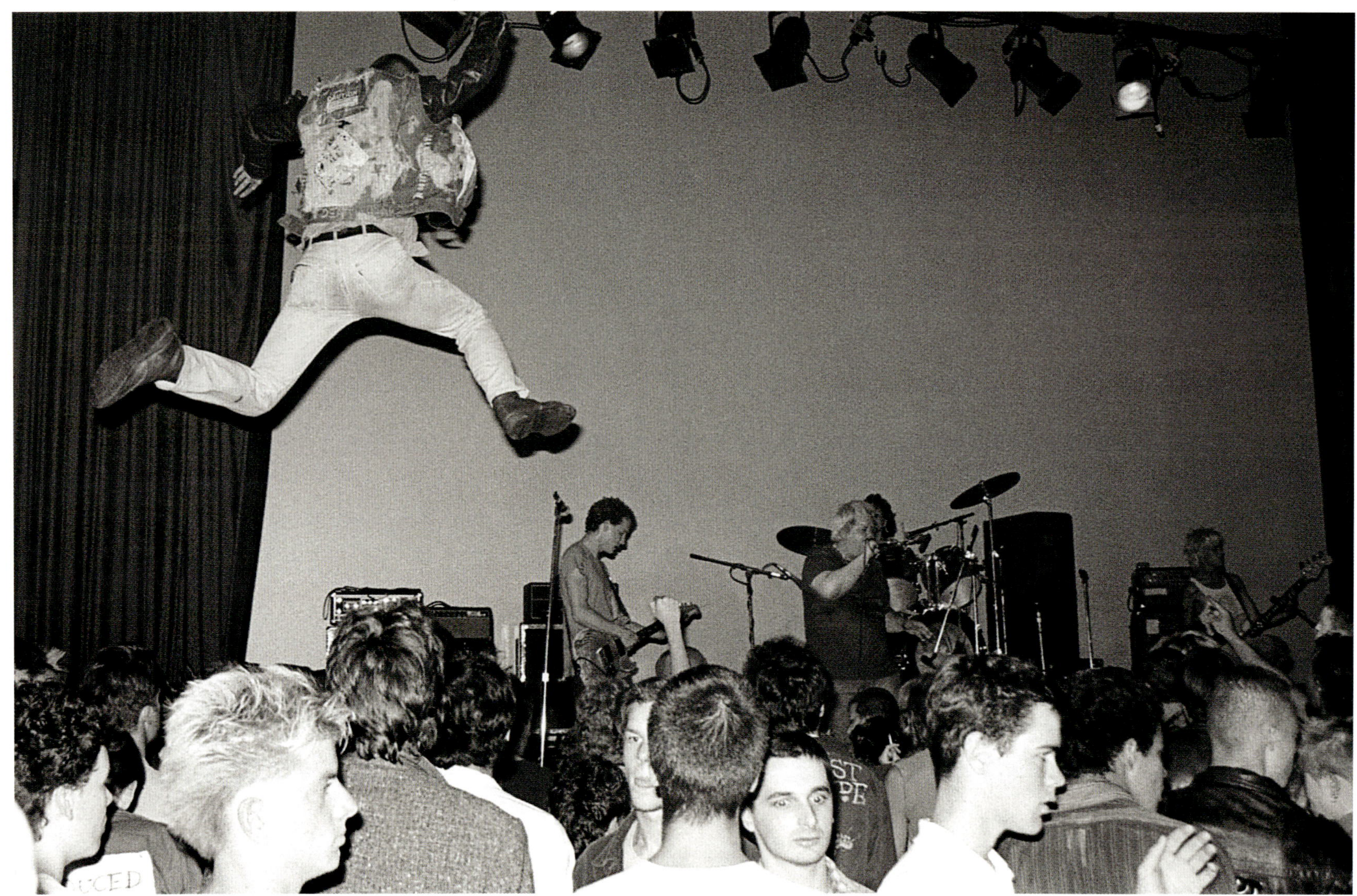

The Dicks
Market Street Cinema, San Francisco, 1984

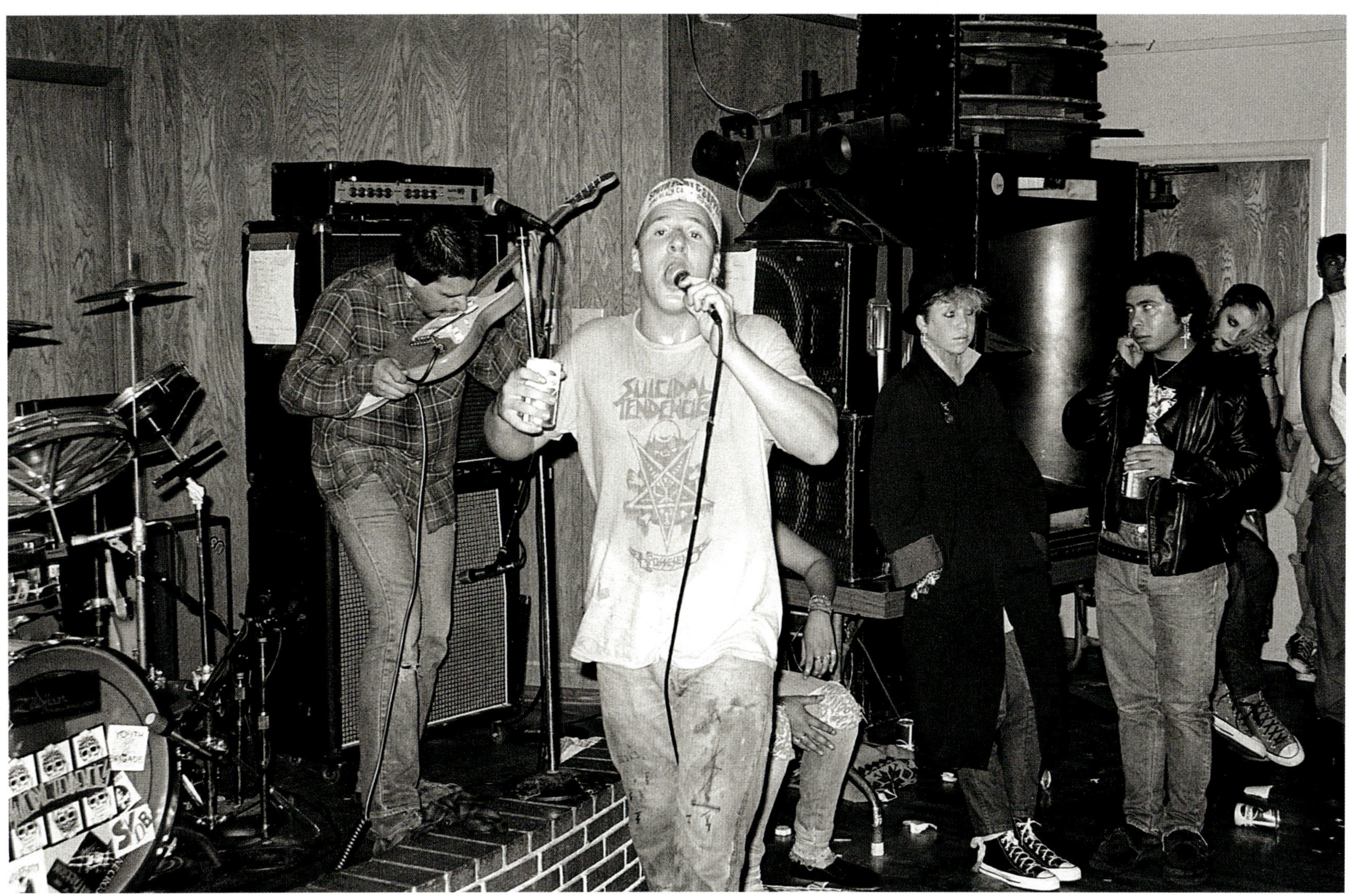

Suicidal Tendencies

San Jose, 1983

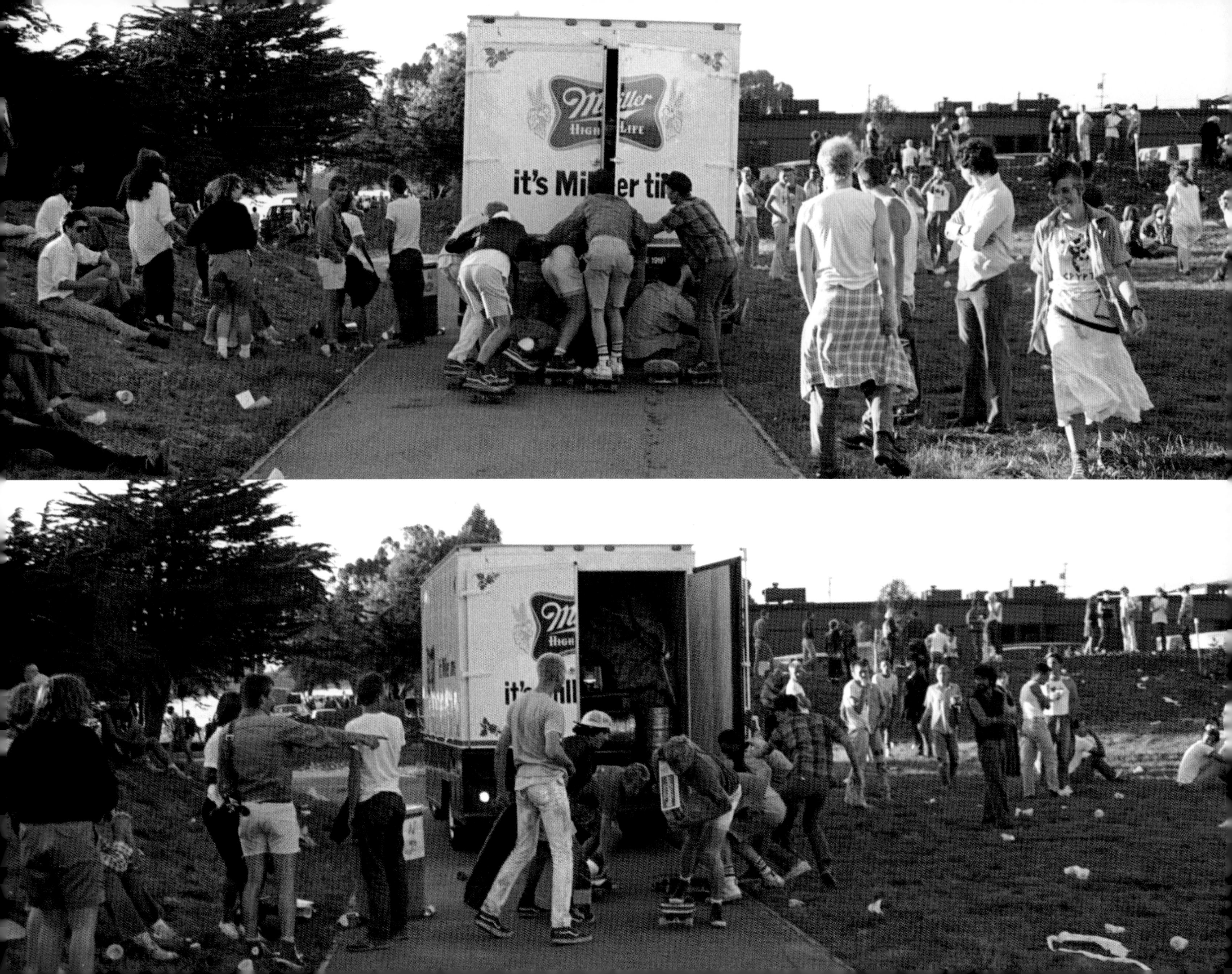
Miller
HIGH LIFE
it's Miller time

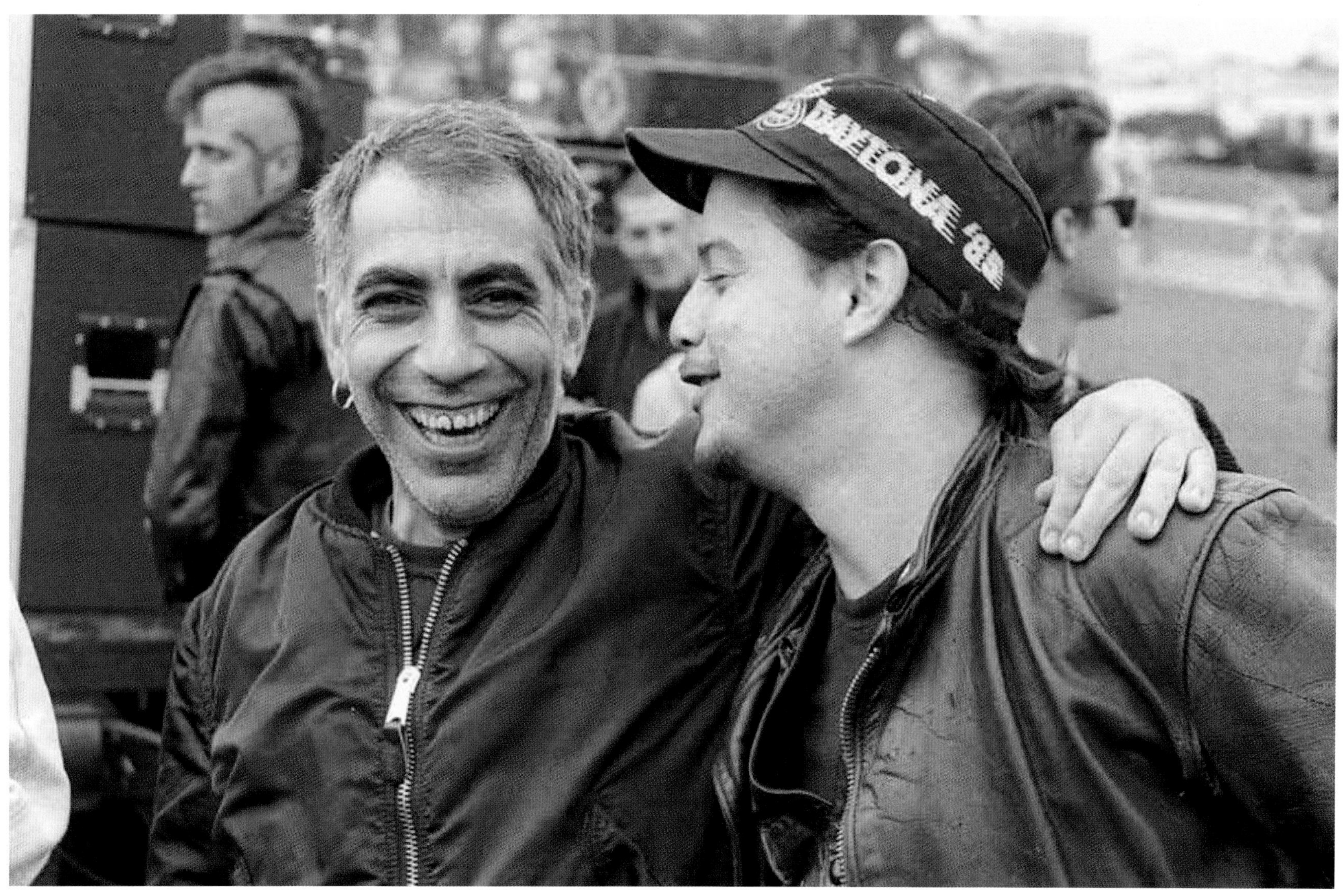

Tim Yohannan and Bob Noxious, San Francisco, 1986

Opposite:
The Heroic Beer Truck Robbery, Aquatic Park, Berkeley, 1984

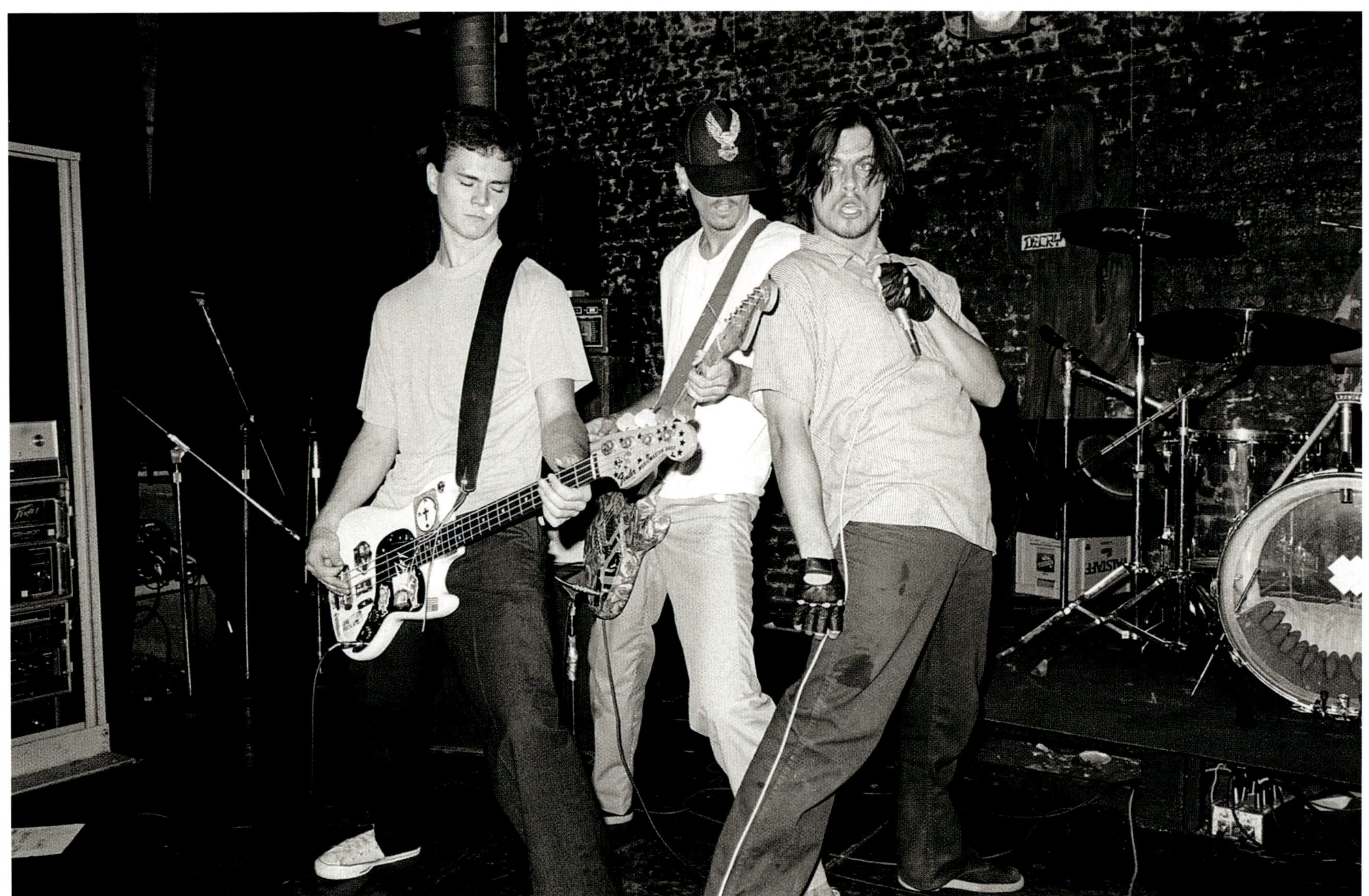

Part Time Christians
Mabuhay Gardens, San Francisco, 1984

Opposite:
Sluglords
People's Park, Berkeley, 1984

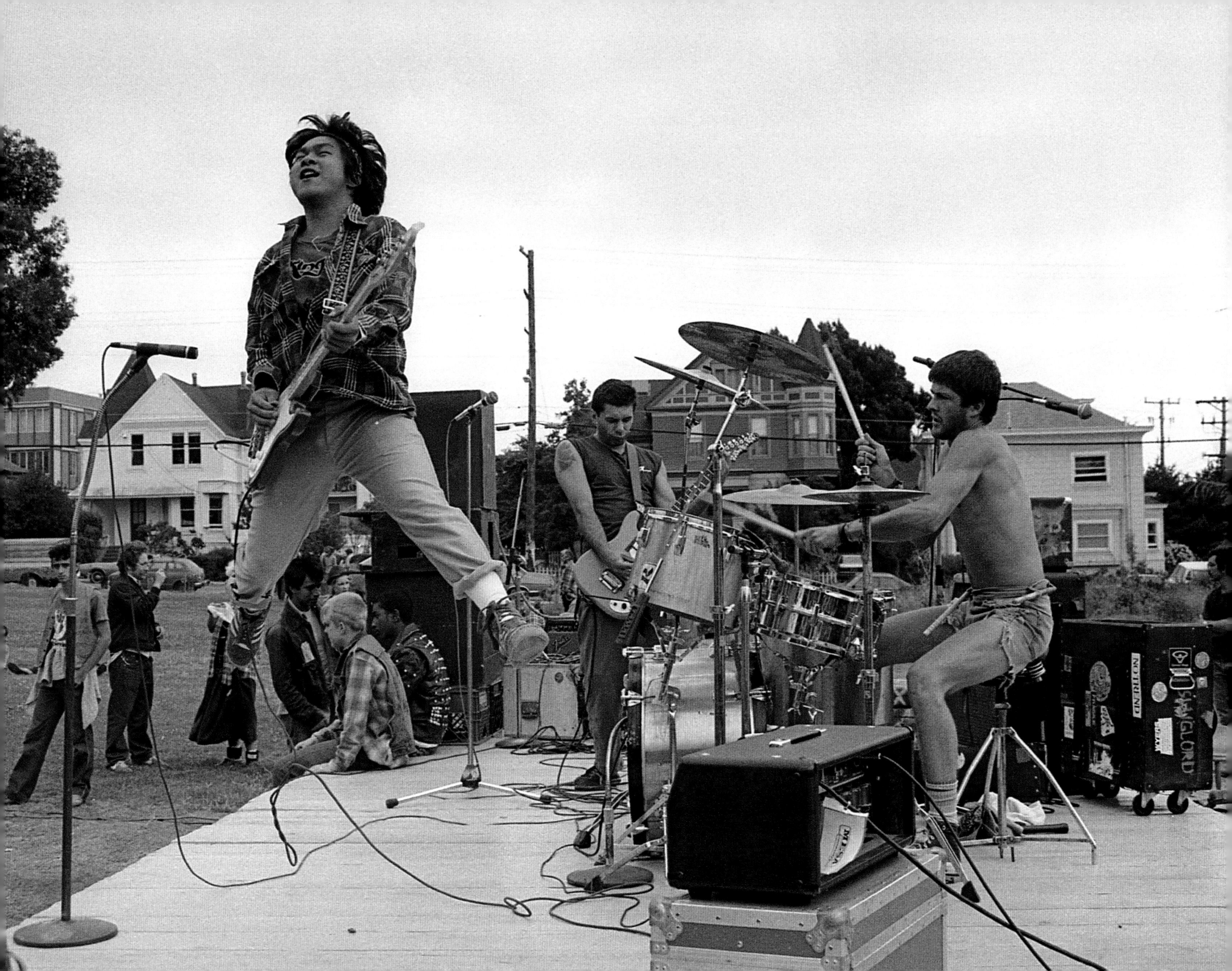

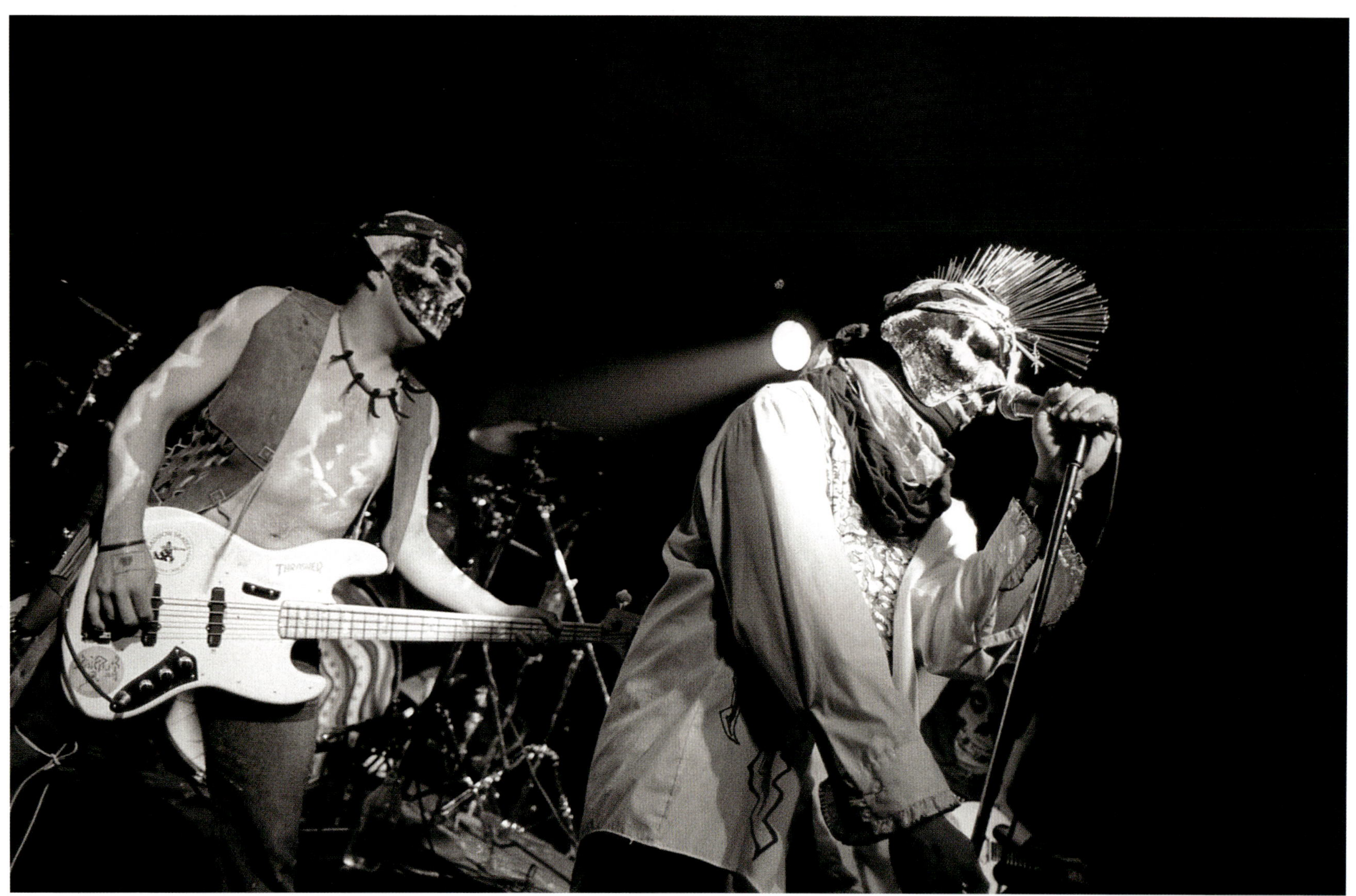

Drunk Injuns

The Farm, San Francisco, 1984

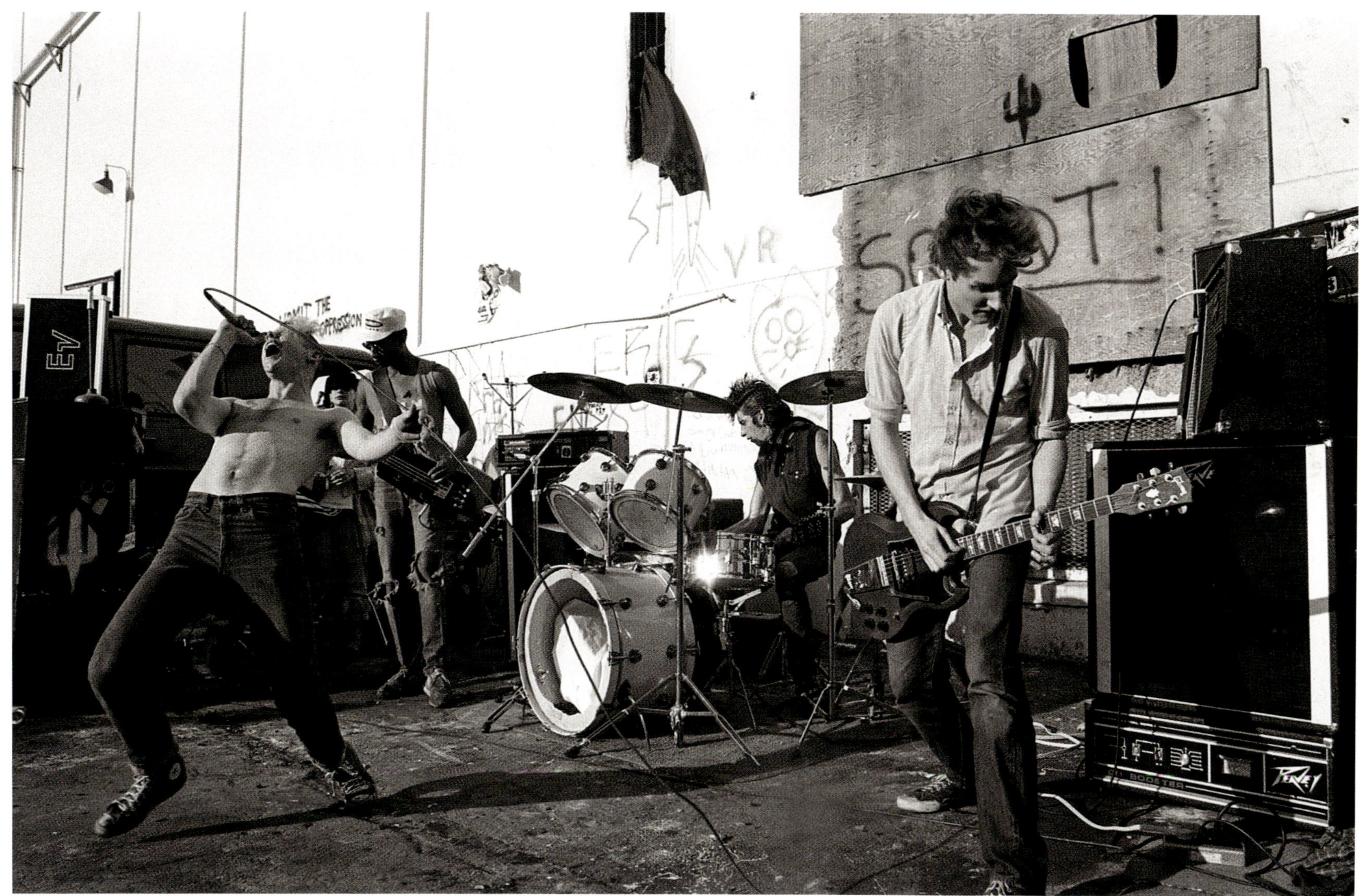

Fang

The Vats, San Francisco, 1984

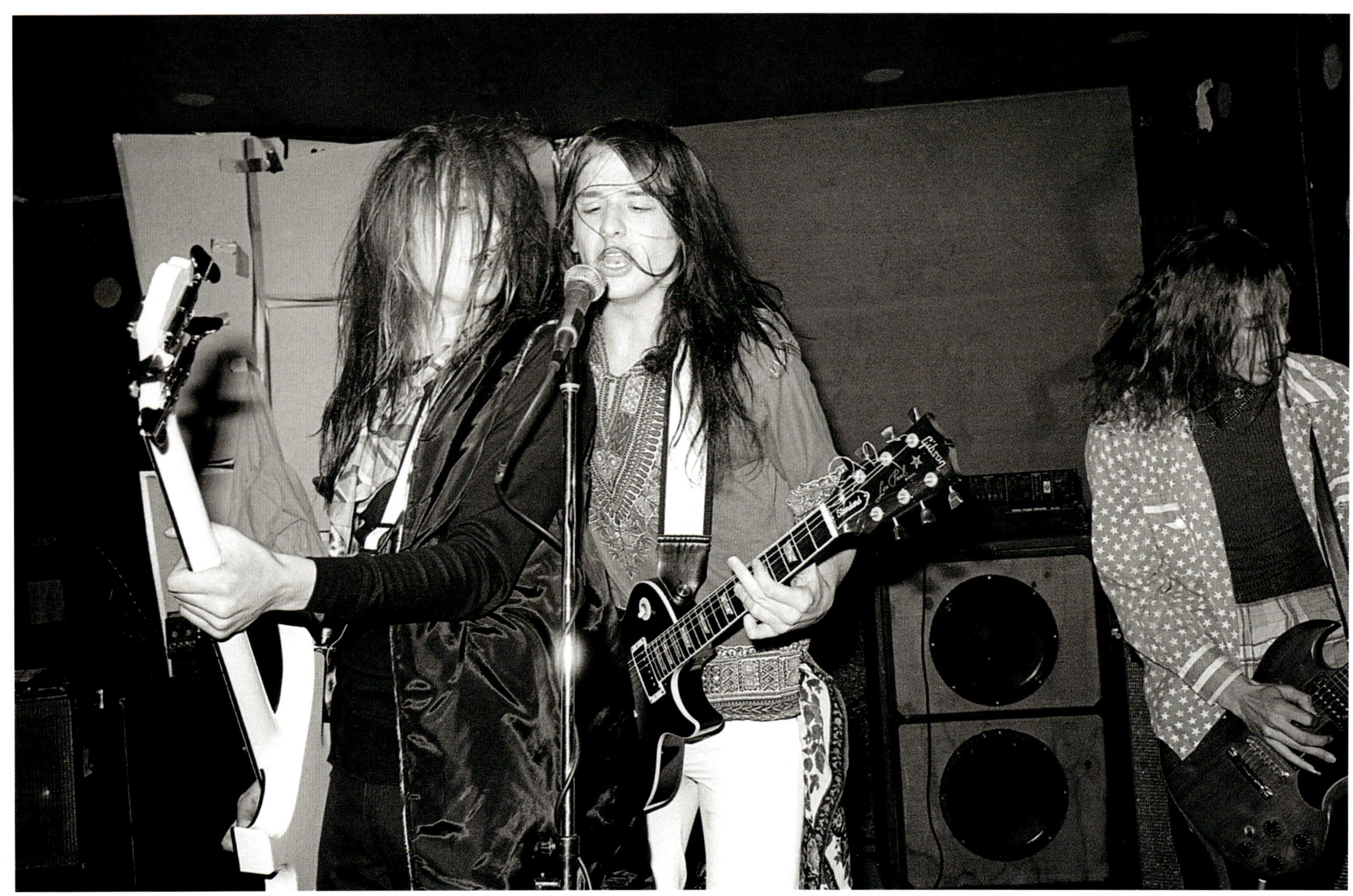

Redd Kross

Al's Bar, Los Angeles, 1985

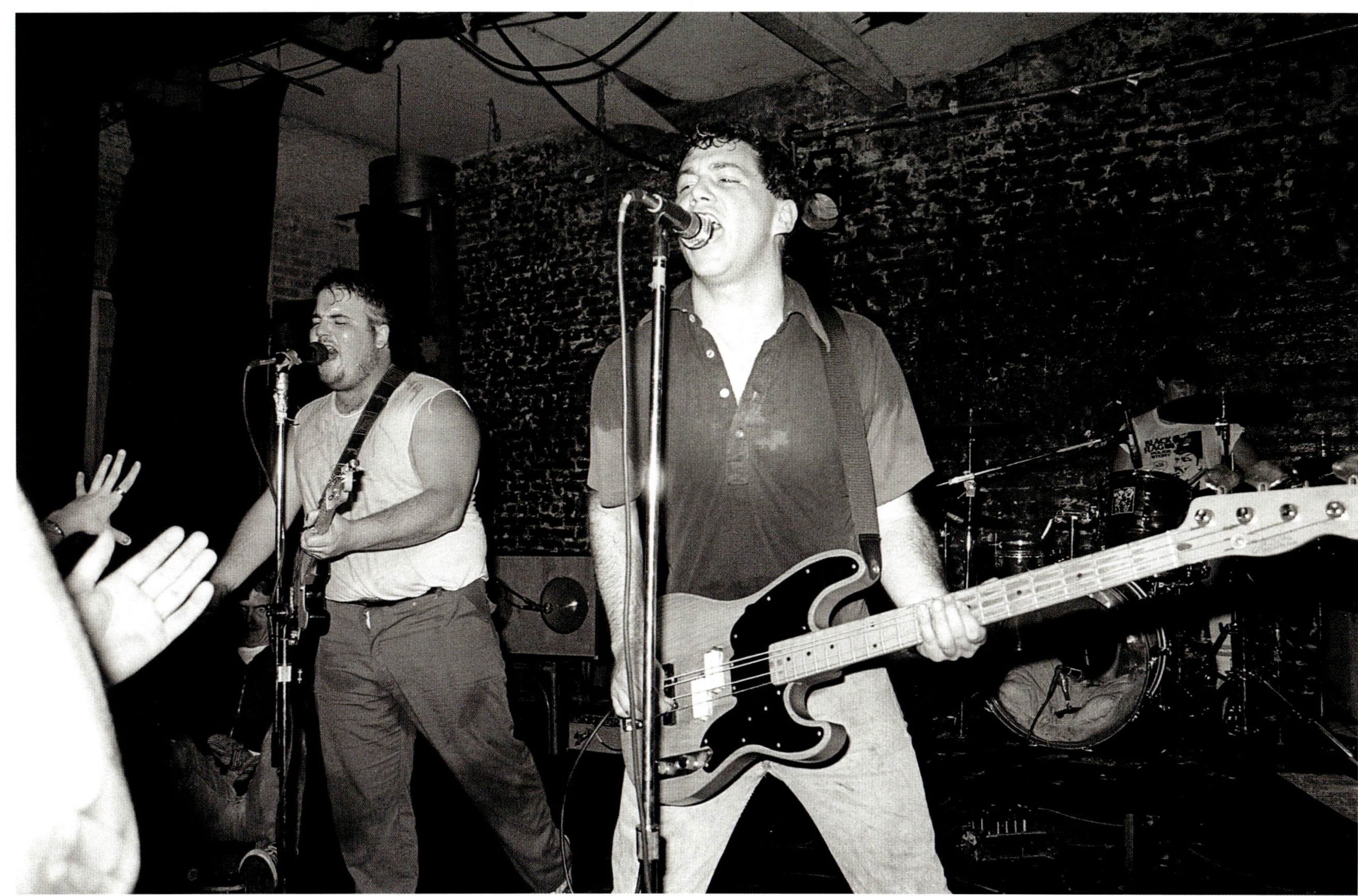

Minutemen
Mabuhay Gardens, San Francisco, 1984

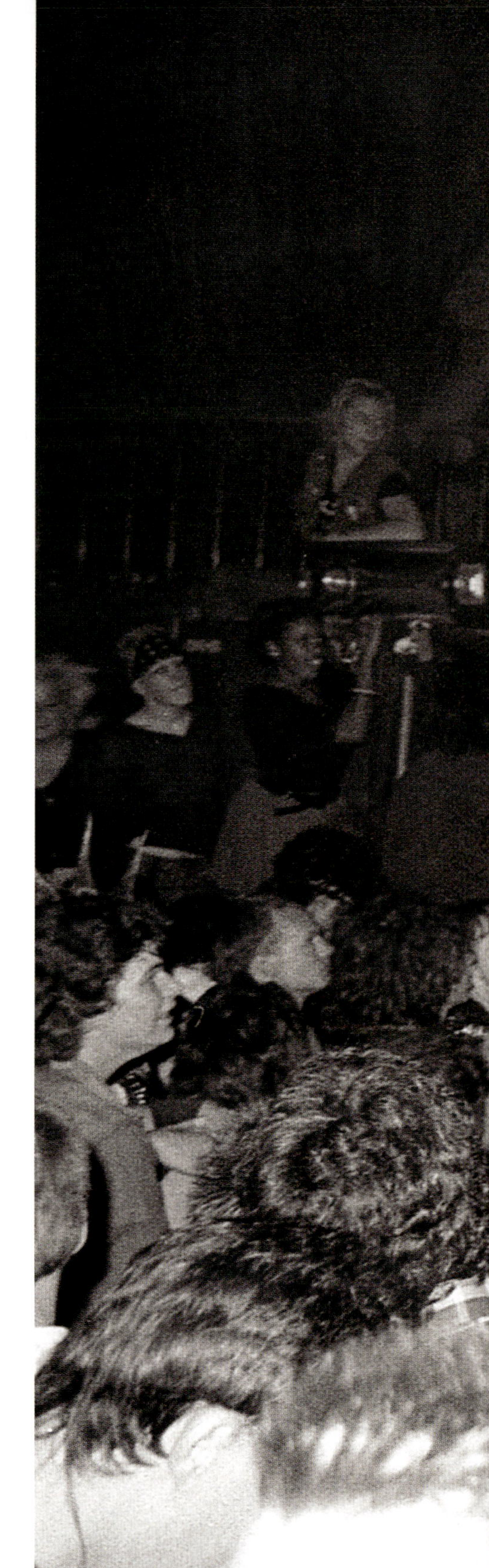

GBH
On Broadway, San Francisco, 1984

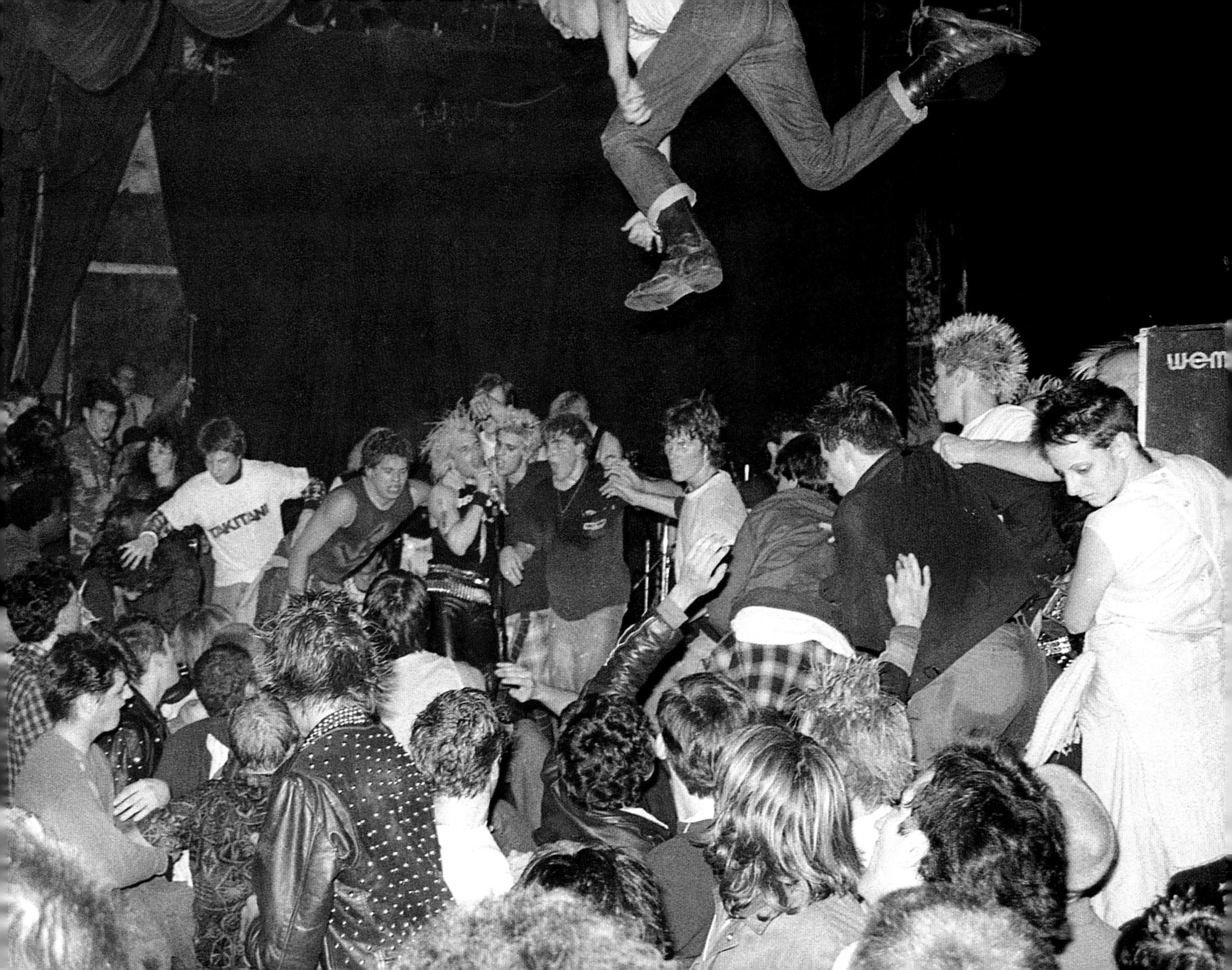

WEM

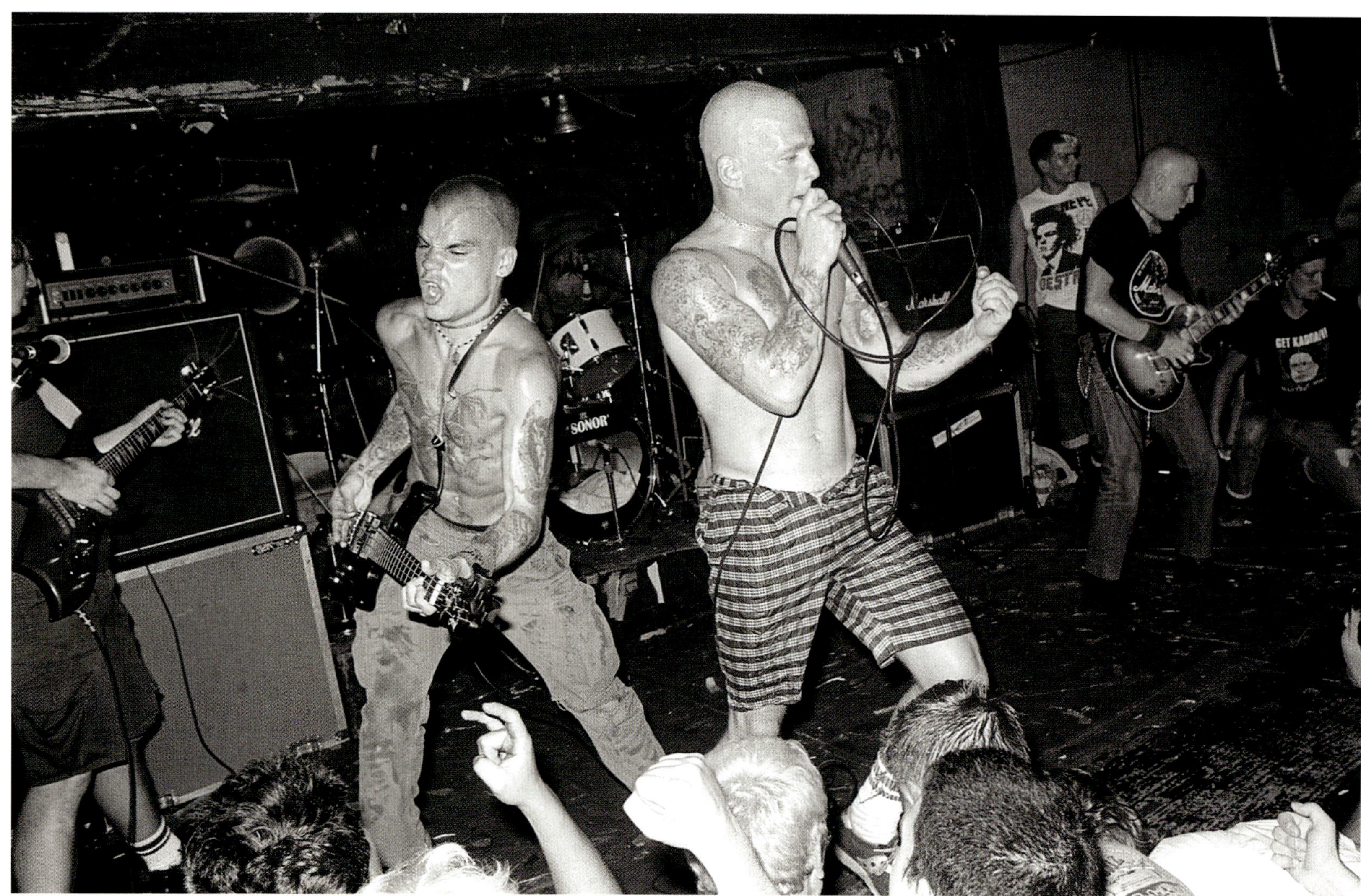

Cro-Mags
Ruthie's Inn, Berkeley, 1985

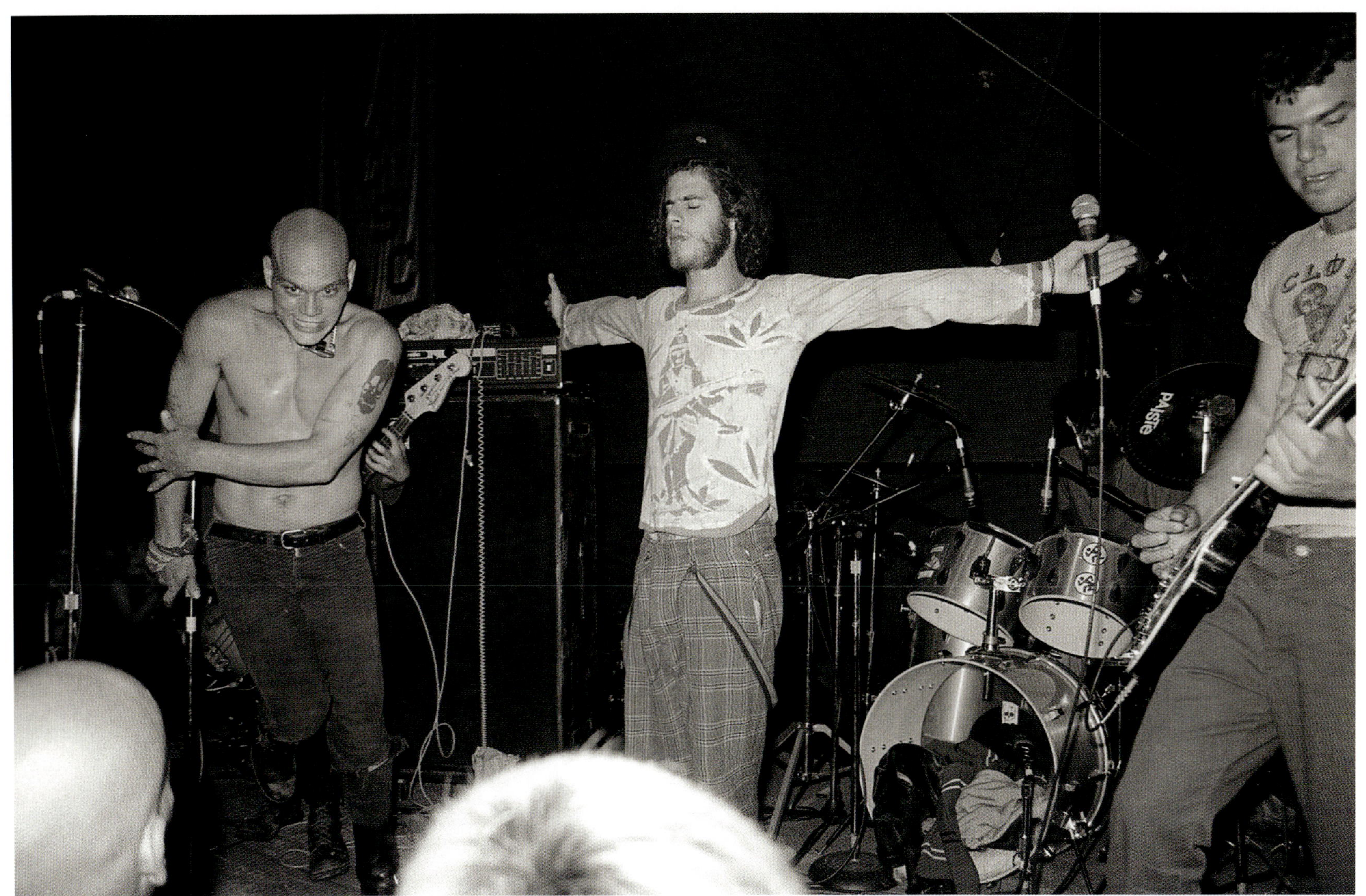

Reagan Youth
Booker T. Washington Community Center, San Francisco, 1984

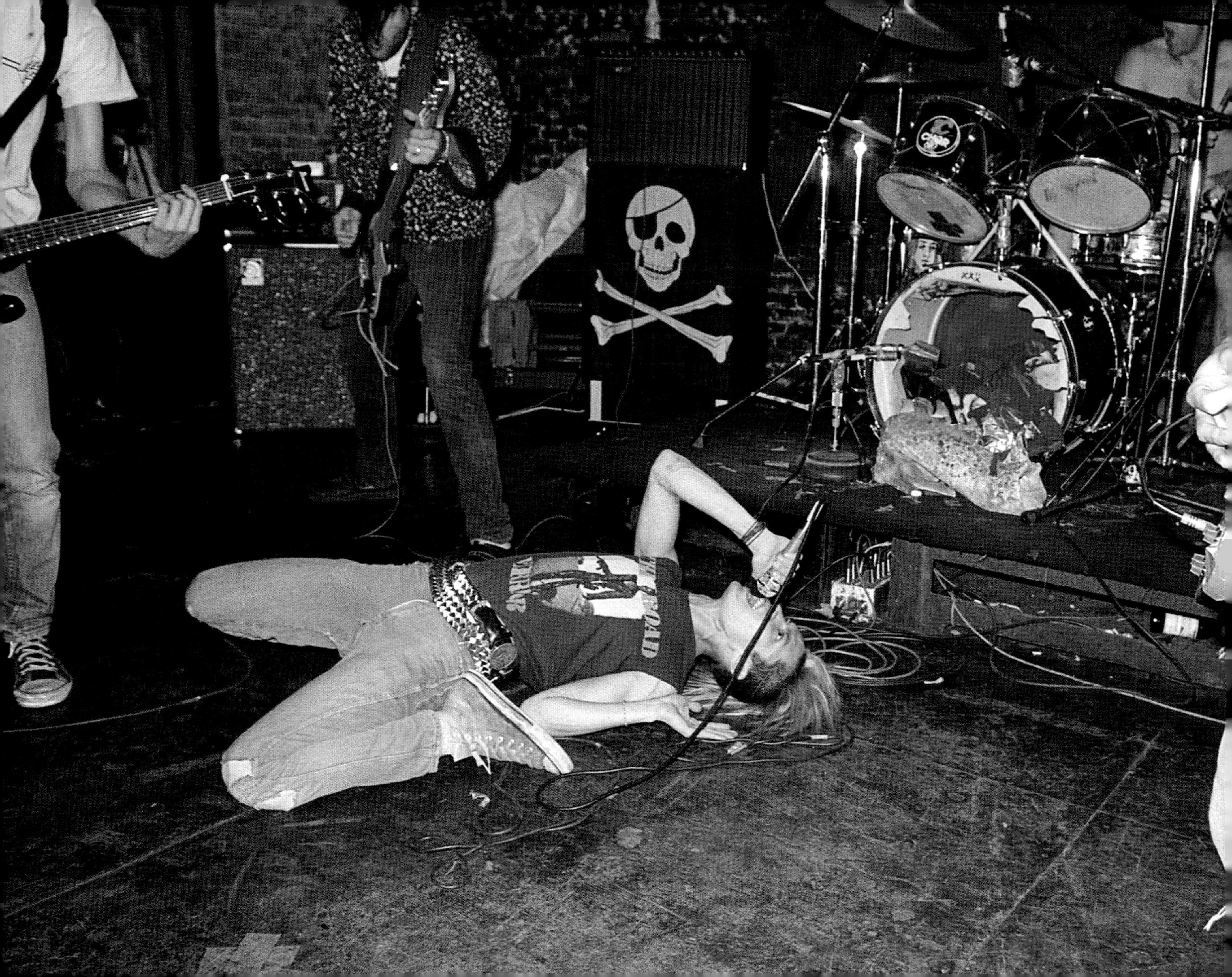

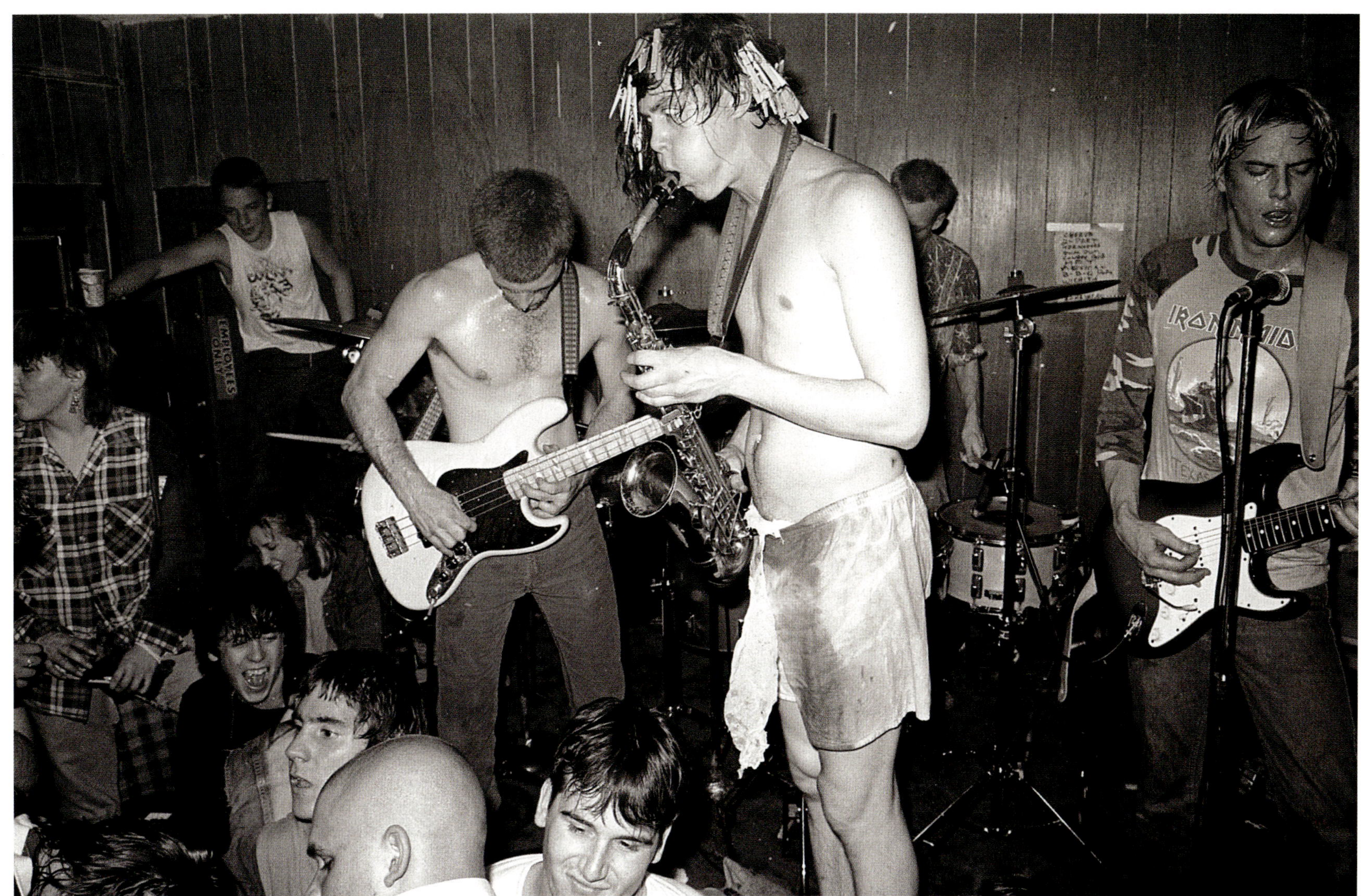

Butthole Surfers
Fiji and Tropical Island Junction, Oakland, 1984

Opposite:
SNFU
Mabuhay Gardens, San Francisco, 1984

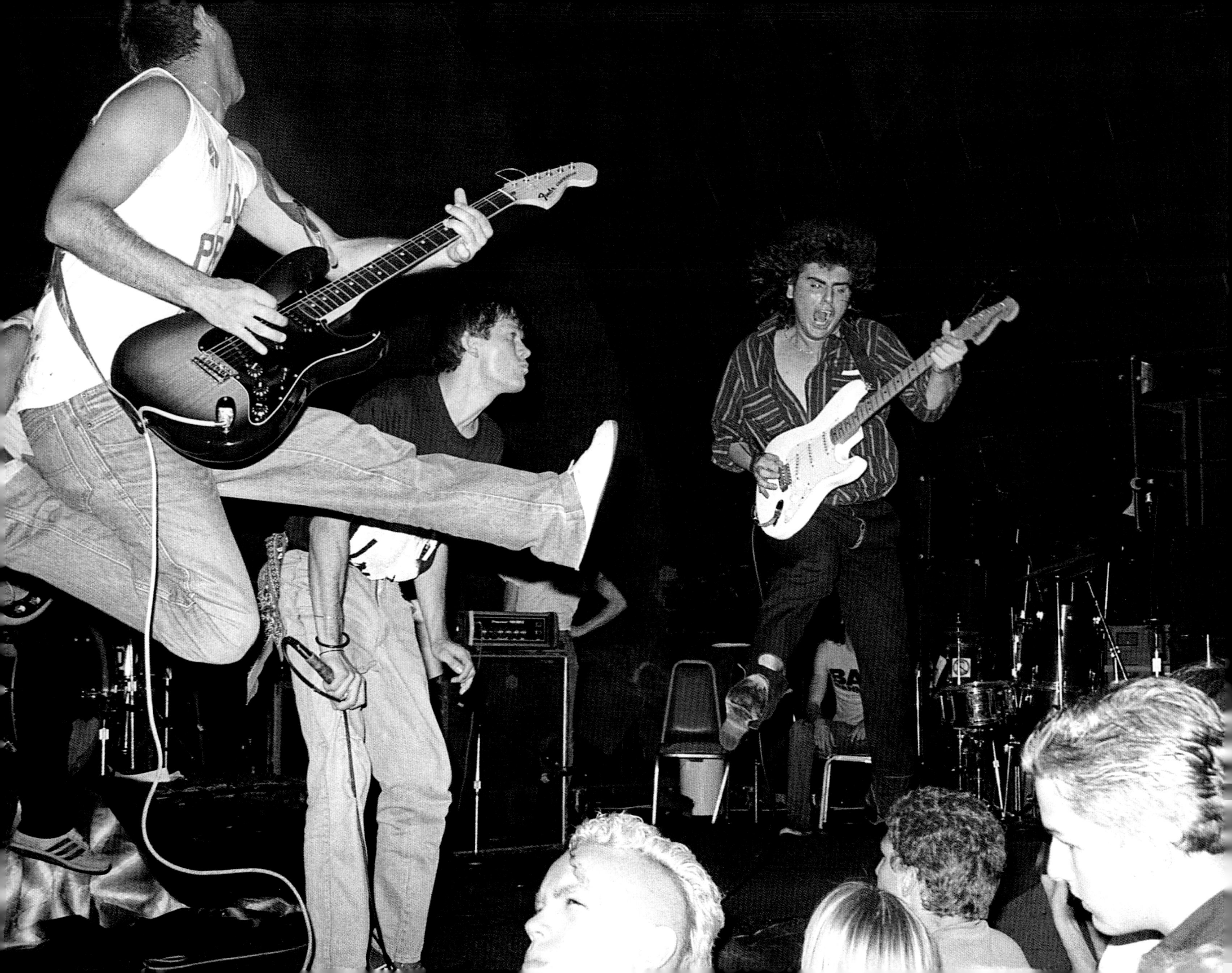

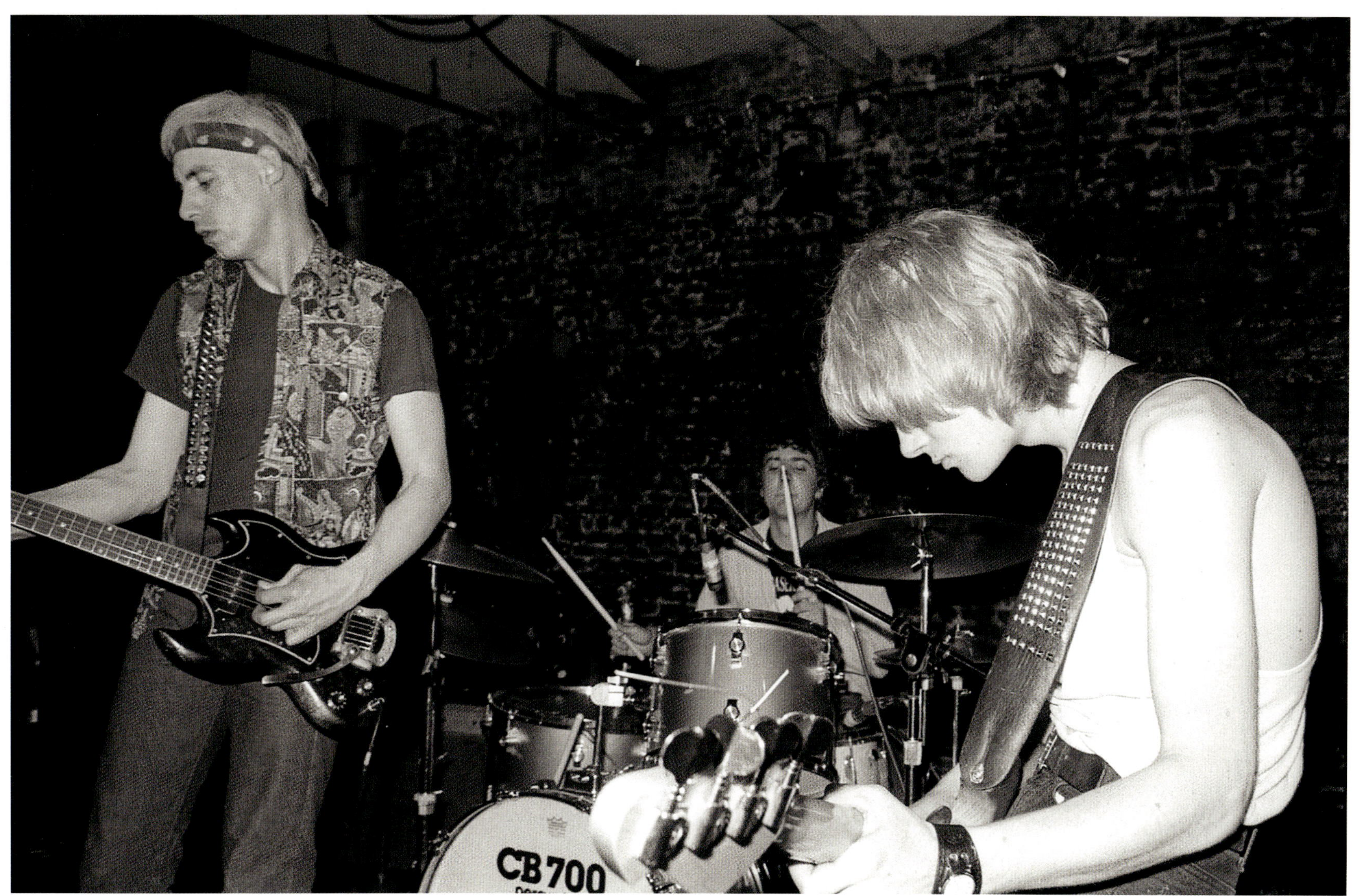

Wipers
Mabuhay Gardens, San Francisco, 1984

Opposite:
Raw Power
On Broadway, San Francisco, 1985

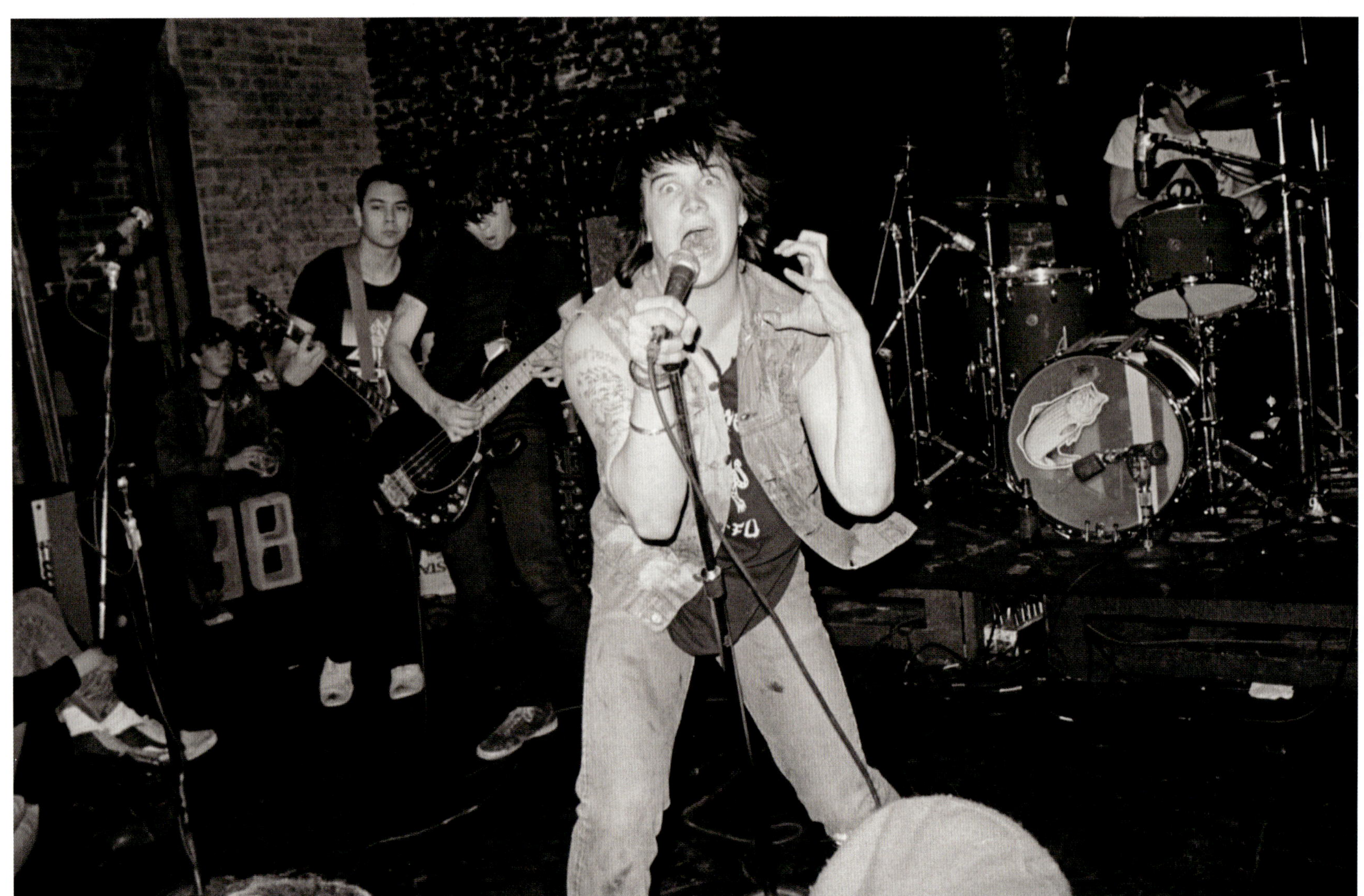

Tales Of Terror
Mabuhay Gardens, San Francisco, 1985

Opposite:
MDC
The Farm, San Francisco, 1985

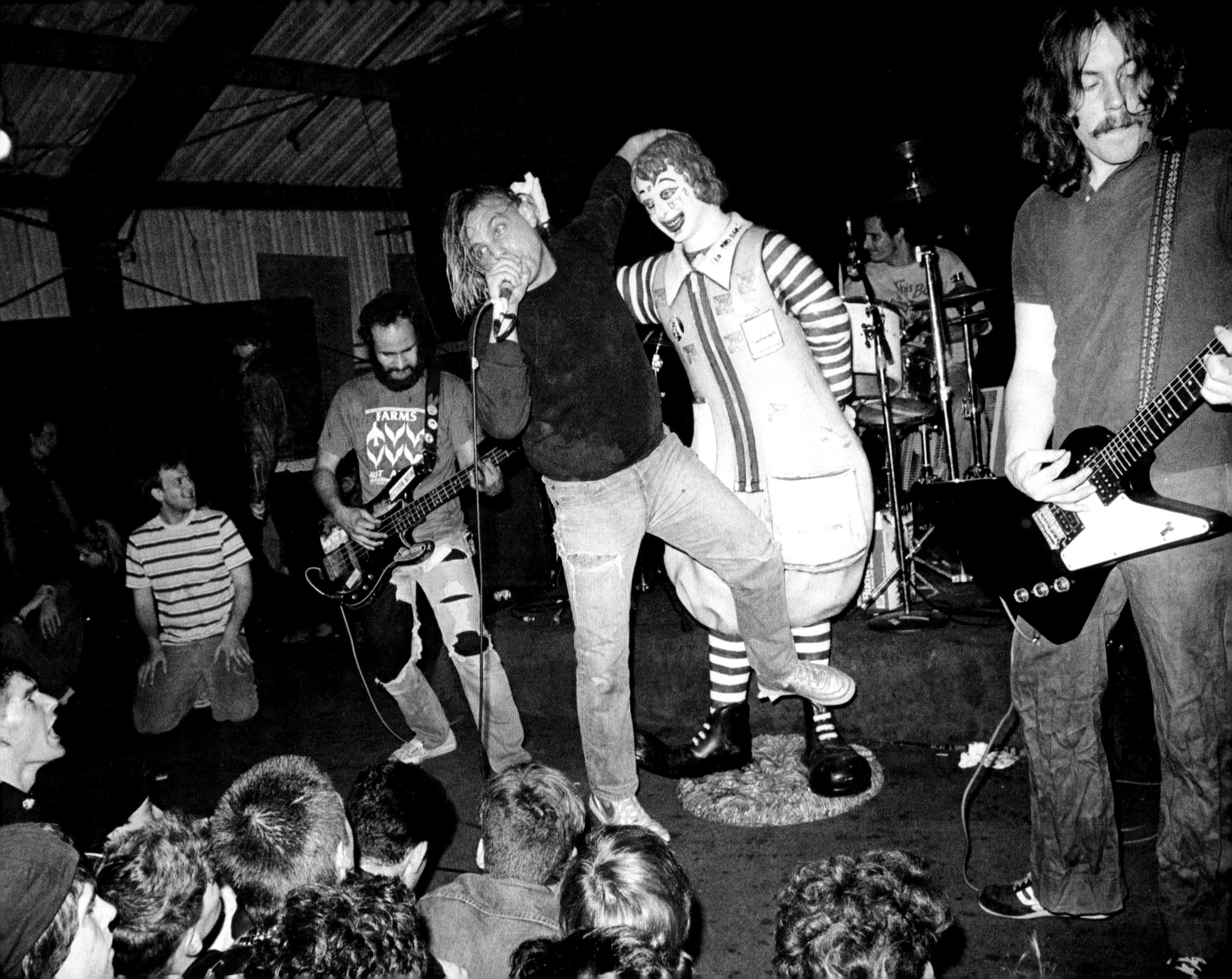

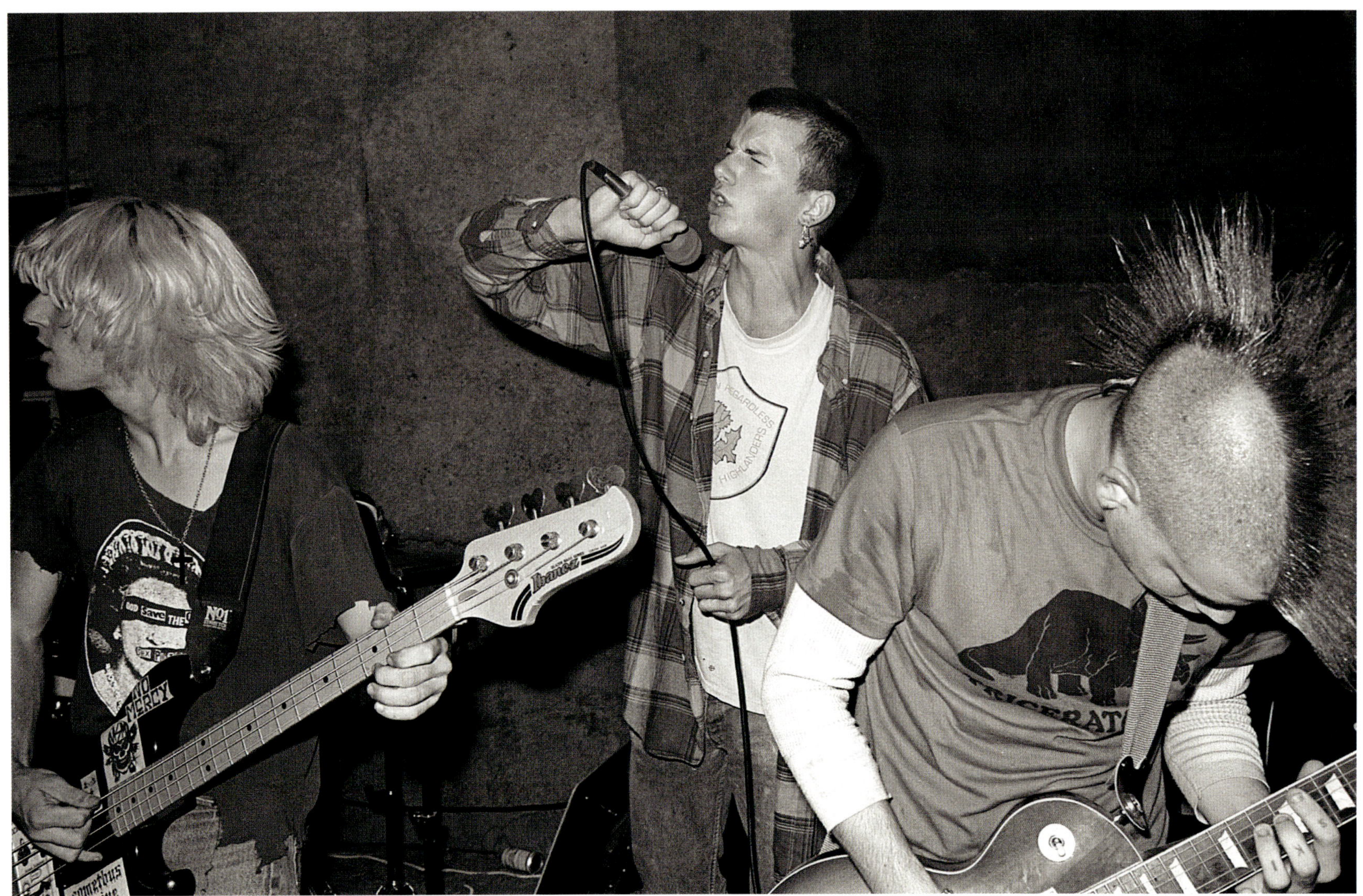

Violent Coercion

New Method, Emeryville, 1985

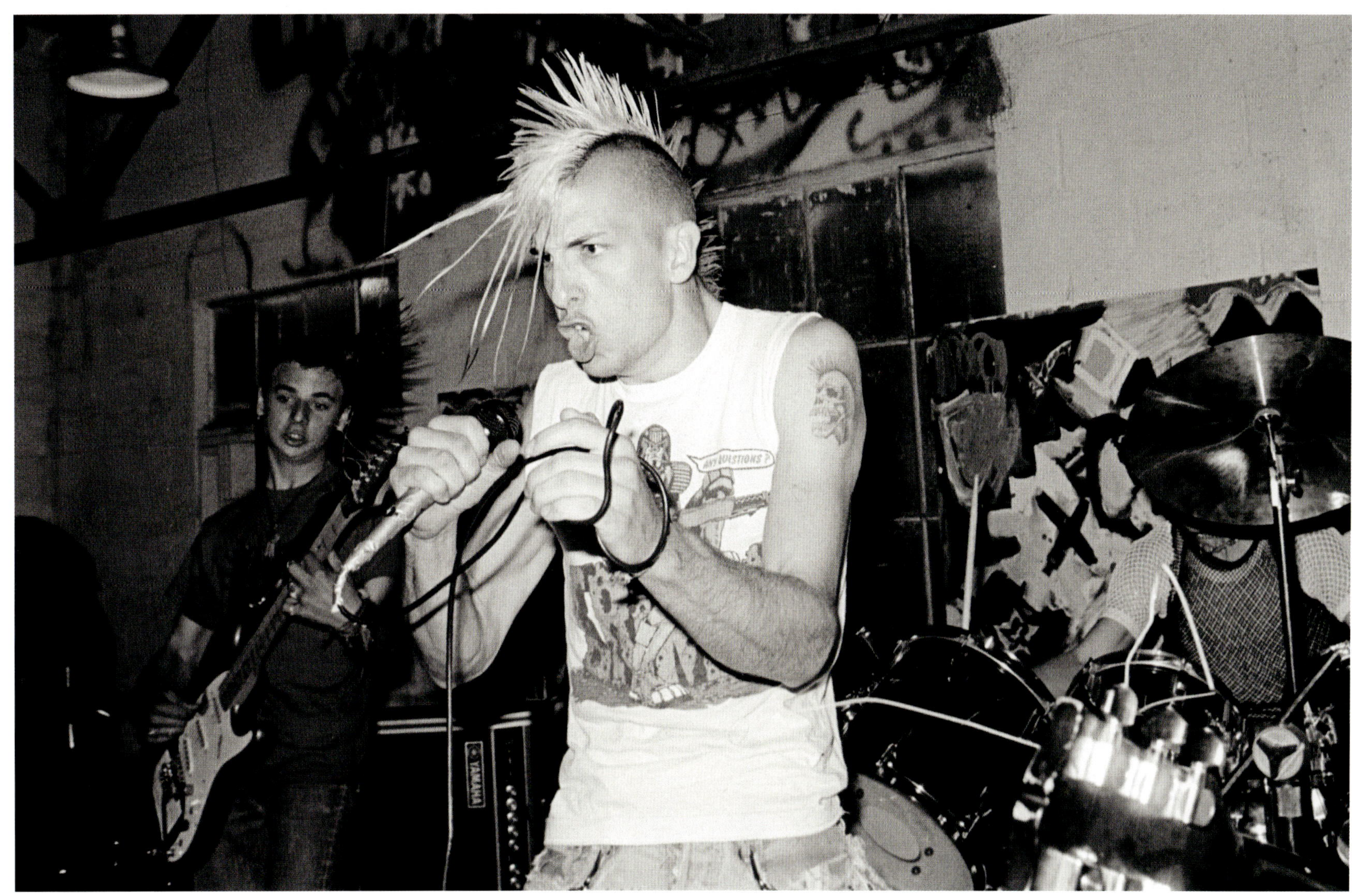

Christ On Parade
Club Culture, Santa Cruz, 1984

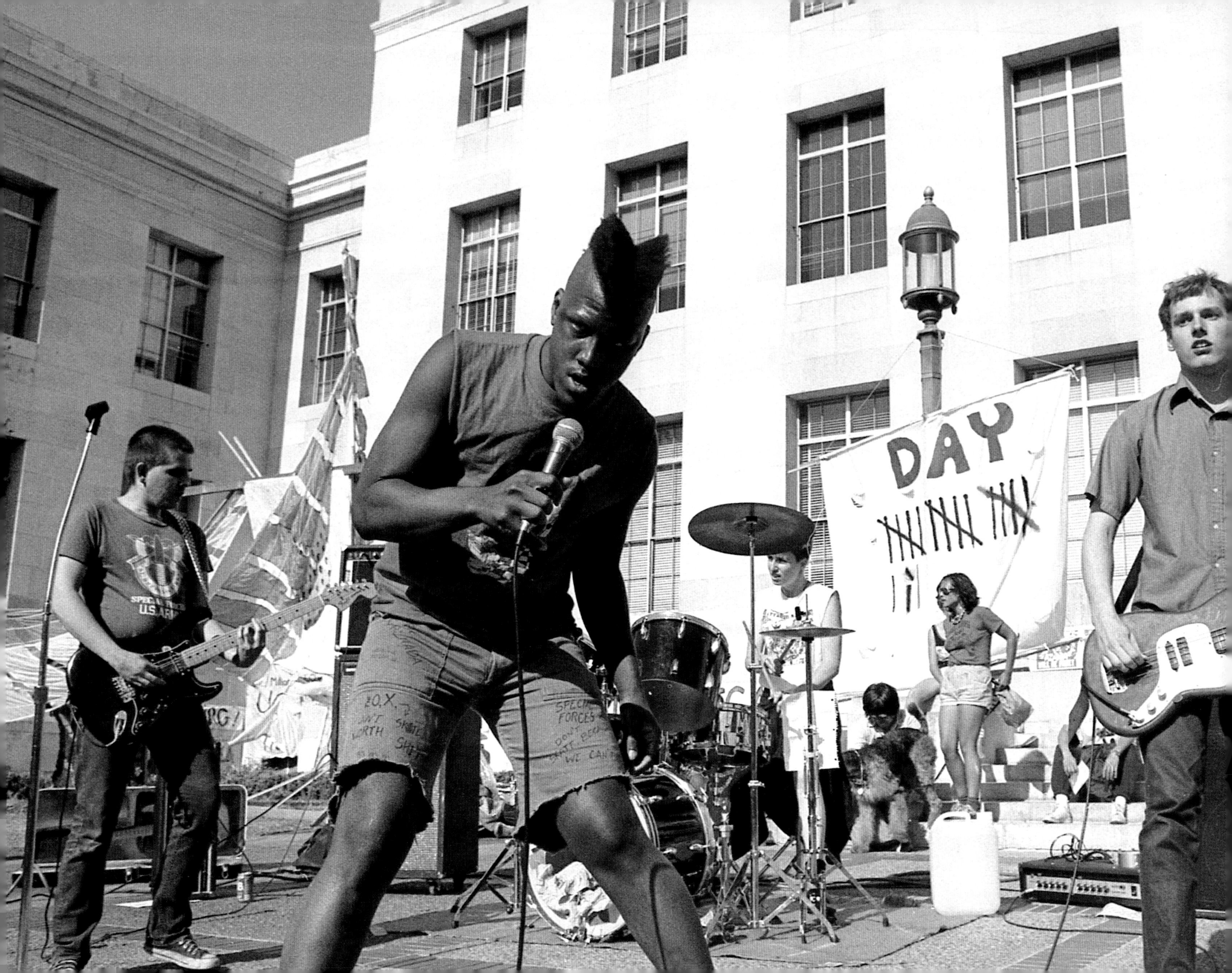
DAY

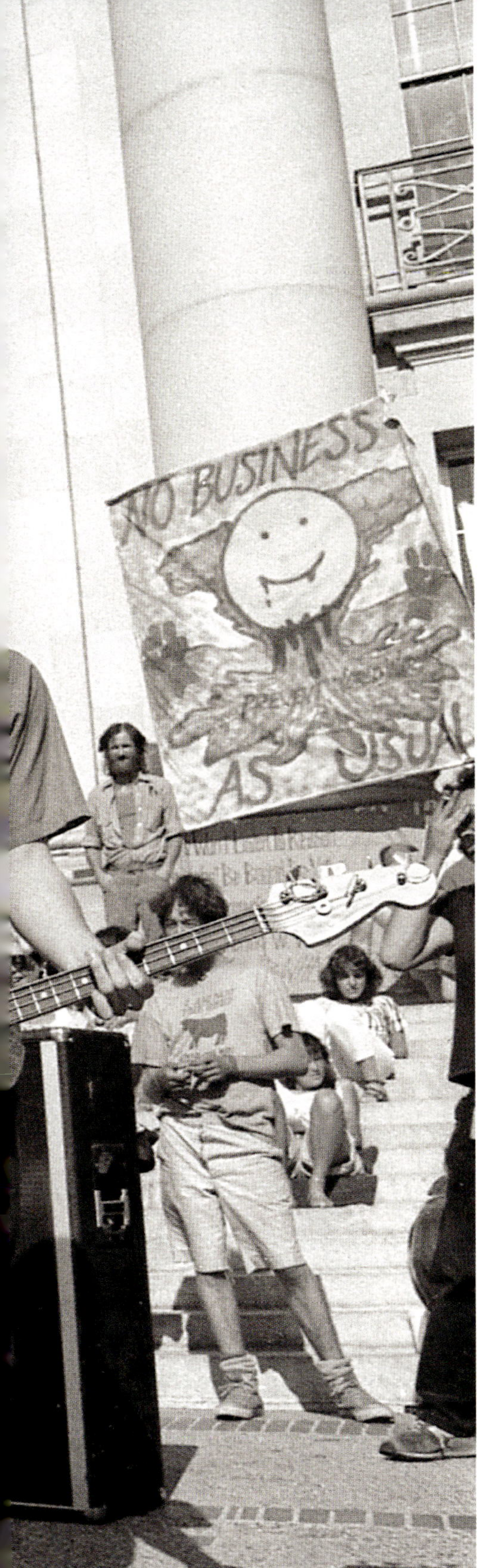

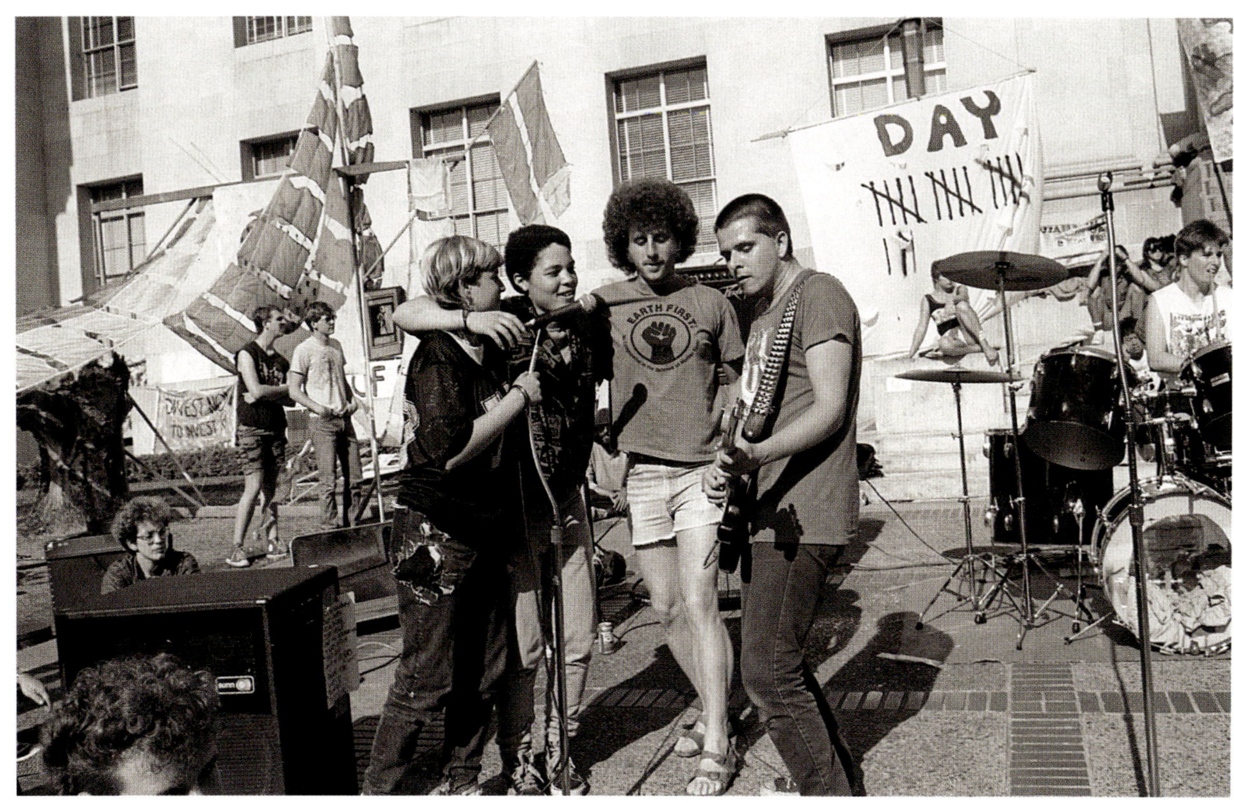

Special Forces
Sproul Plaza, UC Berkeley, 1985

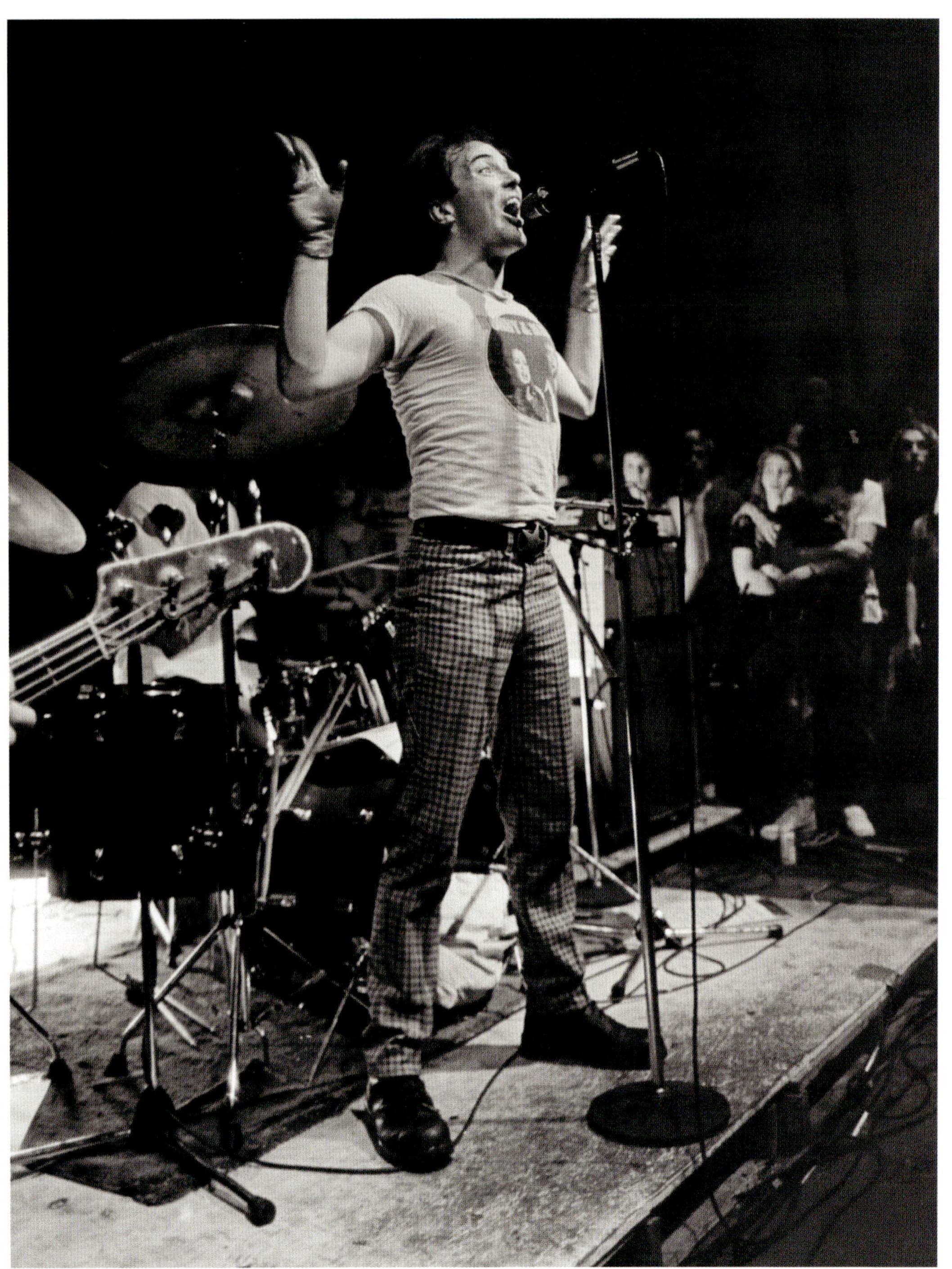

Dead Kennedys
Novato Theater, Novato, 1985

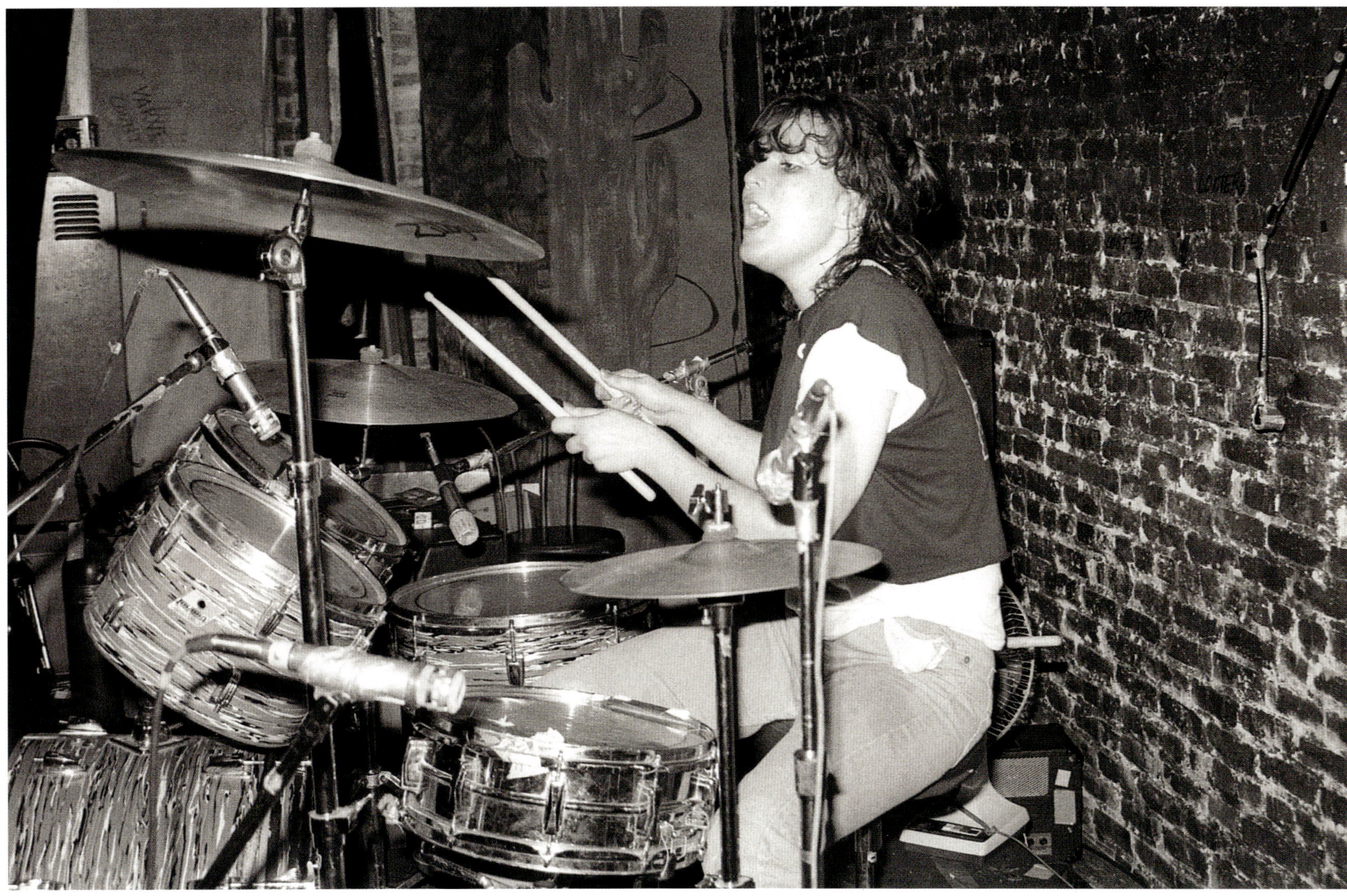

The Dicks

Mabuhay Gardens, San Francisco, 1984

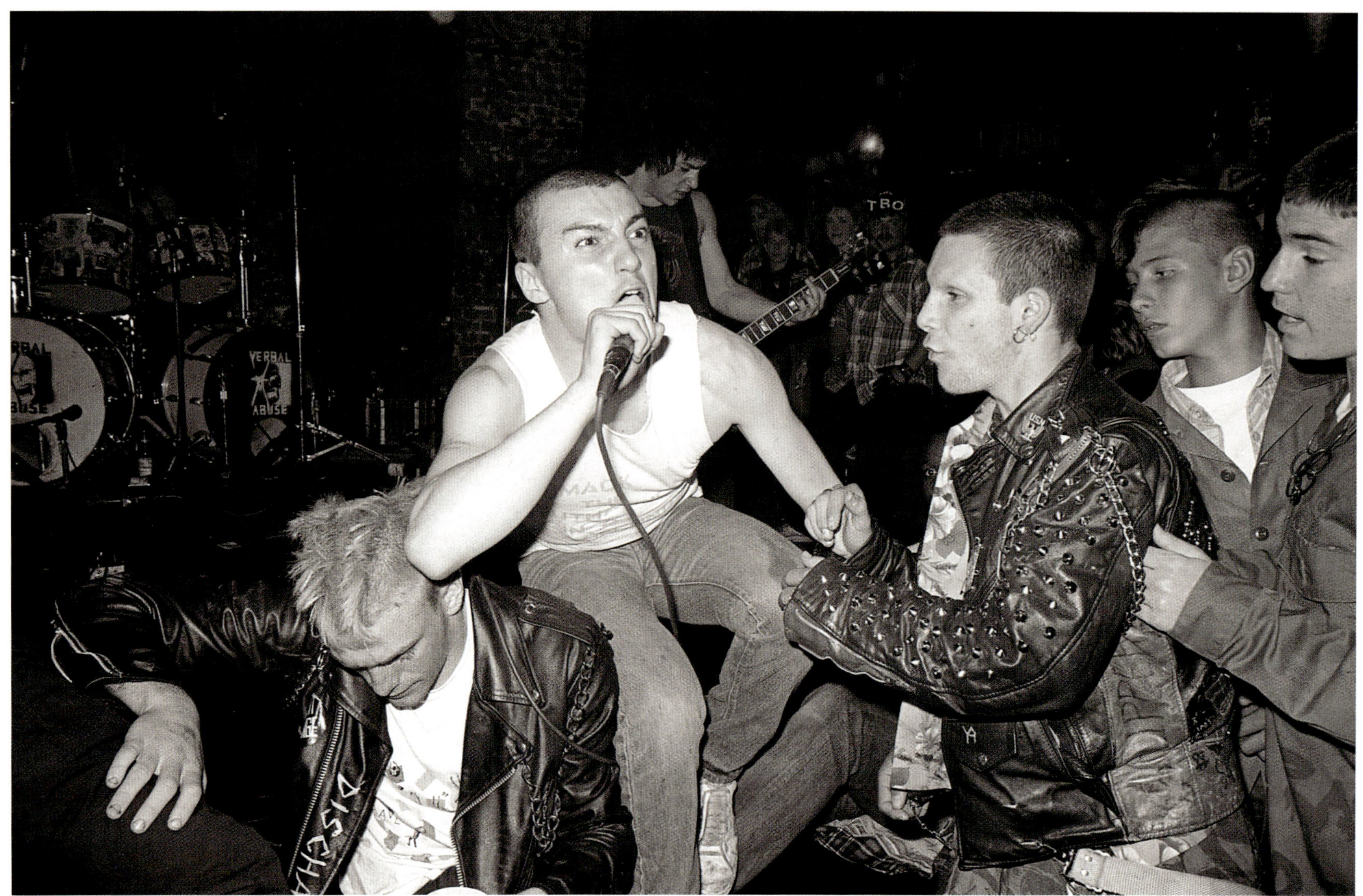

Verbal Abuse
Mabuhay Gardens, San Francisco, 1985

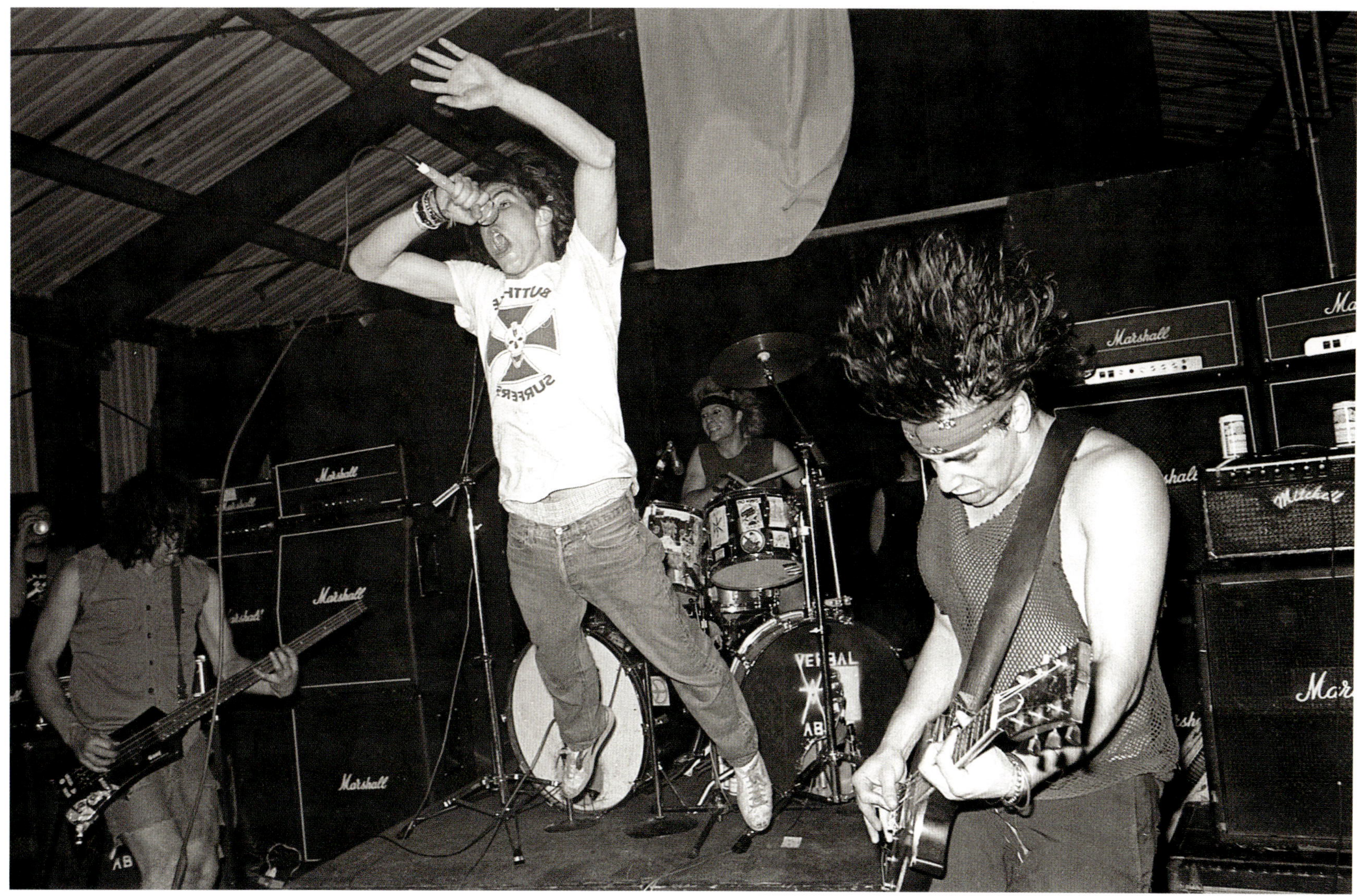

Verbal Abuse
The Farm, San Francisco, 1986

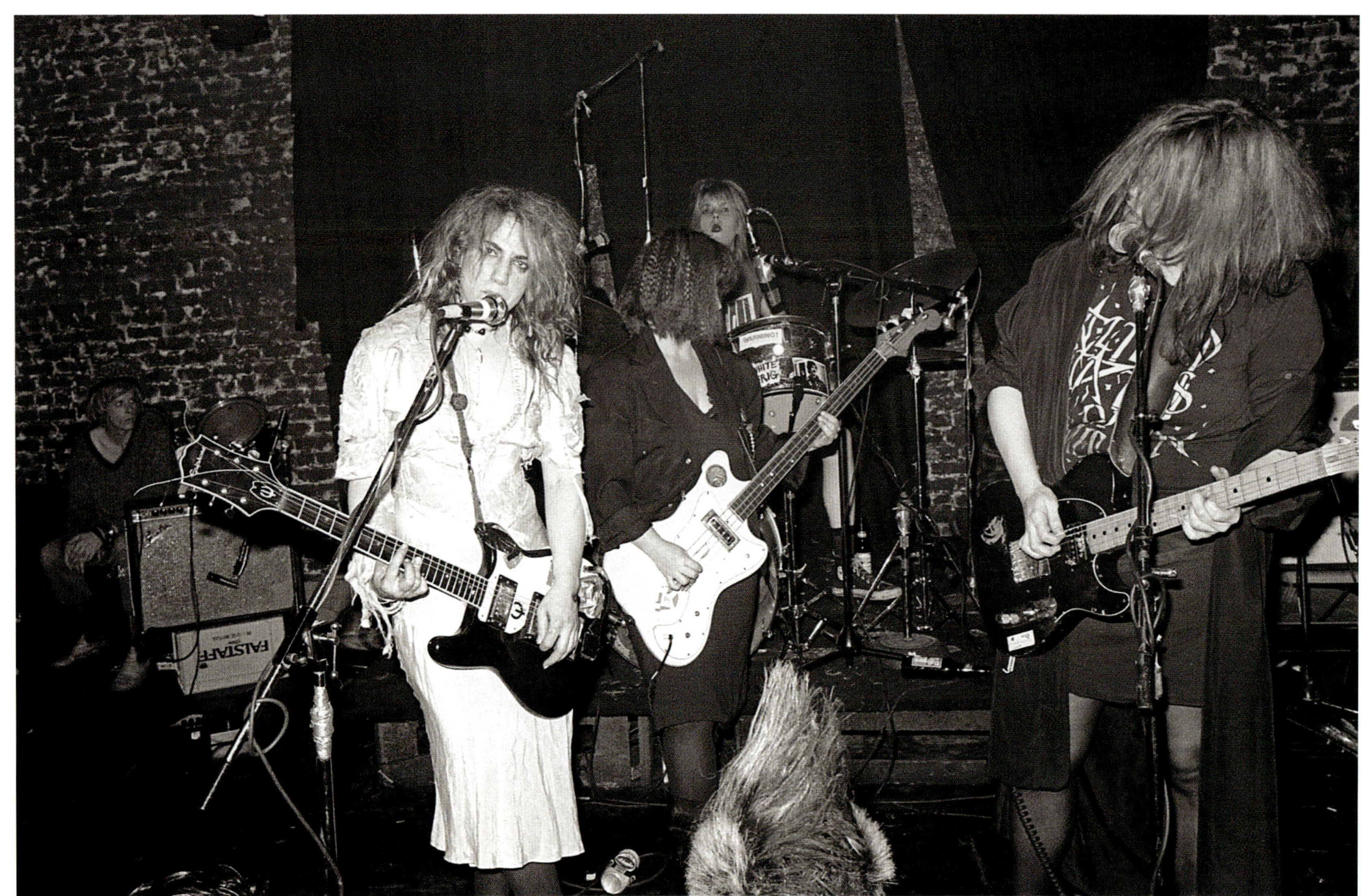

Frightwig
Mabuhay Gardens, San Francisco, 1985

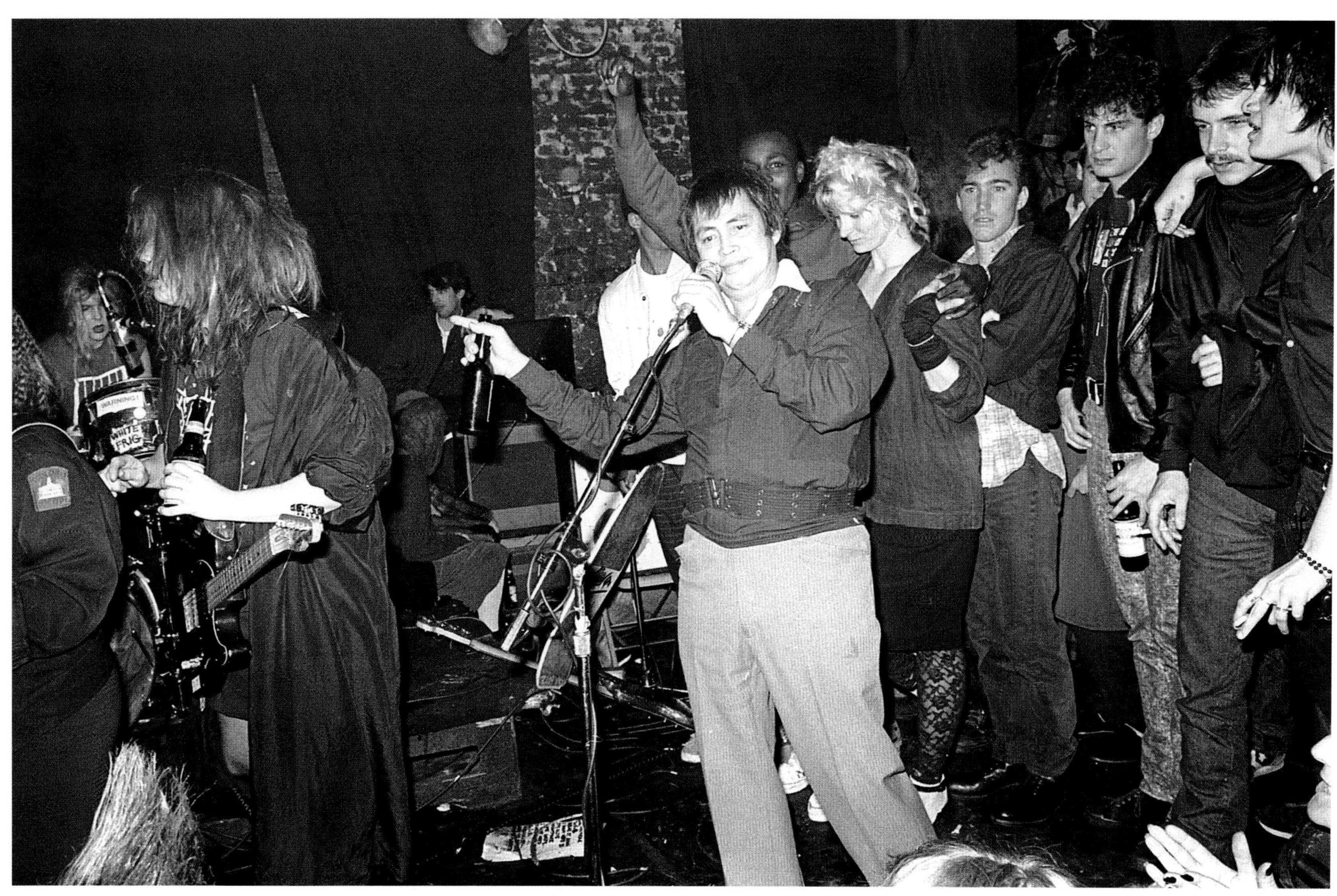

Ness Aquino, Mabuhay Gardens, 1985

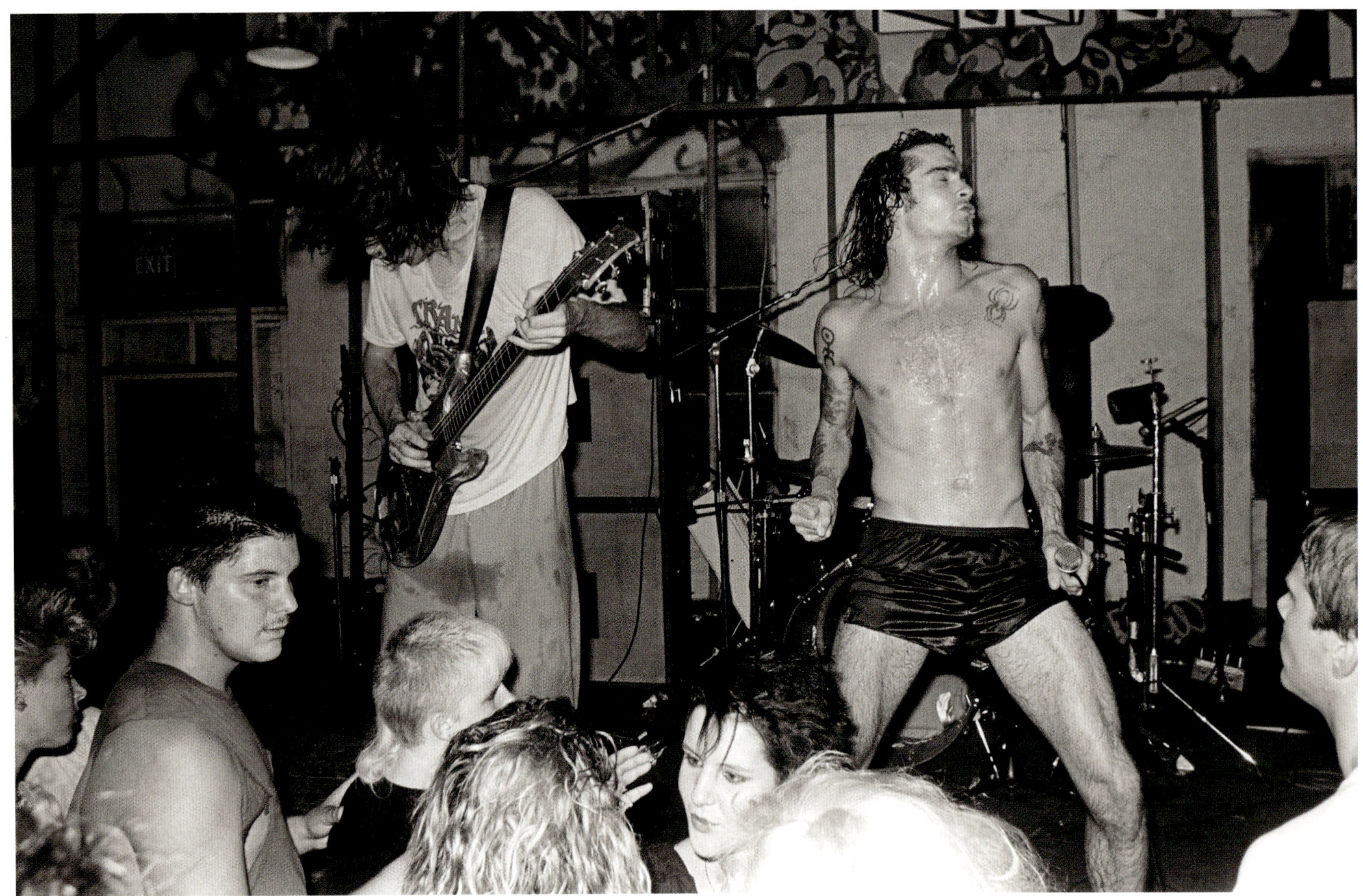

Black Flag

Club Culture, Santa Cruz, 1985

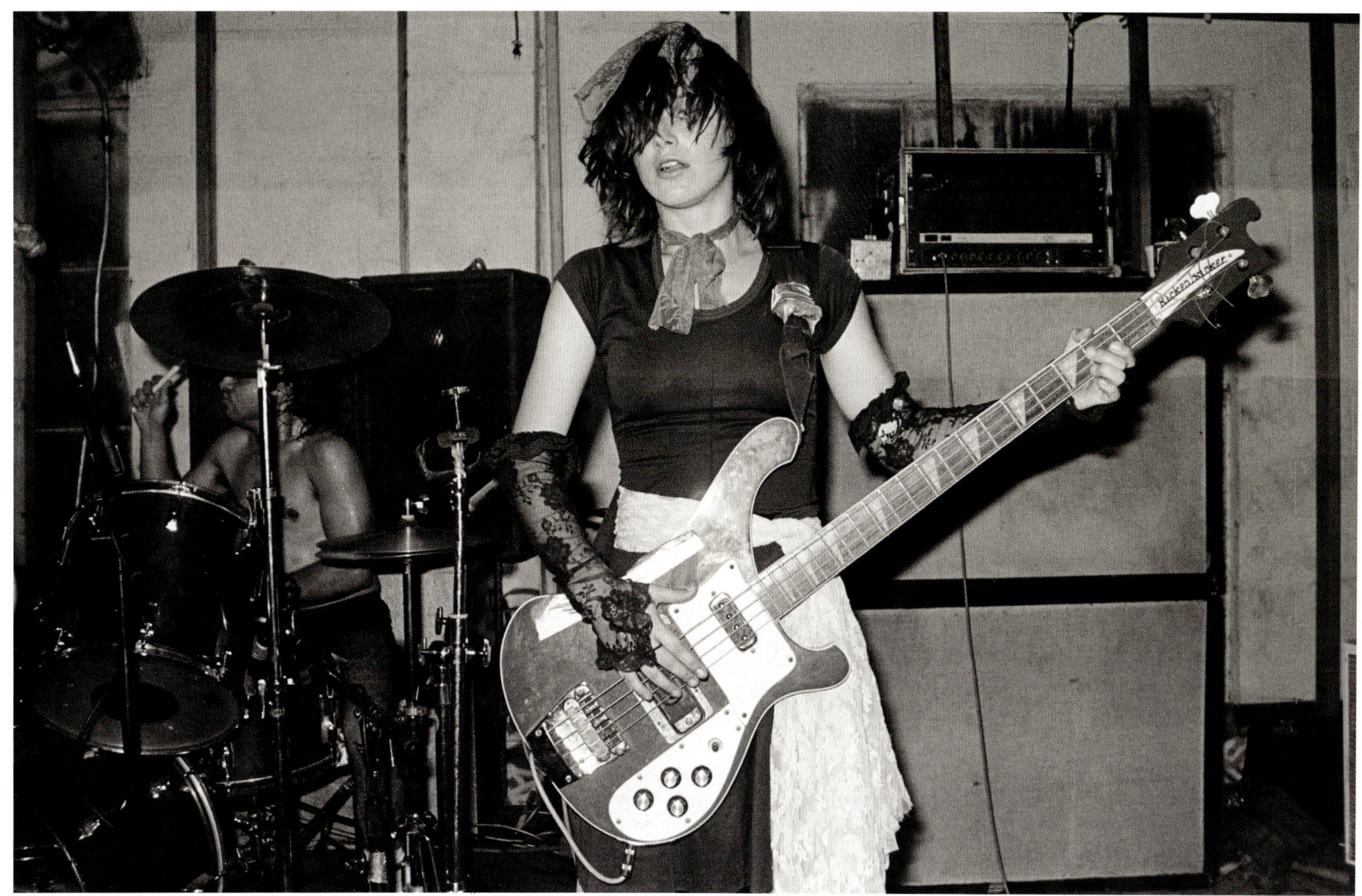

Black Flag
Club Culture, Santa Cruz, 1985

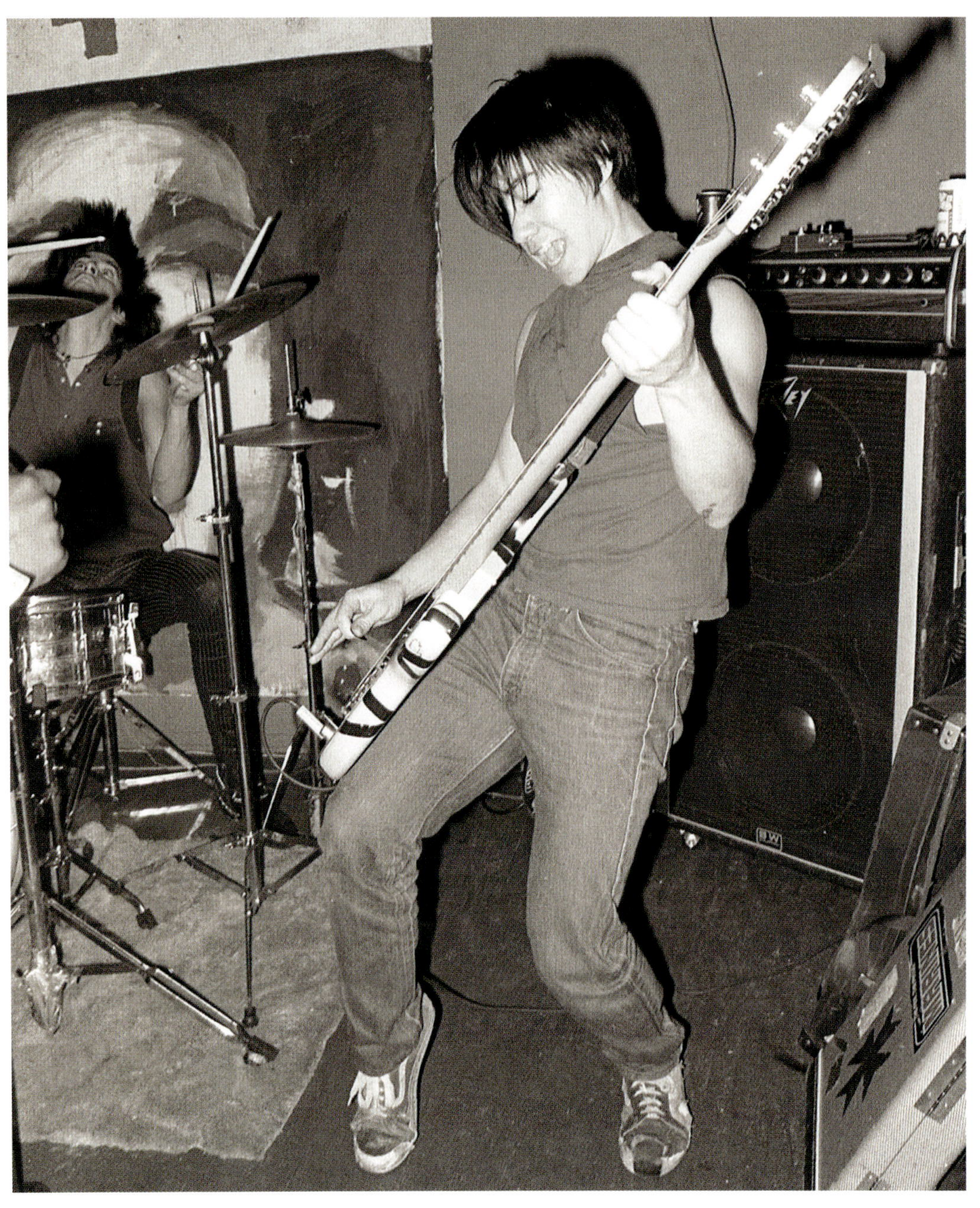

Boneless Ones
Oakland, 1986

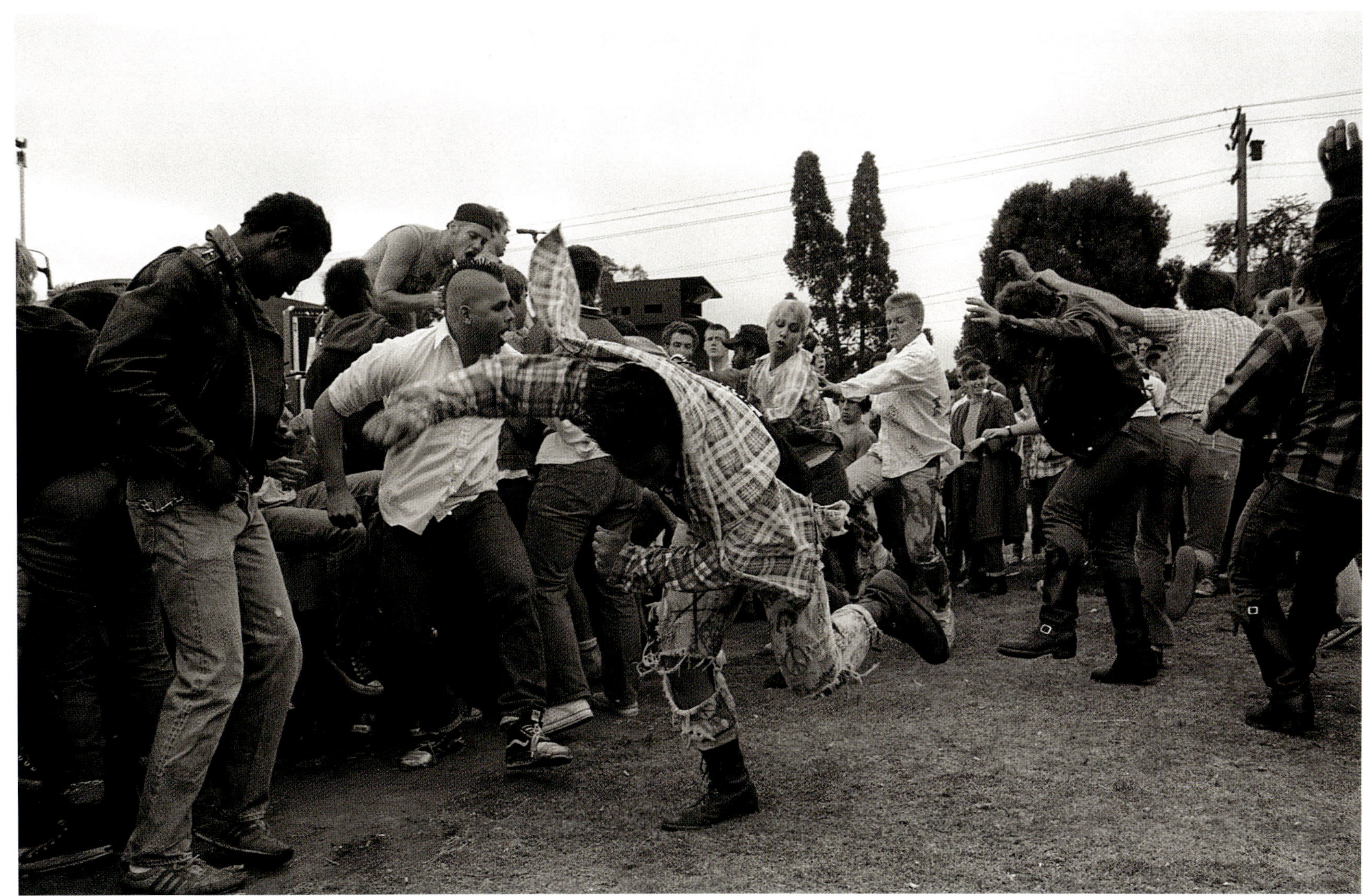

Fang

People's Park, Berkeley, 1985

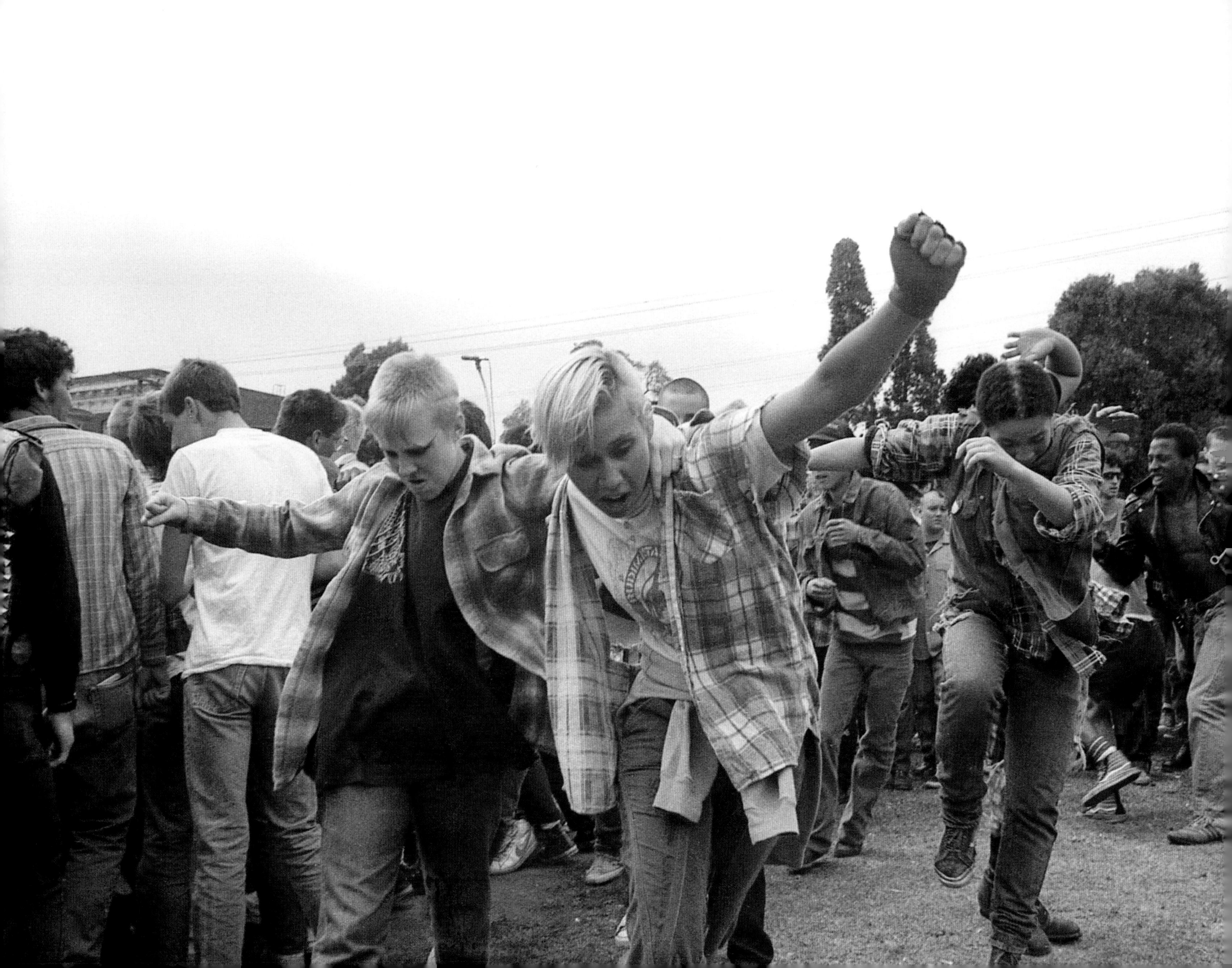

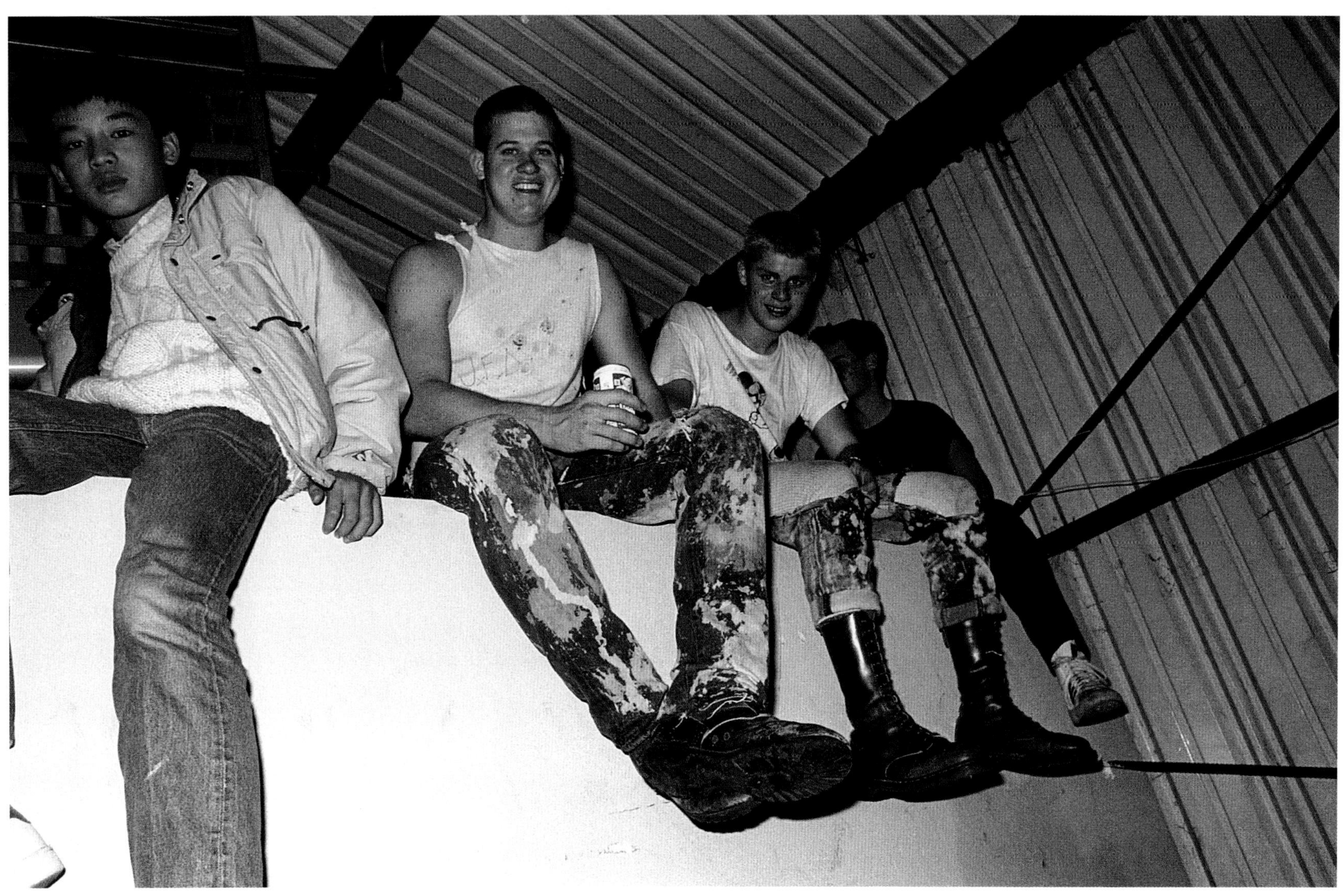

The Farm, San Francisco, 1986

Opposite:
People's Park, Berkeley, 1984

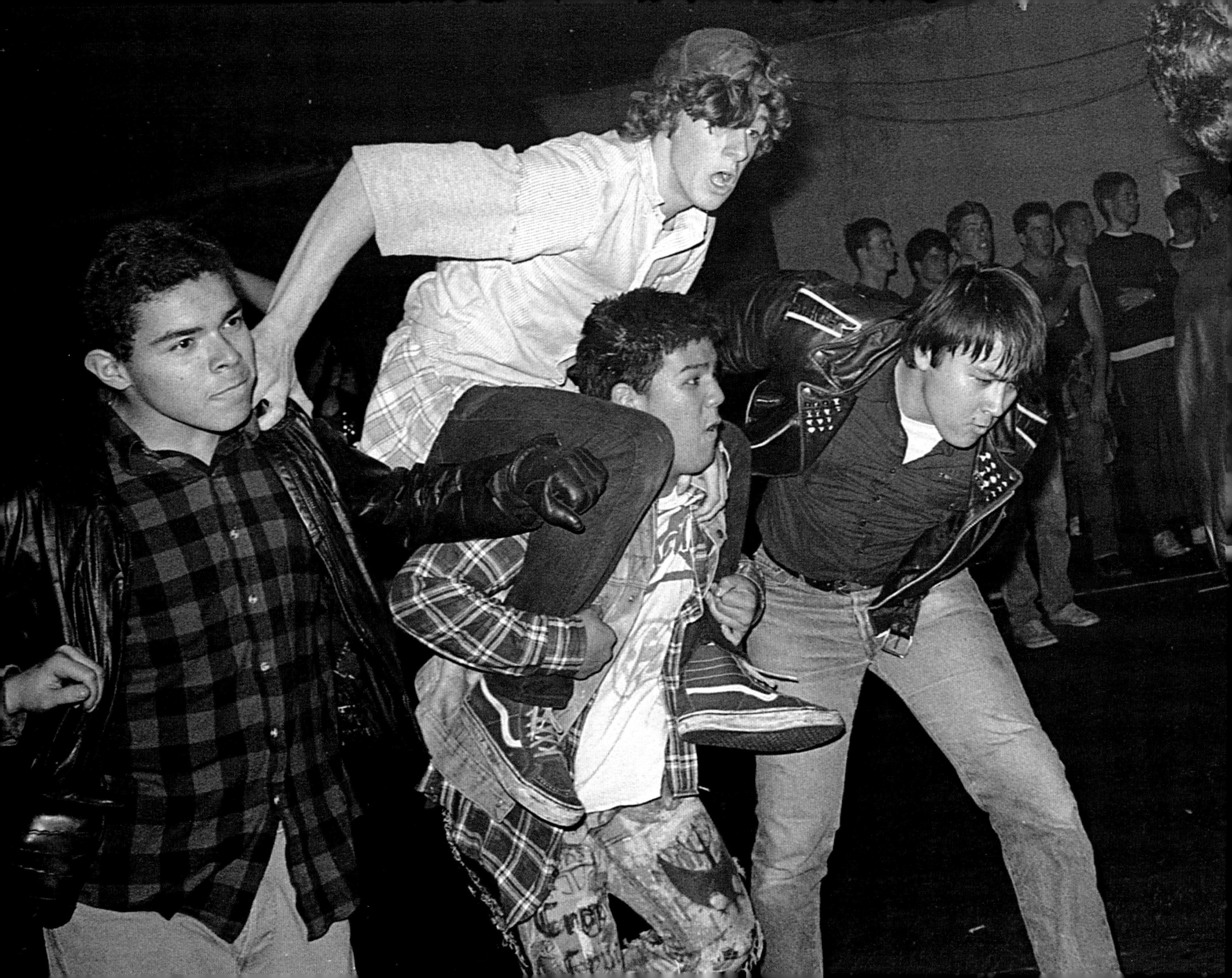

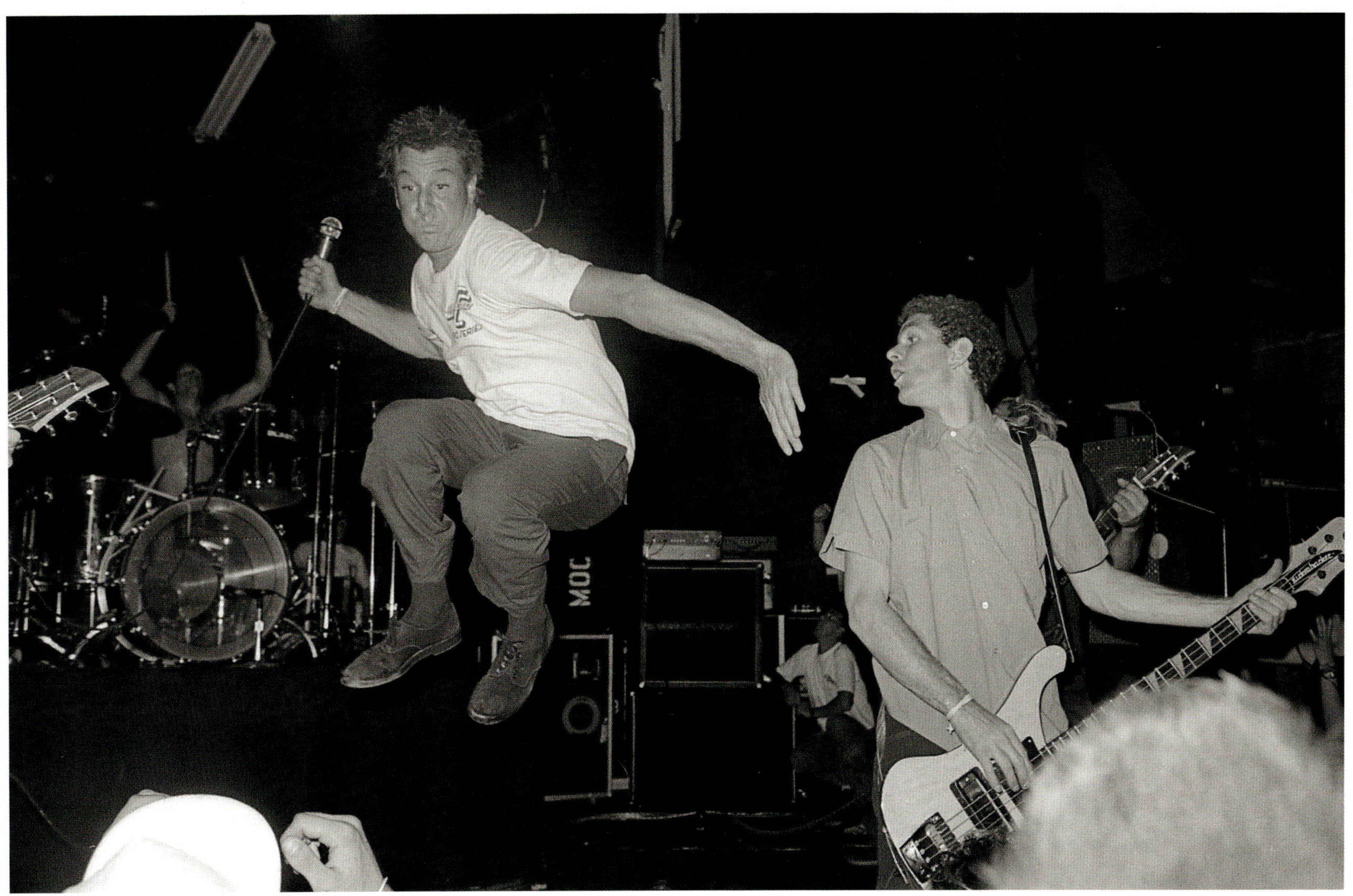

Blast

On Broadway, San Francisco, 1986

Opposite:

Ruthie's Inn, Berkeley, 1984

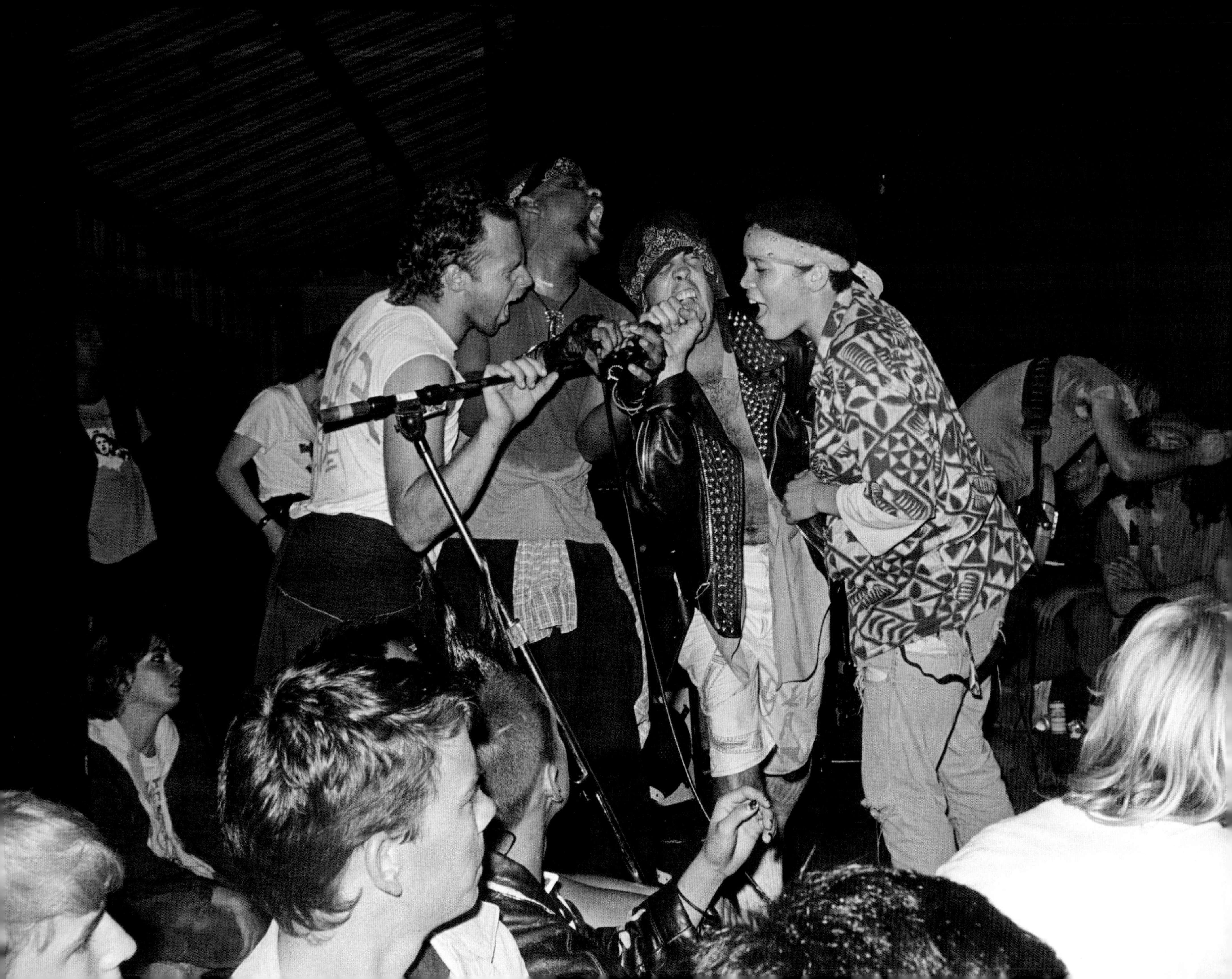

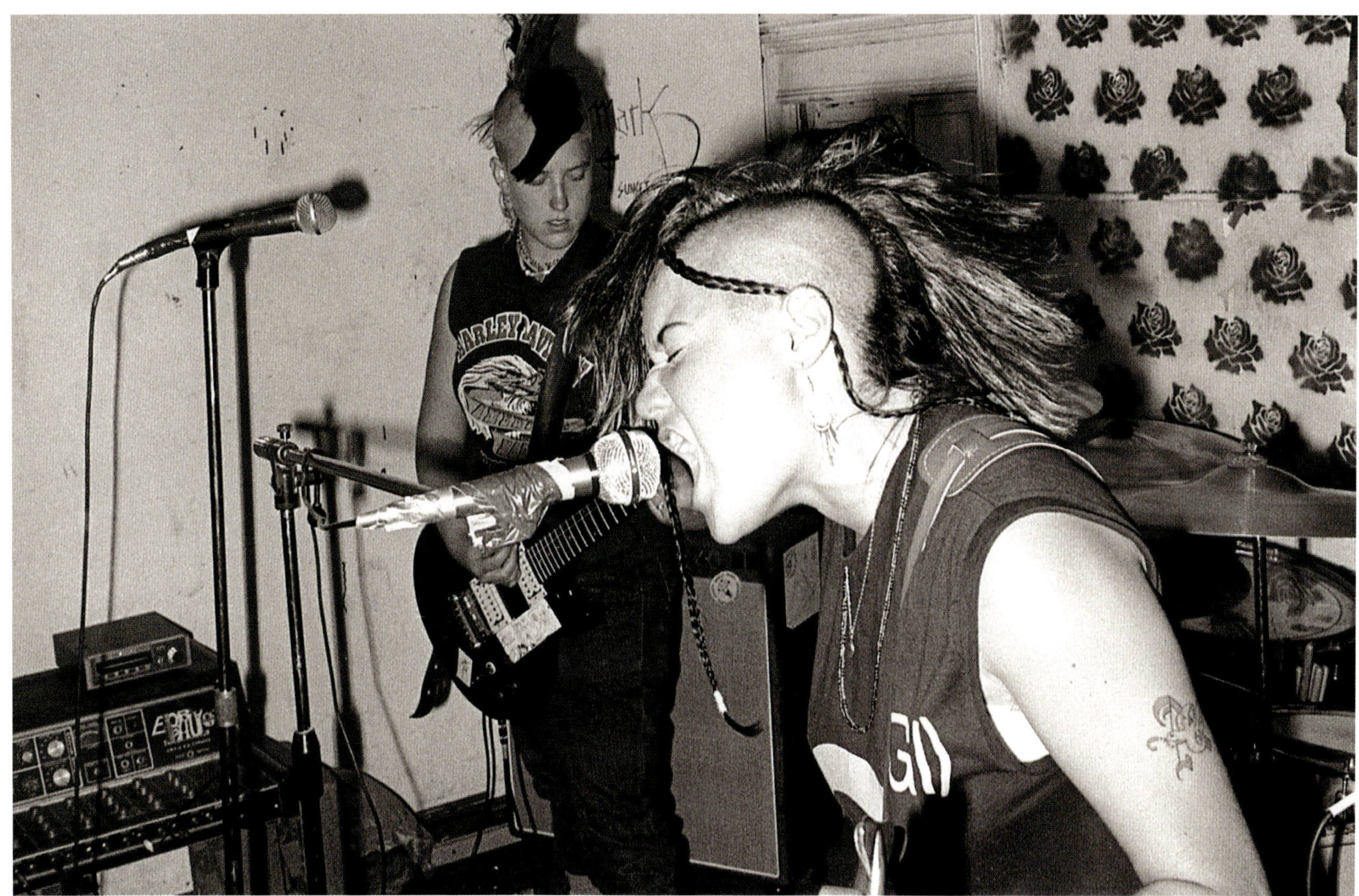

Anti-Scrunti Faction
Club Foot, San Francisco, 1986

Opposite:
Fang
The Farm, San Francisco, 1986

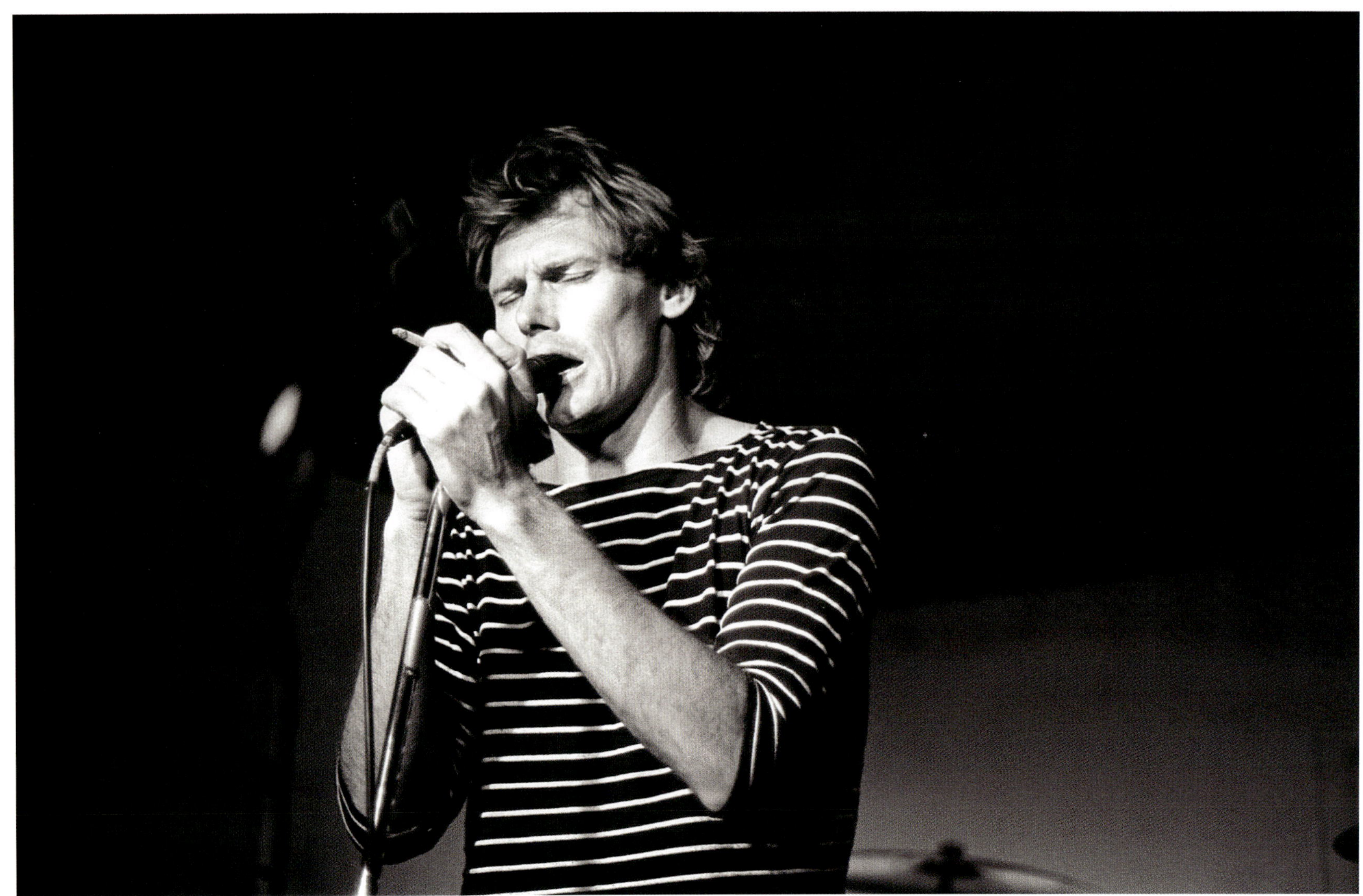

Celibate Rifles

The I-Beam, San Francisco, 1986

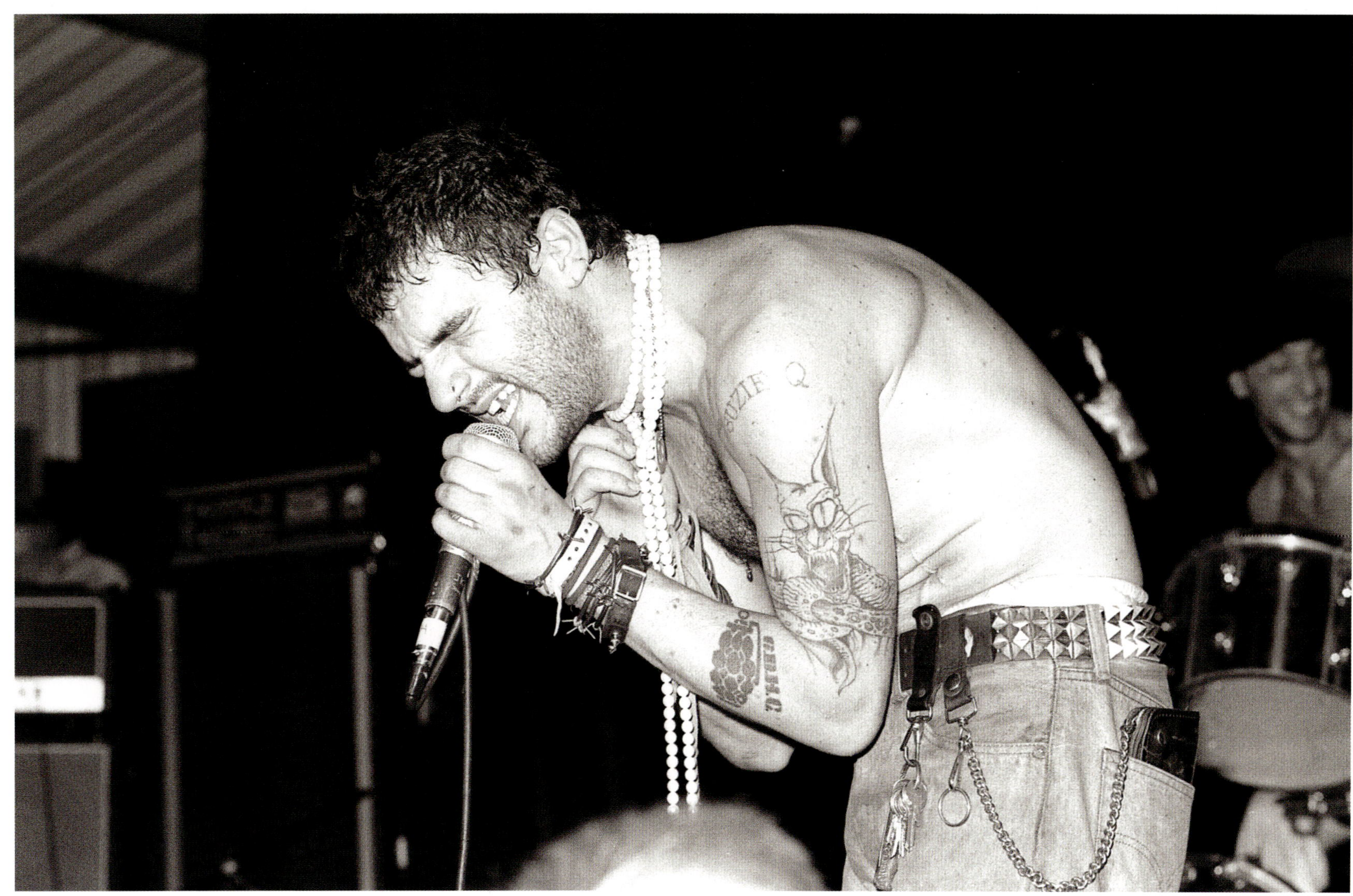

Cheetah Chrome Motherfuckers

The Farm, San Francisco, 1986

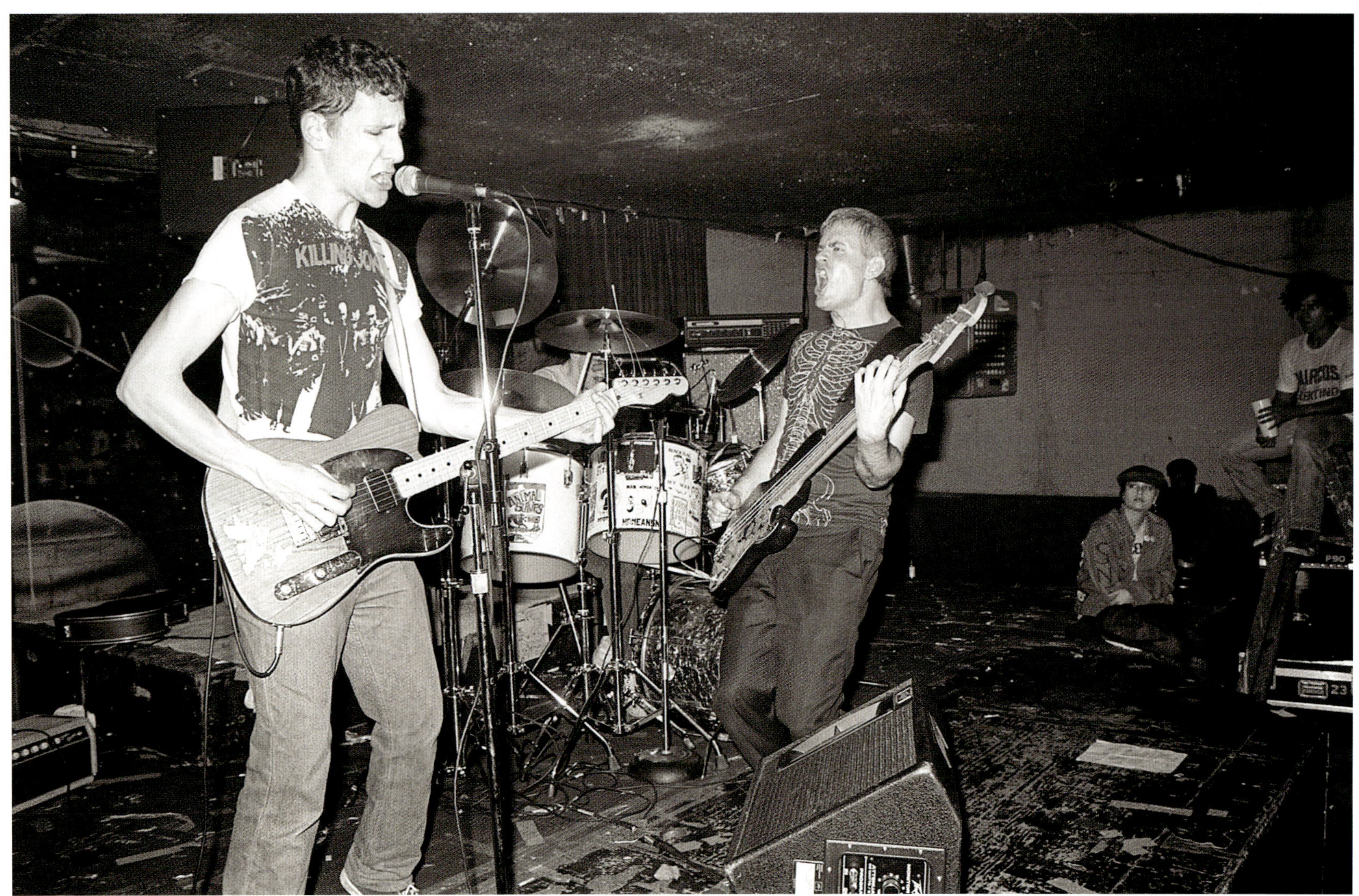

Nomeansno
Ruthie's Inn, Berkeley, 1986

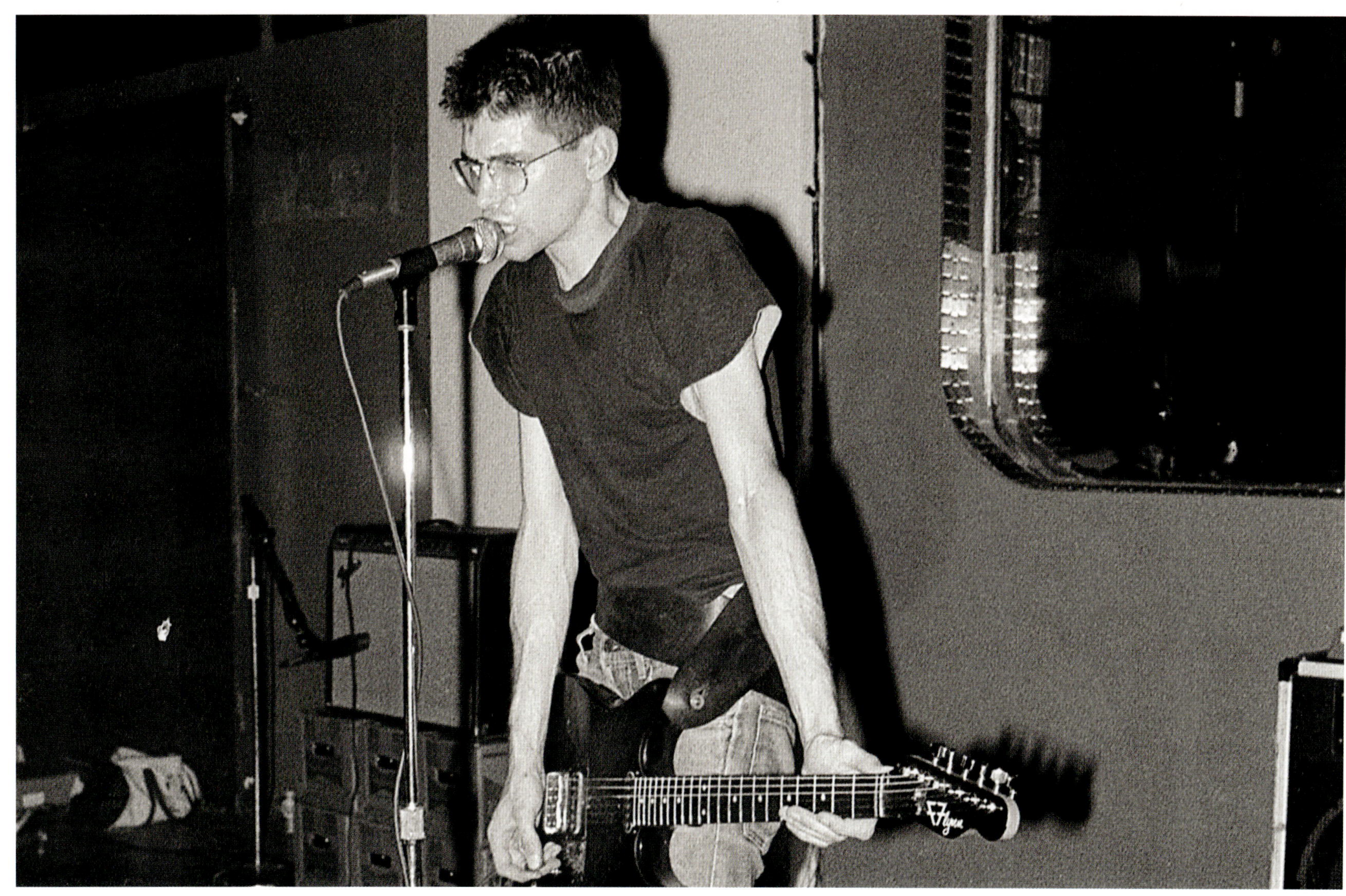

Big Black

The I-Beam, San Francisco, 1987

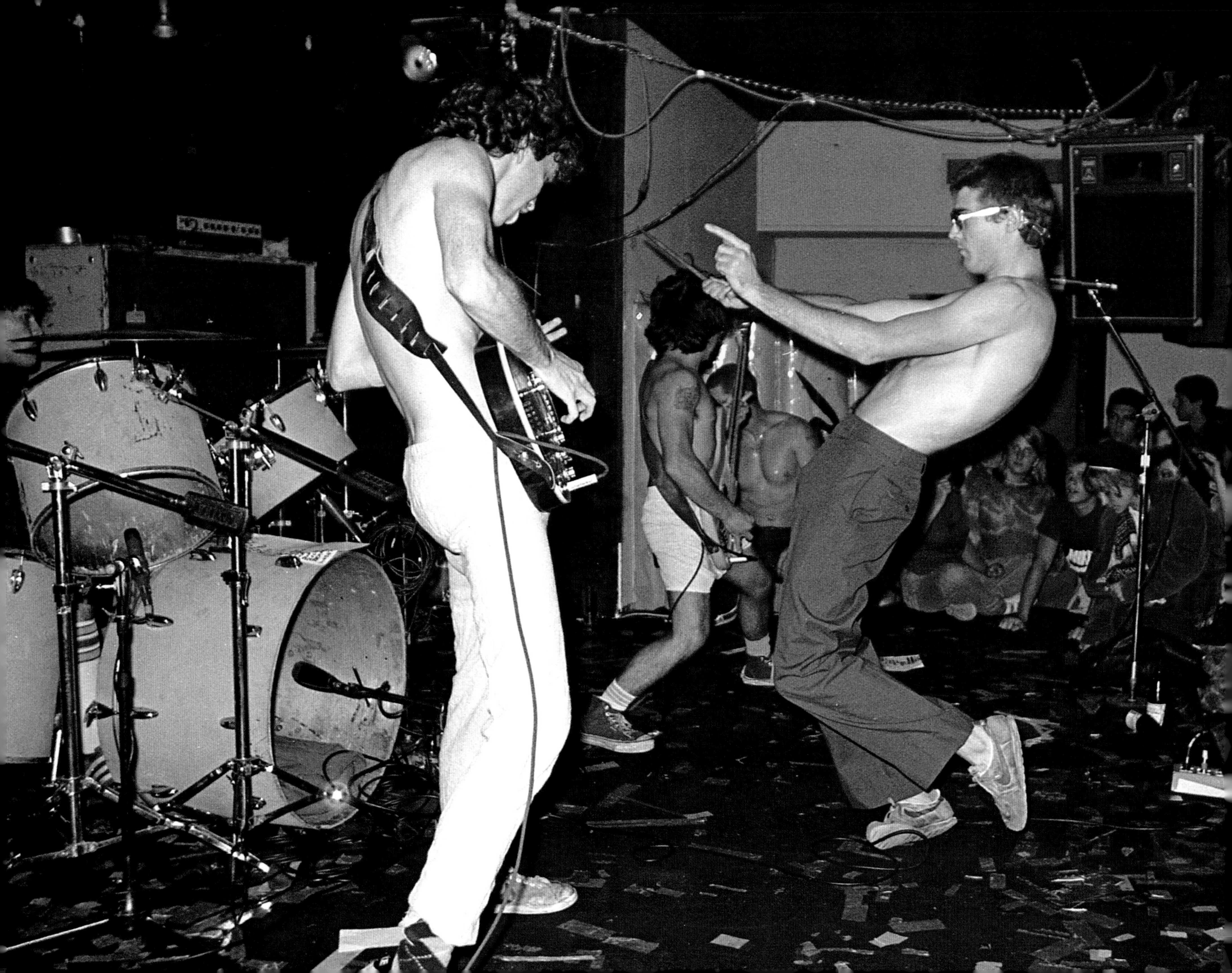

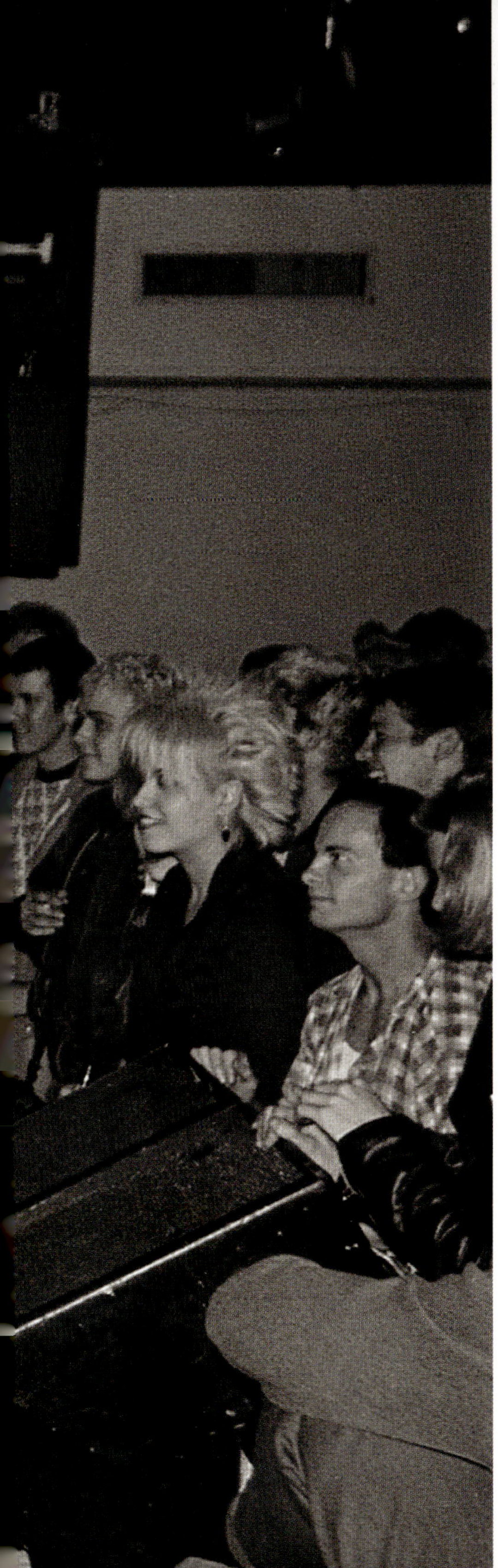

Descendents
Berkeley Square, Berkeley, 1986

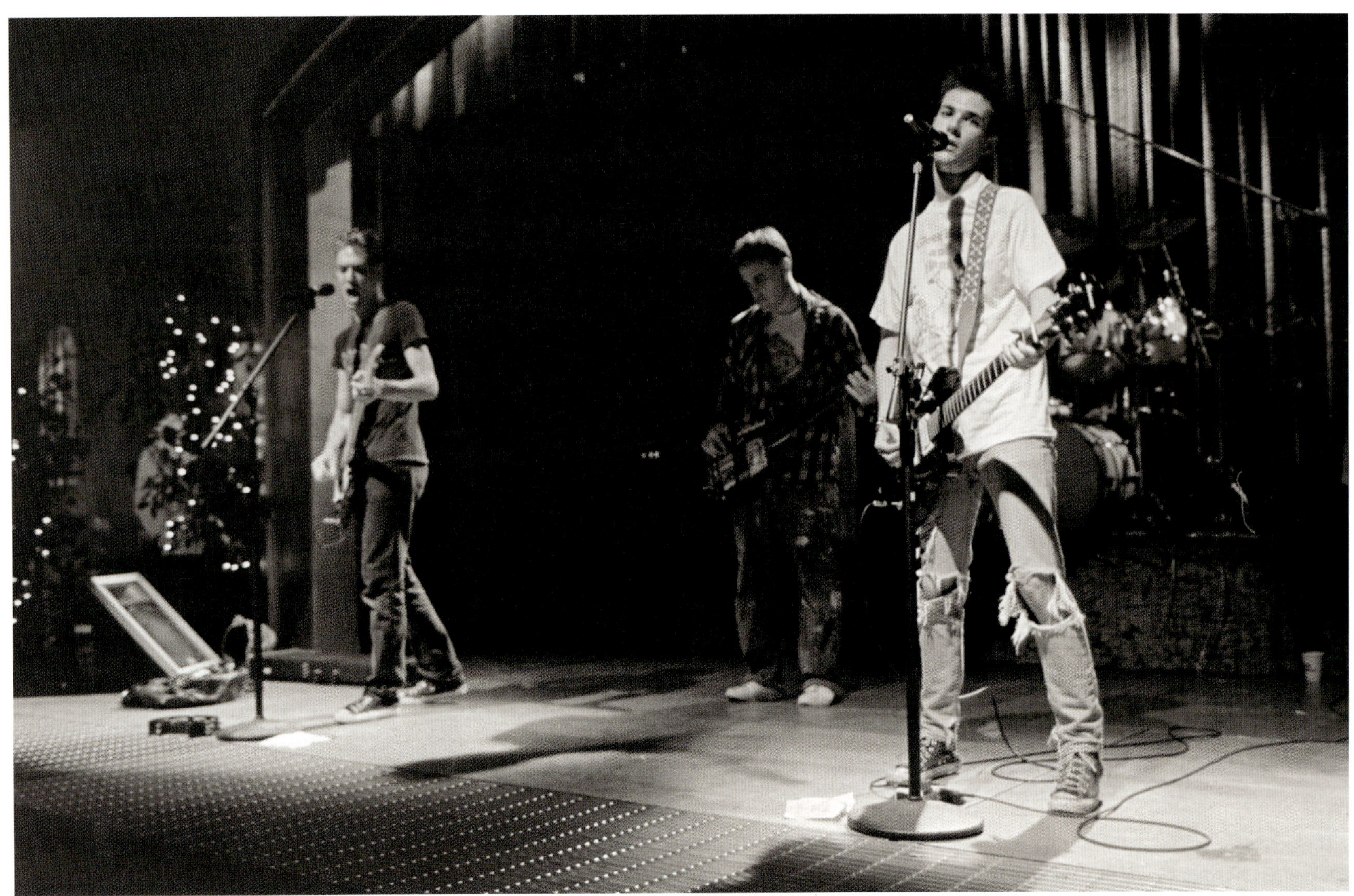

The Mr T Experience
The Omni, Oakland, 1986

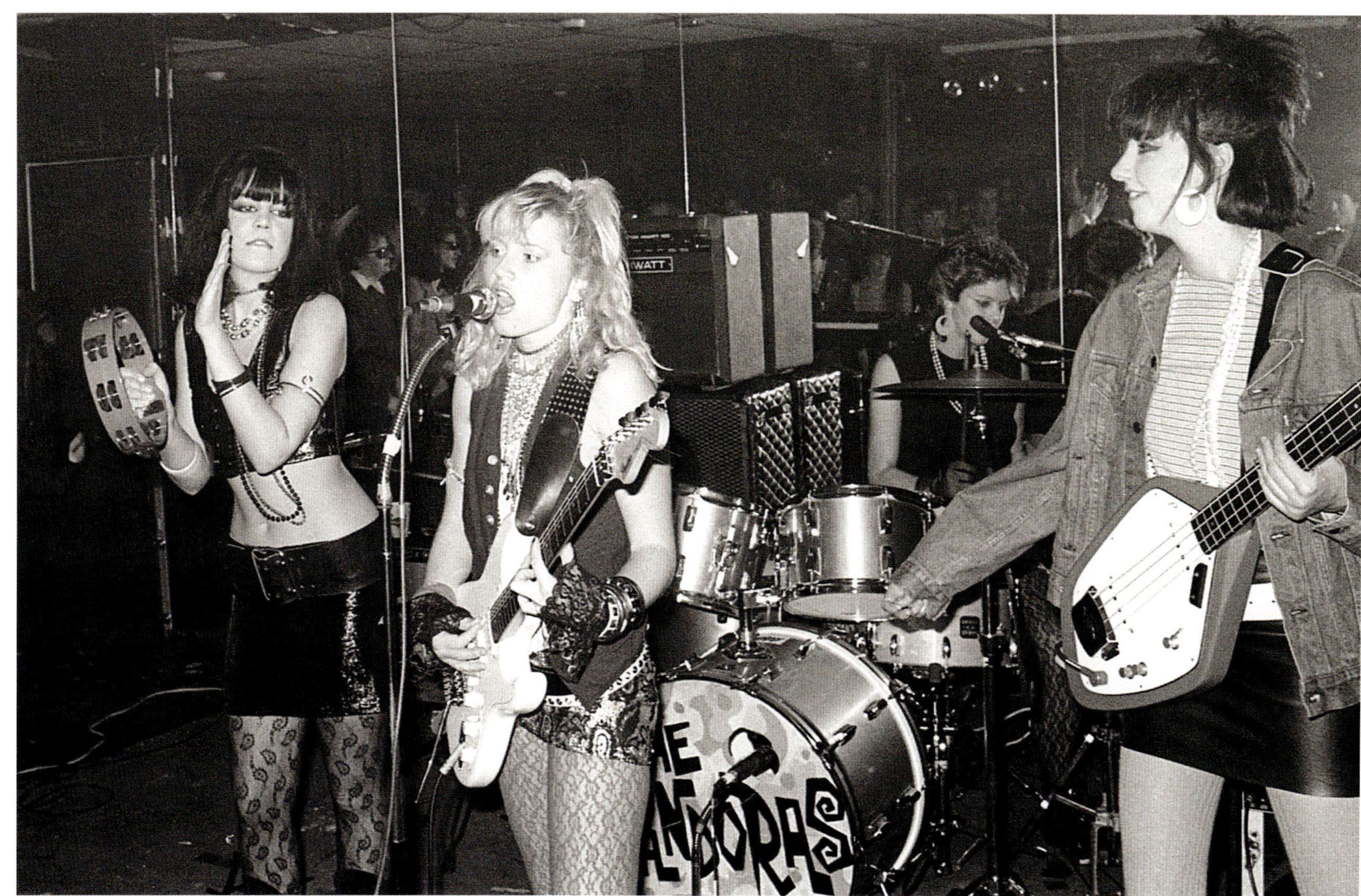

The Pandoras
VIS Club, San Francisco, 1986

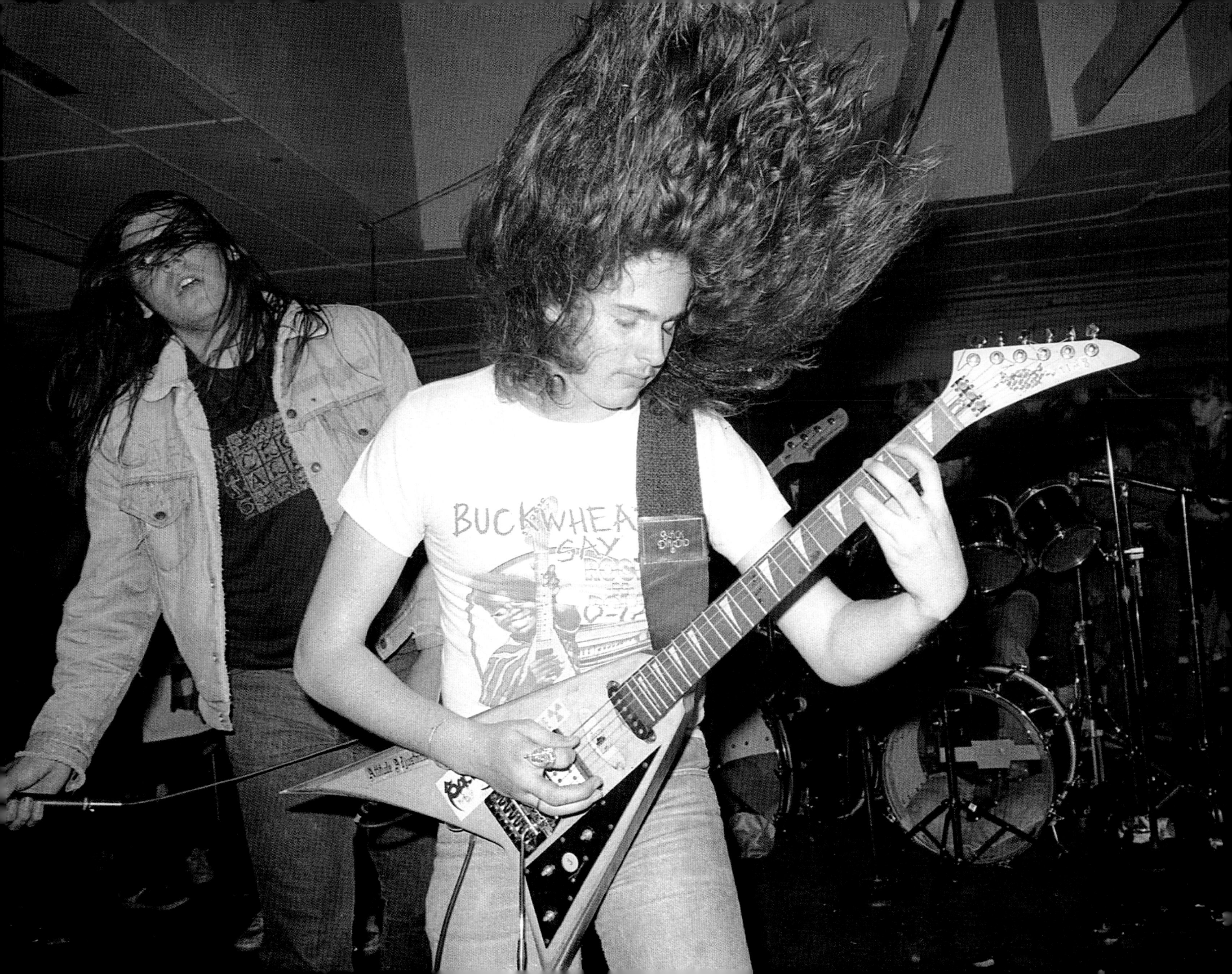

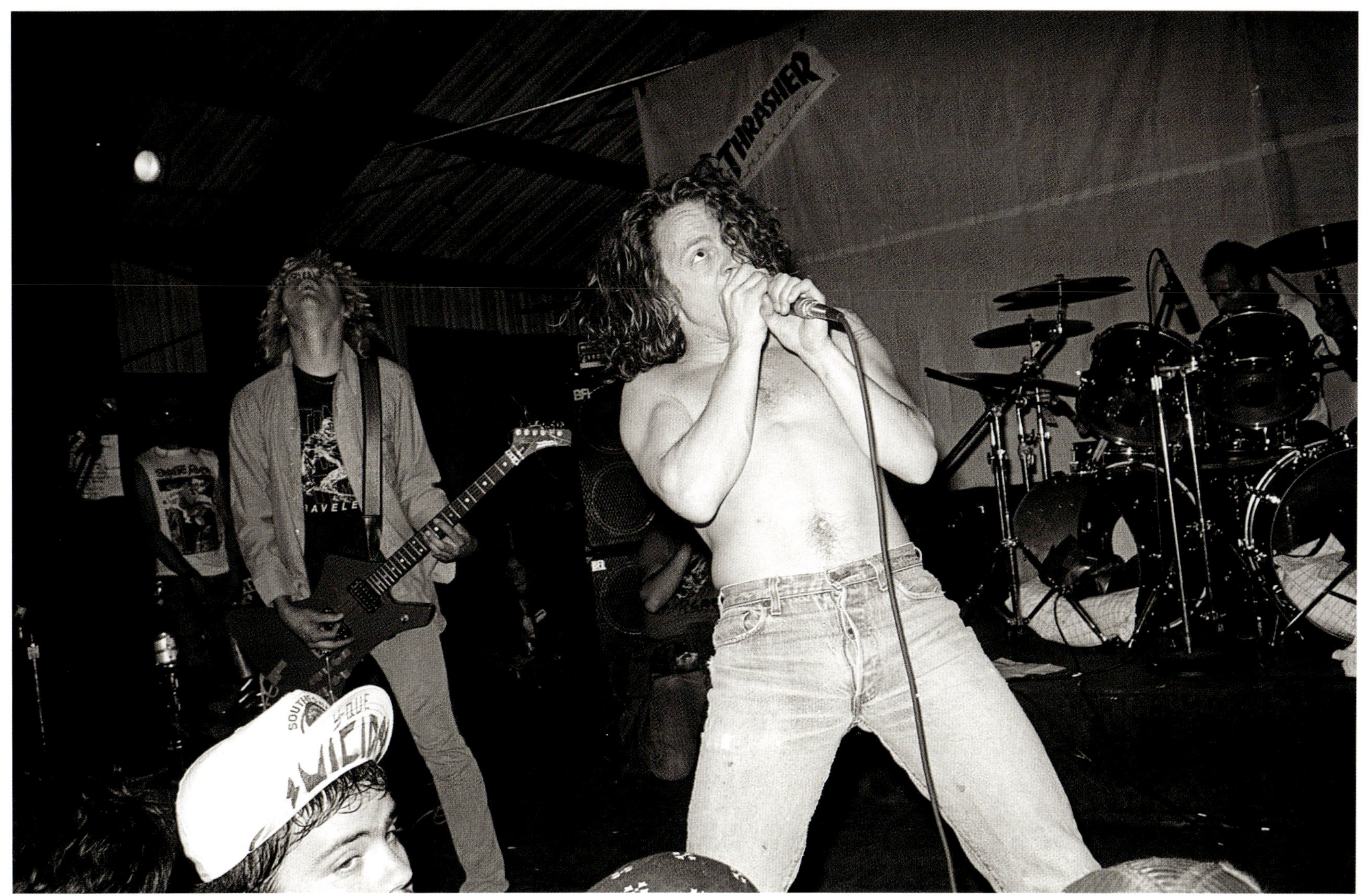

Accüsed
The Farm, San Francisco, 1986

Opposite:
Sacrilege
Berkeley Youth Alternative Center, 1986

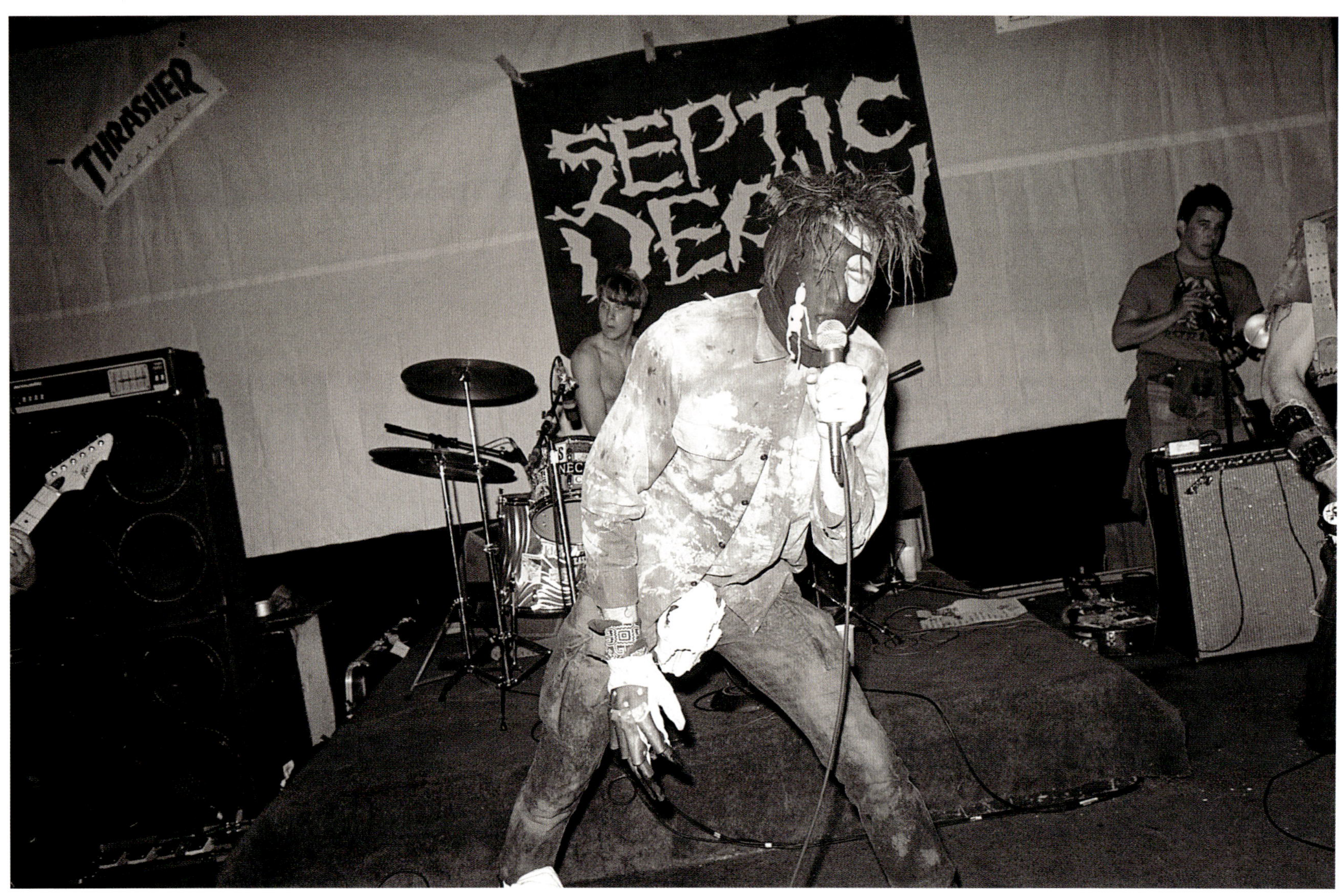

Septic Death

The Farm, San Francisco, 1986

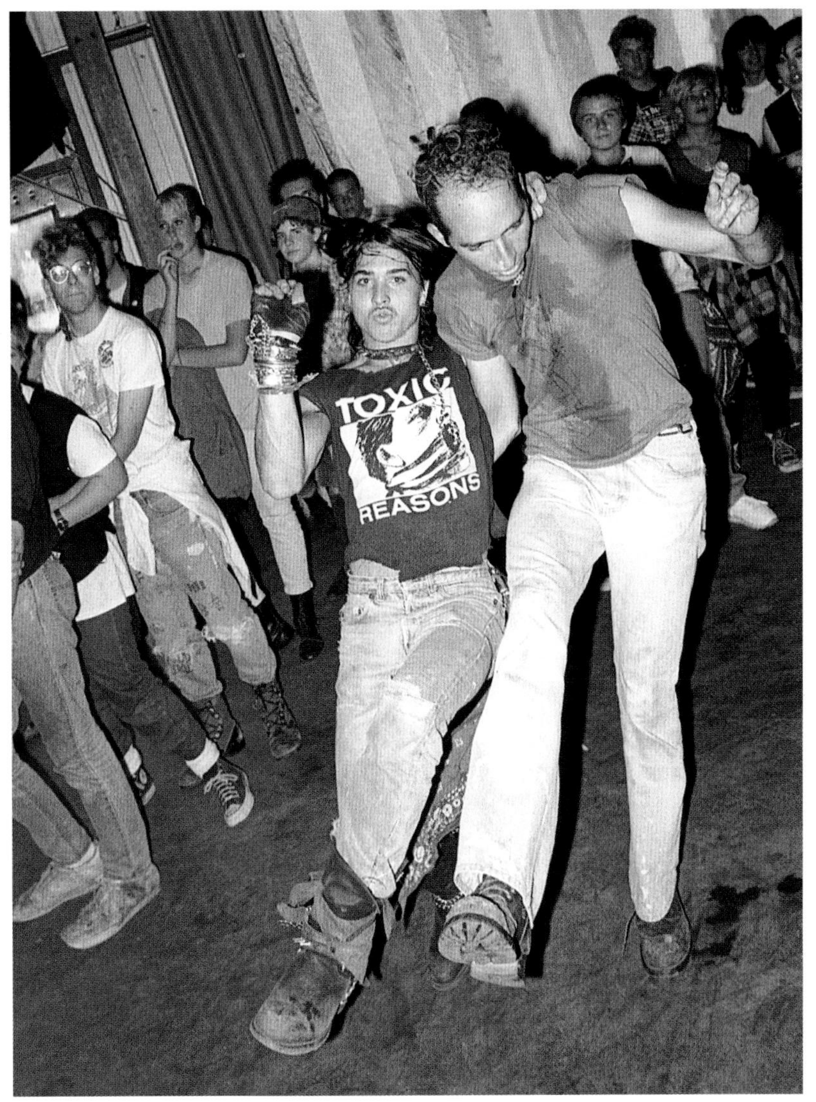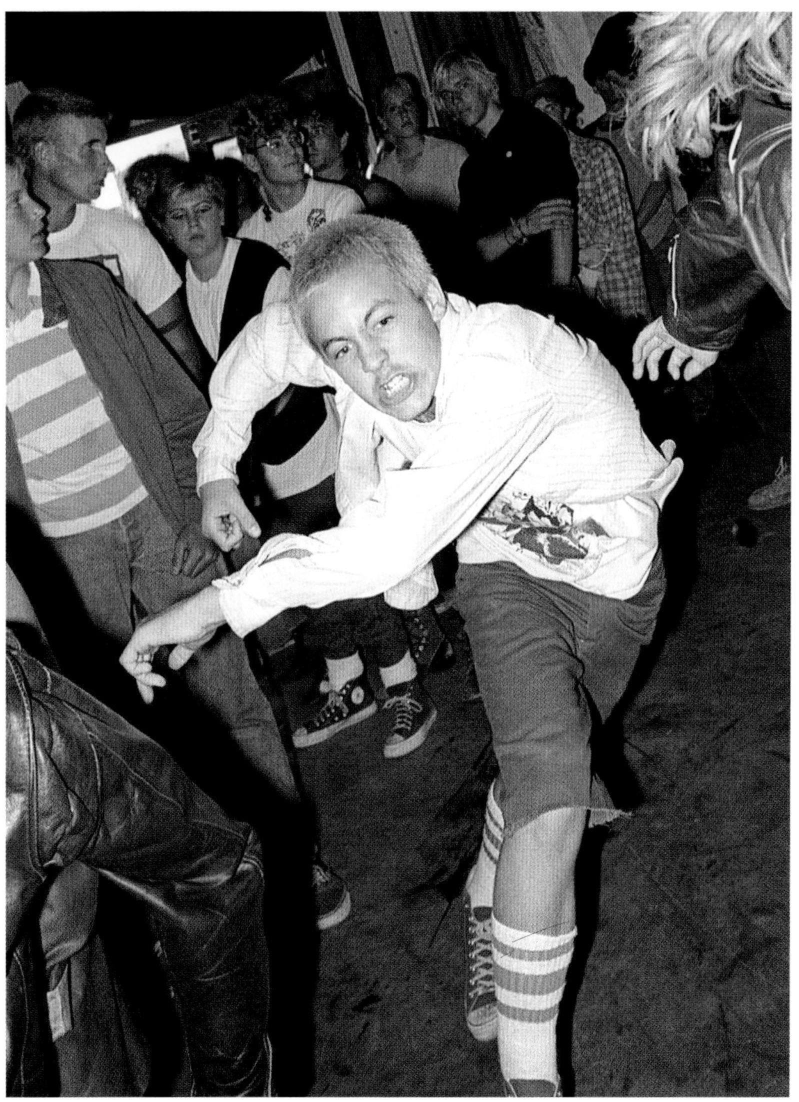

The Farm, 1986

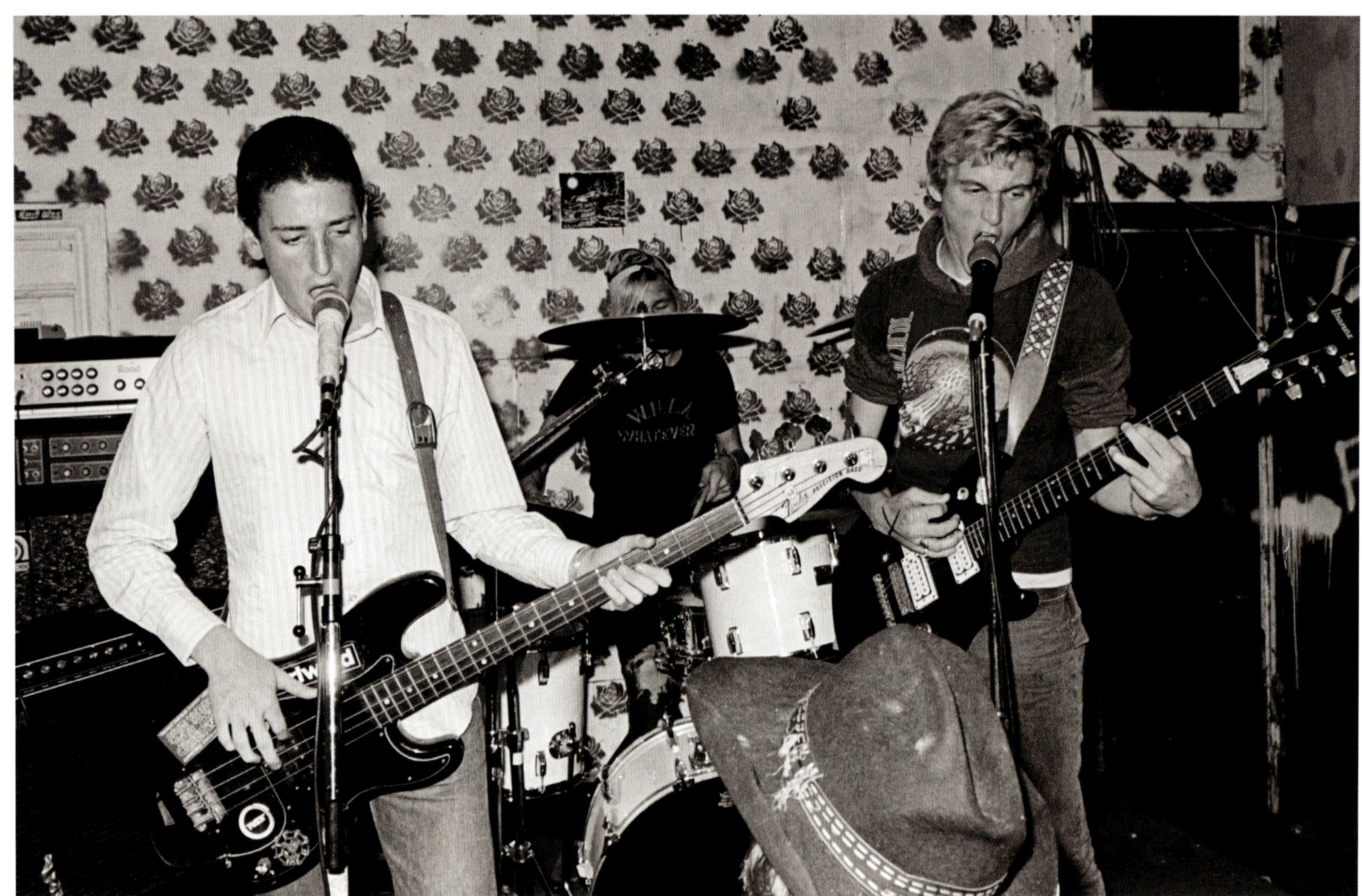

Crimpshrine

Club Foot, San Francisco, 1986

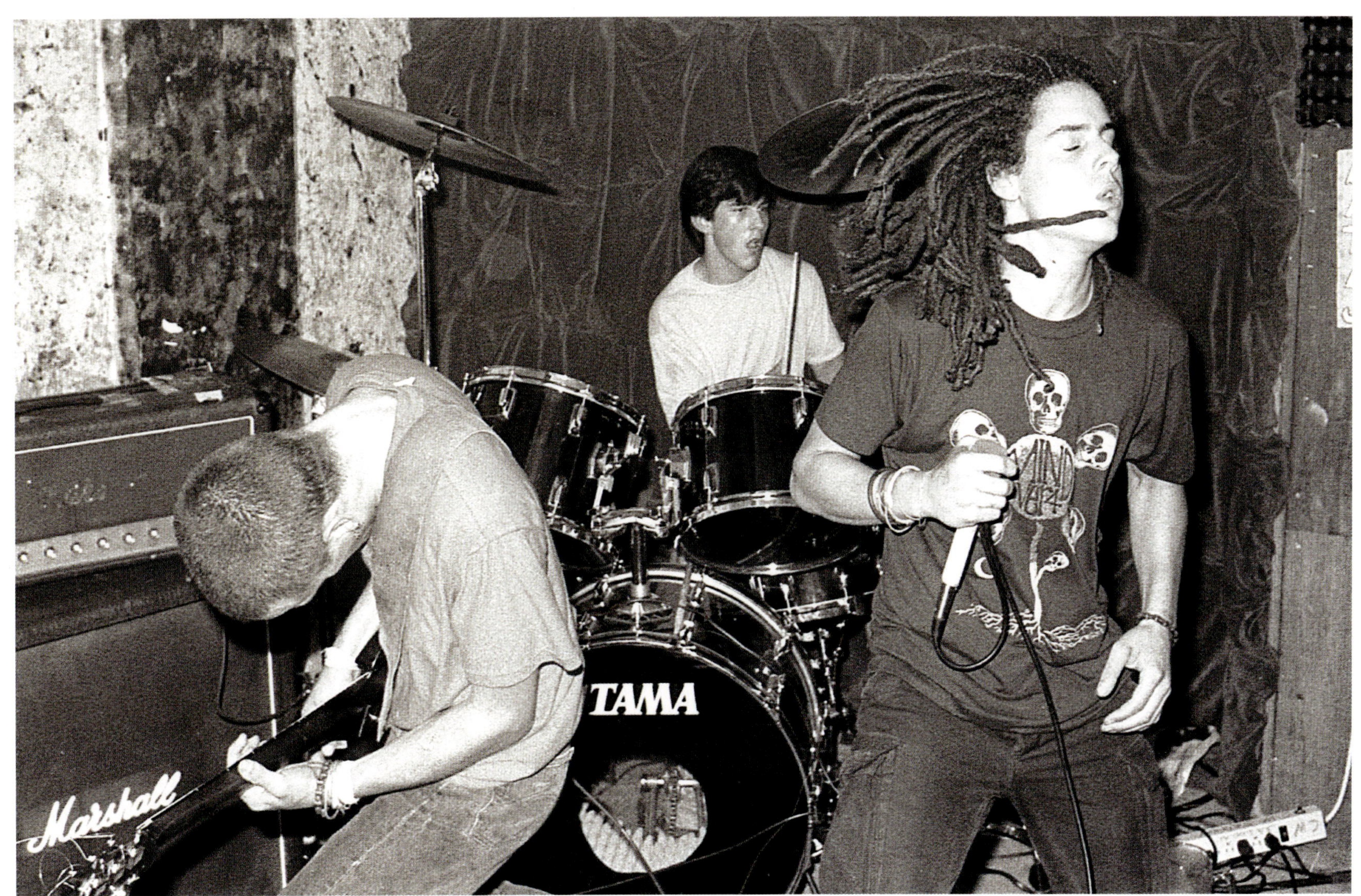

Soulside
Covered Wagon, San Francisco, 1987

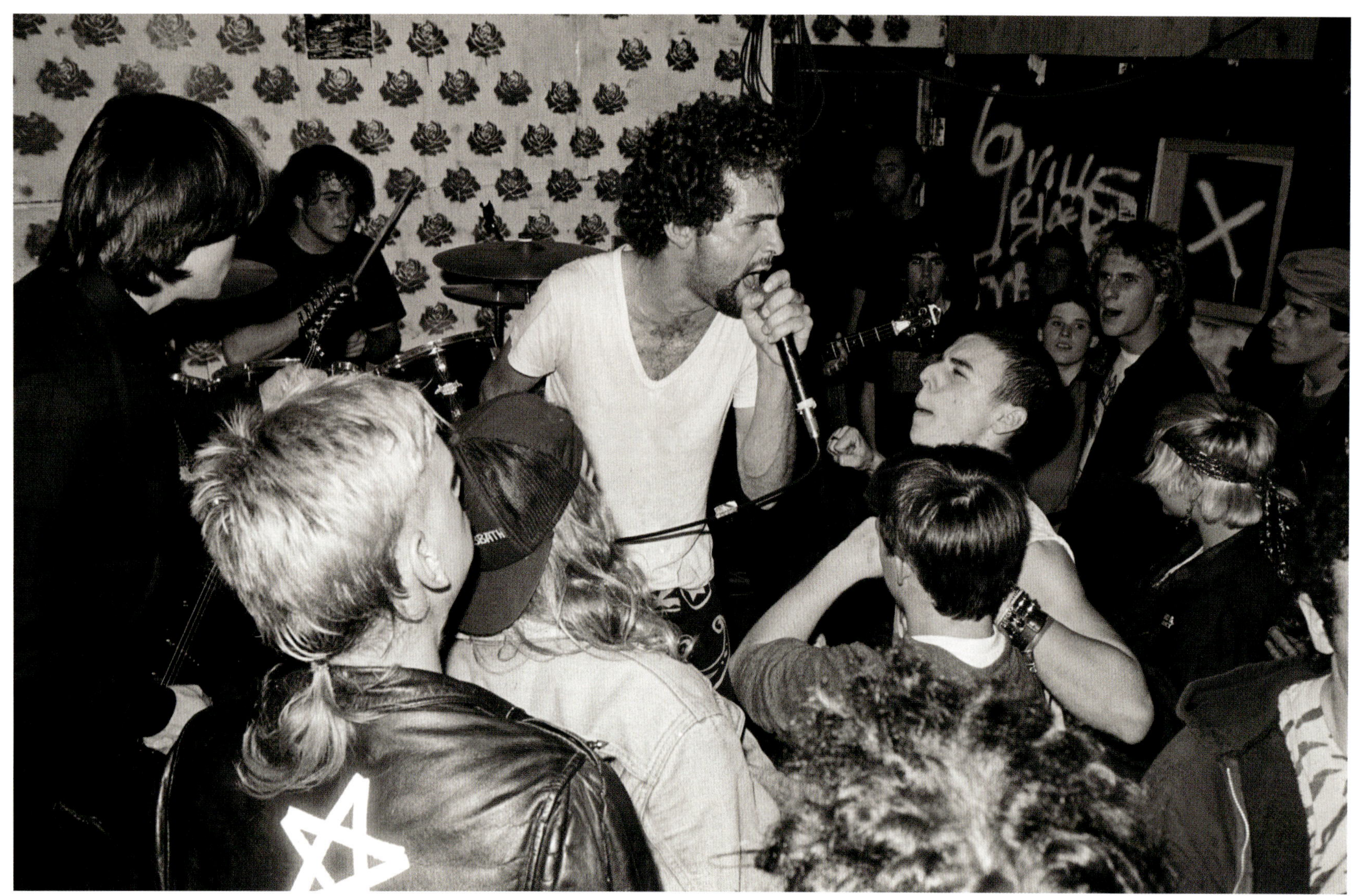

Clown Alley
Club Foot, San Francisco, 1986

Opposite:
Club Foot, 1986

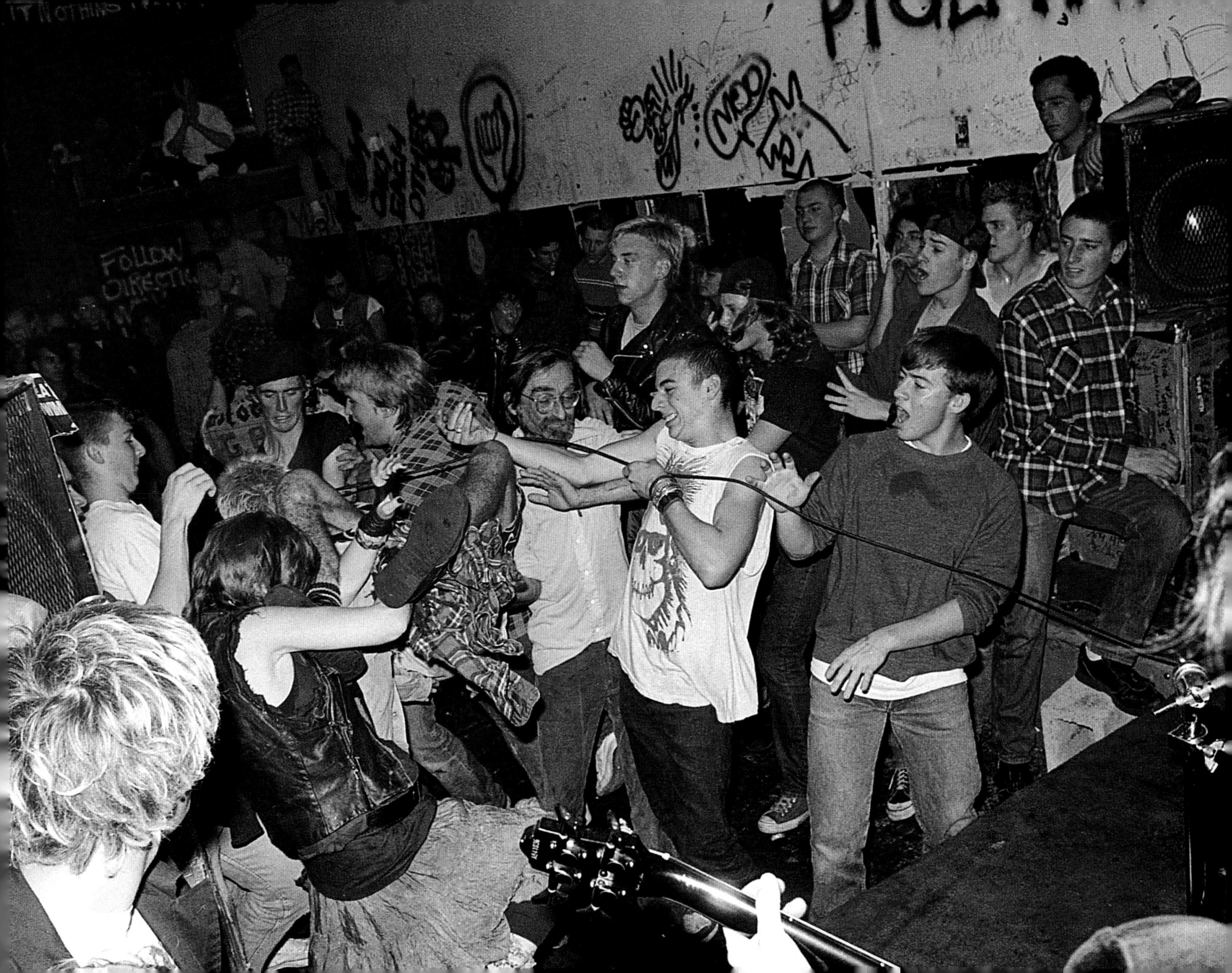

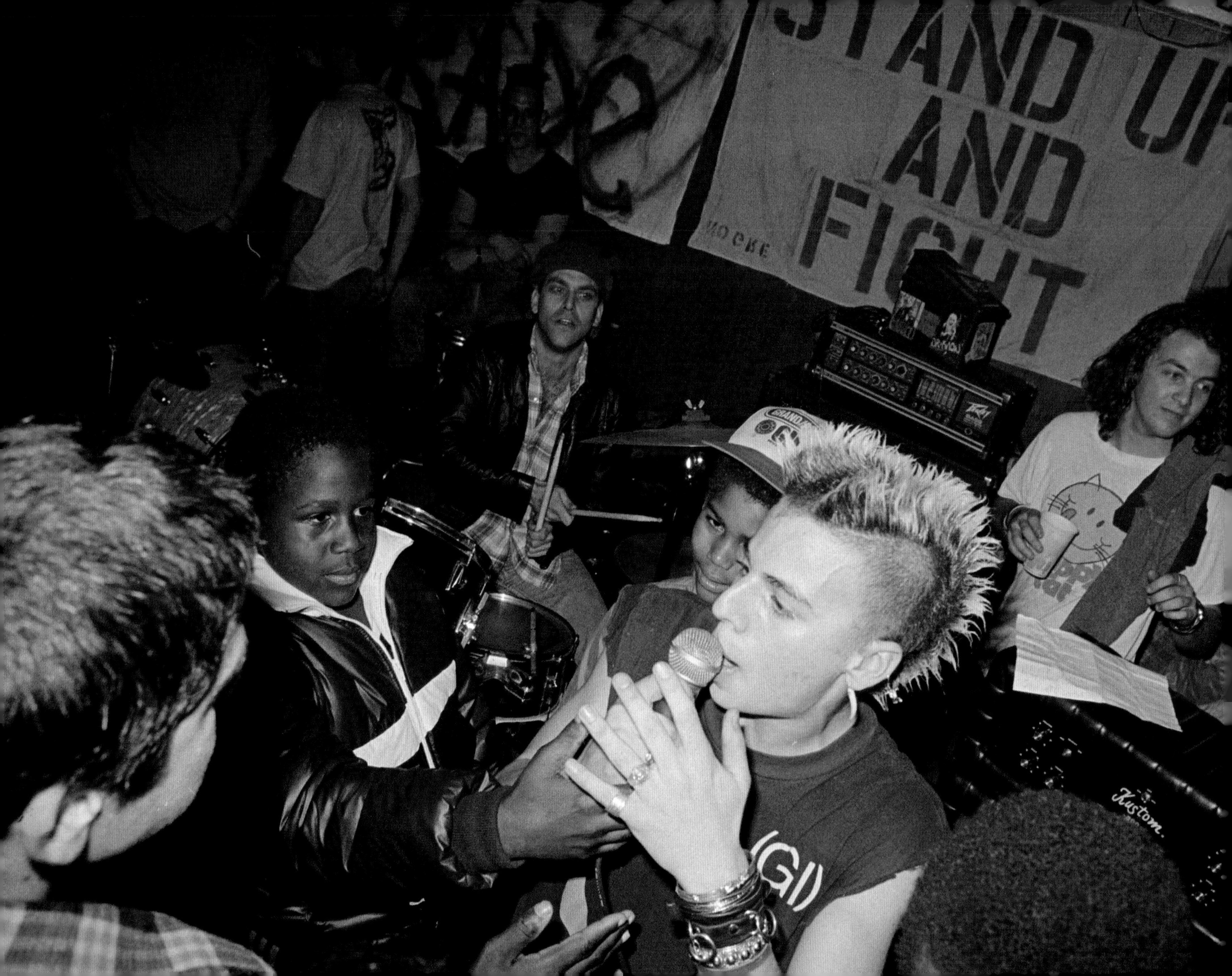
STAND UP
AND
FIGHT

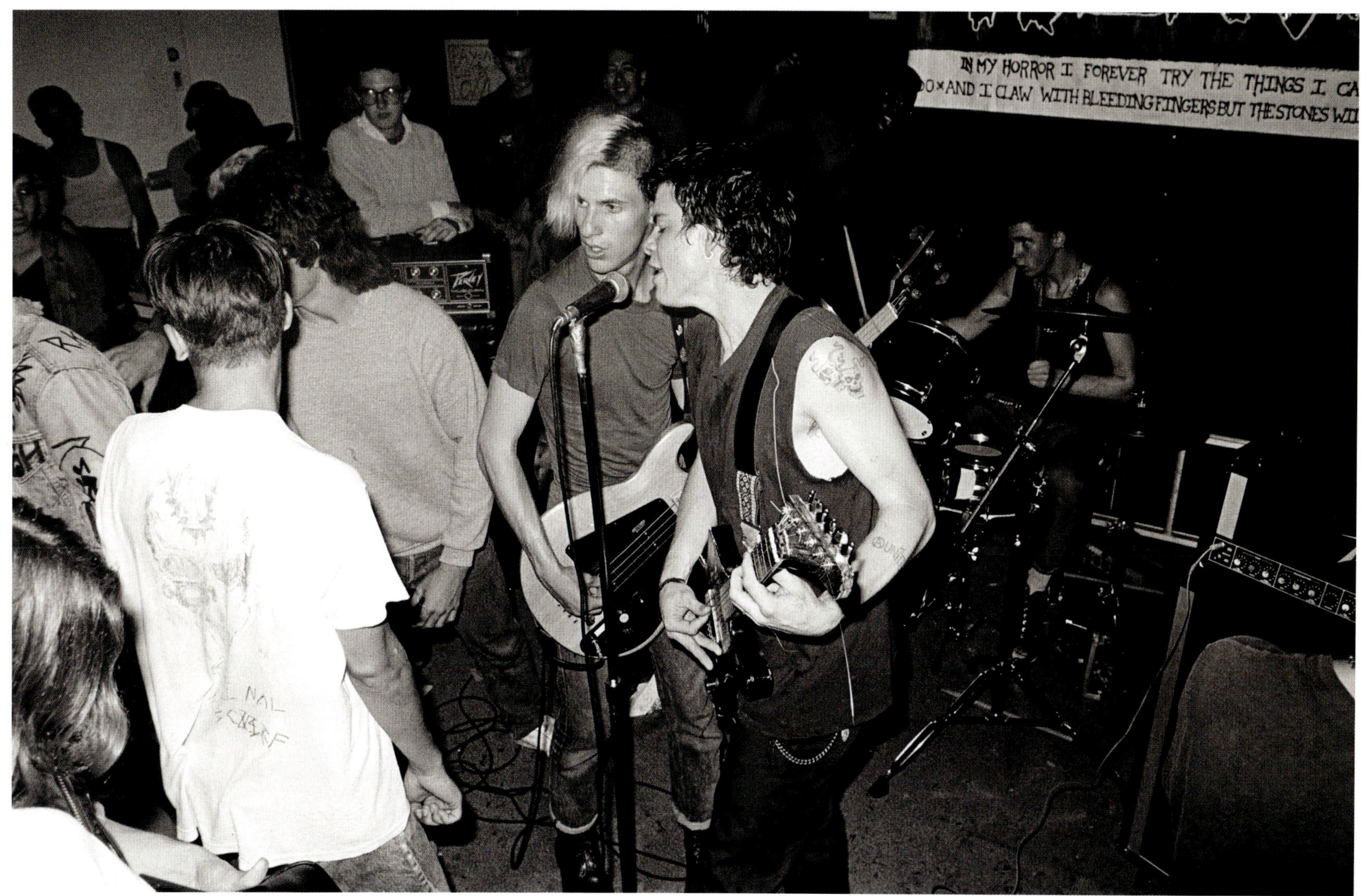

Neurosis
Own's Pizza, Berkeley, 1986

Opposite:
MC Punk
Own's Pizza, 1986

Early Gilman Meeting
Gilman Street, Berkeley, 1986

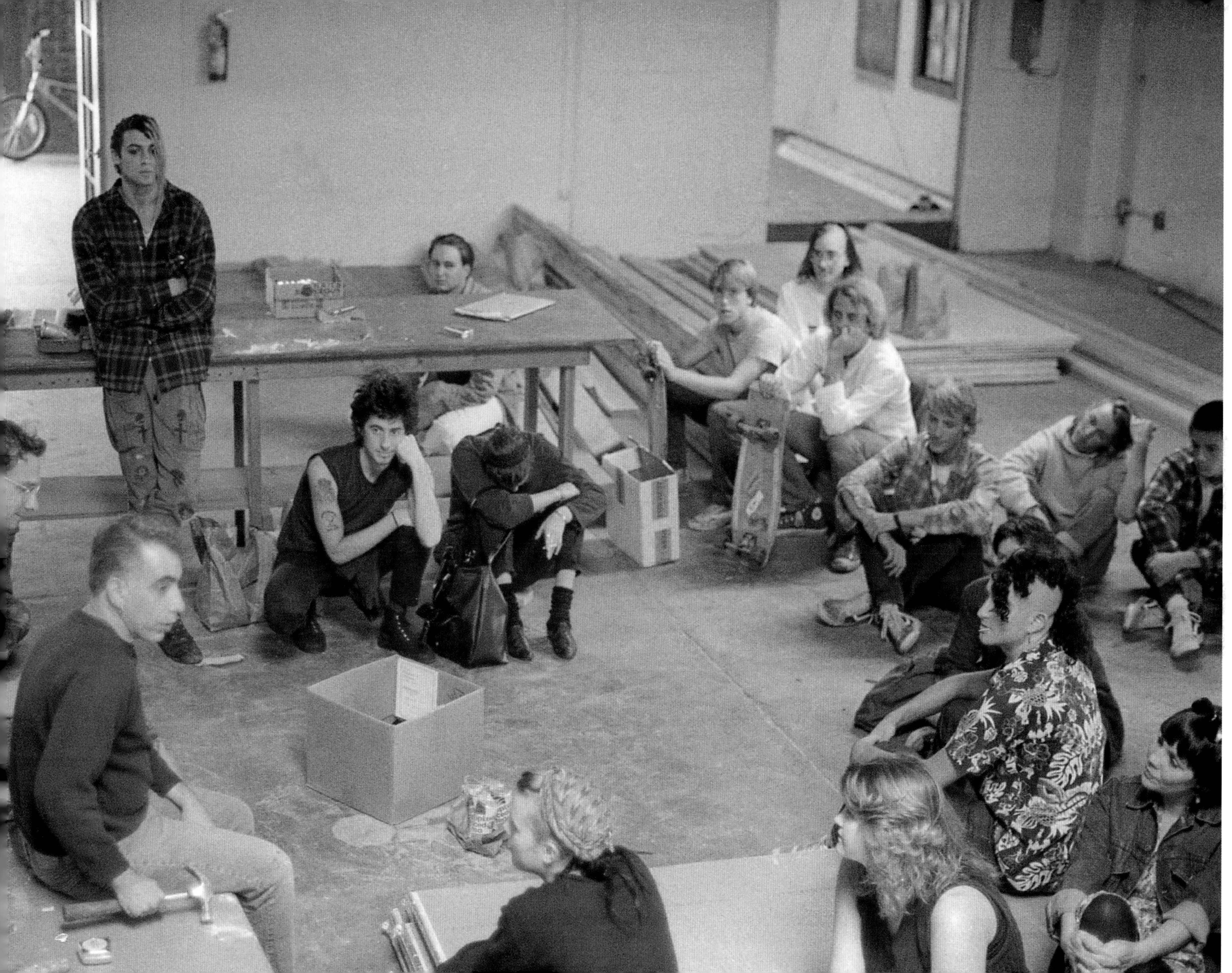

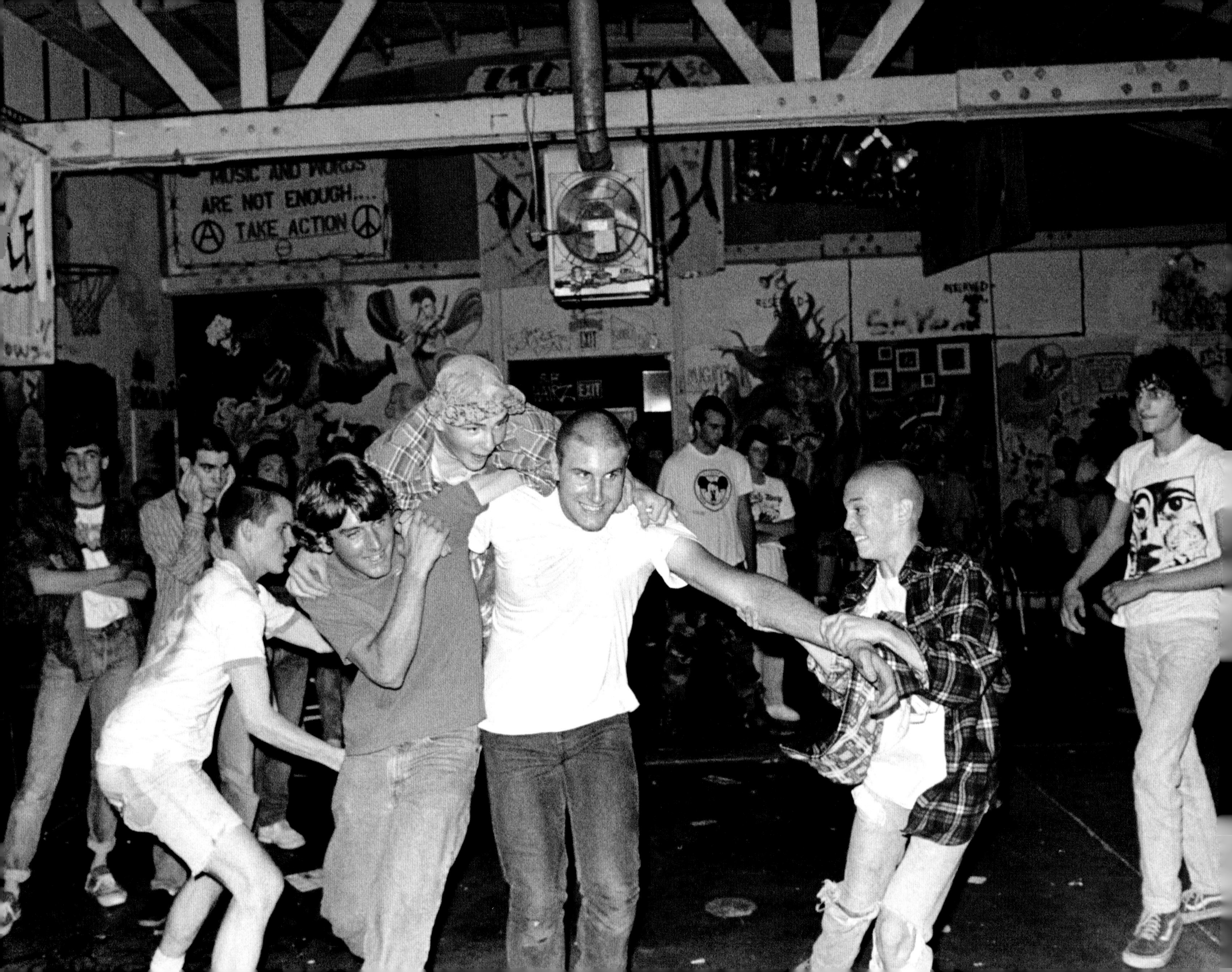
MUSIC AND WORDS
ARE NOT ENOUGH....
TAKE ACTION

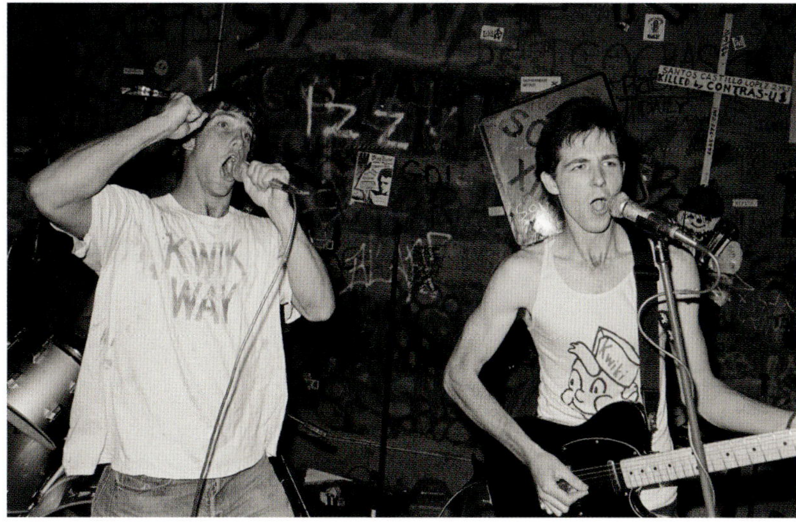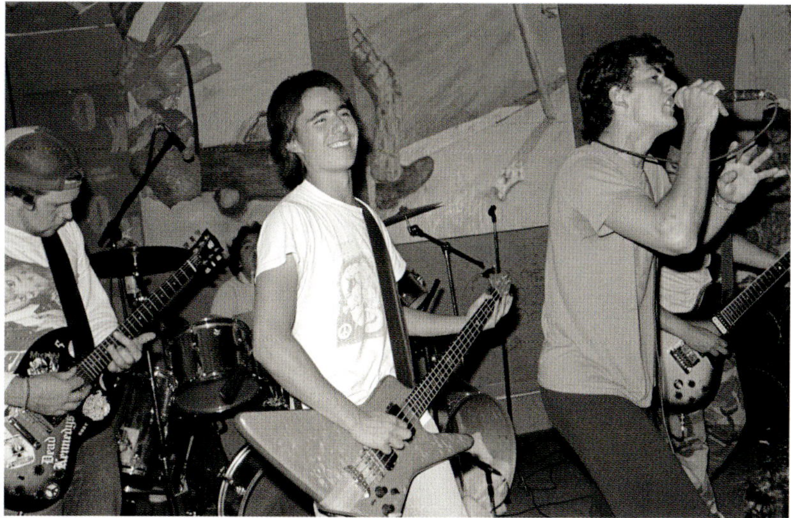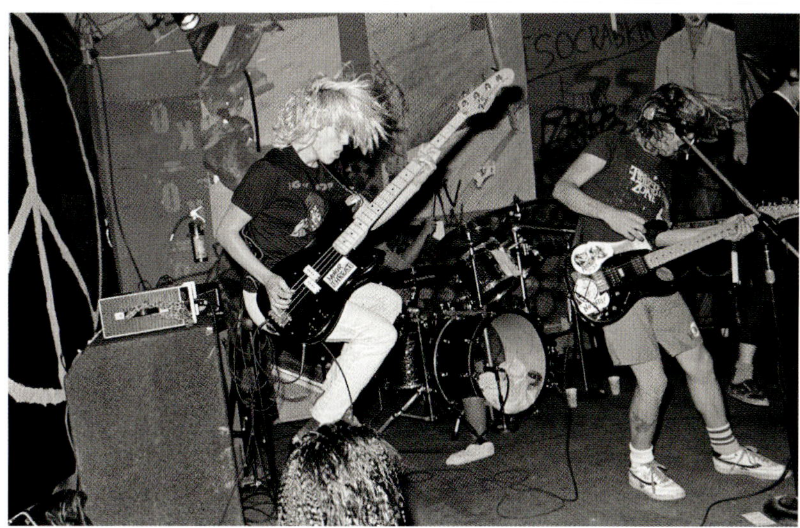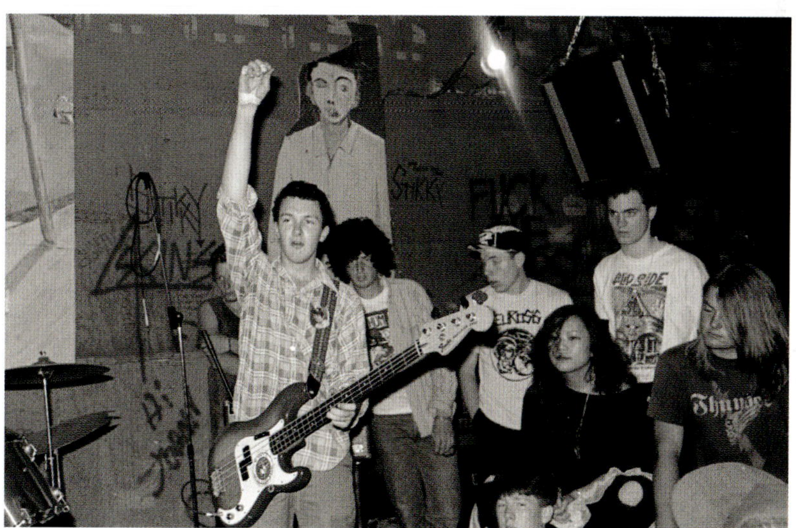

Early Gilman Bands
Clockwise from top left: Kwik Way, 1989; Corrupted Morals, 1987; Soup, 1987; Short Dogs Grow, 1987

Opposite: Gilman Street, Berkeley, 1987

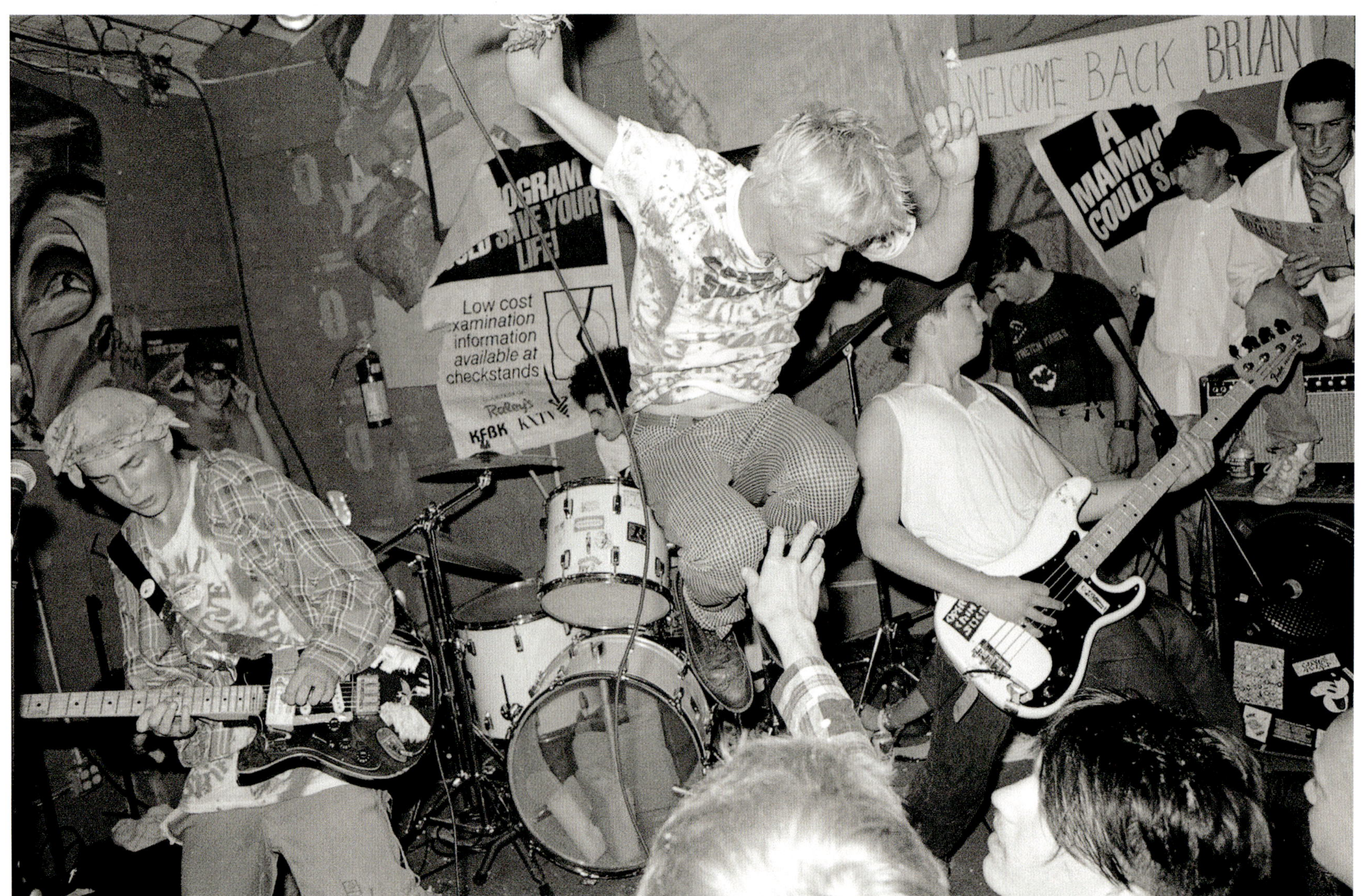

Operation Ivy
Gilman Street, Berkeley, 1987

Opposite:

Crimpshrine
Gilman Street, 1987

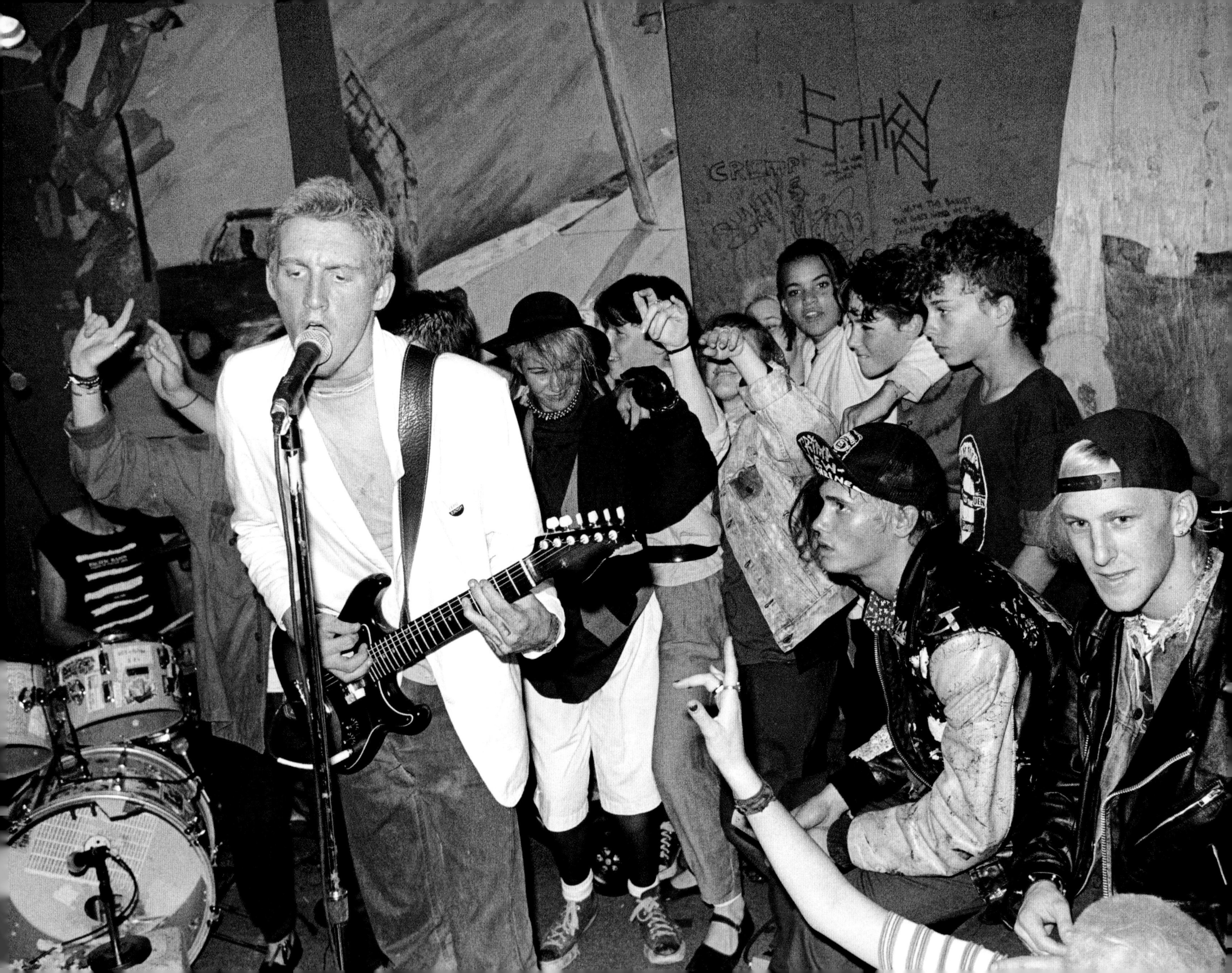

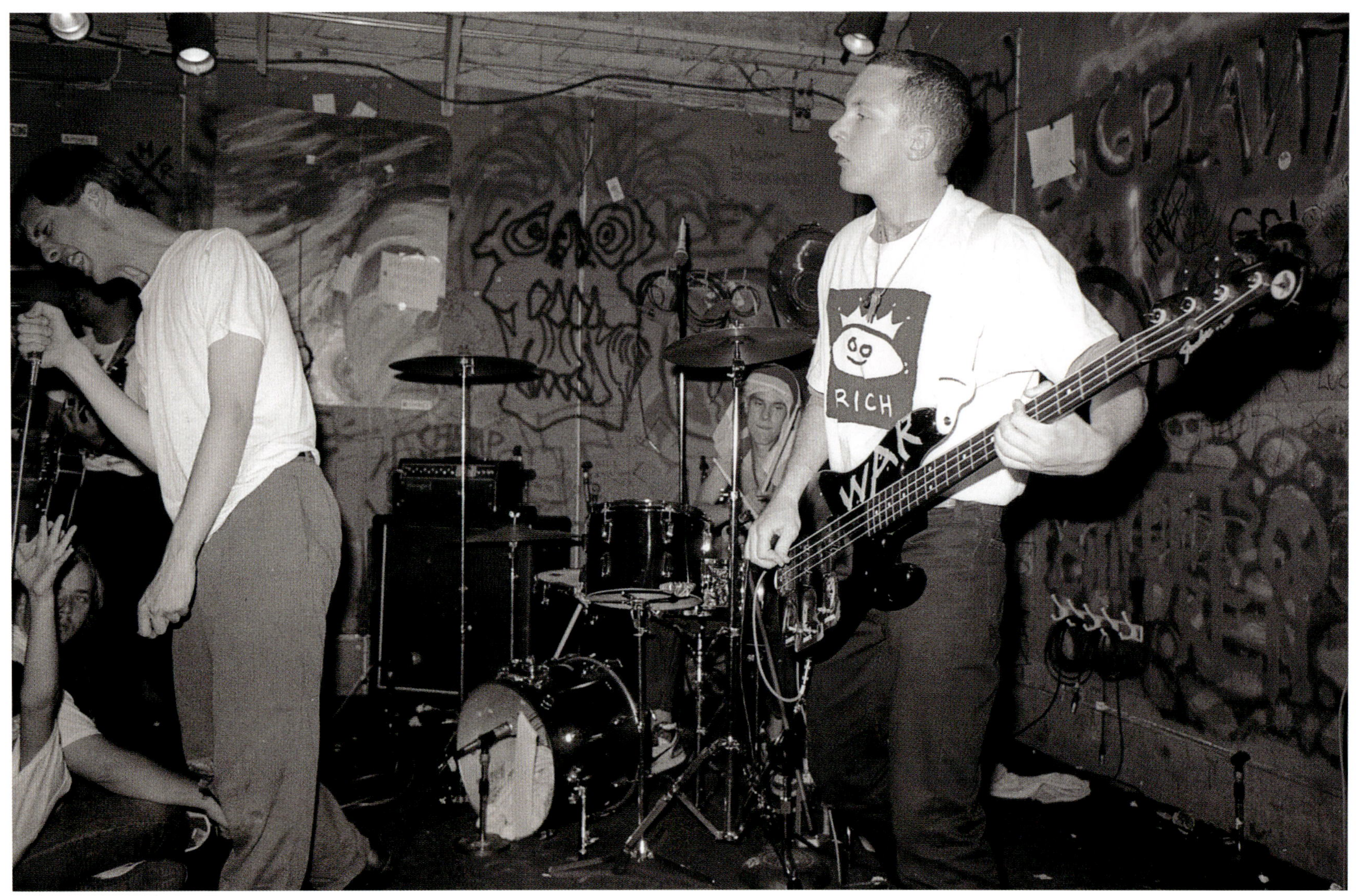

Sweet Baby Jesus
Gilman Street, Berkeley, 1987

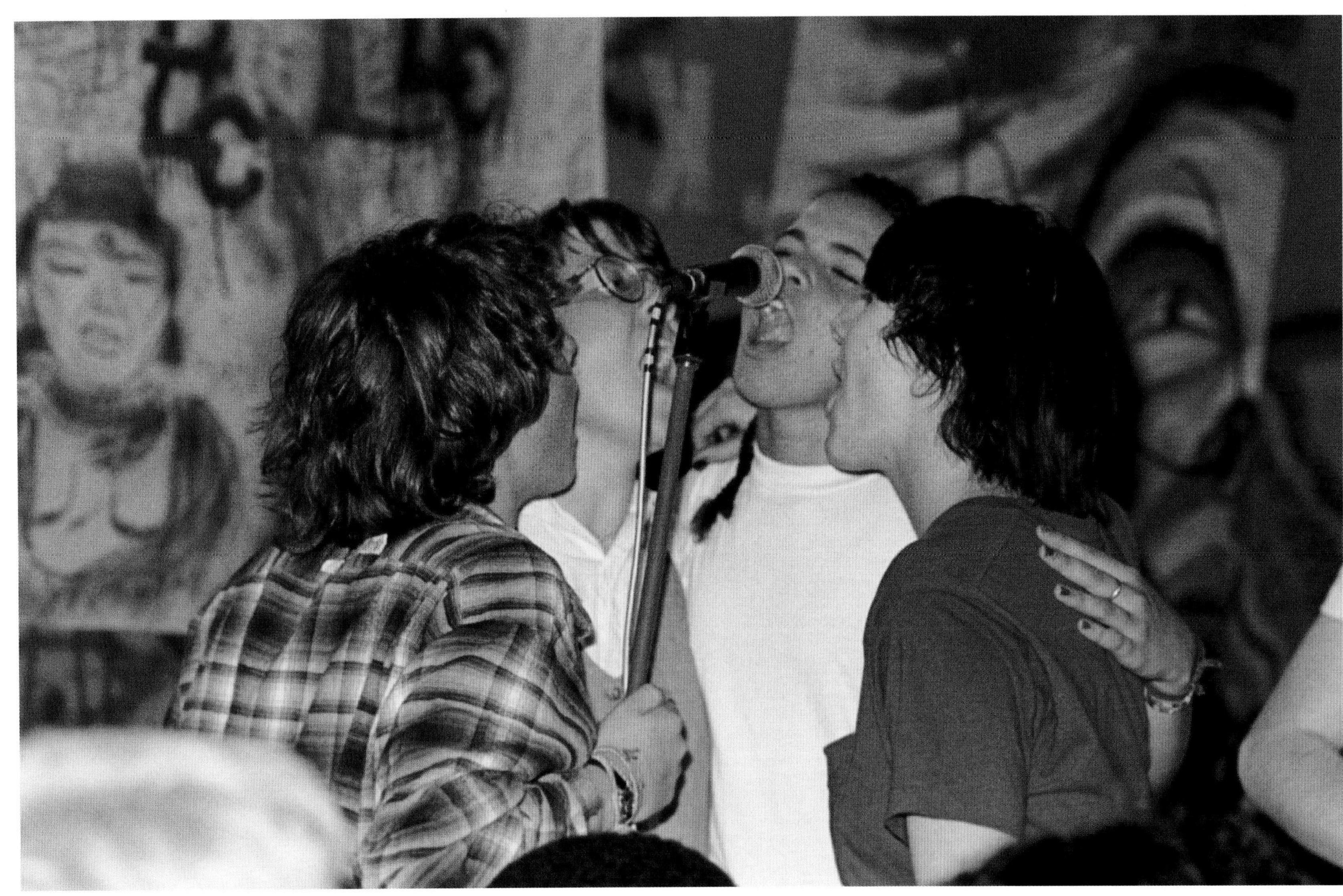

Gilman Street, 1987

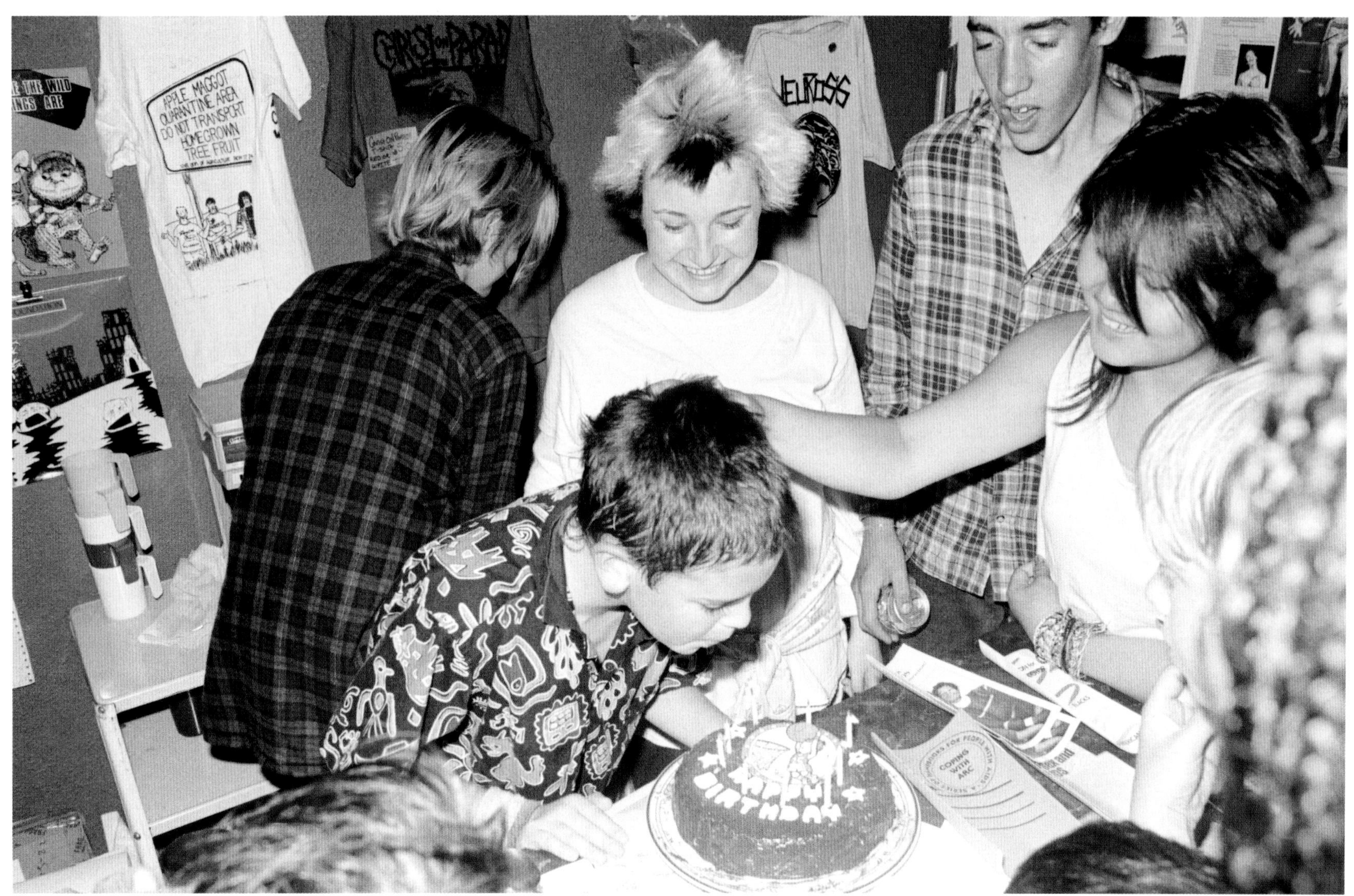

Gilman Street, Berkeley, 1987

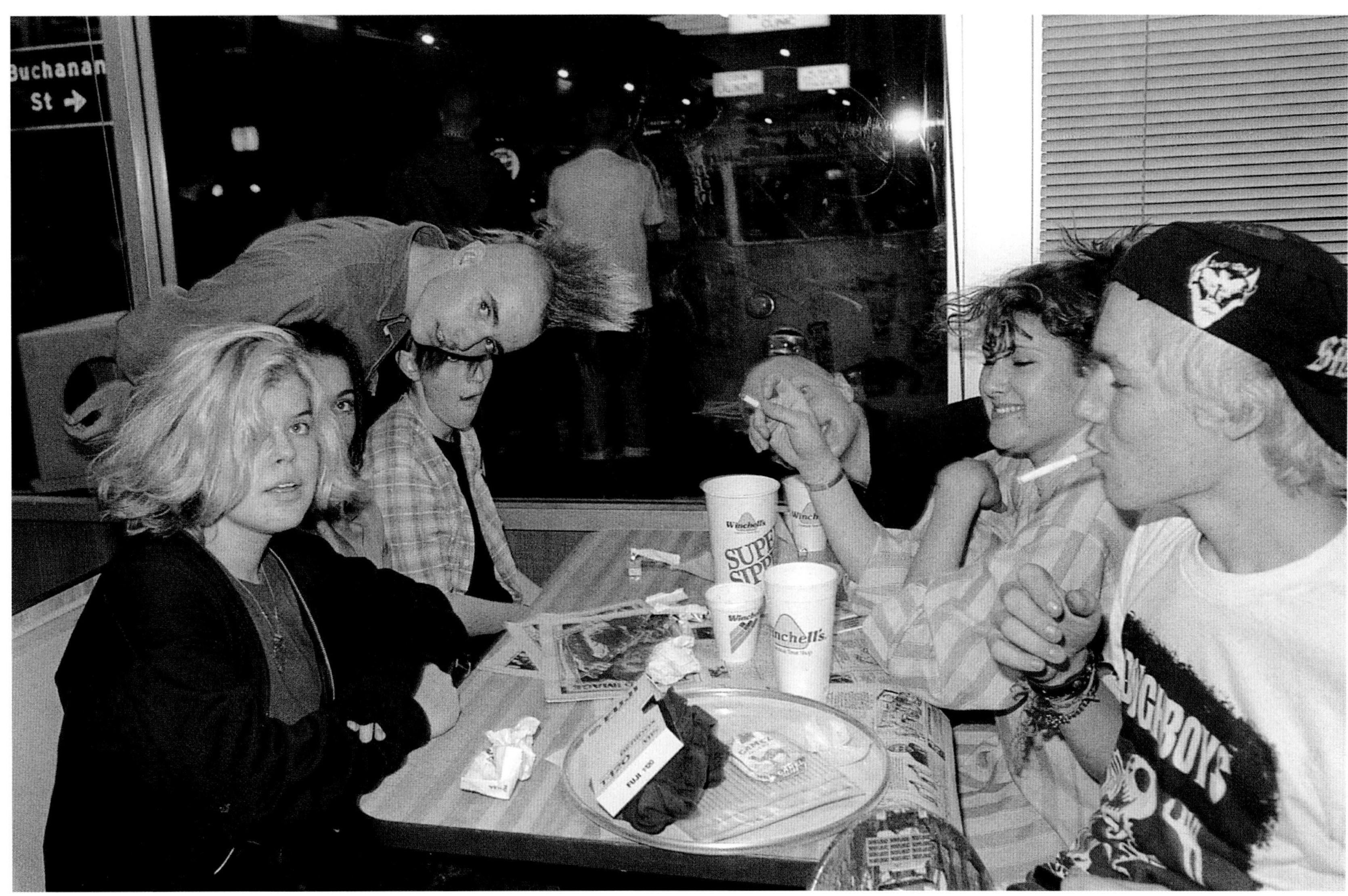

Winchell's Donuts, Albany, 1987

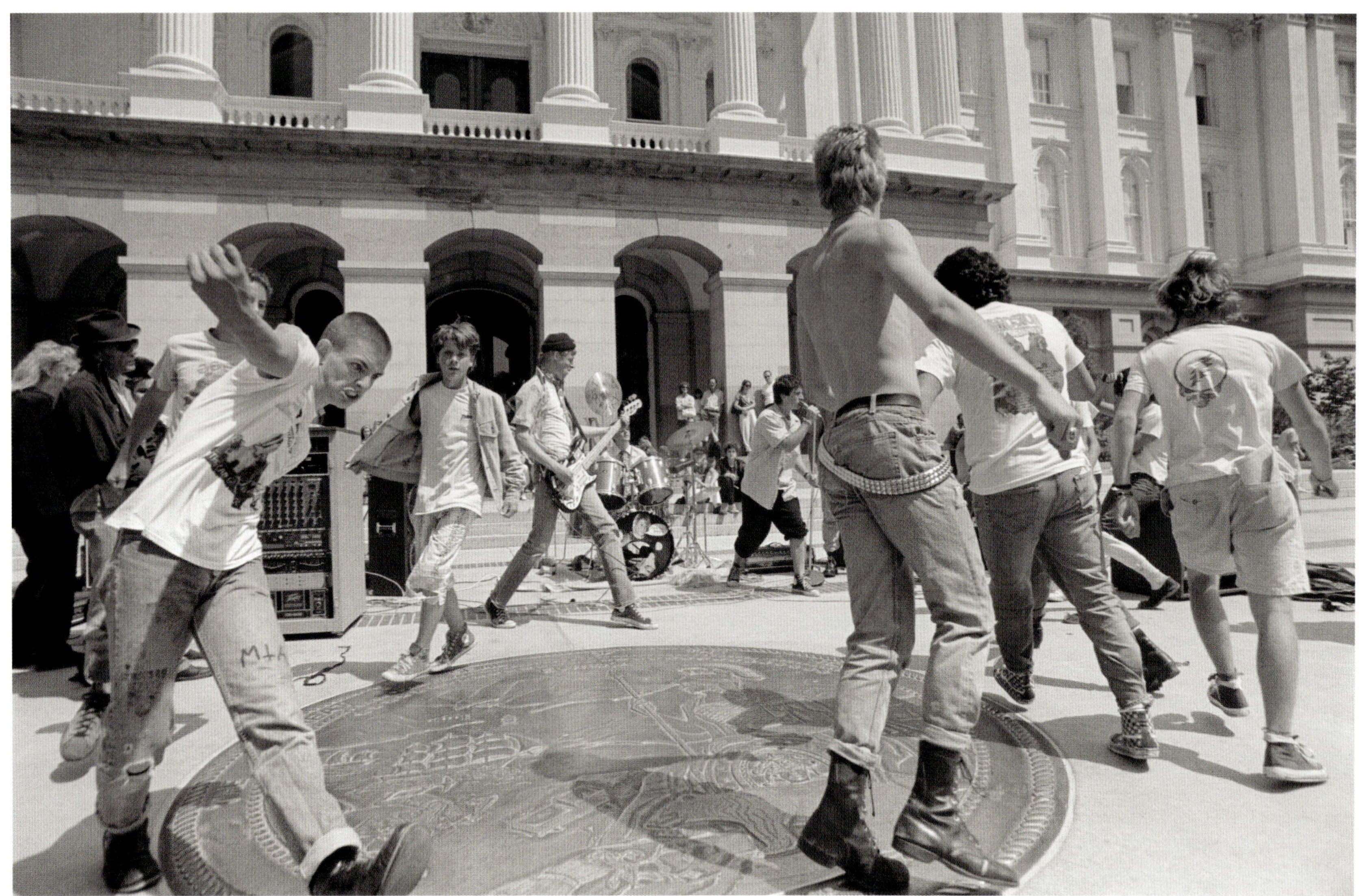

Isocracy

Above: State Capitol, Sacramento, 1987

Opposite: Gilman Street, Berkeley, 1987

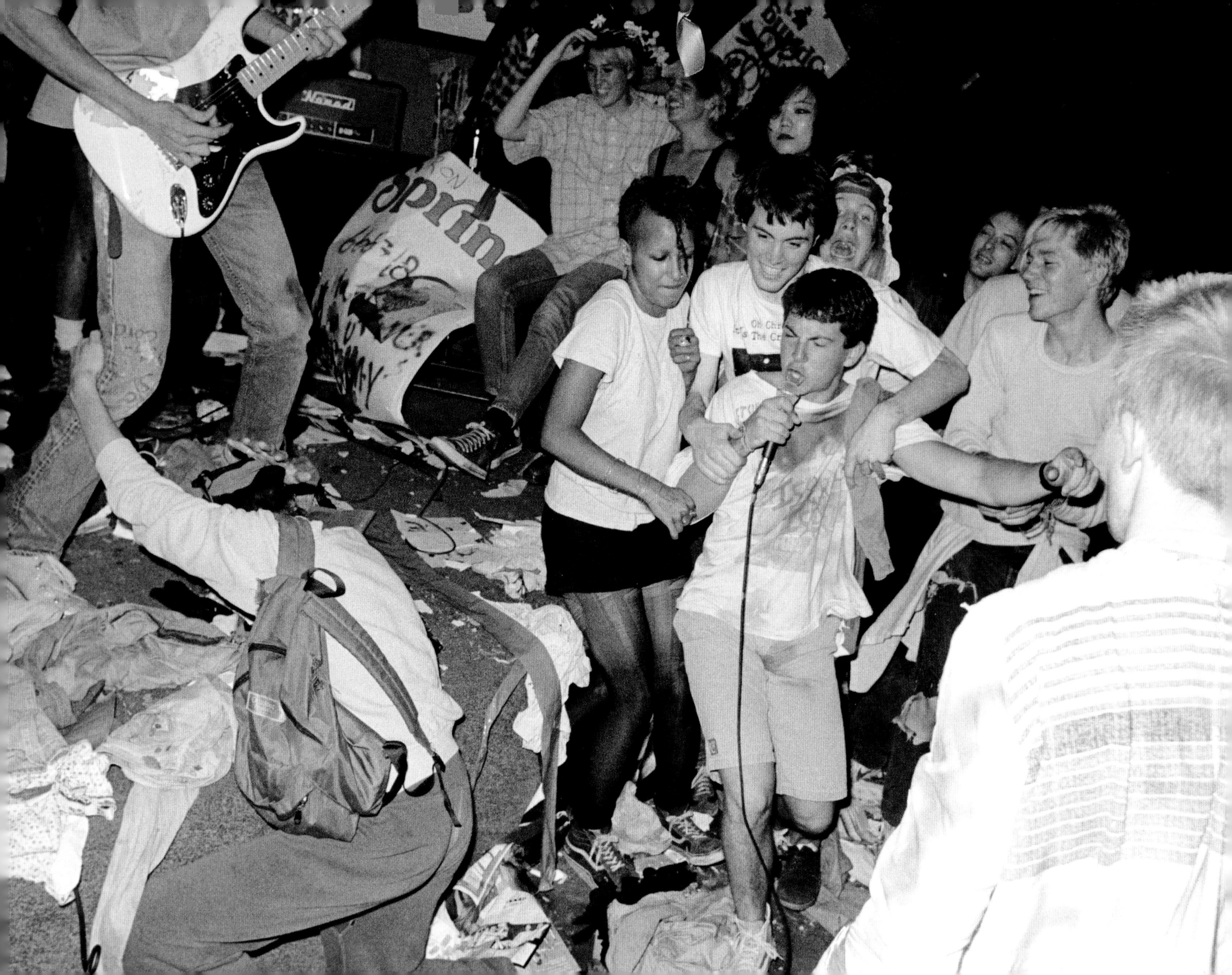

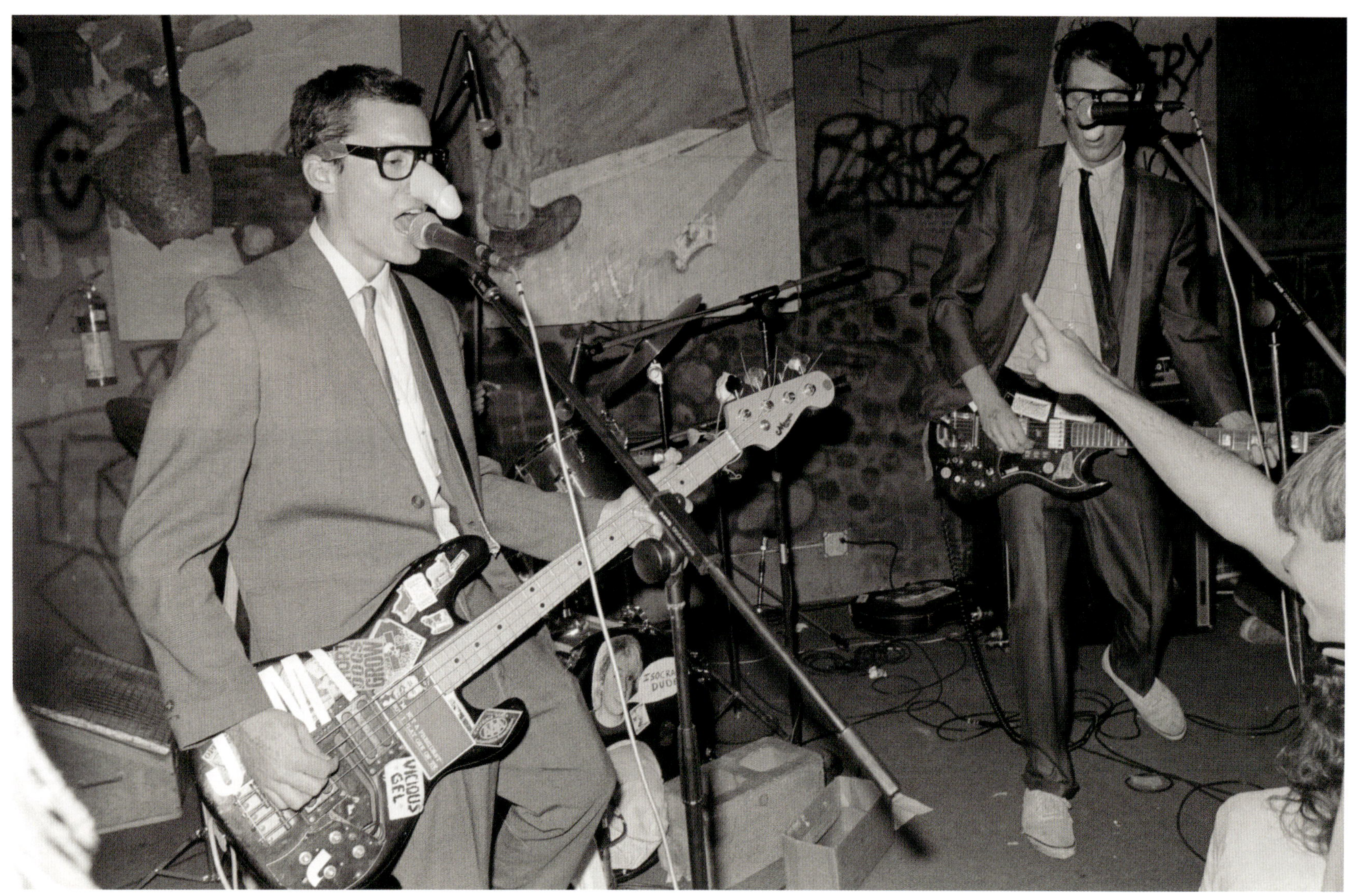

Sewer Trout

Gilman Street, Berkeley, 1987

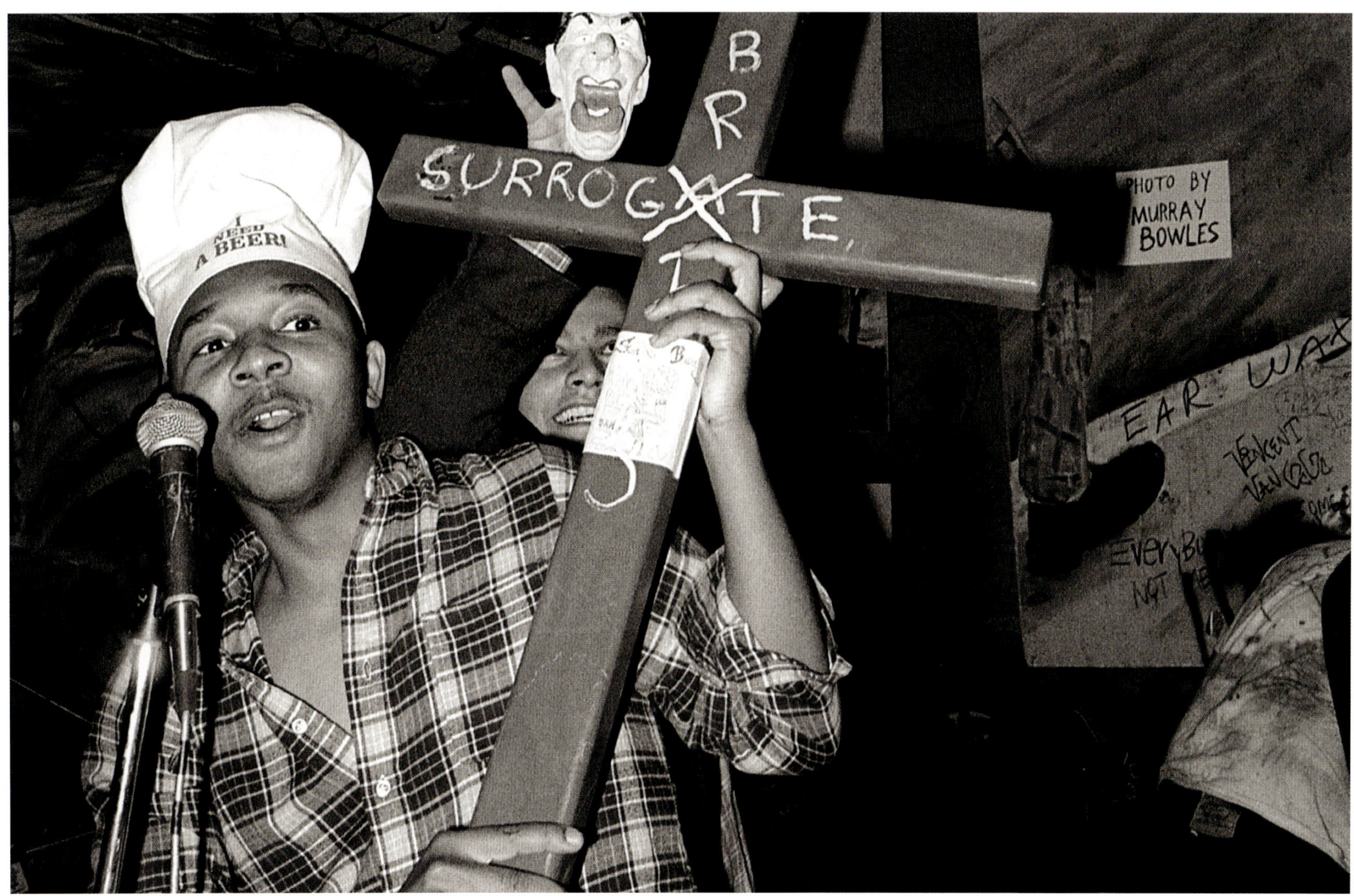

Surrogate Brains
Gilman Street, Berkeley, 1987

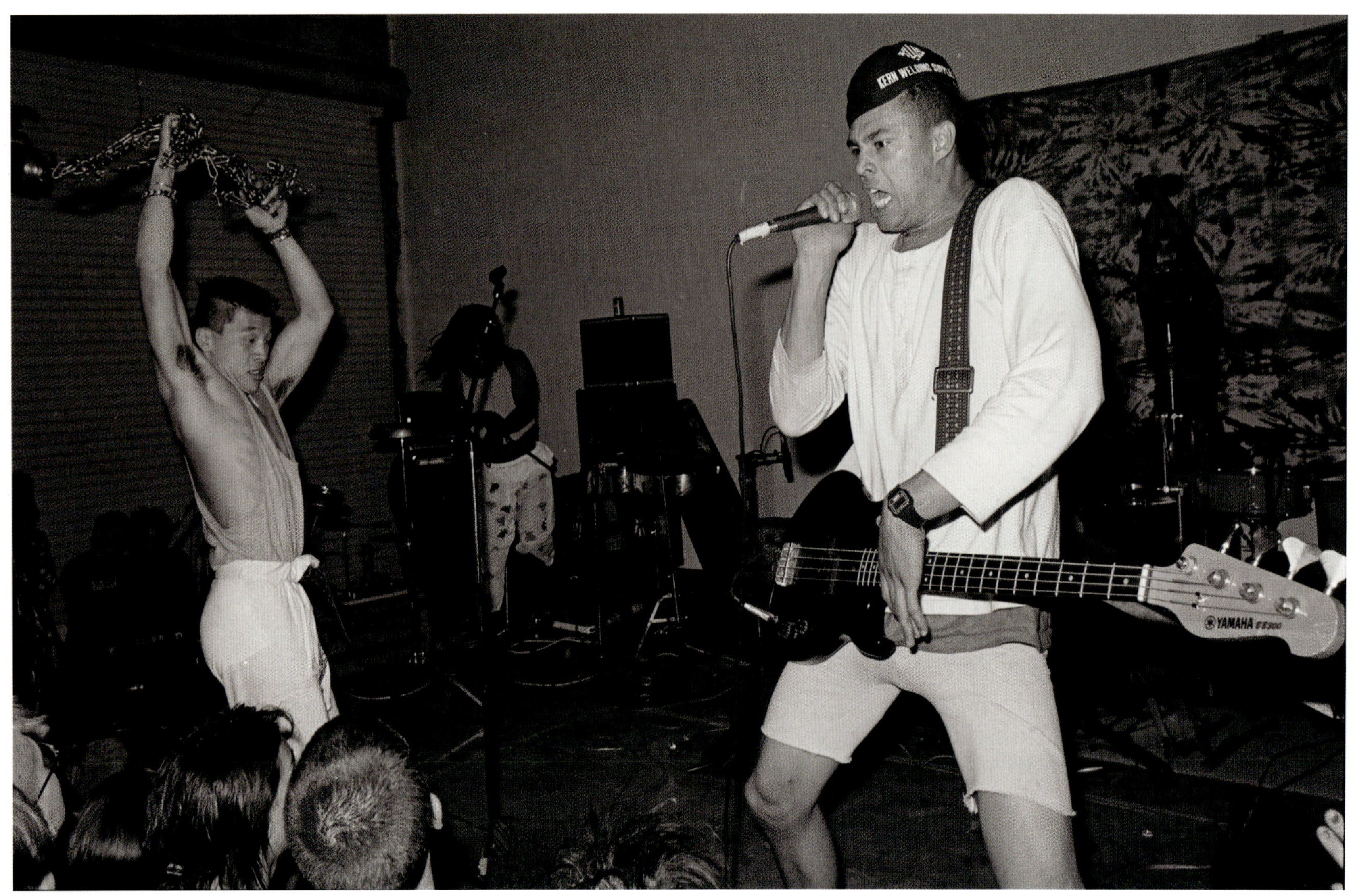

Beatnigs

Santa Rosa, 1988

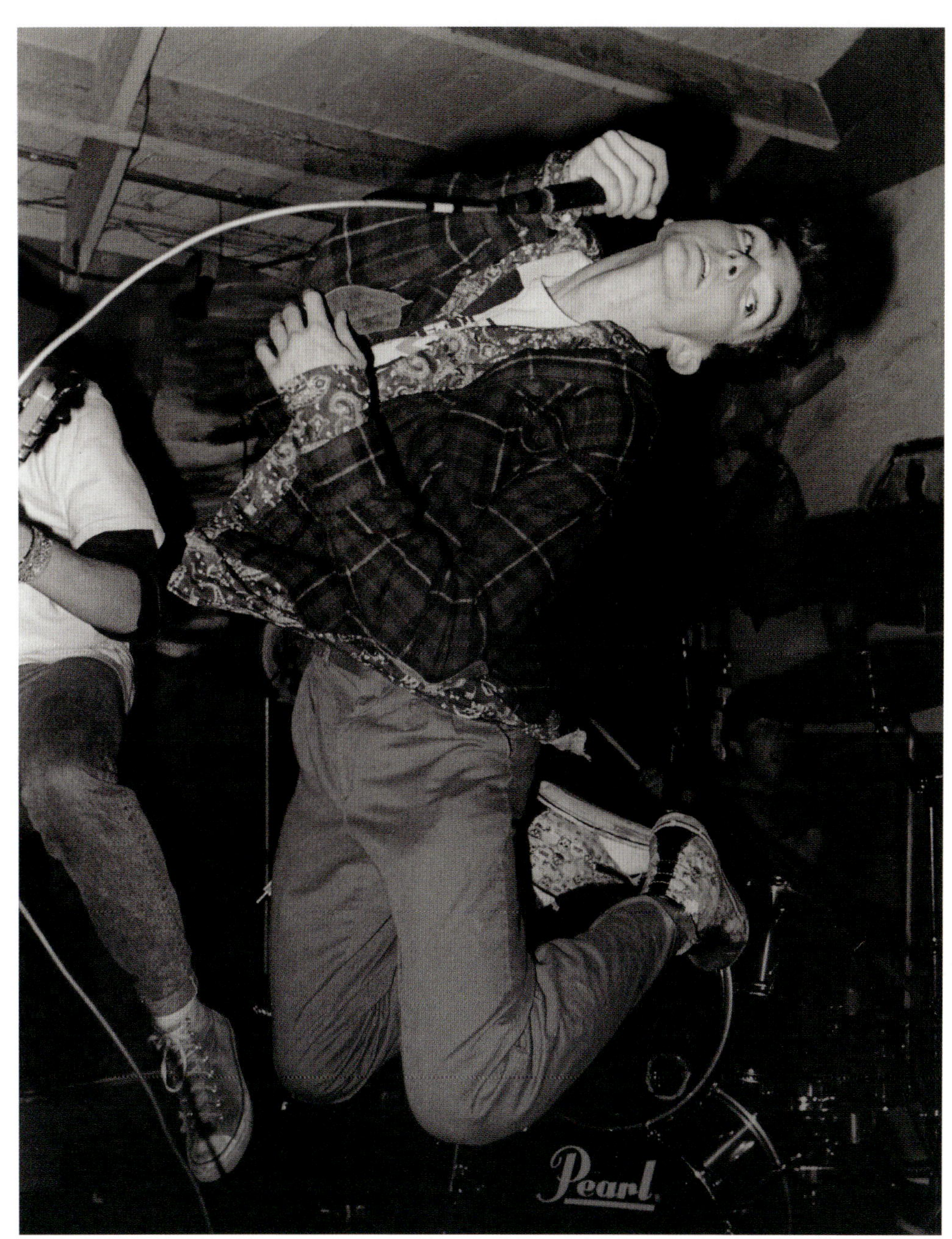

Poultry Magic
Gilman Street, Berkeley, 1987

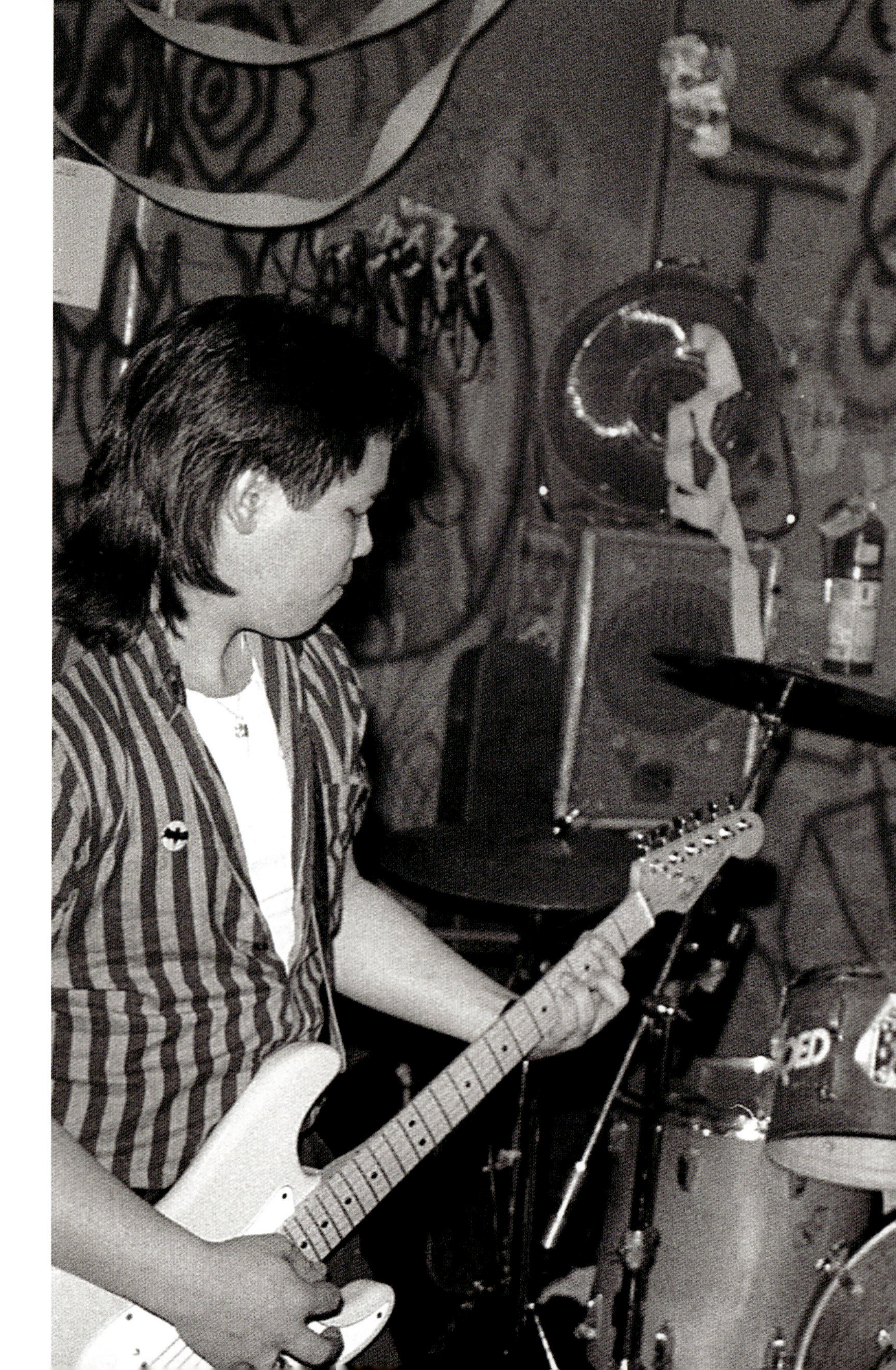

Kamala and the Karnivores
Gilman Street, Berkeley, 1988

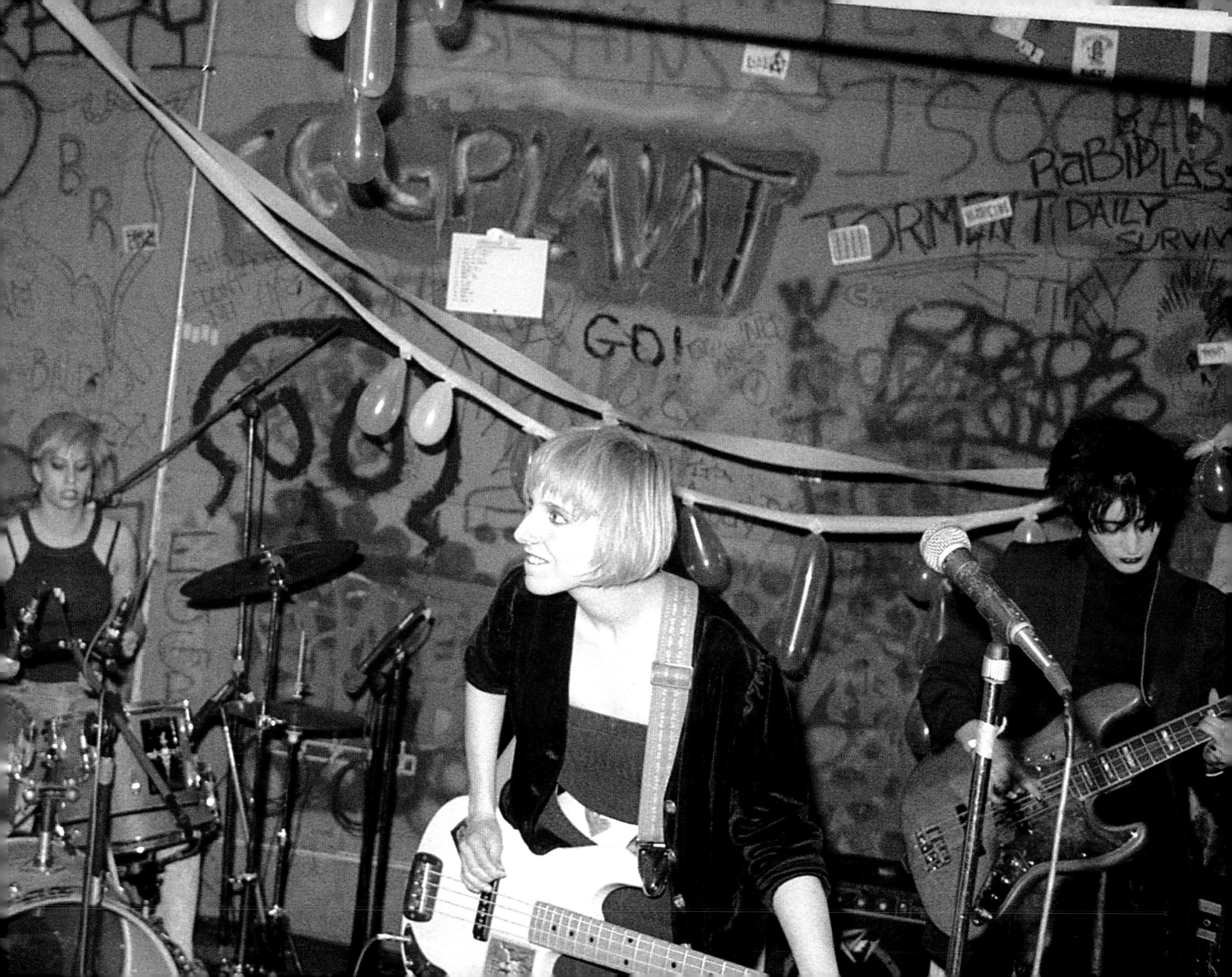

RABID
TORMENT DAILY
SURVIV
GO!

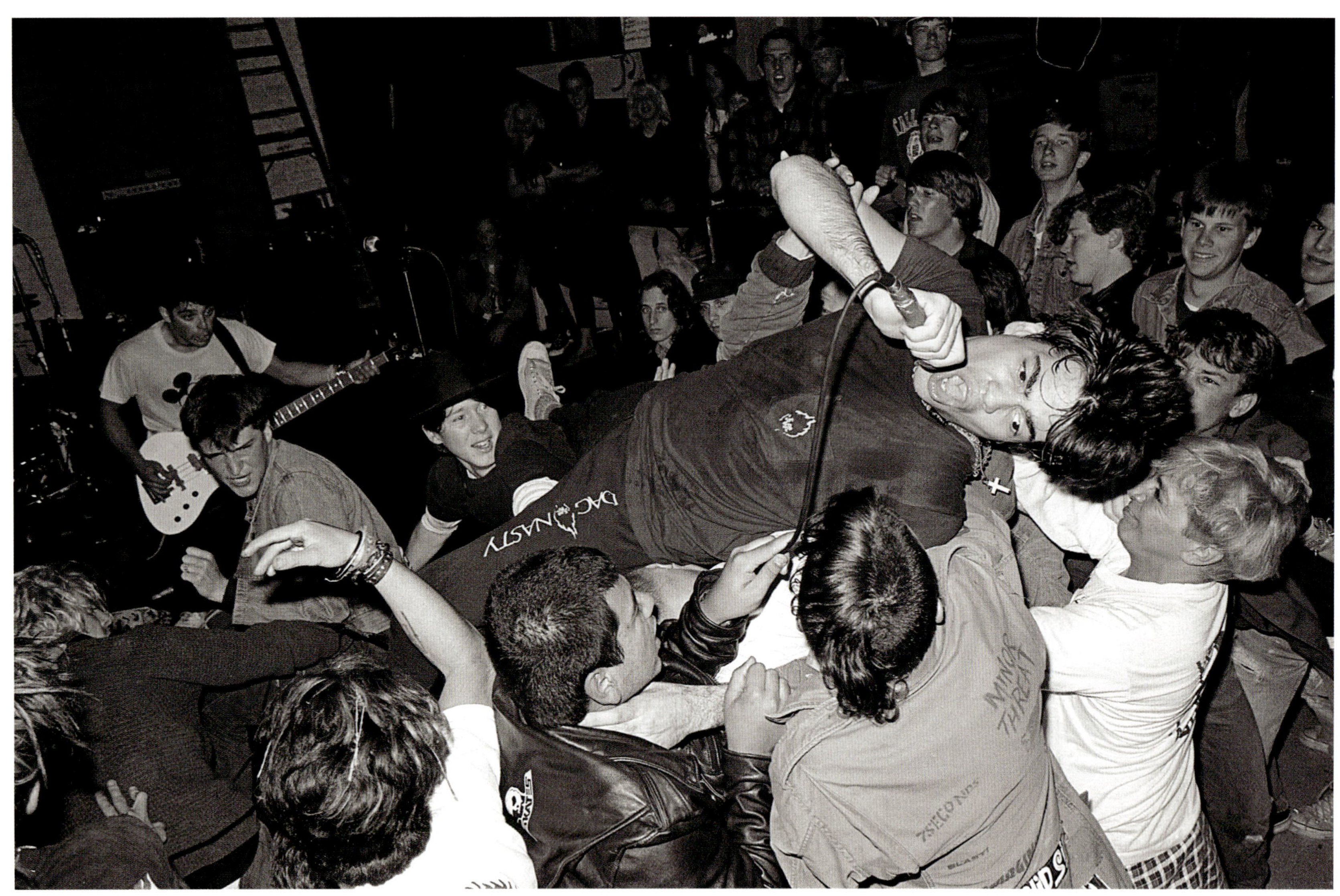

Dag Nasty
Mabuhay Gardens, San Francisco, 1987

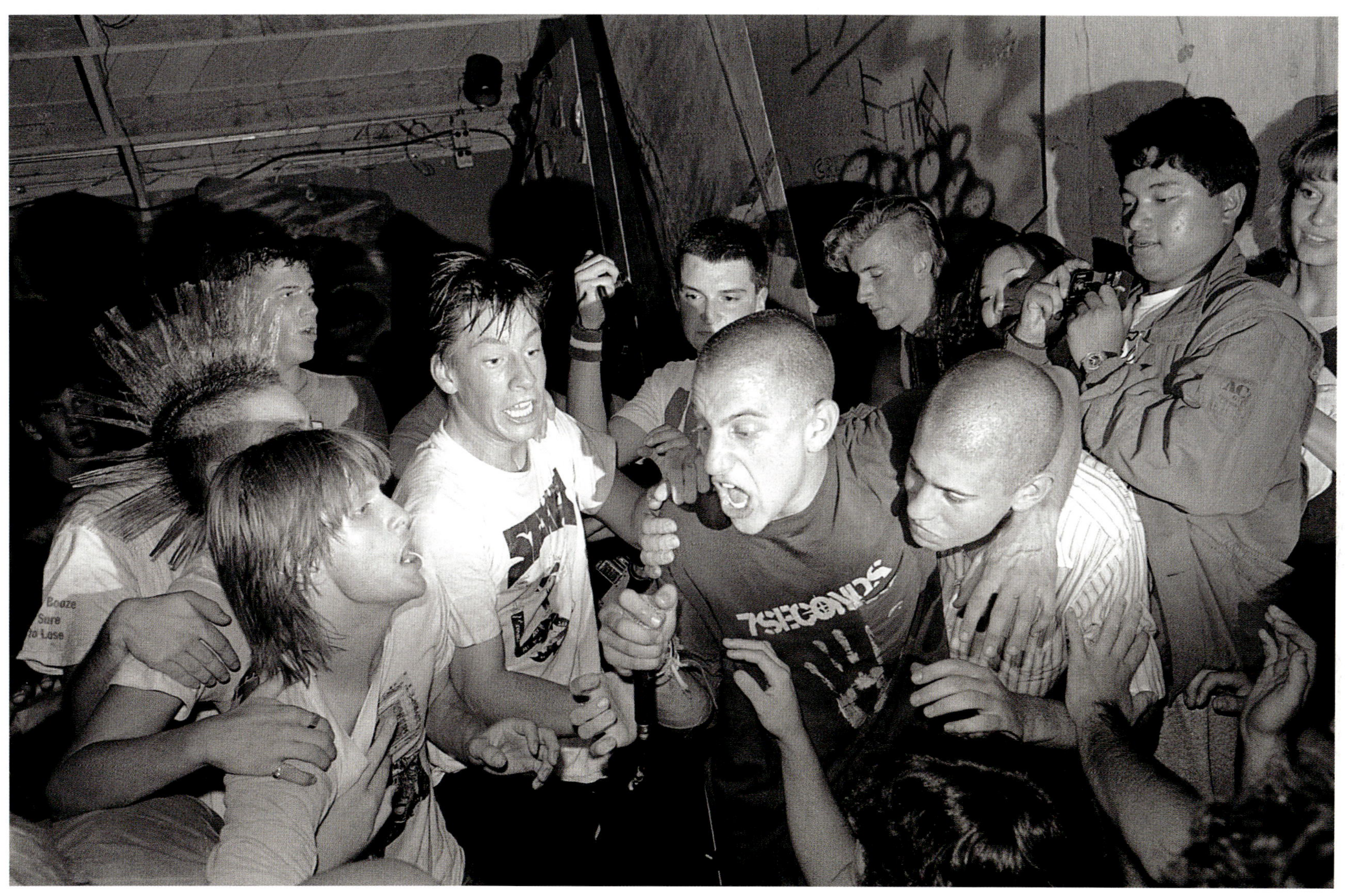

Youth Of Today

Gilman Street, Berkeley, 1987

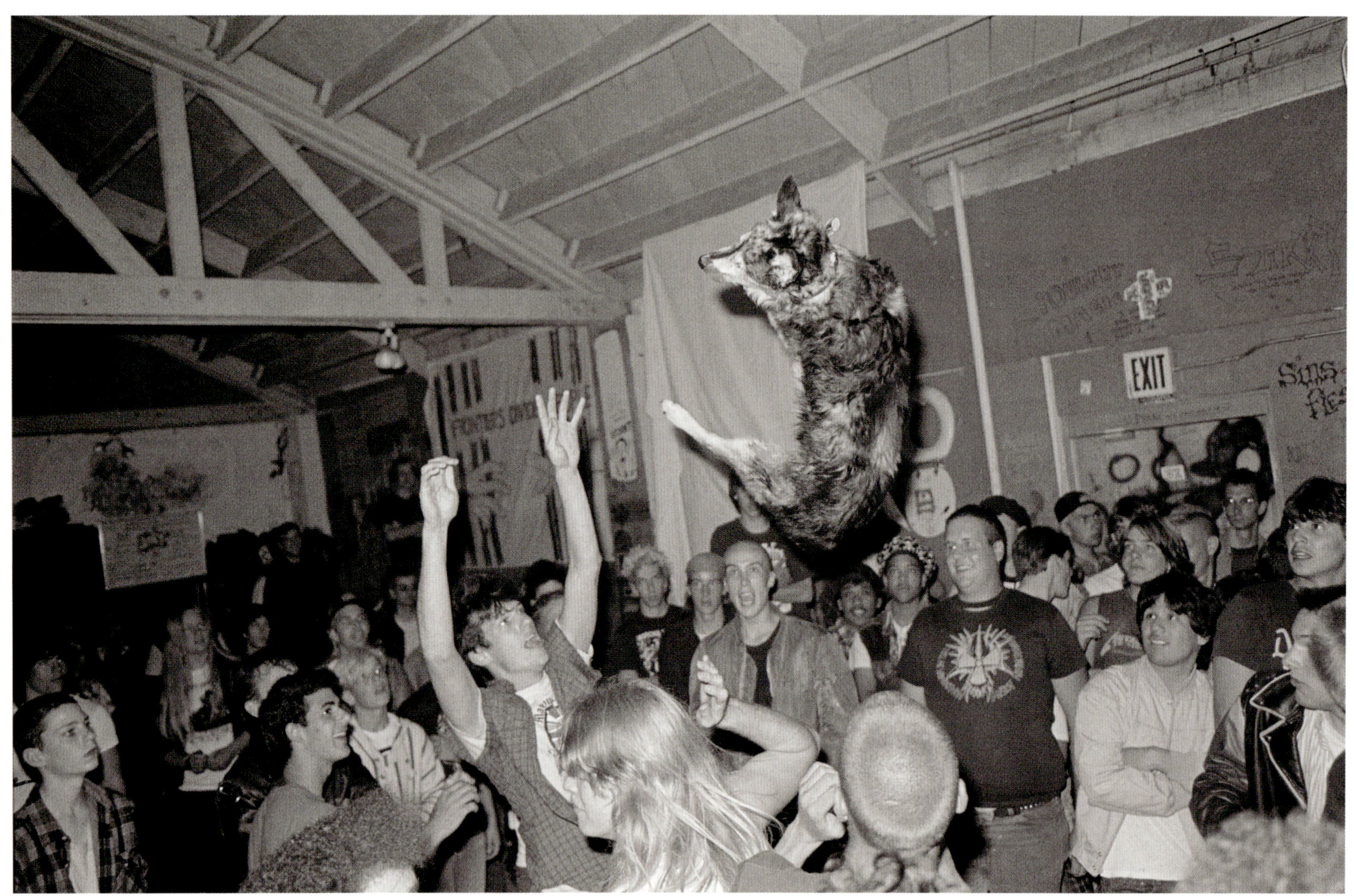

Feederz
Gilman Street, Berkeley, 1987

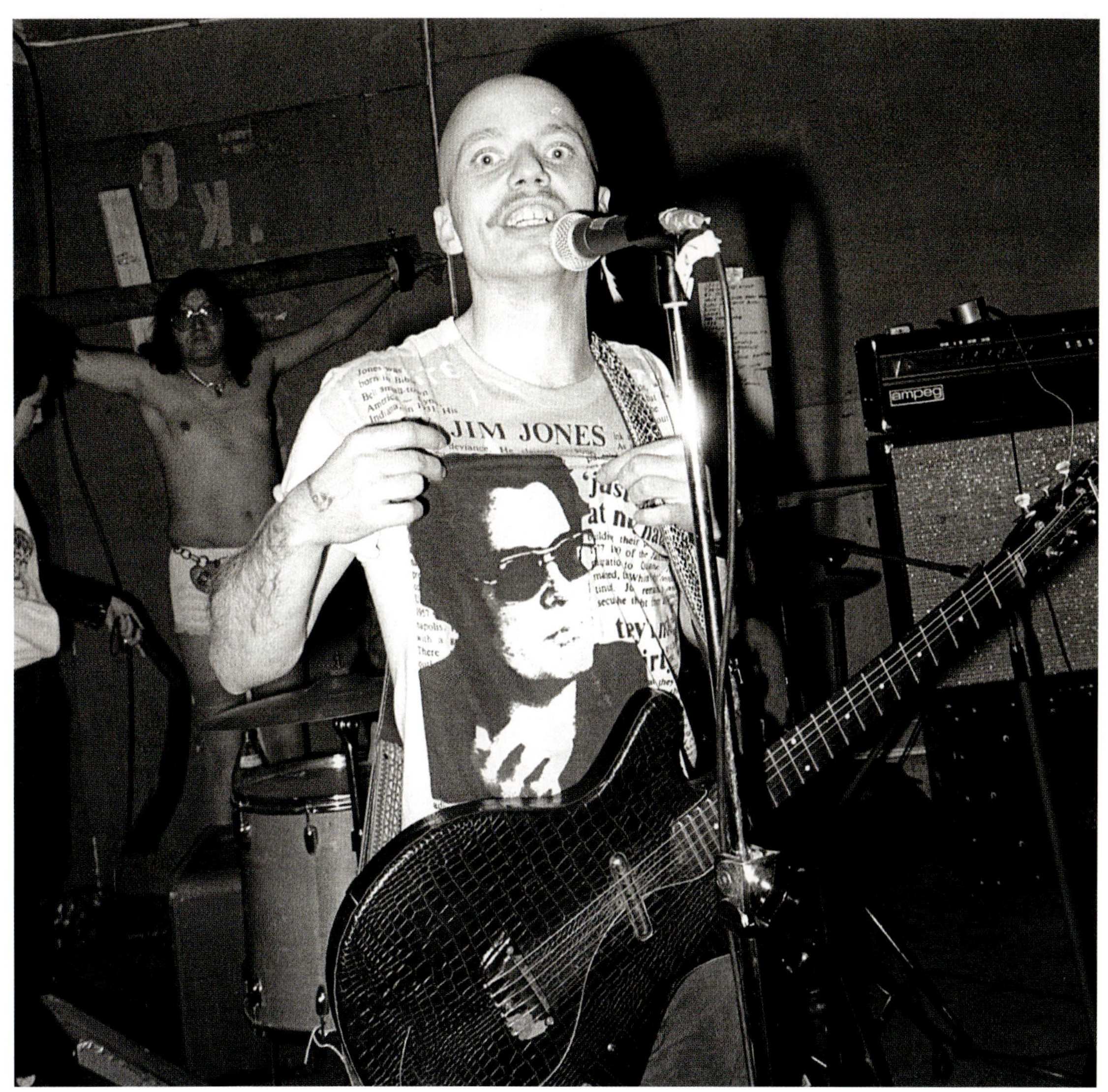

Feederz
Gilman Street, 1987

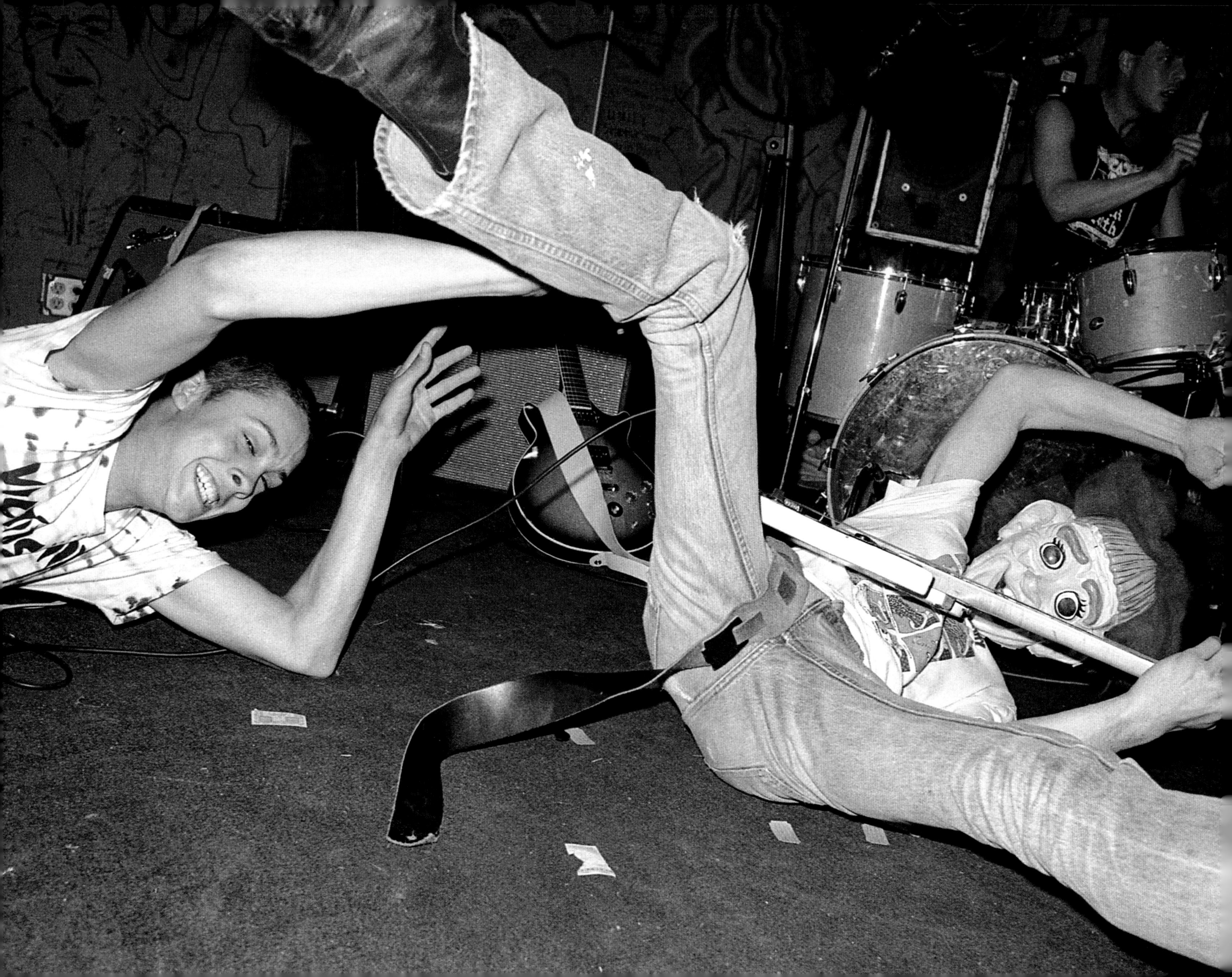

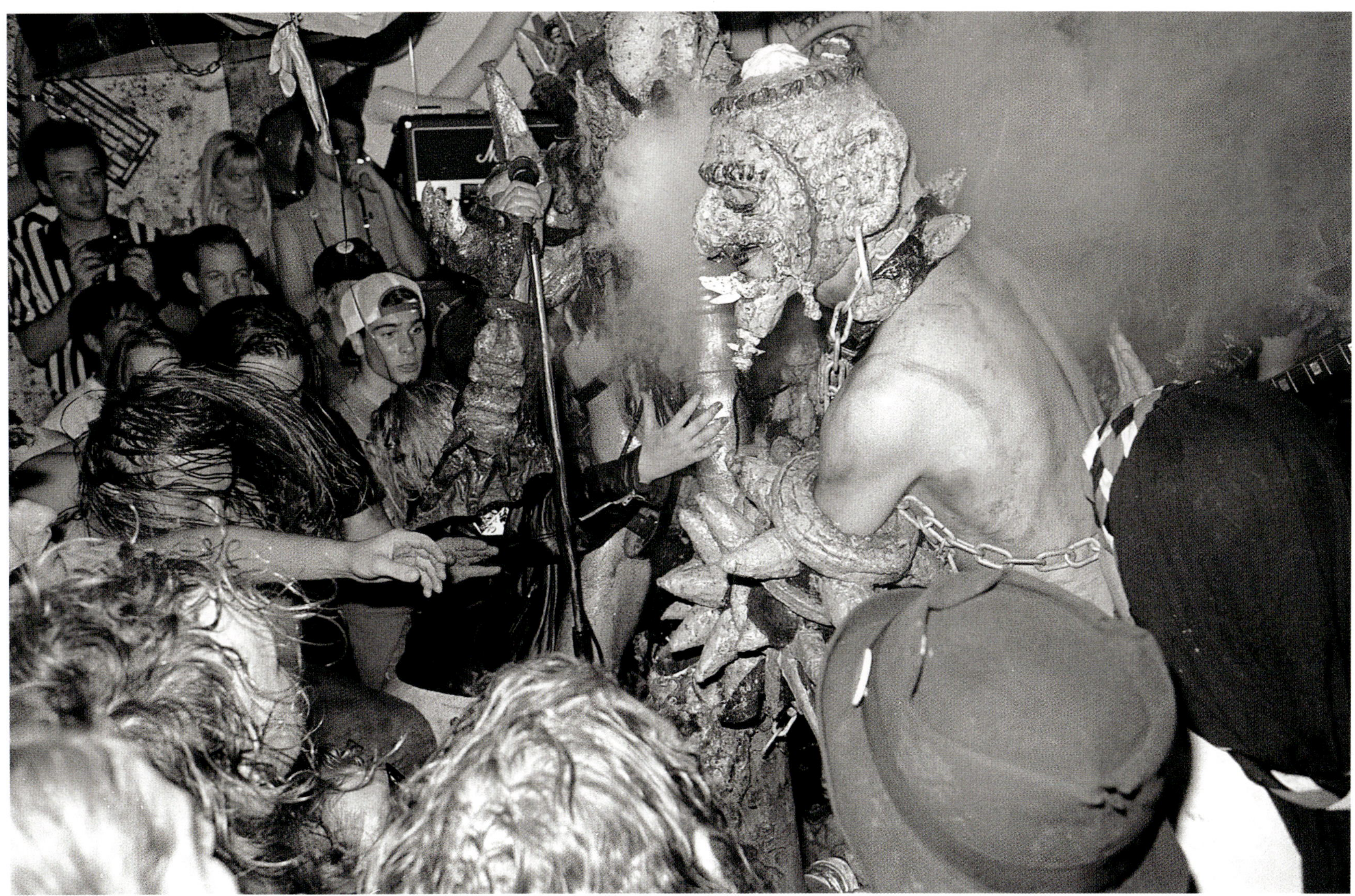

Gwar
Covered Wagon, San Francisco, 1988

Opposite:
Dwarves
Gilman Street, Berkeley, 1988

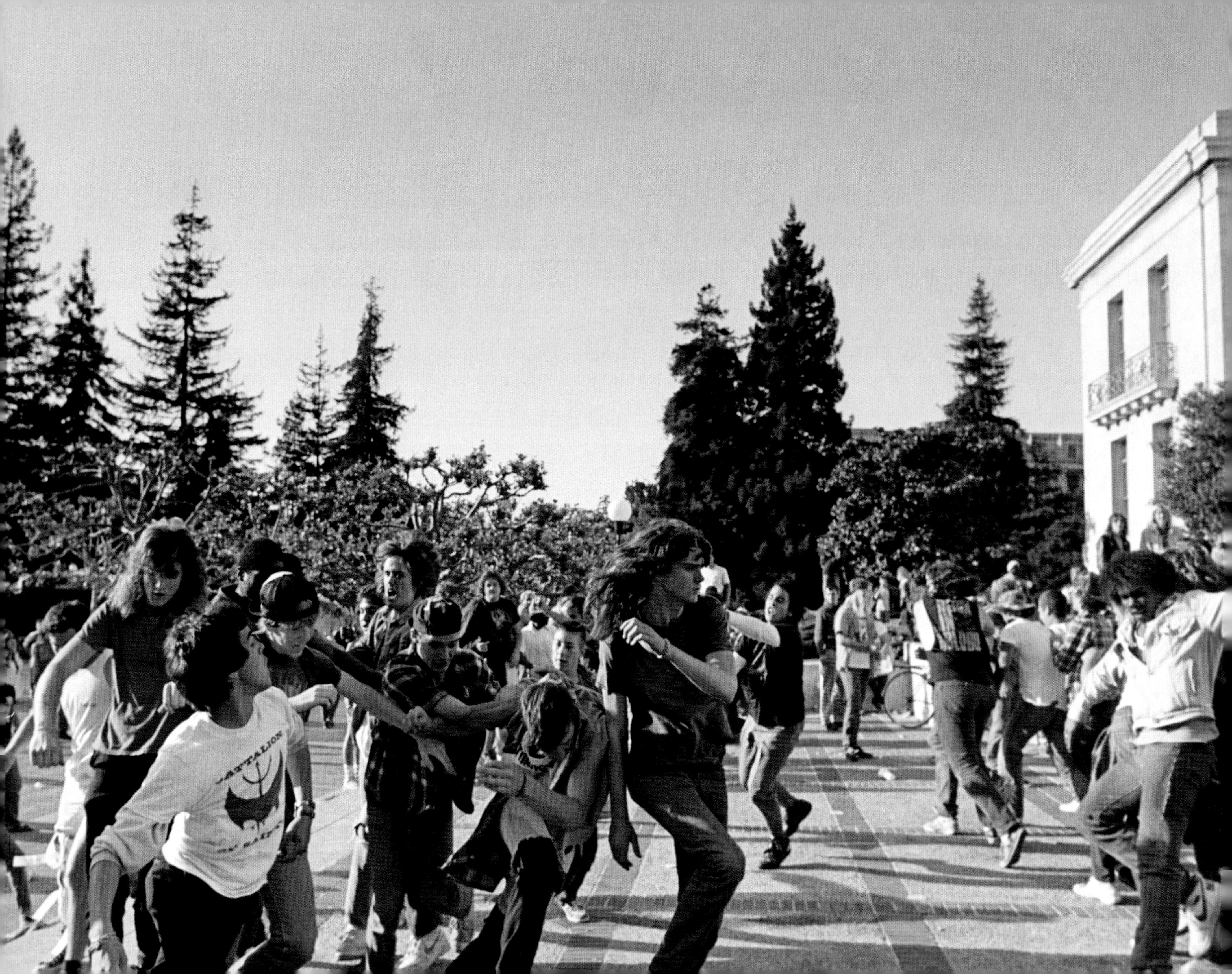

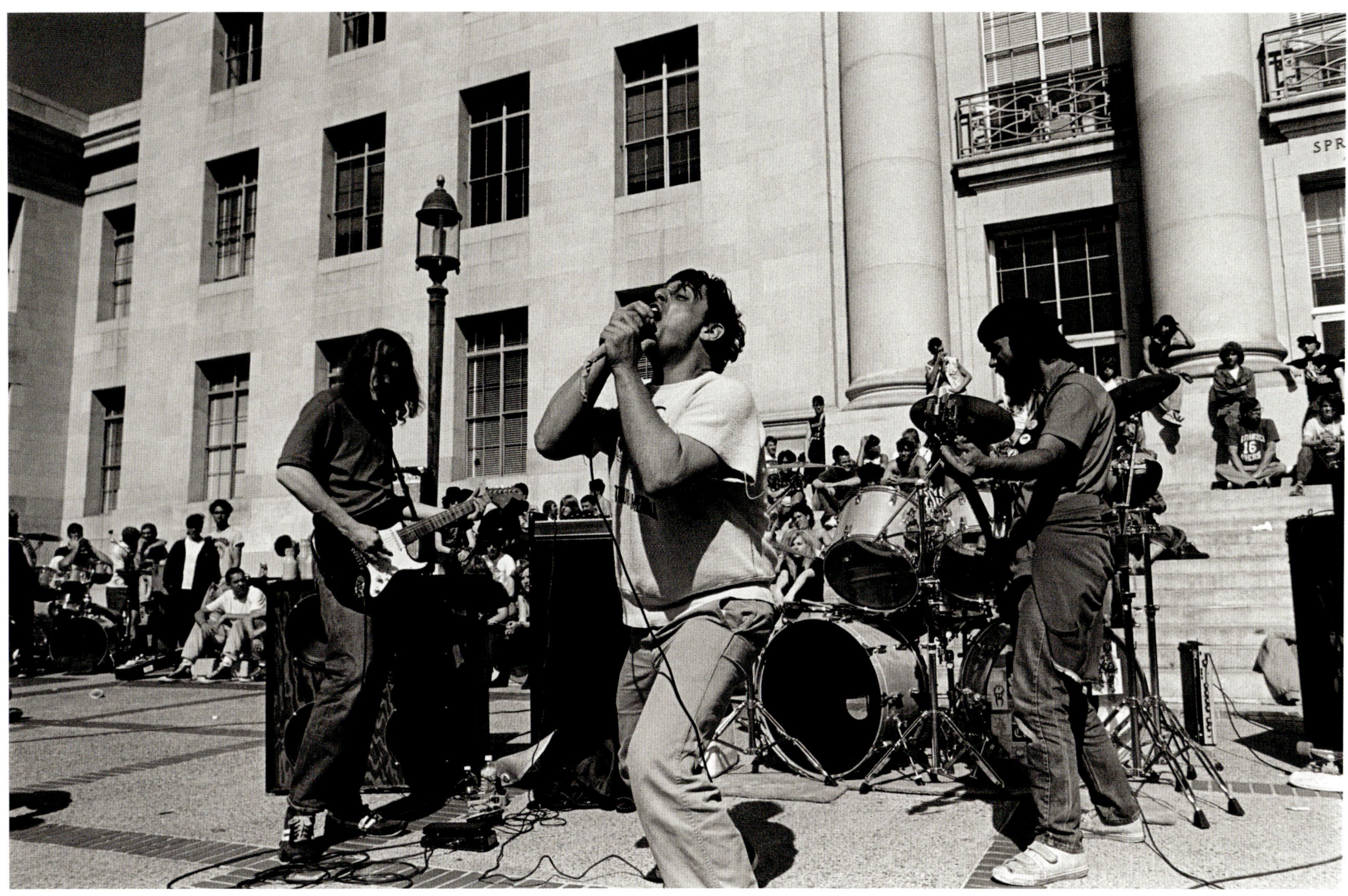

MDC
Sproul Plaza, UC Berkeley, 1987

Opposite:
Sproul Plaza, 1987

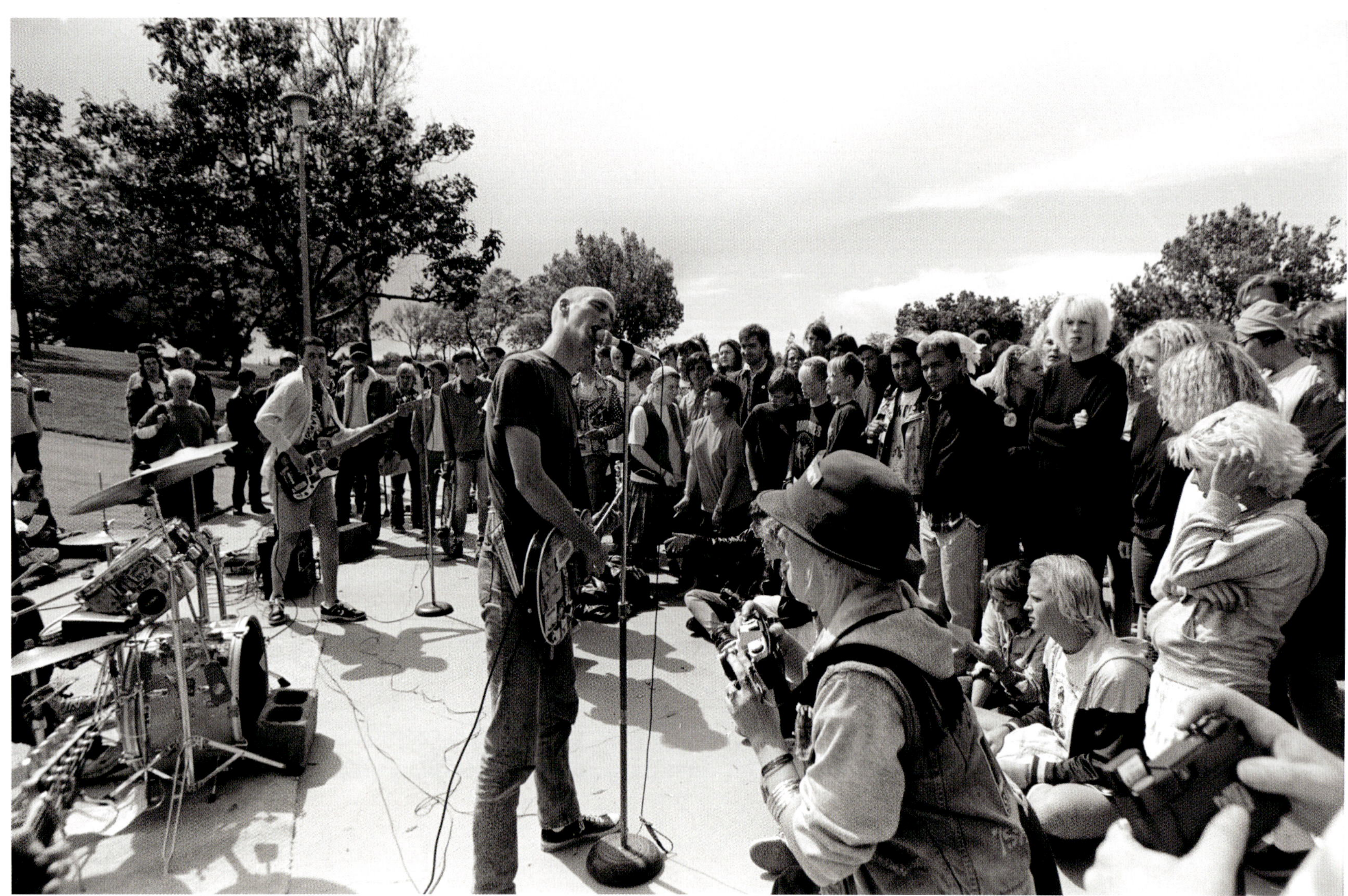

Crimpshrine

Davis, 1988

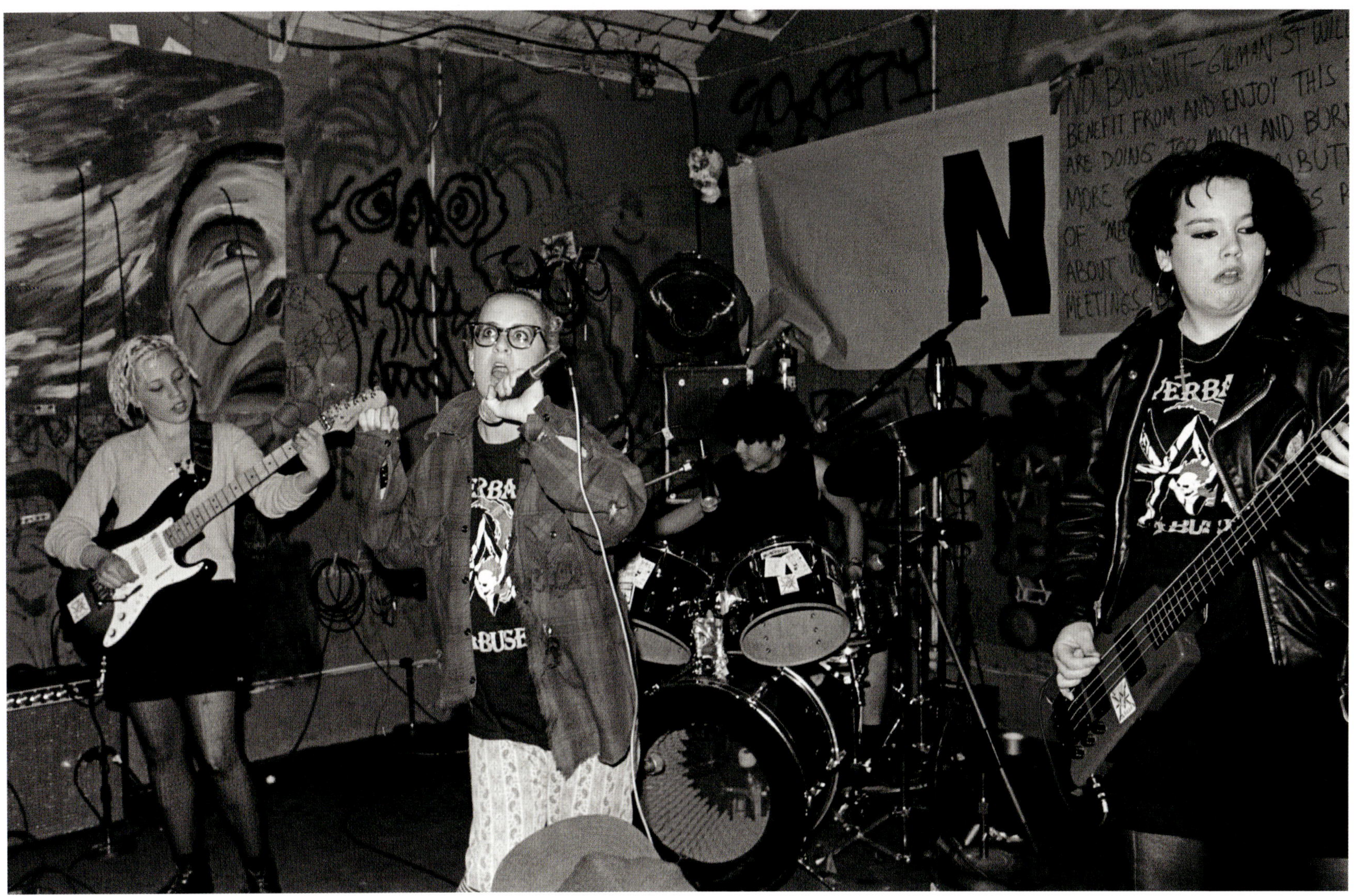

Bitch Fight
Gilman Street, Berkeley, 1988

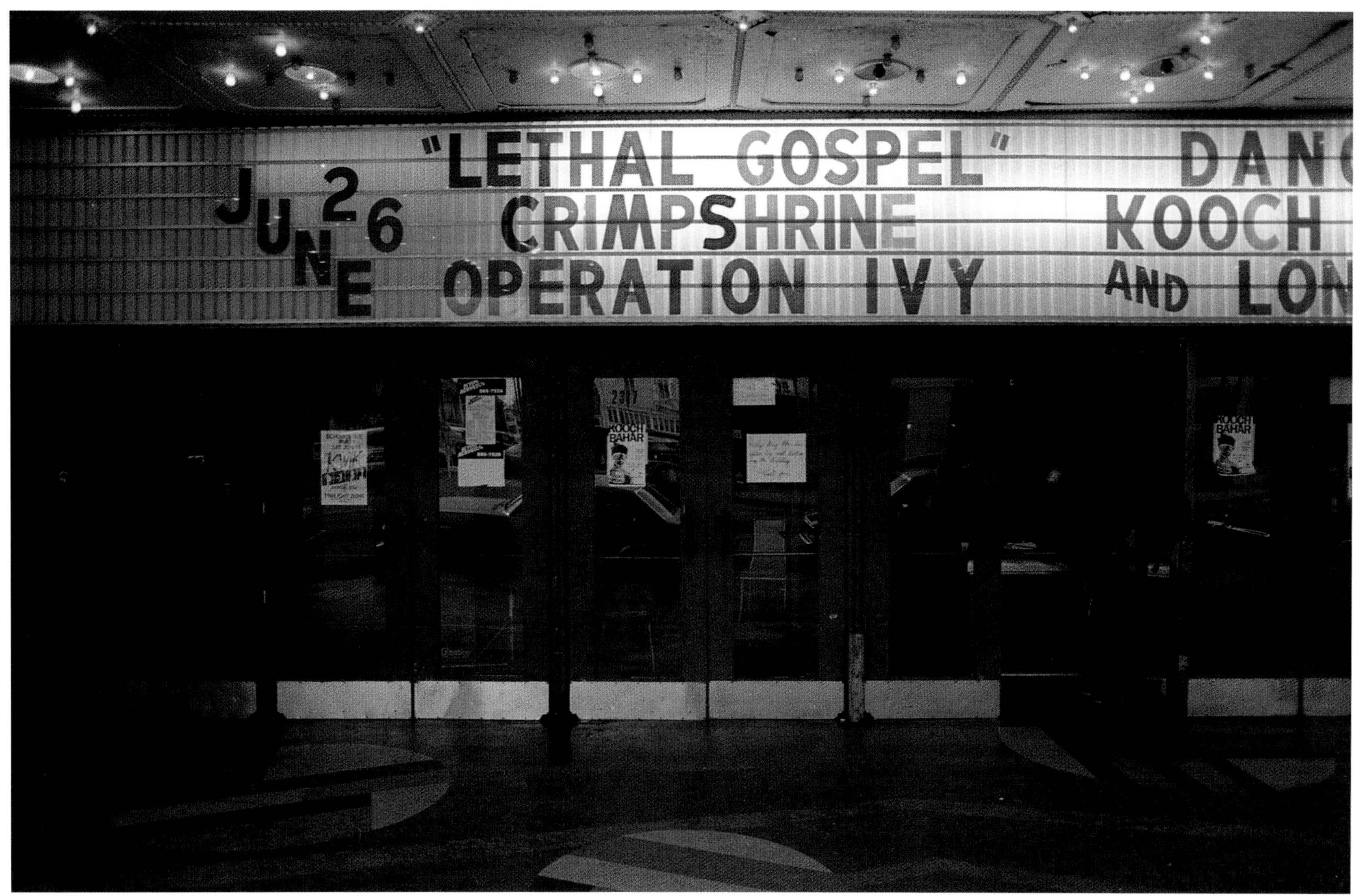

Twighlight Zone, Alameda, 1987

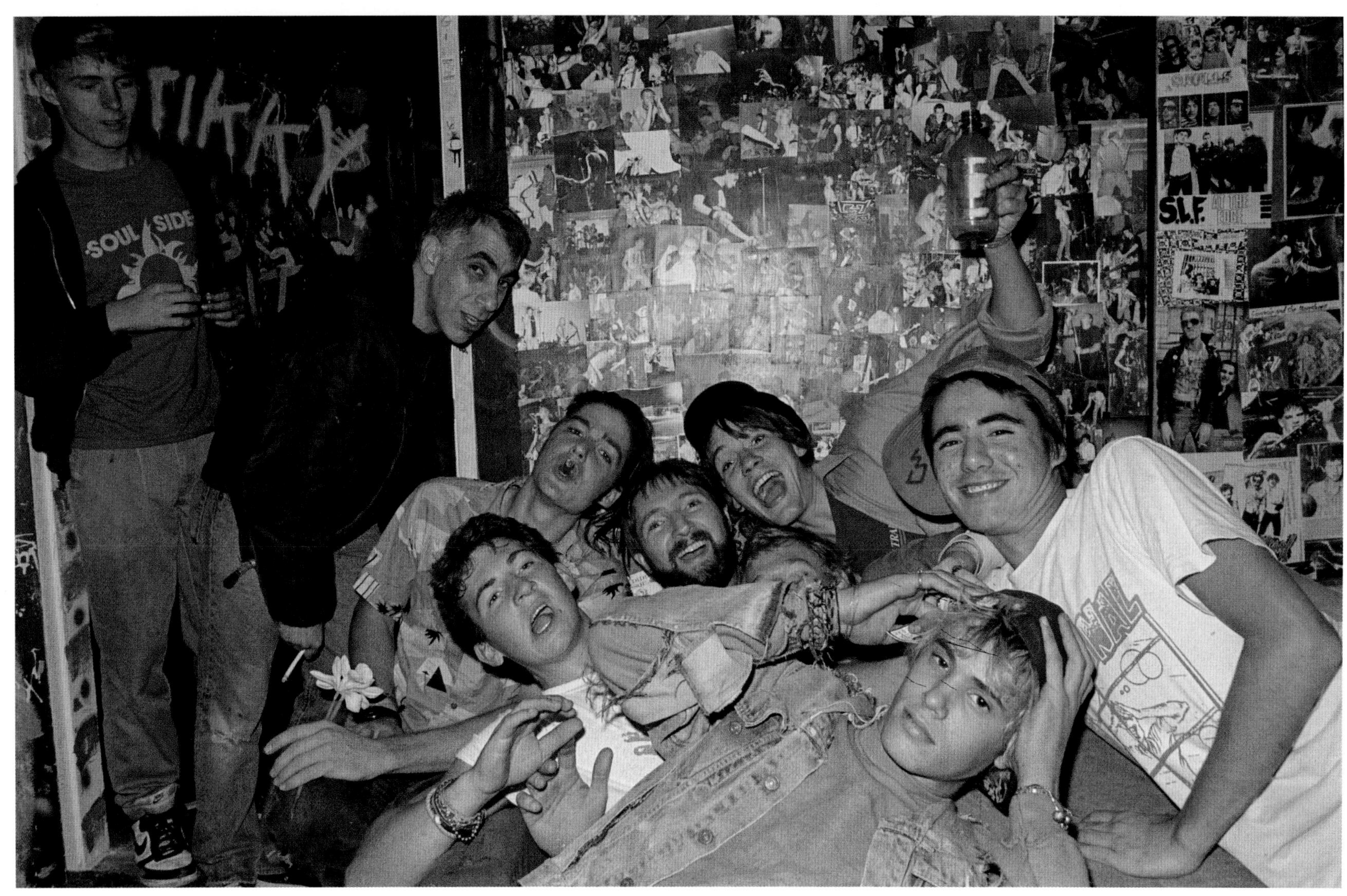

Gilman Street, Berkeley, 1987

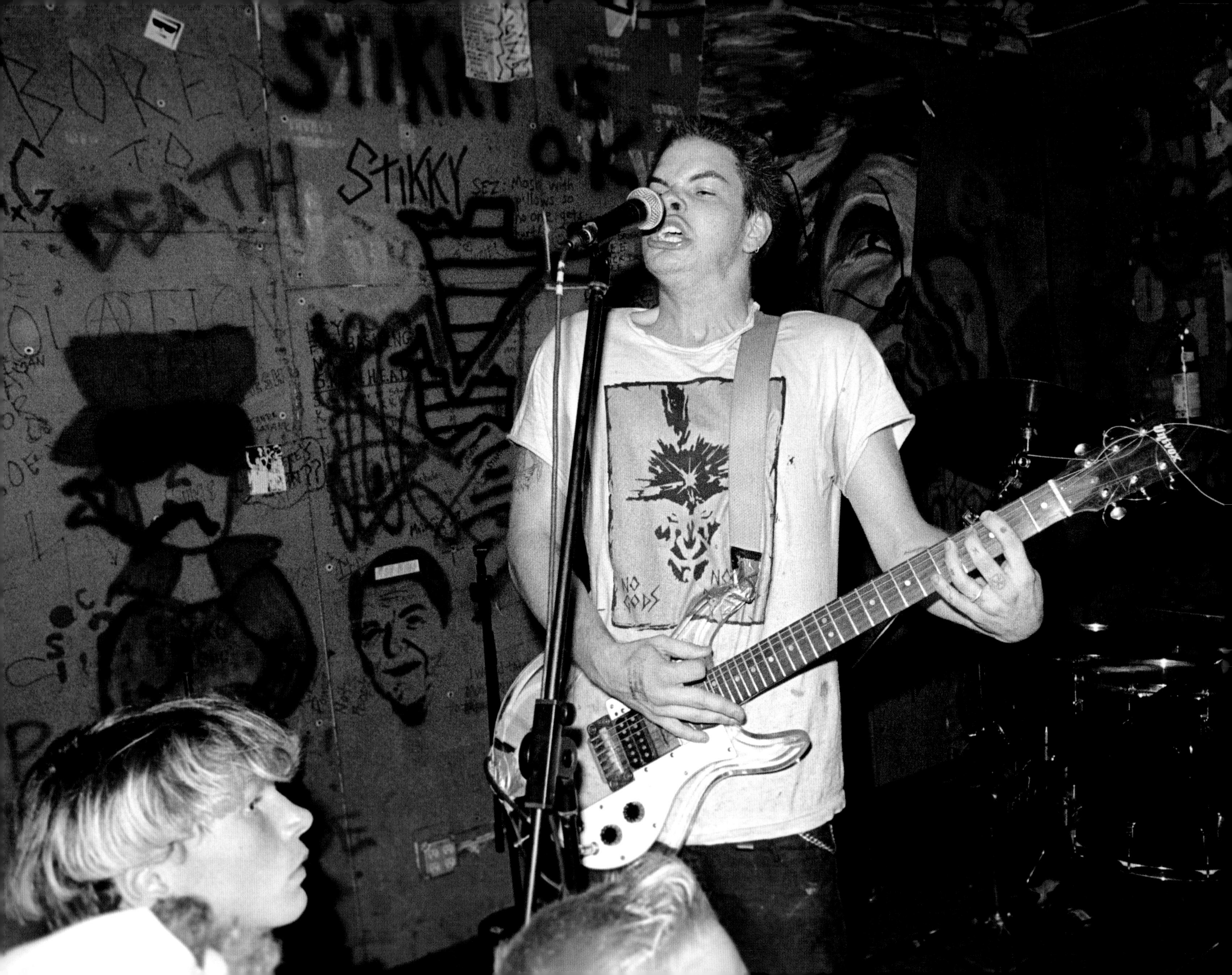

BORED
TO
DEATH
STIKKY
STIKKY
STIKKY SEZ:
NO GODS NO

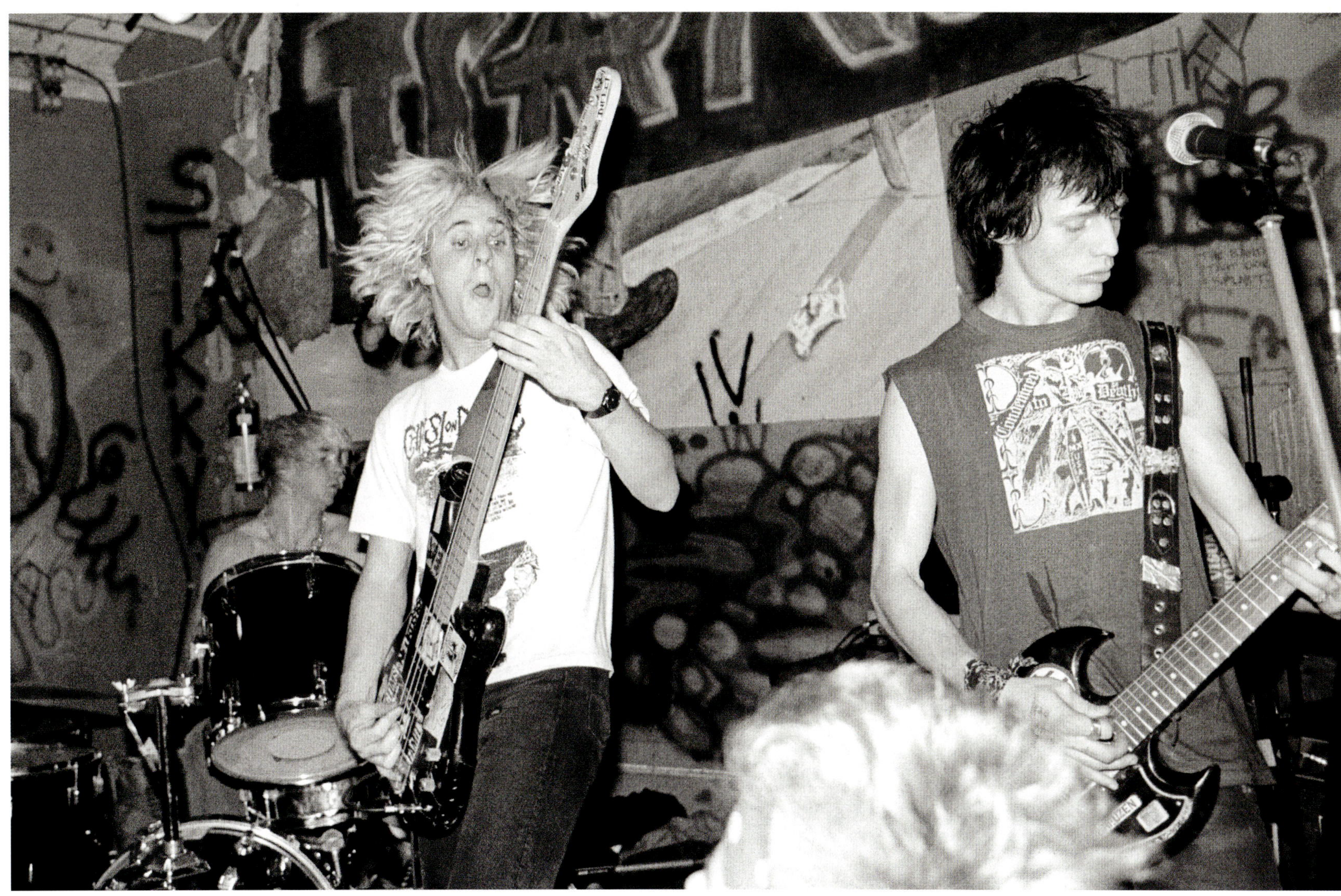

Neurosis

Gilman Street, Berkeley, 1987

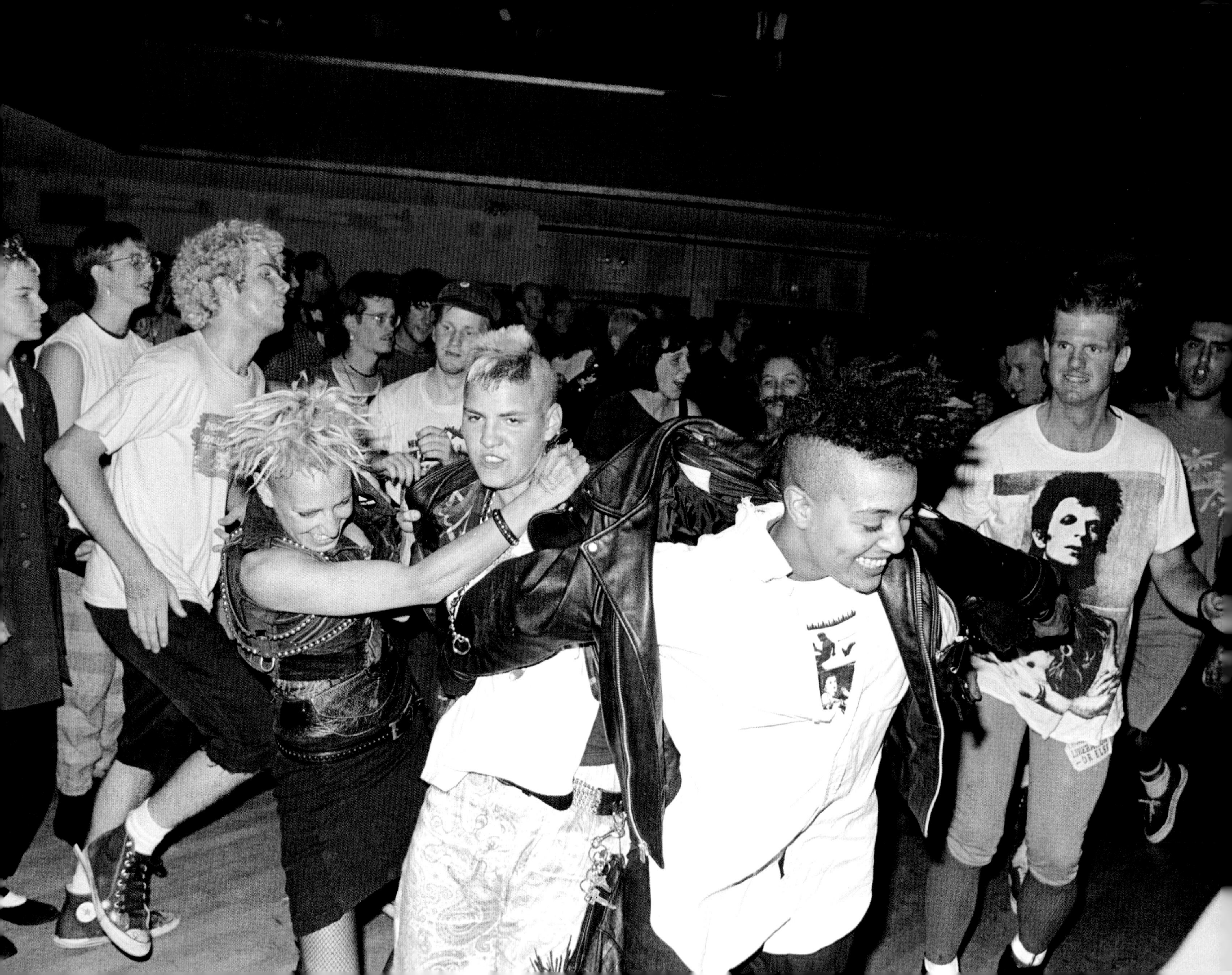

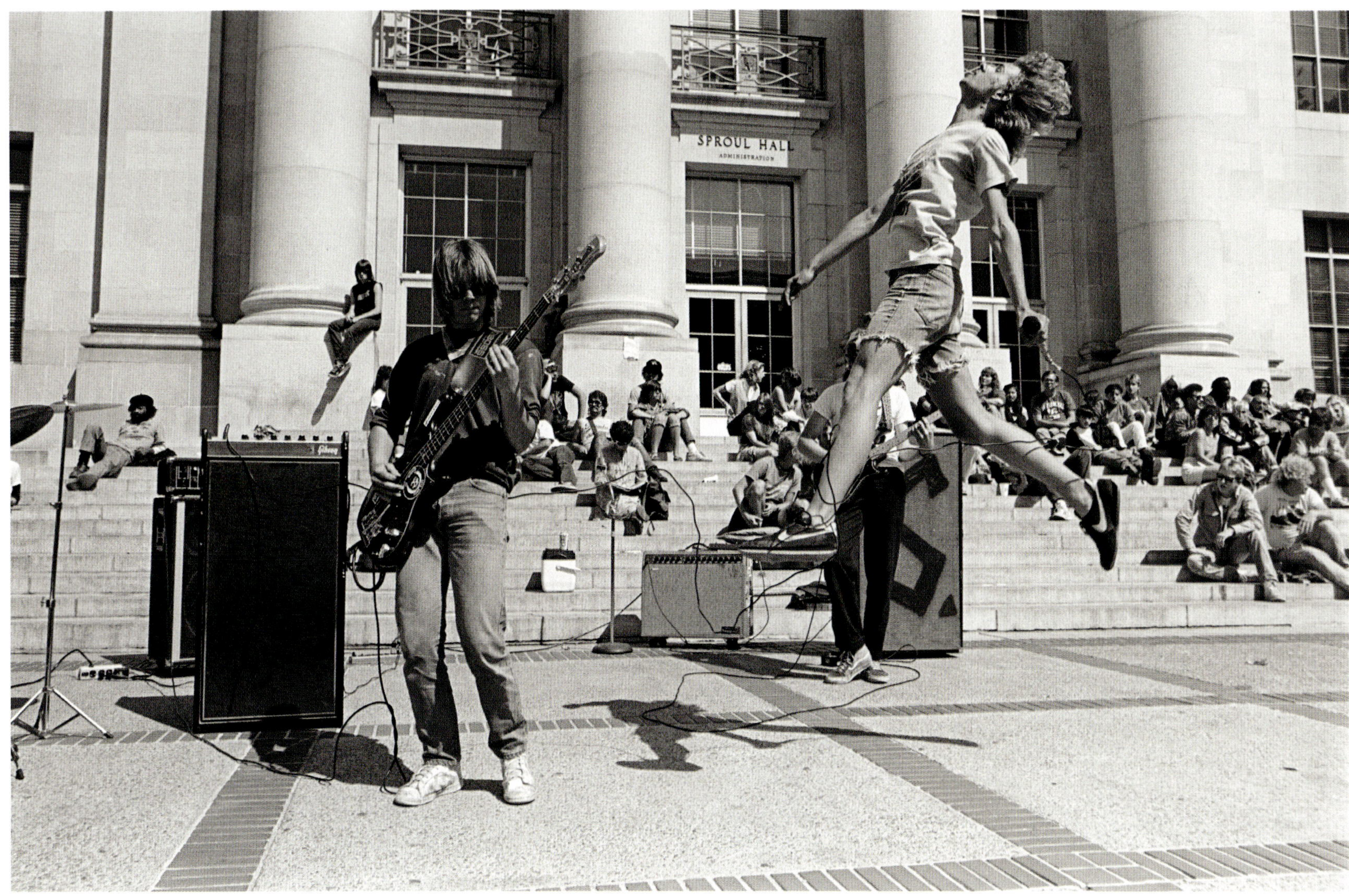

Electric Spaghetti

Sproul Plaza, UC Berkeley, 1987

Opposite:

The Women's Building, San Francisco, 1988

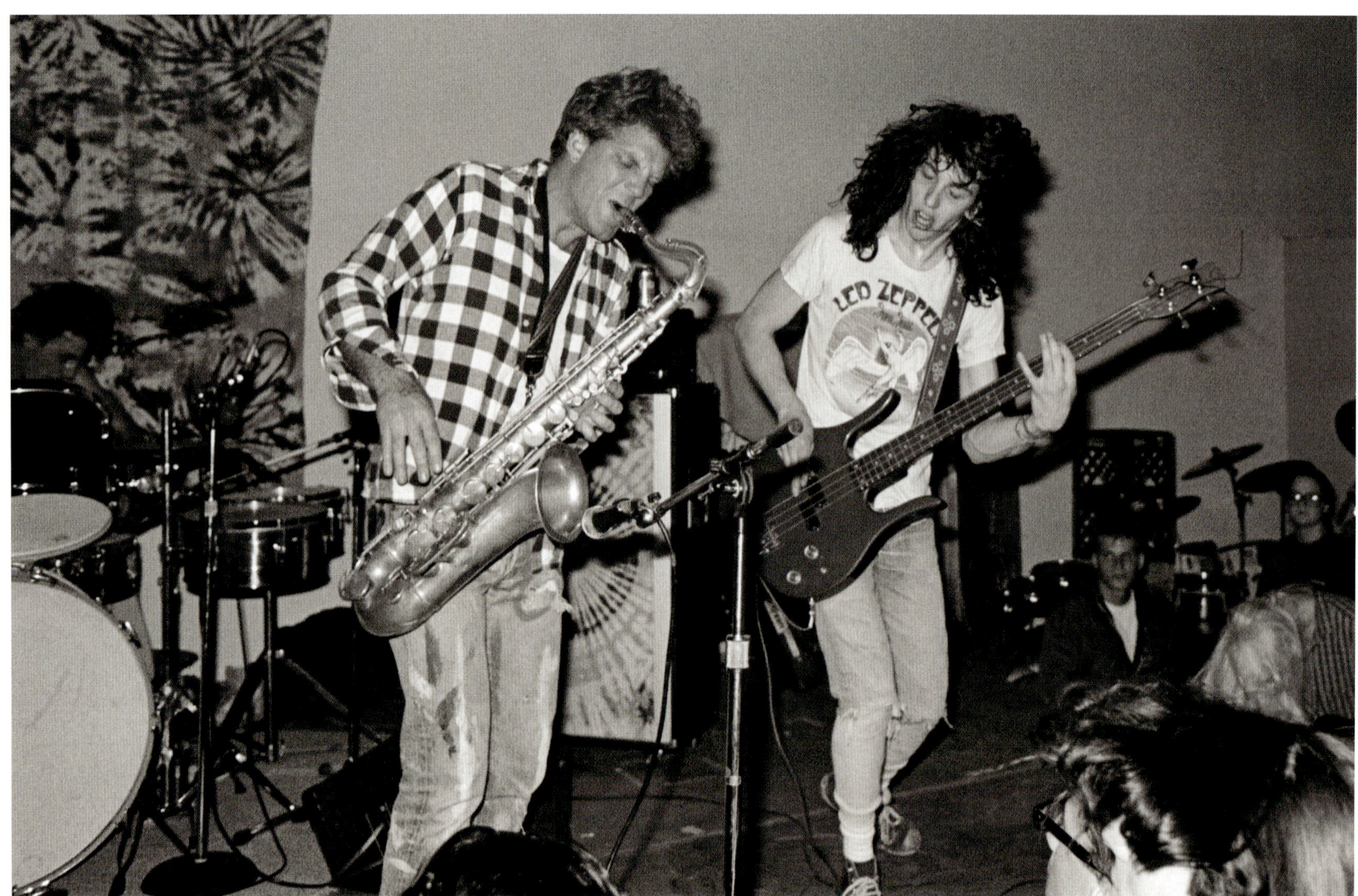

Victim's Family
Santa Rosa, 1988

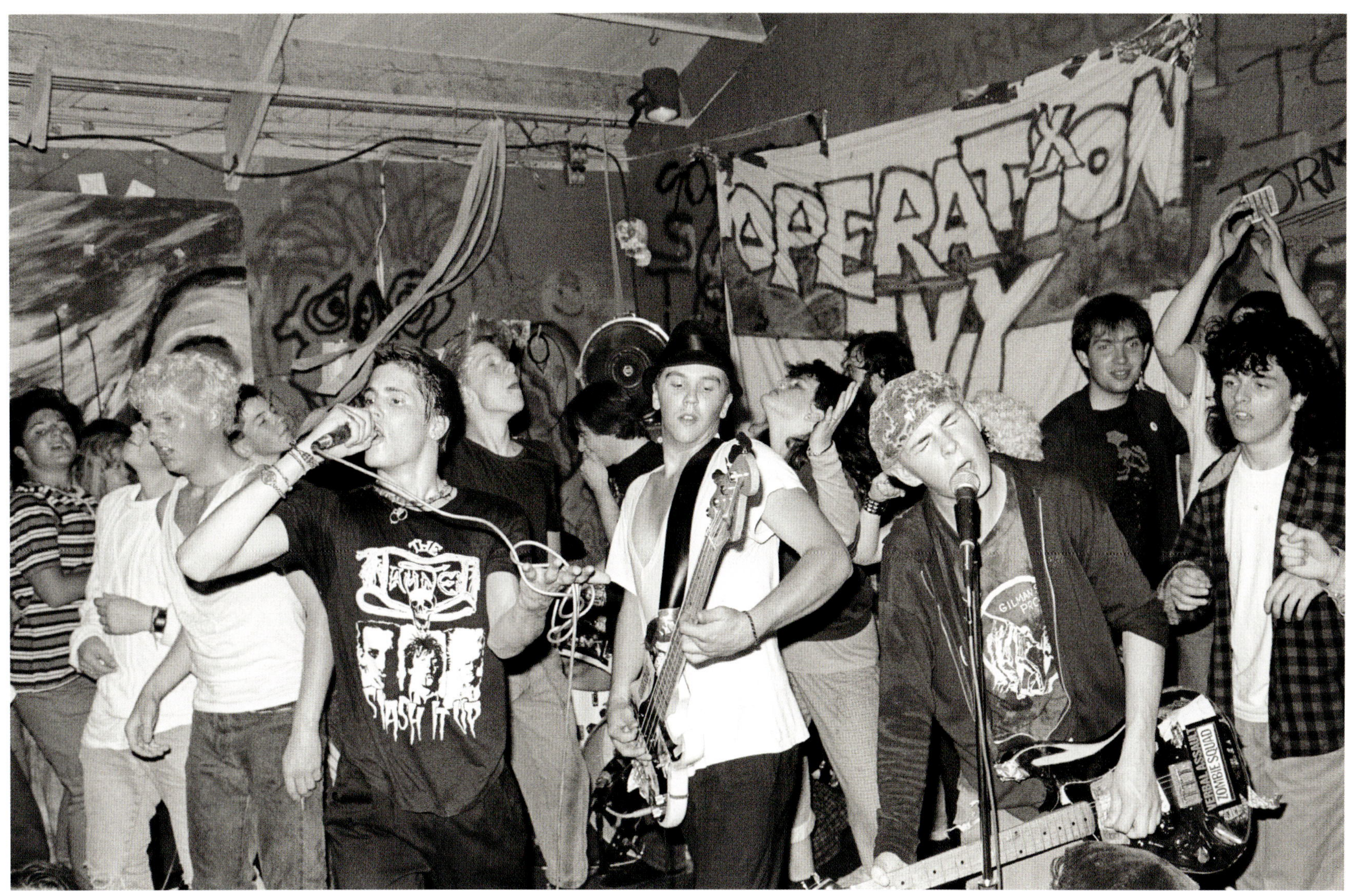

Operation Ivy
Gilman Street, Berkeley, 1988

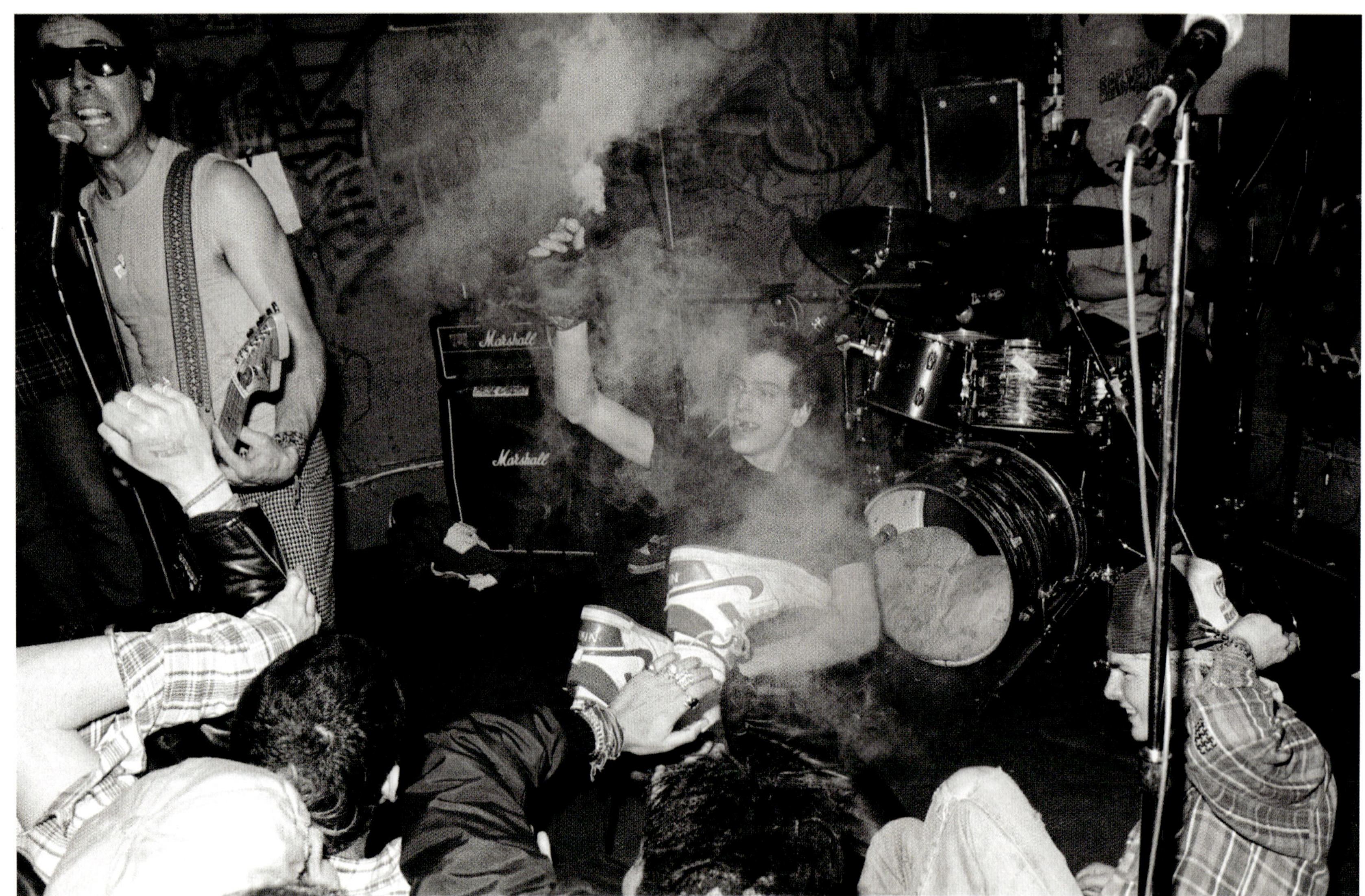

Lookouts

Gilman Street, Berkeley, 1988

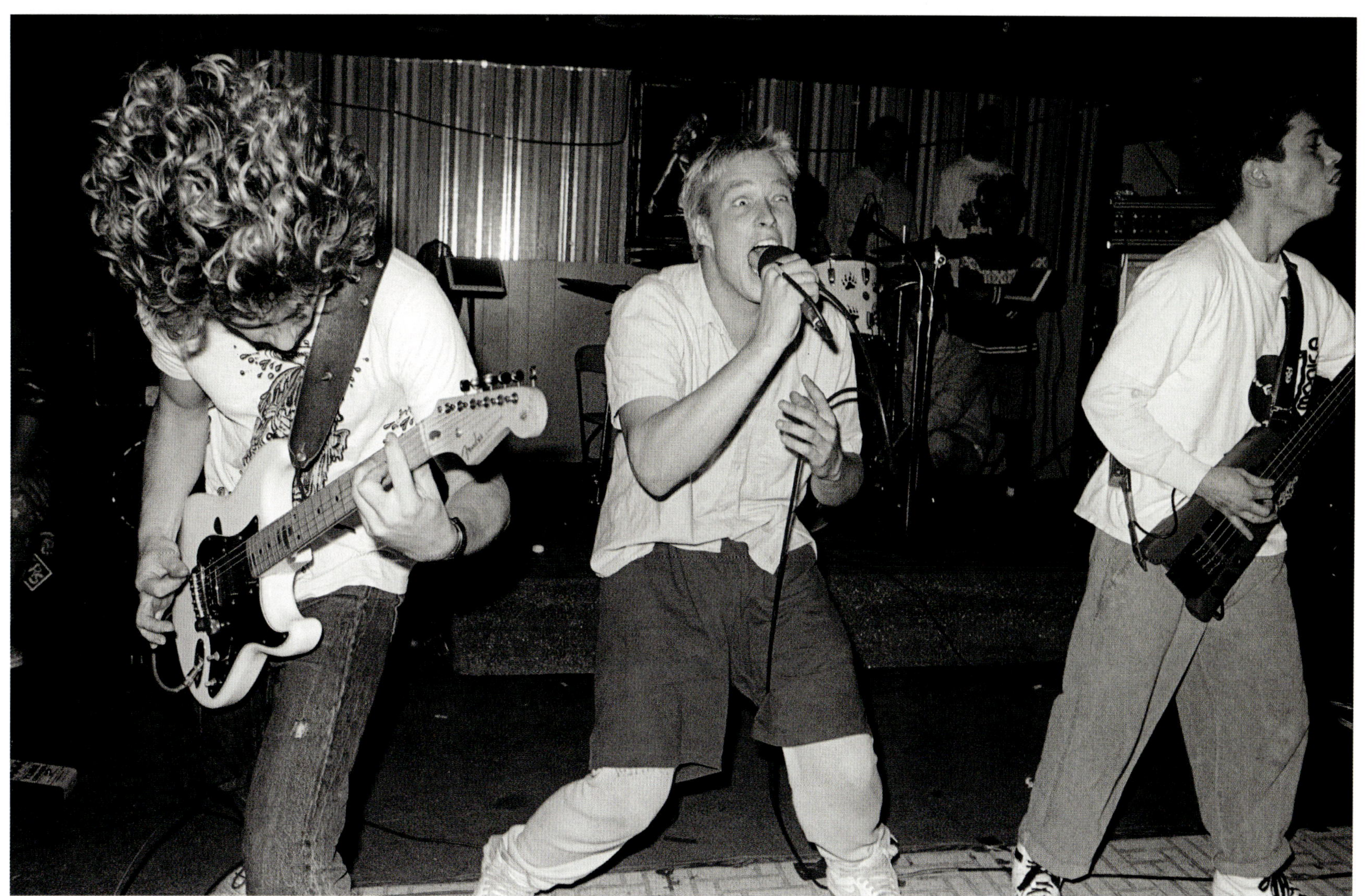

RKL
Covered Wagon, San Francisco, 1988

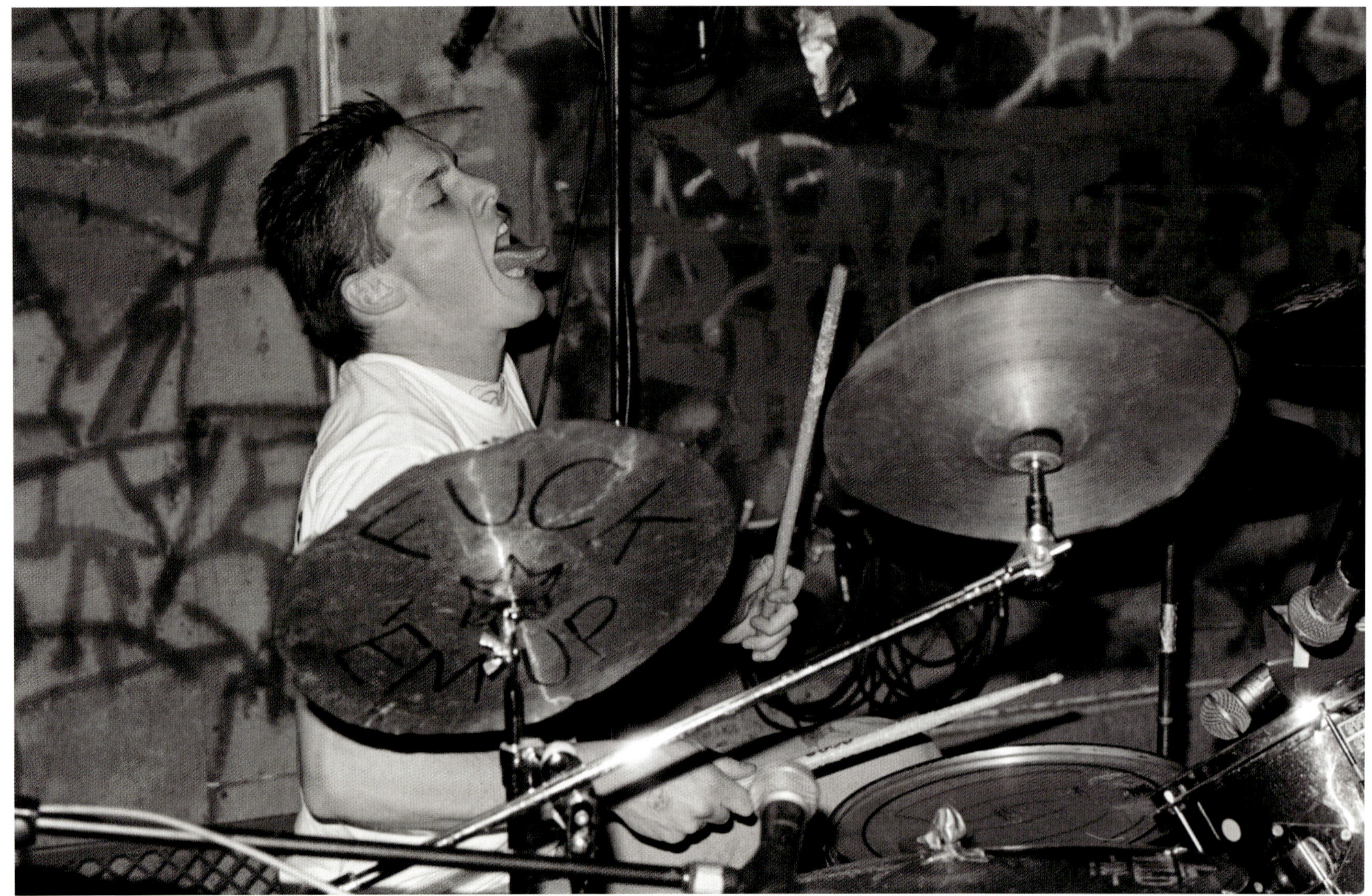

Sewer Trout

Gilman Street, Berkeley, 1989

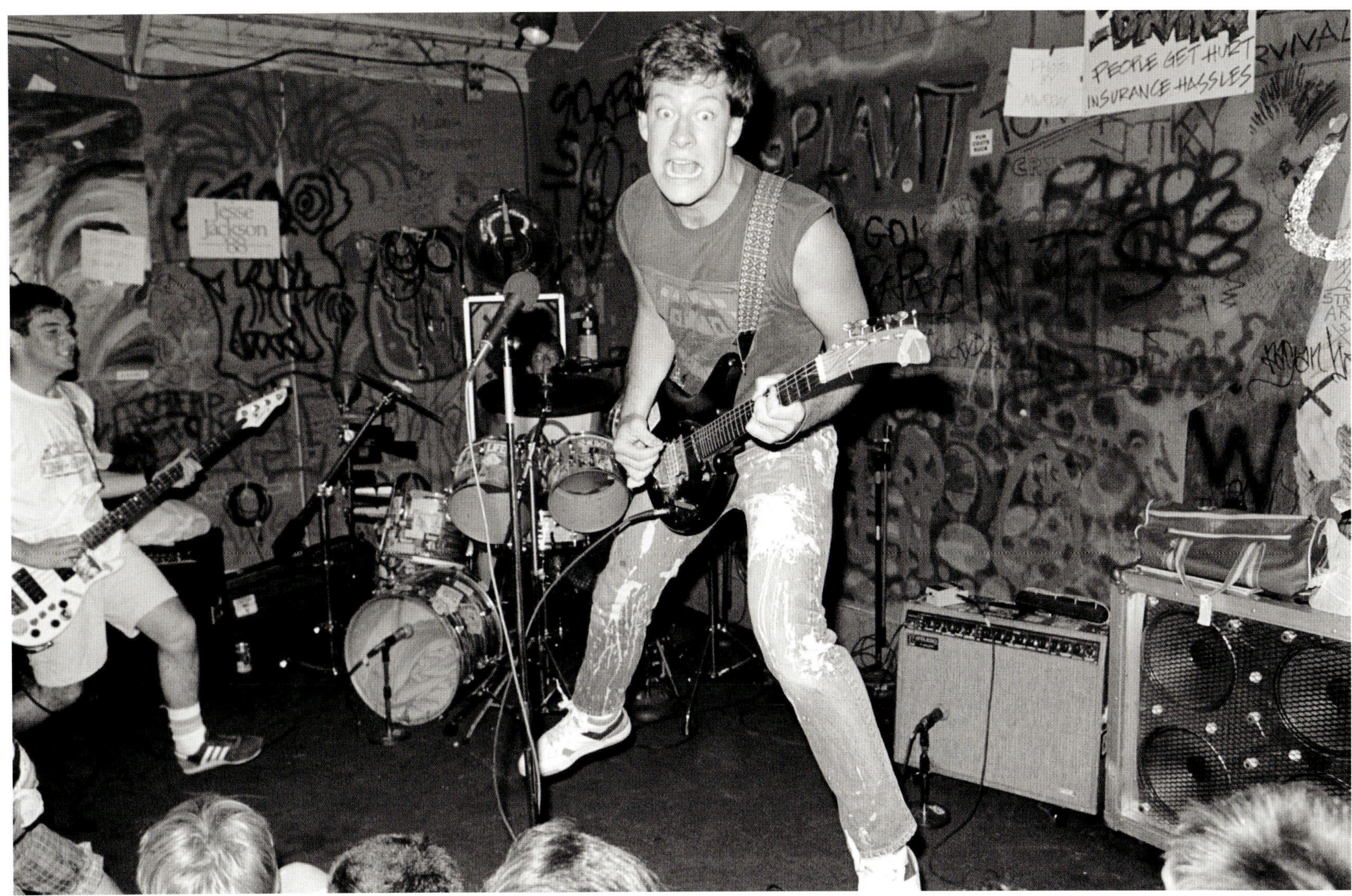

Stikky
Gilman Street, 1988

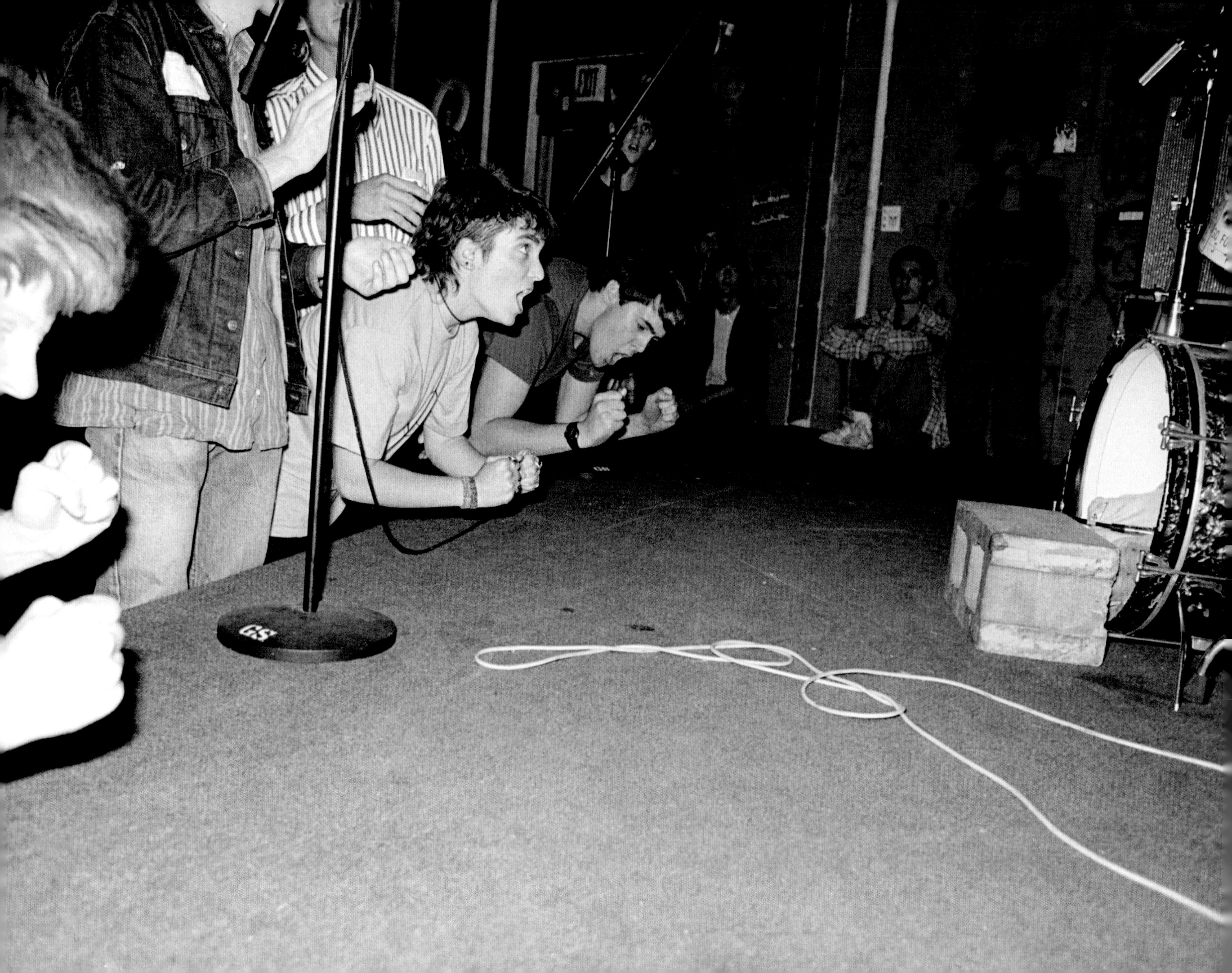

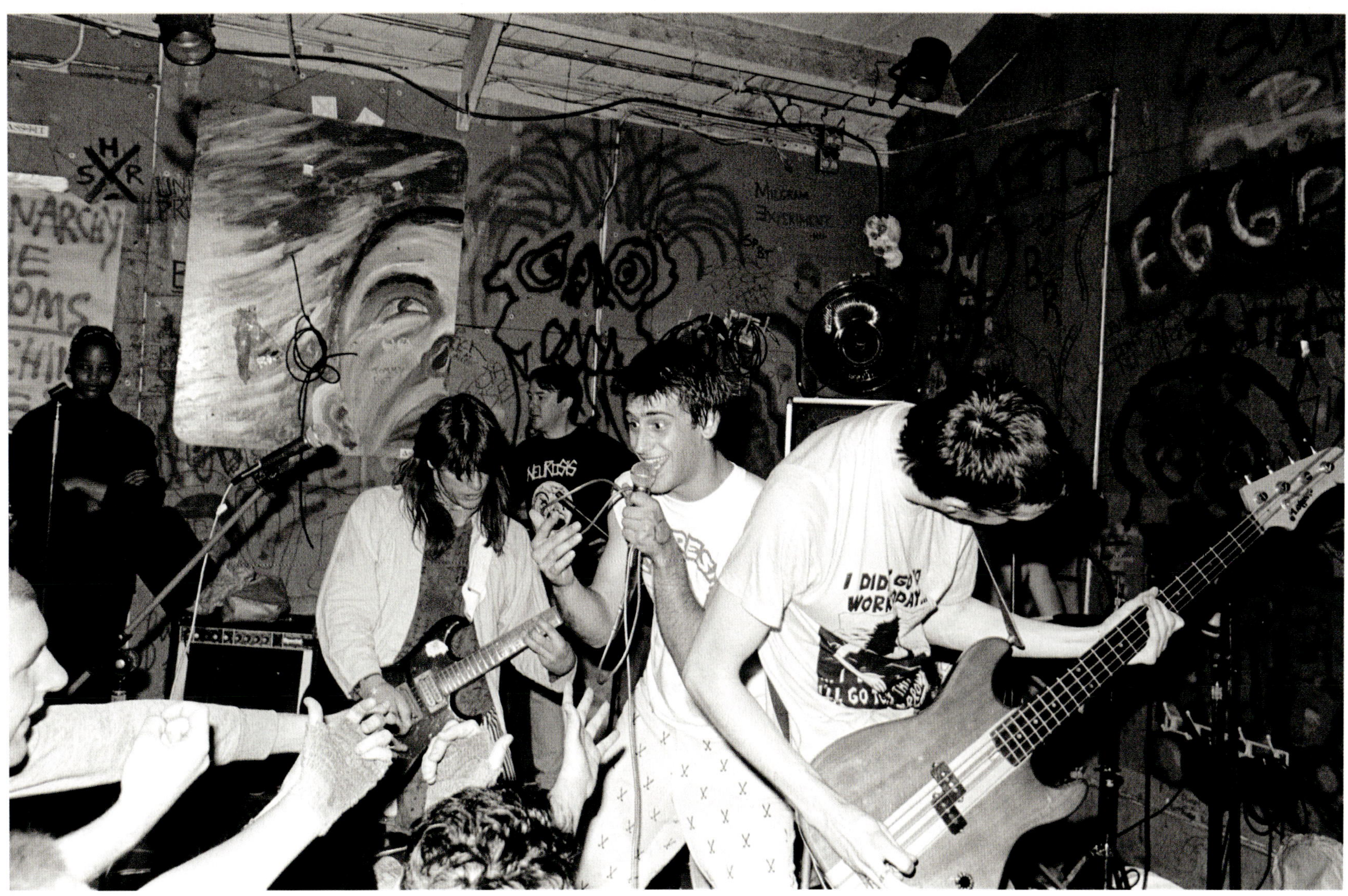

Screeching Weasel

Gilman Street, Berkeley, 1988

Opposite:

Gilman Street, 1987

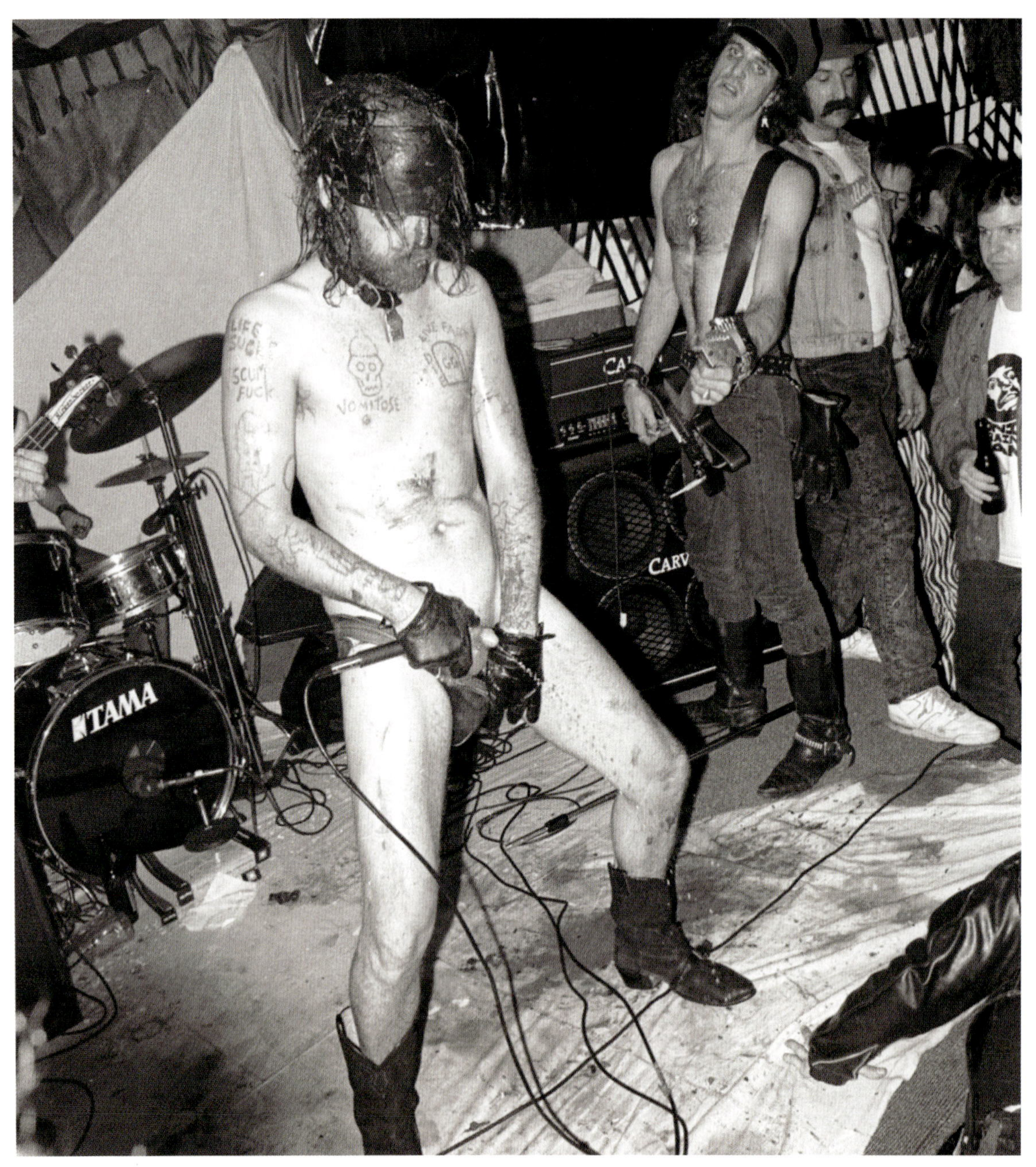

GG Allin
Covered Wagon
San Francisco, 1988

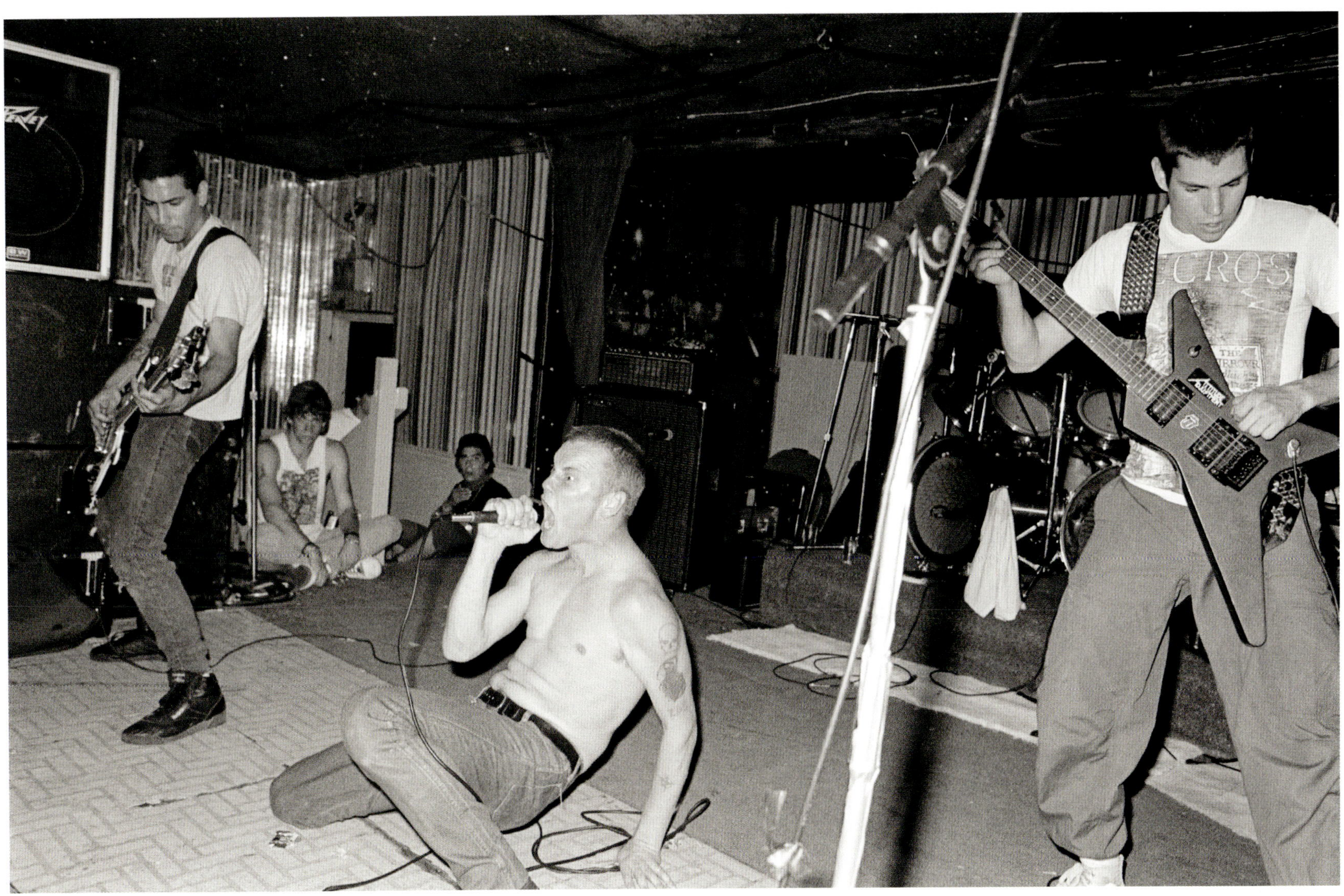

Attitude Adjustment

Ruthie's Inn, Berkeley, 1986

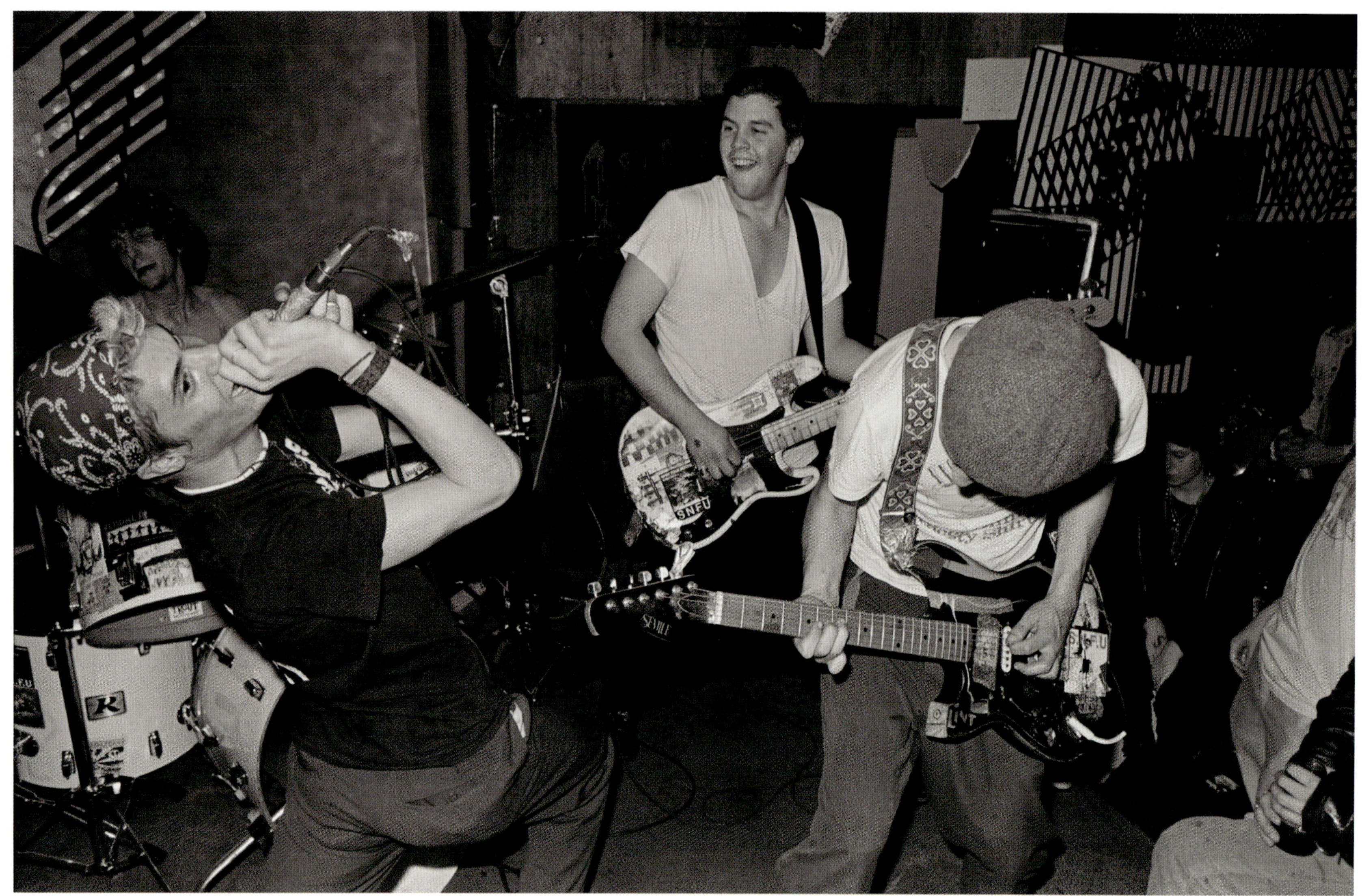

Operation Ivy

Above: **Covered Wagon, San Francisco, 1989**

Opposite: **Ruthie's Inn, Berkeley, 1988**

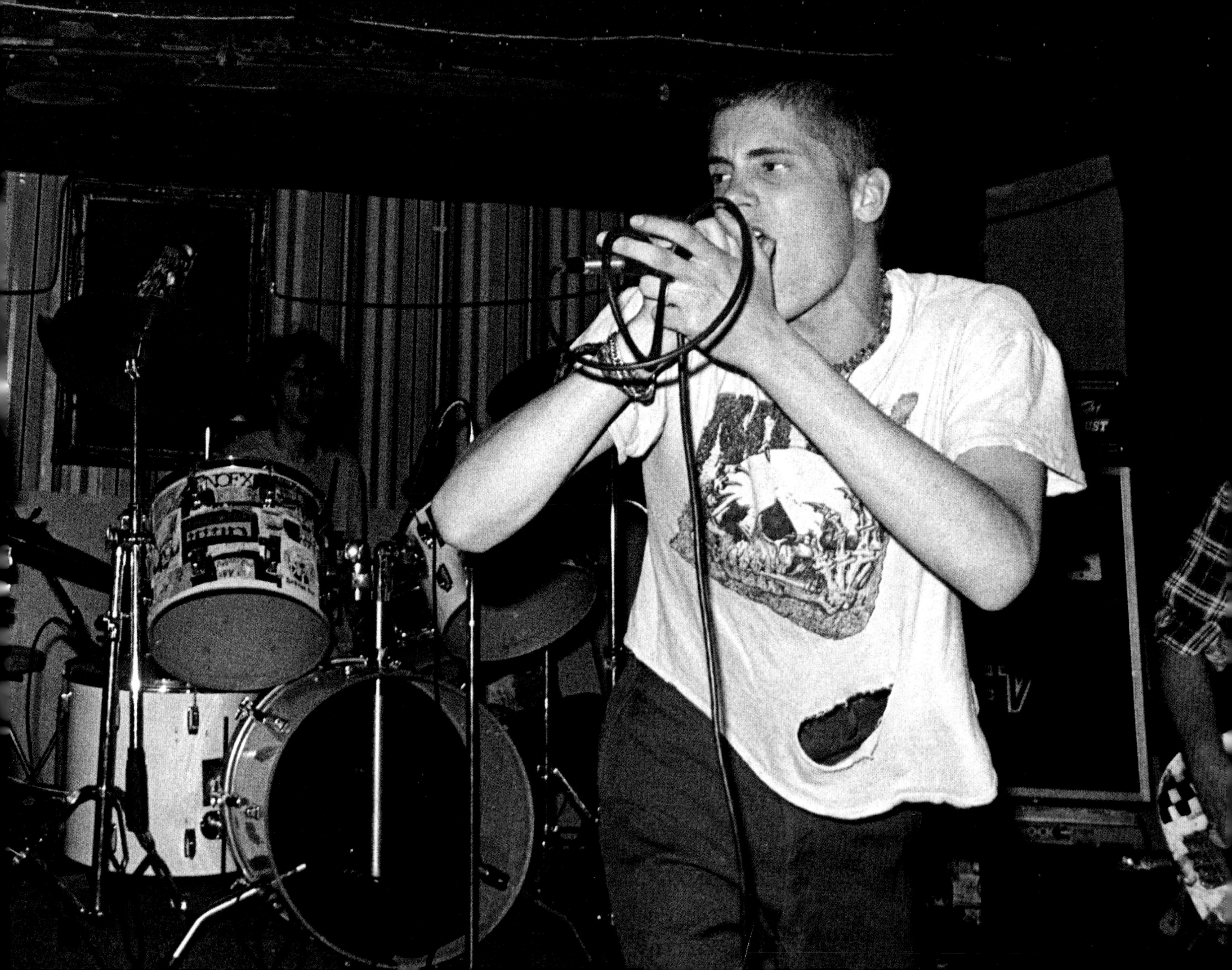

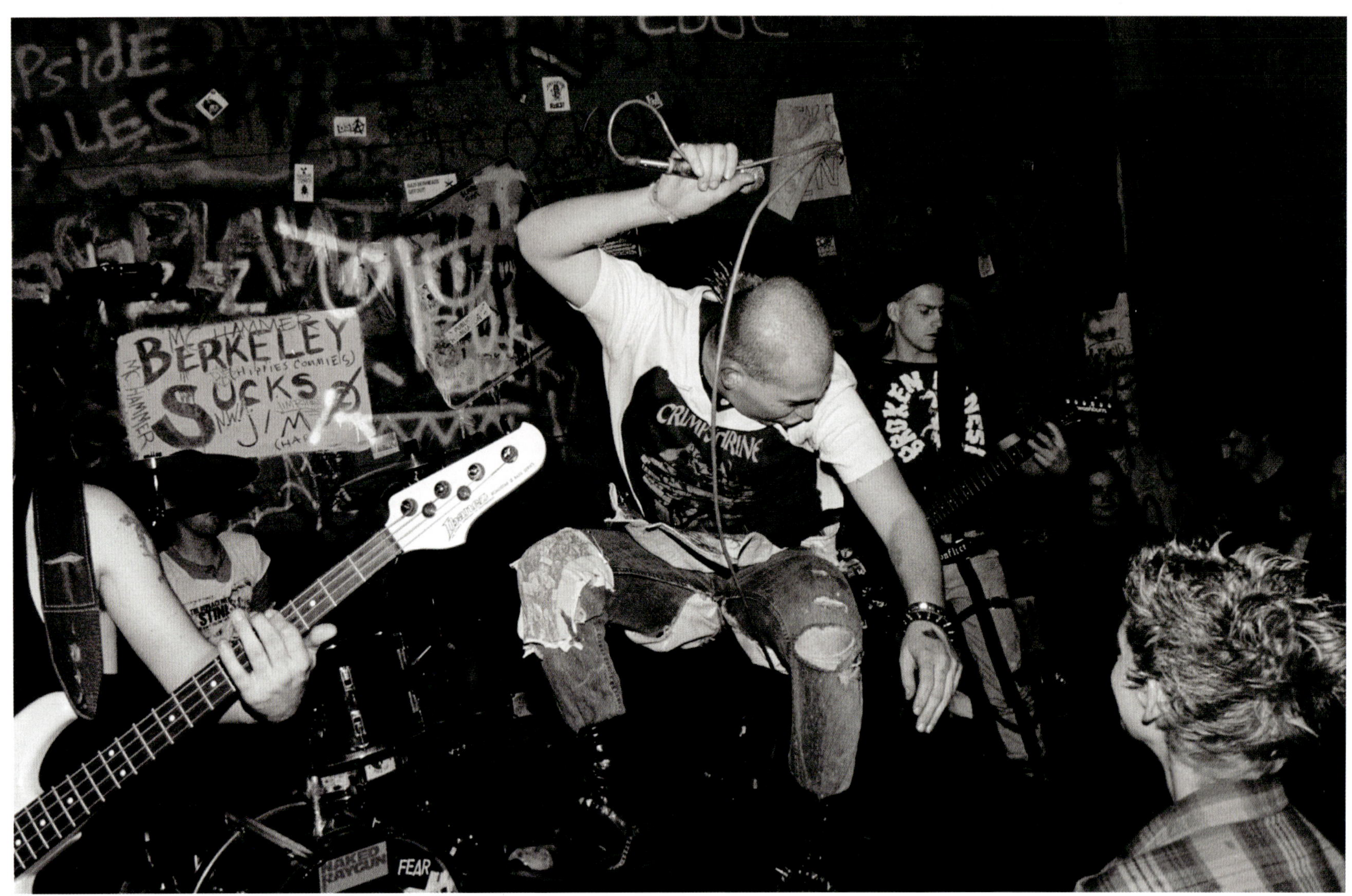

Filth

Gilman Street, Berkeley, 1989

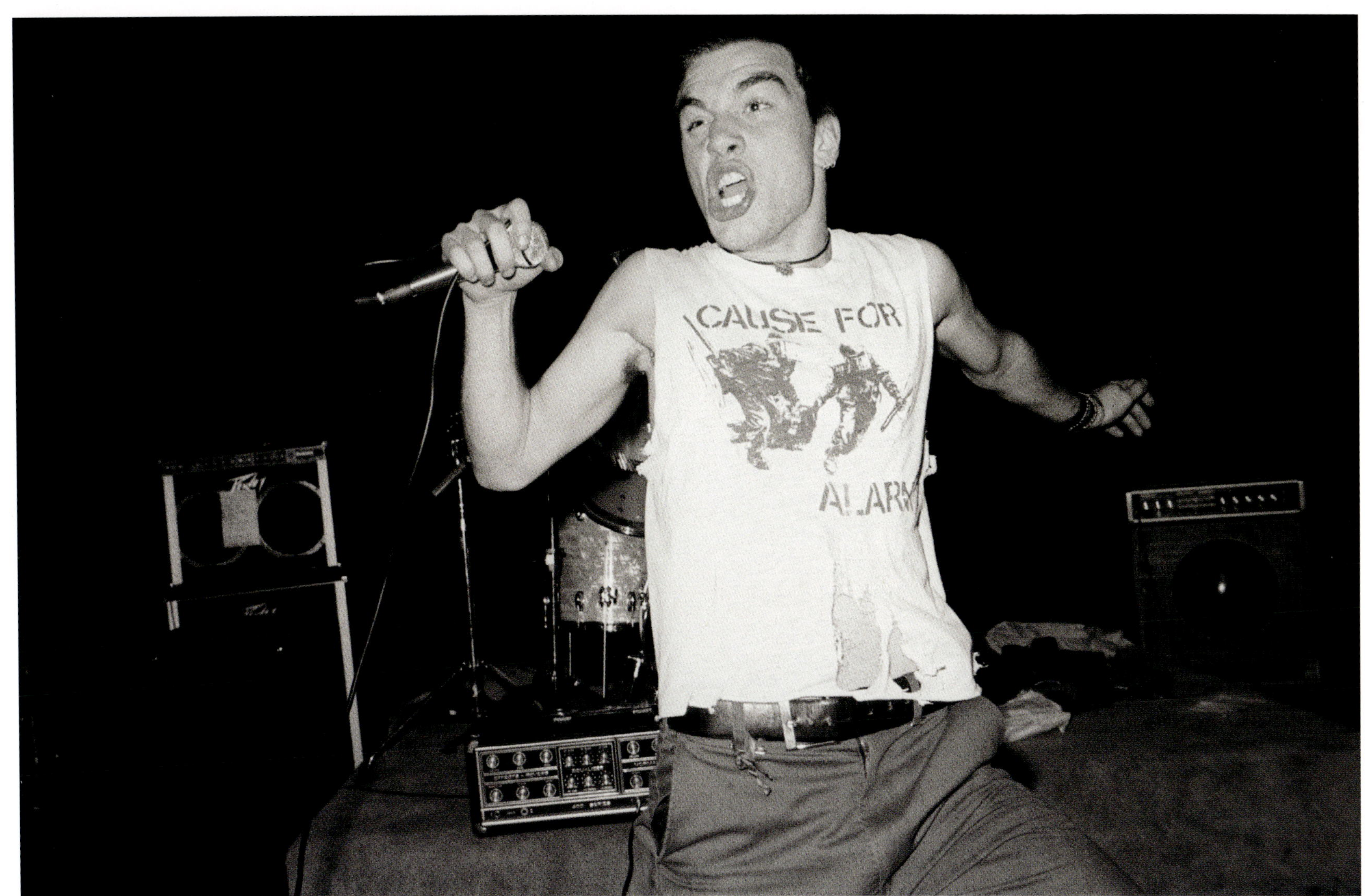

Econochrist
Berkeley Square, Berkeley, 1989

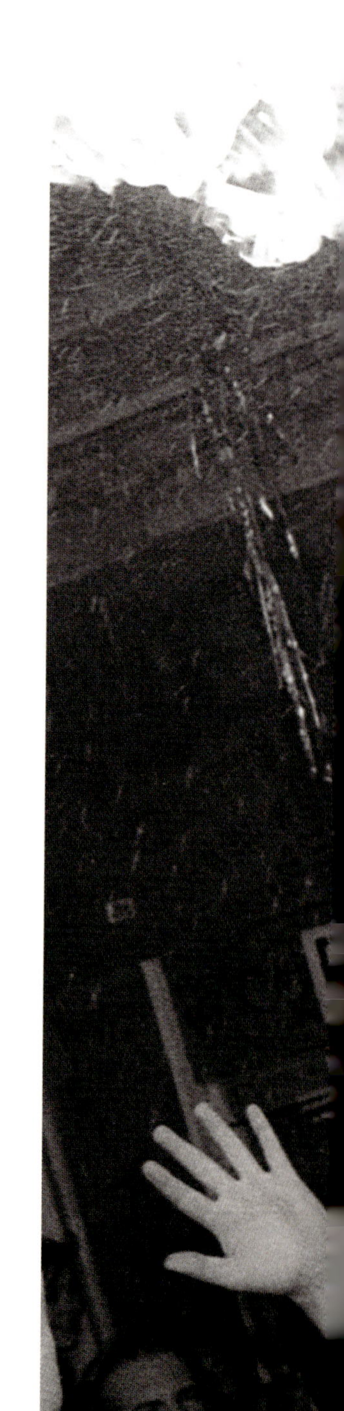

Poison Idea
Gilman Street, Berkeley, 1989

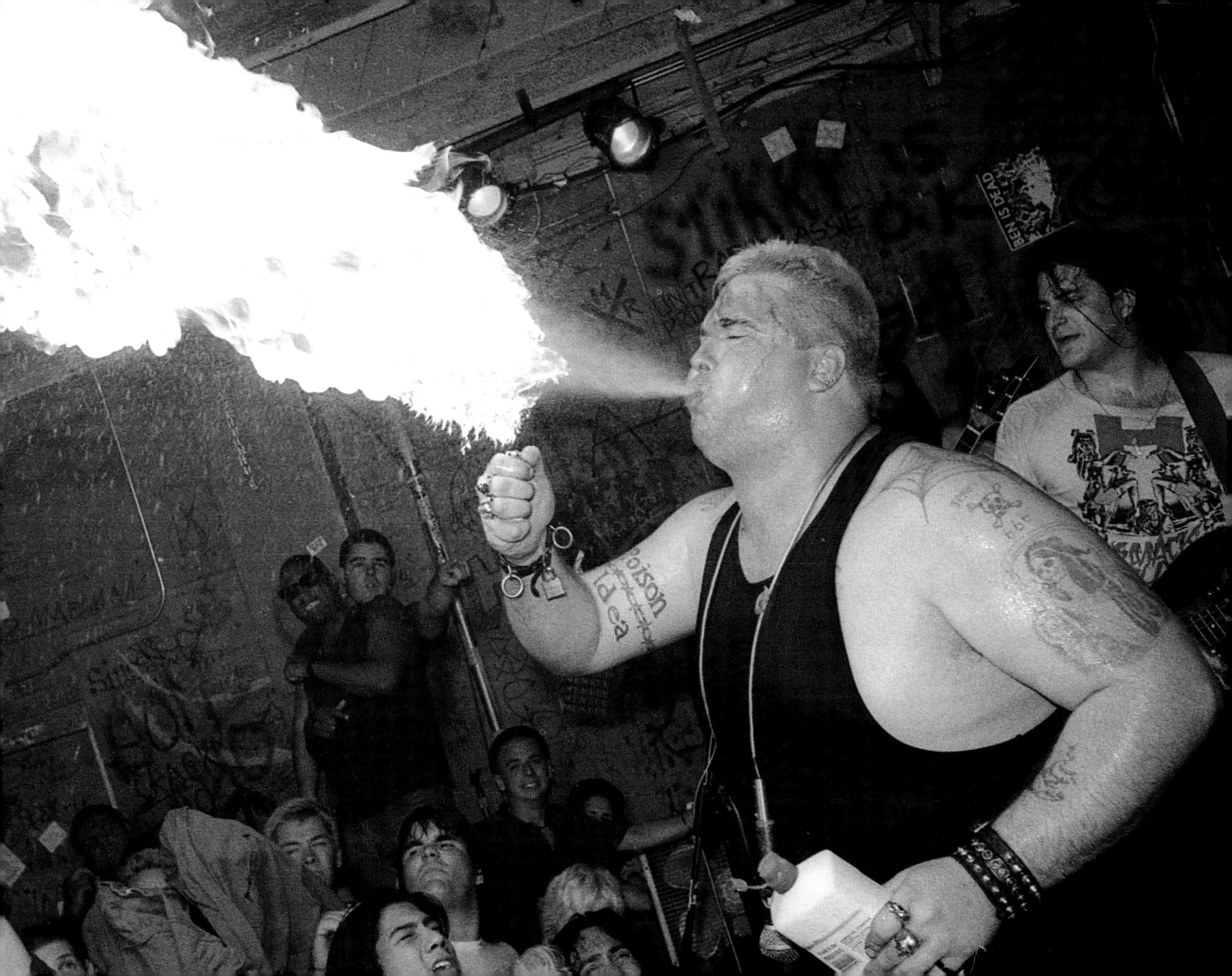
Poison
Idea

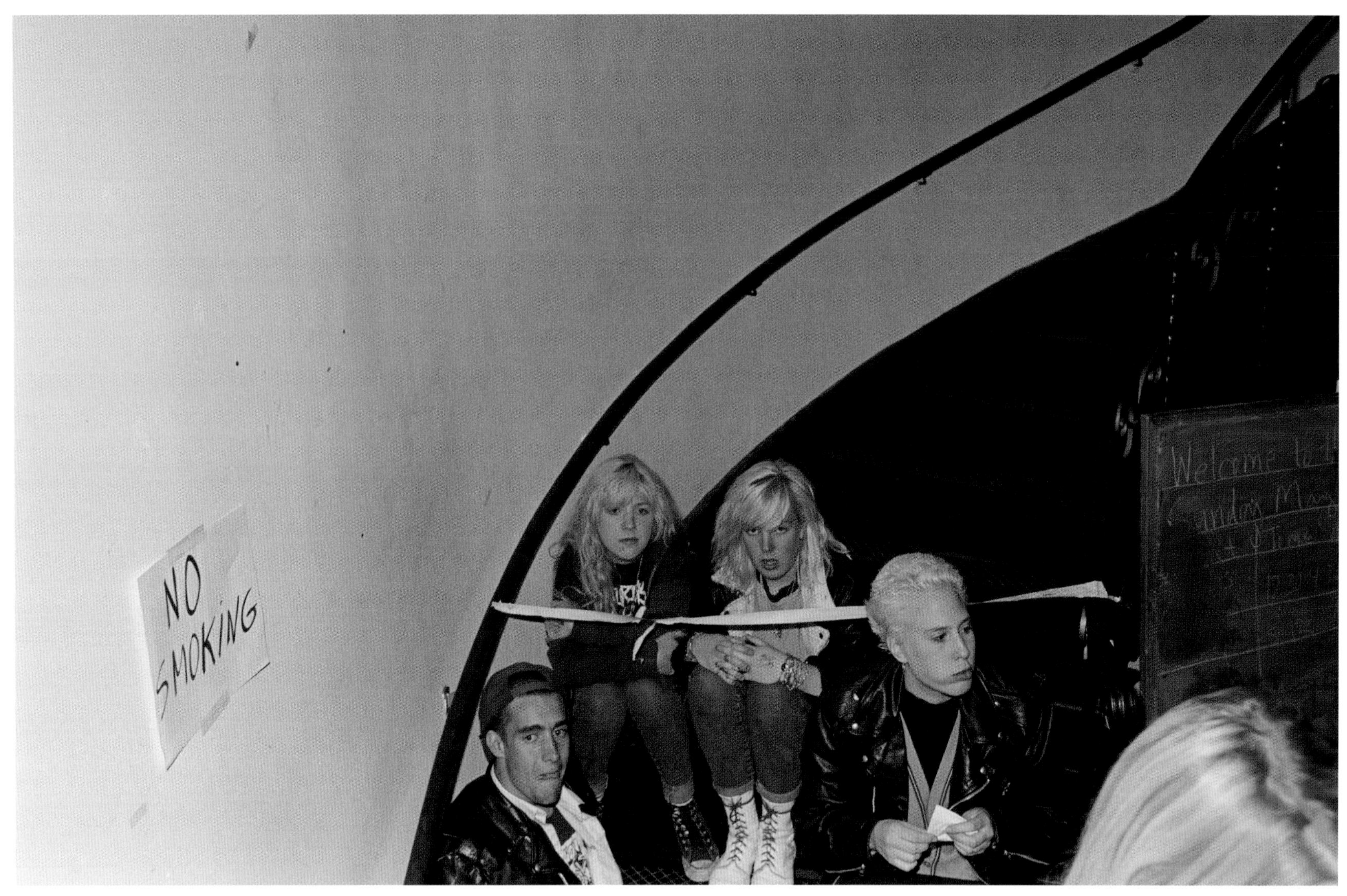

The Women's Building, San Francisco, 1989

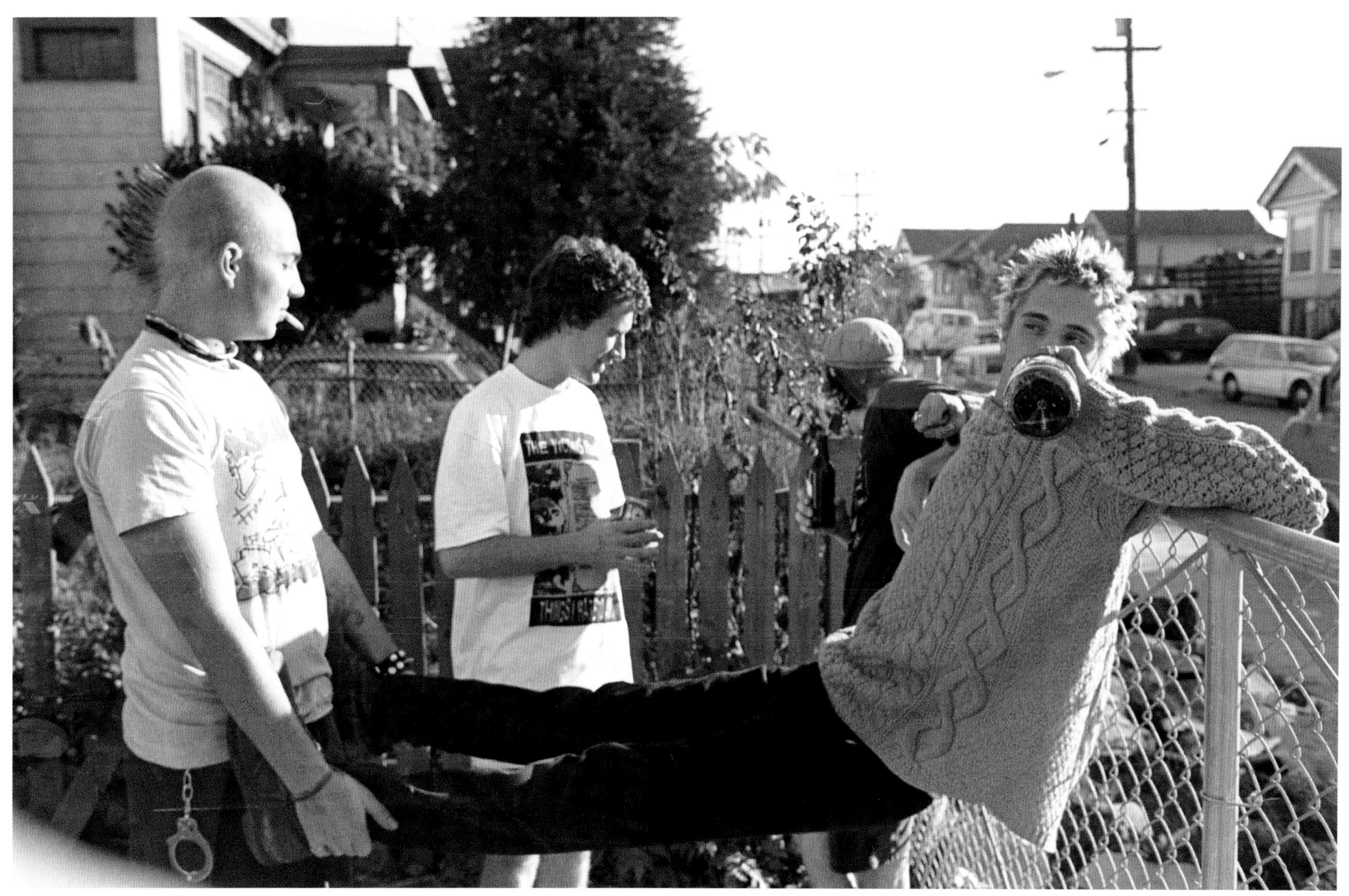

West Oakland, 1989

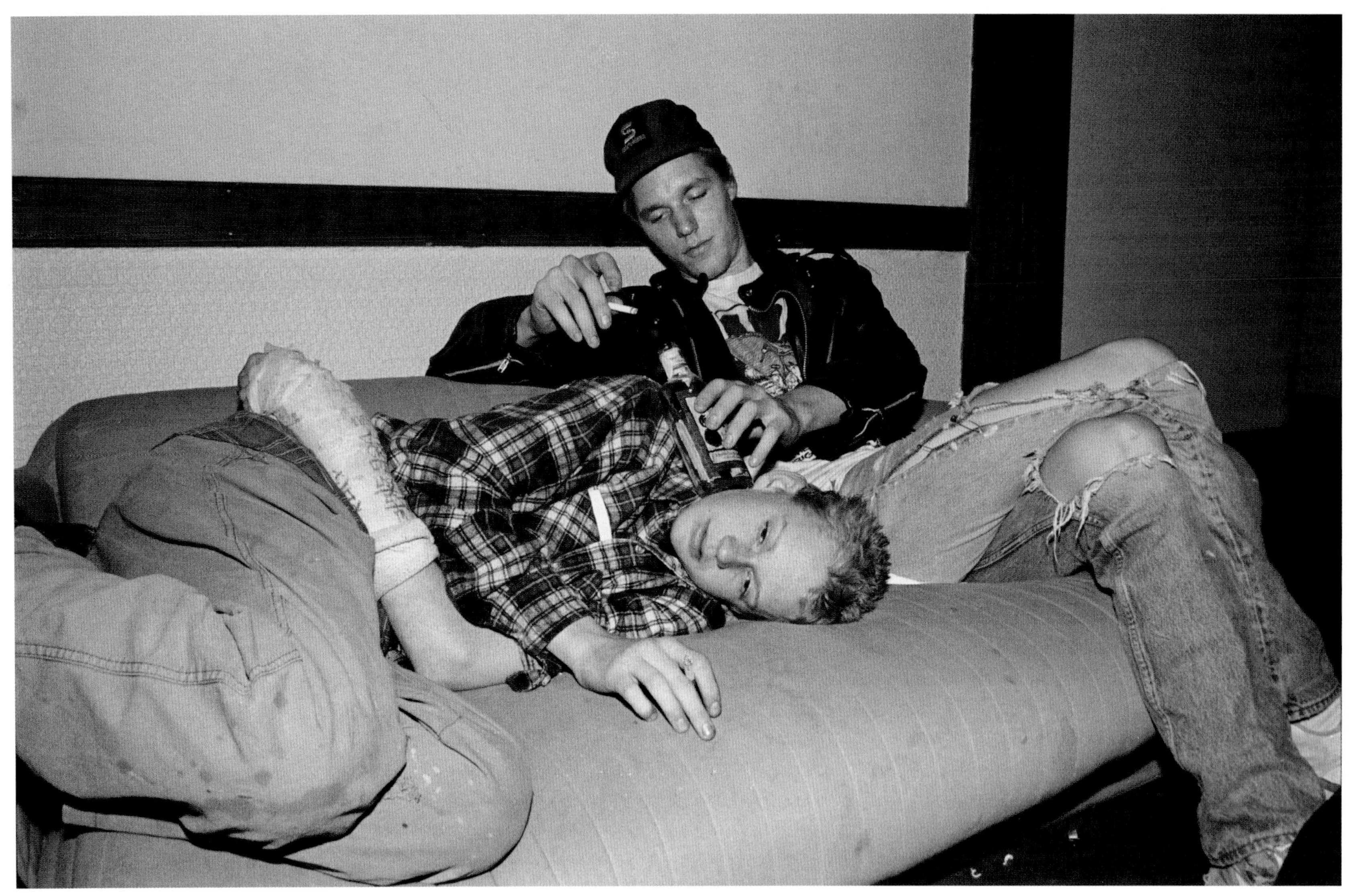

Ewan and Aaron, 1989

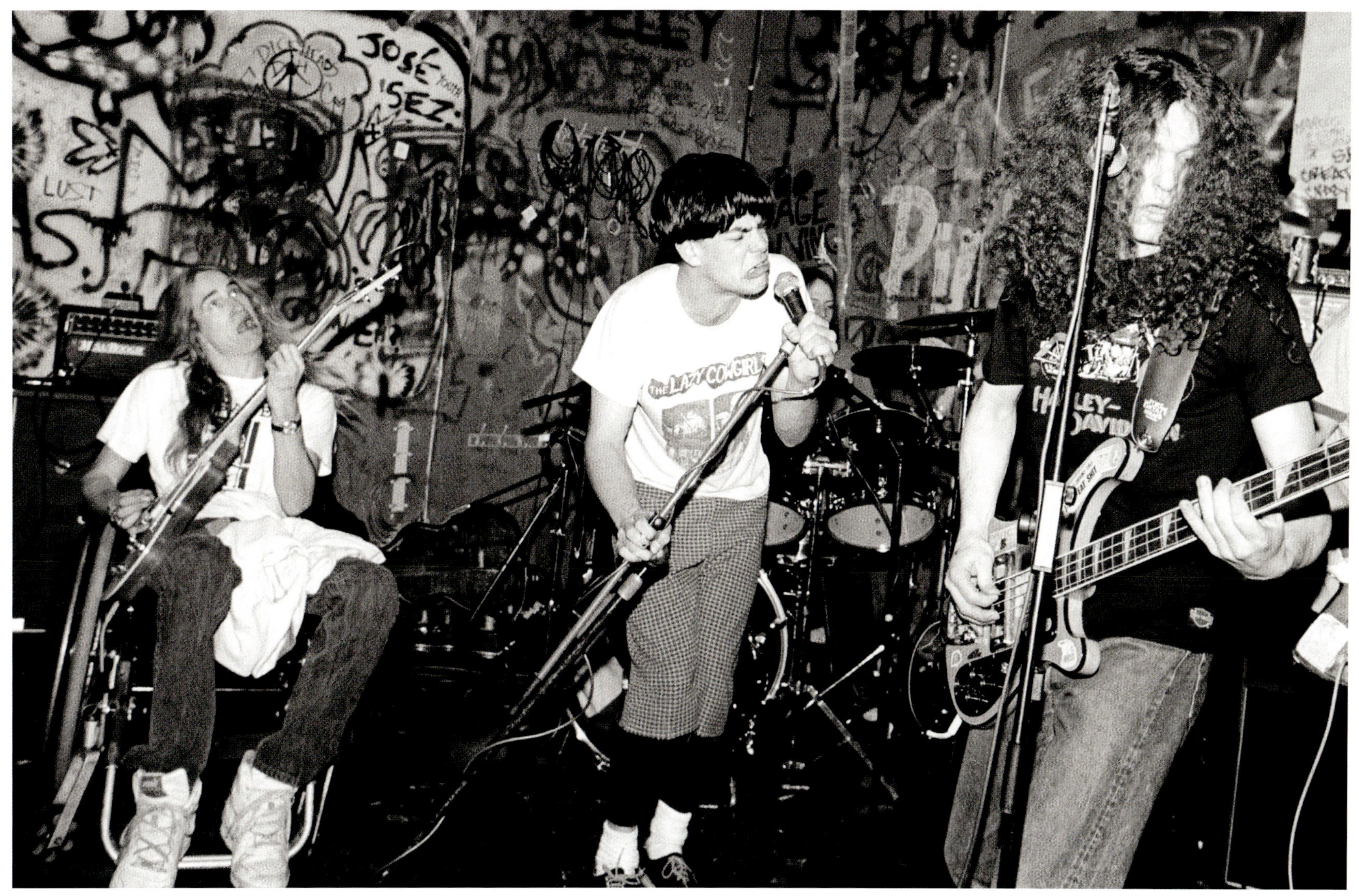

Crutch

Gilman Street, Berkeley, 1989

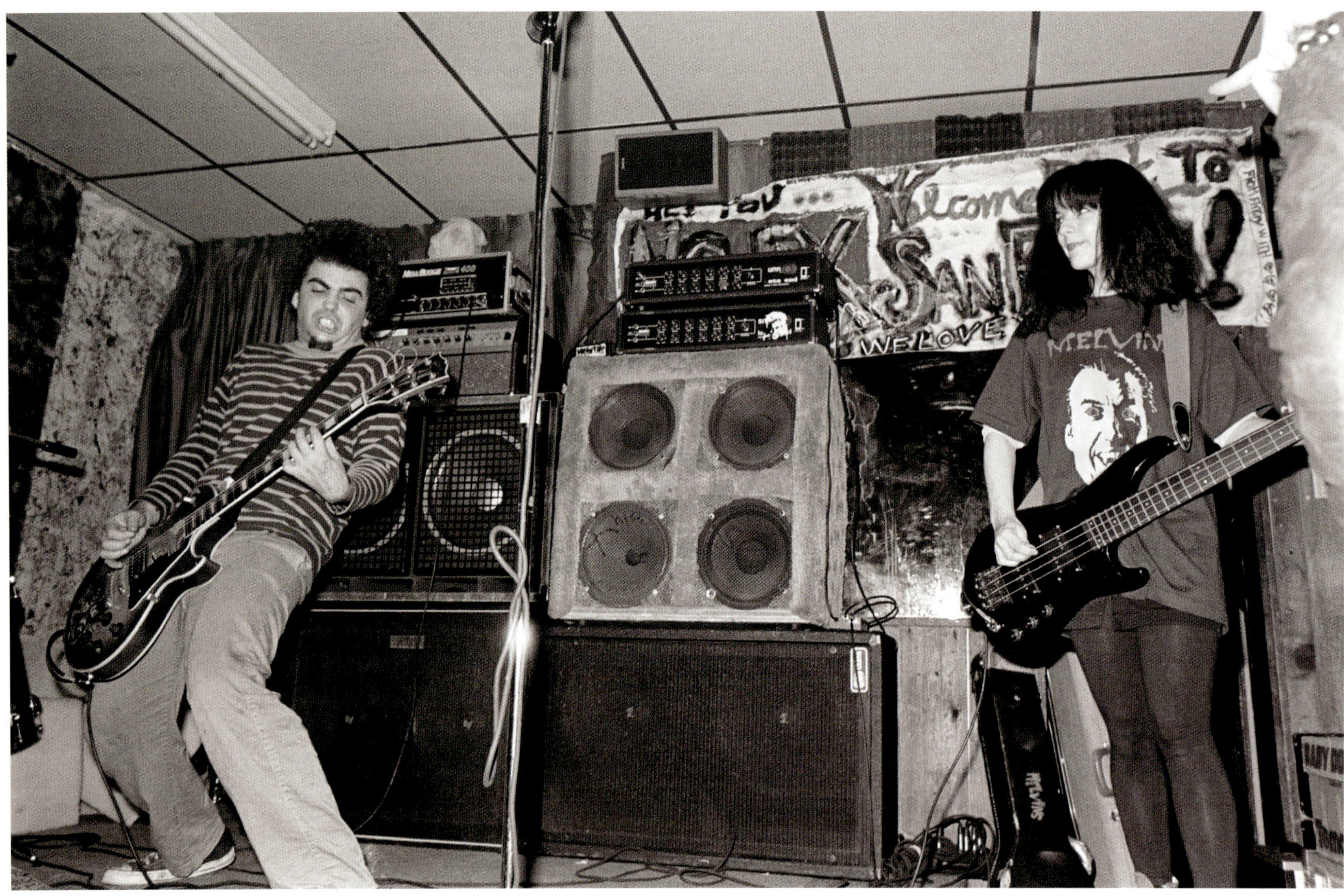

Melvins

Covered Wagon, San Francisco, 1988

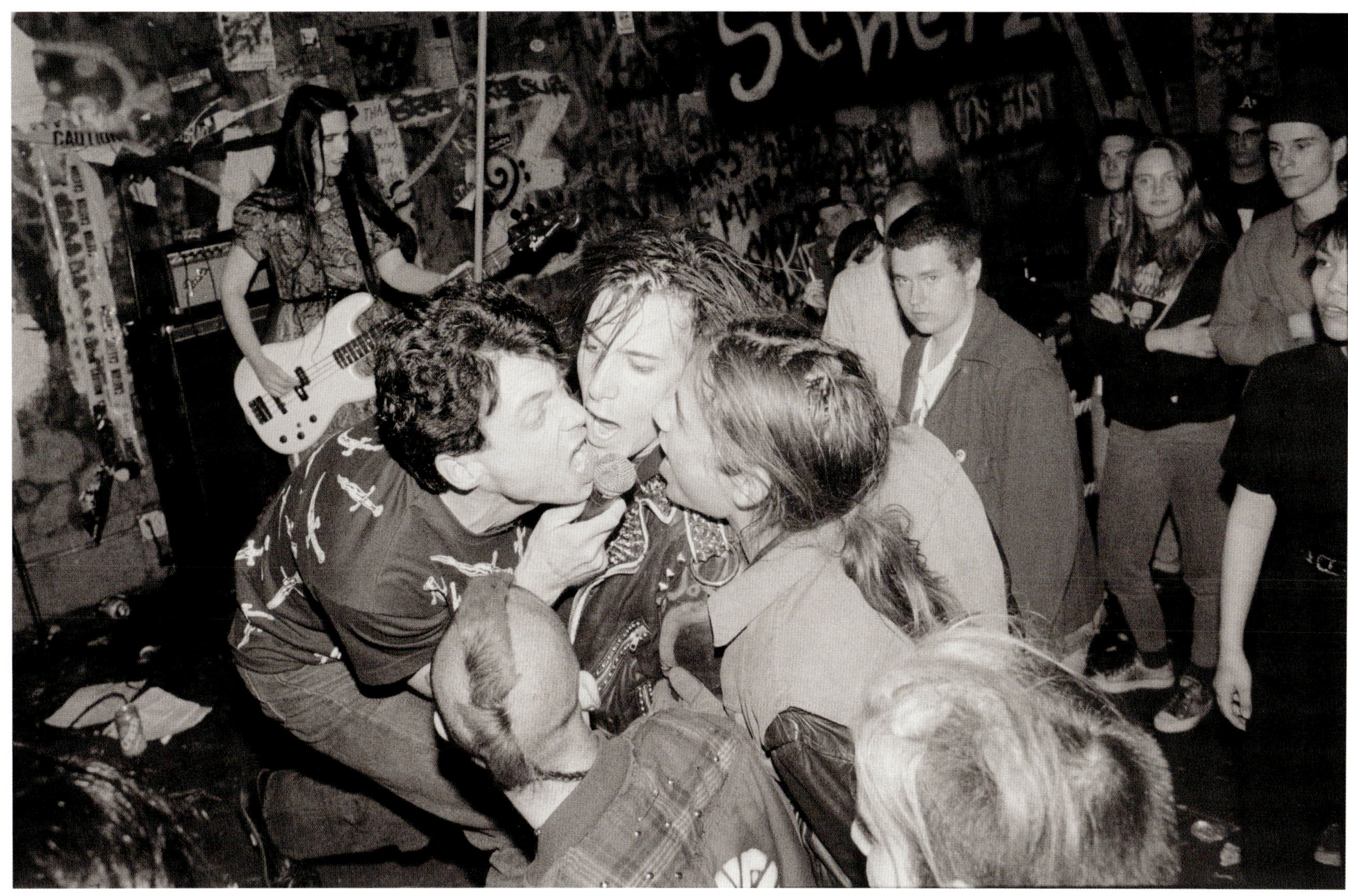

Capitol Punishment

Gilman Street, Berkeley, 1991

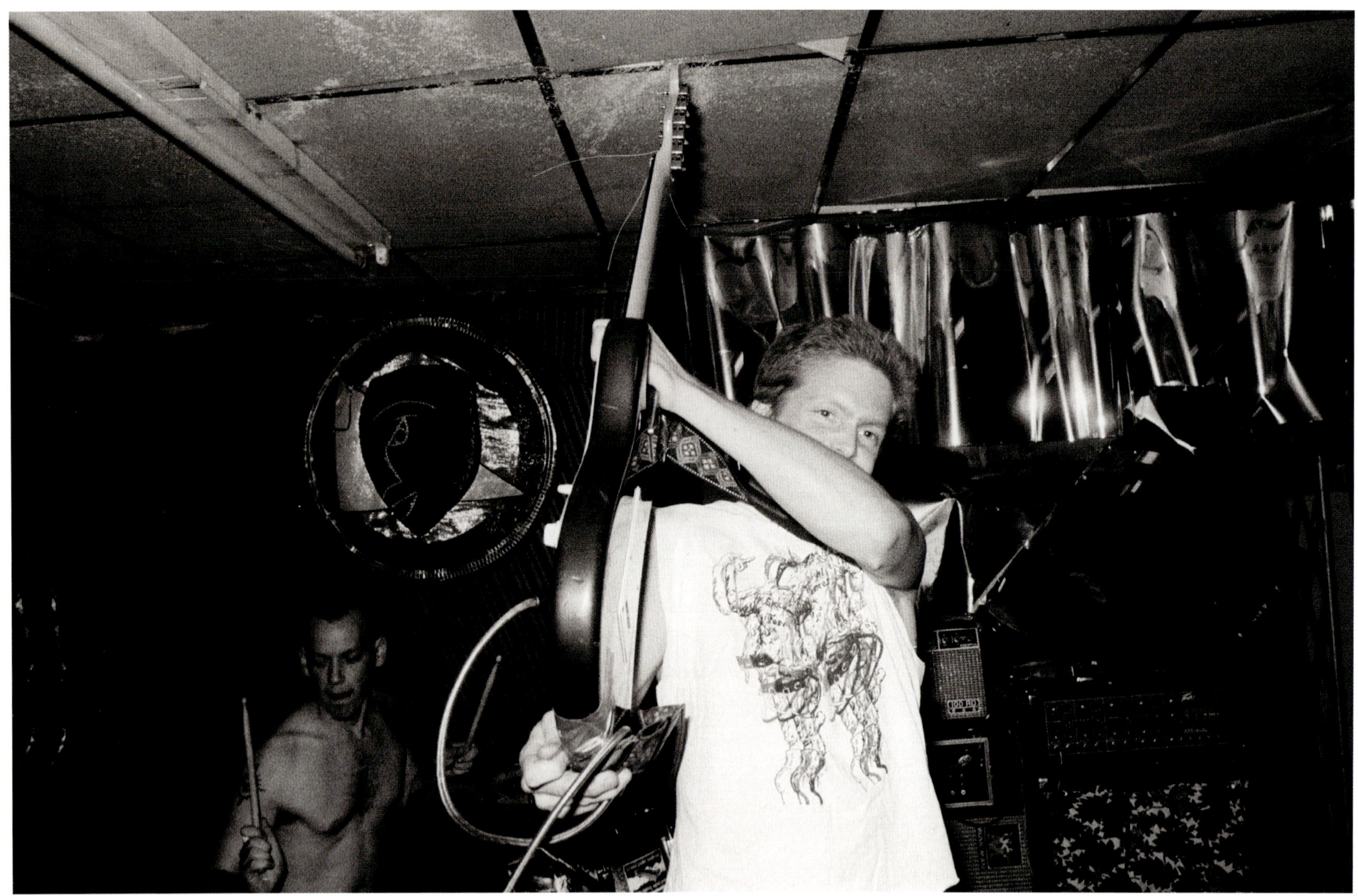

Steelpole Bathtub
Covered Wagon, San Francisco, 1989

Opposite:
Skankin' Pickle
Gilman Street, Berkeley, 1989

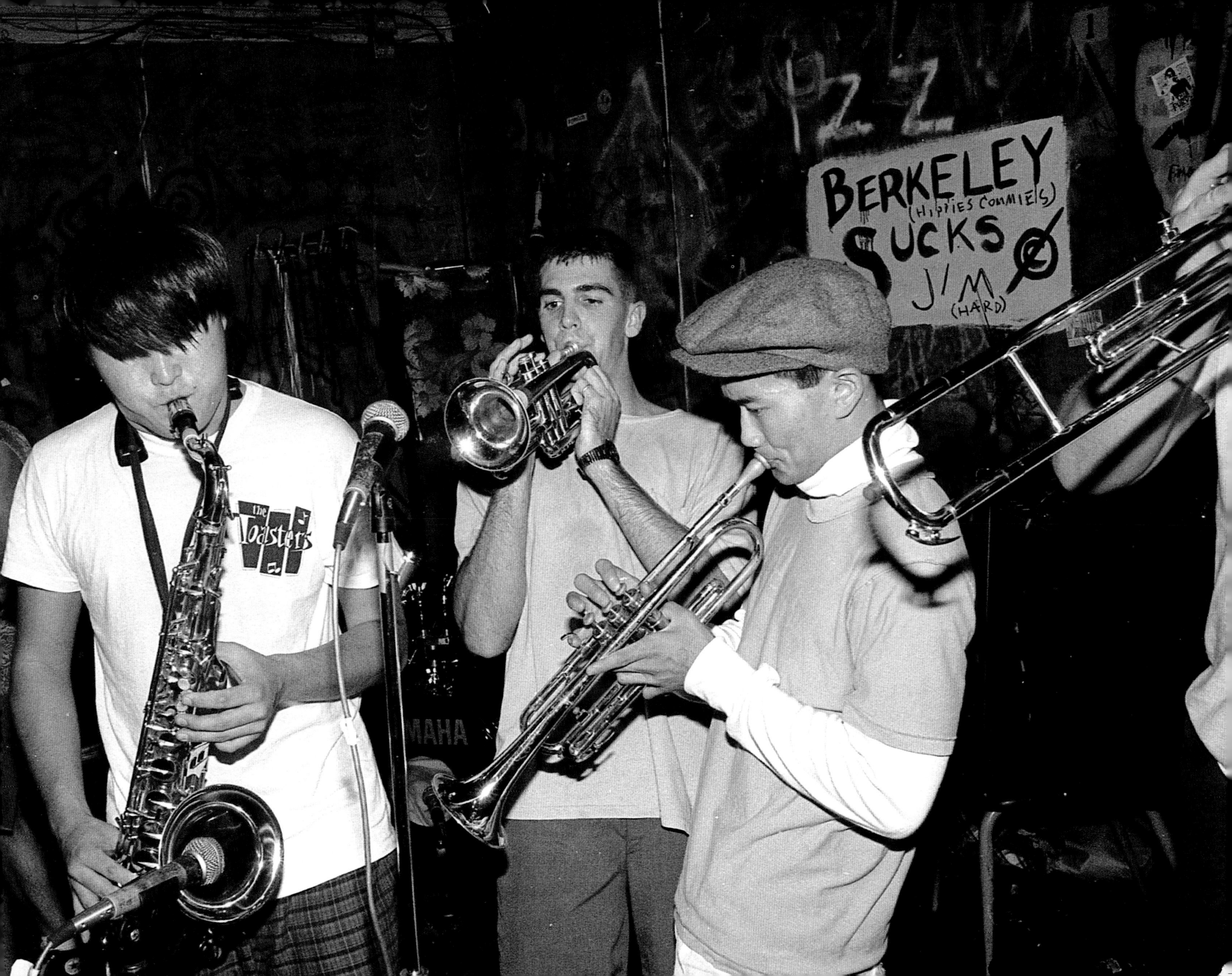
BERKELEY
(HIPPIES COMMIES)
SUCKS
J/M
(HARD)
The
Toasters

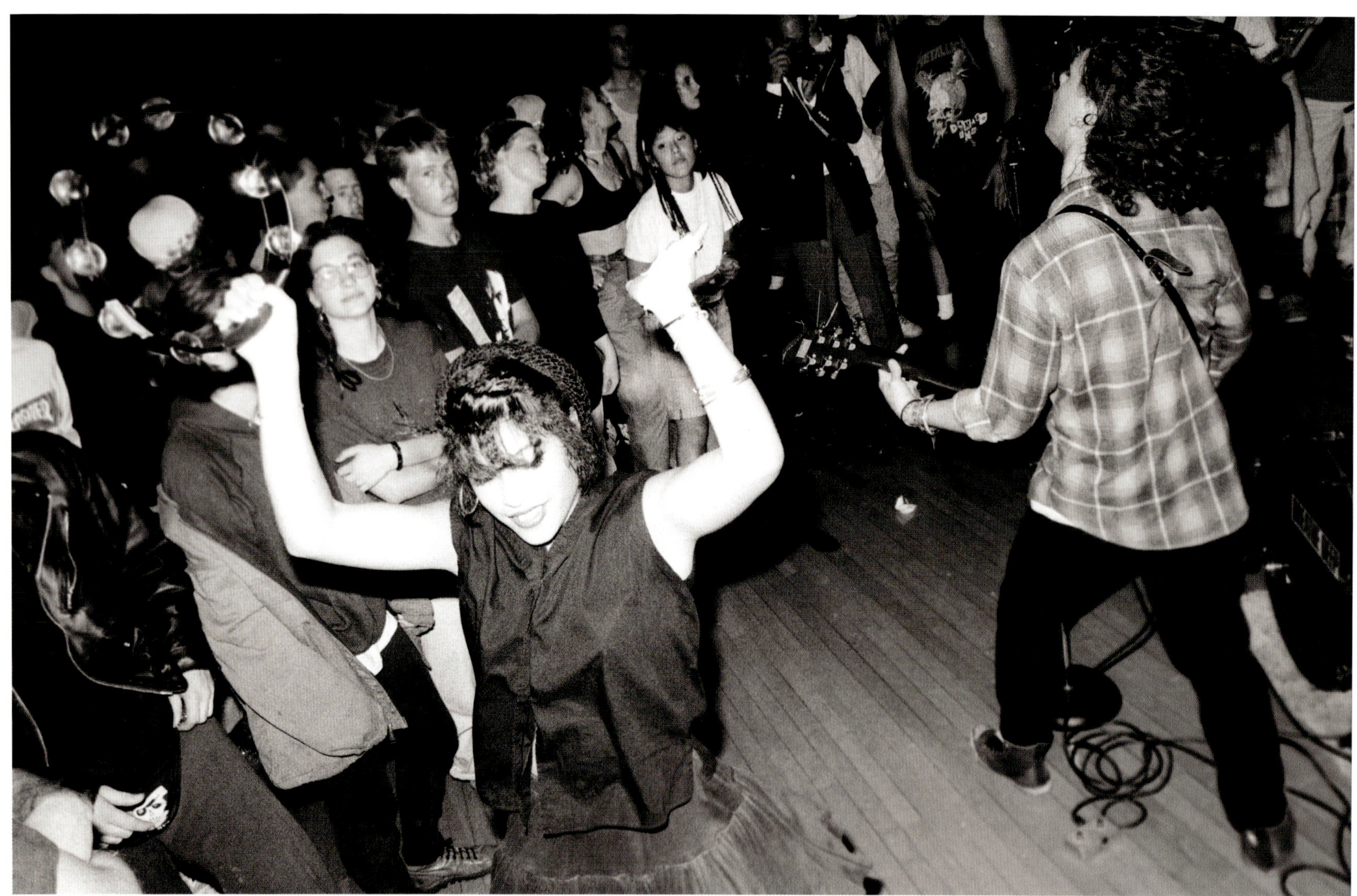

Masonic Temple, Vallejo, 1989

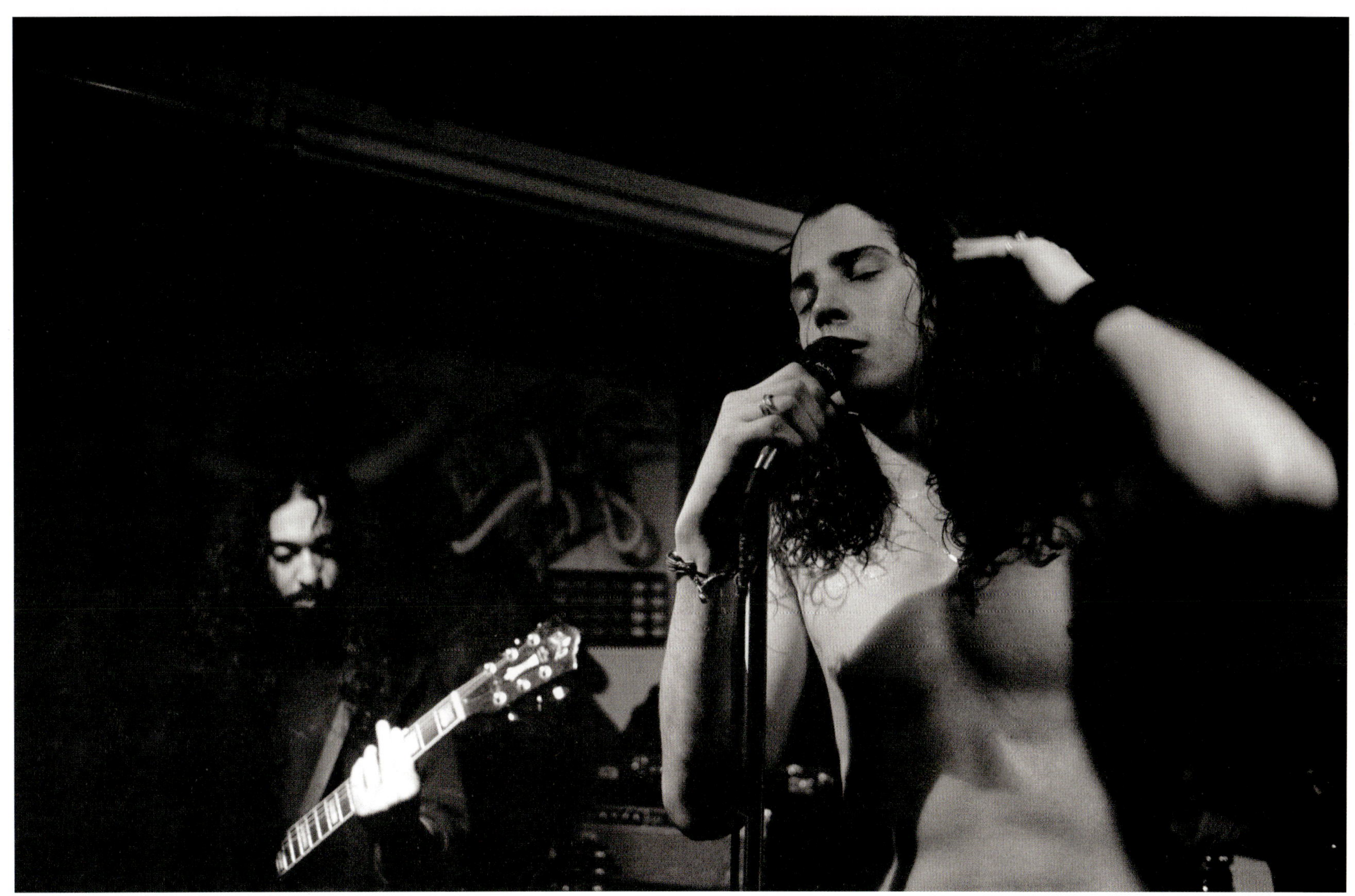

Soundgarden

Covered Wagon, San Francisco, 1989

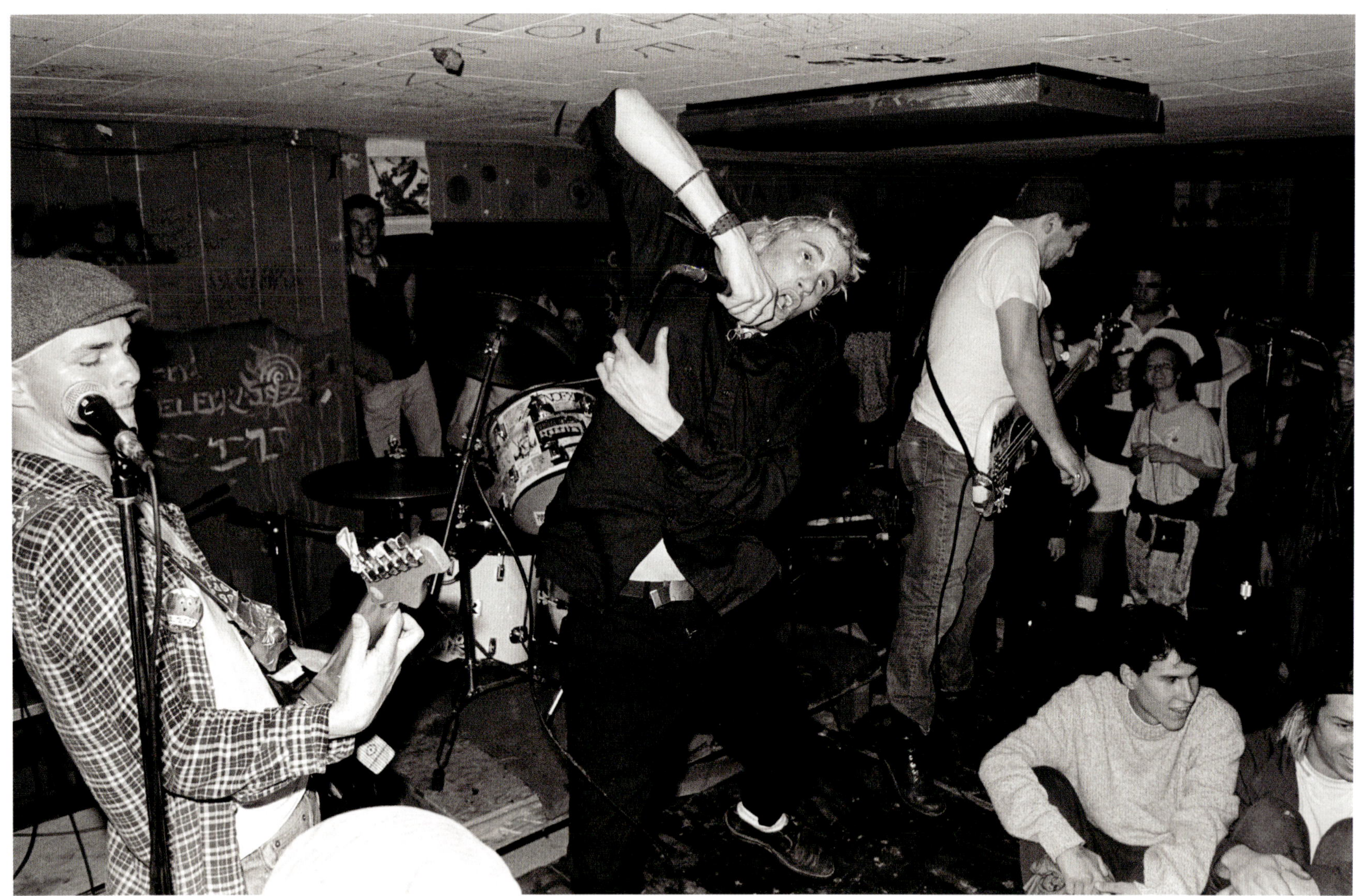

Operation Ivy

Barrington Hall, Berkeley, 1989

Opposite:

Eggplant's Backyard, Pinole, 1989

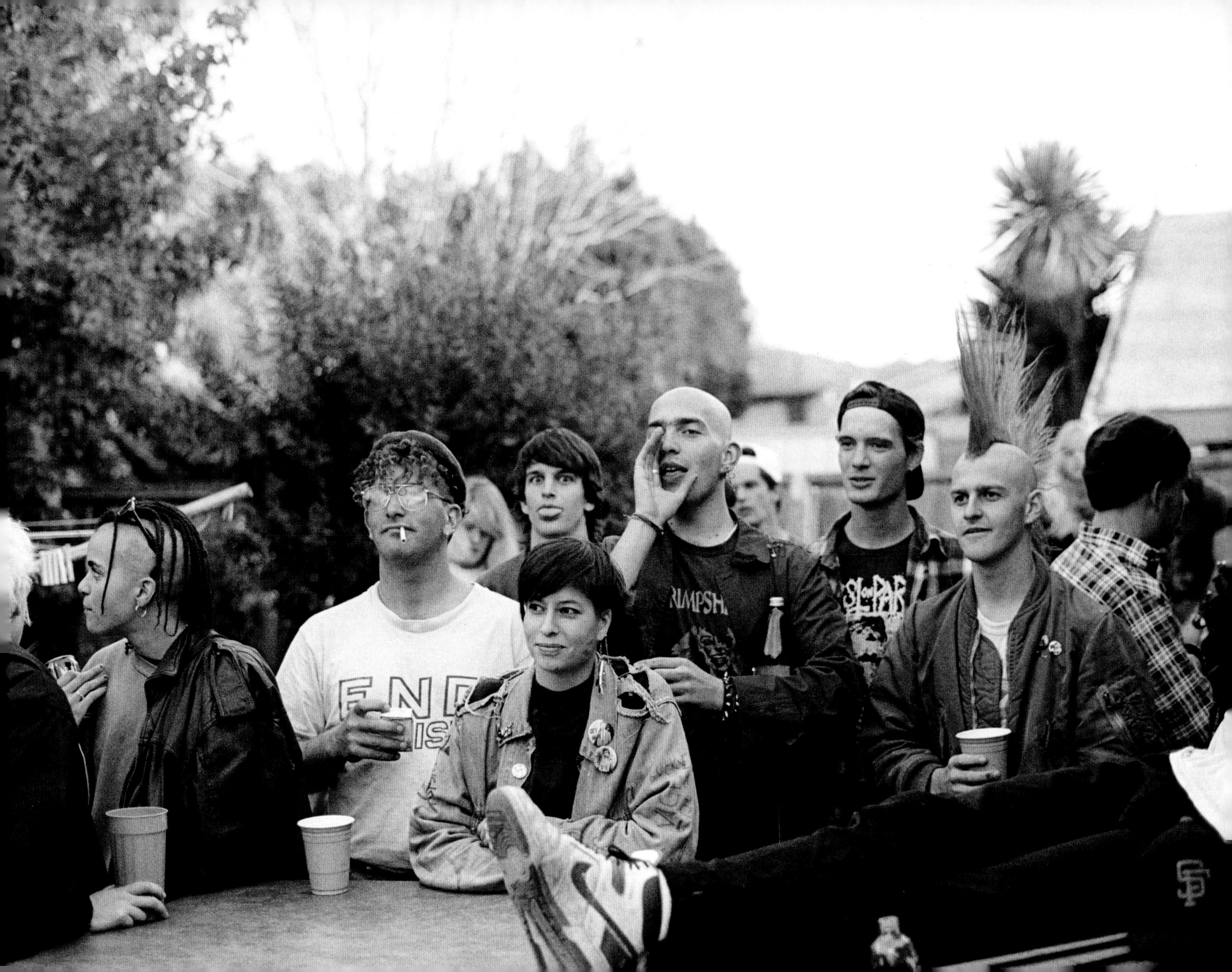

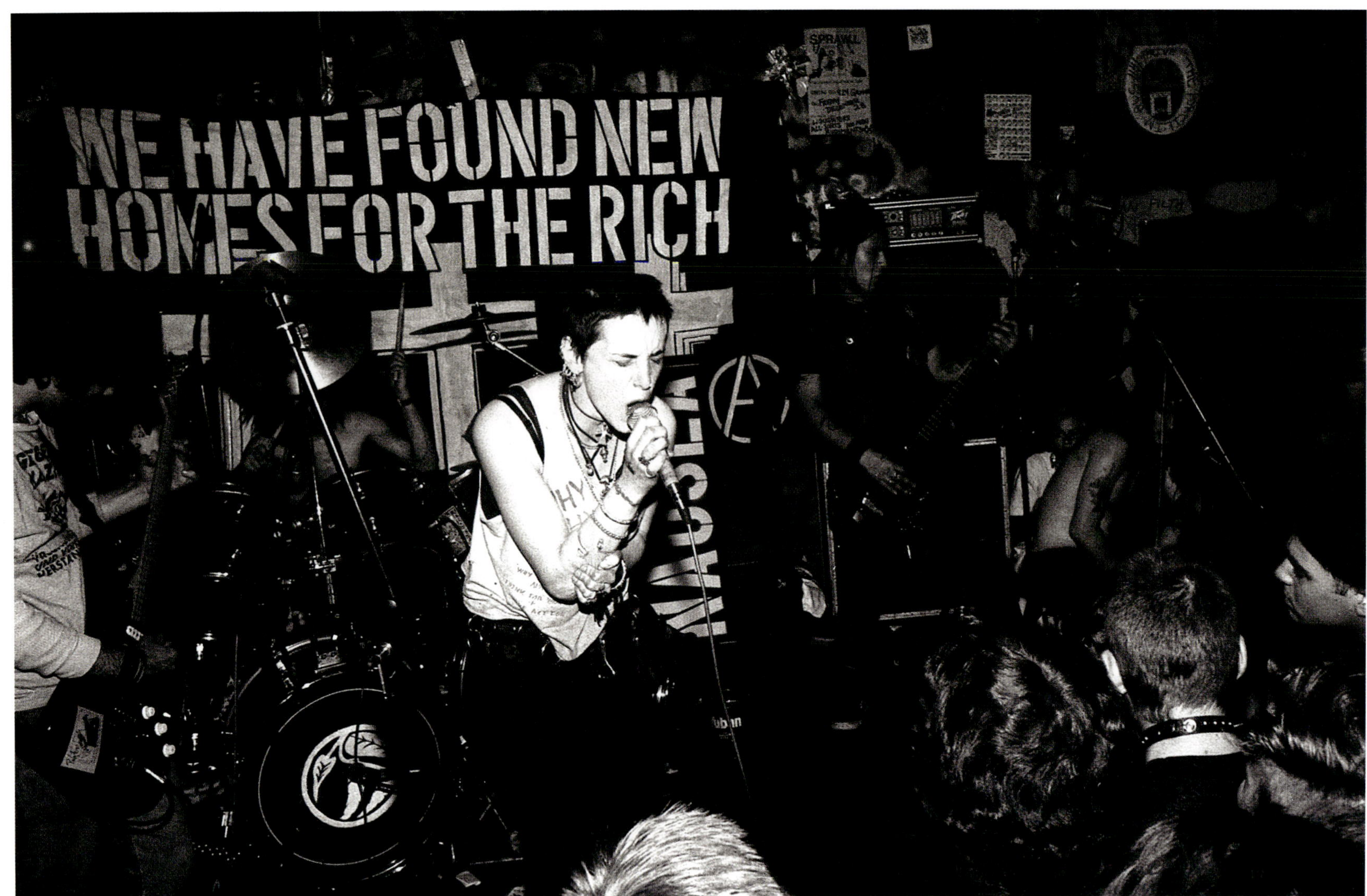

Nausea
Gilman Street, Berkeley, 1990

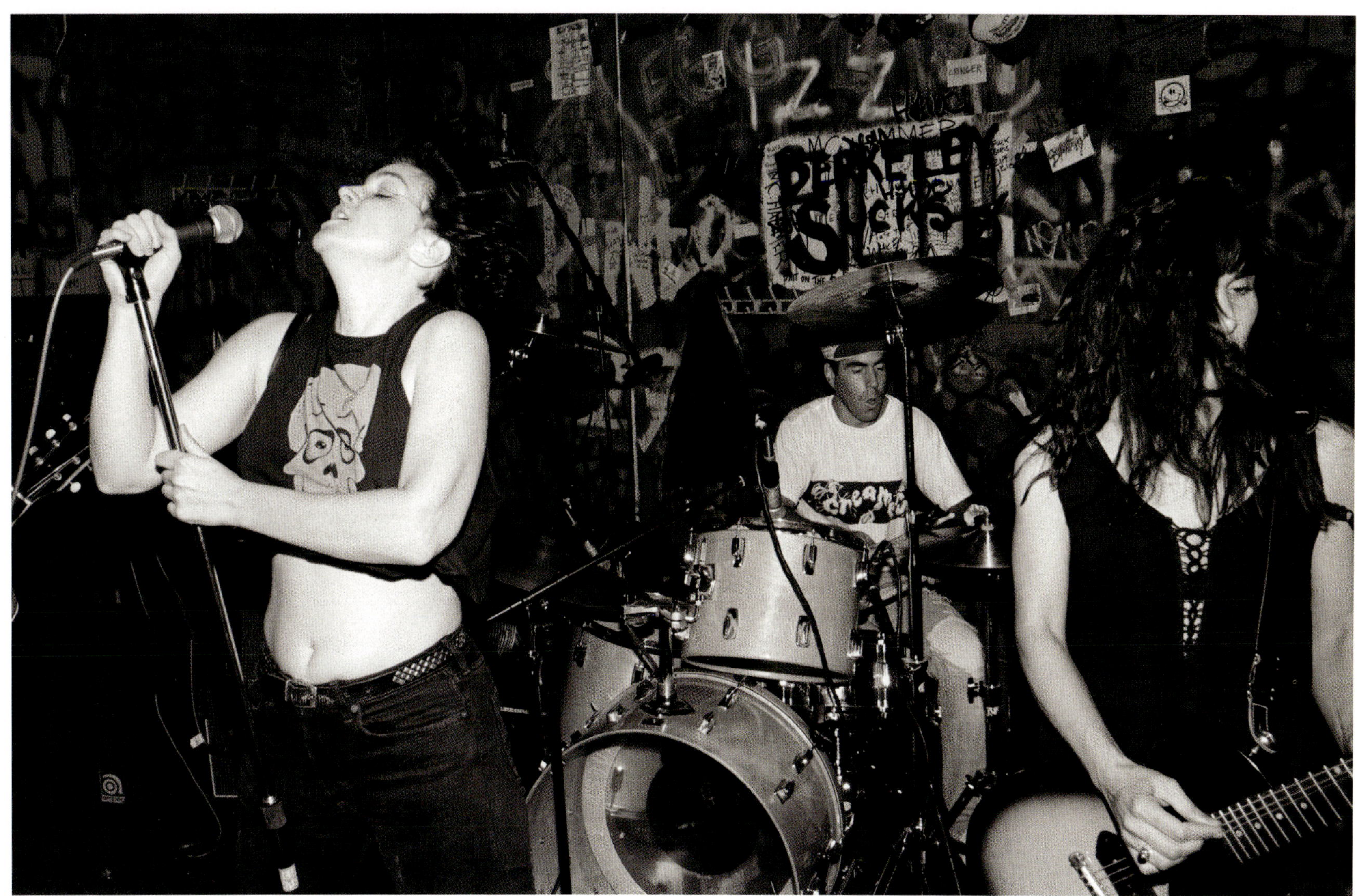

Creamers
Gilman Street, 1990

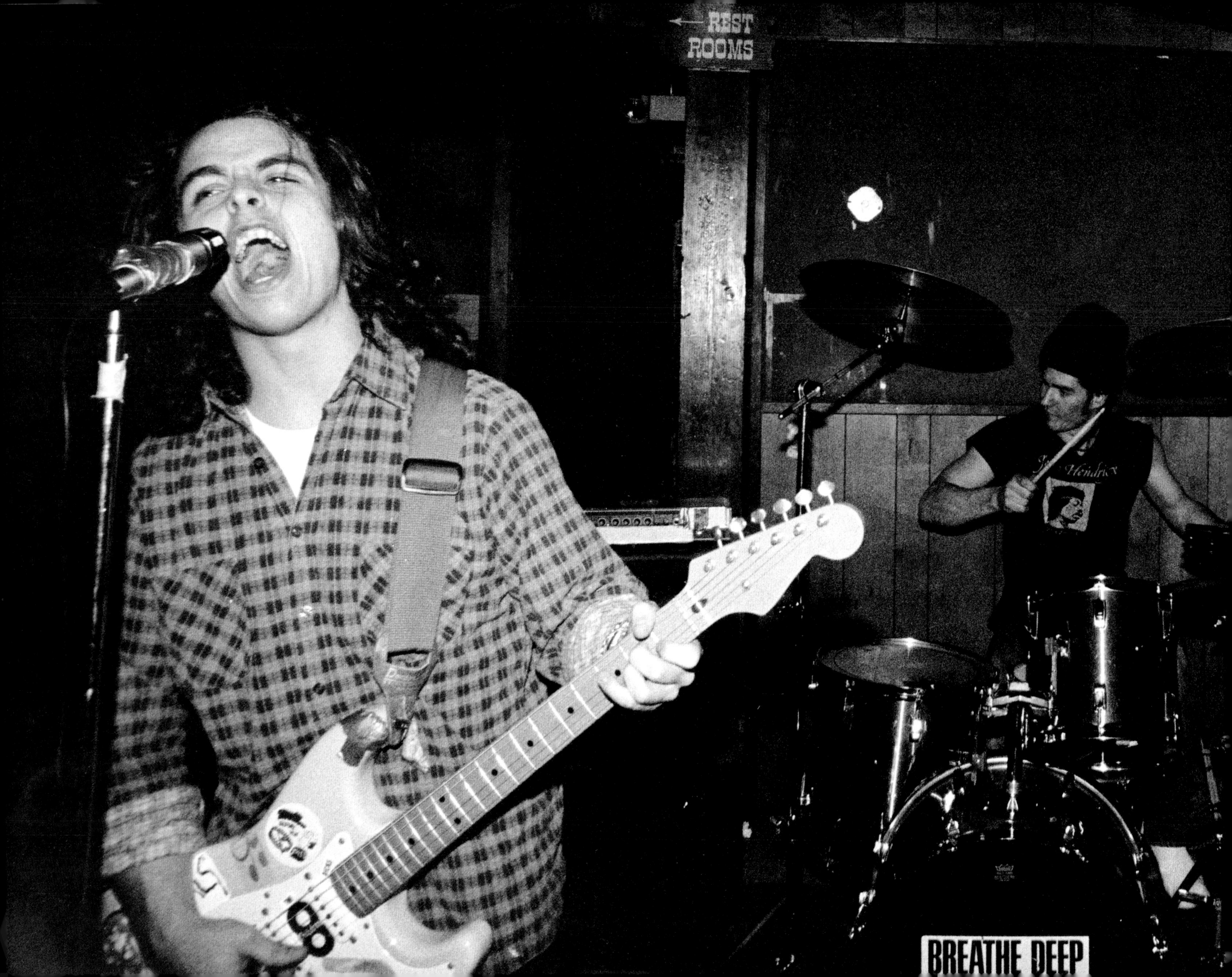
REST
ROOMS
BREATHE DEEP

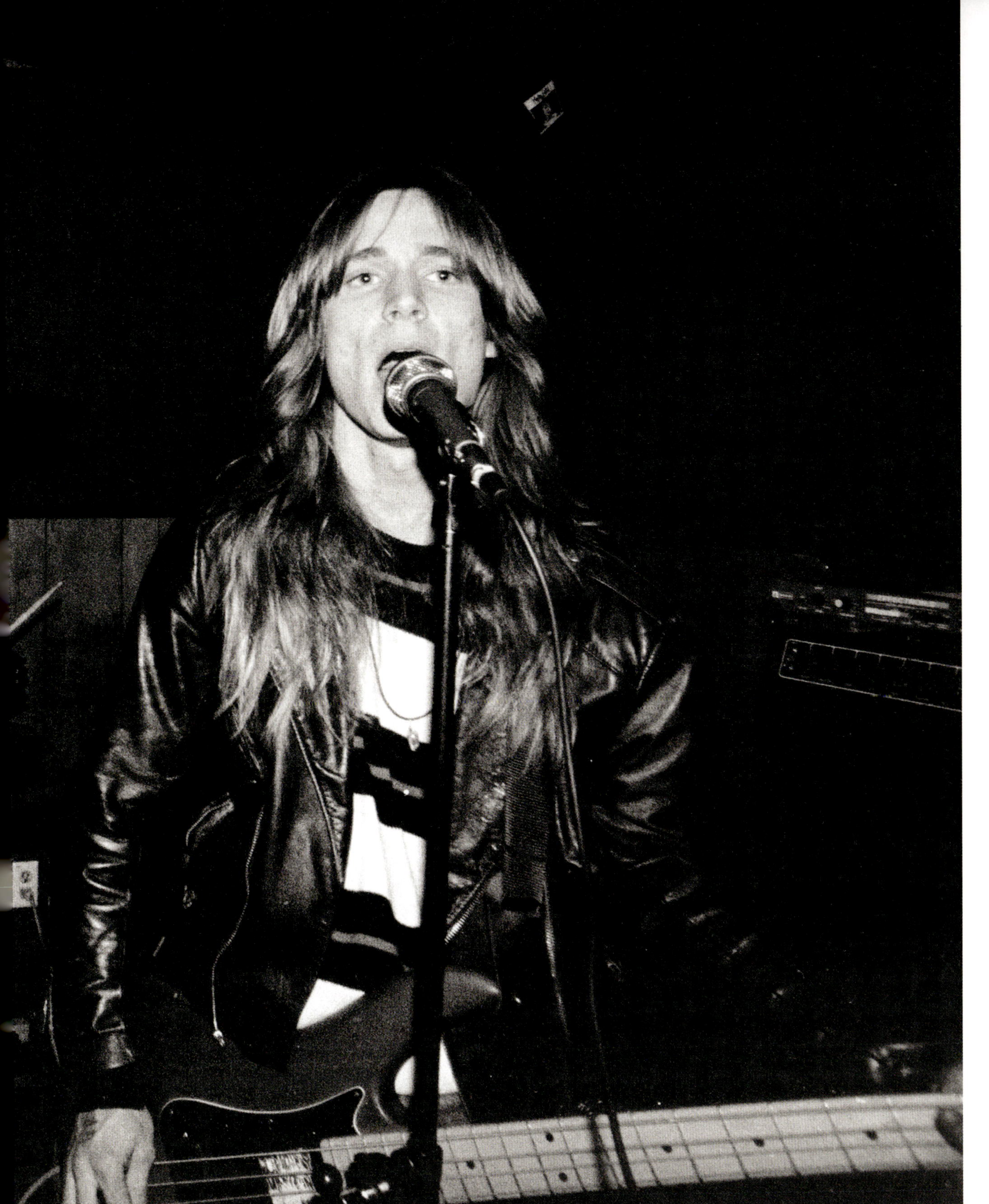

Green Day
Pony Express Pizza, Redwood City, 1990

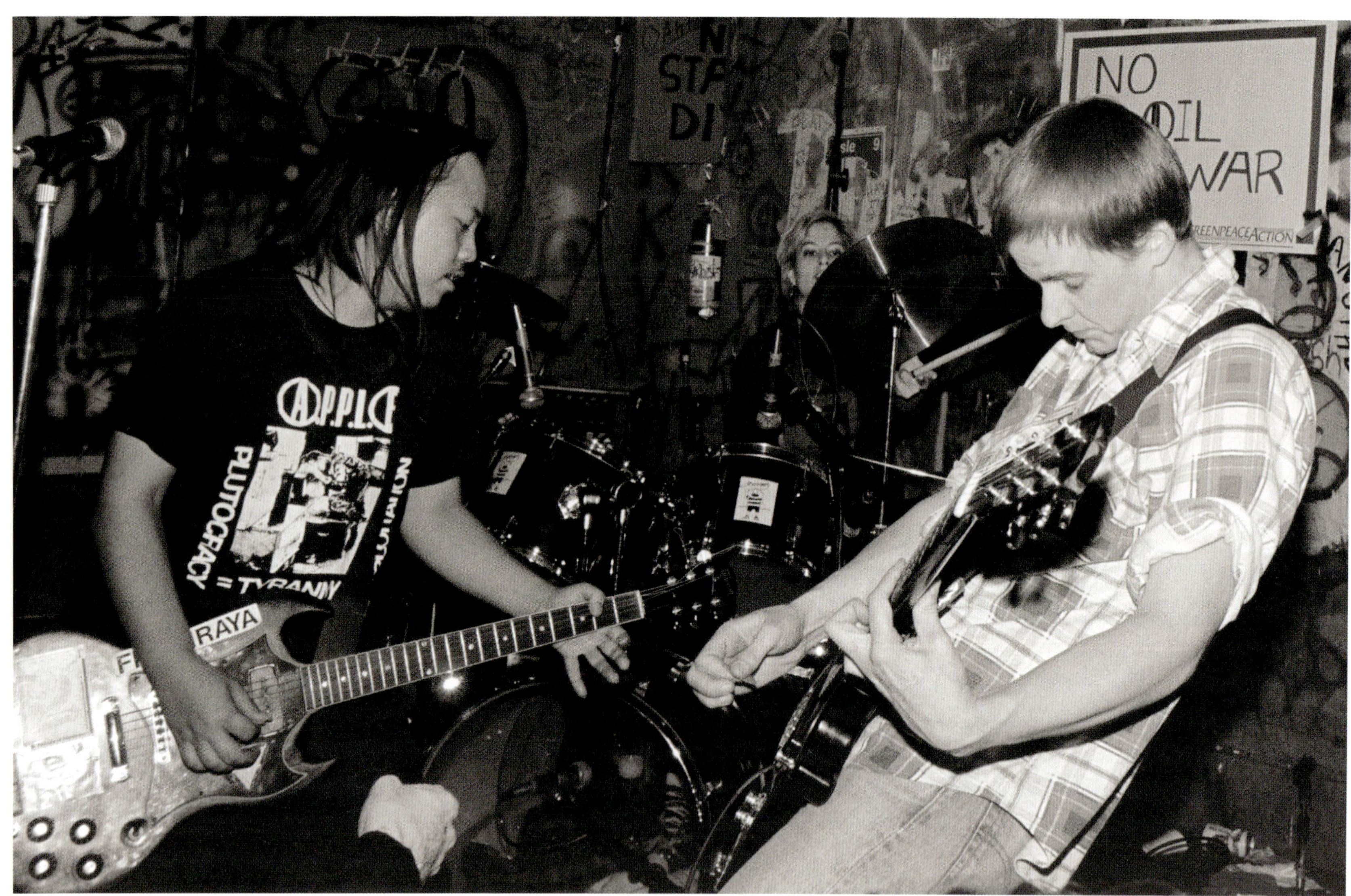

Cringer

Gilman Street, Berkeley, 1991

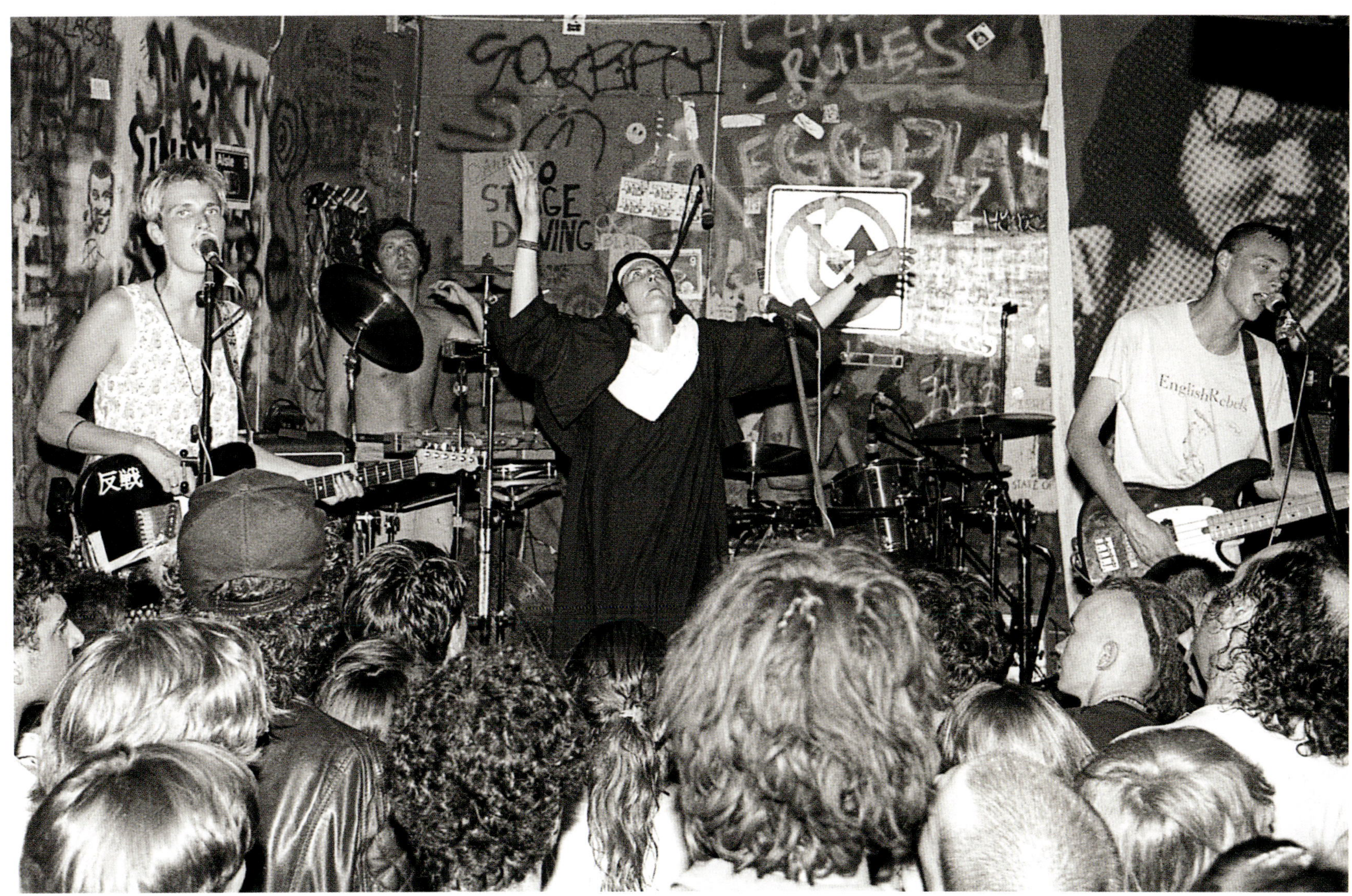

Chumbawamba
Gilman Street, 1990

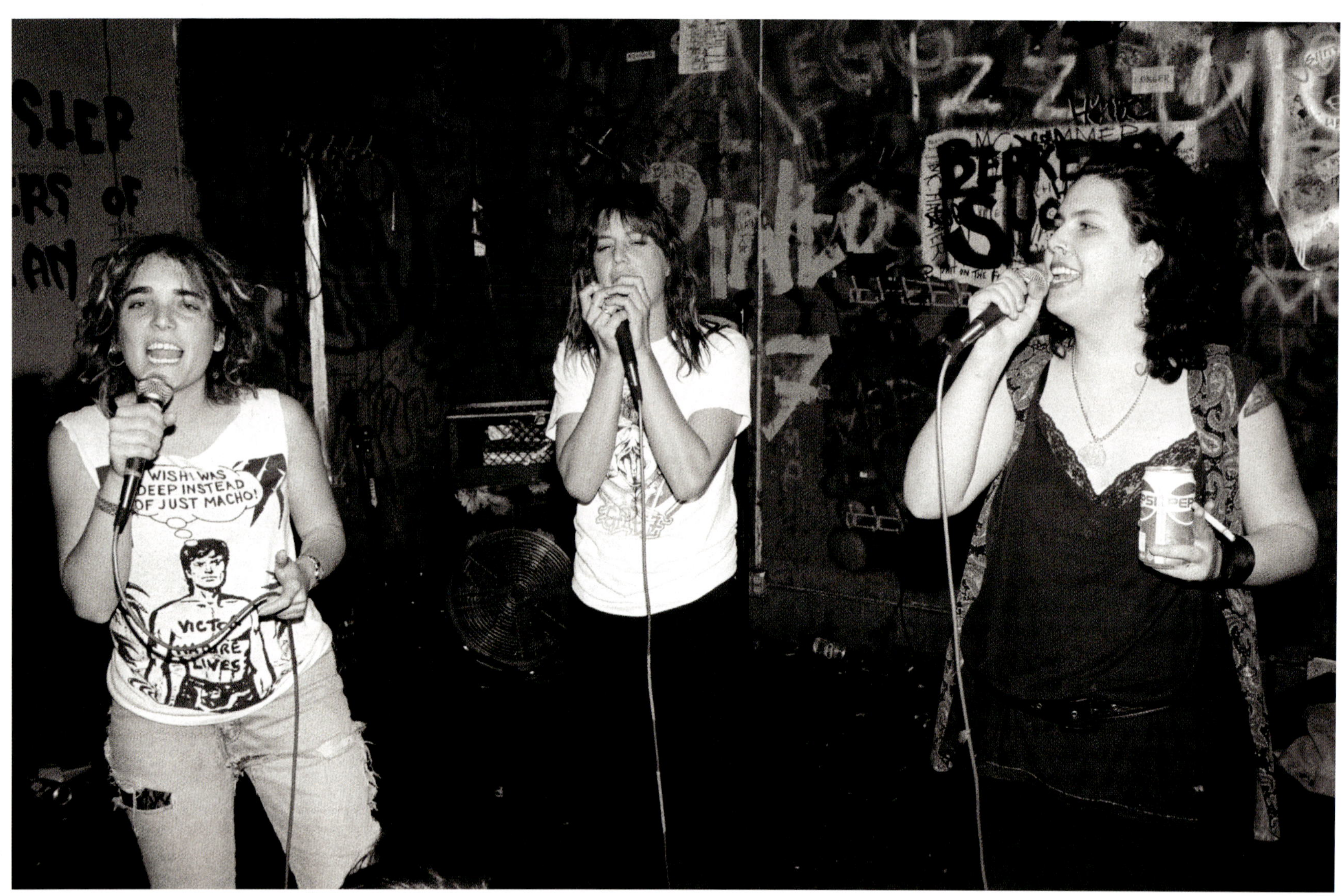

Yeastie Girlz
Gilman Street, Berkeley, 1990

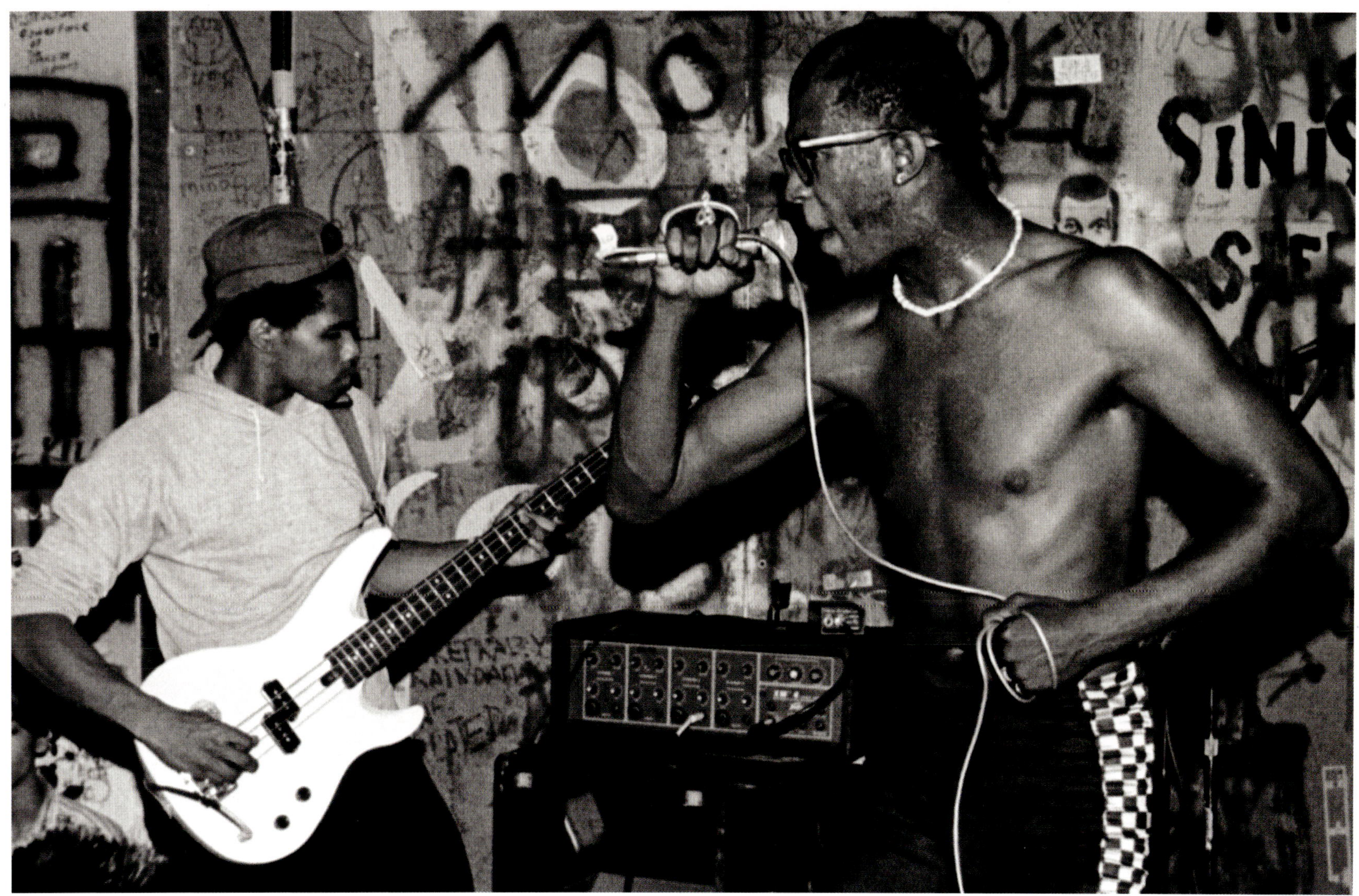

The Hated

Gilman Street, 1990

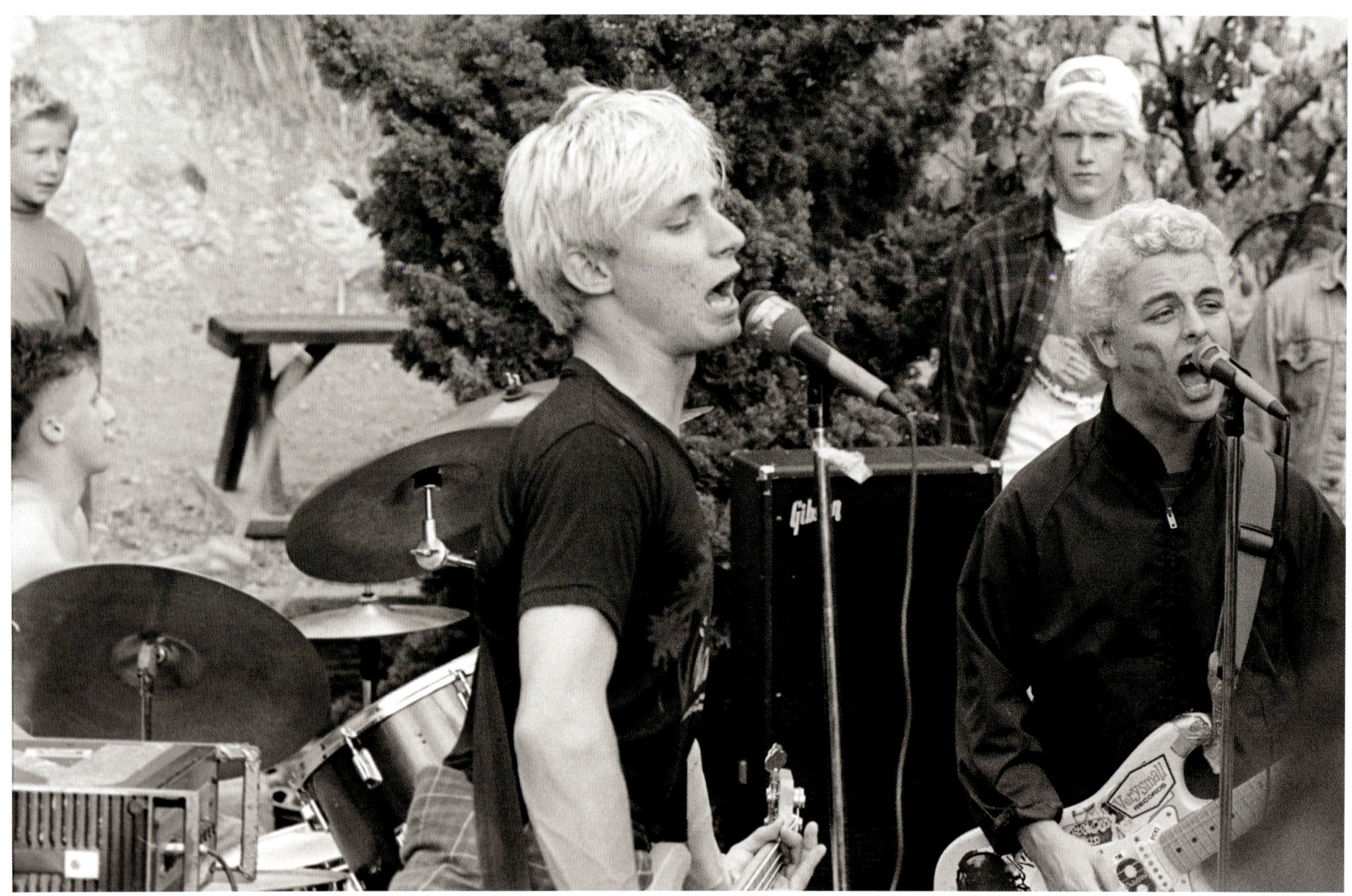

Green Day
Eggplant's Backyard, Pinole, 1990

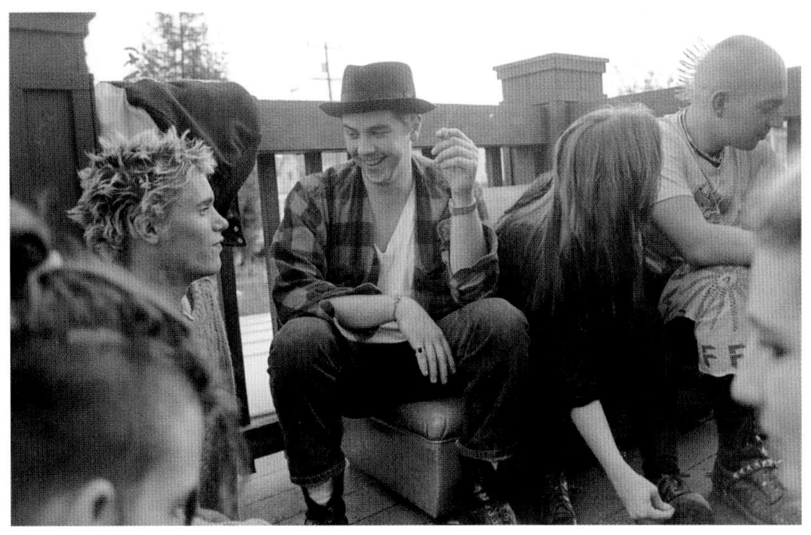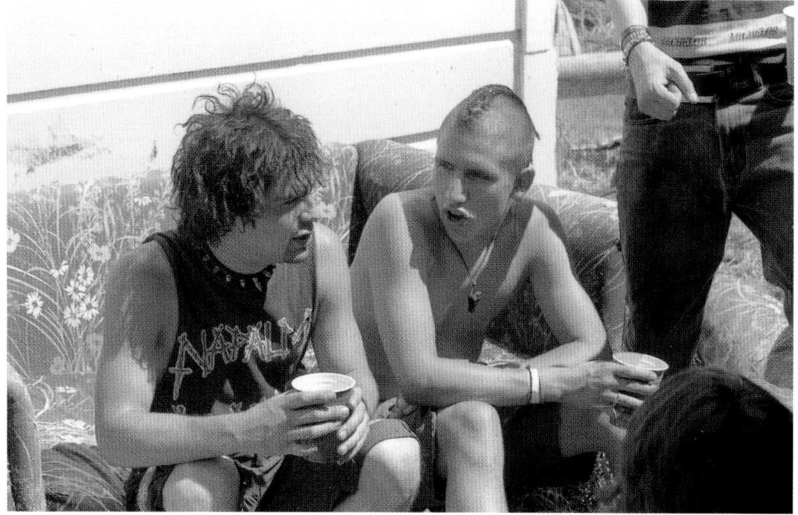

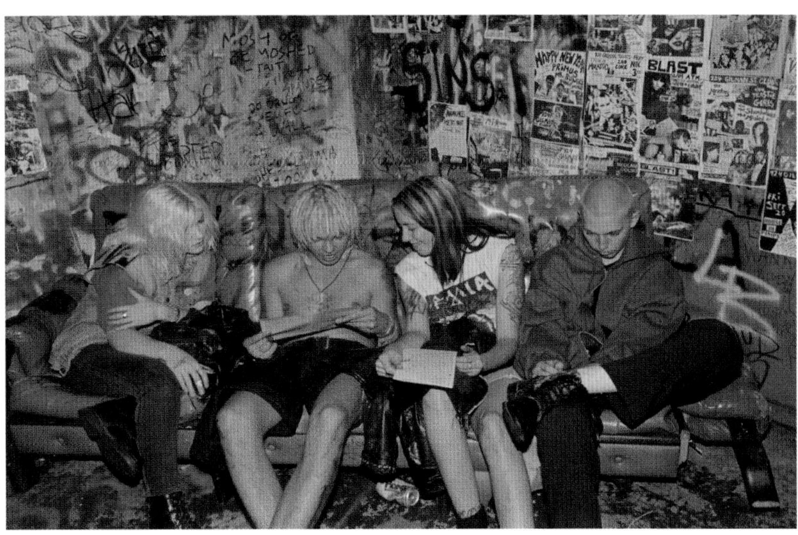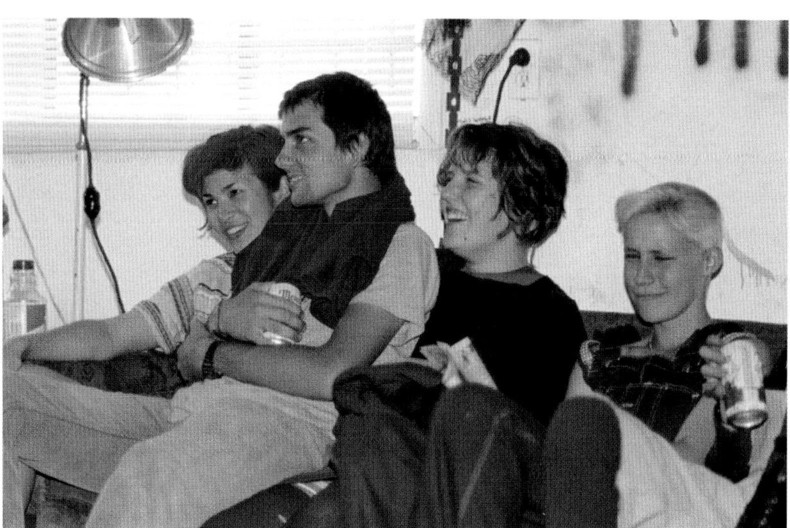

Punks on couches, 1989–1992

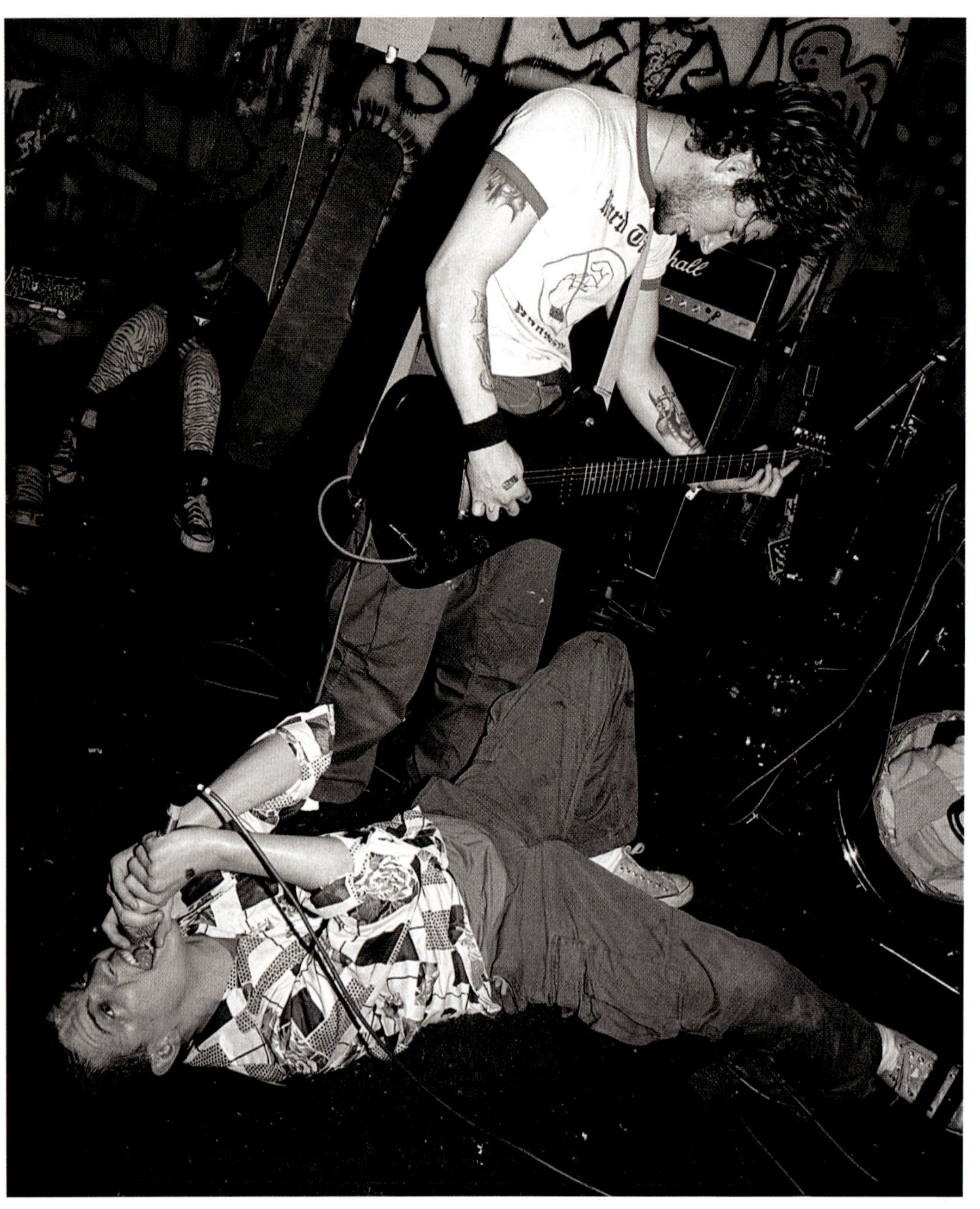

Born Against
Gilman Street, Berkeley, 1991

Opposite:
Spitboy
Gilman Street, 1991

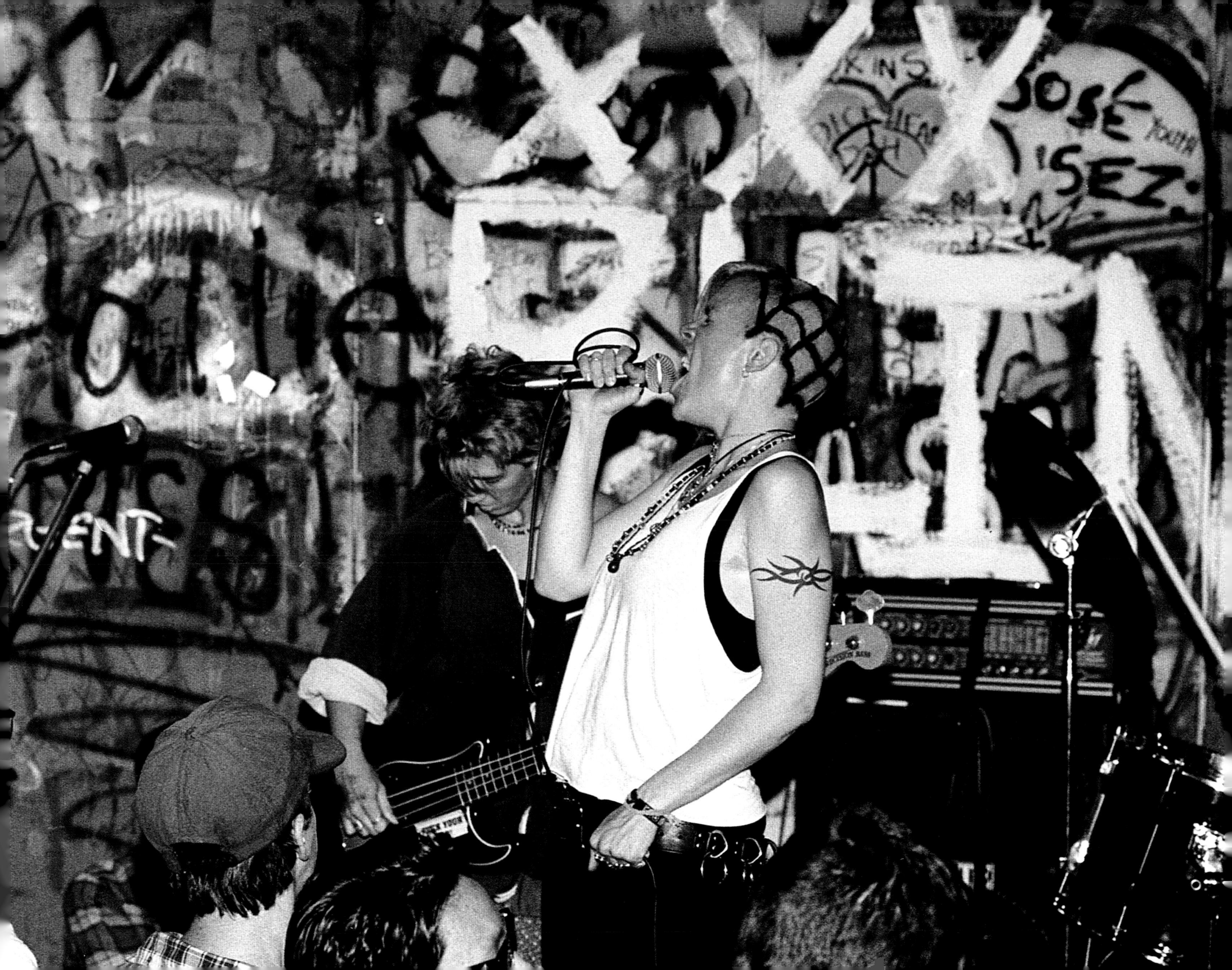
JOSÉ
SEZ.

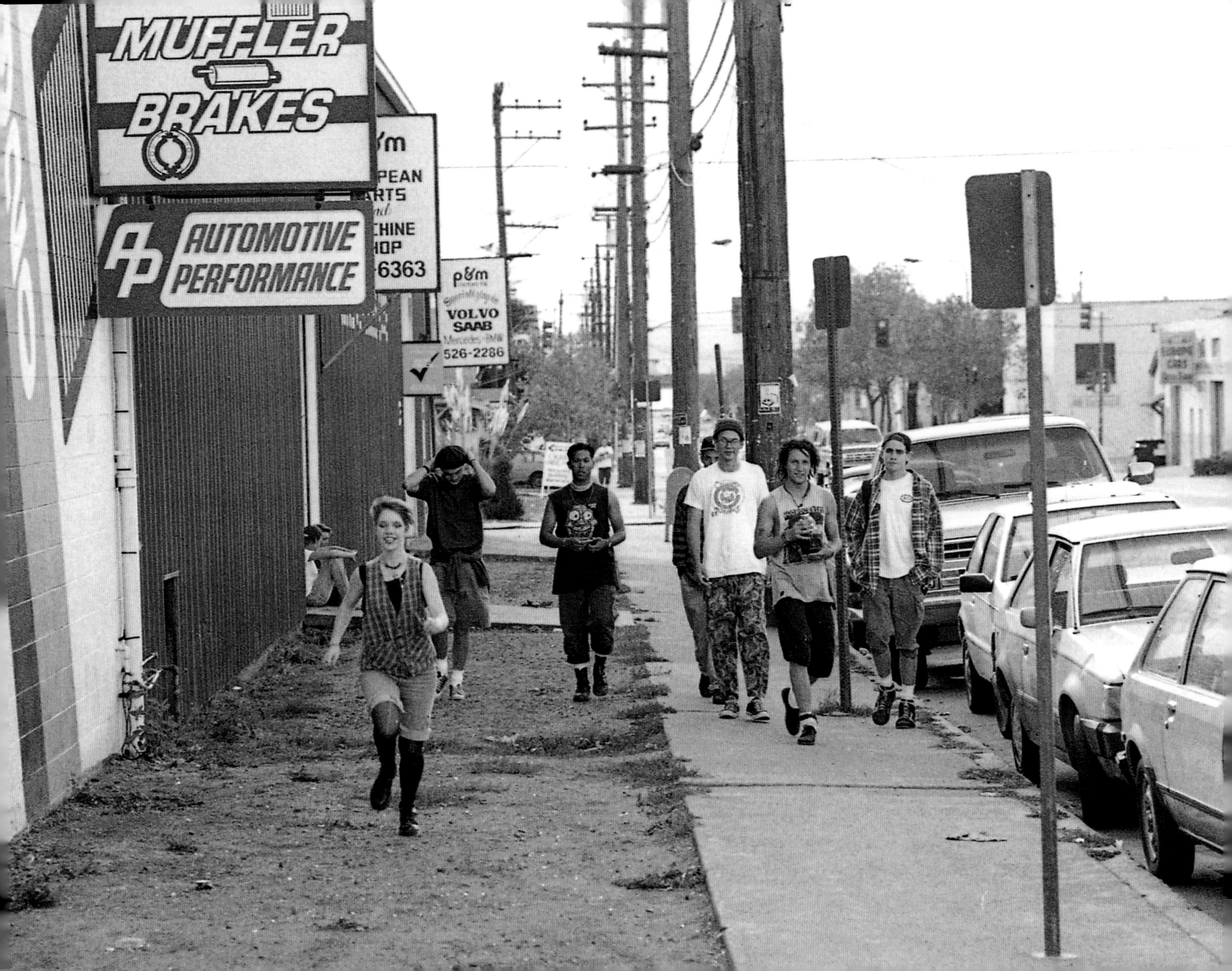

MUFFLER
BRAKES
AUTOMOTIVE
PERFORMANCE
PEAN
ARTS
and
CHINE
HOP
6363
p&m
VOLVO
SAAB
Mercedes-BMW
526-2286

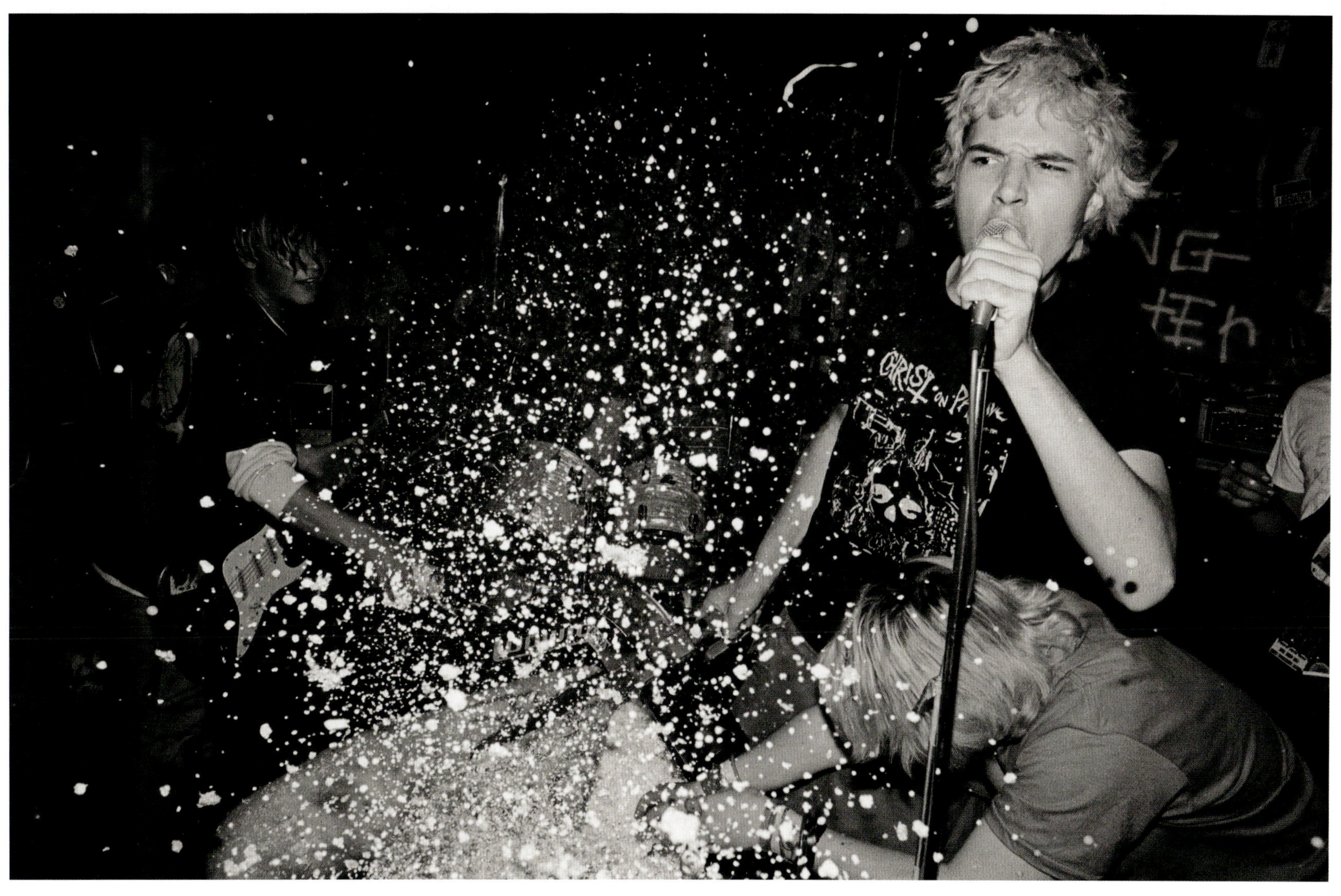

Blatz

Gilman Street, Berkeley, 1990

Opposite:

Gilman Street, 1991

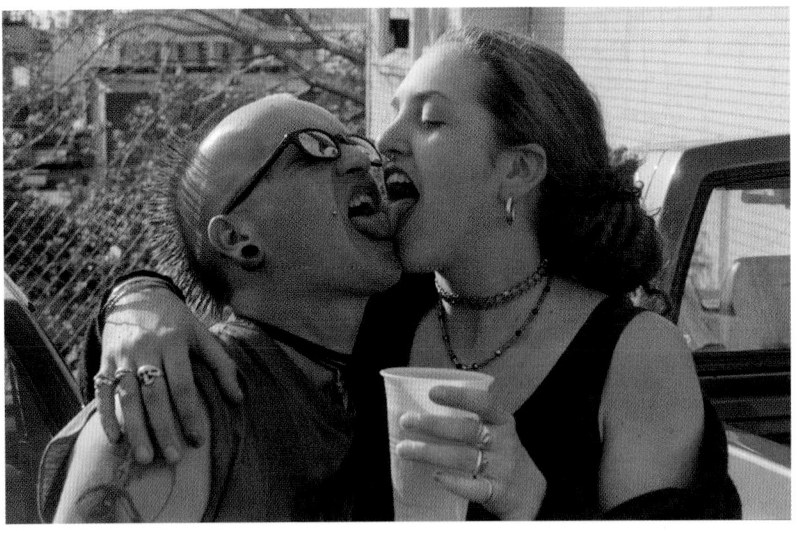
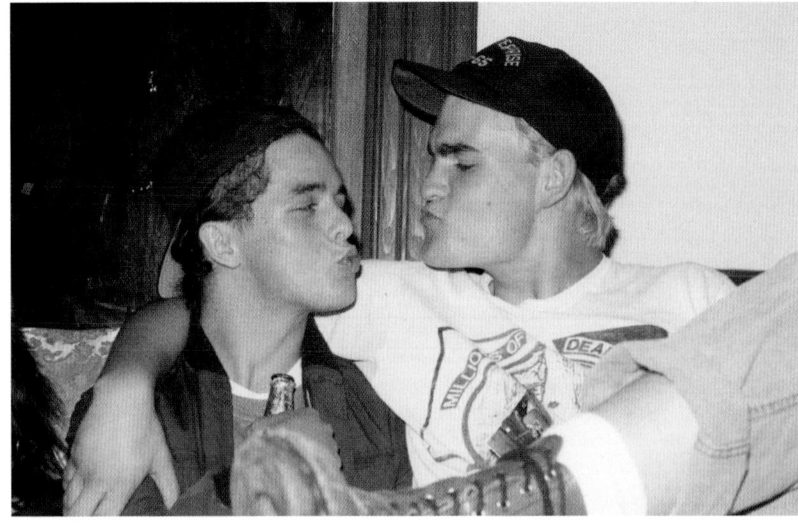
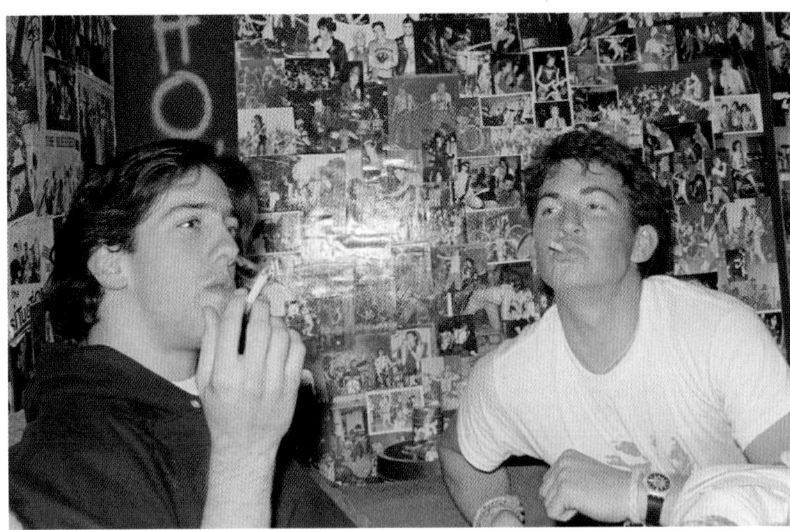
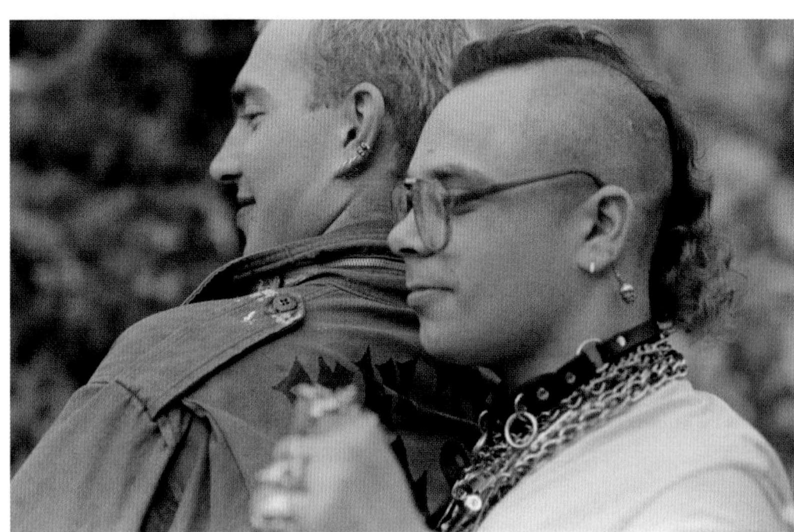

Clockwise from top left: **Trish and Raygun, 1993; Billie Joe and James, 1989; Jake and Fraggle, 1990; Walter and Jason, 1987**

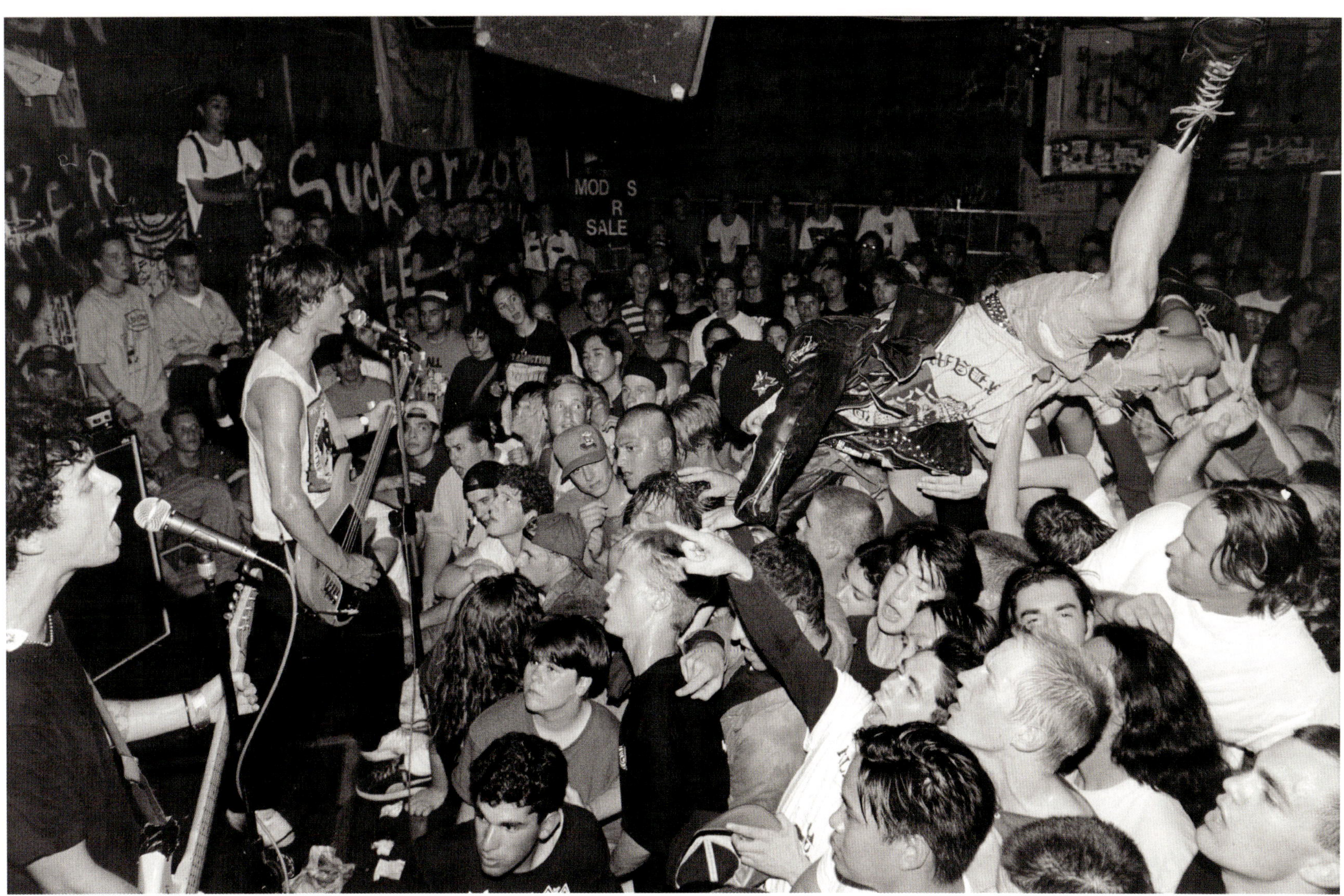

Green Day

Gilman Street, Berkeley, 1992

Following spread:

Neurosis

Anti Club, Los Angeles, 1990

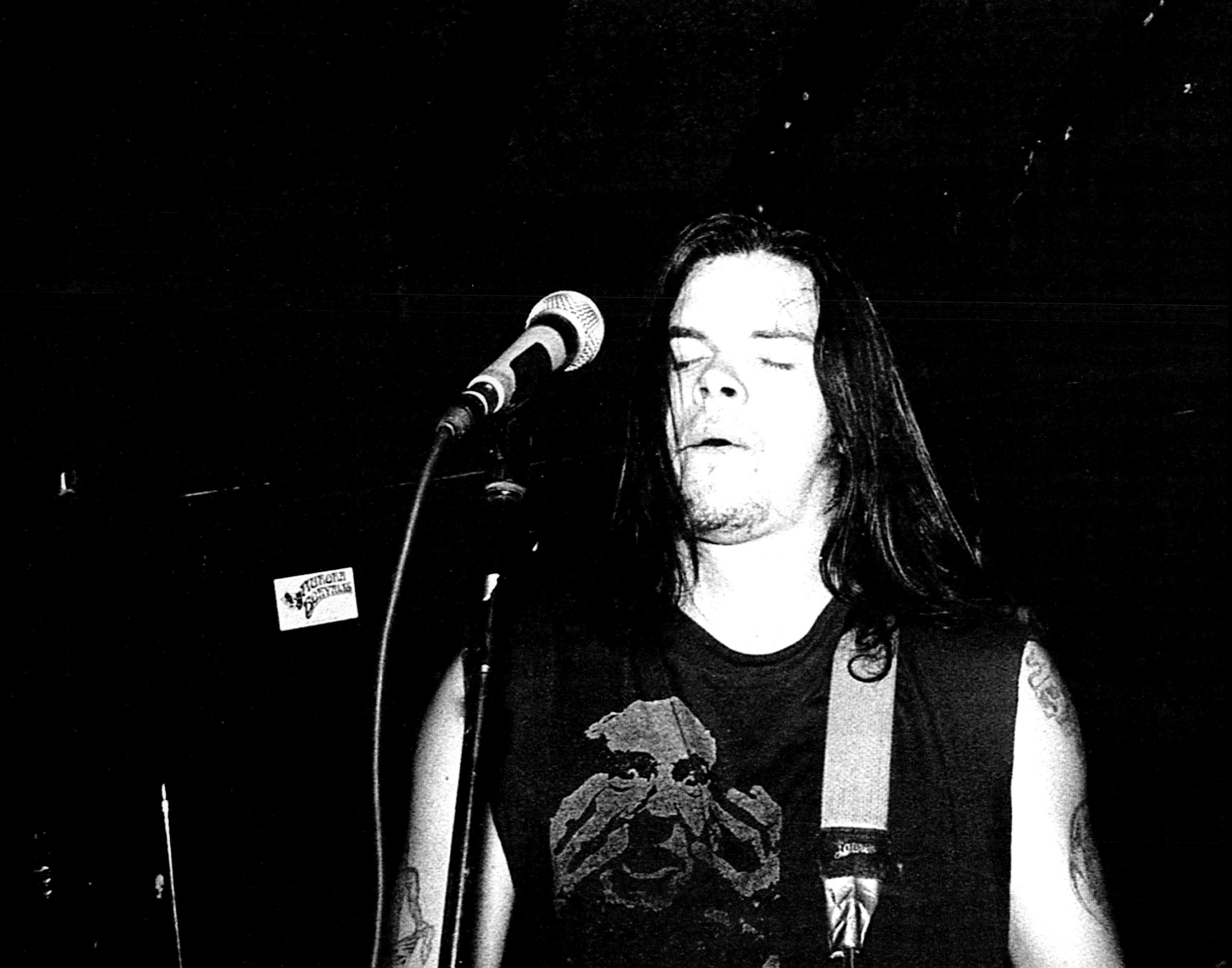

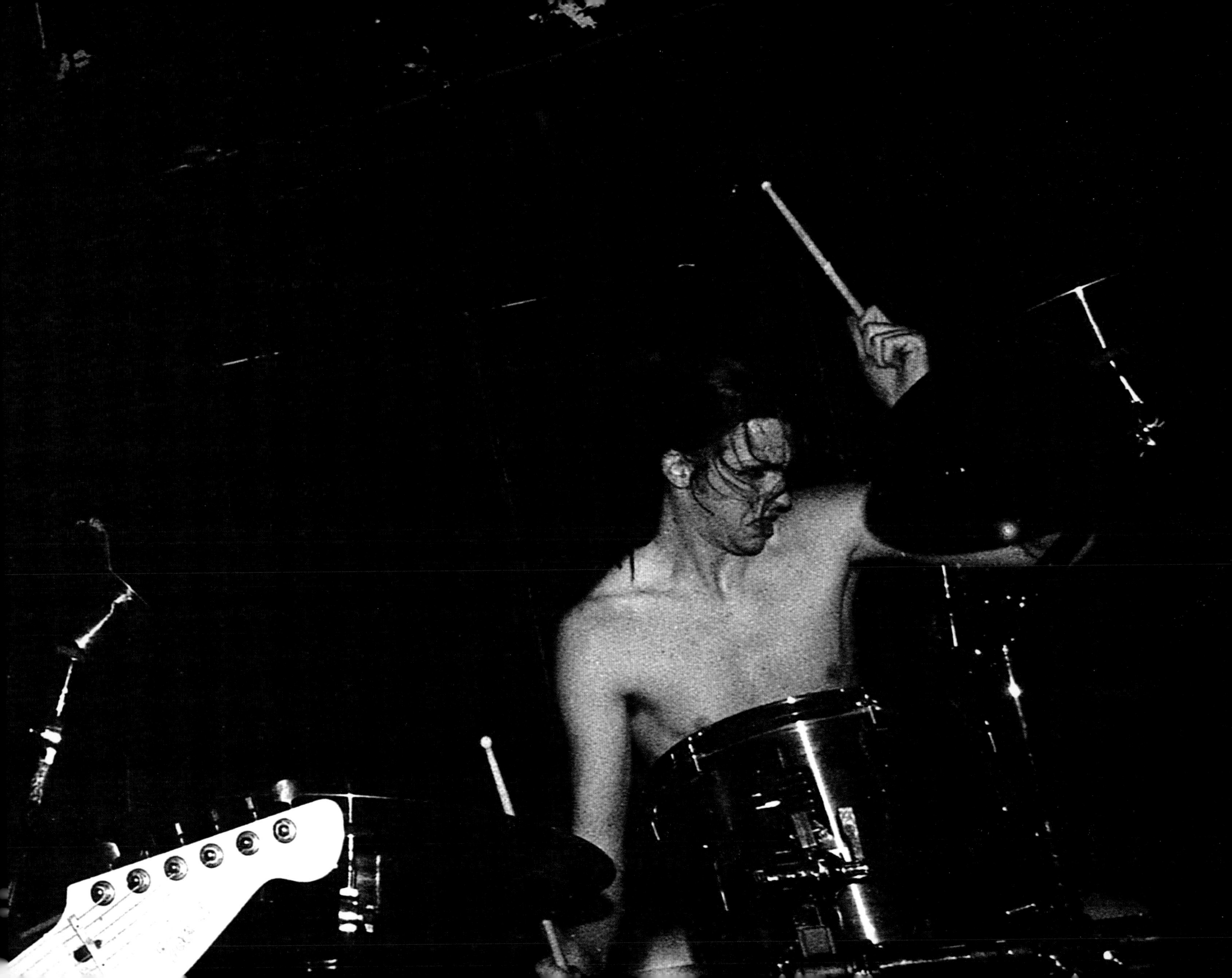

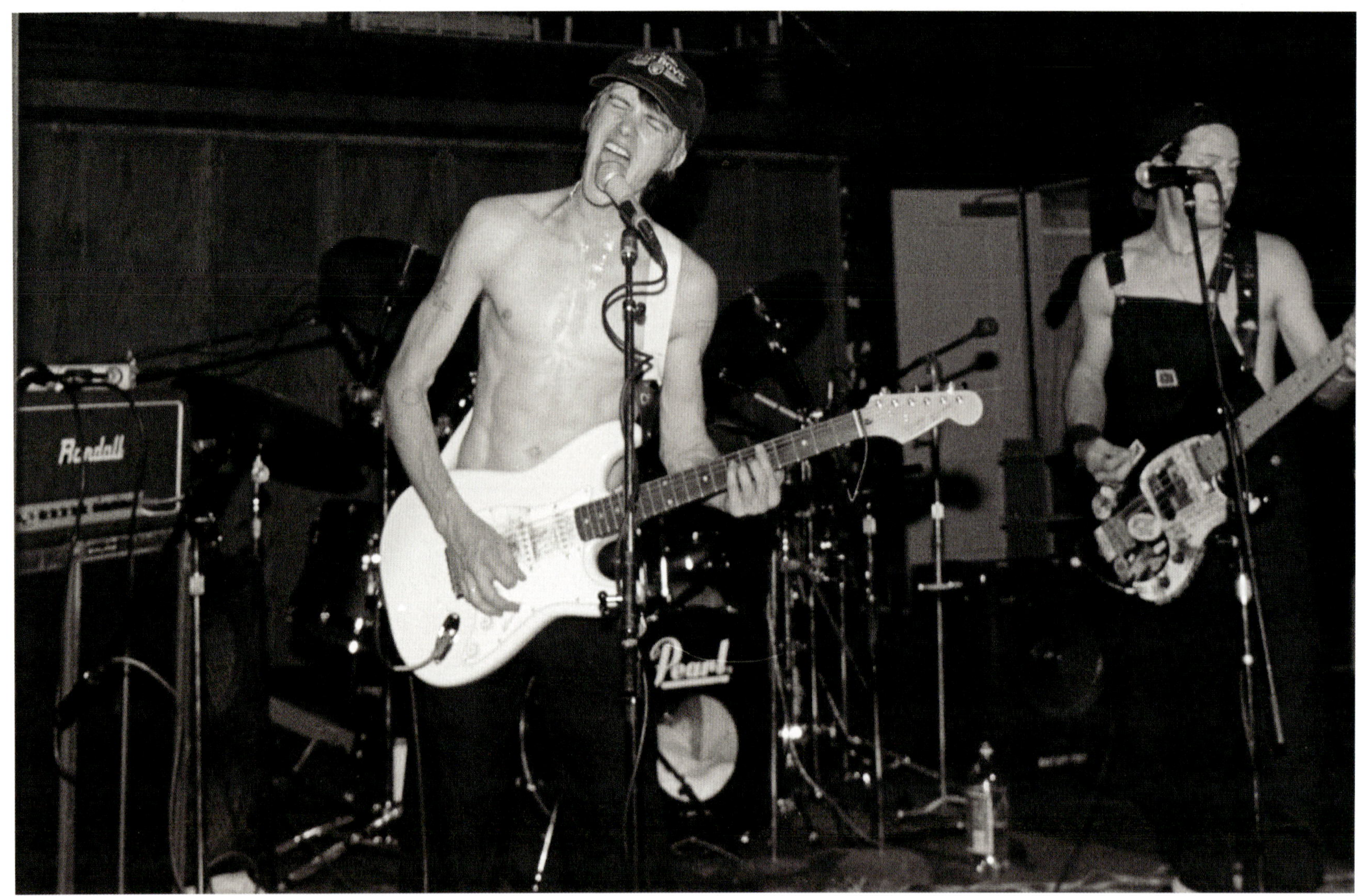

Fifteen
Sonoma, 1992

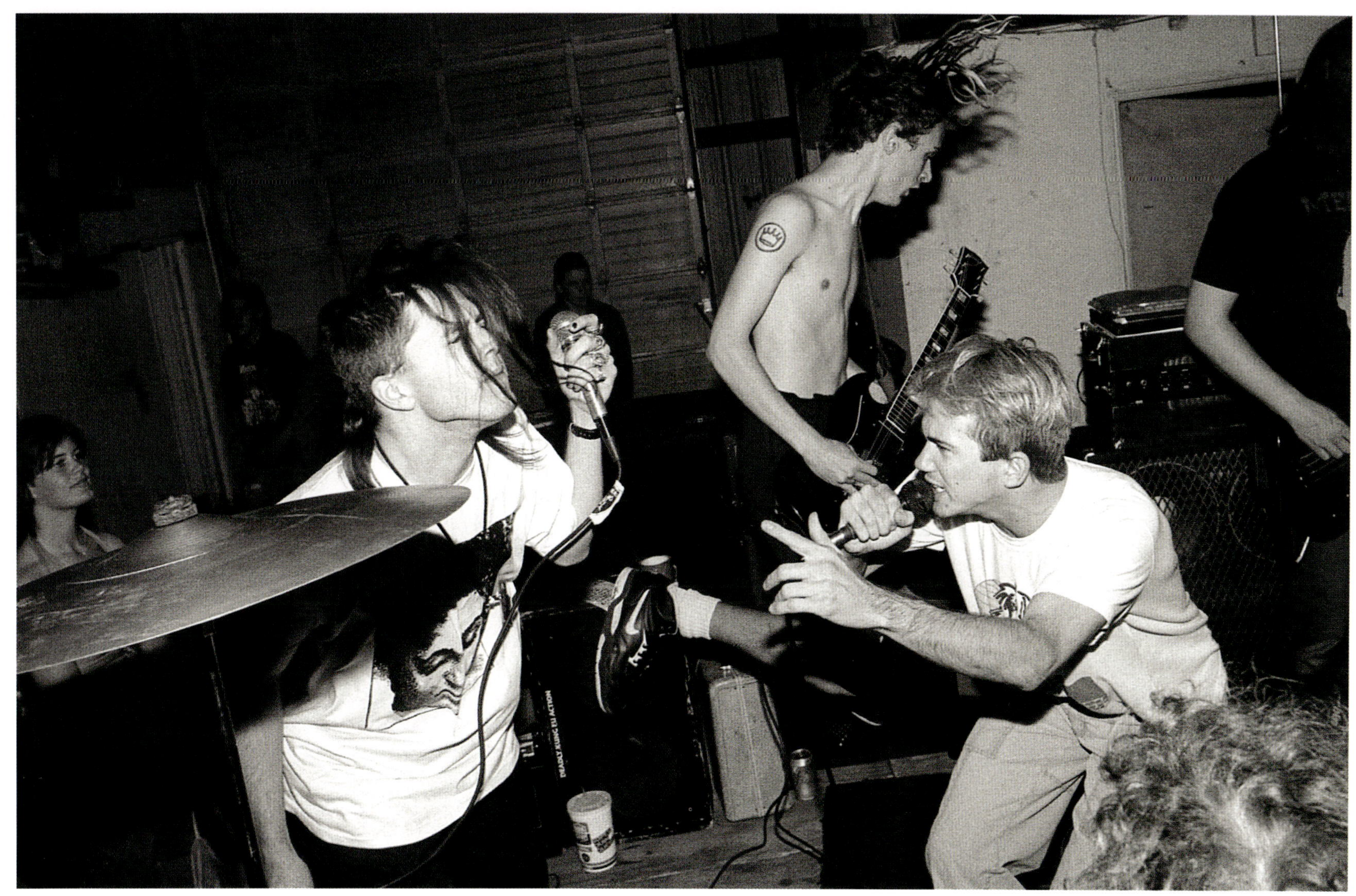

Warlock Pinchers

Petaluma, 1991

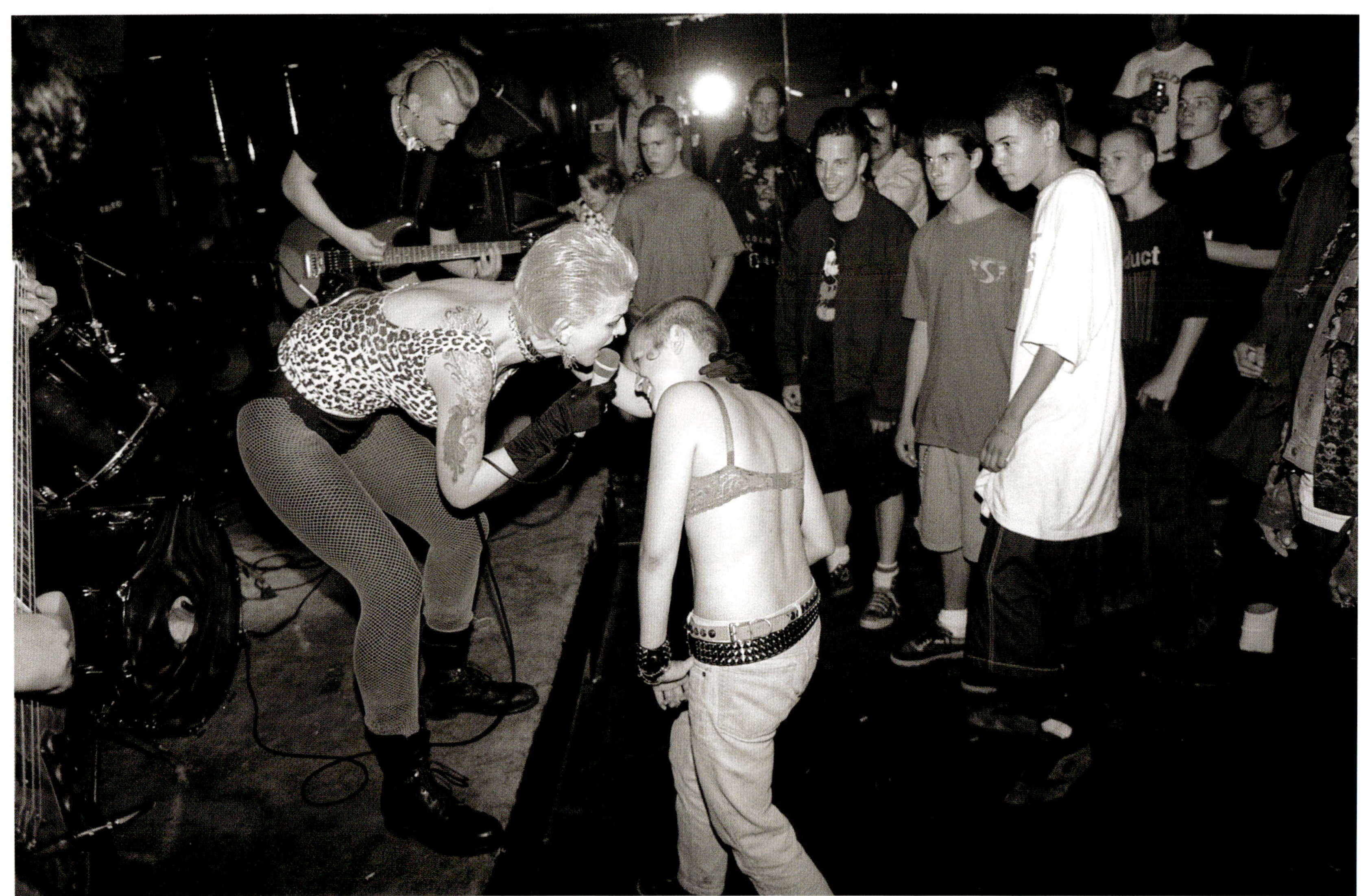

Insaints
Your Place Too, Oakland, 1992

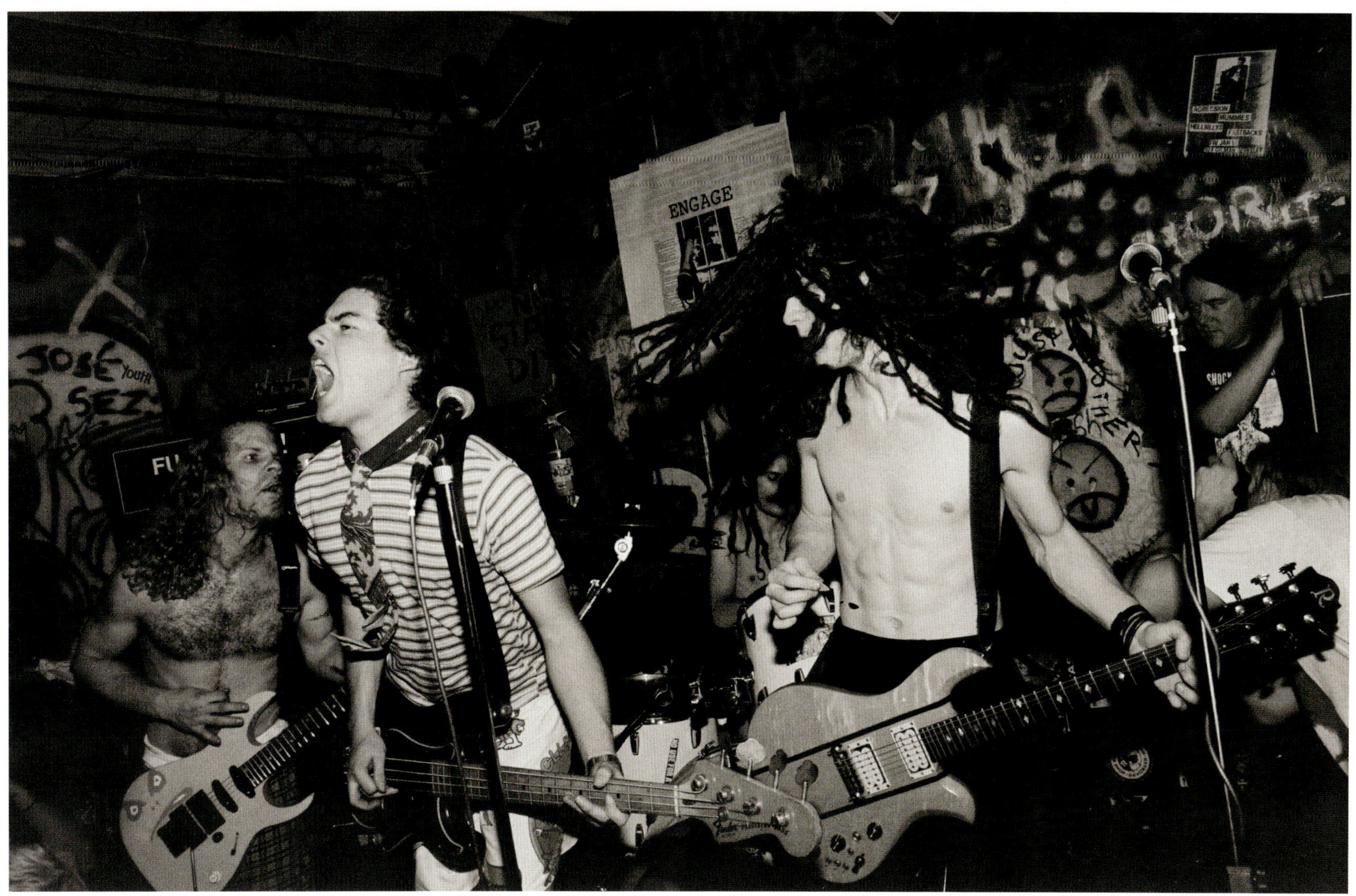

NOFX

Gilman Street, 1991

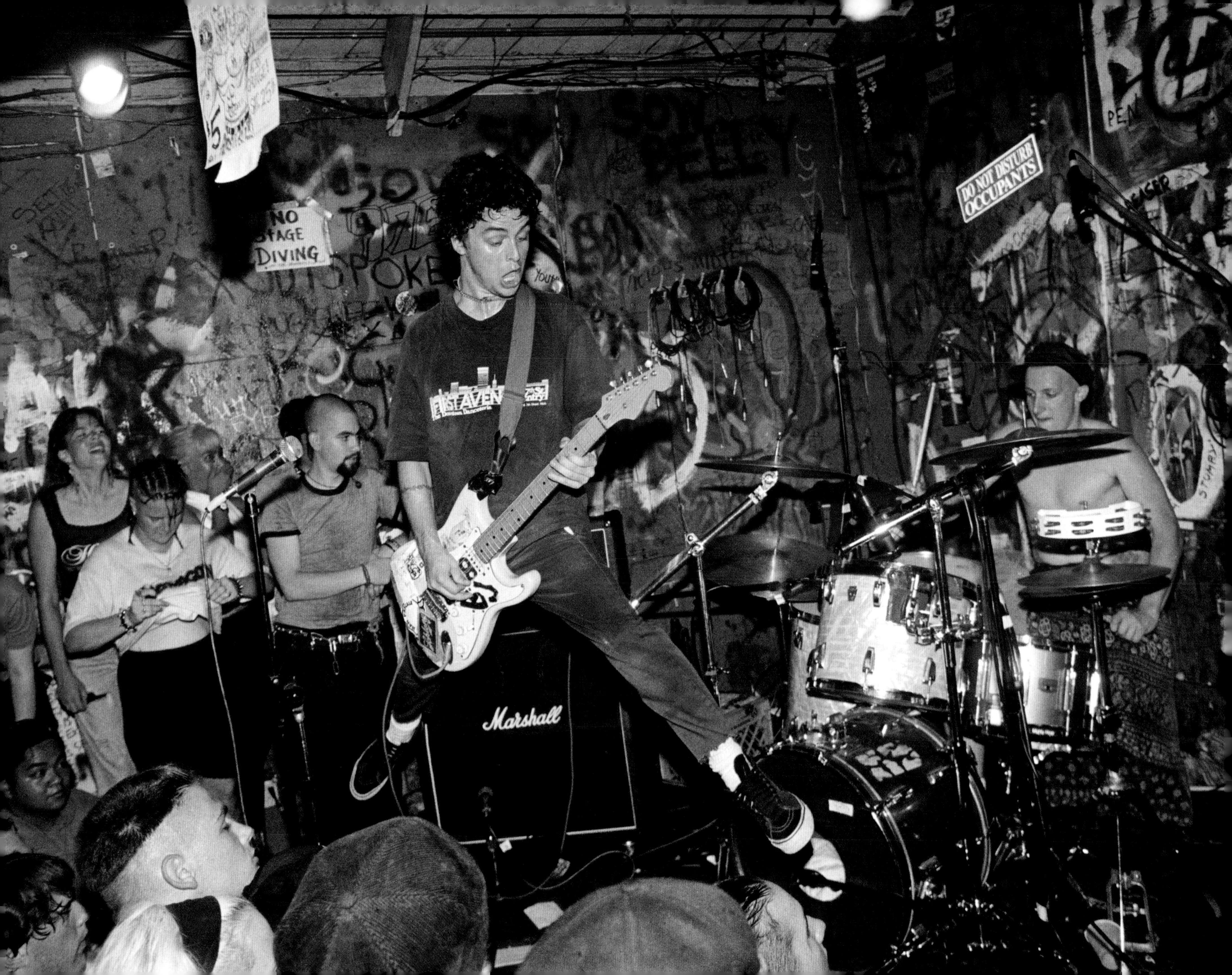

NO
STAGE
DIVING
DO NOT DISTURB
OCCUPANTS
FIRST AVENUE
Marshall

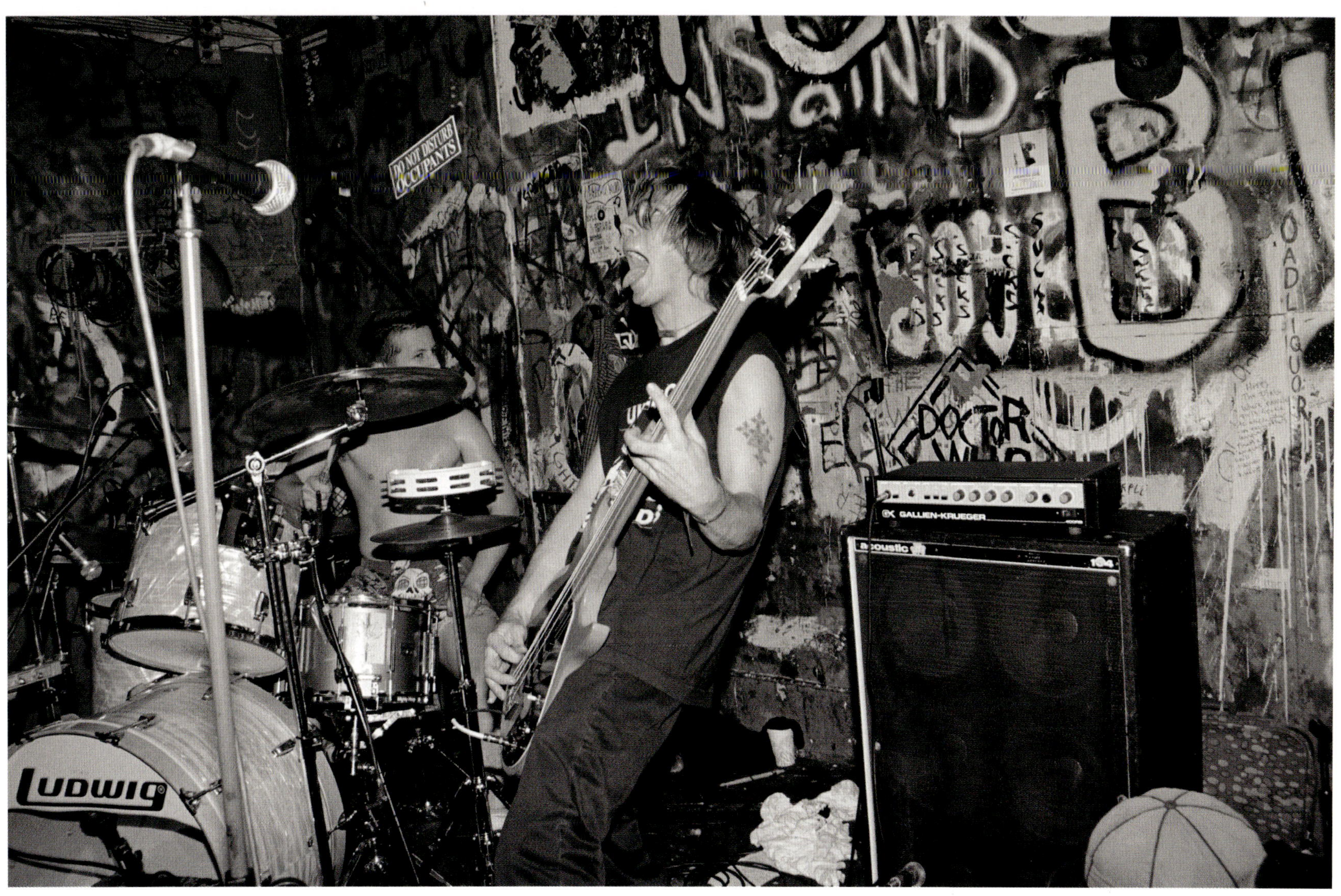

Green Day

Gilman Street, Berkeley, 1992

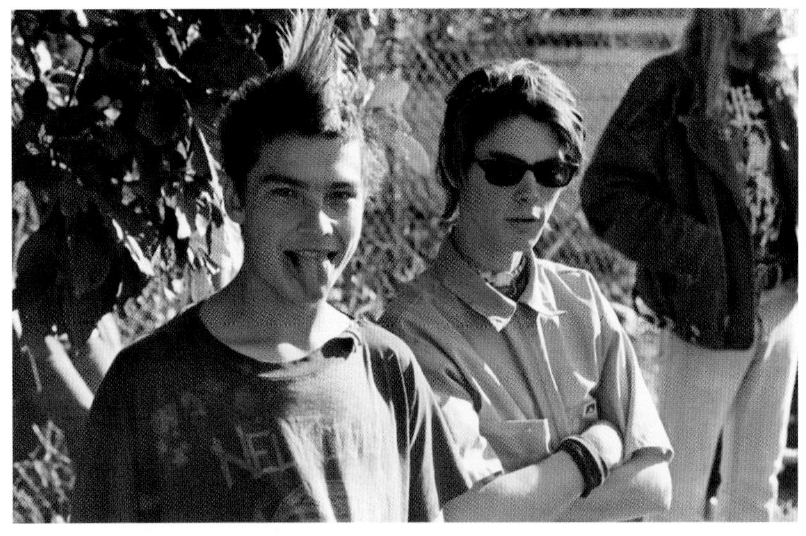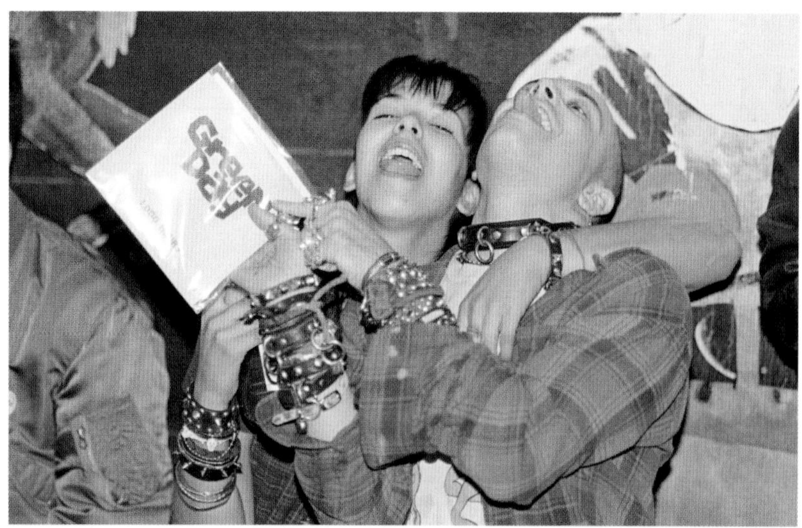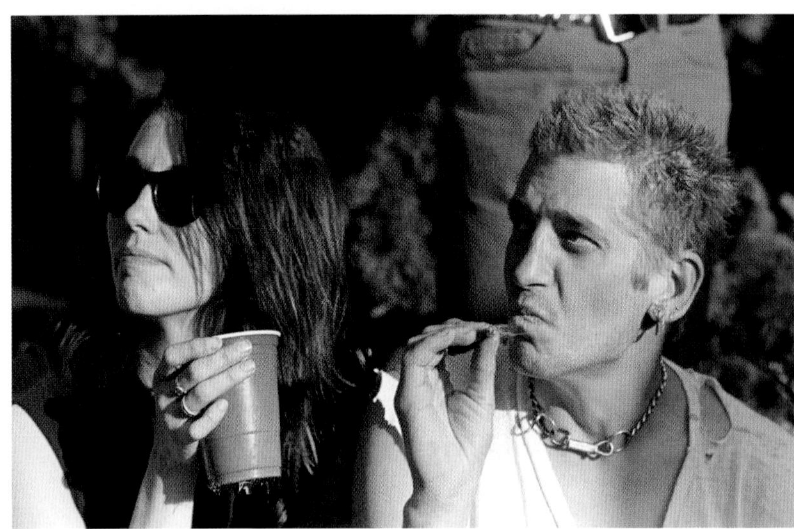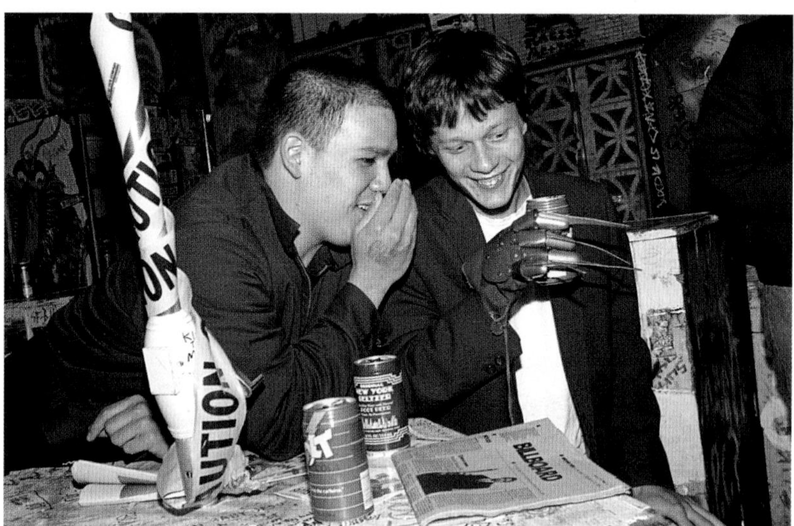

Clockwise from top left: **Eggplant and Joey, 1990; Nana and Fraggle, 1991; Eric and Claude, 1991; Kate and Todd, 1990**

Opposite: **Nando's Backyard, Oakland, 1990**

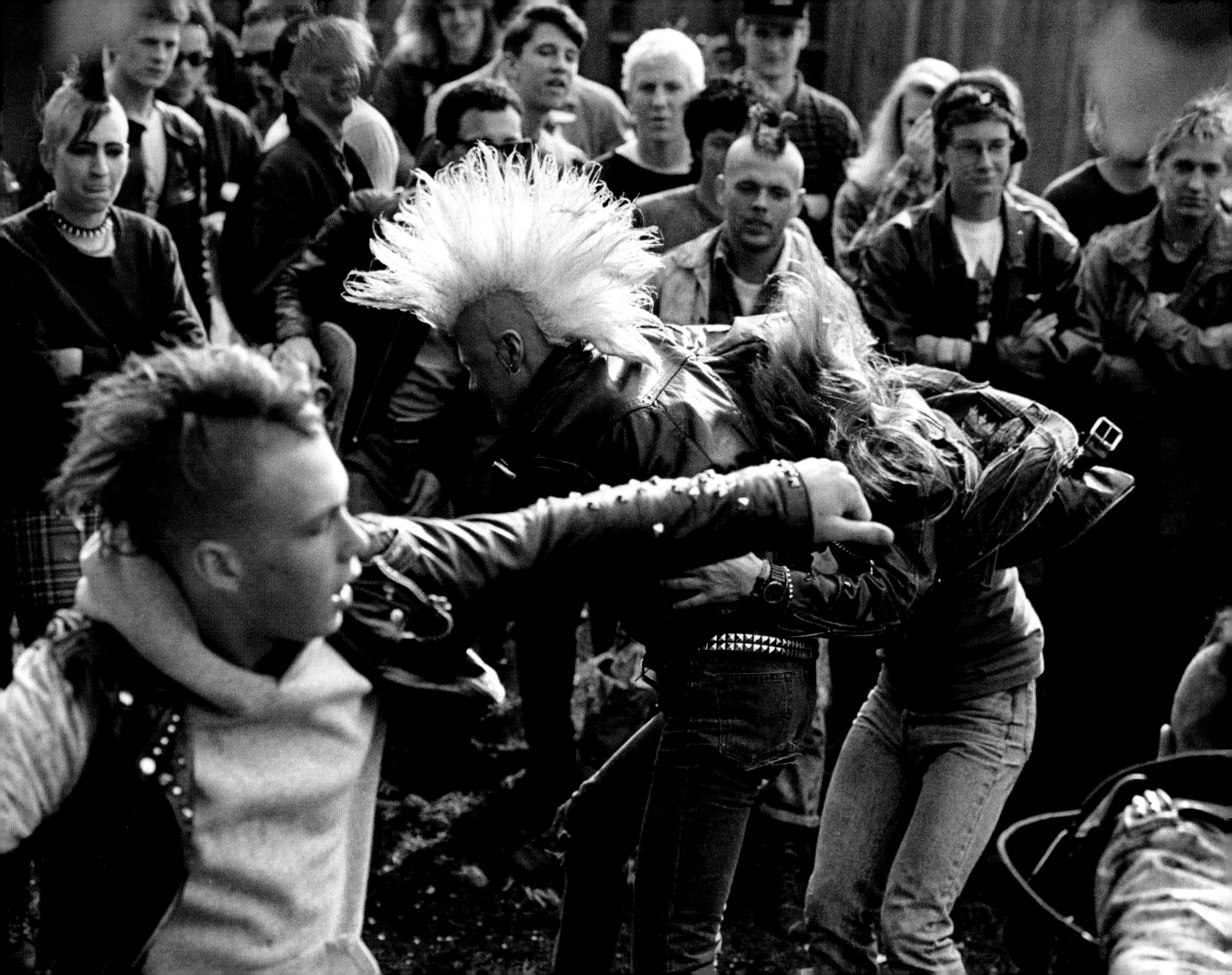

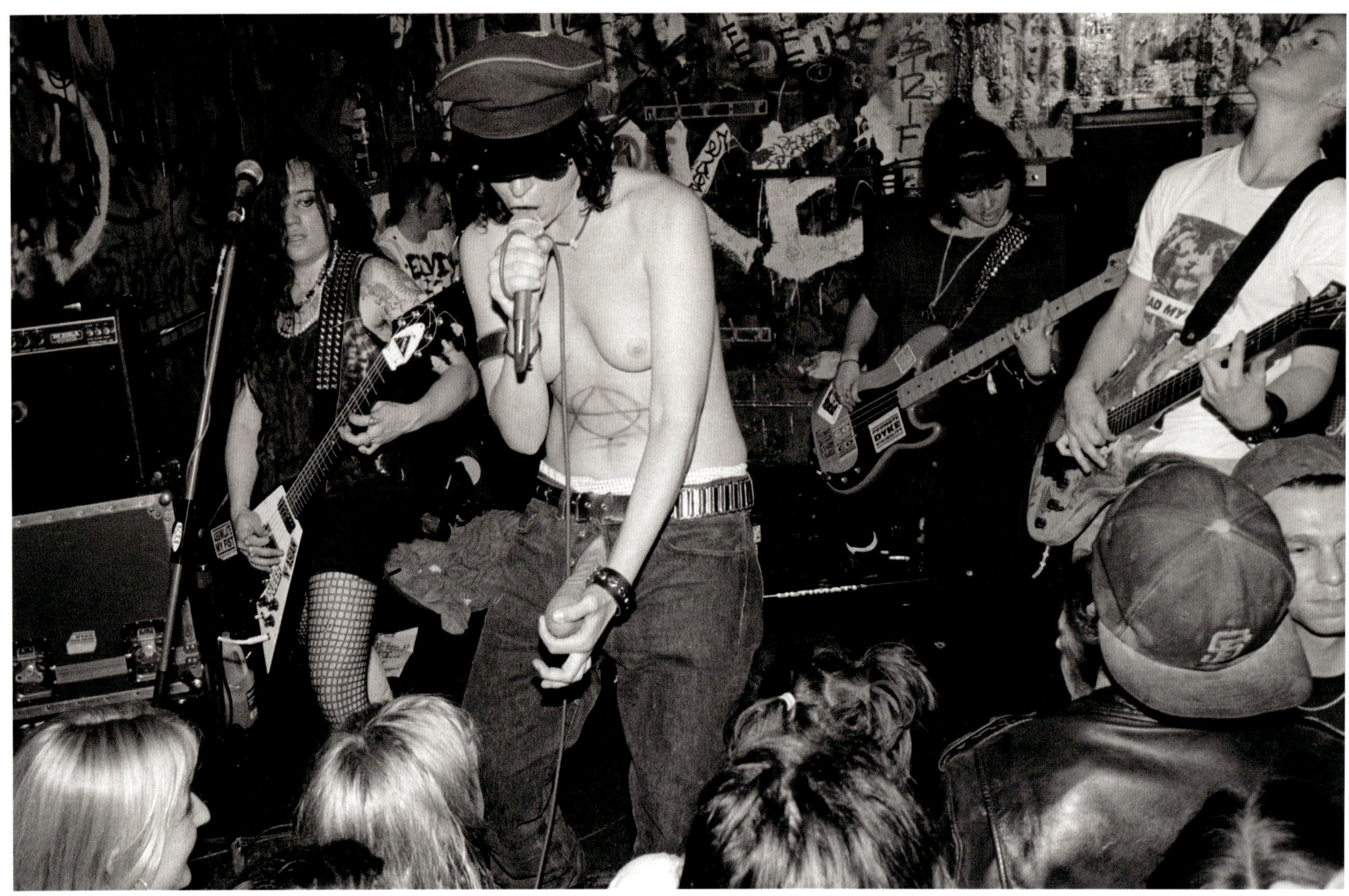

Tribe 8
Gilman Street, Berkeley, 1992

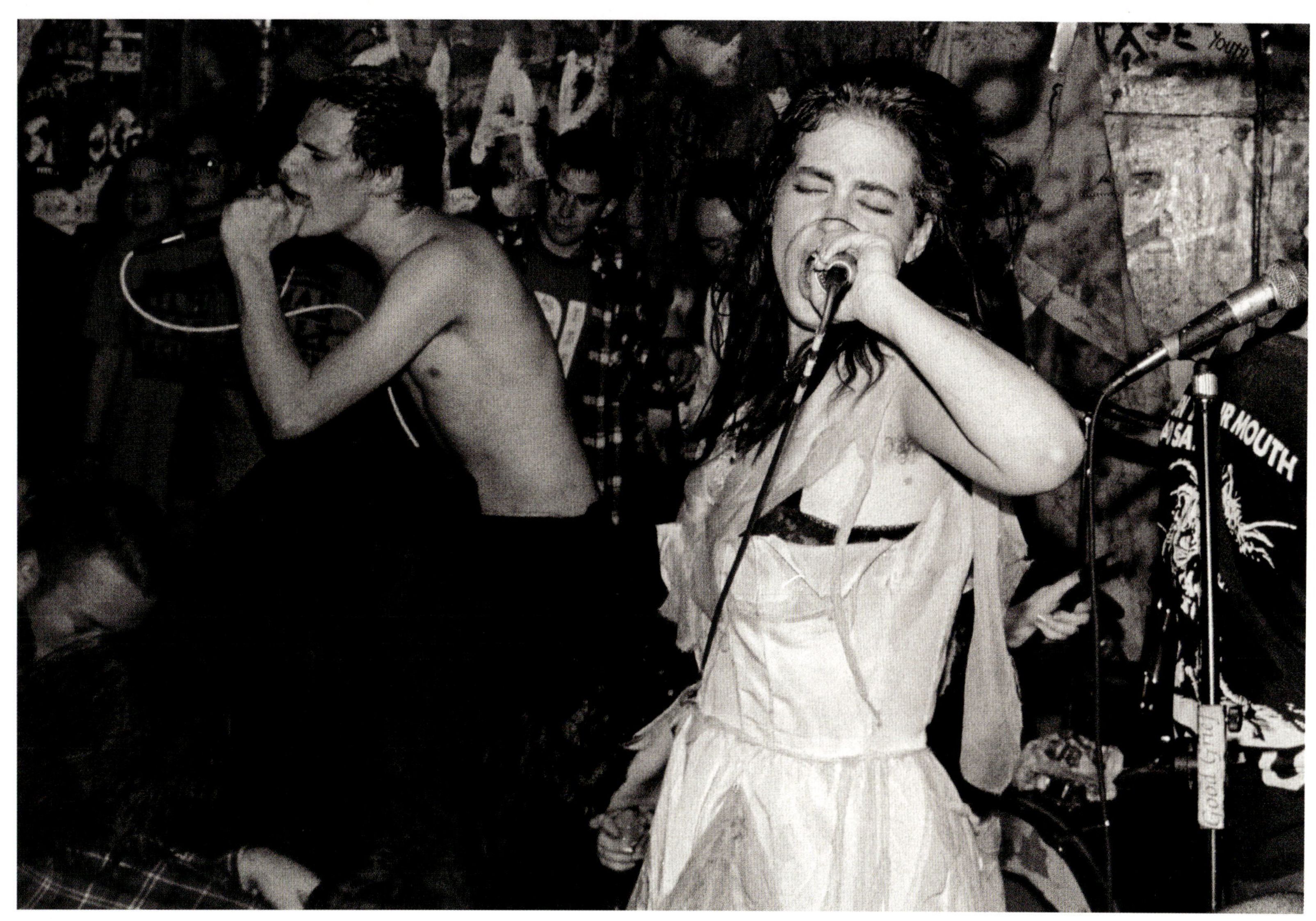

Blatz
Gilman Street, 1991

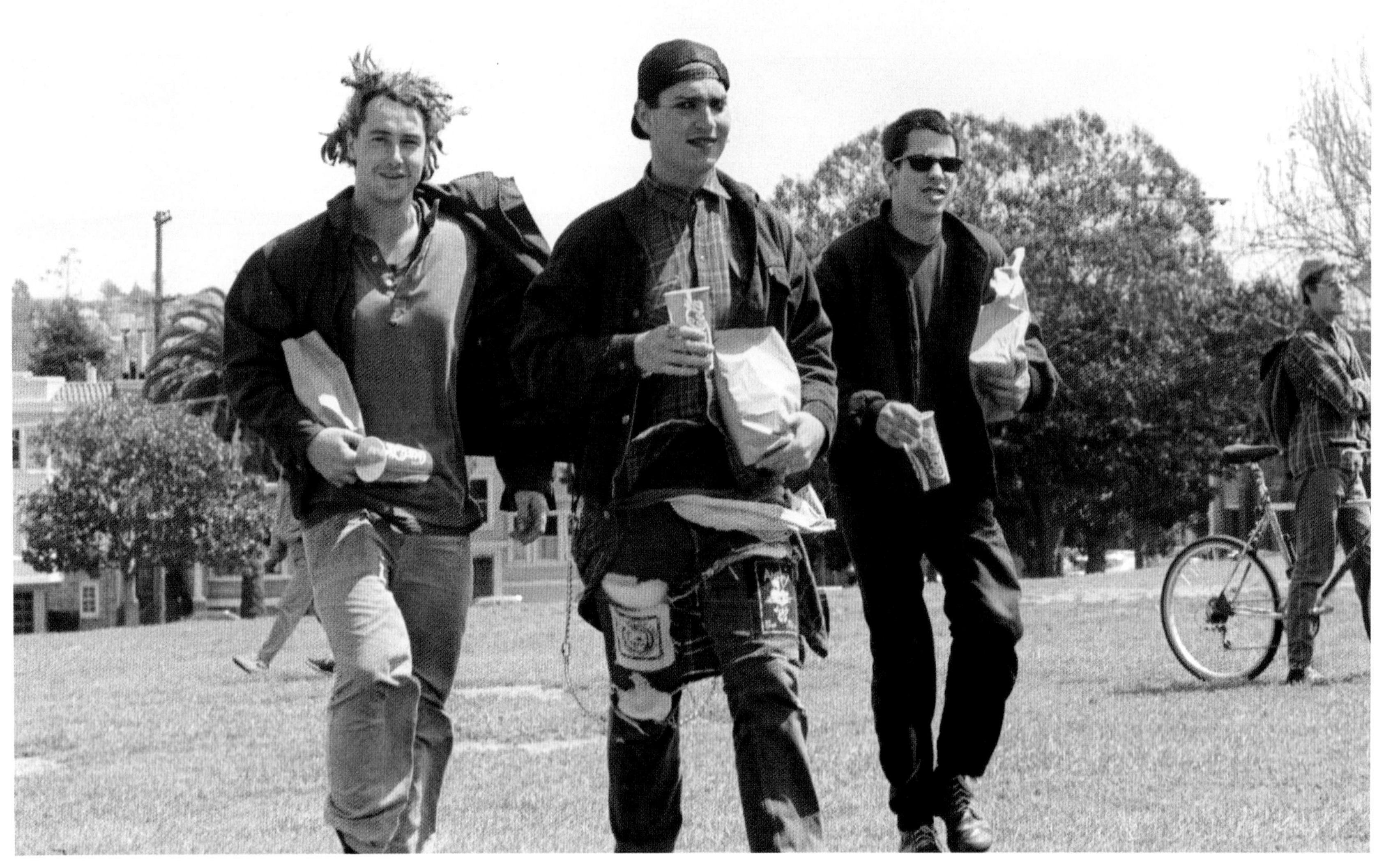

Dolores Park, San Francisco, 1991

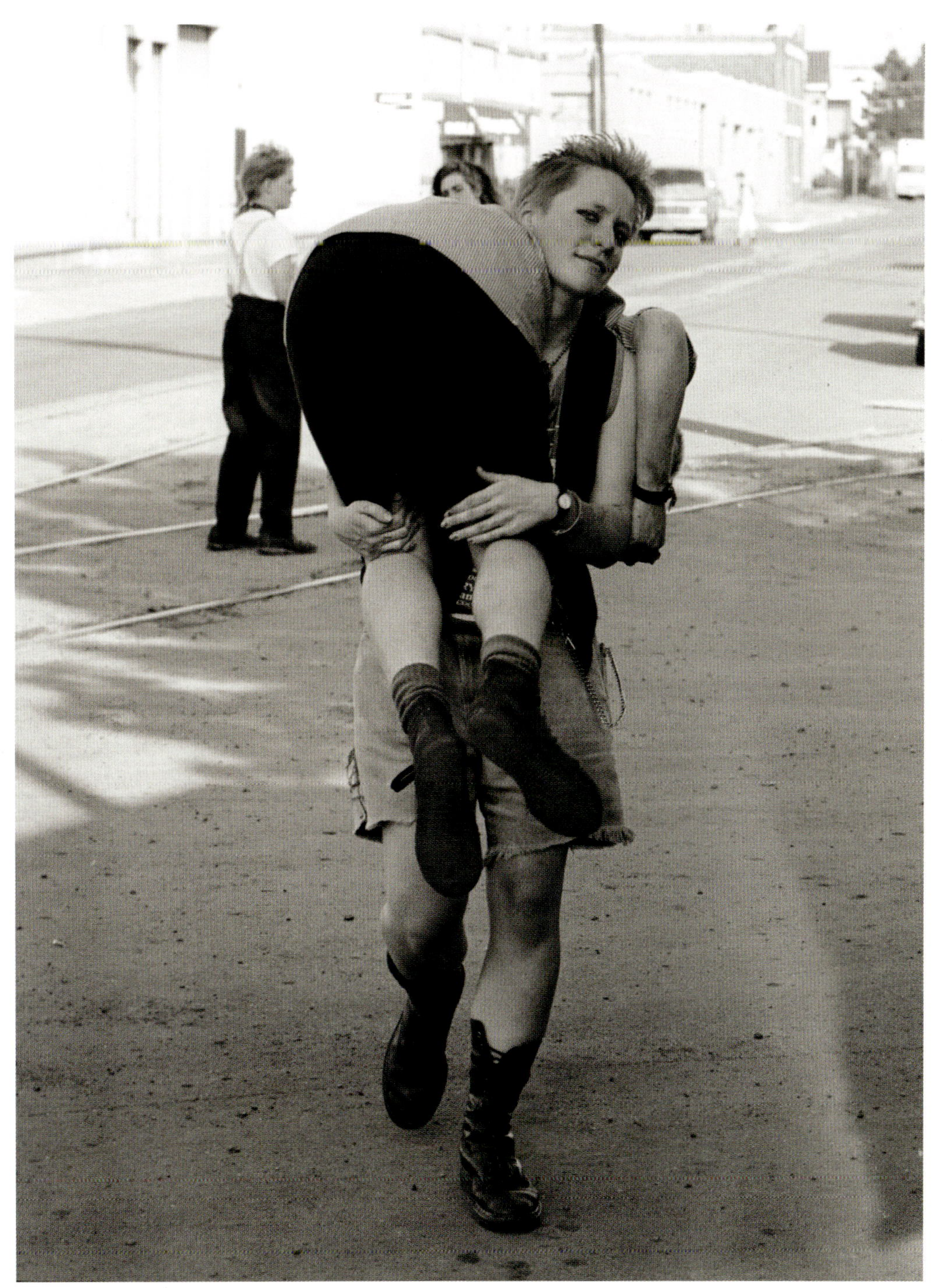

Janelle Blarg
Oakland, 1992

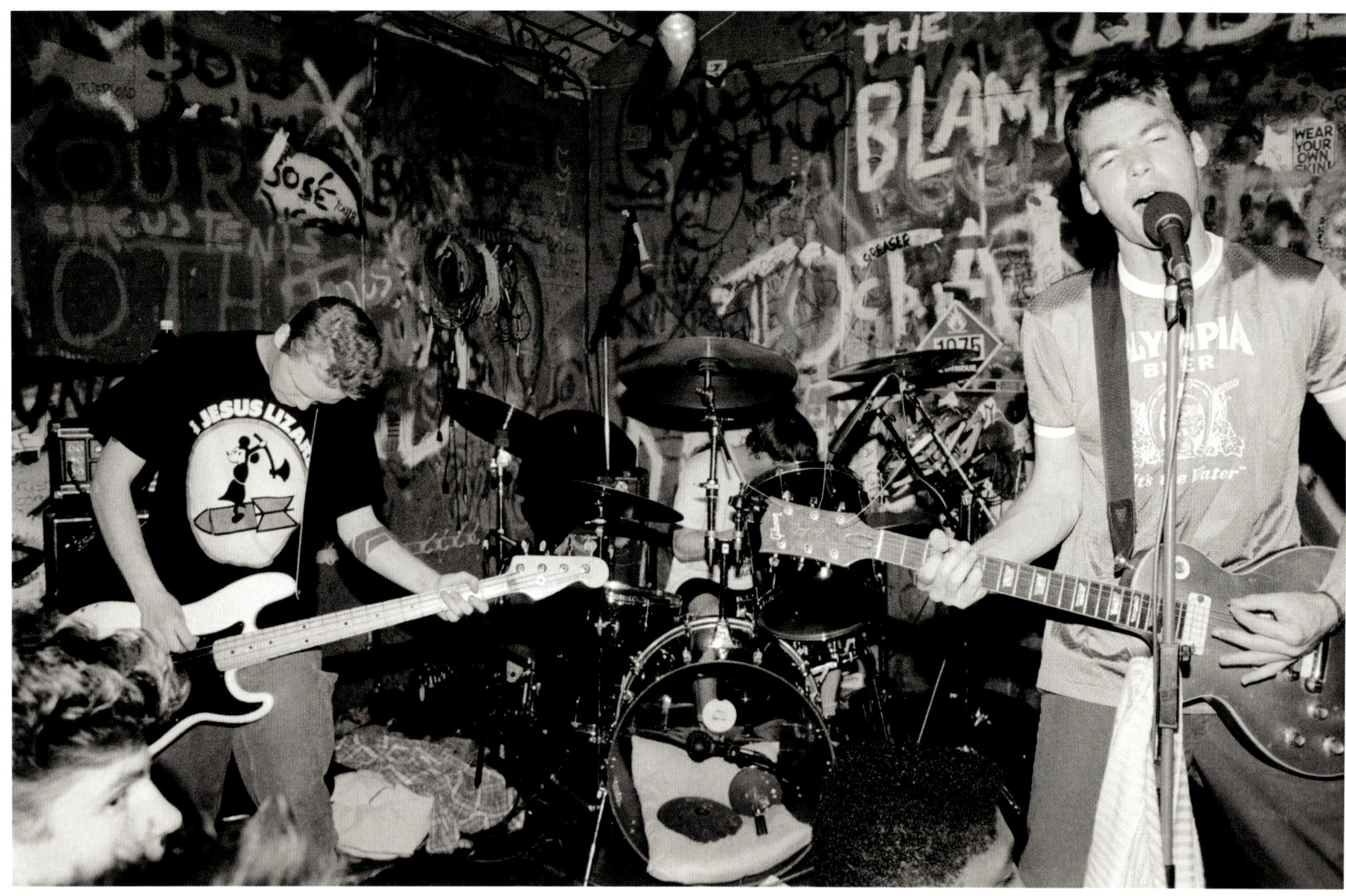

Jawbreaker
Gilman Street, Berkeley, 1991

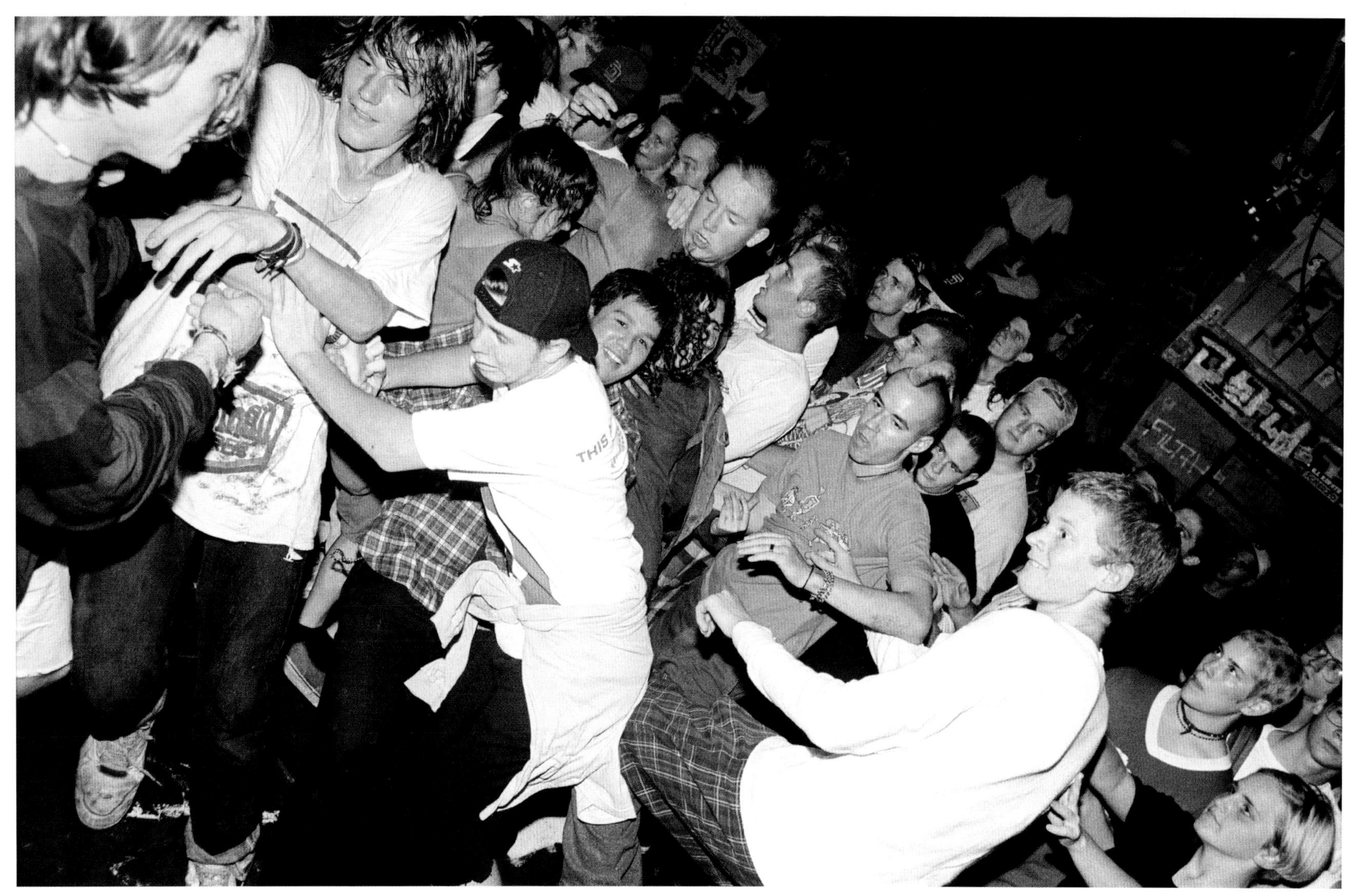

Gilman Street, 1991

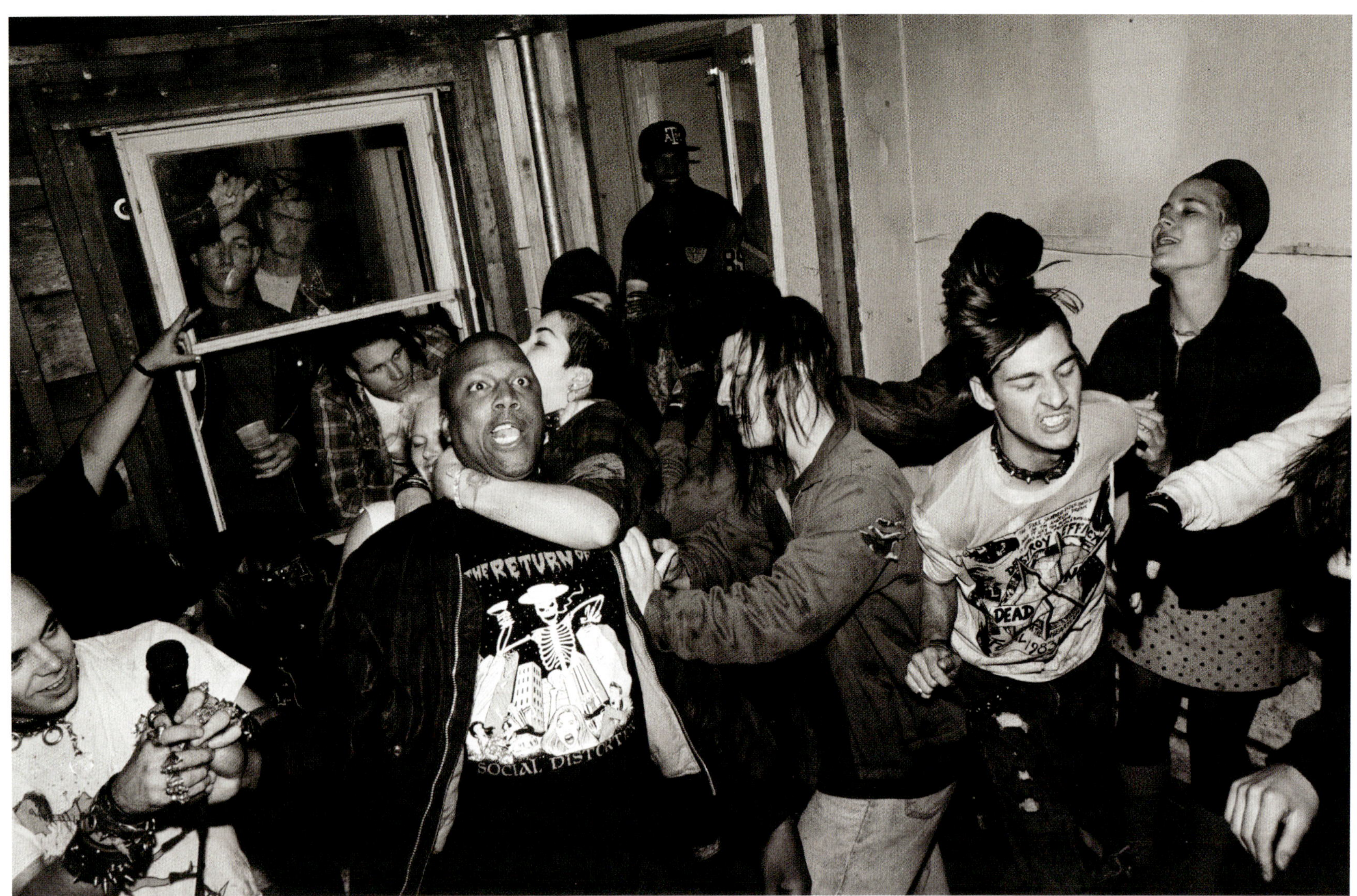

Special Forces
Fraggle's House, Oakland, 1991

Opposite:
Schlong (as The Royal Scam)
Your Place Too, Oakland, 1992

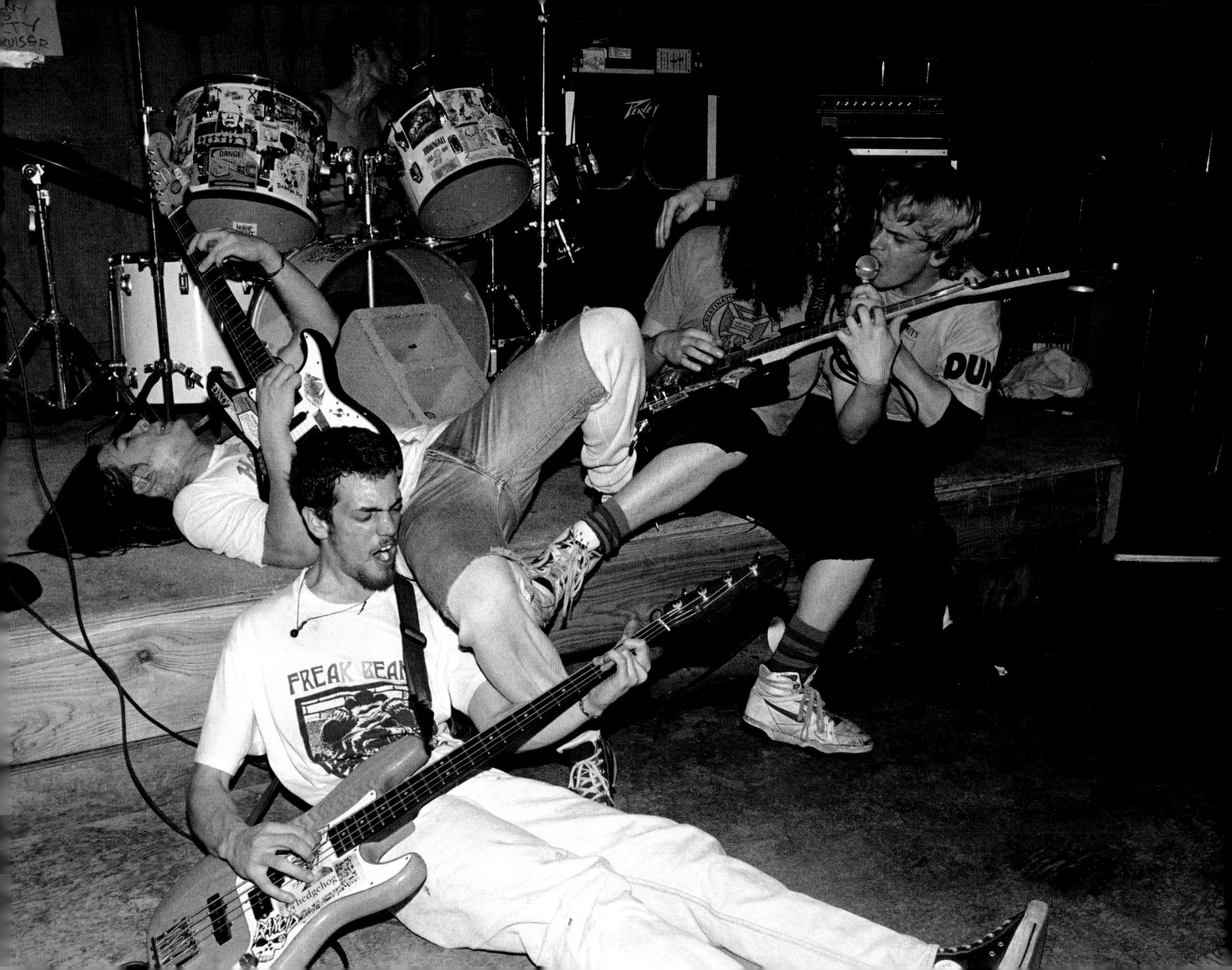

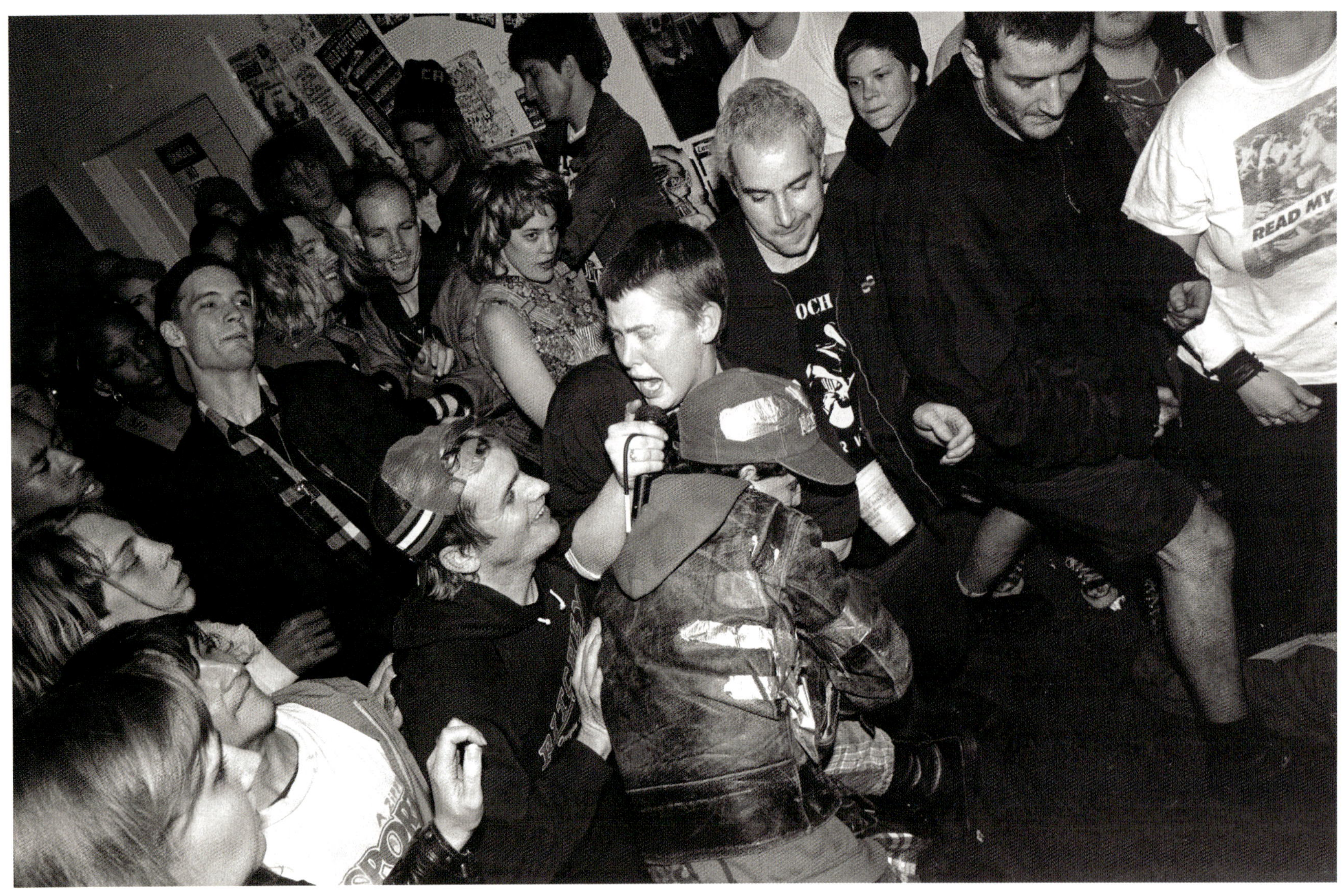

Paxston Quiggley

5th St., Oakland, 1992

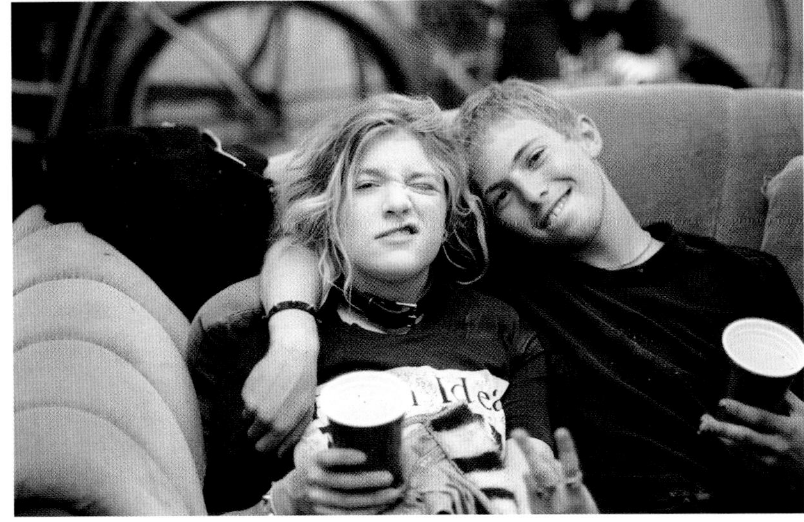
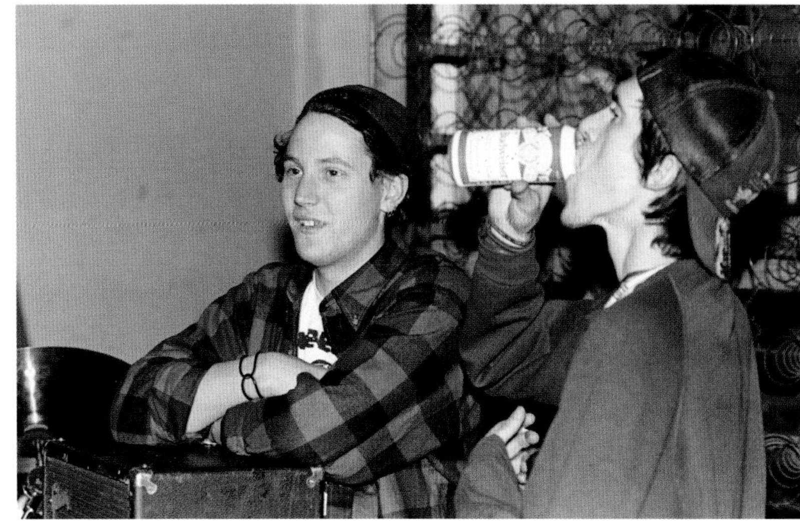
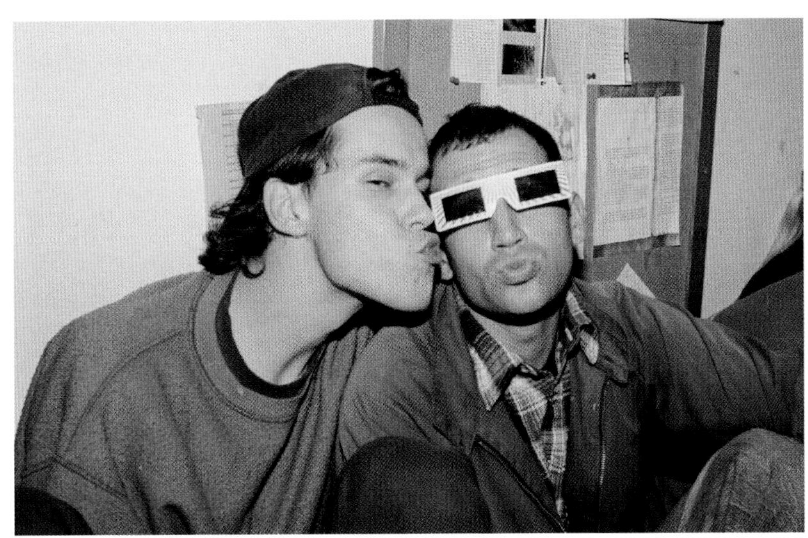
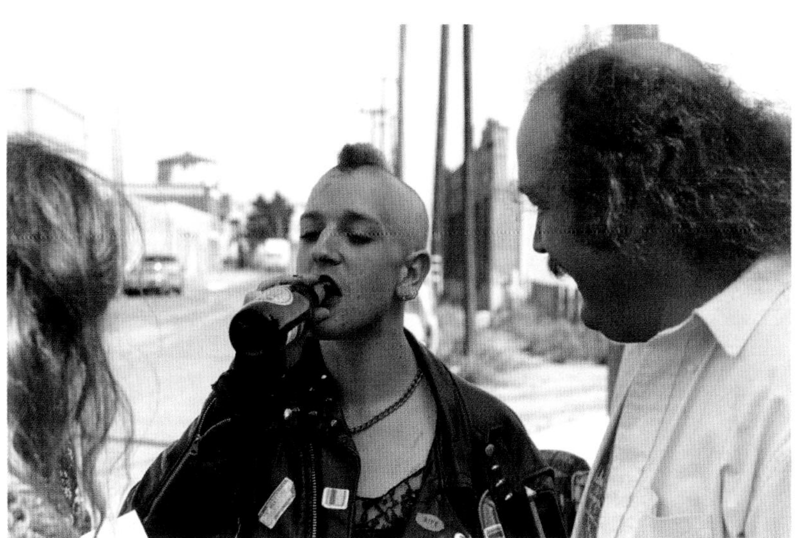

Clockwise from top left: Anna and Aaron, 1993; Lucky and Jack, 1991; Sean and Steve List, 1992; Sergie and Aaron, 1991

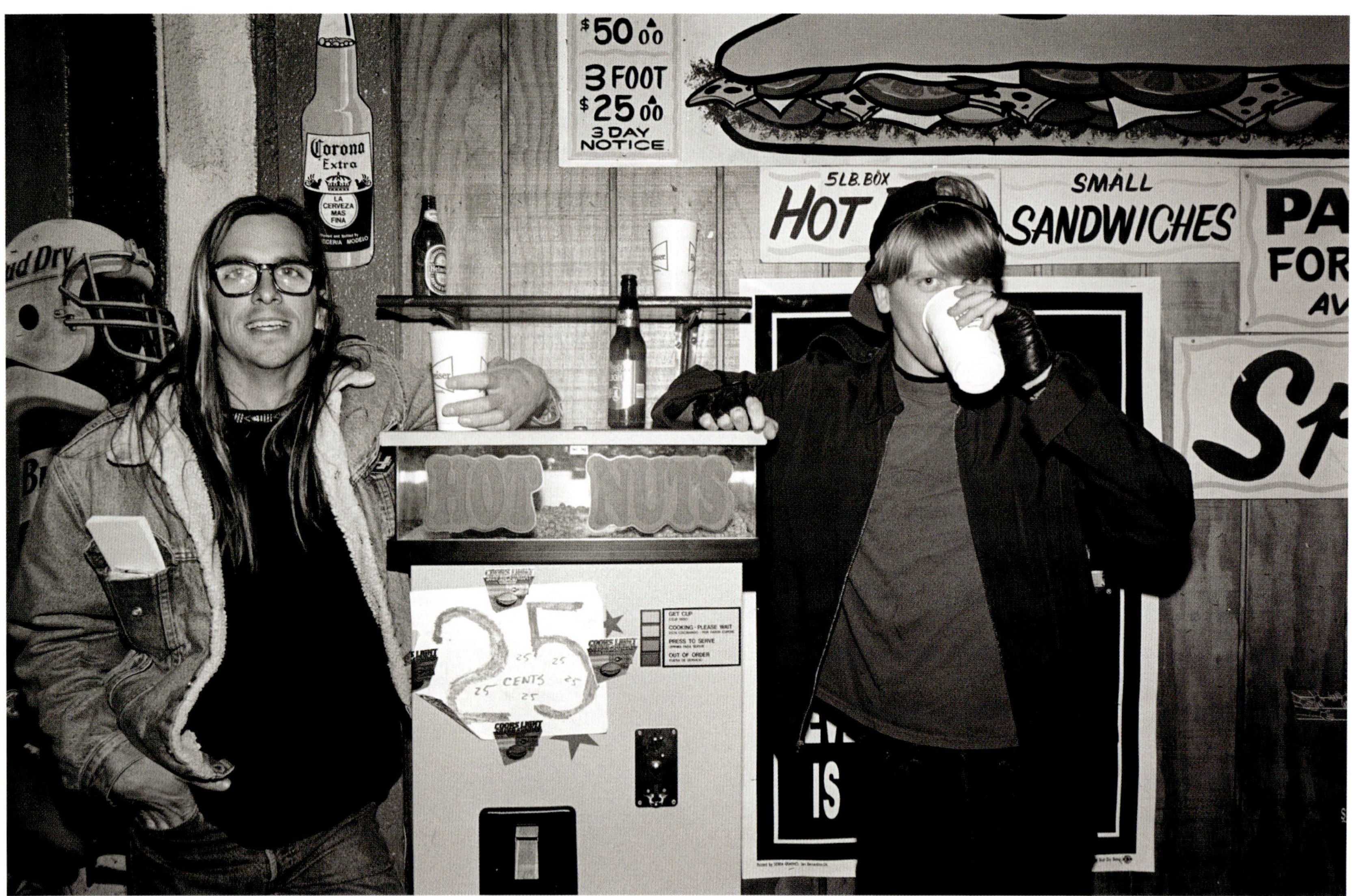

The Offspring
U-Gene's Bar, Pico Rivera, 1991

Opposite:
L7
Gilman Street, Berkeley, 1990

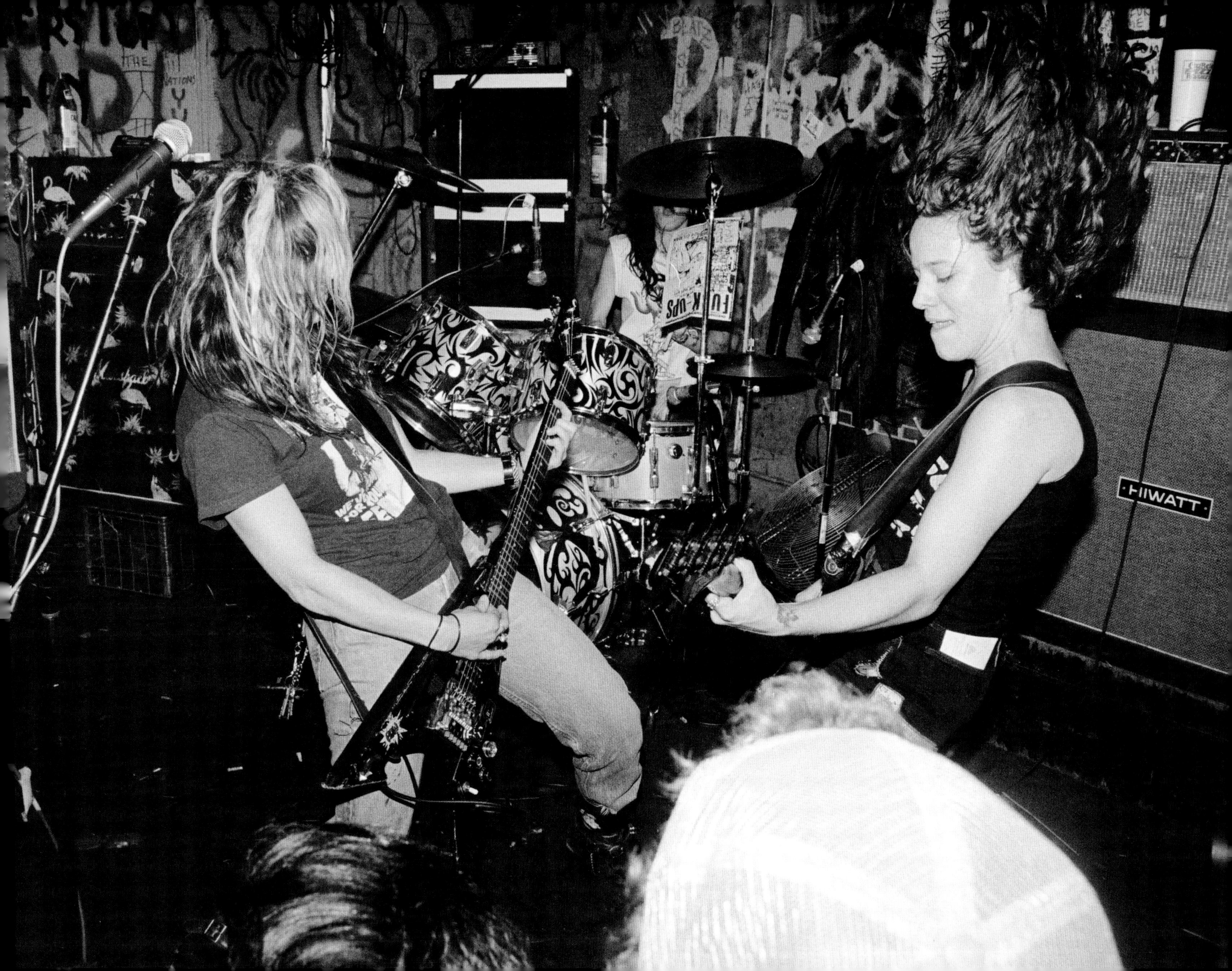

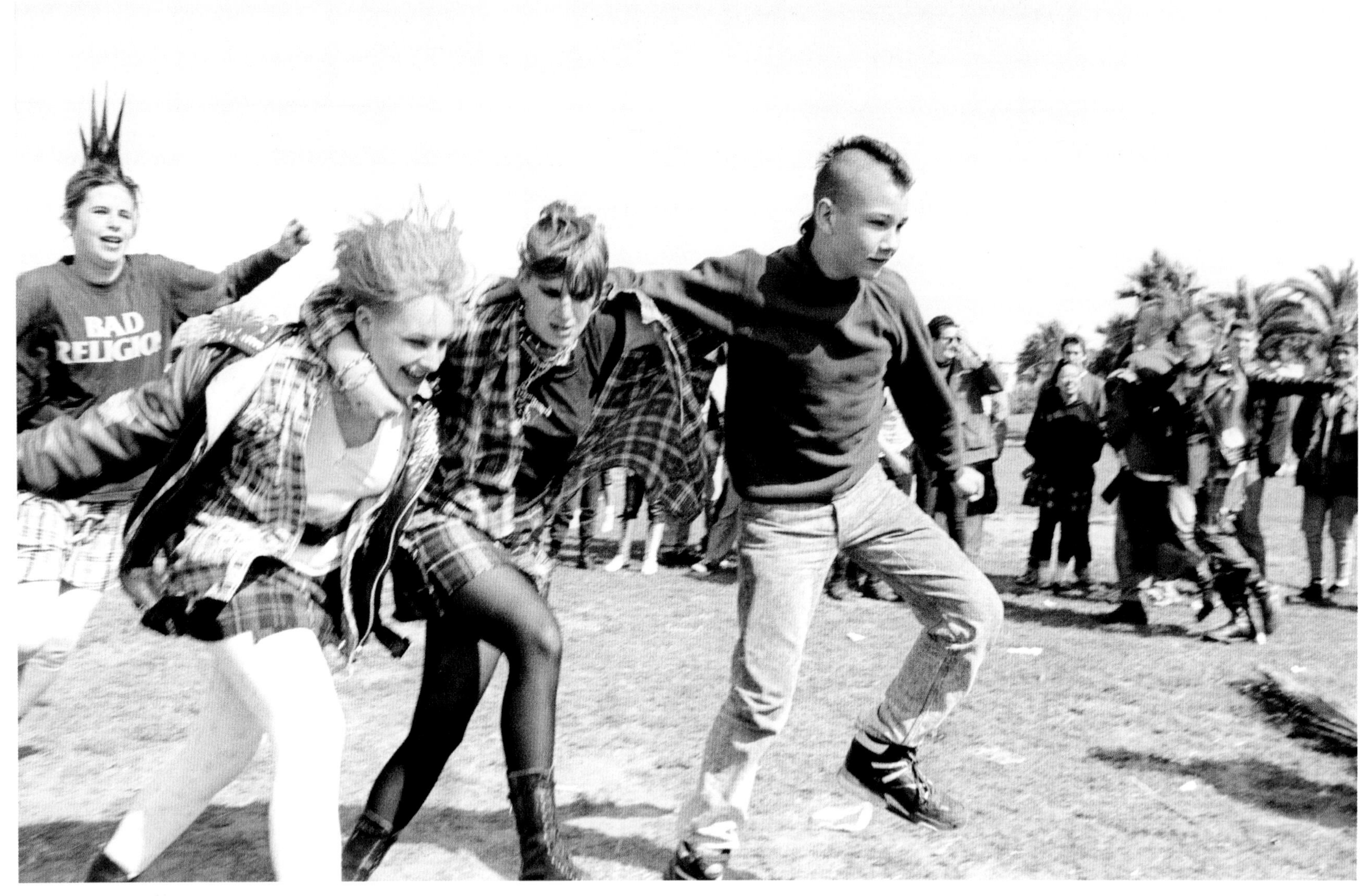

Dolores Park, San Francisco, 1991

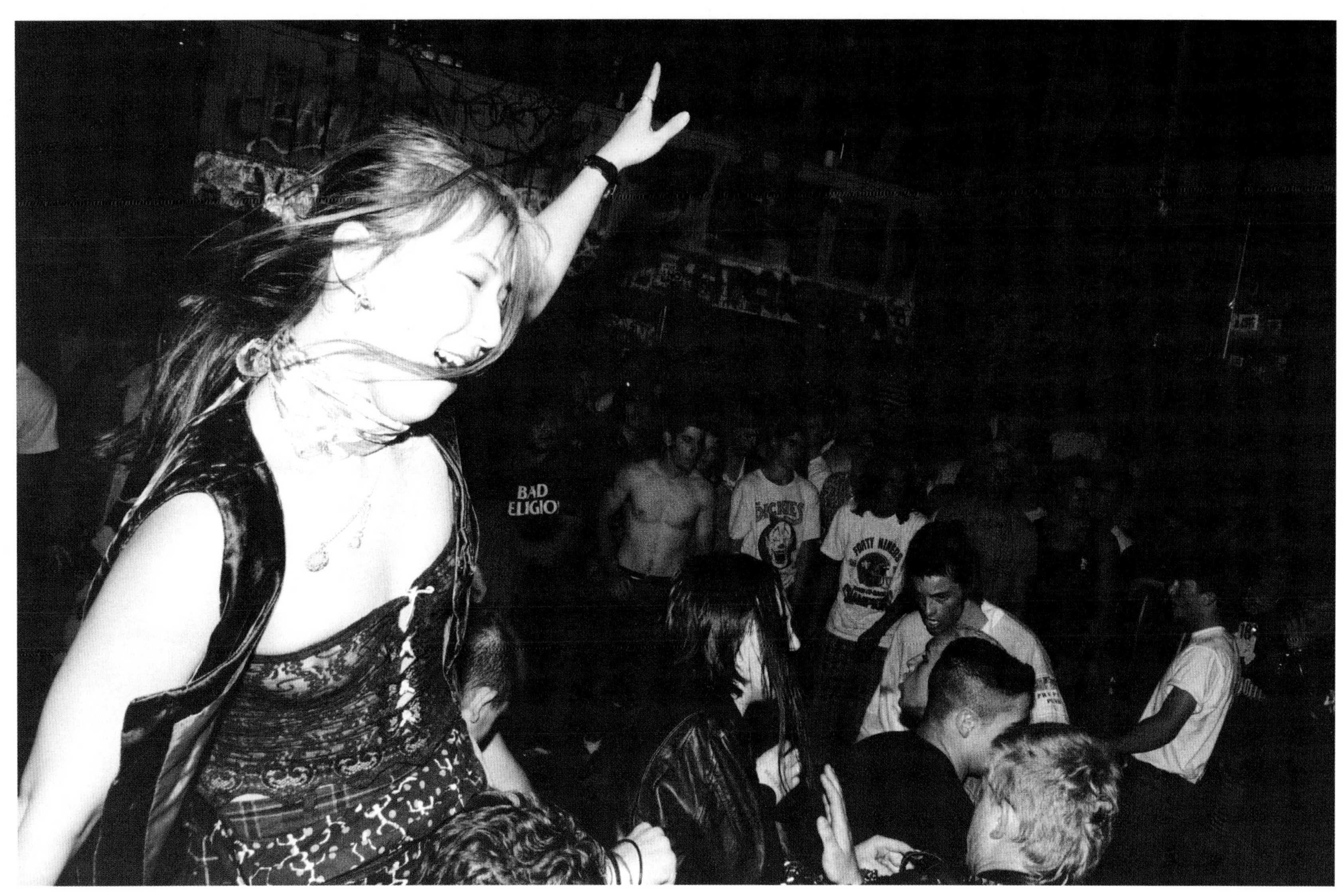

Gilman Street, Berkeley, 1992

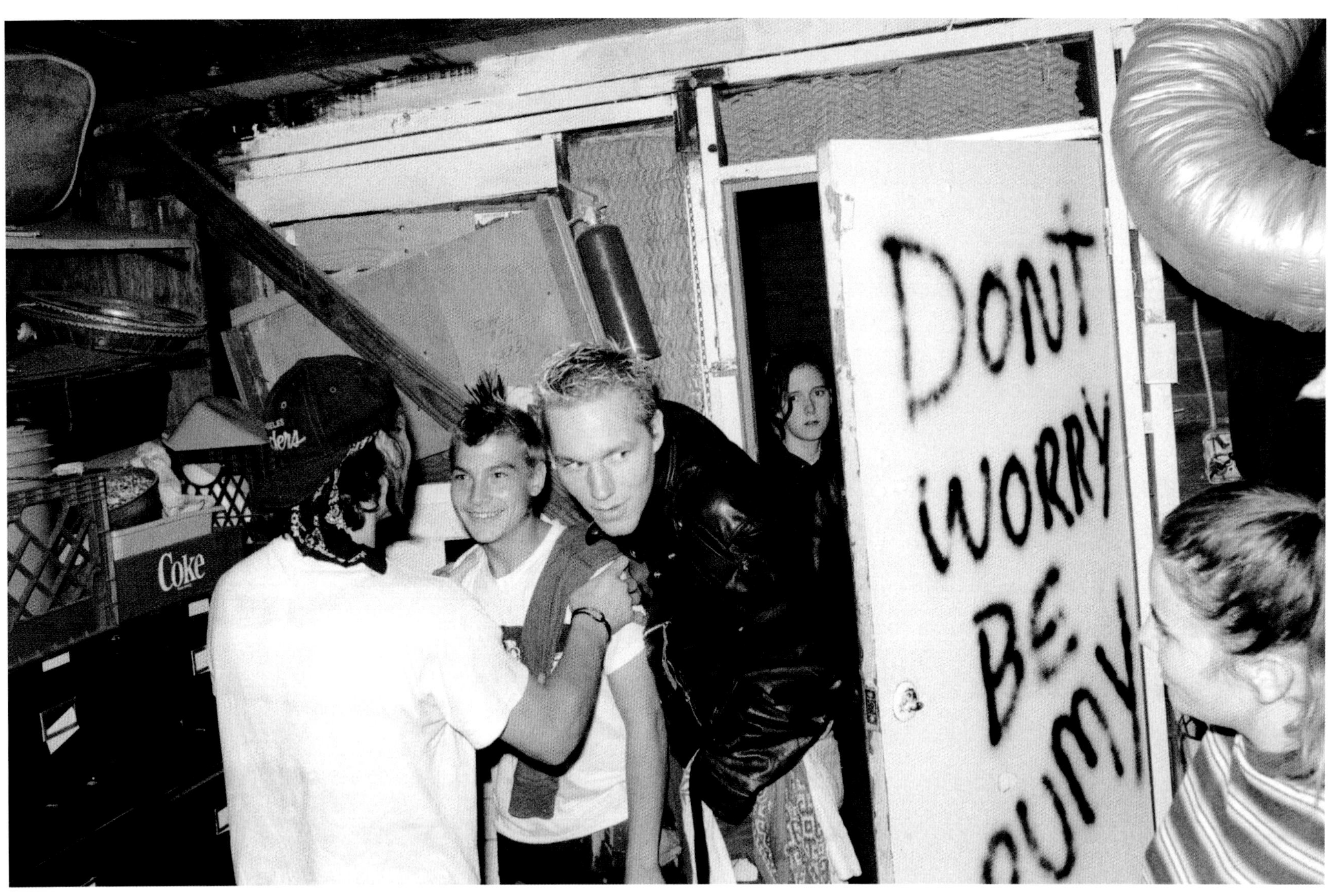

Crummy House, San Pablo, 1995

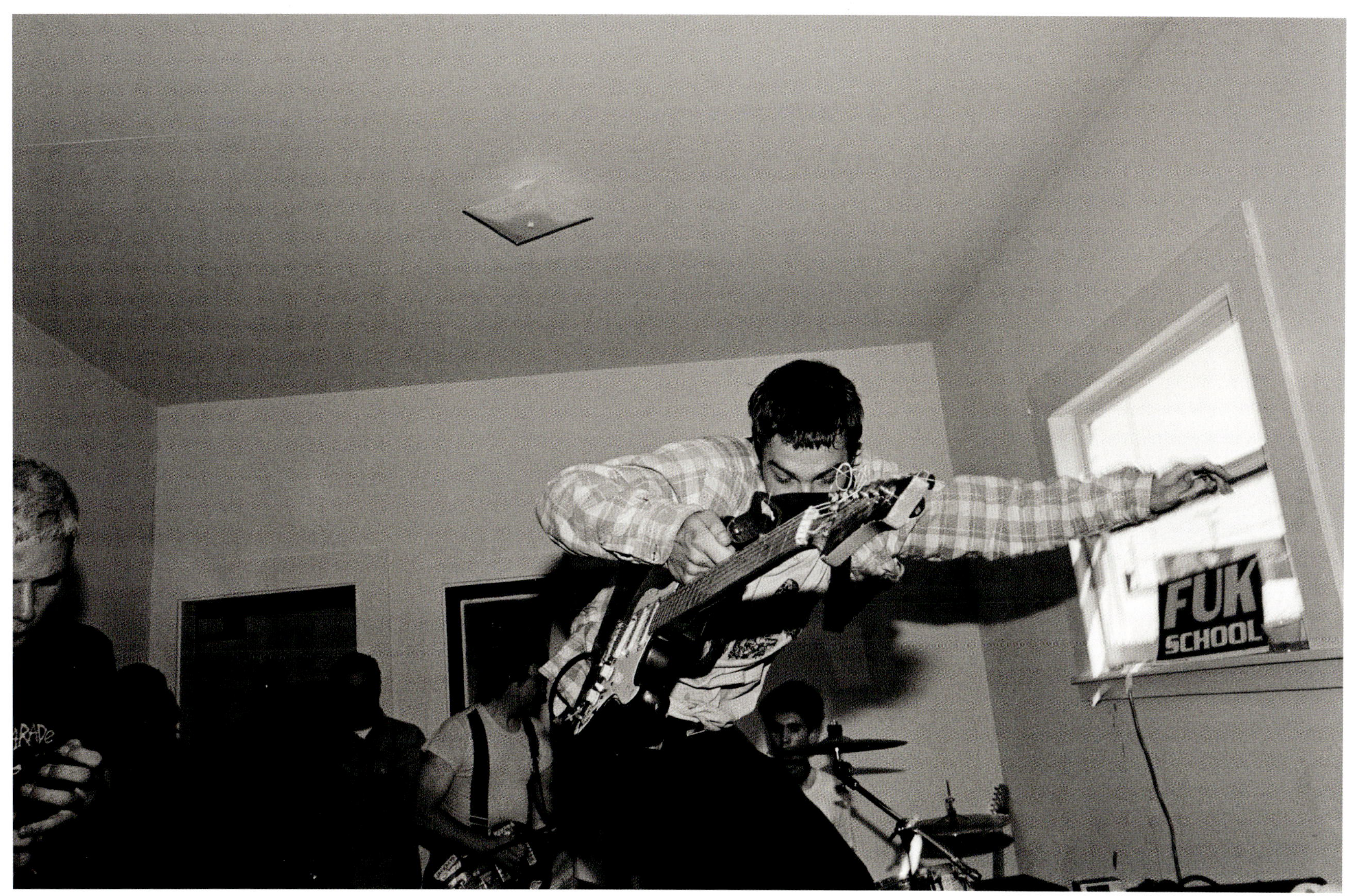

Blatz

West Oakland, 1991

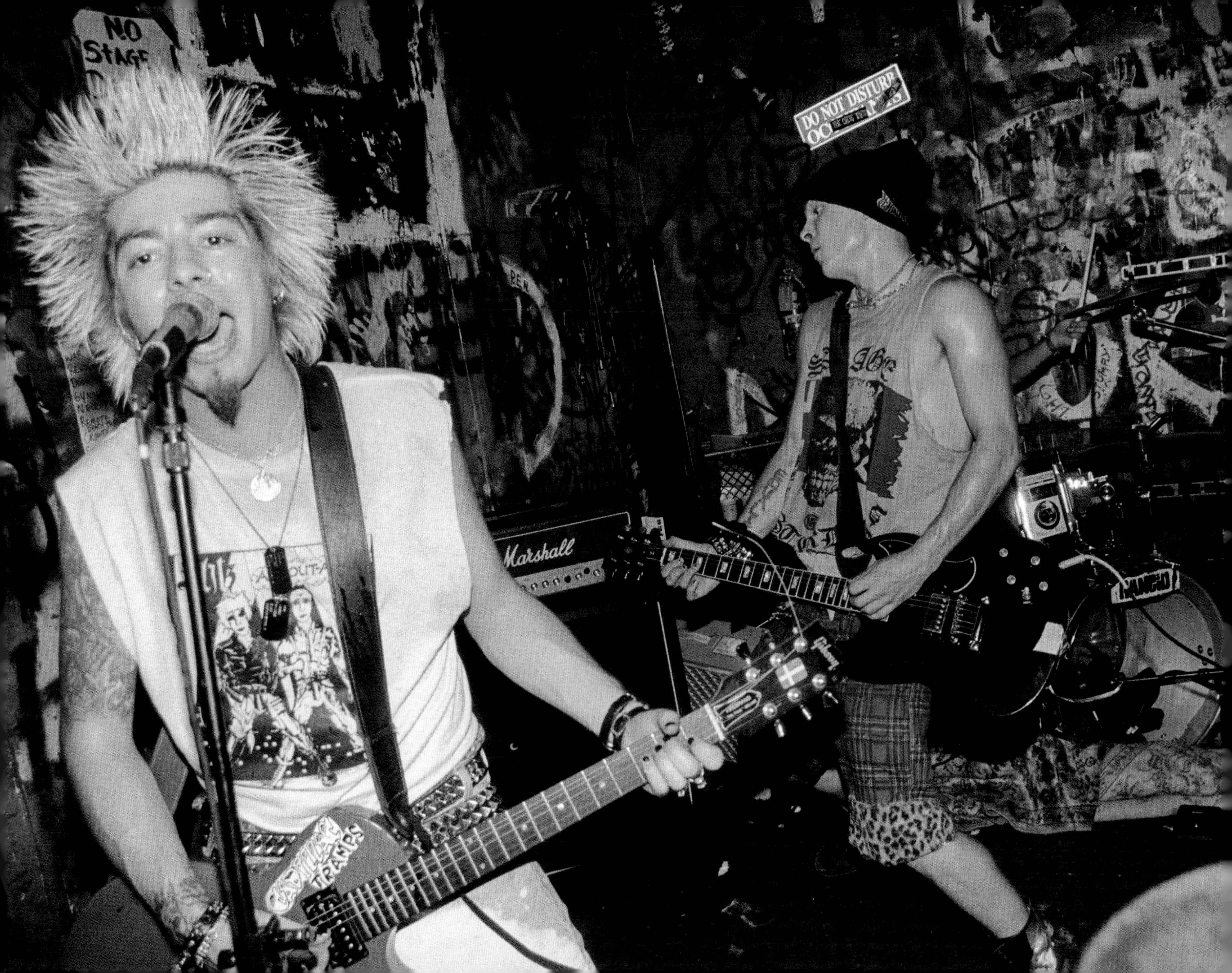
NO STAGE
DO NOT DISTURB
Marshall

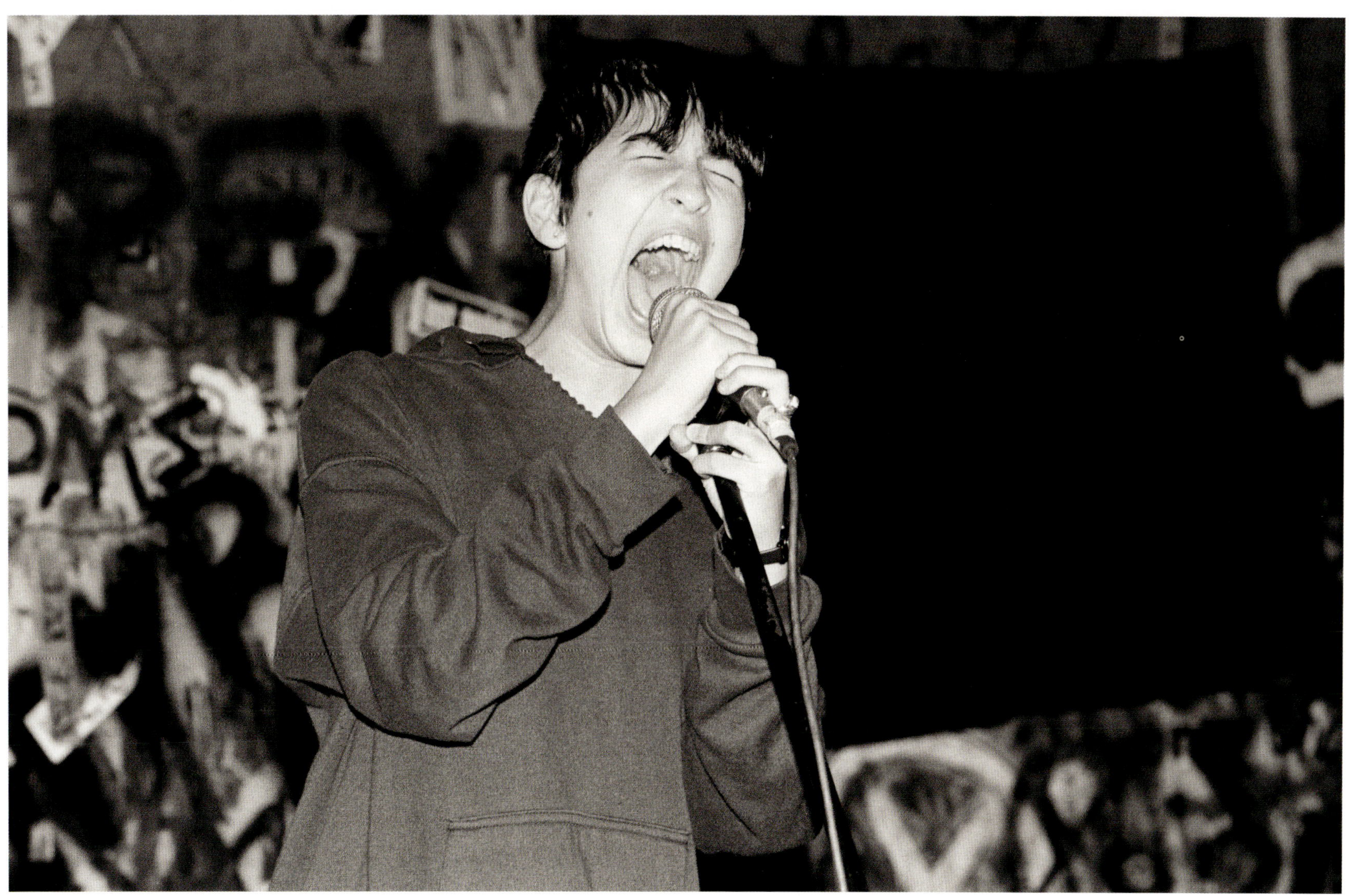

Raooul
Gilman Street, Berkeley, 1992

Opposite:
Rancid
Gilman Street, 1993

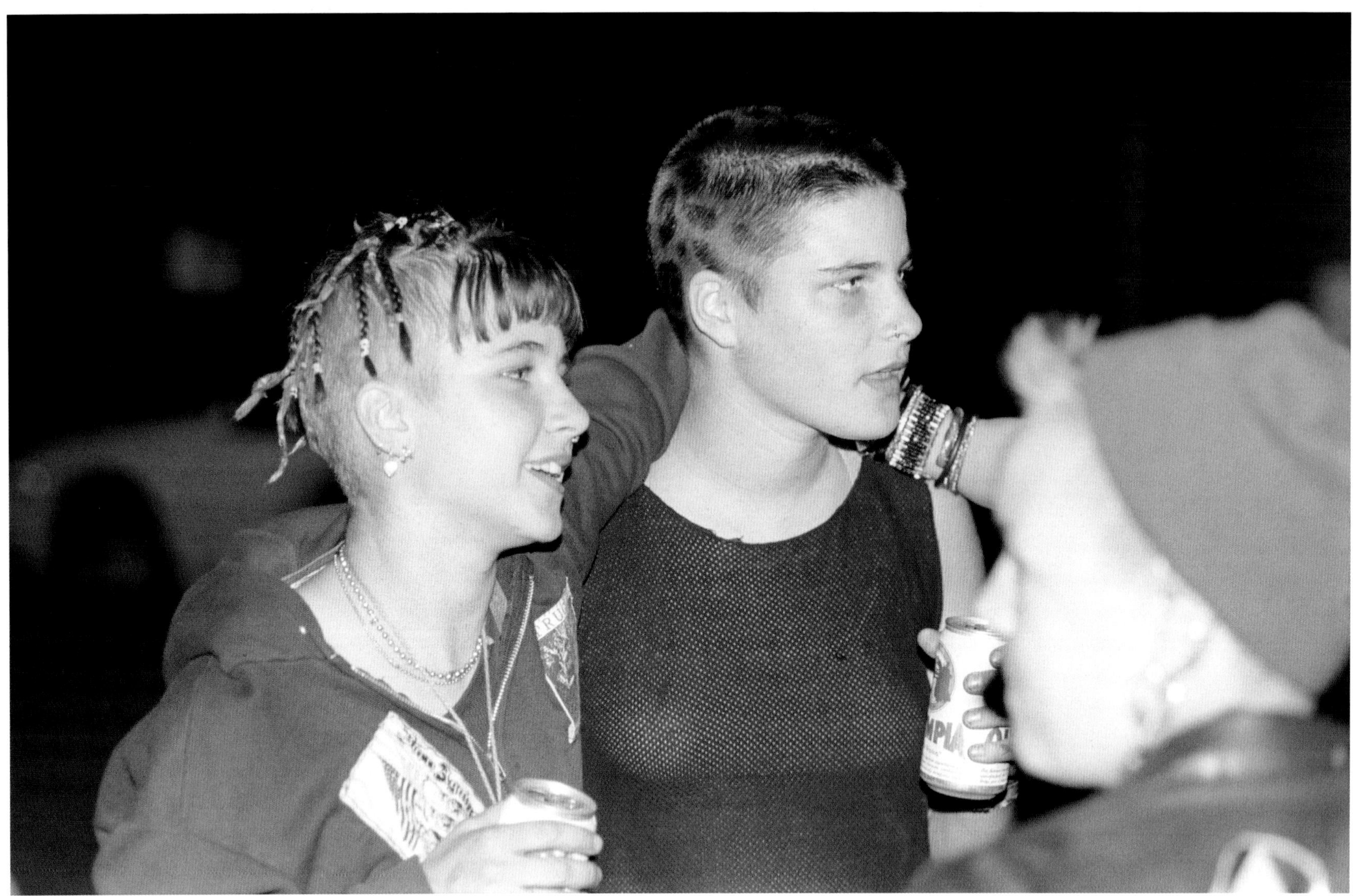

Raina and Daniel, 1992

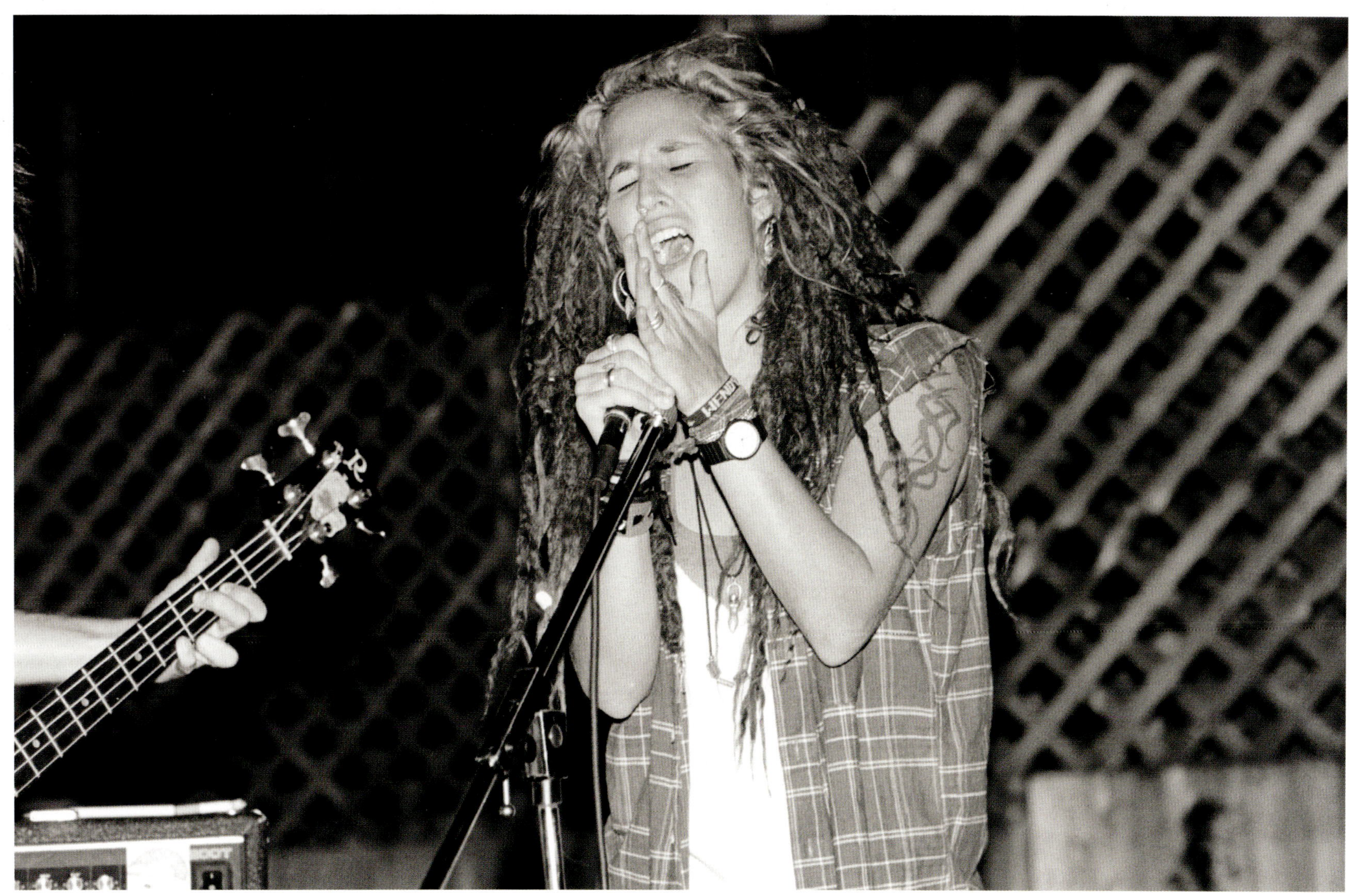

Gag Order
Cloyne Court, Berkeley, 1992

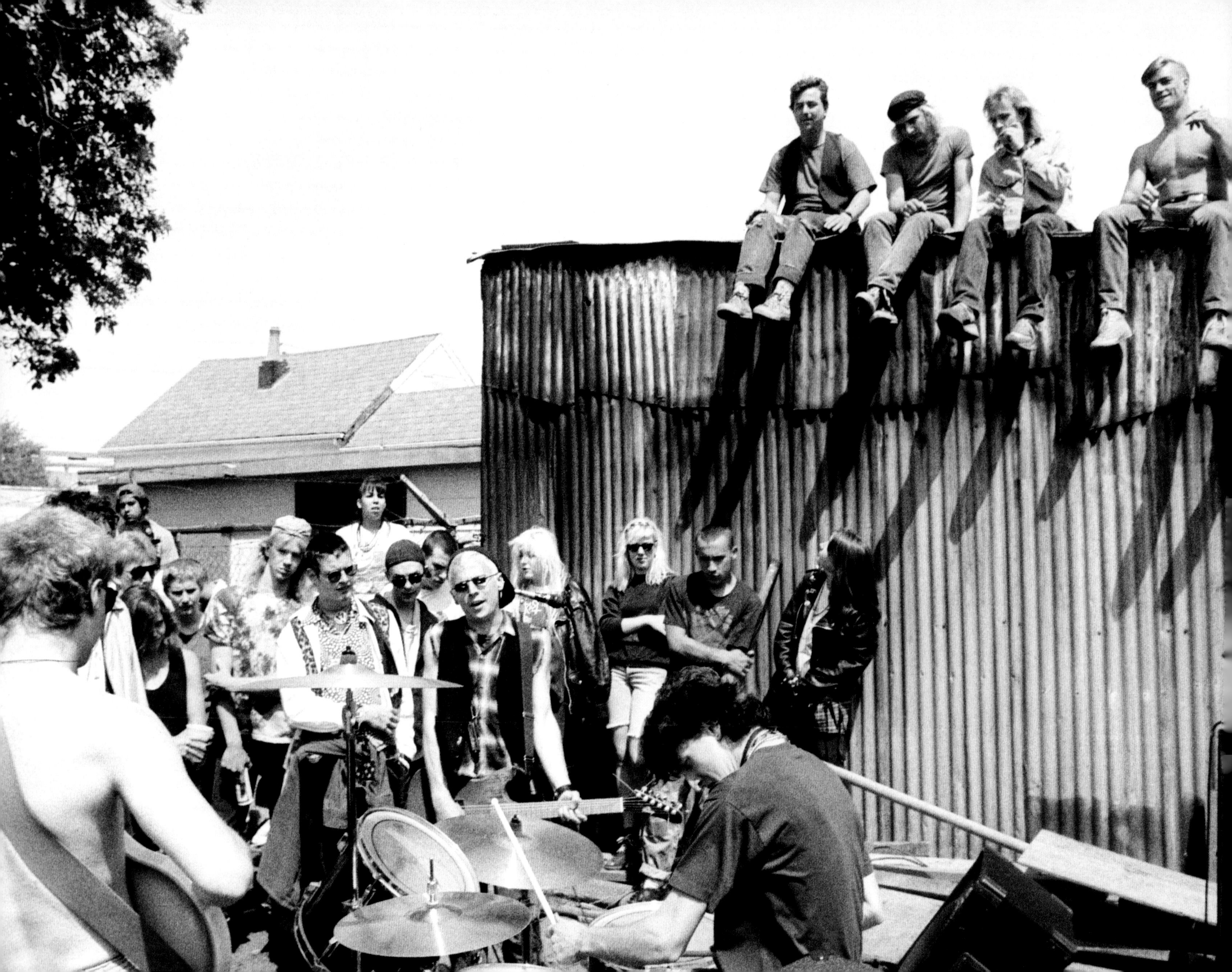

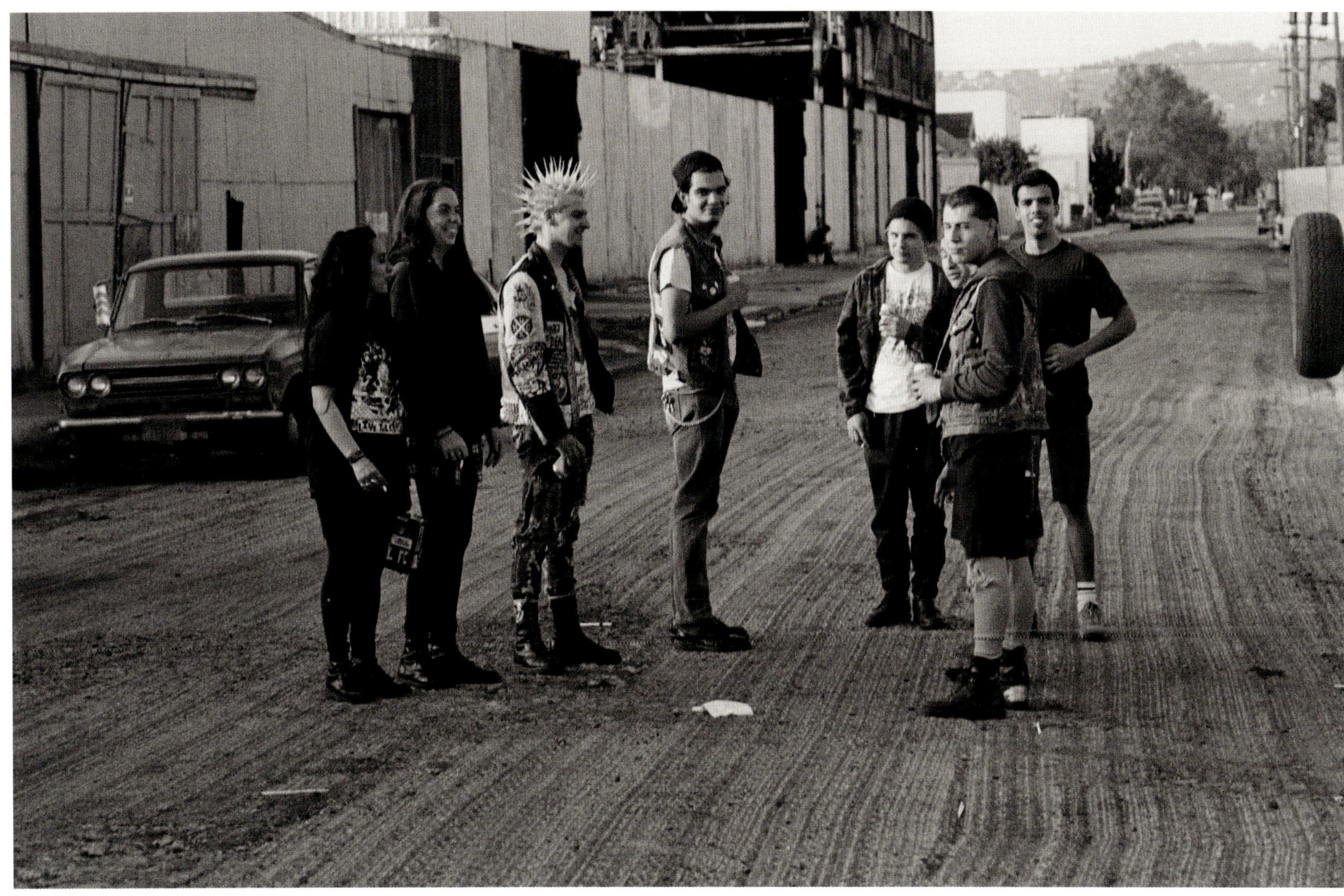

Berkeley, 1992

Opposite:
Blister
5th St. Oakland, 1990

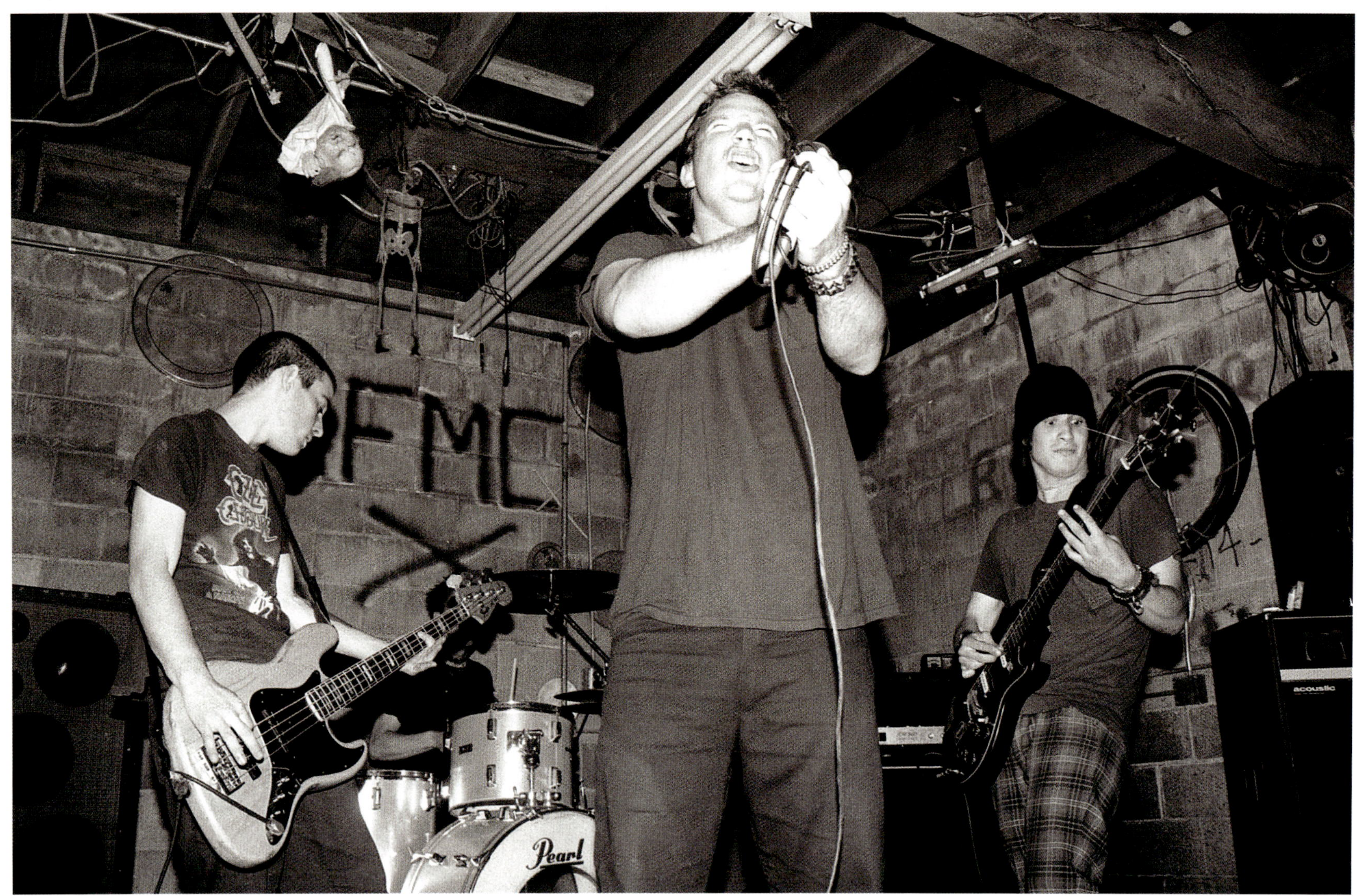

Dead And Gone

The Red Brick Building, Oakland, 1993

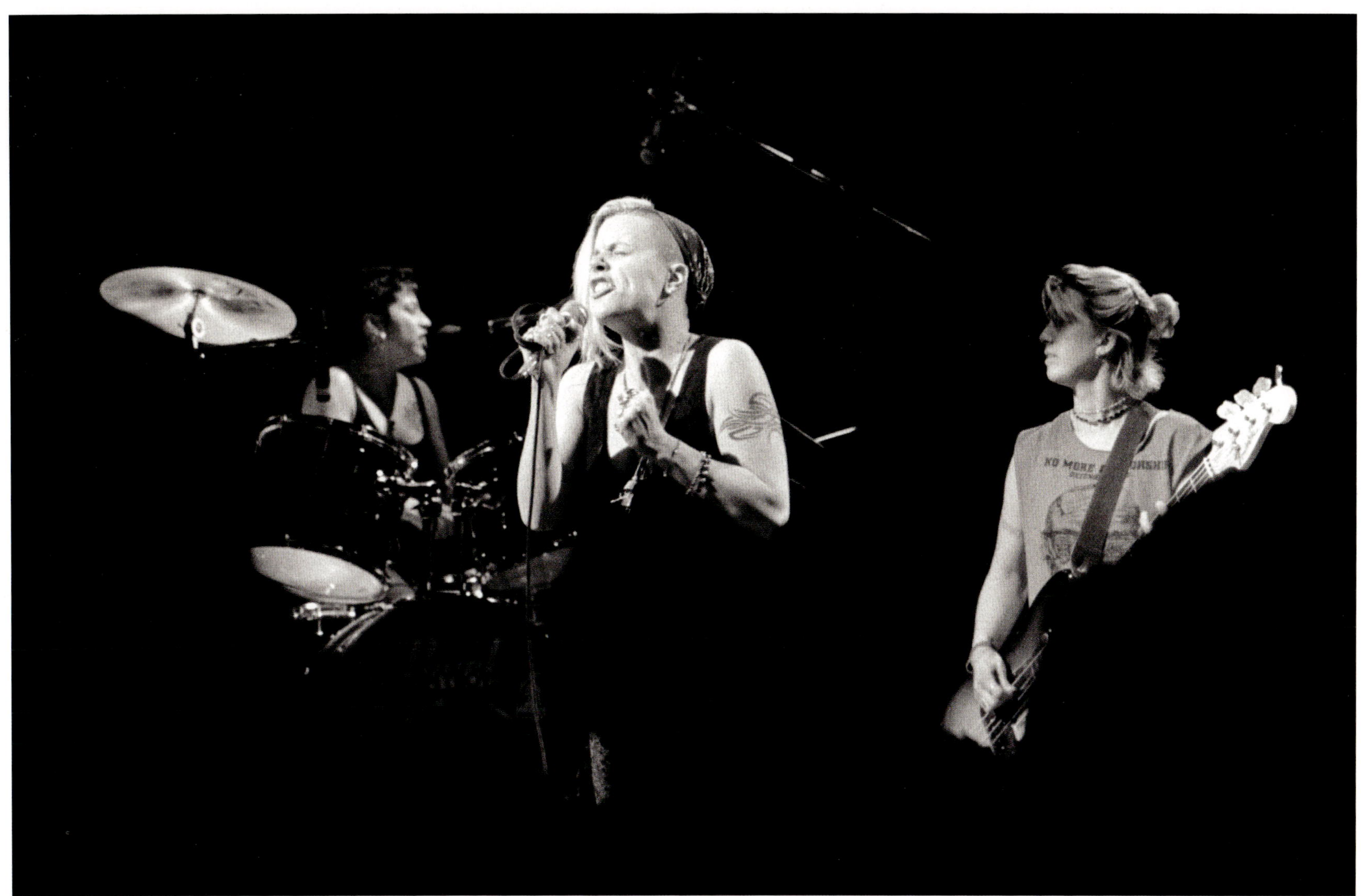

Spitboy
Phoenix Theater, Petaluma, 1992

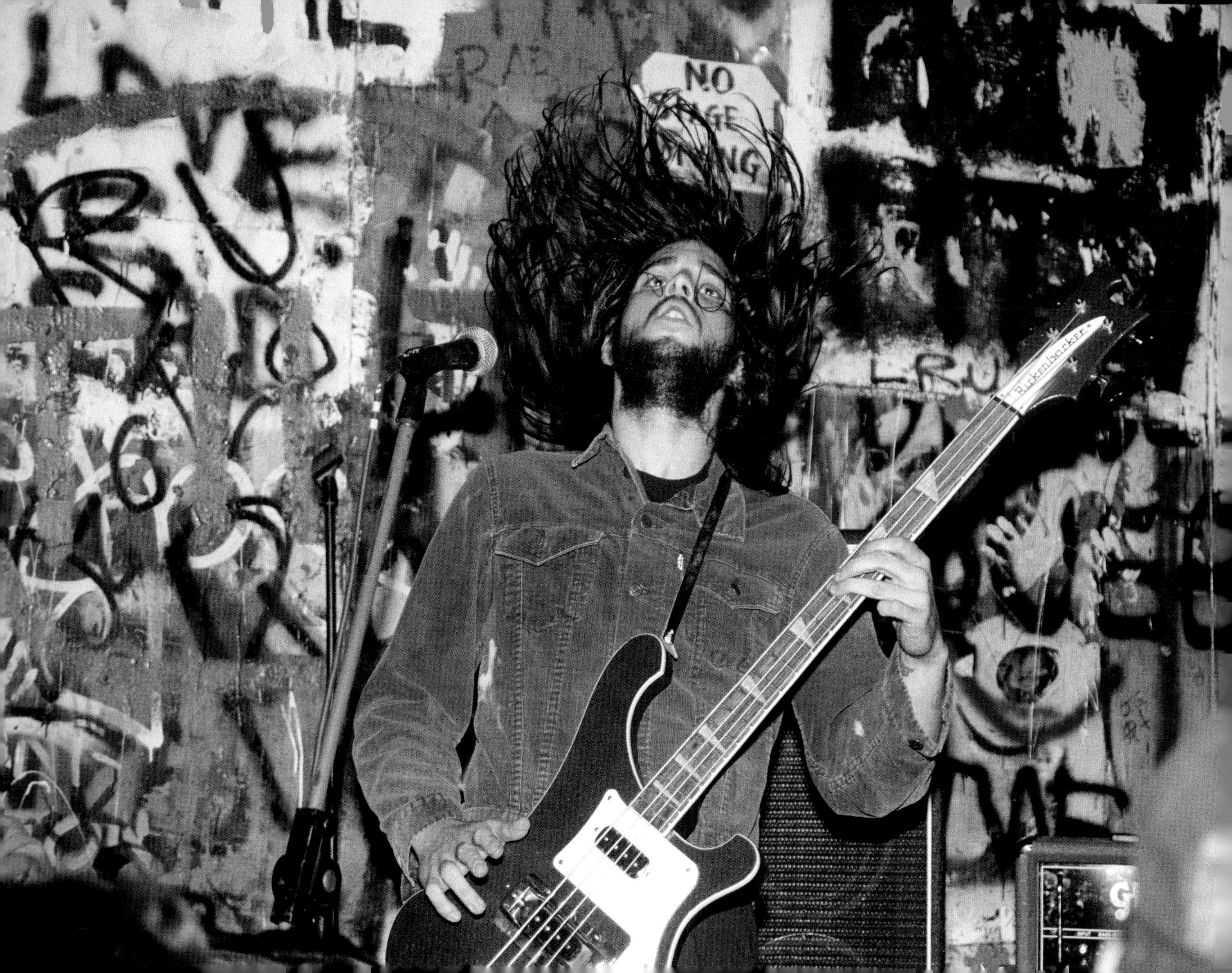

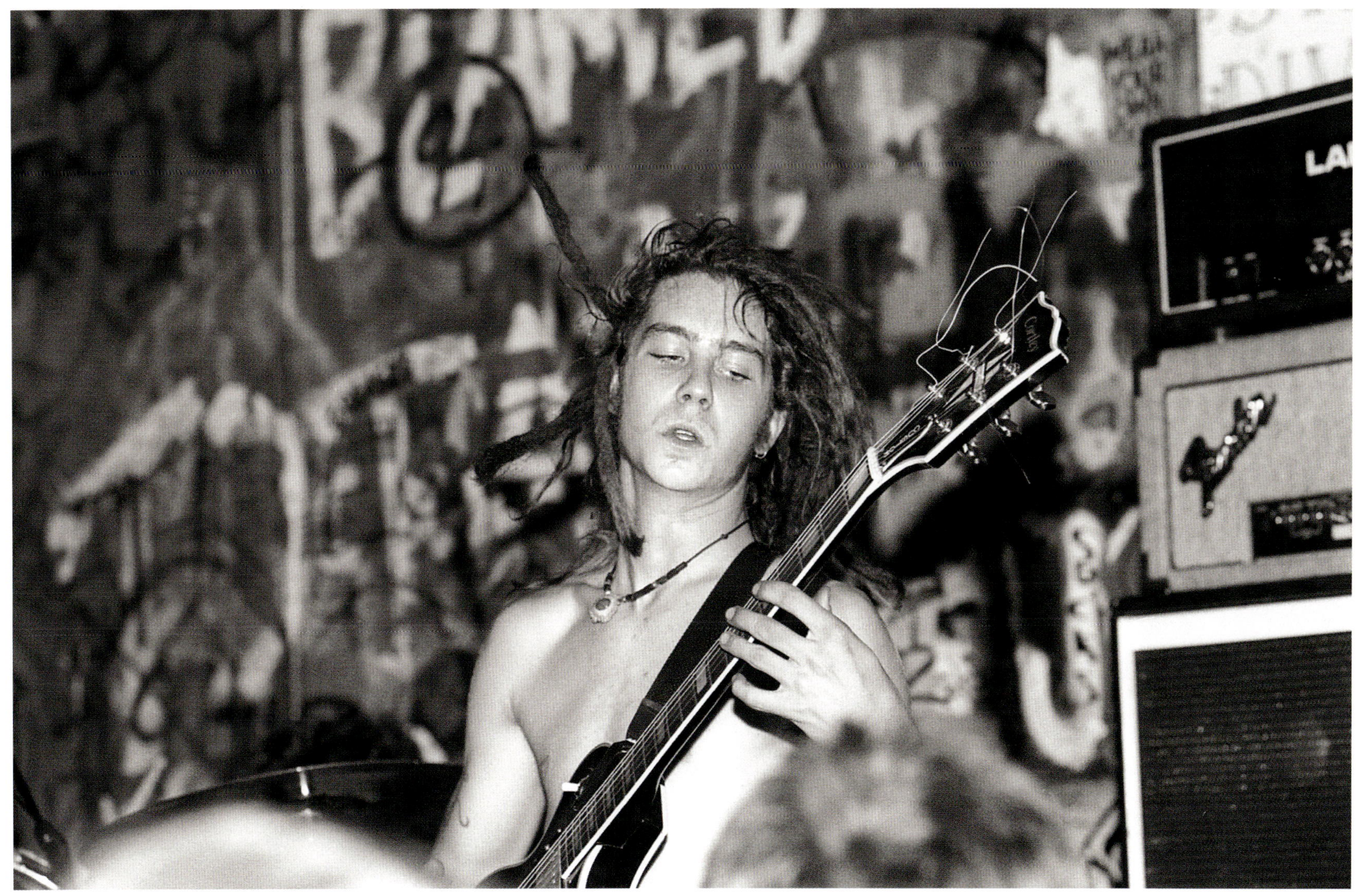

Sleep

Gilman Street, Berkeley, 1993

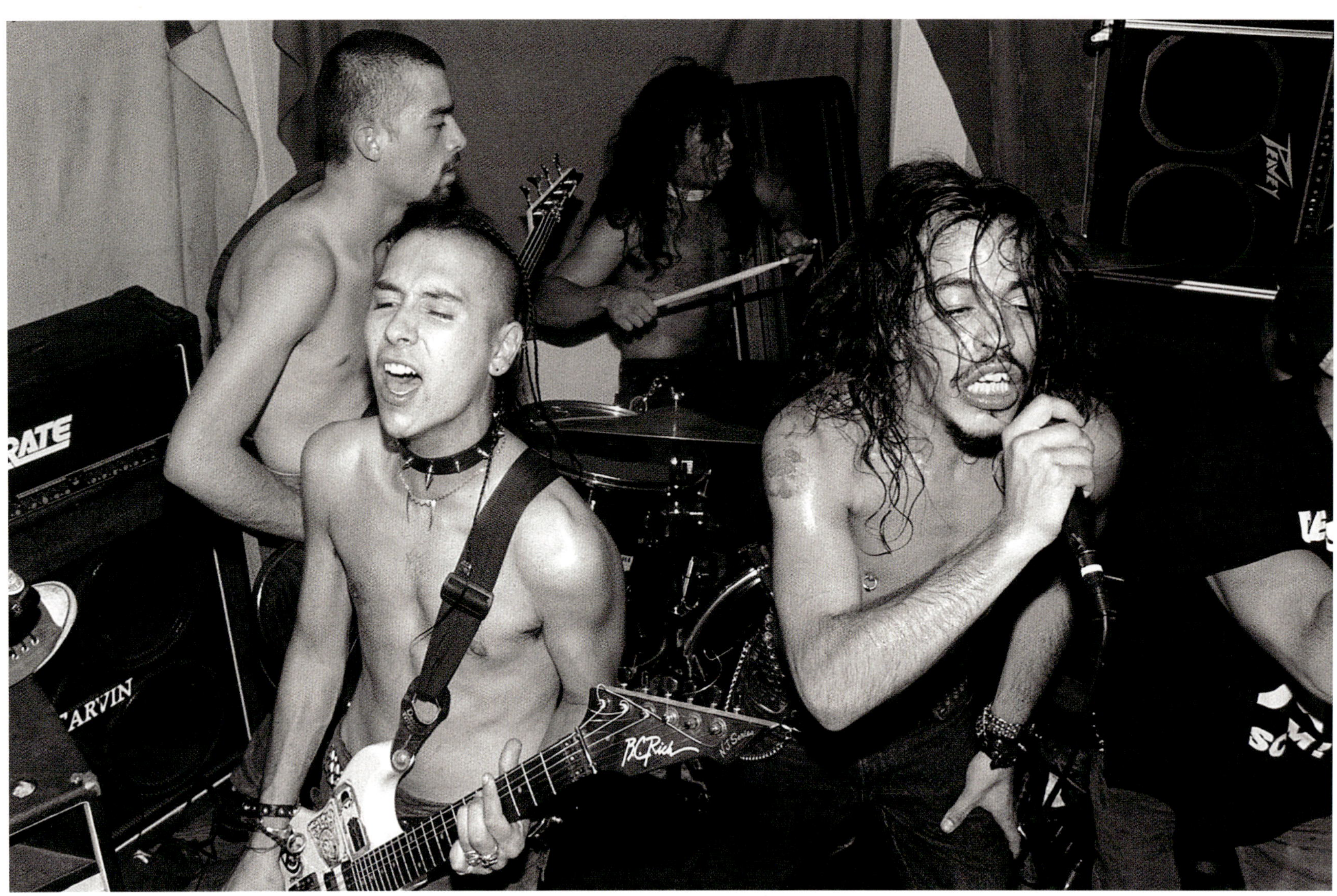

Logical Nonsense
1994

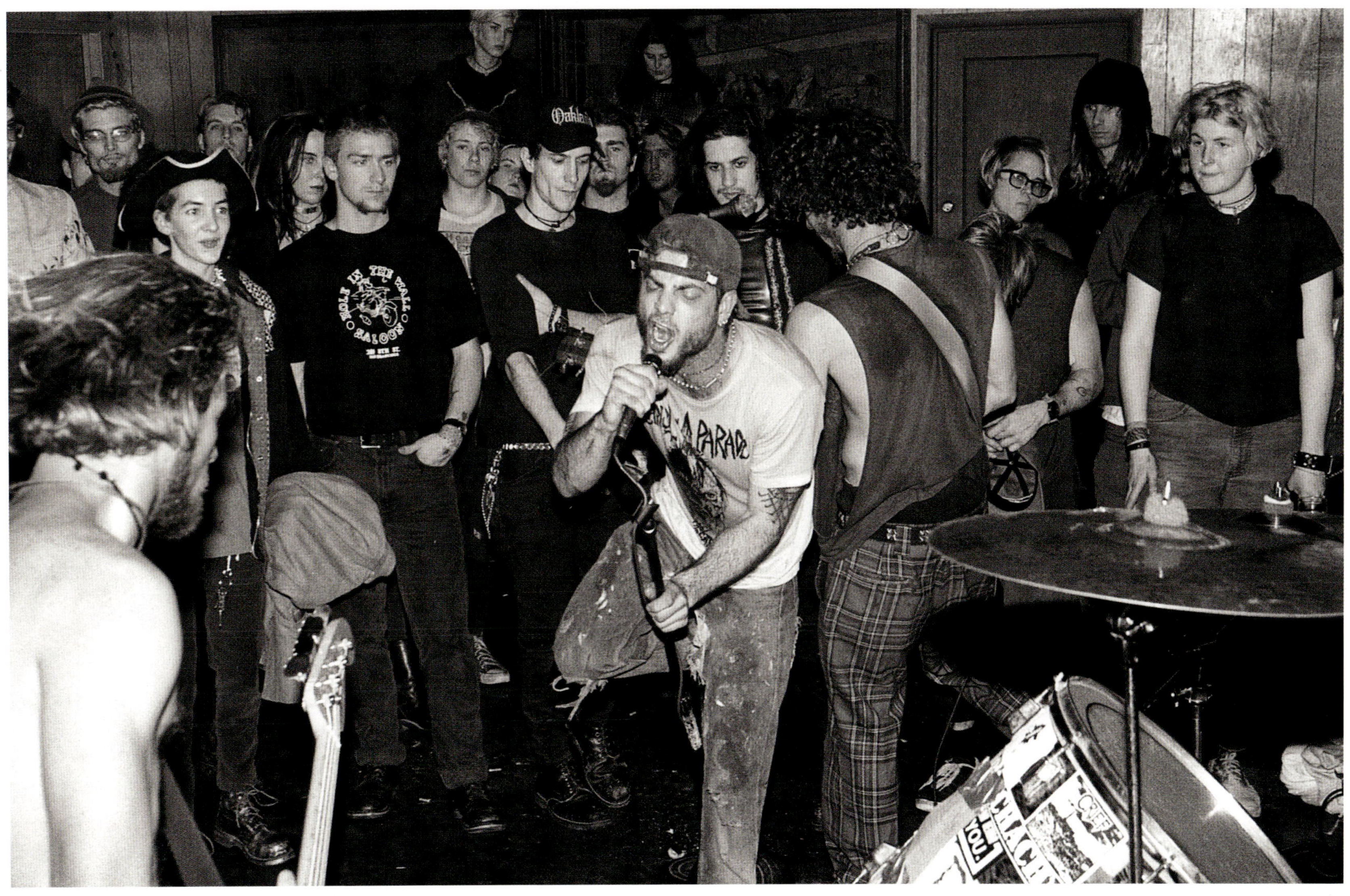

Animal Farm

Hof Brau, Oakland, 1995

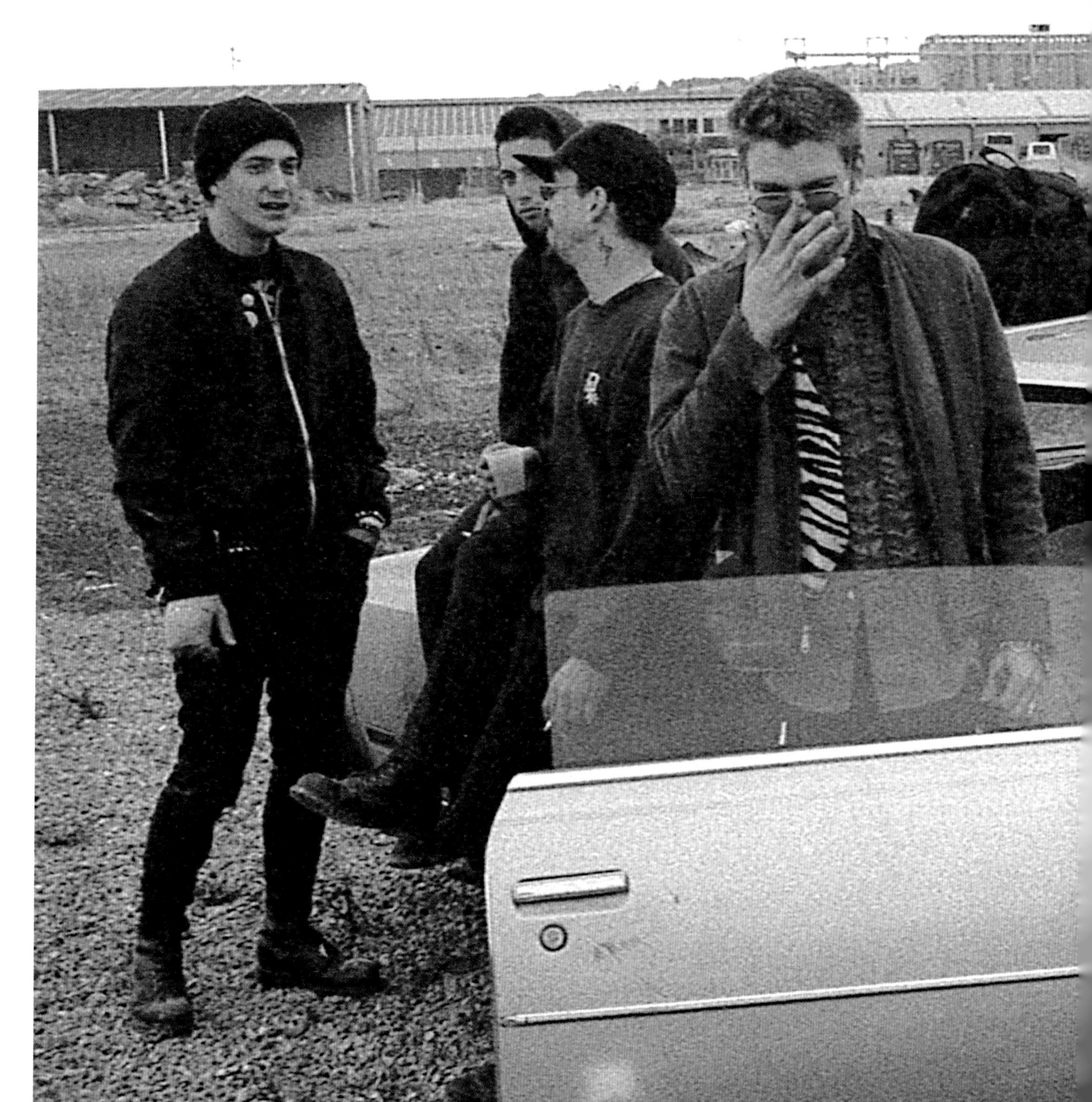

San Francisco, 1995
Left to right: Damon, Aaron, Dave, Jake, Becca,
Ed, and Lenny

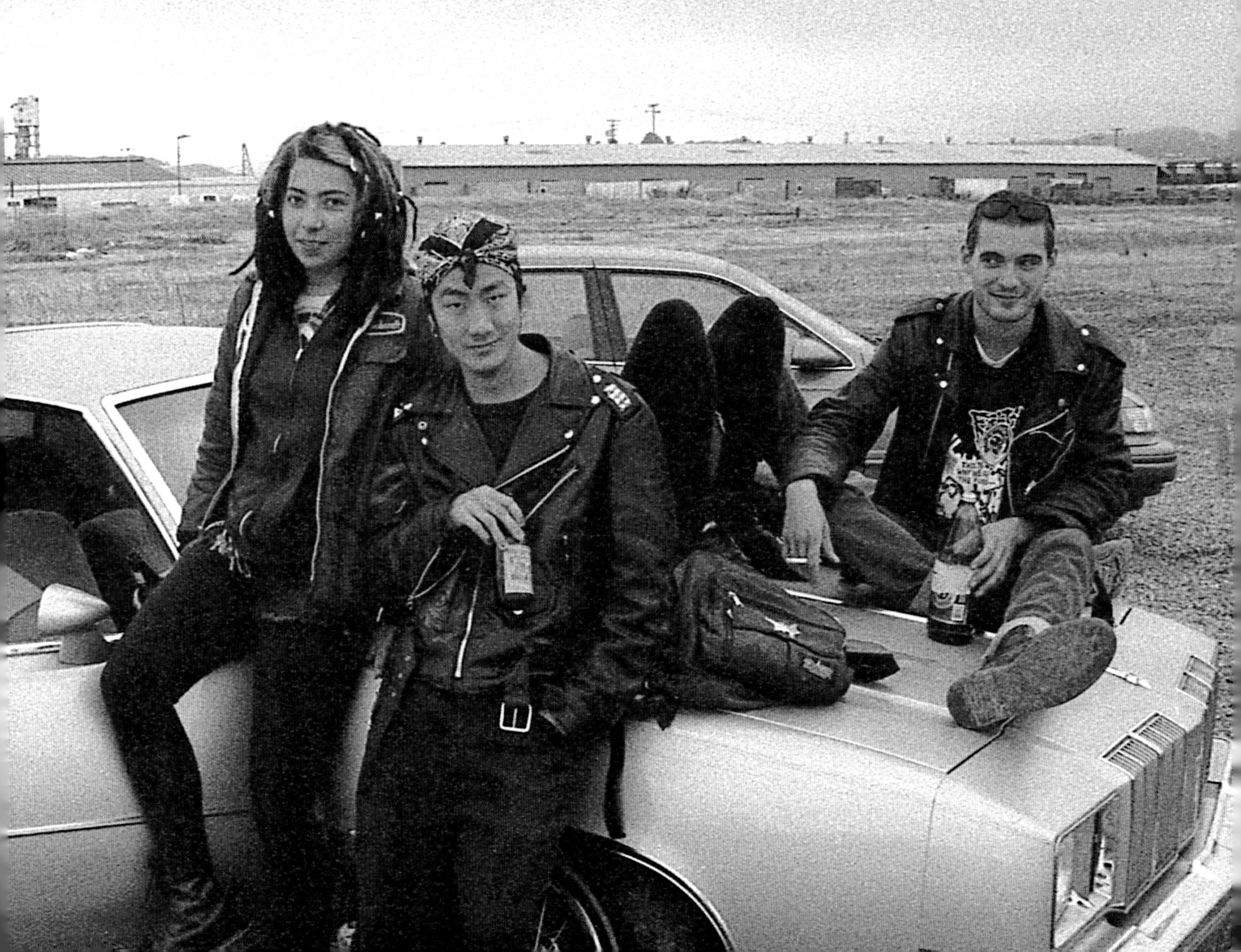

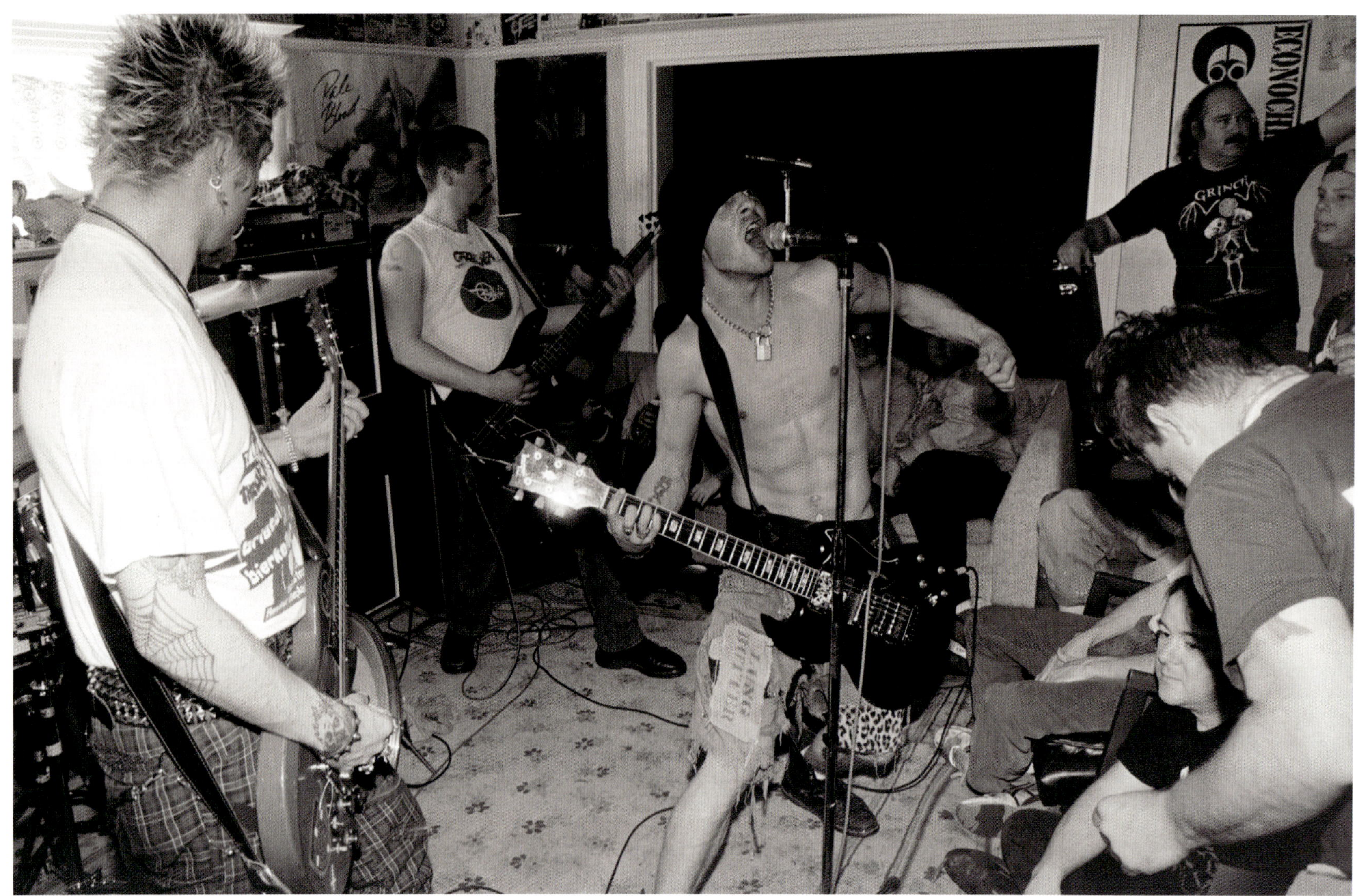

Rancid

Pill Hill House, Oakland, 1993

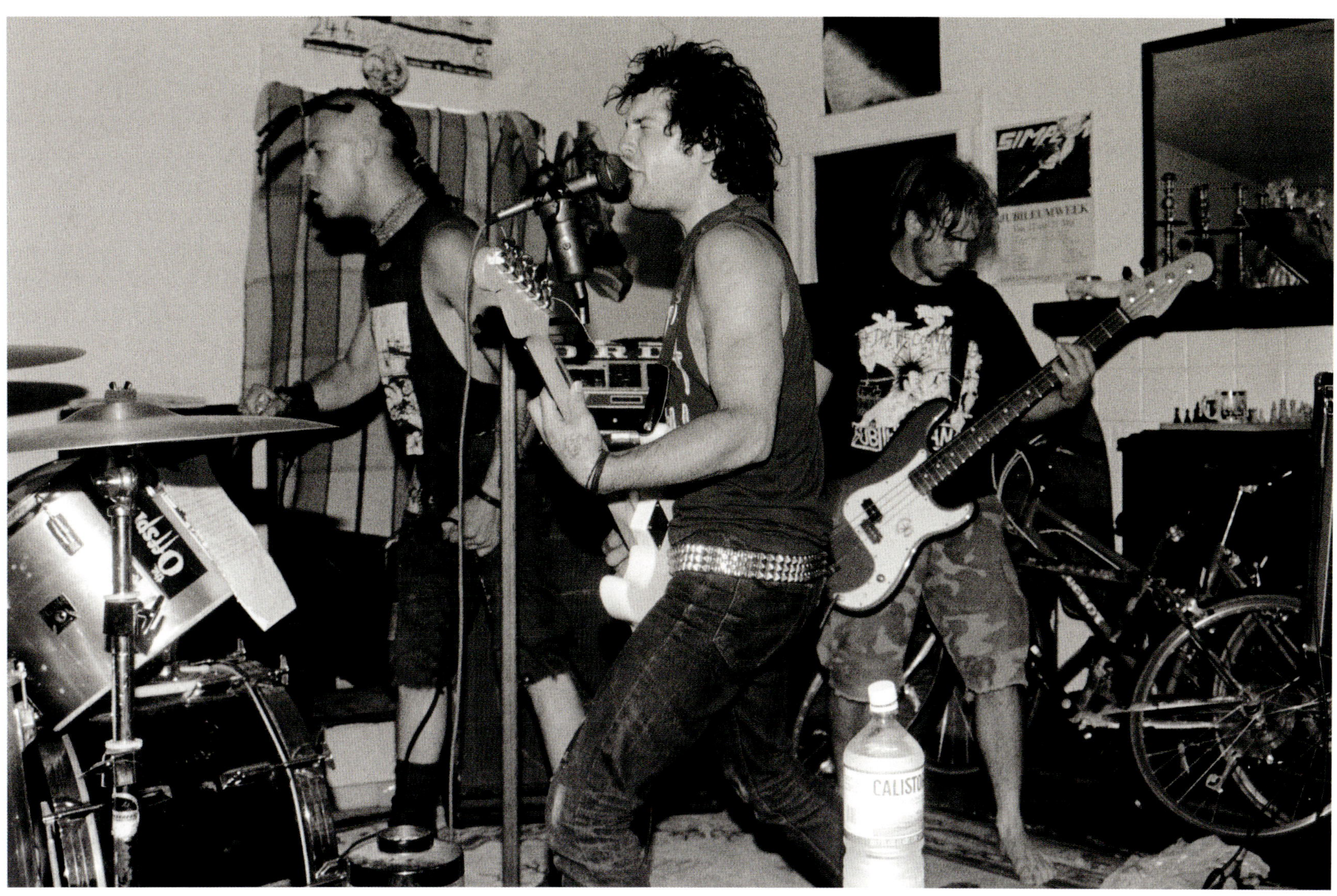

Grimple

Berkeley, 1993

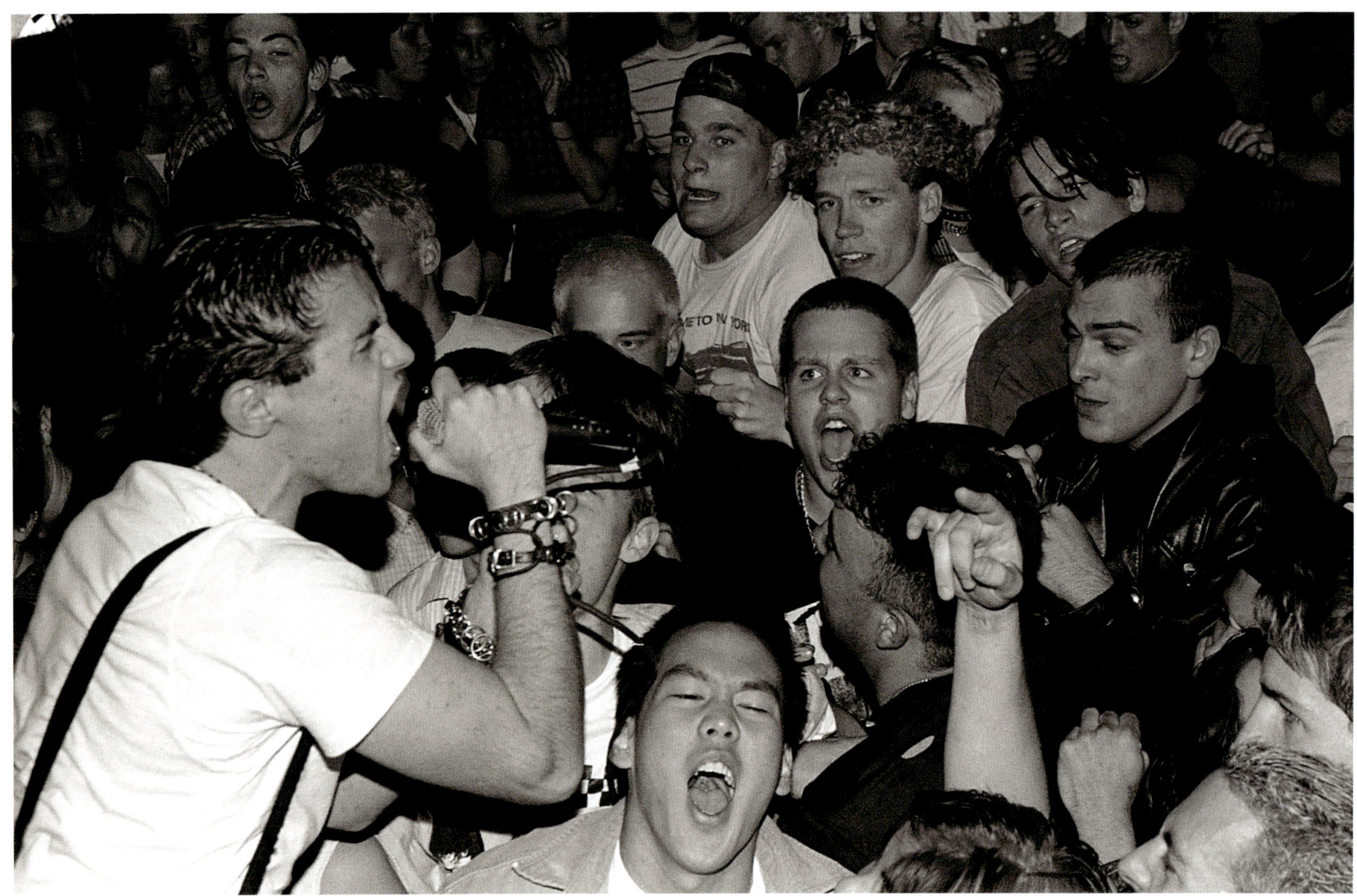

AFI
Gilman Street, Berkeley, 1994

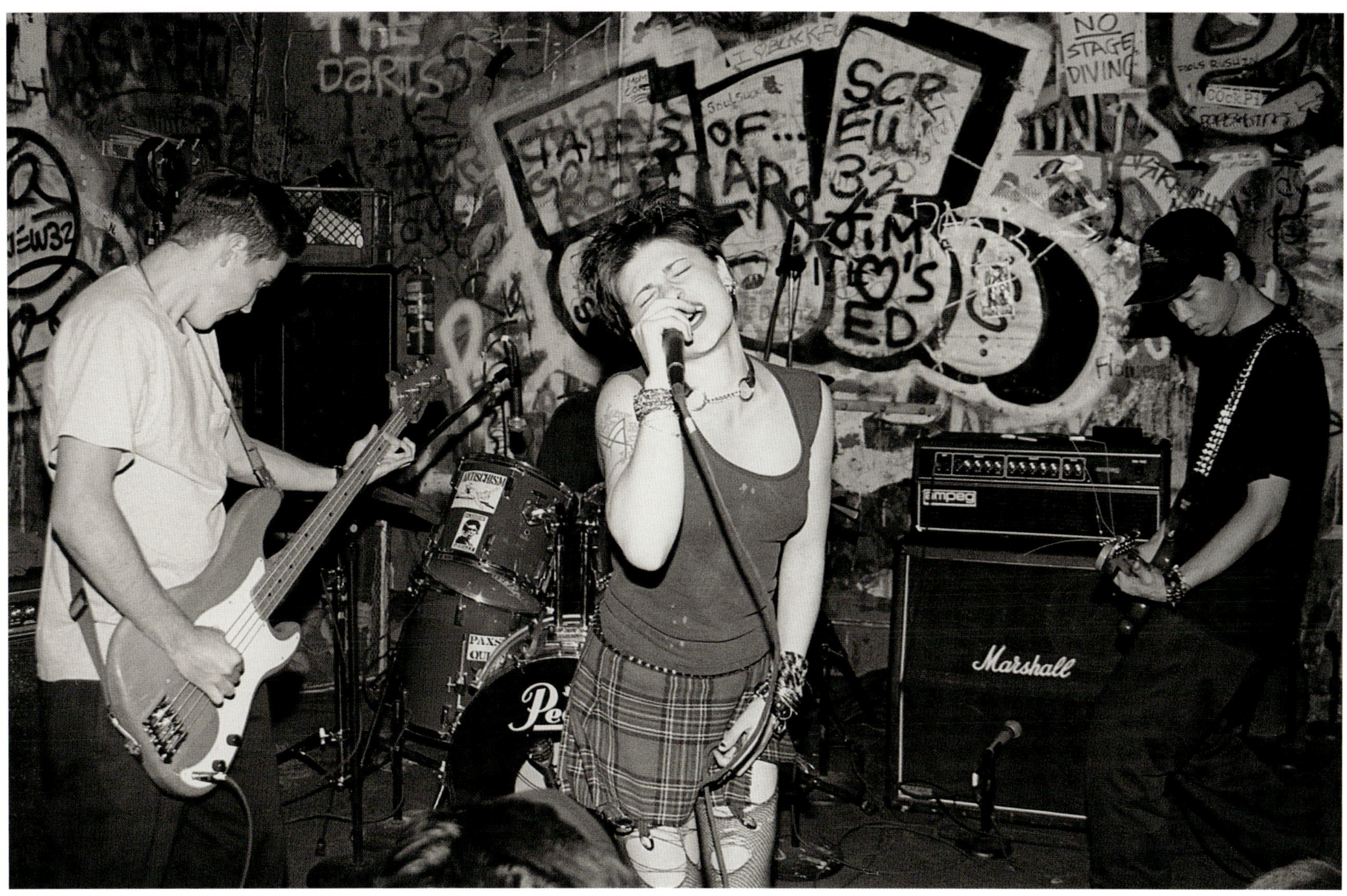

Multi Facet

Gilman Street, Berkeley, 1994

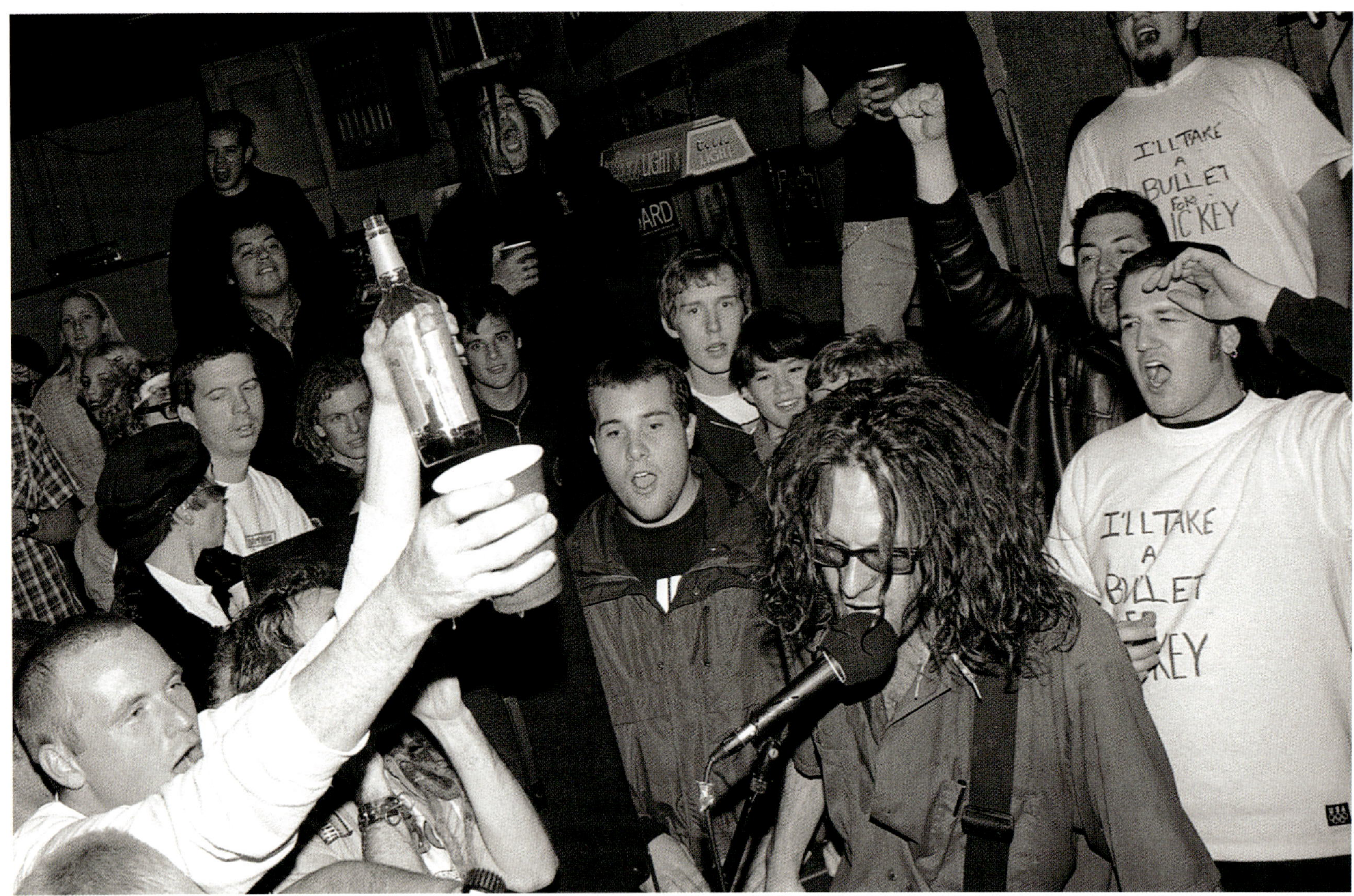

Hickey
San Francisco, 1995

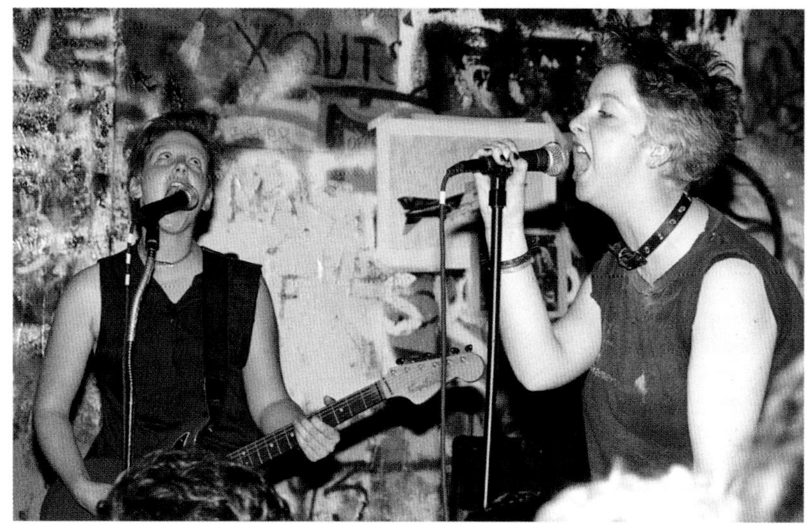
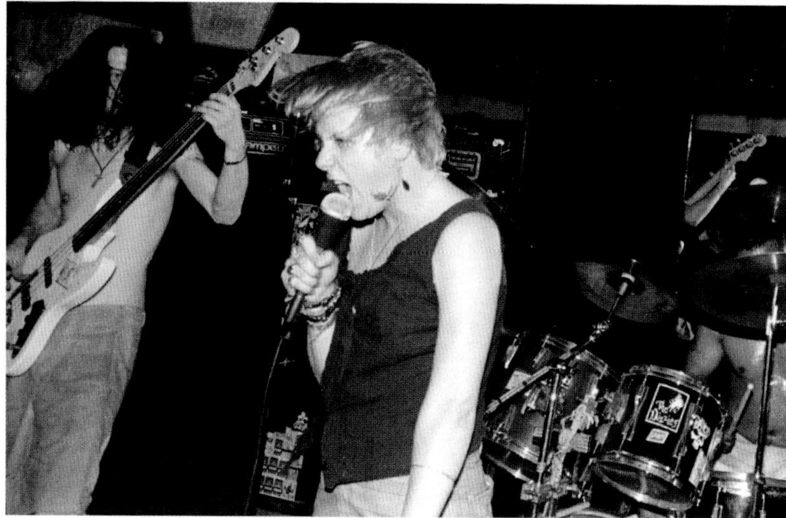
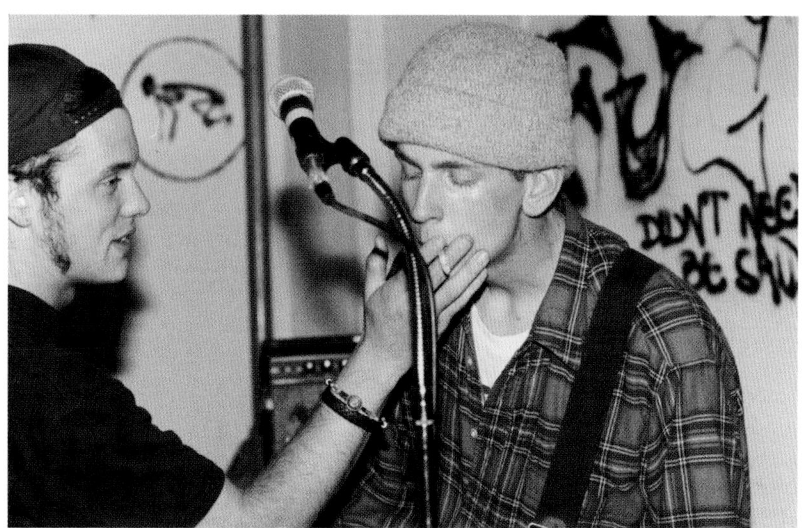
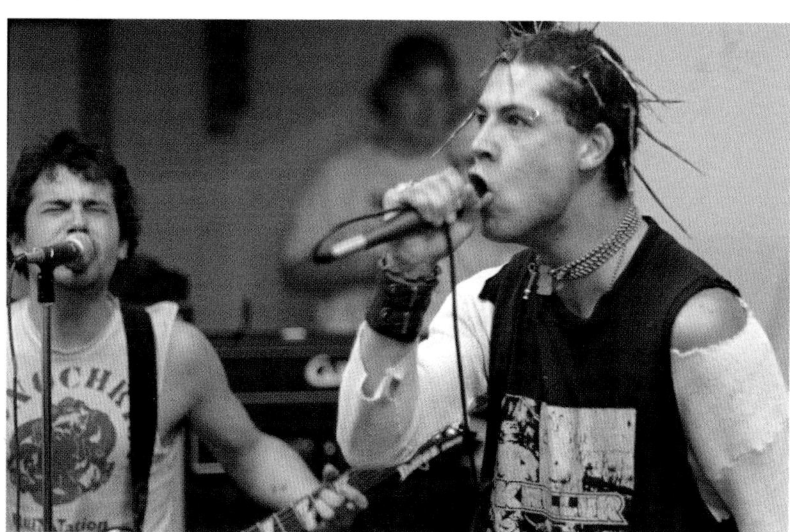

Clockwise from top left: **Hollie and Heather**, 1994; **False Sacrament**, 1992; **Grimple**, 1993; **Nuisance**, 1991

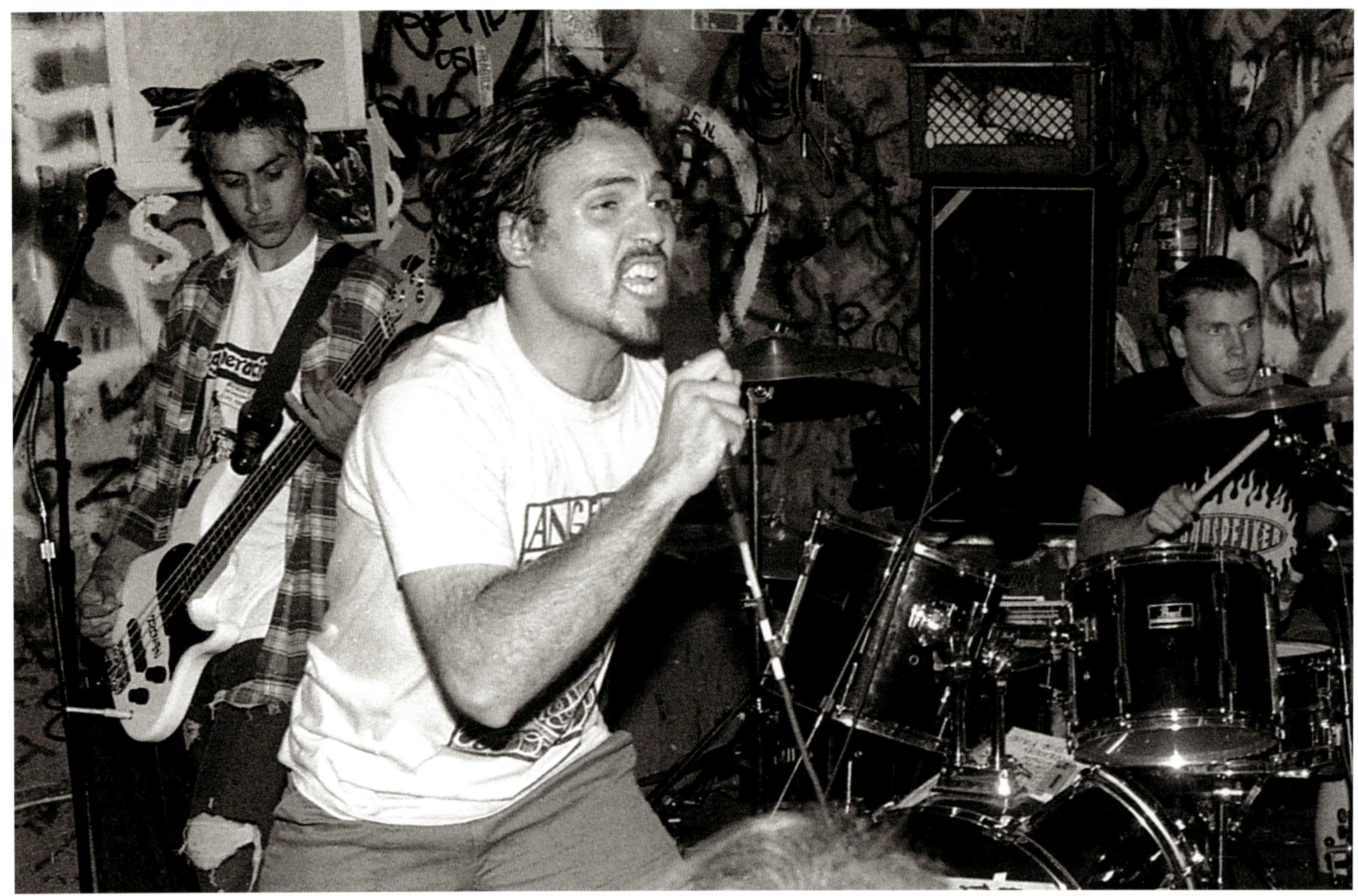

Los Crudos

Gilman Street, Berkeley, 1994

Opposite:

Your Place Too, Oakland, 1994

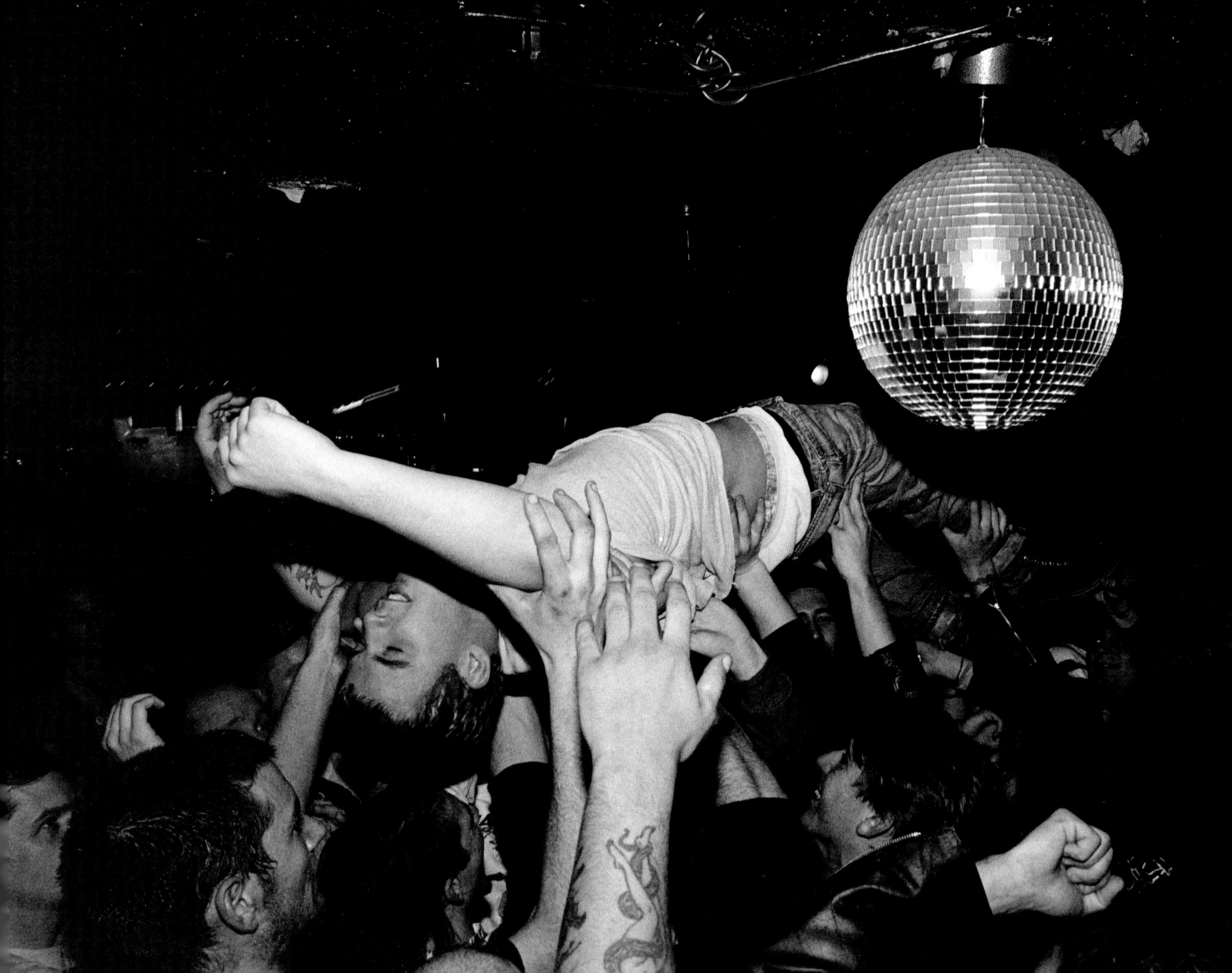

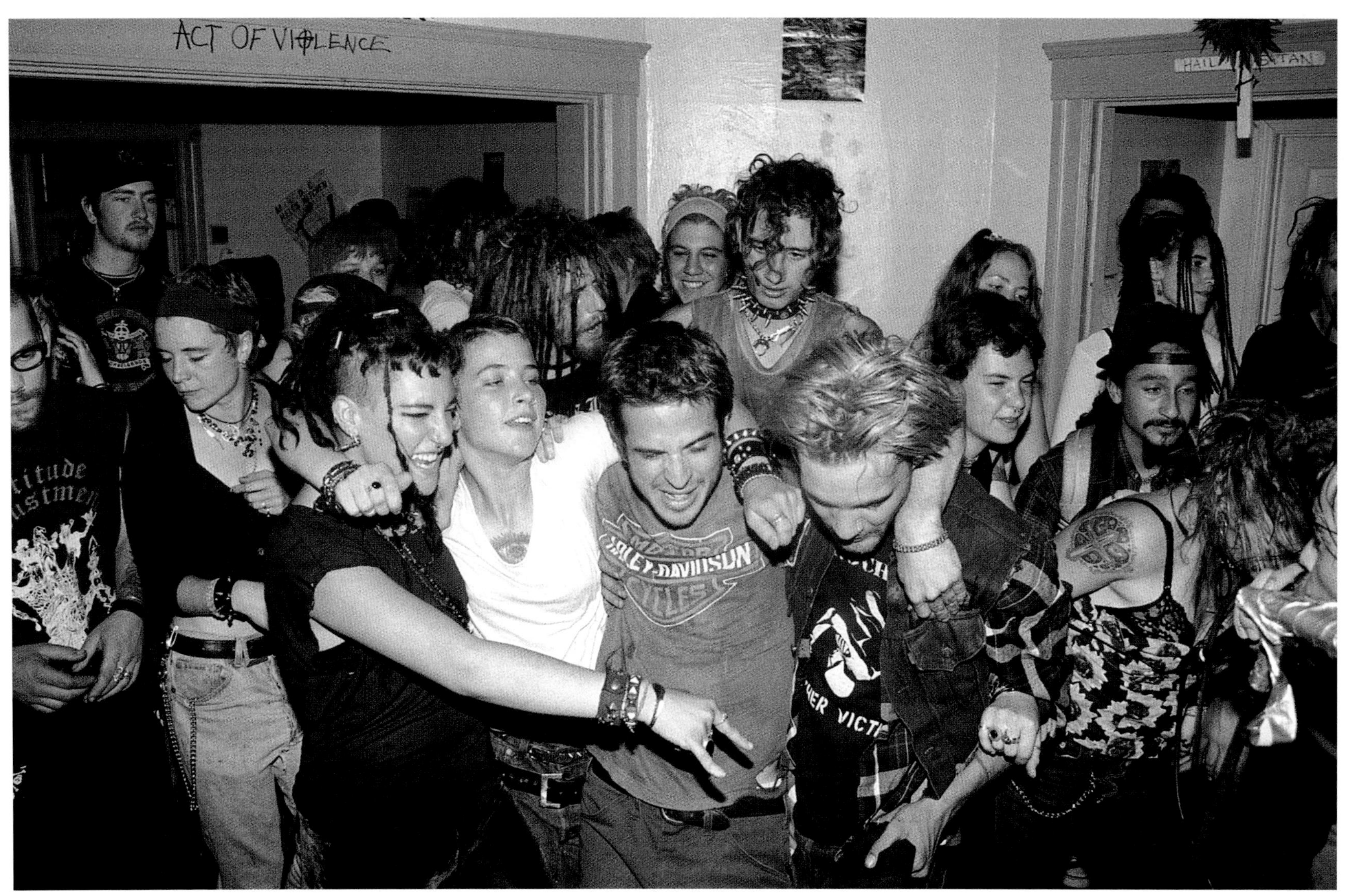

34th Street House, Oakland, 1994

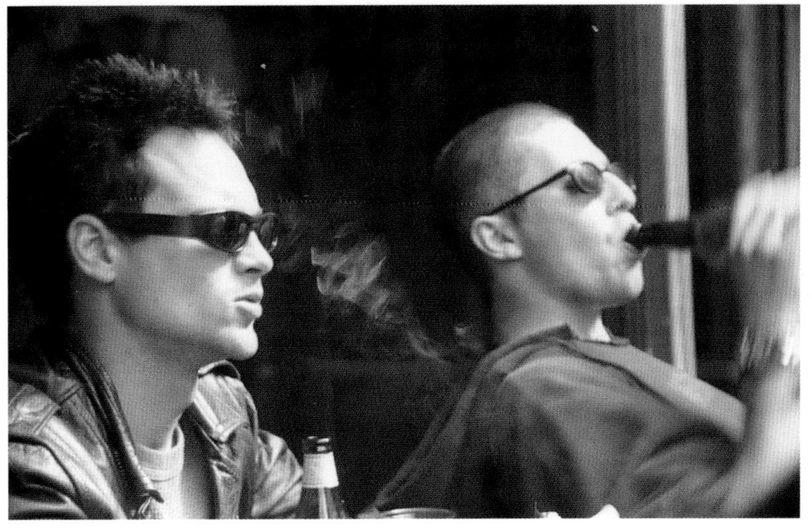

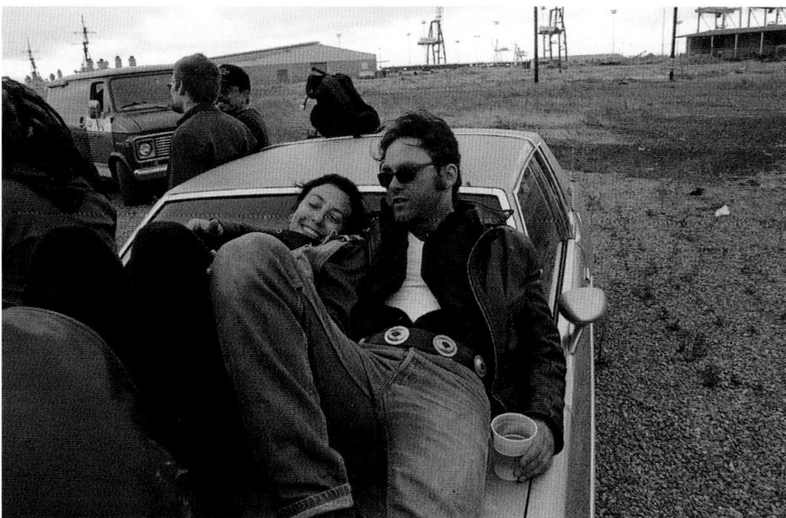

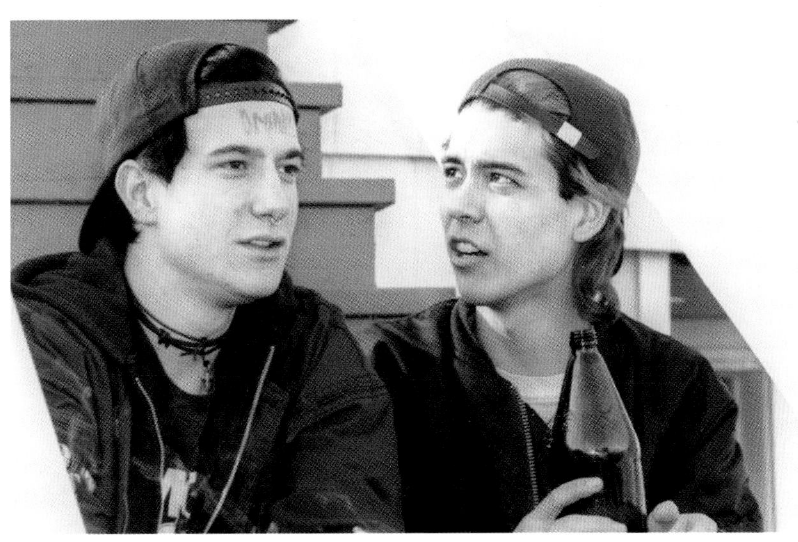

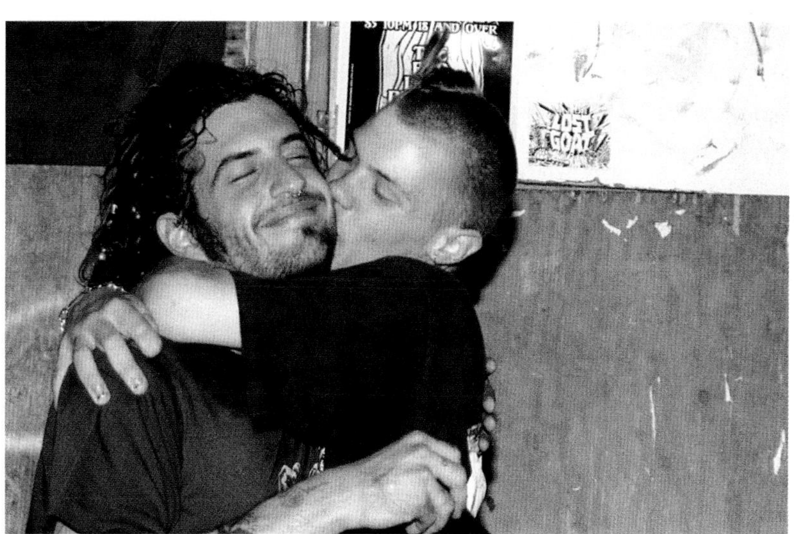

Clockwise from top left: JJ and Aaron, 1995; Kate and Trip, 1995; Aesop and Jason, 1995; Damon and Kaz, 1990

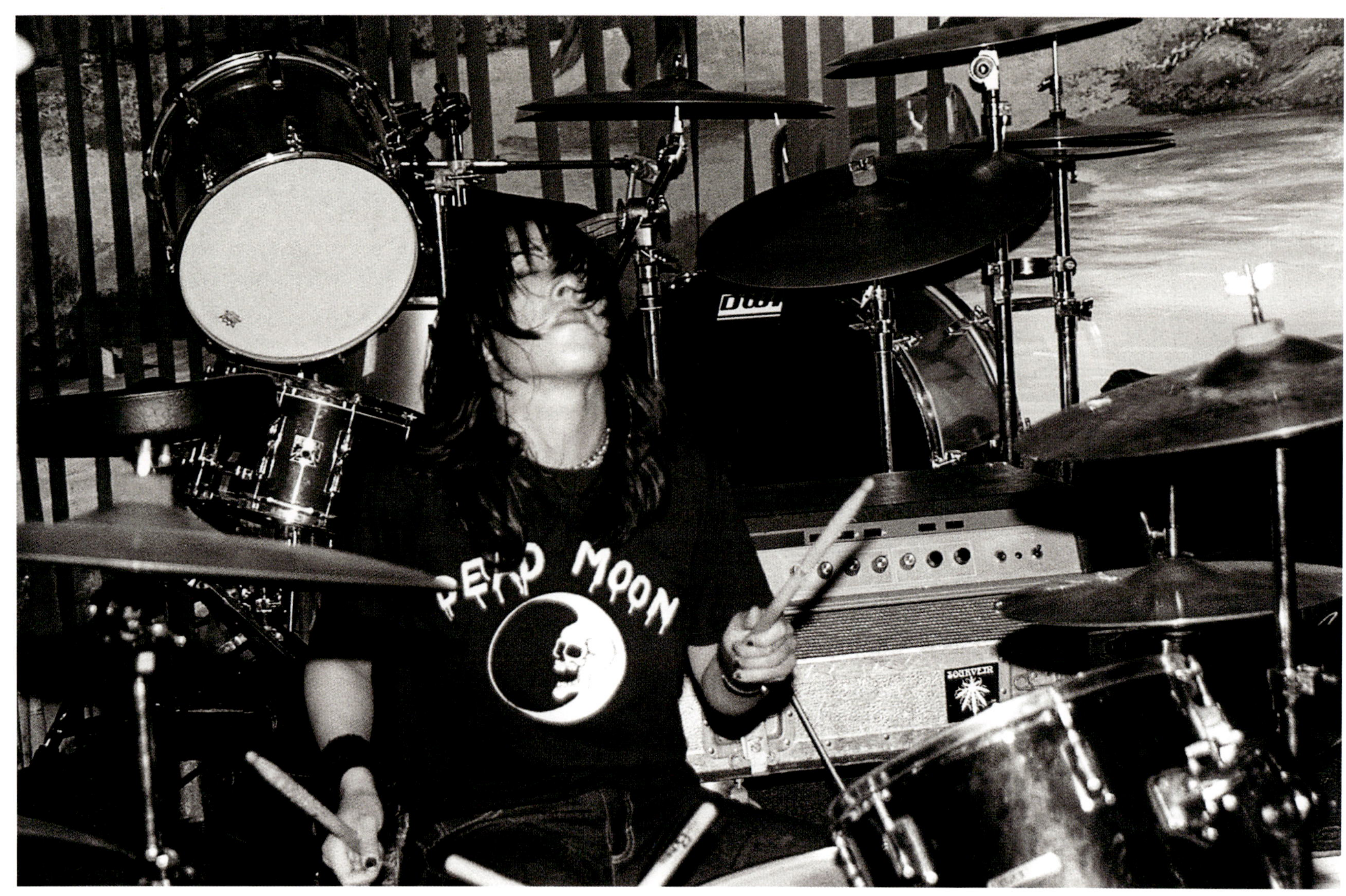

Lost Goat

San Francisco, 1995

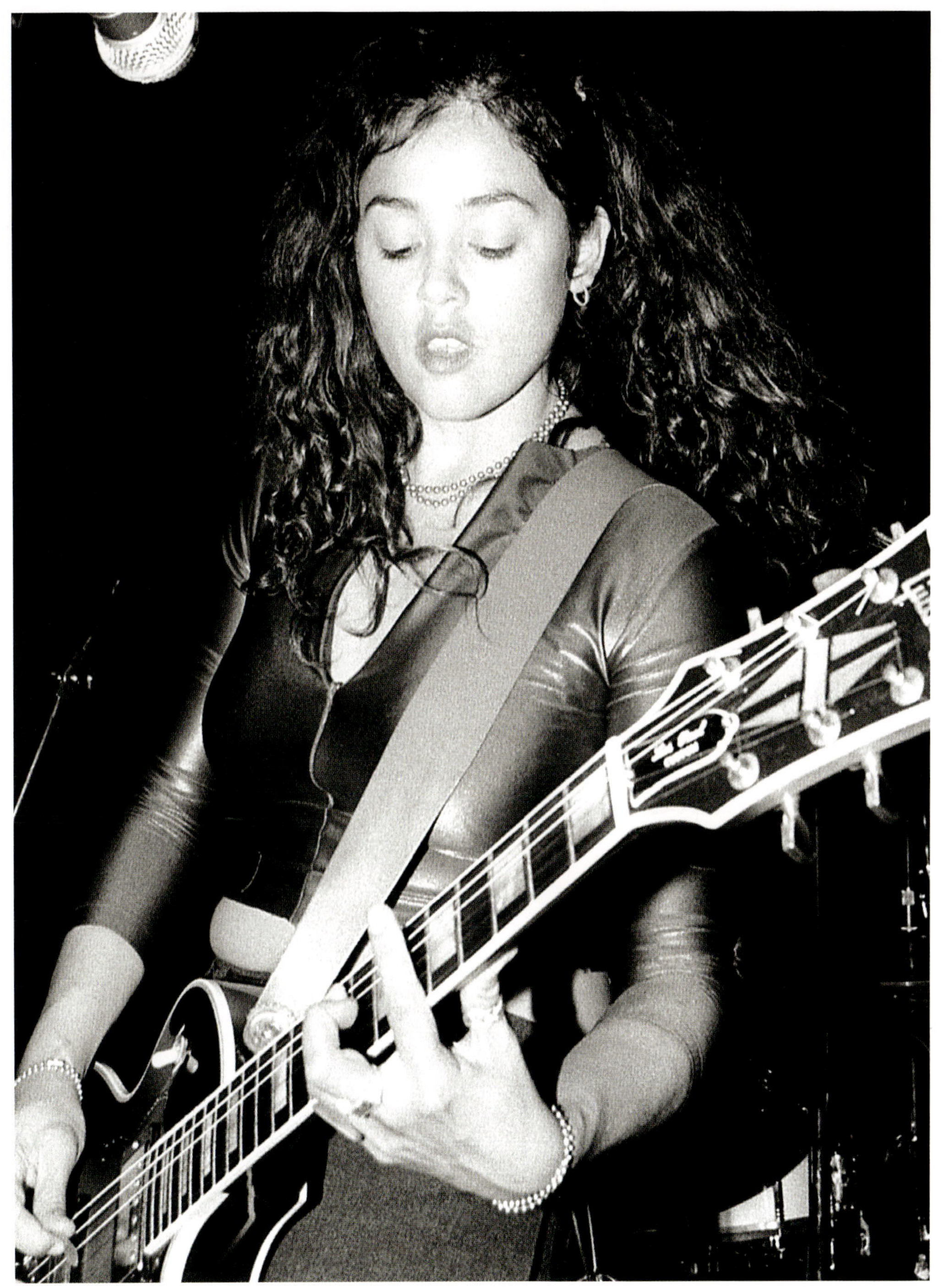

Squat
Nightbreak, San Francisco, 1995

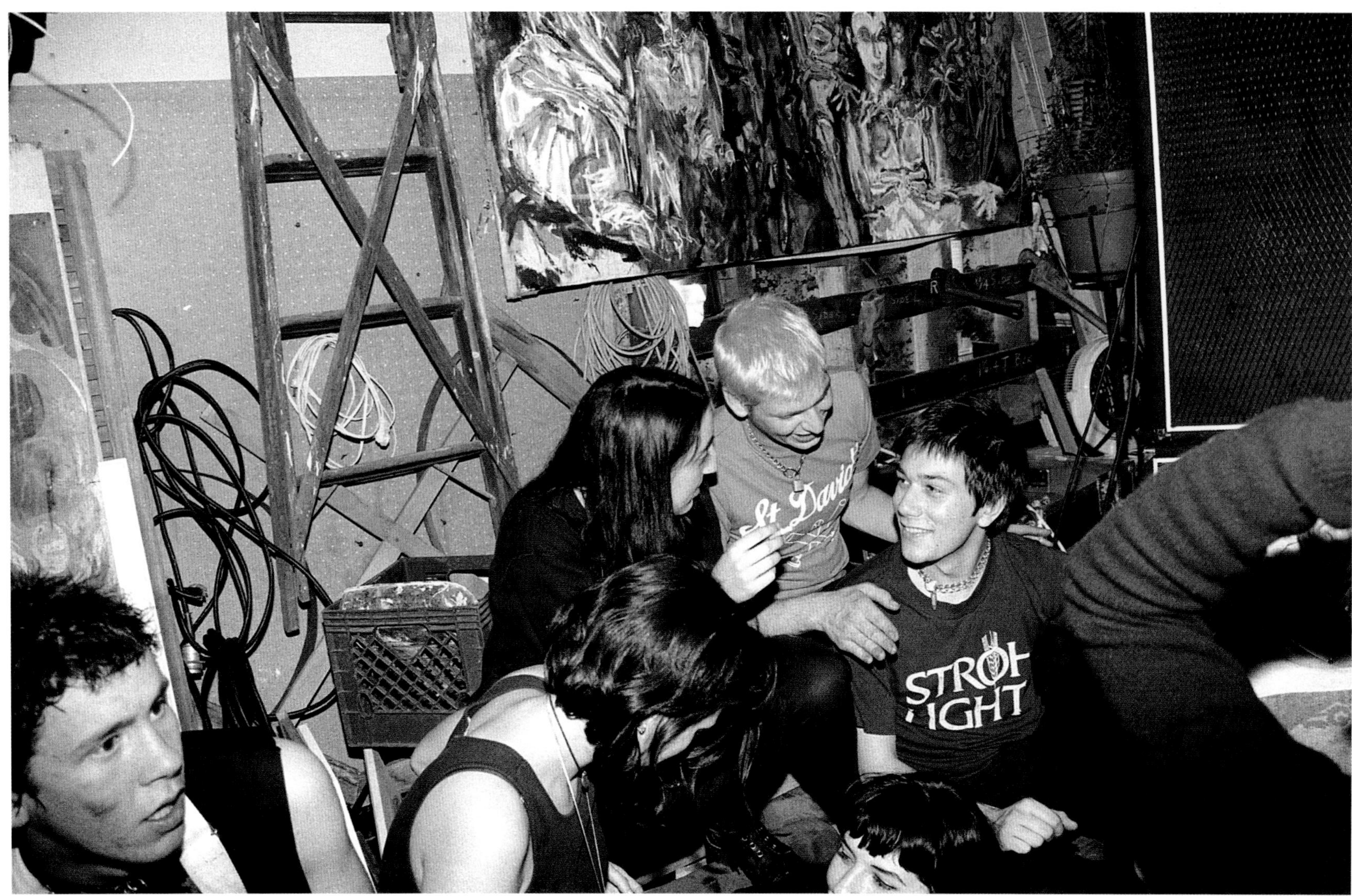

Capp Street, San Francisco, 1995

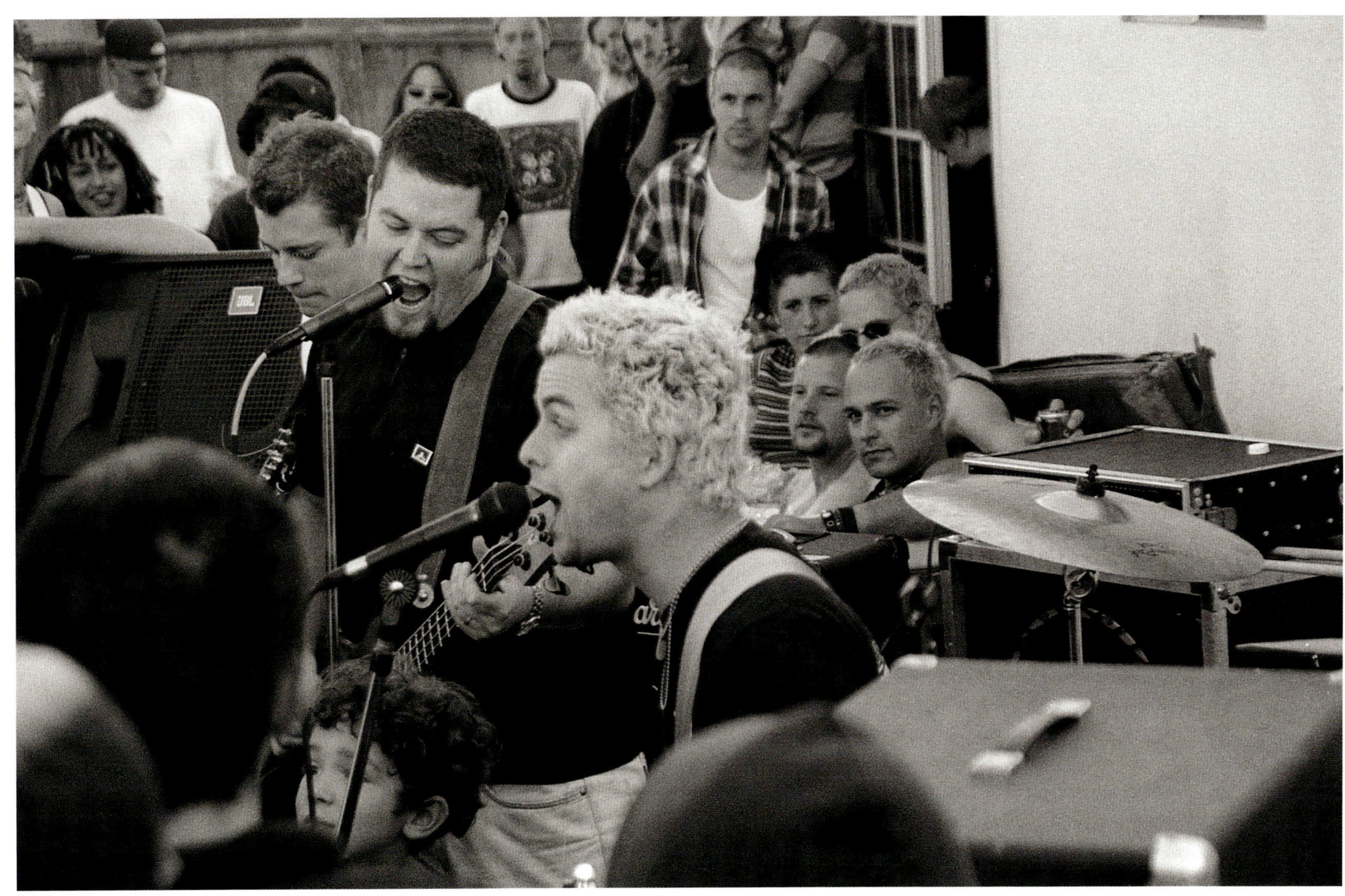

Pinhead Gunpowder

Eggplant's Backyard, Pinole, 1995

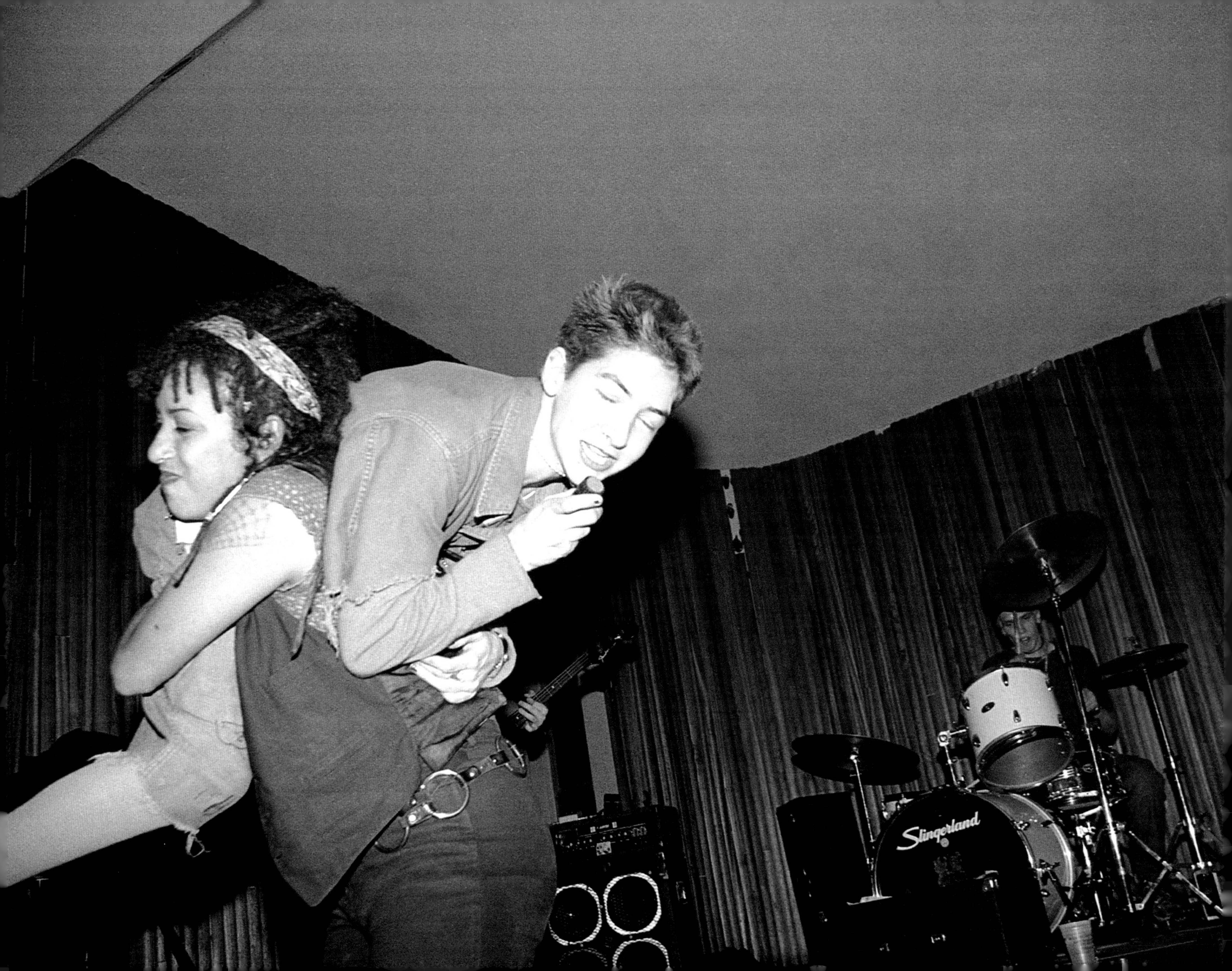

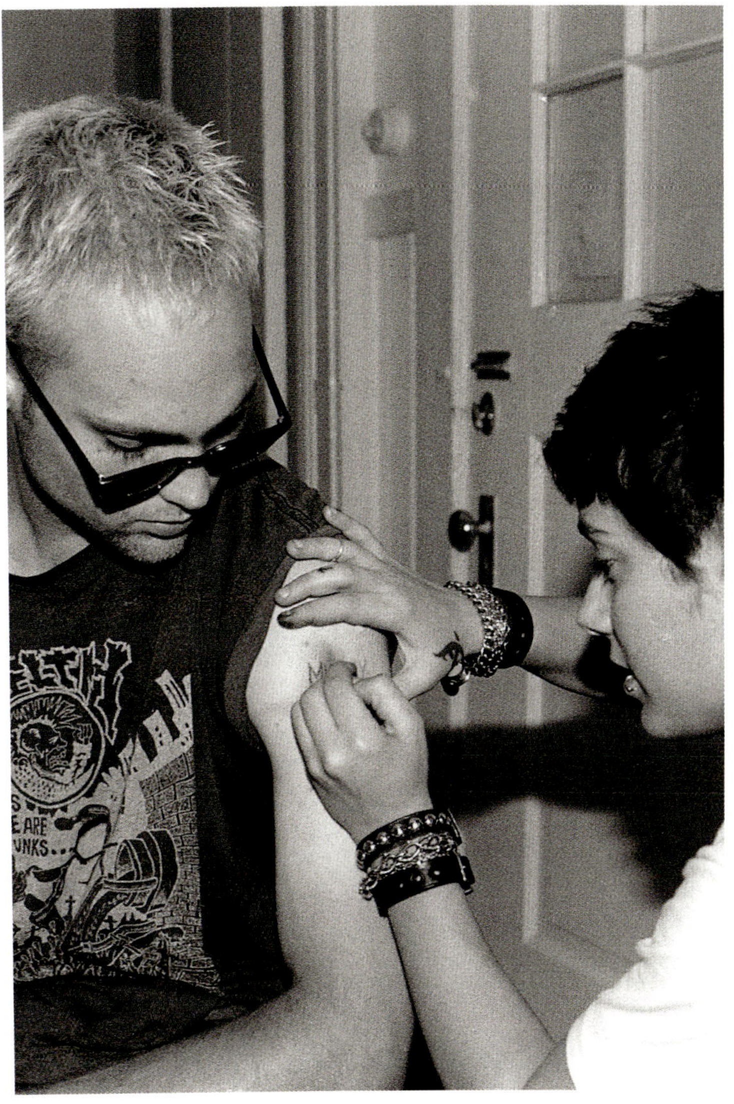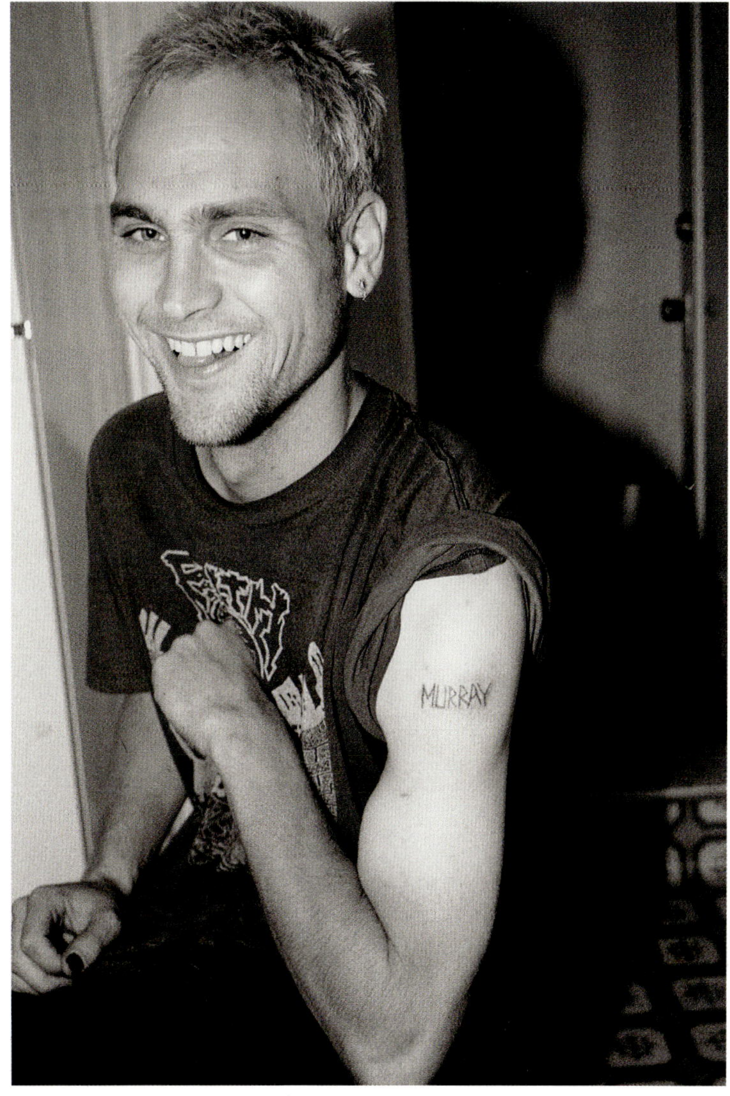

JJ and Alfie, 1995

Opposite:

Black Fork
1995

Acknowledgments

Anna would like to thank:

Kathy Starr, for entrusting me with her brother's work; Jenny and Ryan, for opening the door every time we showed up to dig through Murray's stuff; Corbett Redford, for his boundless generosity, his database and wise counsel, and for the *Turn It Around* interview that captures Murray's voice so well; Caoimhe Carty, for building said database and talking me off the ledge more than once; Paul Curran, for his beautiful layout and collaborative spirit; Eric Yee, for scanning and cataloging countless negatives and for his ability to name even the most obscure bands and venues; Justin Marsh, for recognizing Murray's genius right away and working so hard to preserve his legacy, and for his design vision; Luke Turner, for skillfully retouching the images and all of his thoughtful suggestions; Cammie Toloui, for her priceless pictures of Murray, and the inspired title (Hail Murray!); Christian Larsen, Sally's room alum, for his classic shot of Murray in the pit; Kate Knox, unwavering friend (to Murray and me both), for her all-around toughness, and for orchestrating the launch this behemoth deserves; Dave Ed, Noah Landis, and Brian Stern, for their enthusiastic reviews of early drafts; Heather Brown, for her aesthetic discernment and feedback on the layout; Erin Brown, for all of her time, and for her alchemy turning shit into gold; Arwen Curry, for her knowledge of all things; Robert Eggplant, esteemed historian of East Bay punk, for helping us appraise Murray's vast archive; Aaron Elliott, most of all for being on my side; Ron and Colin Turner, for being the last and the best of the outlaw publishers; Jessica Appelgren, for her PR chops; Bill Schneider and Green Day, for throwing their weight behind this project; Mitchell Klein and Dave Curry, for their insights into Murray's other worlds; Gilman Street, where so much of the magic happened, for keeping the doors open all these years; Sean Naes, for offering up a high-functioning computer; David Schweidel for constant encouragement; Eric Ross, for extracurricular problem solving; Richie Bucher, for his classic portrait; Davey Whitcraft; Bryan Ray and Beta Petrol; Markley Hart and Econopress; Sita Rupe-Lens, for shooting the end paper; Chris, for building me a fortress of solitude and encouraging me to see this through; Flora, for all the pancakes; the whole East Bay punk family, for saving my life; and of course, Murray, for being one in a million, and for being one of us. Thank you.

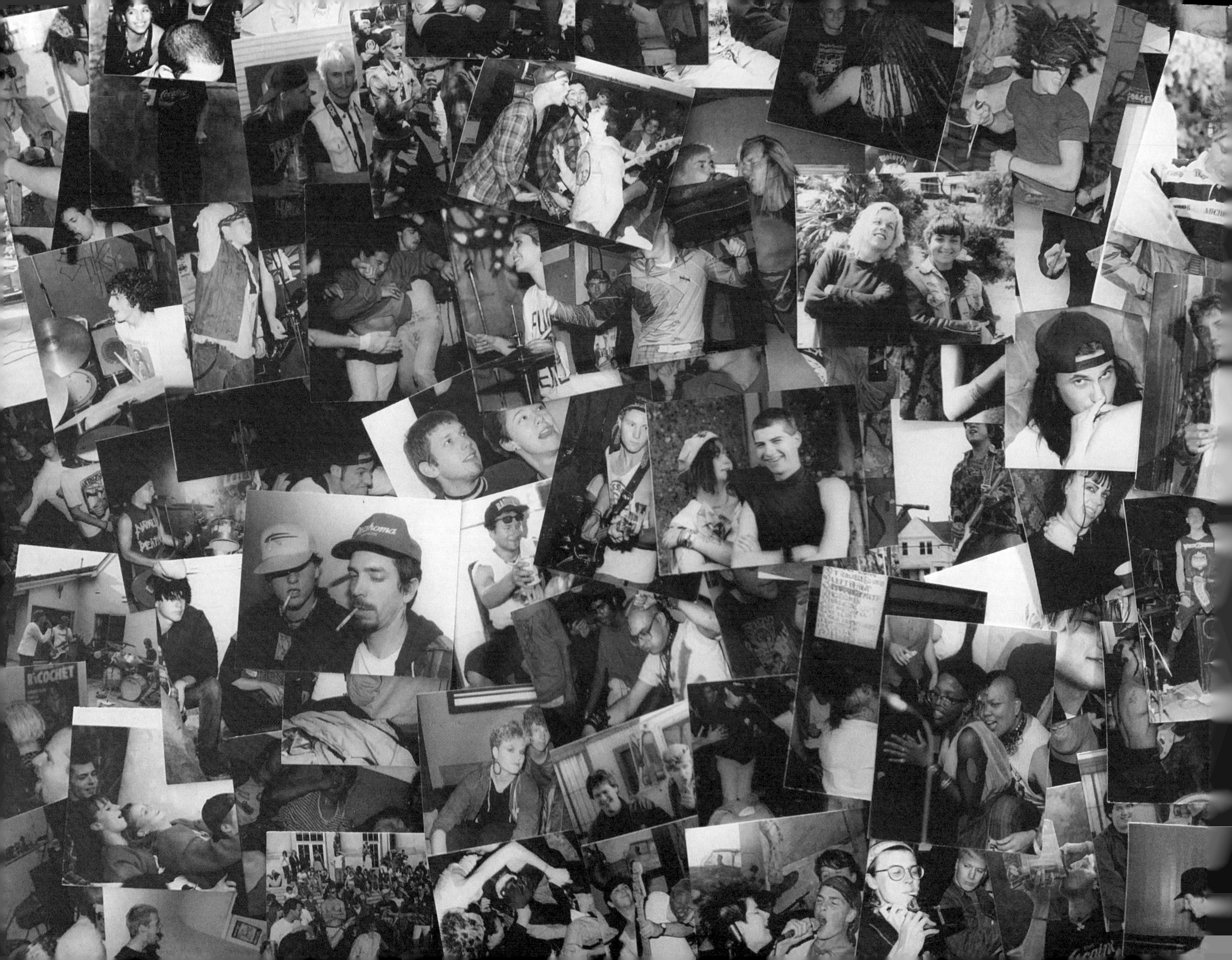